Praise for Children's Writer's & Illustrator's Market

"Sound, hard-headed advice to prospective authors on all aspects of the writing of children's books." **—American Reference Books Annual**

"Remains a useful handbook for those offering creative work in the children's publishing marketplace." **—Library Journal**

"A fine directory packed with listings and advice."
—Children's Bookwatch

"Useful in public libraries, academic libraries that support curricula in illustration, writing, and education, and in school-district professional libraries as well." **—Booklist**

1999
CHILDREN'S WRITER'S & ILLUSTRATOR'S MARKET

800 EDITORS & ART DIRECTORS WHO BUY
YOUR WRITING & ILLUSTRATIONS

EDITED BY
ALICE POPE

WRITER'S DIGEST BOOKS
CINCINNATI, OHIO

Managing Editor, Annuals Department: Cindy Laufenberg
Supervisory Editor: Barbara Kuroff
Production Editor: Tricia Waddell
Writer's Digest Books website: http://www.writersdigest.com

Children's Writer's & Illustrator's Market. Copyright © 1999 by Writer's Digest Books. Published by F&W Publications, 1507 Dana Ave., Cincinnati, Ohio 45207. Printed and bound in the United States of America. All rights reserved. No part of this book may be reproduced in any form or by any electronic or mechanical means including information storage and retrieval systems without written permission from the publisher, except by reviewers who may quote brief passages to be printed in a magazine or newspaper.

International Standard Serial Number 0897-9790
International Standard Book Number 0-89879-877-9

Cover designed by Clare Finney
Cover illustration by David Danz

Contents

The Markets

© 1998 Janie Bynum.

Page 16

© 1998 Joy Allen.

Page 173

The Resources

© 1998 Terry Julien.

Page 225

From the Editor

When I interviewed **Peggy Rathmann** for this edition of *Children's Writer's & Illustrator's Market*, I couldn't help making a confession to her: My whole life I thought "hamster" was spelled with a "p." H-A-M-P-S-T-E-R. (Peggy's latest book, *10 Minutes till Bedtime*, features dozens of hamsters.) I discovered there was no "p" as I spell checked the interview questions I was faxing to her.

Peggy thought this was a riot. "Well," I told her. "Maybe kids across America have the same problem I do, and your book will help them all realize there really is no 'p' in hamster."

A few days later, I was shopping with a friend (an editor, too), and told her, "I just found out there's no 'p' in hamster." "Yes there is," she insisted. "No there's not," I said. "Yes there is." "No there's not." This went on for several minutes. She's still not convinced.

The next week, I was in L.A. at the SCBWI National Conference. I thought I'd see how many writers and illustrators could spell hamster. I found at least three who added a "p," and dozens more who thought I was a little nutty when I said, "Quick—how do you spell hamster?"

This whole hamster experience reminded me of something (besides the fact that I'm a bad speller). For me, every day is full of small revelations. The right way to spell a rodent's name. What Mick Jagger is really saying in any Rolling Stones song. What "html" means. What an agent does all day. That the senior editor from publisher X is now editorial director at publisher Y.

I hope my latest edition of *Children's Writer's & Illustrator's Market* provides you with some small revelations (and maybe some big ones). I learned from every interview I did, every caption I wrote and every article I edited. First Books (page 24) taught me about the value of persistence and peers. Kelly Milner Halls's interview with **Jon Scieszka** and **Lane Smith** (page 78) offered a lesson in partnership (and how to spell Scieszka). The Insider Report with **Nancy Garden** (page 112) showed the importance of fighting for what you know is right. And Meadowbrook editor and publisher **Bruce Lansky**'s Insider Report (page 146) revealed a few magic tricks.

As I began work on my first edition of this book in 1994, I learned something that keeps me enthusiastically working on it year after year. Those who answer the calling to write and illustrate for children are a great bunch. First-time author **Linda R. Rymill** said it better than I could as she talked to me for First Books: "It's a great community. You grow together, share frustration and delight. You love life; you love the simple things in life. You genuinely appreciate the face in a pansy, the coldness of a snowflake, the squish of sand under your feet."

As the year goes by and I'm busy digging up revelations for the 2000 edition of *Children's Writer's & Illustrators' Market*, I'd love to hear from you, appreciators of snowflakes and sandboxes.

Alice Pope
cwim@fwpubs.com

How to Use This Book to Sell Your Work

As a writer, illustrator or photographer first picking up *Children's Writer's & Illustrator's Market*, you may not know quite how to start using the book. Your impulse may be to flip through the book and quickly make a mailing list, then submit to everyone in hopes that someone will take interest in your work. Well, there's more to it. Finding the right market takes time and research. The more you know about a company that interests you, the better chance you have of getting work accepted.

We've made your job a little easier by putting a wealth of information at your fingertips. Besides providing listings, this directory includes a number of tools to help you determine which markets are the best ones for your work. By using these tools, as well as researching on your own, you raise your odds of being published.

USING THE INDEXES

This book lists hundreds of potential buyers of freelance material. To learn which companies want the type of material you're interested in submitting, start with the indexes.

The Age-Level Index

Age groups are broken down into these categories in the Age-Level Index:
- **Picture books** or **picture-oriented material** are written and illustrated for preschoolers to 8-year-olds.
- **Young readers** are for 5- to 8-year-olds.
- **Middle readers** are for 9- to 11-year-olds.
- **Young adults** are for ages 12 and up.

age breakdowns may vary slightly from publisher to publisher, but using them as guidelines will help you target appropriate markets. For example, if you've written an article about the latest teen fashions, check the Magazines Age-Level Index under the Young Adult subheading. Using this list, you'll quickly find the listings for young adult magazines.

The Subject Index

But let's narrow the search further. Take your list of young adult magazines, turn to the Subject Index, and find the Fashion subheading. Then highlight the names that appear on both lists (Young Adult and Fashion). Now you have a smaller list of all the magazines that would be interested in your teen fashion article. Read through those listings and decide which ones sound best for your work.

Illustrators and photographers can use the Subject Index as well. If you specialize in painting animals, for instance, consider sending samples to book and magazine publishers listed under Animals and, perhaps, Nature/Environment. Illustrators can simply send general examples of their style (in the form of tearsheets or postcards) to art directors to keep on file. The indexes may be more helpful to artists sending manuscripts/illustration packages. Always read the listings for the potential markets to see the type of work art directors prefer and what type of samples they'll keep on file, and send for art or photo guidelines if they're available.

The Poetry Index

Brand new this year, the Poetry Index lists book publishers and magazines interested in submissions from poets. Always send for writer's guidelines from publishers and magazines that interest you.

The Photography Index

You'll find lists of book and magazine publishers, as well as greeting card, puzzle and game manufacturers, that buy photos from freelancers in the Photography Index. Copy the lists and read the listings for specific needs. Send for photo guidelines if they're offered.

USING THE LISTINGS

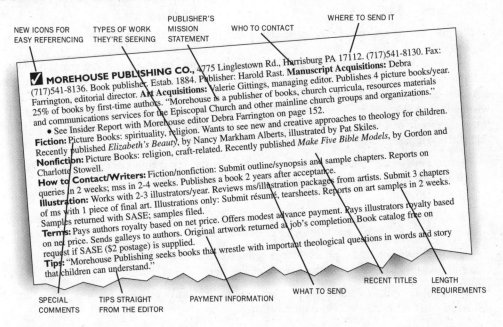

Many listings begin with one or more symbols. (Refer to the inside covers of the book for quick reference.) Here's what each icon stands for:

N indicates a listing is new to this edition.

□ indicates a listing is a book packager or producer.

○ indicates a company publishes educational material.

♣ indicates a listing is Canadian.

✓ indicates a change in contact information from last year's edition.

A indicates a publisher only accepts submissions through agents.

Y indicates a company's publications have received awards recently.

In the Book Publishers section, you'll find contact names after **Manuscript Acquisitions** and **Art Acquisitions**. Contact names in Magazines follow boldface titles such as **Fiction Editor, Articles Editor** or **Art Director**. Following contact information in many of these listings are mission statements. Read these to get a general idea of the aim of certain publishers and magazines to help you decide whether to explore them further.

The subheadings under each listing contain more specific information about what a company needs. In Book Publishers and Magazines, for example, you'll find such things as age levels and subjects needed under the Fiction and Nonfiction subheads. Here's an example from a listing in the Book Publishers section:

Fiction: Picture books: adventure, animal, contemporary, fantasy, humor. Young readers: animal, contemporary, humor, sports, suspense/mystery. Middle readers: adventure, humor, sports. Young adults: humor, problem novels.

Also check the listings for information on how to submit your work and response time. In Book Publishers and Magazines, writers will find this information under the How to Contact/ Writers subhead:

How to Contact/Writers: Query with outline/synopsis and 2 sample chapters. Reports on queries in 6 weeks.

For information on submission procedures and formats, turn to Before Your First Sale on page 6.

Also look for information regarding payment and rights purchased. Some markets pay on acceptance, others on publication. Some pay a flat rate for manuscripts and artwork, others pay advances and royalties. Knowing how a market operates will keep you from being shocked when you discover your paycheck won't arrive until your manuscript is published—a year after it was accepted. This information is found under Terms in Book Publishers, Magazines and Play Publishers. Here's an example from the Magazines section:

Terms: Pays on acceptance. Buys first North American serial rights or reprint rights. Pays $50-100 for stories/articles. Pays illustrators $75-125 for b&w or color inside; $150-200 for color cover.

Under Tips you'll find special advice straight from an editor or art director about what their company wants or doesn't want, or other helpful advice:

Tips: "We are looking for picture books centered on a strong, fully-developed protaganist who grows or changes during the course of the story."

Additional information about specific markets in the form of comments from the editor of this book is set off by bullets (●) within listings:

● This publisher accepts only queries and manuscripts submitted by agents.

Many listings indicate whether submission guidelines are available. If a publisher you're interested in offers guidelines, send for them and read them. The same is true with catalogs. Sending for catalogs and seeing and reading about the books a publisher produces gives you a better idea whether your work would fit in. (You may even want to look at a few of the books in the catalog at a library or bookstore.) Note that a number of publishers offer guidelines and catalogs on their websites.

Especially for artists and photographers

Along with information for writers, listings provide information for photographers and illustrators. Illustrators will find numerous markets that maintain files of samples for possible future assignments. If you're both a writer and illustrator, look for markets that accept manuscript/ illustration packages. You'll find sample illustrations from various publishers sprinkled throughout the listings. These illustrations serve as examples of the kind of art these particular companies buy. Read the captions for additional information about the artwork and the market.

If you're a photographer, after consulting the Photography Index, read the information under the Photography subhead within listings to see what format buyers prefer. For example, some want 35mm color transparencies, others want b&w prints. Note the type of photos a buyer wants to purchase and the procedures for submitting. It's not uncommon for a market to want a résumé and promotional literature, as well as tearsheets from previous work. Listings also note whether model releases and/or captions are required.

Especially for young writers

If you're a parent, teacher or student, you may be interested in Young Writer's & Illustrator's Markets. The listings in this section encourage submissions from young writers and artists. Some may require a written statement from a teacher or parent noting the work is original. Also watch for age limits.

Young people should also check Contests & Awards for contests that accept work by young writers and artists. Some of the contests listed are especially for students; others accept both student and adult work. These listings contain the phrase **open to students** in bold. Some listings in Clubs & Organizations and Conferences & Workshops may also be of interest to students. Organizations and conferences which are open to or are especially for students also include **open to students.**

COMMON ABBREVIATIONS

Throughout the listings, the following abbreviations are used:
- **ms** or **mss** stands for manuscript or manuscripts.
- **SASE** refers to a self-addressed, stamped envelope.
- **SAE** refers to a self-addressed envelope.
- **IRC** stands for International Reply Coupon. These are required with SAEs sent to markets in countries other than your own.

Before Your First Sale

If you're just beginning to pursue your career as a children's book writer or illustrator, it's important to learn the proper procedures, formats, and protocol for the publishing industry. This article outlines the basics you need to know before you head to the post office with your submissions.

FINDING THE BEST MARKETS FOR YOUR WORK

Researching publishers well is a basic element of submitting your work successfully. Editors and art directors hate to receive inappropriate submissions—handling them wastes a lot of their time, not to mention your time and money, and they are the main reason some publishers have chosen not to accept material over the transom. By randomly sending out material without knowing a company's needs, you're sure to meet with rejection.

If you're interested in submitting to a particular magazine, write to request a sample copy, or see if it's available in your local library or bookstore. For a book publisher, obtain a book catalog and check a library or bookstore for titles produced by that publisher. Many publishers and magazines now have websites that include catalogs or sample articles (websites are given within the listings). Studying such materials carefully will better acquaint you with a publisher's or magazine's writing, illustration, and photography styles and formats.

Most of the book publishers and magazines listed in this book (as well as some greeting card and paper product producers) offer some sort of writer's, artist's or photographer's guidelines for a self-addressed, stamped envelope (SASE). Guidelines are also often found on publishers' websites. It's important to read and study guidelines before submitting work. You'll get a better understanding of what a particular publisher wants. You may even decide, after reading the submission guidelines, that your work isn't right for a company you considered. For access to a searchable database of more than 1,000 publishers' guidelines, visit http://www.writersdigest.com.

SUBMITTING YOUR WORK

Throughout the listings you'll read requests for particular elements to include when contacting markets. Here are explanations of some of these important submission components.

Queries, cover letters and proposals

A query letter is a no-more-than-one-page, well-written piece meant to arouse an editor's interest in your work. Many query letters start with leads similar to those of actual manuscripts. In the rest of the letter, briefly outline the work you're proposing and include facts, anecdotes, interviews or other pertinent information that give the editor a feel for the manuscript's premise—entice her to want to know more. End your letter with a straightforward request to write (or submit) the work, and include information on its approximate length, date it could be completed, and whether accompanying photos or artwork are available.

Arthur Levine, editor-in-chief of Scholastic imprint Arthur Levine Books, recommends writers send queries that present their books as a publisher's catalog would present them. Read through a good catalog and examine how the publishers give enticing summaries of their books in a spare amount of words. It's also important that query letters give editors a taste of your writing style. For examples of an effective query letter and cover letter, see pages 7 and 8. For good advice and more samples of queries, cover letters and other correspondence, consult *How*

Good

Floyd Katkin
1234 Published Rd.
Sunny, FL 11111

Jeff Ayers
U*S* Kids
P.O. Box 567
Indianapolis, IN 46205

Dear Mr. Ayers,

Enclosed please find a 500-word nonfiction manuscript titled "The First Horse." I'd appreciate it if you'd consider it for publication. Since this is a printout, in the event of rejection you can discard it and respond via the SASE.

I'm a professional archeologist and freelance writer whose most recent publications include articles in the September 1994 and 1996 issues of _America's Civil War_, the June 1995 issue of _True West_, and the Autumn 1995 issue of _Persimmon Hill_, a publication of the National Cowboy Hall of Fame. I also have pieces appearing in forthcoming issues of _Florida Living and Military History_.

Thanks for your consideration. I look forward to hearing from you on this matter.

Sincerely,

Floyd Katkin

I know right up front that this article will fall within our word count requirements.

I might recommend putting sentence about responding via the SASE toward the end of the query, though it doesn't really bother me here.

Opening paragraph is straightforward and to the point. There are no details that I don't need since the manuscript is included (as specified in our writer's guidelines.) Also the author doesn't waste time telling me how much kids will enjoy reading his article.

I feel more comfortable with the reliability of the factual content of the article because the author has told me that he works in a related field.

The ending is polite and business-like; I like that.

Because the author lists his "most recent publications," I get the impression he has had success over a period of time, and is actively writing and being published at the present time.

The author has also told me that he has been published in other history-oriented publications. Again, my comfort level with the accuracy of the work is increased.

The only thing that should probably be added would be the author's name, address, tel. number, and the date at the top of the letter (though this was included on the manuscript.) Based on his query letter and the accompanying manuscript, this author received a "hold" letter explaining that we wanted to keep the piece for possible publication in a future issue.

Comments provided by Jeff Ayers, editor of _U*S* Kids_.

(Good)

Tess Mallory
P.O. Box 2170
Happy, Texas 78029

Heidi Kilgras
Random House
Books for Young Readers
201 E. 50th St.
New York, NY 10022

October 16, 1997

since this is a children's book submission, it may have been better to state this first, but ok. More relevant.

(Dear Ms. Kilgras,) — *Good*

I am a *(published author)* whose previous works include two time-travel romances, JEWELS OF TIME and CIRCLES IN TIME, one fantasy romance, ''The Fairy Bride'' for MIDSUMMER NIGHT'S MAGIC, an anthology, and one futuristic romance, TO TOUCH THE STARS, all for Leisure/Lovespell Books. *(My credits also include fiction published in Highlights for Children.)*

Great. Target audience is identified right away.

(Enclosed is a brief synopsis detailing a proposed science fiction book series, called MIND WARRIORS, for children ages 8 to 12.) This idea has been formulated with the best possible source of input for such a project—my ten year old son, Jordan. He's my writing ''pardner,'' in as much as he has helped flesh out the characters and ideas for Mind Warriors and will continue to contribute to this series, hence the pseudonym which speaks for us both: J.C. Mallory.

This person clearly knows about book lengths and this information is helpful.

(The series would consist, initially, of 7 books, each about 20,000 to 25,000 words) written from the viewpoint of one of the Mind Warriors, including their pets, Galileo the dog, and Streak the cat. Future books, if the series attains the popularity I think possible, could feature the viewpoint of other characters, such as the good aliens who help the Mind Warriors battle the evil Mindbenders. Actually, the possibilities for new books from new viewpoints are limitless as the Mind Warriors' adventures lead them to make new friends—and new enemies.

Overall series vision is stated clearly (and not overzealously).

MIND WARRIORS will take 8 to 12 year olds on a journey not only into a fantasy of what might lie within our own world and universe, but on a journey inside themselves. Each character in the series will be placed in unusual situations and consequently be forced to deal with problems which will cause each one to draw upon his or her own individual strength, character, and sense of honor. Each character in MIND WARRIORS will also face regular, ''kid'' problems, and realize that it is possible to find the ''hero'' or ''heroine'' within themselves.

Good. Just enough to whet the appetite. There's nothing worse than being overwhelmed by 80 pages of outlines, proposals, plot treatments, sample chapters, etc. It's not an efficient use of my time to have to slog through all that to see if the idea is at all interesting and whether the writer can actually write real narrative prose!

(With science-fiction continuing to soar in popularity, particularly in children's books) for this age group, I believe this series could be a terrific success. I hope you enjoy the synopsis and other material enclosed. If you want to receive the first three chapters of the first book in the series, MIND WARRIORS: *THE BEGINNING*, I would be happy to send them to you. Thank you for your time.

Sincerely,

she is correct! she's done her research.

Tess Mallory (with Jordan Mallory)
aka J.C. Mallory

Comments provided by Heidi Kilgras, editor at Random House.

to Write Attention-Grabbing Query & Cover Letters, by John Wood (Writer's Digest Books).

- **Query letters for nonfiction.** Queries are usually required when submitting nonfiction material to a publisher. The goal of a nonfiction query is to convince the editor your idea is perfect for her readership and that you're qualified to do the job. Note any previous writing experience and include published samples to prove your credentials, especially samples related to the subject matter you're querying about.
- **Query letters for fiction.** More and more, queries are being requested for fiction manuscripts. For a fiction query, explain the story's plot, main characters, conflict and resolution. Just as in nonfiction queries, make the editor eager to see more.
- **Cover letters for writers.** Some editors prefer to review complete manuscripts, especially for fiction. In such cases, the cover letter (which should be no longer than one page) serves as your introduction, establishes your credentials as a writer, and gives the editor an overview of the manuscript. If the editor asked for the manuscript because of a query, note this in your cover letter.
- **Cover letters for illustrators and photographers.** For an illustrator or photographer the cover letter serves as an introduction to the art director and establishes professional credentials when submitting samples. Explain what services you can provide as well as what type of follow-up contact you plan to make, if any.
- **Résumés.** Often writers, illustrators and photographers are asked to submit résumés with cover letters and samples. They can be created in a variety of formats, from a single page listing information, to color brochures featuring your work. Keep your resume brief, and focus on your achievements, including your clients and the work you've done for them, as well as your educational background and any awards you've received. Do not use the same résumé you'd use for a typical job application.
- **Book proposals.** Throughout the listings in the Book Publishers section, publishers refer to submitting a synopsis, outline and sample chapters. Depending on an editor's preference, some or all of these components, along with a cover letter, make up a book proposal.

A *synopsis* summarizes the book, covering the basic plot (including the ending). It should be easy to read and flow well.

An *outline* covers your book chapter by chapter and provides highlights of each. If you're developing an outline for fiction, include major characters, plots and subplots, and book length.

Sample chapters give a more comprehensive idea of your writing skill. Some editors may request the first two or three chapters to see how your material is set up. Find out what the editor wants before writing or revising sample chapters.

Manuscript formats

When submitting a complete manuscript, follow some basic guidelines. In the upper-left corner of your title page, type your legal name (not pseudonym), address and phone number. In the upper-right corner, type the approximate word length. All material in the upper corners should be typed single-spaced. Then type the title (centered) almost halfway down that page, the word "by" two spaces under that, and your name or pseudonym two spaces under "by."

The first page should also include the title (centered) one-third of the way down. Two spaces under that type "by" and your name or pseudonym. To begin the body of your manuscript, drop down two double spaces and indent five spaces for each new paragraph. There should be one-inch margins around all sides of a full typewritten page. (Manuscripts with wide margins are more readable and easier to edit.)

Set your computer or typewriter on double-space for the manuscript body. From page two to the end of the manuscript, include your last name followed by a comma and the title (or key words of the title) in the upper-left corner. The page number should go in the top right corner. Drop down two double spaces to begin the body of each page. If you're submitting a novel, type each chapter title one-third of the way down the page. For more information on manuscript formats, read *Writer's Digest Guide to Manuscript Formats*, by Dian Buchman and Seli Groves, or *Manuscript Submissions*, by Scott Edelstein (both Writer's Digest Books).

Picture book formats

The majority of editors prefer to see complete manuscripts for picture books. When typing the text of a picture book, don't include page breaks. And unless you are an illustrator, don't worry about supplying art. Editors will find their own illustrators for picture books. Most of the time, a writer and an illustrator who work on the same book never meet. The editor acts as a go-between in case either the writer or illustrator has any problems. *How to Write and Sell Children's Picture Books*, by Jean E. Karl (Writer's Digest Books), offers advice on preparing text and marketing your work.

If you're an illustrator who has written your own book, create a dummy or storyboard containing both art and text. Then submit it along with your complete manuscript and sample pieces of final art (color photocopies or slides—never originals). Publishers interested in picture books specify in their listings what should be submitted. For a step-by-step guide on creating a good dummy, see to How to Make a Smart Dummy on page 18. Also refer to *How to Write and Illustrate Children's Books and Get Them Published*, edited by Treld Pelkey Bicknell and Felicity Trotman (North Light Books), or Frieda Gates's book, *How to Write, Illustrate, and Design Children's Books* (Lloyd-Simone Publishing Company).

Writers may also want to learn the art of dummy making to help them through their writing process with things like pacing, rhythm and length. For a great explanation and helpful hints, see *You Can Write Children's Books*, by Tracey Dils (Writer's Digest Books).

Mailing submissions

Your main concern when packaging material is to be sure it arrives undamaged. If your manuscript is less than six pages, simply fold it in thirds and send it in a #10 (business-size) envelope. For a SASE, either fold another #10 envelope in thirds or insert a #9 (reply) envelope which fits in a #10 neatly without folding.

Another option is folding your manuscript in half in a 6×9 envelope, with a #9 or #10 SASE enclosed. For larger manuscripts use a 9×12 envelope both for mailing the submission and as a SASE (which can be folded in half). Book manuscripts require sturdy packaging for mailing. Include a self-addressed mailing label and return postage.

If asked to send artwork and photographs, remember they require a bit more care in packaging to guarantee they arrive in good condition. Sandwich illustrations and photos between heavy cardboard that is slightly larger than the work. The cardboard can be secured by rubber bands or with tape. If you tape the cardboard together, check that the artwork doesn't stick to the tape. Be sure your name and address appear on the back of each piece of art or each photo in case the material becomes separated. For the packaging use either a manila envelope, foam-padded envelope, brown paper or a mailer lined with plastic air bubbles. Bind non-joined edges with reinforced mailing tape and affix a typed mailing label or clearly write your address.

Mailing material first class ensures quick delivery. Also, first-class mail is forwarded for one year if the addressee has moved, and can be returned if undeliverable. If you're concerned about your original material safely reaching its destination, consider other mailing options, such as UPS or certified mail. If material needs to reach your editor or art director quickly, use overnight delivery services.

Remember, companies outside your own country can't use your country's postage when returning a manuscript to you. When mailing a submission to another country, include a self-addressed envelope and International Reply Coupons or IRCs. (You'll see this term in many Canadian listings.) Your postmaster can tell you, based on a package's weight, the correct number of IRCs to include to ensure its return.

If it's not necessary for an editor to return your work (such as with photocopies) don't include return postage. You may want to track the status of your submission by enclosing a postage-paid reply postcard with options for the editor to check, such as "Yes, I am interested," "I'll keep the material on file," or "No, the material is not appropriate for my needs at this time."

Some writers, illustrators and photographers simply include a deadline date. If you don't hear from the editor or art director by the specified date, your manuscript, artwork or photos are automatically withdrawn from consideration. Because many publishing houses and companies are overstocked with material, a minimum deadline should be at least three months.

Unless requested, it's never a good idea to use a company's fax number or e-mail address to send manuscript submissions. This can disrupt a company's internal business.

Keeping submission records

It's important to keep track of the material you submit. When recording each submission, include the date it was sent, the business and contact name, and any enclosures (such as samples of writing, artwork or photography). You can create a record-keeping system of your own or look for record-keeping software in your area computer store. The 1999 *Writer's Market: The Electronic Edition* CD-ROM features a submission tracker that can be copied to your hard drive.

Keep copies of articles or manuscripts you send together with related correspondence to make follow-up easier. When you sell rights to a manuscript, artwork or photos you can "close" your file on a particular submission by noting the date the material was accepted, what rights were purchased, the publication date and payment.

Often writers, illustrators and photographers fail to follow up on overdue responses. If you don't hear from a publisher within their stated response time, wait another month or so and follow up with a note asking about the status of your submission. Include the title or description, date sent, and a SASE for response. Ask the contact person when she anticipates making a decision. You may refresh the memory of a buyer who temporarily forgot about your submission. At the very least you'll receive a definite "no," and free yourself to send the material to another publisher.

Simultaneous submissions

If you opt for simultaneous (also called "multiple") submissions—sending the same material to several editors at the same time—be sure to inform each editor your work is being considered elsewhere. Many editors are reluctant to receive simultaneous submissions but understand that for hopeful freelancers, waiting several months for a response can be frustrating. In some cases, an editor may actually be more inclined to read your manuscript sooner if she knows it's being considered by another publisher. The Society of Children's Book Writers and Illustrators cautions writers against simultaneous submissions. The official recommendation of SCBWI is to submit to one publisher at a time, but wait only three months (note you'll do so in your cover letter). If no response is received, then send a note withdrawing your manuscript from consideration. SCBWI considers simultaneous submissions acceptable only if you have a manuscript dealing with a timely issue.

It's especially important to keep track of simultaneous submissions, so if you get an offer on a manuscript sent to more than one publisher, you can instruct other publishers to withdraw your work from consideration.

AGENTS AND REPS

Most children's writers, illustrators and photographers, especially those just beginning, are confused about whether to enlist the services of an agent or representative. The decision is strictly one that each writer, illustrator or photographer must make for herself. Some are confident with their own negotiation skills and believe acquiring an agent or rep is not in their best interest. Others feel uncomfortable in the business arena or are not willing to sacrifice valuable creative time for marketing.

About half of children's publishers accept unagented work, so it's possible to break into children's publishing without an agent. Some agents avoid working with children's books because traditionally low advances and trickling royalty payments over long periods of time make children's books less lucrative. Writers targeting magazine markets don't need the services of an agent. In fact, it's practically impossible to find an agent interested in marketing articles and short stories—there simply isn't enough financial incentive.

One benefit of having an agent, though, is it may speed up the process of getting your work reviewed, especially by publishers who don't accept unagented submissions. If an agent has a good reputation and submits your manuscript to an editor, that manuscript may actually bypass the first-read stage (which is done by editorial assistants and junior editors) and end up on the editor's desk sooner.

When agreeing to have a reputable agent represent you, remember that she should be familiar with the needs of the current market and evaluate your manuscript/artwork/photos accordingly. She should also determine the quality of your piece and whether it is saleable. When your manuscript sells, your agent should negotiate a favorable contract and clear up any questions you have about payments.

Keep in mind that however reputable the agent or rep is, she has limitations. Representation does not guarantee sale of your work. It just means an agent or rep sees potential in your writing, art or photos. Though an agent or rep may offer criticism or advice on how to improve your work, she cannot make you a better writer, artist or photographer.

Literary agents typically charge a 15 percent commission from the sale of writing; art and photo representatives usually charge a 25 to 30 percent commission. Such fees are taken from advances and royalty earnings. If your agent sells foreign rights to your work, she will deduct a higher percentage because she will most likely be dealing with an overseas agent with whom she must split the fee.

Be advised that not every agent is open to representing a writer, artist or photographer who lacks an established track record. Just as when approaching a publisher, the manuscript, artwork or photos, and query or cover letter you submit to a potential agent must be attractive and professional looking. Your first impression must be as an organized, articulate person.

For a detailed directory of literary agents, refer to *Guide to Literary Agents*; for listings of art reps, consult *Artist's & Graphic Designer's Market*; and for photo reps, see *Photographer's Market* (all Writer's Digest Books).

For Illustrators: What Should I Submit?

BY MARY COX

Your success as an illustrator can depend largely on the quality of your promotional material. Each week, busy art directors receive hundreds of promotional mailings from illustrators who have just a few seconds to impress them. There are a number of choices when it comes to submitting material to children's publishers and magazines. Many freelance illustrators send a cover letter and one or two samples in initial mailings. Others prefer a simple postcard showing their illustrations. Here are a few of your options:

Postcard. Choose one (or more) of your illustrations that is representative of your style, then have the image printed on postcards. Have your name, address and phone number printed on the front of the postcard, or in the return address corner. Somewhere on the card should be printed the word "Illustrator." If you use one or two colors you can keep the cost below $200. Art directors like postcards because they are easy to file or tack on a bulletin board. If the art director likes what she sees, she can always call you for more samples.

Promotional sheet. If you want to show more of your work, you can opt for an 8½×11 color or black and white photocopy of your work.

Tearsheets. After you complete assignments, acquire copies of any printed pages on which your illustrations appear. (Ask the art director if you can have some printed copies, called tearsheets, of the published work. Usually, art directors can arrange for extra copies—you might even negotiate for extra tearsheets as part of your fee if the publisher is on a tight budget.) Tearsheets impress art directors because they are proof that you are experienced and have met deadlines on previous projects.

Photographs and slides. Some illustrators have been successful sending photographs or slides, but printed or photocopied samples are preferred by most art directors.

Query or cover letter. A query letter is a nice way to introduce yourself to an art director for the first time. One or two paragraphs stating you are available for freelance work is all you need. Include your phone number, samples or tearsheets. If you send 8½×11 photocopies or tearsheets, do not fold them in thirds. It is more professional to send them flat, not folded, in a 9×12 envelope, along with a typed query letter, preferably on your own professional stationery.

To see a few examples of simple yet effective promo pieces, see pages 15-17.

ARE PORTFOLIOS NECESSARY?

You do not need to send a portfolio when you first contact a publisher. But after buyers see your samples they may want to see more, so have a portfolio ready to show. Many successful illustrators started their careers by making appointments to show their portfolios. But it is often enough for art directors to see your samples.

Some publishers have drop-off policies, accepting portfolios one or two days a week. You will not be present for the review and can pick up the work a few days later, after they've had

MARY COX *is editor of* Artist's & Graphic Designer's Market, *published annually by Writer's Digest Books, which includes listings for publishers, magazines, galleries, greeting card companies and more. She can be reached by e-mail at artdesign@fwpubs.com.*

a chance to look at it. Most companies are honorable and you don't have to worry about your case being stolen. However, since things do get lost, include only good-quality duplicates—only show originals when you can be present for the review. Label your portfolio with your name, address and phone number.

WHAT SHOULD I INCLUDE IN MY PORTFOLIO?

The overall appearance of your portfolio affects your professional presentation. Your portfolio need not be made of high-grade leather to leave a good impression. Neatness and careful organization are essential, whether you are using a three-ring binder or a leather case. The most popular portfolios are simulated leather with puncture-proof sides that allow the inclusion of loose samples. Choose a size that can be handled easily. Avoid the large "student"-size books which are too big and bulky to fit easily on an art director's desk. Most artists choose 11×14 or 18×24.

Don't include everything you've done in your portfolio—select only your best work. In reviewing portfolios, art directors at children's publishers are often interested in seeing characters in different scenes from different angles, children, people of different ethnicities and animals. They also look for consistency of style and skill.

When presenting your portfolio, allow your work to speak for itself. It's best to keep explanations to a minimum and be available for questions if asked. Prepare for the review by taking along notes on each piece. If the art director asks a question, take the opportunity to talk a little bit about the piece in question. Don't ever walk out of a portfolio review without leaving the art director a business card or sample to remember you by. A few weeks after your review, follow up by sending a small promo postcard or other sample as a reminder.

For more information, see *The Ultimate Portfolio*, by Martha Metzdorf (North Light Books) and *Writing with Pictures*, by Uri Shulevitz (Watson-Guptill Publications).

SELF-PROMOTION STRATEGIES

Self-promotion is an ongoing process of building name recognition and reputation by introducing yourself to new clients and reminding past clients you are still available. Experts suggest artists spend about one-third of each week and up to ten percent of their gross income on self-promotion. Whether you decide to invest this much time is up to you, but it is important to build time into your schedule for promotional activities. It's a good idea to supplement your mailings with other forms of self-promotion. Consider some of these options:

Talent directories. Many illustrators buy pages in illustration annuals such as *Picturebook*, *Black Book* and *The American Showcase*. These go to thousands of art directors and many keep their directories up to five years. A page in one of these directories can run from $2,000 to $3,500 and you have no control over who receives them. Yet some artists who buy pages claim they make several times the amount they spend. One bonus to these directories is they provide you with up to 2,000 loose pages, depending on the book, to use as samples.

Media relations. The media is always looking for good public interest stories. If you've done something unique with your work, send a press release to magazines, newspapers and radio stations. This exposure is free and will increase public awareness of you and your work.

Networking. Attending conferences, seminars, organization meetings and trade shows is a good way to get your name out. It doesn't hurt to keep business cards on hand. Volunteering to work on committees gives you an even better opportunity to make contacts. For networking tips, see Only Connect: A Beginner's Guide to Networking on page 53.

Contests. Even if you don't win, contests provide good exposure. Judges of illustration contests are usually art directors and editors who may need work in the future. See the Contests & Awards section for listings of competitions that might interest you.

James Bret Blevins
Illustrator

2805 Frisco Peaks Dr.
Prescott, AZ 86301

520 776-4216
(Phone/Fax)

E-mail:
bblevins@primenet.com

James Bret Blevins's watercolor and pencil piece featuring a tiny family on a flying chair is unpublished and created especially for this promotional postcard and to display at the 1998 SCBWI National Conference. "I had 500 6 × 14¼ cards printed for $95, plus tax and shipping. I'll mail out a different set of samples every four months or so," says Blevins, who has begun to pursue work in children's book illustration after making a living doing comic book pages (including Batman and Superman), narrative illustration, portraits and sculpture for 16 years. "If your work has passion and is realized with sufficient skill, it will do most of its own promotion. You can help it along best by taking the time and care to find editors and art directors likely to be in sympathy with your vision and target your work to them."

Illustrator Janie Bynum's promo postcards are actually Giclée fine art prints cut to postcard size. Bynum produced about 100 sets of 4 postcard images. The ballooning baboon is from her book *Altoona Baboona* (Harcourt Brace, 1999). "Laughing Pig" is an unpublished promo piece, "but he served as a springboard idea for a character I recently developed, wrote a book about, and signed with Harcourt." Bynum's marketing strategy consists of researching publishers through *Children's Writer's & Illustrator's Market*, and putting together a packet for the appropriate art directors or editors. "My packet includes these postcards and additional promo pieces. I put it all in a cast-coated pocket folder, affixing a label on the front with my name and a small four-color illustration printed from my Epson printer." See Bynum's portfolio at http://www.grafika.com.

Joy Allen's 8½ × 11 promotional flier "Tasty Morsels" was created with unpublished images. "It was my first promo. I ended up using it in *California Images* directory," she says. Allen had 2,000 copies of the piece printed, and later created a folder using published pieces to house her flier. "I send my flier inside my folder and am sending out postcards [postcard-size fine art Giclée prints] to show my new work. I try to send out promos about every three to four months." Allen advises illustrators to "keep sending new material to those who are interested and have put you in their files. Good color photocopies are fine. Remember that it often takes a while before a publisher will have something they feel is just right for your type of art—promos are a good way to jog their memory."

How to Make a Smart Dummy

BY KATIE DAVIS

So, you have a story you think would make a great picture book. You're an illustrator, too . . . or not. Either way, you have no idea how to submit your picture book to a publisher. Okay, you know where the post office is—you just can't figure out in what form to send the project. There is, however, an industry standard: It's called a dummy. For years I've been writing and illustrating stories—really bad ones. (There was the 7-page book I made for my brother's 22nd birthday. And the epic illustrated limerick for Mother's Day my mom pulled out of her scrapbook when she heard I was writing this article.)

I had some "real" stories too, and even had some paintings to go along with them, but instinctively I felt an obstacle blocking my path. I thought they looked too unprofessional, even though I put my manuscript in a snappy little folder, with a couple of color copies of the art stuck in back. There was something specific I sensed I didn't know, and not knowing stopped me cold.

Then in August 1996, I found out about The Society of Children's Book Writers and Illustrators (SCBWI) and their annual conference. I signed up and headed over. Walking into the conference, I felt I had come home. I made invaluable contacts and friends, including an incredibly bright group of people who invited me into their critique group.

I also discovered the secret that had alluded me (drum roll, please) . . . the dummy. The dummy is a mock-up of a book. Dummies can be crucial when submitting a picture book to a publisher. You want an editor to read your story with all the drama and suspense, set-up and punch line that is revealed through rhythm and pacing—and you get that with the page turn.

Even if you aren't an illustrator and you're submitting text only, a manuscript might read better in dummy form. My editor told me reading from a dummy sometimes helps her evaluate a picture book manuscript because it can slow her down when she's reading it. They don't necessarily expect it from a writer, but it can help. Now you may be thinking, "But how will they know which illustrations should go with my text?" These editors are experts. Trust that. If, however, your text reads, "He was a normal boy," and you want an illustration of an alien child, make a note so the editor is aware of the intended irony.

Finding out about dummies was like being given "the key." It made all my ideas flood forth onto the pages. When I saw my stories in book form, I could see what worked—and what didn't. Some things I thought were hysterically funny were about as funny as a rock when I saw them in book format.

After the conference, I got to work. In about six months, a literary agent heard about one of my stories from a mutual friend (whom I met at the conference), and after seeing my dummies, he signed me! Obviously, it wasn't my beautiful dummies that got me signed, but a good presentation that looks professional can only help the cause.

Over the last few years I've collected some very smart dummy constructing methods from

KATIE DAVIS's first book Who Hops? was published by Harcourt Brace. A member of the Society of Children's Book Writers and Illustrators, she was a presenter at the organization's 1998 national conference along with her agent and editor. Davis, a native New Yorker, lives in Southern California with her husband and two children, whose car-seat-diversion game inspired Who Hops?. Visit her webpage at http://www.ber genstein.com/SCBWI/kdavis/davis.html.

some very talented people. This is basic stuff, but it may help make your picture book dummy stand out from the rest. It'll last longer if it needs to be sent and re-sent to many editors, if it's passed around a lot within a company or, the best reason, if an editor buys it, it'll last the year(s!) she works on it.

The first stage is making what I call the "skeleton." This is a mock-up book into which you will be gluing your story. I use white card stock and cardboard. You can buy posterboard and cut it to size, or go to your local office supply and get actual card stock. What you use will depend on the size of your dummy. The size you choose should be within the industry standards. To learn what those are, go to a bookstore and check out what's selling. Just remember, you want your dummy to look and feel as close to a real book as possible, without it being too finished—you don't want a prospective editor to think you're married to the thing; a dummy is simply a blueprint for the book it will become.

I write my books on computer, scan in rough sketches, and bring everything into Quark, a page layout program especially suited to book production. I then print out each page of my book so it looks clean—with the illustration and text on one page.

If you don't work on a computer, type out your text, cut it out and paste it onto the appropriate pages. You can do the sketches directly on those pages or make copies of the text pages, do sketches and then photocopy the whole thing. Make another photocopy of that and use it to make the dummy. You definitely should not be working with your original—mistakes will and do happen!

I like to do one finished piece of art, or at least something close to finished. And most editors/ art directors like to see that. I prefer doing the cover as my color piece because to me it announces, "Ta-da! Here is Katie's book!" and also, it may make mine stand out from the rest. (And though I'm sure you thought of this on your own, make a color copy of your art and use that in your dummy—*not your original*!) Depending on the story, I might also choose to paint the last spread, but no more than that.

The average picture book is 32 pages, including what is called front matter. Incorporate the front matter, which is the copyright/dedication and title pages, in your dummy. You want it to read like a real book and front matter will enhance that effect. If you're designing end papers (the very first and very last pages in the book), include those as well. Check out your favorite picture books for examples of front matter and end papers.

KATIE'S RECIPE FOR MAKING A SMART DUMMY

Ingredients:
- cardboard that's white on both sides (enough for your front and back cover)
- poster board or card stock (enough for your pages of text)
- big fat nails
- white embroidery thread
- embroidery needle
- white duct tape
- spray adhesive
- ruler
- sharp cutting blade of some sort
- binder clips
- old newspapers
- removable scotch tape (optional)
- a scrap piece of wood (also optional)
- a pinch of oregano (only kidding)

First-time author/illustrator Katie Davis's dummy for her book *Who Hops?* (pictured left) held up well as her agent shopped it around and later as her editor at Harcourt Brace referred to it throughout the year-long editing process. The final cover of *Who Hops?* is pictured right. *Kirkus Reviews* calls Davis's debut "a sharp introduction to the animal world" asking young readers which animals hop, fly, slither, swim and crawl, "with each section suggesting three of the usual suspects, and one odd man out: anteaters swim? giraffes crawl?," encouraging kids to shout along with the book, "NO THEY DON'T!"

Try your best to adhere to the 32-page count. Sometimes, if a book is absolutely fabulous and you positively *must* have 34 or 36 or even 40 pages to make it work, an editor will see that, but these are exceptions.

Step 1: Gather poster board or card stock for your dummy pages and two separate pieces of white (on both sides) cardboard to serve as your covers. Make the covers slightly larger than the pages (this protects the pages better). Stack the pages between the cover pieces.

Step 2: Flip the top cover over. Using a ruler as a guide, score the inside of the cover with a blade. Do this about an inch from the outer edge of the spine. This enables the book to lay flat when the pages are being turned. Do the same to the back cover.

Step 3: Tap everything, spine down, against your work surface to make both the pages and the covers flush at the spine. Secure them with a few big black binder clips.

Step 4: Take about six fat nails (this is the technical name, I'm pretty sure) and hammer them about one-half-inch in from the outer edge of the spine. These holes will accommodate the thread you'll use to bind the book—you'll get really sore fingers is you try to sew a book without pre-punched holes. Tip: Hammer into a board and leave the nails in until you've make all your holes to hold the pages together while you're banging.

Step 5: Take out nails, and take off clips.

Step 6: Thread a big embroidery needle with white embroidery thread. This is very strong thread. (I've heard of people using dental floss, but in my experience, it breaks a lot, so I'd stick with embroidery thread.) Sew the heck out of the thing. I usually do three times up and back with different stitches.

Step 7: Using a single piece of white duct tape, cover the thread and the spine.

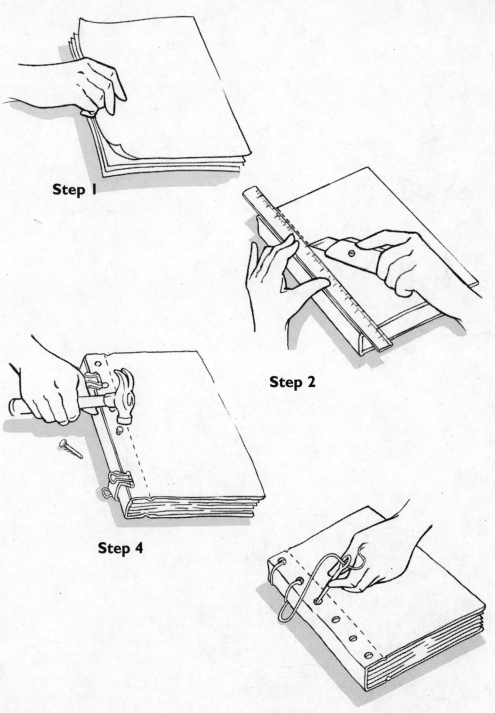

Step 1

Step 2

Step 4

Step 6

Step 7

Step 8

Step 9

Step 10

Step 8: Trim the computer layout pages or copies of pasted-up pages of your book so they'll easily fit on the blank dummy pages you've created. After trimming, slip them into the appropriate corresponding pages of the skeleton (where they will soon be glued down). I hate doing this, but I've made enough mistakes to know it's a worthwhile step in case you forget a page or mispaginate. You may want to use removable tape for this step to keep the pages in place. At this stage, go through the book and read it aloud to make sure it's all correctly placed.

Step 9: Spread out a bunch of newspaper and take out the first six pages of your book, placing them face down (in the correct and same order every time). Spray them all with spray adhesive—this saves time, and the more pages you spray at once, the less mess you make. I prefer Super 77 spray glue . . .the permanent stuff. Moveable glue is a hassle because pages start peeling up after a short while.

Step 10: Take your first page and place it in the skeleton. Continue, one by one, placing each page in ascending order. Then, finally, glue on the front and back covers. This is my own preferred method. There are certainly many other ways to do it including folding 16 sheets in half, or gluing the pages accordion style. I know a guy who submitted a photocopy of his book in storyboard form and got published. It was a great story and very well written.

Of course, the key is not the dummy, but the story within. No matter how gorgeous your dummy is, it won't sell a badly written or inappropriate story. Whatever method you use, remember what they said in first grade . . .neatness counts. Experiment with different methods or ask other illustrators how they put their dummies together—but make it neat and make it strong. Present a great dummy showcasing your terrific, irresistible, Caldecott-worthy, potential bestseller, and you should have it published in no time!

First Books

BY ALICE POPE

Childhood is filled with "firsts"—your first step, your first day of school, the first time you rode your bike without training wheels. Your first kiss . . . can't you remember that fluttery feeling in your stomach, the excitement and the apprehension, the joy and the nervousness?

Adults have firsts, too. The four authors and one illustrator featured here have fresh memories of an important first for each of them—their first published book. Their stories are all a bit different, but they offer much of the same advice—love the process, have support of peers, and be eager to revise. Thank goodness for all of them, their publishing experiences went much better than my first kiss did (but I'm sure they all had at least a few butterflies). Here are their stories.

PATRICK JENNINGS
Faith and the Electric Dogs (Scholastic Inc.)

"*Faith and the Electric Dogs* was my first book and my first book published," says author Patrick Jennings. Set in Mexico and starring a transplanted American girl and her newly adopted stray dog, Edison (the narrator), *Faith* is a middle reader fantasy featuring communicating canine characters, and a trip in a homemade rocket ship to a bone-shaped island. "Neil Armstrong stepped down onto the moon when I was in second grade. When the principal announced it over the intercom, a feeling of excitement overcame me that I have never forgotten. Ever since then, rockets have loomed large in my imagination," says Jennings.

Faith also provides definitions of Spanish words and phrases used throughout the story, as well as translations of Edison's thoughts in his dog language called Bowwow. (The Mexican expression *un perro corriente* or *electric dog* refers to a mutt.)

Jennings, who in college studied literature, photography, cinema and early childhood education, among other things, was always interested in writing, but got the call to write for children when he began his first teaching job. "The first class I taught—a motley crew of preschoolers—were ravenous for books. I mean that both figuratively and literally," he says. "Many of our books had tooth imprints in them; some had entire bites taken out of them. I had never witnessed such sincere and unbridled book-love before."

As Jennings read his little students books by Maurice Sendak, William Steig, Margaret Wise Brown and Kevin Henkes, he says, "I realized what, and to whom, I wished to be writing. For kids, anything can happen between the covers of a book because, to them, anything can happen outside the covers of the books. The day is a blank page."

He got the initial idea for a story about "a dog, his master and a rocketship" in 1991. When he lived in Mexico in 1993, "where the dog became electric—and, consequently, Edison," Jennings decided to put it down on paper. He returned to Bisbee, Arizona, and worked on a rough draft for about a month, and showed it to a writer friend who helped him "whip it into shape" over the next year.

"I've moved around a bit, and I'm sure that influenced Faith's story. I understand how it

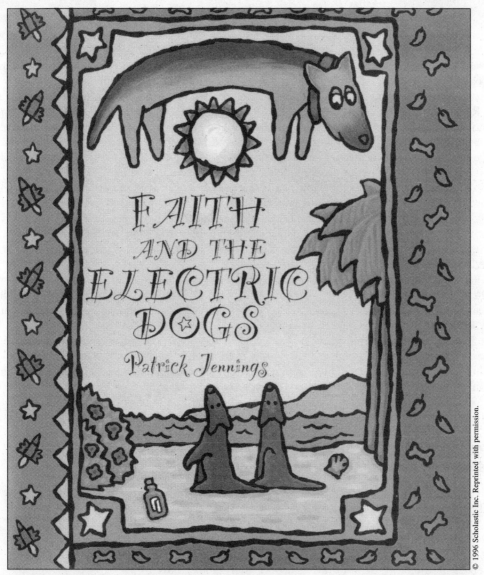

Patrick Jennings's first book *Faith and the Electric Dogs* (Scholastic Press) is a middle reader fantasy set in Mexico featuring dogs who communicate in Bowwow (their own language), and a journey on a homemade rocket ship to a bone-shaped island. As he wrote, Jennings felt very close to his characters, Edison (the dog narrator) and Faith (Edison's master). "The challenge when writing is to be empathetic to your characters enough to be able to fill not only their mouths with words, but their thoughts as well," he says. "Once you begin to understand their interior worlds, they will speak to you. Then all you have to do is scribble it down."

feels to be suddenly transplanted into a new environment, and how difficult it can be to adjust," says Jennings. "Let it be known for the record, however, that I never fled any of those situations in a rocket ship."

Referring to *Children's Writer's & Illustrator's Market* and several books on manuscript submission, Jennings began sending the manuscript for *Faith* to publishers. "One of the books suggested keeping a chart noting to which publishers copies of the manuscript had been sent, and pragmatically, on what date the rejection slips had been received. I made a chart, I chose ten publishers. I readied three copies of my manuscript for mailing and wrote cover letters."

At the same time, Jennings says, his writer friend suggested he mail a copy to an agent she knew. "The agent called me a week later, and said she liked the story and wanted to take it with her to New York. Another week passed, and she called to say Scholastic had expressed interest in the book. Before she was finished, two other houses were interested as well. I threw my chart away."

After his story was accepted, it went through only one revision before it went to galleys. "Regina Griffin, my editor at Scholastic, offered comments that were both sensitive and constructive. The revision helped the story immeasurably." After its release in 1996, *Faith* received starred reviews in *Publishers Weekly*, *Booklist* and *Kirkus Reviews*. Jennings received an offer from Scholastic for the sequel he was writing—*Faith and the Rocket Cat* was published in August 1998. He's currently working on another novel and a picture book.

"The best part about being published is that the story that lived in your head, the one you felt so sure children would like, actually finds its way into their hands," says Jennings." I've received many letters from readers and met with groups of them on many occasions where I've been able to hear their impressions firsthand and undiluted. You know you're on the right track when a child not only has read your book all the way through, but also smiles when he or she tells you so."

Kids like animal stories in general, says Jennings, "because, one, they love animals, and two, they are animals. William Steig once said about his book *Dominic*—one of my favorite middle readers—that when you write about a dog, 'you're writing about a child, because a dog's mature when it's only a year old.' Ah to be young *and* grown up *and* four-legged!

"As for anthropomorphism and realistic plots and any other thing that get touted or trounced as salable or unsalable—people will always have a lot of ideas about what kinds of books children are reading or should be reading or don't like reading, and which kinds are fresh and which have been done to death. If you listen to these voices, you'll go mad. Just follow your story and stay true to it and to yourself. Then when you have a book in front of you that you like, send it off and hope for the best. In the meantime, start another one."

PATRICIA CURTIS PFITSCH
Keeper of the Light (Simon & Schuster)

"I'd been writing novels and trying the get them published for about 11 years when I got my first acceptance. I'm a great example of the lesson that persistence does finally pay off," says author Patricia Curtis Pfitsch.

Her first published book, *Keeper of the Light*, was actually accepted by Simon & Schuster a few weeks after another novel, *The Deeper Song*, but *Keeper* was released first. After years of submitting on her own, Pfitsch's first sales came with the help of an agent.

"I first sent *Song* to Simon & Schuster on my own. The editor sent a wonderful letter telling me how much he liked the book, but that others in the department weren't so sure, so he had to turn it down," says Pfitsch. "I was very discouraged, but kept on sending it out and working on *Keeper*."

photo: George H. Curtis

After her brush with acceptance, a friend suggested Pfitsch submit her work to a new agent who had been an editor for many years. "I wrote him a letter asking if he'd consider looking at *The Deeper Song*, and I included the letter from Simon & Schuster about how much they'd liked the book—sometimes a rejection letter can help in an acceptance."

The agent was interested in seeing Pfitsch's work, but asked, "Do you have anything else—any other novels you've written?" She told him she had three more, "and I could hear by the

Patricia Curtis Pfitsch's first published novel, *Keeper of the Light* (Simon & Schuster), set in the 1870s, tells the story of a strong young heroine, Faith, a lighthouse keeper. "Since I was a small child I have always wanted to live in an earlier century," says Pfitsch. "In fact, what I *really* wanted was to be Laura Ingalls Wilder. My favorite books when I was growing up were historical fiction and biographies." *Keeper* was well-received, making the *American Bookseller* Pick of the Lists and the 1998 Books for the Teen Age (a list compiled by the New York Public Library). The book also won the Friends of American Writers First Place Juvenile Award and was nominated for the American Library Association Best Books for Young Adults.

tone of his voice that information made him even more interested."

For Pfitsch this offers a lesson to writers: "Once you have a novel written and you begin to submit it, don't stop writing. Focus on marketing that book, of course, but start another project. When you find an editor or agent who's interested in your work, he's going to ask you, 'What else have you got?' You want to show him right off that you're a committed professional."

At a Society of Children's Book Writers and Illustrators conference, Pfitsch ran into the Simon & Schuster editor who had previously turned down *Song*. "He asked me about it, and told me that if I revised it, adding a subplot, he could look at it again. After some discussion between my agent and this editor, I rewrote the book, and S&S bought it. By this time, I'd finished *Keeper* and when my agent sent it to him, he bought it right away."

Keeper of the Light is set in 1872 on the upper peninsula of Michigan. Faith, the main character, is the daughter of a lighthouse keeper killed in a storm. She takes over the duties of keeping the light burning until she's replaced by a young man. Faith is a strong, determined heroine who isn't ready to trust the important lighthouse duties to a novice keeper.

For Pfitsch historical fiction is a passion. She loves history and she loves research. "I like writing about women who did significant things. We get so much information in school and in textbooks about what men did. In my fiction I like to give women some recognition."

Pfitsch got the idea for a story centered on a lighthouse as she visited Au Sable Point Lighthouse on Lake Superior. "I'd never even been close to a lighthouse before, but as soon as I saw it, I knew my novel was going to be set at a lighthouse like that one." She also stumbled upon a book called *Women Who Kept the Lights* at a gift shop. "I was on my way," she says.

" 'Keeping the lights burning' was almost a religion to many keepers, and they taught their spouses and children about how important it was. That's why many lighthouse keepers came from families who had kept the lights—they already had a strong sense of the importance of the job.

"While I was researching, I read part of a letter [written by lighthouse keeper Abby Burgess]. She talked about how anxious she felt whenever she was away from the lighthouse—she worried constantly about whether the lights were lit, and even dreamed about them," says Pfitsch. "It was that emotional response that really connected me with Faith—I knew that in my story, Faith would be taken away from the lighthouse. I knew how she would feel, and that she would be almost frantic to get back."

Pfitsch was fascinated by the research she did for *Keeper* and happy to have an excuse to spend hours on end in the library. "Though it's hard to stop researching, at some point I find the story that's building in my head becomes more compelling than the research, so I have to start writing. But I keep researching as I write, because I'm always running into things I don't know."

To balance her solitary time spent poring through books and clicking away at her keyboard, Pfitsch corresponds over e-mail with seven other writers. "We 'talk' at least once a day by copying our messages to everyone on the list. We're all member of SCBWI, but live in different parts of the country."

As she worked on her manuscript for *Keeper*, Pfitsch says her online group "helped me celebrate good writing days and empathized with bad ones. When my editor asked me to change the title, they all gave me suggestions. I e-mailed some people chapters for critique—that's a huge help and much faster than mail."

This constant contact with other writers is an essential part of Pfitsch's writing life. "You can sustain each other and learn from each other. If you're not in contact with writers, you might think you're the only one getting rejections."

Most important to Pfitsch is loving the process. "I got to the point where I was convinced I'd never sell a novel, and it was then I realized I wanted to keep on writing novels anyway. I couldn't imagine not writing."

RHONDA GOWLER GREENE
When a Line Bends . . . A Shape Begins (Houghton Mifflin)

For picture book author Rhonda Gowler Greene, rejection became an accepted part of her writing life, but didn't deter her from submitting her work. "In the fall of 1991, I bought my first *Children's Writer's & Illustrator's Market*, studied the list of children's book publishers, and began sending out picture book manuscripts," she says. "Over the next three and a half years, I circulated several stories simultaneously to different publishers. After receiving more than 200 rejections, I finally made my first sale the summer of 1995.

photo: Gary W. Greene

"The last year I was getting rejections, many of the letters I received had personal comments on them from editors saying they liked my writing. Many asked to see more of my work, and some were asking me to revise stories I had sent them. This made me keep submitting. I could tell I was getting close to selling something."

Greene's book *When a Line Bends . . . A Shape Begins* (which received a starred review in *Publishers Weekly*) was turned down 23 times—and went through several revisions—before it was finally accepted for publication by Houghton Mifflin. "It first began as a manuscript about things that are round. An editor from a major house called me about that manuscript, said she liked the idea and my writing, and asked if I could come up with poems for other shapes." Greene did as the editor requested, creating more concrete poems (poems typed in the shapes they are describing), sent them in and waited several months. The editor finally decided to pass on the project.

Greene began sending the revised version of *When a Line Bends* to other publishers and got

Picture book author Rhonda Gowler Greene's first title *When a Line Bends . . . A Shape Begins* teaches various shapes through a series of concrete poems. The book went through several revisions and was rejected 23 times before its publication by Houghton Mifflin. "I revised immediately when an editor asked me to. I persisted and kept submitting," says Greene. "I sent manuscripts simultaneously, which made the process go faster. And I did my homework—read all the how-to books and did what they said so I came across as a professional." Her third book, *The Stable Where Jesus Was Born*, will be published in Fall 1999. "All the manuscripts I've sold were pulled from the slush pile."

good comments from editors. "I got a basic form rejection from Houghton Mifflin, however."

In the meantime, another editor interested in her book asked Greene to add poems about even more shapes. "Each time an editor would ask for a major revision, I thought it sounded too difficult," Greene says. "But I would come up with something, which always made my manuscript stronger." She added poems for crescent, pentagon, hexagon, heptagon, octagon, semicircle and spiral. But again, the editor asking for revisions eventually turned down her manuscript.

"I didn't give up because I felt my manuscript was strong. I decided to try Houghton Mifflin again with my newest version and randomly chose a different editor there. Nearly two years after sending out my original version, the editor called and said she wanted to buy my manuscript. I still had to do significant revisions. The number of shapes was cut to ten."

A few weeks before she got the good news from Houghtom Mifflin, another of her manuscripts, *Barnyard Song*, was accepted by Atheneum. "I was so excited by both calls. The call from Houghton Mifflin was every bit as exciting, because I had worked harder on that manuscript [*Barnyard Song*, a *School Library Journal* Best Book of '97, had been rejected just six times before it sold], and I couldn't believe that, after trying so long, I sold two things to major houses within such a short time."

"Working with the two editors was a very similar experience. Both my editors were very good. They didn't tell me how to change something, but said what didn't work for them in the manuscripts and then pretty much left it up to me to come up with something better," says Greene. "I've read that editors not only look for authors who can write well, but ones who can revise. Since my manuscripts were in rhyme, they were especially difficult to revise, but they always became stronger after I had revised them."

Indeed, writing good rhyme can be difficult, but it's something Greene loves to do. "I love alliteration and trying to find the exact word to fit a story." She advises writers to study the best rhyme out there in children's poetry and picture books. (Some of her favorites children's poets are Karla Kuskin, Mary Ann Hoberman and Aileen Fisher.) She often types out the texts to get a feel for the writing.

"It's been said often that writing picture books is much like writing poetry. It takes tight, rhythmical writing. That doesn't always mean the writing is in rhyme. You can have rhythm to your writing without using rhyme. If you're a picture book writer, I think it's essential that you read your manuscripts aloud. Even better, have someone else read them aloud. Then you can hear what doesn't work or flow well."

For Greene, finally having stories published has been a learning experience. "The whole process is a very long one, even after signing the contract. It's a group project—author, illustrator, editor, copy editor, art director (maybe even more). And most of the time you never meet these people in person, but everyone has the same goal—to make the book the best it can be."

JAMES KACZMAN
When a Line Bends . . . A Shape Begins (Houghton Mifflin)

After 11 years as a freelance illustrator, James Kaczman got his first picture book project. "I had wanted to do one for a long time," he says. "I had brought my portfolio to publishers in New York and Boston, and I'd gotten calls and met with art directors at different publishers who liked my work. They basically said they had to wait for the right book to come along."

For Kaczman, the right book was *When a Line Bends . . . A Shape Begins*. "I did get an offer to work on another book first, but I read it and didn't think I was appropriate for it. *When a Line Bends* came up right after that. I really liked this book, and I thought it would be great for my style and a lot of fun to do."

As he got into doing the illustrations for *When a Line Bends*, Kaczman found that working on a picture book was quite different than the magazine and business assignments he was used to doing. "I hadn't done this many full-color illustrations. Planning and executing them was really different. Like good art directors on other projects, the art director gave me a lot of freedom, but steered me in certain directions."

Author Rhonda Gowler Greene's poems in *When a Line Bends* are about shapes. "A diamond sits upon a point./ Its four sides are the same./ A giant green one is the infield of a baseball game./ Yellow ones along the road serve as warning signs./ Black and white ones stand out bold in fancy floor designs./ Babies' gates are wooden ones that you can stretch or squeeze./ A ballerina's legs form one when bending at the knees."

This illustration by James Kaczman is half of a spread from his first book *When a Line Bends . . . A Shape Begins* featuring a poem about things that are square. "A square is four sides all the same—the boxes of a hopscotch game, a patch to cover up your knee, a present sent from you to me, a checkerboard of red and black, blocks to build with, share and stack./ A cracker is a square to eat./ A square dance is for happy feet." Kaczman faced the challenge of creating a number of scenes featuring an array of items named in author Rhonda Gowler Greene's poems.

Kaczman found presenting the elements of each poem in full-bleed two-page spreads a challenge. "There were so many different elements, I couldn't always redraw and move something. The only way I could work on all the different elements was to get a few large ones in place, then take drawings of the other ones and move then around like a puzzle, trying to fit them in different areas, and sometimes pulling out my hair. You know how puzzles are—sometimes really fun and sometimes frustrating."

Kaczman also found he had to draw images he'd never tried before. "I hadn't drawn a ballerina–it just wasn't something I'd worked out in my style before. I had to do a lot of drawings of that and make the legs not look deformed, but still have the diamond shape. That was really hard."

When the author received the unbound folded and gathered pages for *When a Line Bends*, she was very happy with the final product. "I didn't know James was going to draw some of the things in the book so tiny, almost like hidden pictures. The first week, I looked through the book each day and found something I hadn't seen the day before. I think his artwork enhances my text. I like the whimsicalness of his work—that was my intent with my verse—to give a sense of playfulness. I really feel James captured that in his art."

Although he currently doesn't have any picture book projects in the works, Kaczman would like to do more—and next time, he'd like to write the text as well. "I have a few ideas. I want to come up with 32 pictures I want to draw, so I'm in control—so I'm starting with the pictures. When you come up with an idea for a picture, there's kind of a story already going on, there's something happening."

Kaczman has two reps, one for publishing projects and one for his other illustration work. "There's so much involved. Just keeping up with all the art directors and creative directors is a big job—they're always changing. It's hard to keep an up-to-date mailing list. I wouldn't have thought giving up a percentage of my fees was worth it, until I saw how much reps do. They're doing a much better job than I ever could. What I'm good at is drawing pictures."

For illustrators starting out on their own, Kaczman says persistence is key. "Give it some time. It's really rare for a person to jump into illustration full-time and make a living. Talented people get discouraged and give up before they give it a fair shot. Some will make a living just because they stick to it. I didn't want to make a living doing anything else. I felt like I didn't have a choice."

LINDA R. RYMILL
Good Knight (Henry Holt)

"I approached writing much as I would any other area of my life. I sought education and set personal goals," says picture book author Linda R. Rymill, who submitted her first manuscript in 1989. "My first goal was to collect 286 rejections. And once I collected them, I'd re-address my goal. In the meantime, at least I would have written a lot and submitted; I would have made progress."

Rymill has yet to reach 286 rejections. Her first book *Good Knight* (which *Publishers Weekly* called "a well-observed story of a boy whose 'knightly' activities are interrupted by nightly rituals") was a manuscript in progress when Rymill read it at an SC-BWI conference open mike. "I hadn't planned to read *Good Knight*, but I thought my character might wake up the audience. He did. Simone Kaplan, then a Holt editor, approached me and requested I submit it to her for consideration. Two weeks (and an ending) later, I submitted it." And Henry Holt accepted it.

"The whole process was exciting and I loved it," Rymill says. "I had heard horror stories of how publishers keep authors and illustrators separate. They don't tell you anything. One day your book will show up, and, 'Here you go—hope you like it.' I never felt that way. I really felt included in the process."

Rymill expected her manuscript to be "returned with red lines and hieroglyphics all over the place. Instead, Simone called me, offered her input, and after a short chat, I rewrote the parts she felt weren't working.

"Written correspondence followed, a word here, a sentence there—and endless conversation about the title. Mid-book, Simone called; she had taken a position at HarperCollins and a letter from Holt soon arrived introducing my new editor. Margaret Garrou was as delightful as Simone. Holt was a pleasure to work with."

When all the revisions for *Good Knight* were completed and Rymill felt it was perfect, she

Linda R. Rymill's first book, *Good Knight* (Henry Holt), a rhyming picture book, stars a boy who isn't quite ready to abandon his playtime adventures for bedtime rituals. Rymill studies publishers catalogs and reads tons of books in her genre before submitting her work, and encourages other writers to do the same. "If every year you make an effort to read all the books in your genre you can, soon you'll have a handle on who might want what you write. And you will have learned more about your genre as well."

submitted it to Holt. "I got a letter weeks later from my editor saying they had gotten the final art from illustrator G. Brian Karas, and they felt, 'Your text doesn't seem to match the pictures in this one area.' I thought about it. The pictures were wonderful, and I rewrote the text on one page of my manuscript, and they were pleased with it. I think it works better—but that was a surprise."

When the process started, Rymill had been very interested in who would be hired to illustrate her manuscript. " 'Curious' would be such an understatement. When Simone told me, 'We're thinking about using Karas,' I rushed out and picked up every book he had illustrated, carting at least a dozen home from the library. I was pleased Holt shared the process with me. I remember seeing the first sketches and being so surprised. It took me three days to get used to the idea, and I've been in love with the illustrations ever since. Reviewers have agreed it was a good match. A picture book is true teamwork.

"I think that a lot of picture book authors feel it's 'my book,' but it's not. It's 'our book.' It's certainly the illustrator's as much as the writer's, and it's certainly a great deal the house's and the editor's."

Throughout *Good Knight* "Holt decided to play with and enlarge the type in some areas, and they sent it to me and asked what I thought of it. I thought about it for a couple days," says Rymill. "There were three or four places where I felt strongly they had enlarged the wrong words, and I wrote back and picked the points that were most important to me, and described why I felt there should be different words highlighted. They made every change I suggested.

"I think you have to pick. If you want to change everything, you're likely to not get anything. And if you can't explain why you want a change, then maybe your reason is not good. When you're forced to explain anything, you're forced to really think about it."

The text of *Good Knight* is rhyming. ("No./ You can't make me./ I don't want a bath I say./ I'm busy putting flames out./ I'm Fire Chief today.") When writing in rhyme, "you have to be honest with yourself, and not delighted that you can rhyme," says Rymill. "If you can write your story in prose using fewer words, do it. Ax every sentence—every word—that doesn't move the story. Ax any sentence with manipulated, awkward structure. Then if it still seems perfect—and still rhymes—submit it."

For Rymill, crafting the best story possible before submitting is essential. "I spend more time on craft than marketing. Without strong writing, even dynamite marketing is useless. Picture books have such pacing. Turning the page seems much like a pause in speech; it says a lot. Rewriting, honing, pruning is my favorite part of writing. In picture books, this seems especially crucial."

Participating in a writing network is also important to Rymill. She's the regional advisor for the Michigan Society of Children's Book Writers and Illustrators, and several years ago, through SCBWI contacts, formed a writing group which she calls "the best thing I ever did." Without a network of peers, Rymill says, "Writers are really handicapped. They're totally on their own. They're not going to have objective feedback that would make their road quicker. They're not going to have information that other people will willingly share with them. When you don't have support, when you don't have peers who are doing what you're doing, it's really easy to just quit—and you won't get there if you quit.

"Writers are a neat bunch. It's a great community. I've formed so many friendships and learned so much just from meeting other children's writers. You grow together, share frustration and delight. You love life; you love the simple things in life. You genuinely appreciate the face in a pansy, the coldness of a snowflake, the squish of sand under your feet.

"Unless you self- or vanity-publish, becoming an author is not within your control. Strive to be the best writer you can be. Recognize and take delight in your improvements. Enjoy the journey. Attaining 'authordom' is like eating dessert. Tastes scrumptious but it's not lasting nourishment."

First Books Follow-Up

BY ANNE BOWLING

For its sheer power to thrill, probably no event in a writer's or illustrator's career can compare with first publication. In the mailbox is the envelope—tearing it open you find the watermarked publisher's letterhead notifying you your work has been accepted. Or the phone rings unexpectedly on an otherwise ordinary day, and the editor you've contacted two—or was it three?—times is on the line with the good news. Regardless of the scenario, it's a defining moment, and once you have been published there's no turning back.

But what happens next? Will first publication be an isolated event, or can you parlay it into a long-term, satisfying career as a working children's author or illustrator? We decided to revisit six authors and illustrators featured in First Books in years past to check the pulse of their careers—and in each case we found that first publication was a prelude to second, third and fourth contracts. Here they generously shared the details of their progress for your inspiration and instruction. We'll continue to revisit one author per edition in future issues of *Children's Writer's & Illustrator's Market*.

ROB THOMAS, young adult novelist
First Books 1997

Rob Thomas lined up a publisher for his first book *Rats Saw God* on his own, unagented, despite its controversial content. Four or five publishing houses turned Thomas's book down before Simon & Schuster Books for Young Readers scooped it up and signed Thomas to write three more young adult novels.

That was 1996 and, as Thomas will attest, a lot can happen in three years. He followed publication of that first book with *Slave Day*, *Doing Time: Notes from the Undergrad* and *Satellite Down*. Both *Slave Day* and *Satellite Down* are being considered for motion pictures, and Thomas has moved on to writing for television. After his debut as a screenwriter for *Dawson's Creek*, he moved on to his own series, *Cupid*, which premiered in September 1998 on ABC.

"I knew nothing about the publishing business and no one in the publishing business," Thomas says. "When I finished *Rats Saw God*, I went out and bought *Writer's Market* and *Guide to Literary Agents* and just followed the steps, and ended up getting a book deal. So it can happen. The thing about writing, at least from my experience, is I was given a fair shake. You're judged by what's on the page, and there's nothing else they can judge you by."

As you progressed through your book contract, did you find the process got easier?

The need to write faster didn't necessarily mean I was writing better books. After the first book, I quit my day job, and my advances were so small I was literally writing to eat. So not only was I doing the novels, but I was also ghost writing anything that people would let me. I wrote *Rats Saw God* writing a page a day for a year, and since then I've been writing five pages a day, and certainly immediately after quitting my job it became necessary to write very fast. I think I became a better writer, but probably a less observant editor. With *Rats Saw God* I would let myself stay on one sentence forever, and by the time I was writing *Doing Time*, I didn't have that luxury.

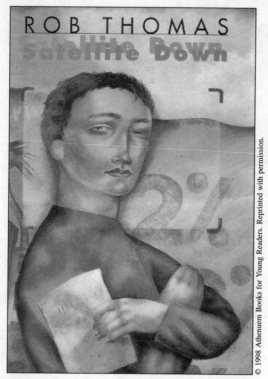

© 1998 Atheneum Books for Young Readers. Reprinted with permission.

Exciting things have been happening in young adult novelist Rob Thomas's writing career. His fourth book from Simon & Schuster, *Satellite Down*, is being considered for a motion picture, and Thomas is writing for television. After his debut as a screenwriter for the popular teen drama *Dawson's Creek*, he moved on to his own series, *Cupid*, which premiered September 1998 on ABC. Despite his recent TV successes, Thomas says, "I really look forward to writing another novel, because a novel is all you, and writing for television and film is a collaboration, it's a democracy. I miss knowing that what I put down on the page is going to be what people read."

How do your skills in fiction writing translate to screenwriting?

What I enjoy most in writing is voice, and that's essentially what screenwriting is—having a voice and writing dialogue. In screenplays you don't spend a page describing the dew on the grass by the barn, or whatever, which is stuff that I'm not that good at anyway. So it plays to my strengths, I think.

Do you plan to return to novels or stay with television?

I really look forward to writing another novel, because a novel is all you, and writing for television and film is a collaboration, it's a democracy. I miss knowing that what I put down on the page is going to be what people read. In television, you write something and then the studio puts in their two cents, the network puts in their two cents, the director puts in his two cents, and . . . I've had to please a lot of different masters. You don't have to do that with books, and I miss that. However, I can make more on one television script than I can on a novel, and a television script takes me two weeks. A novel will take five months. I could write two feature screenplays in the time it takes me to write a novel, and it would pay me ten times what I make on a novel.

So is it love or is it money?

The good news is it can be both. I just wrote the adaptation of *Slave Day* for Universal, and the nice thing there is I get paid not only for screenwriting but for the book. So at the end of a day it can be real possible. And I do have an offer for *Satellite Down* as well. I love writing books, but it's tough to say, "Okay, for the next four or five months I'm going to not take any of this money people are offering me."

Before *Rats Saw God* was published, did you expect that your career would head in this direction?

No, not at all. It amazes me on a daily basis—I'm in Chicago right now where we film the series, and if I go downstairs there are 200 employees, and all these sets built that essentially I wrote. There are famous actors who are doing lines that I wrote. There's a chair that has my name stitched to it down there. Thirteen months ago I lived in Texas and I was ghostwriting X-Files novels. It boggles my mind sometimes.

KAREN CUSHMAN, young adult novelist
First Books 1996

Author Karen Cushman wasn't looking for a niche when she penned her first novel, *Catherine, Called Birdy*, the story of a teenage girl told in diary form set in medieval England. An instructor in the museum studies department at John F. Kennedy University in San Francisco, Cushman had long been drawn to the past, and found a place to indulge that interest in writing historical fiction. "I never said, 'That's what I write and that's what I'm going to write and that's all I want to write,' but whenever I get an idea for a story it seems to be in the past," Cushman says. "And I've got a whole bunch of ideas for five or six more books, and they're all historical fiction. It's very dramatic and colorful, and I get kind of caught up in the setting, in the milieu."

Although writing that first book was a stop-and-start process, once published, *Catherine, Called Birdy* was a critical success. It was named a Newbery Honor book the year after publication, and Cushman followed that performance with *The Midwife's Apprentice* (Clarion, 1995), which was awarded the Newbery Medal. And in spite of a "quite chaotic" publicity schedule for those books, Cushman managed to complete *The Ballad of Lucy Whipple* (Clarion, 1996), and move well along on her upcoming novel *Mathilda Bone*, set again in medieval England, about an orphan girl who lives with a bone setter on Blood and Bone Alley.

Perhaps more important to Cushman than critical success is the connection she has made with her readers. "I am constantly surprised by what some people will read into the book, or how they will use it in their own lives," she says. "There's this line between me and them, almost a telephone line, and I don't even know who they are or where it's going in the world. I've gotten letters from Russia, Thailand and Vietnam. I've even gotten one from Iraq. I enjoy hearing from them."

How did receiving the Newbery Honor for your first book affect your writing in subsequent novels?

It's a little scary. It makes you a little more scared as a writer—I felt more public. I had the second book finished before the Honor, and I had *Lucy Whipple* finished before *Midwife's Apprentice* won the Newbery, so really what I'm working on now is the first post-Newbery book. I think I feel like more people are looking at me. I question myself more, "Is this worthy of a Newbery winner?" And so instead of being a more confident writer, I think I'm a little more questioning.

Do you recommend that new writers find an agent?

It certainly worked for me. I didn't want to spend my time being in the business of submitting fiction, and I knew that with an unusual kind of book by a first-time writer it would have been a business. I was going to have to send it a lot of different places, and keep track of that, and research the right publishers, and I really didn't want to do that.

If you don't have an agent, you're the one who has to do the research, to look at all the publishers, who's publishing what, who might like the kind of thing you're writing, who publishes the age group you're writing for, then keep track of who you are submitting to and what they say and if they have any recommendations and if you want to go with what they are

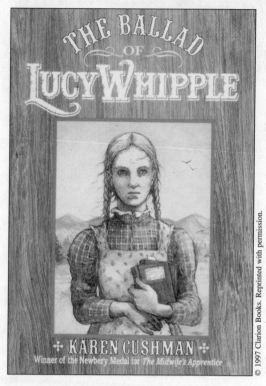

The Ballad of Lucy Whipple (Clarion) follows up two critical successes for author Karen Cushman. Her first book, Catherine, Called Birdy was named a Newbery Honor book, and her next novel, The Midwife's Apprentice, was awarded the Newbery Medal. Winning the Newbery, she says, "makes you a little more scared as a writer—I felt more public. Instead of being a more confident writer, I question myself more, 'Is this worthy of a Newbery winner?'" Cushman is moving well along on her upcoming novel Mathilda Bone, set in medieval England about an orphan girl who lives with a bone setter on Blood and Bone Alley.

© 1997 Clarion Books. Reprinted with permission.

recommending or not. I came to this late—I was 50 years old—and I didn't want to spend a lot of time getting myself established. I was in a hurry. I just wanted to go back and get started on something else.

How is children's publishing different from your expectations?

I think the big difference is how wonderful people are. I had heard stories about publishing—you read things about publishers and agents and other authors—but I have found in children's publishing everybody I have talked to is supportive, friendly and encouraging. Everybody from interviewers to media people to other authors and editors and publishers. I was really surprised by that. Maybe it's because people don't go into it for the money and the prestige, because there really isn't any. They go into it because they love it, and they love other people who love it.

How has your writing changed since your first novel?

I would hope it's gotten better, that I've developed a certain facility. I believe the more you write the better you write, whether you're in school or writing a book, it's just a kind of ease that comes. I think in terms of writing a sentence or paragraph, it's gotten easier, but in terms of writing a book it's gotten a little harder because I expect more of myself. I think my last book is more complicated in structure. It's more a traditional narrative, not a diary, and I think that diary format was a lot easier for a first-time writer.

What do you know now that you could have benefitted from knowing before your first book was published?

For me, it's been incredibly satisfying to finally be doing what I kept saying I wanted to do and didn't. I put it off and I procrastinated and I started Catherine, Called Birdy and I put it in a drawer and said, "I can't do this—there are millions of people who submit novels to publishers who can only accept 20. They'll never pick mine." I would say to new writers be more confident in following your dream. The realization of having achieved something and being able to live a life that you could only imagine is really satisfying.

SHELLEY MOORE THOMAS, picture book author
First Books 1996

For Shelley Moore Thomas, success in children's publishing is a matter of matching the right manuscript with the right publisher. "I've been lucky," says Thomas, whose first book was *Putting the World to Sleep* (Houghton Mifflin, 1995), a gentle, lilting bedtime story. Thomas has never hired an agent, preferring instead the personal contact of pinpointing her publishers and getting to know the editors. "I don't know that people necessarily know what they're looking for until they read it," she says. "So you never really know if what you're writing is the right thing or the wrong thing—you just have to try it and see if other people enjoy it as well."

Moore followed publication of her first book with *Somewhere Today: A Book of Peace* (Albert Whitman, 1998), which uses rhyme and a gentle spirituality to "quietly make readers aware of the kindness and pleasures around us," wrote a critic in *Publishers Weekly*. That book will also be reprinted in a basal reader for use in schools, Thomas says, and "being a teacher, I'm really excited that more kids will get to read the book because it's being recognized by the educational market."

Coming next is an easy reader titled *Good Night, Good Knight*, to be published by Dutton (Thomas also has a fourth book in negotiation stages with Dutton). "I try to at least have two manuscripts out there, and if I have more ready to go, I'll send out more," Thomas says of her submission process. "I'm not very scientific about how I send things out. I kind of just look through *Children's Writer's & Illustrator's Market*, and highlight the publishers who might be interested in the kind of things I do, and then I send things out to them. And I've been very lucky."

How do you balance teaching, writing and managing the business of your publishing?
I think that when there are things you want to do you just find time to do them. I have two children, and I'm pregnant with the third. My husband is in law school right now, so it's rather crazy around here. Writing helps me manage the other things in my life. It gives me time for the things that are in my head. It allows me just to have some time to myself, and with this busy life that's very important. So I make the time to write.

Is it time-consuming to target your publishers, send out your manuscripts and follow their progress?
Again, it's one of those things you make time to do. I love having things out in the mail and not knowing if right now someone might be reading one going, 'Hey, this is what we've always been looking for!' I like knowing what is going on with my work. It is important to me, so I would be hesistant to give it up, the knowledge and the connections that I have been able to make personally with editors. I enjoy that and appreciate it.

How did you find Albert Whitman to publish *Somewhere Today: A Book of Peace*?
It just goes to show that if you do decide you're going to be your own agent, and keep some kind of records of where you send things, good things can happen. I had sent them a manuscript back in 1993, and the editor sent it back to me and said, "We liked this, but we're not going to publish it, and please try us again." In the meantime I had a book published by Houghton Mifflin and another accepted by Dutton, but I remembered that letter. And when I wrote this book I thought, "Albert Whitman does concept books, kind of simple things—this is the kind of book

Shelly Moore Thomas's second book *Somewhere Today: A Book of Peace* (Albert Whitman) came three years after her first book *Putting the World to Sleep* (Houghton Mifflin). Next for the author is an easy reader titled *Good Night, Good Knight*, to be published by Dutton. Thomas also has a fourth book in negotiation. "I try to at least have two manuscripts out there, and if I have more ready to go, I'll send out more," she says. "I'm not very scientific about how I send things out. I kind of just look through *Children's Writer's & Illustrator's Market* and highlight the publishers who might be interested in the kind of things I do, and then I send things out to them. And I've been very lucky."

they might be interested in." So I sent the editor a letter saying, "Back in 1993 . . . so here's another piece of mine. You're the first editor to see this, and if you're interested, let me know." And she called pretty shortly to say she was. That was just from having positive encouragement from an editor, and then trying to find the right piece. You do really get to know the market a lot better if you send your things off, including what specific publishers might be more inclined to buy.

What to you is the most useful piece of advice an unpublished writer could use?

Persistence is very important. It is the key to getting published. I would say, to be honest, it's not any easier now. I thought once I was published one time doors would be opening, but that's not true. I learn how to do things better and more professionally through experience, and how to have connections with different editors, but it is not really any simpler. It doesn't all of a sudden come easily and everyone is banging down my door saying, "Gee, what words did she come up with today?" It's still work. But I would say that being published gave me the confidence that it can happen, and if it can happen once, it can happen again. So you keep working at it.

KAYTA KRENINA, illustrator
First Books 1997

Since her first book was published in 1996, illustrator Katya Krenina has not had much time between assignments to catch her breath. A trip to New York City to show her portfolio yeilded her assignment for *The Magic Dreidels* (Holiday House), by Eric Kimmel. Since that first book, she has been illustrating projects steadily for publishers such as Simon & Schuster, Charlesbridge and Dutton.

A Ukranian-born illustrator with a dreamlike style reminiscent of painter Marc Chagall, Krenina credits both her background and style with several assignments which have paired her with Kimmel, known for retelling folktales in picture book form. Working sometimes long hours in her home studio, Krenina is happy for the work both with Kimmel and on a variety of other projects.

When her schedule permits, Krenina says, she hopes to both write and illustrate for children. Attending a Society of Children's Book Writers and Illustrators conference in 1998 inspired her to try her hand at writing, although "I can't be committed to both writing and illustrating to the same extent," she admits. "I know that if I worked on my writing as much as I work on my illustration, then maybe something would come out of it, but I just don't have time to do that now. But that is something I plan on doing, and I'm working on it."

You have worked on three books with author Eric Kimmel. How did that partnership get started?

After I illustrated my first book, I wrote to Eric Kimmel, and we started a correspondence. Eric told me he really liked the book that I did, *The Magic Dreidels,* and he asked me which stories I would like to illustrate myself. And then he retold them for me. He's a wonderful writer, full of warmth and humor, and there's always enough space for me to be creative within the stories—he leaves space for illustration and fantasy. I'm really lucky to be working with him.

So it's a happy coincidence?

Maybe it's a coincidence, maybe not. Usually when I finish an illustration project, I write a note to the author thanking him for writing the story and giving me an opportunity to illustrate it. And that's how it happened with Eric Kimmel. It doesn't always work that way. His stories really appeal to me—they have those folkloristic roots—and I'm really lucky to be able to illustrate the stories I want to illustrate that he retold for me. That doesn't happen very often.

Were you surprised and pleased by the volume of work you were assigned after your first book was published?

I was very pleased but I can't say I was surprised, because basically from the first time I went to New York there were already two contracts. I did my best on each book, hoping that more

The House of Boo, by J. Patrick Lewis (Athenuem), is one of the latest titles illustrated by Katya Krenina. Since illustrating her first book in 1996, Krenina has had steady work from publishers like Simon & Schuster, Charlesbridge and Dutton, and has chosen to get assignments without the aid of an agent. "I think I'm doing quite well without an agent so far. I do enjoy the business part of my illustrating. I don't mind calling art directors and editors, writing letters, negotiating contracts," says Krenina. "I like to be able to be in control of things, and talk to the publisher directly."

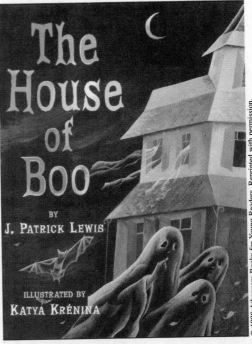

projects would come out of that, and that's exactly what happened. And yes, I have been very, very busy. It's more than a full-time job. I often work during weekends, and I work long hours. I'm pretty disciplined. I think I have been planning my work well, but sometimes an unexpected project comes up, or a publisher moves a deadline, and then things can get complicated.

Have you hired an agent?

I think I'm doing quite well without an agent so far. I do enjoy the business part of my illustrating. I don't mind calling art directors and editors, writing letters, negotiating contracts. I know many illustrators prefer not to deal with the business part, and want just to be able to do the creative work. But I found that even though such aspects of, say, negotiating a contract might not be pleasant at first, it's very rewarding in the end. I like to be able to be in control of things, and talk to the publisher directly.

What's the most challenging aspect of illustrating children's books full time?

For me, it's the isolation part. I am my own coworker and boss, but I do need contact with other illustrators and people who share the same problems and joys in their work as I do. I am a member of an illustrator's Internet group, but I do need human contact. Having a computer list of people is great, but it's not exactly the same.

How has the process of illustration changed for you since you were first published?

With the first book, I did worry about what the editor would think, and that's not so good. Now, I think more abut the vision of the book, and less about what an editor will think, or if they will like it. Whenever I start thinking about other, outside things like what other people will think about my work, I stop working, because usually it will show in the artwork if you start thinking like that. So I take a little break and get away from it, and start working again. I know that later they will critique my work, and they will have comments, but at the stage when I'm working on my illustrations I can't be thinking that.

YUMI HEO, illustrator/author
First Books 1996

Although Yumi Heo has been drawing and painting since she was four, a coincidence led her to what has become a flourishing career in children's books. At the suggestion of a teacher at the School for Visual Arts in New York City, Heo created a book based on stick puppets she had created for another project. That dummy led her to publication of *The Rabbit's Judgement*, a Korean folktale, published by Henry Holt & Co. in 1994.

That same year, Heo followed her first book with publication of *One Afternoon* (Orchard Books), which she wrote and illustrated. A Korean native, Heo faced a language barrier in putting together the book, which features onomatopoeic words representing the sounds of a street scene in New York. ("When I hear a sound, I think in Korean," she says.) The effort paid off with a starred review in *Publishers Weekly*, and a series of books subsequently written and published by Heo, including *Father's Rubber Shoes* (Orchard, 1995), *The Green Frogs, A Korean Folktale* (Houghton Mifflin, 1996), and the upcoming *One Sunday* (Orchard, 1999). She has had six titles published that she illustrated for other authors, including *So Say the Little Monkeys* by Nancy Van Laan (Atheneum, 1998).

While her style has evolved considerably from the dumpling-headed puppets that launched her career, in many ways Heo has remained true to the simple, whimsical characters that first caught a publisher's eye. "There are so many styles you can do, and there is so much freedom," Heo says. "There is no limit to what you can do."

Since the publication of the first book she illustrated in 1994, Yumi Heo's career has taken off. Among her titles are *The Green Frogs, A Korean Folktale* (Houghton Mifflin) and *One Sunday* (Orchard), both of which she wrote and illustrated. She's had six titles published that she illustrated for other authors, including her latest *So Say the Little Monkeys*, by Nancy Van Laan (Atheneum). Through all these projects, Heo has remained true to the simple, whimsical characters that first caught a publisher's eye. "There are so many styles," says Heo. "Artists starting out need to find their own style, beyond traditional watercolors and oil paintings. Editors are always looking for something different."

Do you prefer both writing and illustrating your work to illustrating others' stories?

I like to do both, but I guess I like doing my own books better. But sometimes my schedule does not allow me to. Sometimes I just don't have time to write, although I have a couple of things already written that I haven't had a chance to show to editors yet.

Have you hired an agent?

I like to work with people directly, the art directors or editors. I like the freedom and control. I wouldn't mind having an agent for my contracts, but there aren't agents who will only take care of the contract. At one point there was an agent who really wanted to represent me, and she talked to me a littleabout it, but through the whole thing I wasn't quite [convinced an agent.

would be right for me]. I wouldn't have much freedom, because an agent would tell me what to do.

Does it benefit an illustrator to hit on a particular style they become known for?

Yes, I definitely think so. I think artists starting out need to find their own style, whatever that is, beyond the traditional watercolors and oil paintings. I think that's a good way to go. That's how I started—when I was in school, as my thesis project, I made a doll with a dumpling shaped head and a stick body. Those were my characters, and I put them together as a book. People really liked them a lot; they hadn't seen anything like that before. Editors are always looking for something different.

Is the market healthy for new illustrators trying to break in?

It's always competitive, but there are always books that need or demand certain styles, and there are always books that need the traditional watercolor styles. It's competitive, but always a good time to break in with a new style.

SUSAN MIDDLETON ELYA, picture book author
First Books 1997

Persistence is an important ally for aspiring children's authors, as Susan Middleton Elya will tell you. A junior high school Spanish teacher, Elya wrote for eight years before her first book, *Say Hola to Spanish*, was published by Lee & Low in 1996. By that time, Elya had written a young adult novel and several picture books. Her current count is 24 manuscripts in various stages of completion—some submitted to publishers, others awaiting revision. "I write a lot of different things, but I've only sold the Spanish-English combination," Elya says. "So I will probably continue to write a lot of different things and just hope that someday I'll sell something other than the *Say Hola* books."

Say Hola to Spanish, a nonfiction Spanish-English primer presented in a rhyming format, became a Children's Book of the Month Club Selection. *Say Hola to Spanish Otra Vez*, the second book of the series, was called "another bright-eyed dose of Spanish vocabulary" by *Kirkus Reviews*. And Lee & Low has agreed to publish a third volume tentatively titled *Say Hola to Spanish at the Circo*.

The most surprising aspect of life after publication to Elya is the way others have changed their perception of her. "I had been writing for 10 years, and no one really acknowledged that I was a writer until I was published," she says. "I always thought of myself as a writer even though I wasn't published, but once I became published it was so different. People's reactions were so different: 'Oh, here comes the author, Susan Elya.' You just get treated on a whole different level when you finally have something in your hand that you've published. That was a surprise to me."

Have you started working with an agent?

My agent represents the book that is next closest to publication. I've had that for nine years and it has gotten very close a couple of times. It's one of those you know is going to make it, but you just don't know when. That's how I feel about it—it is going to be a book, but it just can't quite get there. My agent thinks it's the strongest one I have, and that's why she's representing it. The others—she didn't do a lot for me with them, so I thought I should be marketing those. I think they're good, so I pulled them back from her.

Are you still in your writing group, and has the dynamic of the group changed now that you've been published?

Oh yes. We have a lot of published members, so I think no, it hasn't really changed. I think it's encouraging for those who aren't published because they see that we made it, and they will too.

Say Hola to Spanish, Otra Vez is the second in a series of books teaching Spanish vocabulary written by Susan Middleton Elya for Lee & Low. A third volume is in the works, tentatively titled Say Hola to Spanish at the Circo. For Elya, the most surprising aspect of life after publication is the way others have changed their perception of her. "I always thought of myself as a writer even though I wasn't published, but once I became published it was so different," she says. "You get treated on a whole different level when you finally have something in your hand that you've published."

Say Hola to Spanish, Otra Vez (Again!)

by Susan Middleton Elya • Illustrated by Loretta Lopez

I know for me it was encouraging when I wasn't published to meet every month with people who were, because they were so willing to help and make comments.

Was the first book you sent to Lee & Low accepted as is, or were there revisions to the manuscript?

No, it was not accepted as is. I had probably seven couplets they fooled around with extensively. Of those seven couplets, two of them I argued to keep and five of them I agreed to change. They wanted a very universal book, and so they were trying to weed out anything that would offend anybody—for instance, a lot of people just say 'computer' in Spanish, but in some countries they don't, so they pulled that out. The same with 'blue jeans.' They were probably minor, but to me it was really a big thing, because they were my words. But then I thought well, if they say this would be better, I'll just have to go along with them. And I'm really glad I did, because we got great reviews on that first book.

What advice would you share with children's writers aspiring to publication?

Don't work on just one thing. If you've got something that's out there just sitting somewhere, don't wait for it to come back. Be working on something else. And any kind of encouragement you get—no matter how small—take it as a really big compliment. Whatever you need to keep going, focus on that, and forget all the other stuff. I had somebody say to me you're never going to sell this book because you're not a native speaker. And I'm happy to report he was wrong. You just can't listen to the negative stuff. Focus on the positive things you hear about your writing.

The Business of Writing & Illustrating

A career in children's publishing involves more than just writing skills or artistic talent. Successful authors and illustrators must be able to hold their own in negotiations, keep records, understand contract language, grasp copyright law, pay taxes and take care of a number of other business concerns. Although agents and reps, accountants and lawyers, and writers' organizations offer help in sorting out such business issues, it's wise to have a basic understanding of them going in. This article offers just that—basic information. For a more in-depth look at the subjects covered here, check your library or bookstore for books and magazines to help you, some of which are mentioned. We also tell you how to get information on issues like taxes and copyright from the federal government.

CONTRACTS & NEGOTIATION

Before you see your work in print or begin working with an editor or art director on a project, there is negotiation. And whether negotiating a book contract, a magazine article assignment, or an illustration or photo assignment, there are a few things to keep in mind. First, if you find any clauses vague or confusing in a contract, get legal advice. The time and money invested in counseling up front could protect you from problems later. If you have an agent or rep, she will review any contract.

A contract is an agreement between two or more parties that specifies the fees to be paid, services rendered, deadlines, rights purchased and, for artists and photographers, whether original work is returned. Most companies have standard contracts for writers, illustrators and photographers. The specifics (such as royalty rates, advances, delivery dates, etc.) are typed in after negotiations.

Though it's okay to conduct negotiations over the phone, get a written contract once both parties have agreed on terms. Never depend on oral stipulations; written contracts protect both parties from misunderstandings. Watch for clauses that may not be in your best interest, such as "work-for-hire." When you do work-for-hire, you give up all rights to your creations.

Some reputable children's magazines, such as *Highlights for Children*, buy all rights, and many writers and illustrators believe it's worth the concession in order to break into the field. However, once you become more established in the field, it's in your best interest to keep rights to your work. (Note: magazines such as *Highlights* may return rights after a specified time period, so ask about this possibility when negotiating.)

When negotiating a book deal, find out whether your contract contains an option clause. This clause requires the author to give the publisher a first look at her next work before offering it to other publishers. Though it's editorial etiquette to give the publisher the first chance at publishing your next work, be wary of statements in the contract that could trap you. Don't allow the publisher to consider the next project for more than 30 days and be specific about what type of work should actually be considered "next work." (For example, if the book under contract is a young adult novel, specify that the publisher will receive an exclusive look at only your next young adult novel.) For more tips on contracts, Society of Children's Book Writers and Illustrators members can send a SASE to SCBWI, 345 N. Maple Drive, Suite 296, Beverly Hills CA 90210 and request their publication "Answers to Some Questions About Contracts."

Book publishers' payment methods

Book publishers pay authors and artists in royalties, a percentage of either the wholesale or retail price of each book sold. From large publishing houses, the author usually receives an advance issued against future royalties before the book is published. Half of the advance amount is issued upon signing the book contract; the other half is issued when the book is finished. For illustrations, one-third of the advance should be collected upon signing the contract; one-third upon delivery of sketches; and one-third upon delivery of finished art.

After your book has sold enough copies to earn back your advance, you'll start to get royalty checks. Some publishers hold a reserve against returns, which means a percentage of royalties is held back in case books are returned from bookstores. If you have a reserve clause in your contract, find out the exact percentage of total sales that will be withheld and the time period the publisher will hold this money. You should be reimbursed this amount after a reasonable time period, such as a year. Royalty percentages vary with each publisher, but there are standard ranges.

Book publishers' rates

According to the latest figures from the Society of Children's Book Writers and Illustrators, picture book writers can expect advances of $3,500-5,000; picture book illustrators' advances range from $7,000-10,000; text and illustration packages can score $8,000-10,000. Royalties for picture books are generally about five percent (split between the author and illustrator) but can go as high as ten percent. Those who both write and illustrate a book, of course, receive the full royalty.

Advances for chapter books and middle-grade novels vary slightly from picture books. Hardcover titles can fetch authors advances of $4,000-6,000 and 10 percent royalties; paperbacks bring in slightly lower advances of $3,000-5,000 and royalties of 6-8 percent. Fees for young adult novels are generally the same, but additional length may increase fees and royalties.

As you might expect, advance and royalty figures vary from house to house and are affected by the time of year, the state of the economy and other factors. Some smaller houses may not even pay royalties, just flat fees. First-time writers and illustrators generally start on the low end of the scale, while established and high-profile writers are paid more.

Pay rates for magazines

For writers, fee structures for magazines are based on a per-word rate or range for a specific article length. Artists and photographers have a few more variables to contend with before contracting their services.

Payment for illustrations and photos can be set by such factors as whether the piece(s) will be black and white or four-color, how many are to be purchased, where the work appears (cover or inside), circulation, and the artist's or photographer's prior experience.

Remaindering

When a book goes out of print, a publisher will sell any existing copies to a wholesaler who, in turn, sells the copies to stores at a discount When the books are "remaindered" to a wholesaler, they are usually sold at a price just above the cost of printing. When negotiating a contract with a publisher you may want to discuss the possibility of purchasing the remaindered copies before they are sold to a wholesaler, then you can market the copies you purchased and still make a profit.

KNOW YOUR RIGHTS

A copyright is a form of protection provided to creators of original works, published or unpublished. In general, copyright protection ensures the writer, illustrator or photographer the power to decide how her work is used and allows her to receive payment for each use.

Essentially, copyright also encourages the creation of new works by guaranteeing the creator power to sell rights to the work in the marketplace. The copyright holder can print, reprint or copy her work; sell or distribute copies of her work; or prepare derivative works such as plays, collages or recordings. The Copyright Law is designed to protect work (created on or after January 1, 1978) for her lifetime plus 50 years.

If you collaborate with someone else on a written or artistic project, the copyright will last for the lifetime of the last survivor plus 50 years. The creators' heirs may hold a copyright for an additional 50 years. After that, the work becomes public domain. Works created anonymously or under a pseudonym are protected for 100 years, or 75 years after publication. Under work-for-hire agreements, you relinquish your copyright to your "employer."

Copyright notice and registration

Some feel a copyright notice should be included on all work, registered or not. Others feel it is not necessary and a copyright notice will only confuse publishers about whether the material is registered (acquiring rights to previously registered material is a more complicated process).

Although it's not necessary to include a copyright notice on unregistered work, if you don't feel your work is safe without the notice, it is your right to include one. Including a copyright notice—© (year of work, your name)—should help safeguard against plagiarism.

Registration is a legal formality intended to make copyright public record, and can help you win more money in a court case. By registering work within three months of publication or before an infringement occurs, you are eligible to collect statutory damages and attorney's fees. If you register later than three months after publication, you will qualify only for actual damages and profits.

Ideas and concepts are not copyrightable, only expressions of those ideas and concepts. A character type or basic plot outline, for example, is not subject to a copyright infringement lawsuit. Also, titles, names, short phrases or slogans, and lists of contents are not subject to copyright protection, though titles and names may be protected through the Trademark Office.

You can register a group of articles, illustrations or photos if it meets these criteria:
- the group is assembled in order, such as in a notebook;
- the works bear a single title, such as "Works by (your name)";
- it is the work of one writer, artist or photographer;
- the material is the subject of a single claim to copyright.

It's a publisher's responsibility to register your book for copyright. If you've previously registered the same material, you must inform your editor and supply the previous copyright information, otherwise, the publisher can't register the book in its published form.

For more information about the proper way to register works, contact the Copyright Office, Library of Congress, Washington DC 20359. The forms available are TX for writing (books, articles, etc.); VA for pictures (photographs, illustrations); and PA for plays and music. (To order copyright forms by phone, call (202)707-9100.) For information about how to use the copyright forms, request a copy of Circular I on Copyright Basics. All of the forms and circulars are free. Send the completed registration form along with the stated fee and a copy of the work to the Copyright Office.

For specific answers to questions about copyright (but not legal advice), call the Copyright Public Information Office at (202)707-3000 weekdays between 8:30 a.m. and 5 p.m. EST. Forms can also be downloaded from the Library of Congress website: http://lcweb.loc.gov/copyright. The site also includes tips on filling out forms, general copyright information, and links to other sites related to copyright issues. For members of SCBWI, information about copyrights and the law is available. Send a SASE to SCBWI and request "Copyright Facts for Writers."

The rights publishers buy

The copyright law specifies that a writer, illustrator or photographer generally sells one-time rights to her work unless she and the buyer agree otherwise in writing. Many publications will want more exclusive rights to your work than just one-time usage; some will even require you to sell all rights. Be sure you are monetarily compensated for the additional rights you relinquish.

If you must give up all rights to a work, carefully consider the price you're being offered to determine whether you'll be compensated for the loss of other potential sales.

Writers who only give up limited rights to their work can then sell reprint rights to other publications, foreign rights to international publications, or even movie rights, should the opportunity arise. Artists and photographers can sell their work to other markets such as paper product companies who may use an image on a calendar, greeting card or mug. Illustrators and photographers may even sell original work after it has been published. And there are now galleries throughout the U.S. that display the work of children's illustrators.

Rights acquired through the sale of a book manuscript are explained in each publisher's contract. Take time to read relevant clauses to be sure you understand what rights each contract is specifying before signing. Be sure your contract contains a clause allowing all rights to revert back to you in the event the publisher goes out of business. (You may even want to have the contract reviewed by an agent or an attorney specializing in publishing law.)

The following are the rights you'll most often sell to publishers, periodicals and producers in the marketplace:

First rights. The buyer purchases the rights to use the work for the first time in any medium. All other rights remain with the creator. When material is excerpted from a soon-to-be-published book for use in a newspaper or periodical, first serial rights are also purchased.

One-time rights. The buyer has no guarantee that she is the first to use a piece. One-time permission to run written work, illustrations or photos is acquired, then the rights revert back to the creator.

First North American serial rights. This is similar to first rights, except that companies who distribute both in the U.S. and Canada will stipulate these rights to ensure that another North American company won't come out with simultaneous usage of the same work.

Second serial (reprint) rights. In this case newspapers and magazines are granted the right to reproduce a work that has already appeared in another publication. These rights are also purchased by a newspaper or magazine editor who wants to publish part of a book after the book has been published. The proceeds from reprint rights for a book are often split evenly between the author and his publishing company.

Simultaneous rights. More than one publication buys one-time rights to the same work at the same time. Use of such rights occurs among magazines with circulations that don't overlap, such as many religious publications.

All rights. Just as it sounds, the writer, illustrator or photographer relinquishes all rights to a piece—she no longer has any say in who acquires rights to use it. All rights are purchased by publishers who pay premium usage fees, have an exclusive format, or have other book or magazine interests from which the purchased work can generate more mileage. If a company insists on acquiring all rights to your work, see if you can negotiate for the rights to revert back to you after a reasonable period of time. If they agree to such a proposal, get it in writing.

Note: Writers, illustrators and photographers should be wary of "work-for-hire" arrangements. If you sign an agreement stipulating that your work will be done as work-for-hire, you will not control the copyrights of the completed work—the company that hired you will be the copyright owner.

Foreign serial rights. Be sure before you market to foreign publications that you have sold only North American—not worldwide—serial rights to previous markets. If so, you are free to market to publications that may be interested in material that's appeared in a North American-based periodical.

Syndication rights. This is a division of serial rights. For example, if a syndicate prints portions of a book in installments in its newspapers, it would be syndicating second serial rights. The syndicate would receive a commission and leave the remainder to be split between the author and publisher.

Subsidiary rights. These include serial rights, dramatic rights, book club rights or translation rights. The contract should specify what percentage of profits from sales of these rights go to the author and publisher.

Dramatic, television and motion picture rights. During a specified time the interested party tries to sell a story to a producer or director. Many times options are renewed because the selling process can be lengthy.

Display rights or electronic publishing rights. They're also known as "Data, Storage and Retrieval." Usually listed under subsidiary rights, the marketing of electronic rights in this era of rapidly expanding capabilities and markets for electronic material can be tricky. Display rights can cover text or images to be used in a CD-ROM or online, or may cover use of material in formats not even fully developed yet. If a display rights clause is listed in your contract, try to negotiate its elimination. Otherwise, be sure to pin down which electronic rights are being purchased. Demand the clause be restricted to things designed to be read only. By doing this, you maintain your rights to use your work for things such as games and interactive software.

RUNNING YOUR BUSINESS

An important part of being a freelance writer, illustrator or photographer is running your freelance business. It's imperative to maintain accurate business records to determine if you're making a profit as a freelancer. Keeping correct, organized records will also make your life easier as you approach tax time.

When setting up your system, begin by keeping a bank account and ledger for your business finances apart from your personal finances. Also, if writing, illustration or photography is secondary to another freelance career, keep separate business records for each.

You will likely accumulate some business expenses before showing any profit when you start out as a freelancer. To substantiate your income and expenses to the IRS, keep all invoices, cash receipts, sales slips, bank statements, canceled checks and receipts related to travel expenses and entertaining clients. For entertainment expenditures, record the date, place and purpose of the business meeting as well as gas mileage. Keep records for all purchases, big and small—don't take the small purchases for granted; they can add up to a substantial amount. File all receipts in chronological order. Maintaining a separate file for each month simplifies retrieving records at the end of the year.

Record keeping

When setting up a single-entry bookkeeping system, record income and expenses separately. Use some of the subheads that appear on Schedule C (the form used for recording income from a business) of the 1040 tax form so you can easily transfer information onto the tax form when filing your return. In your ledger include a description of each transaction—the date, source of income (or debts from business purchases), description of what was purchased or sold, the amount of the transaction, and whether payment was by cash, check or credit card.

Don't wait until January 1 to start keeping records. The moment you first make a business-related purchase or sell an article, book manuscript, illustration or photo, begin tracking your profits and losses. If you keep records from January 1 to December 31, you're using a calendar-year accounting period. Any other accounting period is called a fiscal year.

There are two types of accounting methods you can choose from—the cash method and the accrual method. The cash method is used more often: you record income when it is received and expenses when they're disbursed.

Using the accrual method, you report income at the time you earn it rather than when it's actually received. Similarly, expenses are recorded at the time they're incurred rather than when you actually pay them. If you choose this method, keep separate records for "accounts receivable" and "accounts payable."

Satisfying the IRS

To successfully—and legally—work as a freelancer, you must know what income you should report and what deductions you can claim. But before you can do that, you must prove to the IRS you're in business to make a profit, that your writing, illustration or photography is not merely a hobby.

The Tax Reform Act of 1986 says you should show a profit for three years out of a five-year period to attain professional status. The IRS considers these factors as proof of your professionalism:

- accurate financial records;
- a business bank account separate from your personal account;
- proven time devoted to your profession;
- whether it's your main or secondary source of income;
- your history of profits and losses;
- the amount of training you have invested in your field;
- your expertise.

If your business is unincorporated, you'll fill out tax information on Schedule C of Form 1040. If you're unsure of what deductions you can take, request the IRS publication containing this information. Under the Tax Reform Act, only 30 percent of business meals, entertainment and related tips, and parking charges are deductible. Other deductible expenses allowed on Schedule C include: car expenses for business-related trips; professional courses and seminars; depreciation of office equipment, such as a computer; dues and publications; and miscellaneous expenses, such as postage used for business needs.

If you're working out of a home office, a portion of your mortgage interest (or rent), related utilities, property taxes, repair costs and depreciation may he deducted as business expenses—under special circumstances. To learn more about the possibility of home office deductions, consult IRS Publication 587, Business Use of Your Home

The method of paying taxes on income not subject to withholding is called "estimated tax" for individuals. If you expect to owe more than $500 at year's end and if the total amount of income tax that will be withheld during the year will be less than 90% of the tax shown on the current year's return, you'll generally make estimated tax payments. Estimated tax payments are made in four equal installments due on April 15, June 15, September 15 and January 15 (assuming you're a calendar-year taxpayer). For more information, request Publication 533, Self-Employment Tax.

The Internal Revenue Service's website (http://www.irs.ustreas.gov/) offers tips and instant access to IRS forms and publications.

Social Security tax

Depending on your net income as a freelancer, you may be liable for a Social Security tax. This is a tax designed for those who don't have Social Security withheld from their paychecks. You're liable if your net income is $400 or more per year. Net income is the difference between your income and allowable business deductions. Request Schedule SE, Computation of Social Security Self-Employment Tax, if you qualify.

If completing your income tax return proves to be too complex, consider hiring an accountant (the fee is a deductible business expense) or contact the IRS for assistance (look in the White Pages under U.S. Government - Internal Revenue Service). In addition to numerous publications to instruct you in various facets of preparing a tax return, the IRS also has walk-in centers in some cities.

Insurance

As a self-employed professional be aware of what health and business insurance coverage is available to you. Unless you're a Canadian who is covered by national health insurance or a full-time freelancer covered by your spouse's policy, health insurance will no doubt be one of your biggest expenses. Under the terms of a 1985 government act (COBRA), if you leave a job with health benefits, you're entitled to continue that coverage for up to 18 months—you pay 100 percent of the premium and sometimes a small administration fee. Eventually, you must search for your own health plan. You may also need disability and life insurance. Disability insurance is offered through many private insurance companies and state governments. This insurance pays a monthly fee that covers living and business expenses during periods of long-term recuperation from a health problem. The amount of money paid is based on the recipient's annual earnings.

Before contacting any insurance representative, talk to other writers, illustrators or photographers to learn which insurance companies they recommend. If you belong to a writers' or artists' organization, ask the organization if it offers insurance coverage for professionals. (SCBWI has a plan available. Look through the Clubs & Organizations section for other groups that may offer coverage.) Group coverage may be more affordable and provide more comprehensive coverage than an individual policy.

Only Connect: A Beginner's Guide to Networking

BY FRANCESS LANTZ

Networking doesn't come naturally to me. Growing up, I was taught that if you worked hard and did a good job, you would be rewarded. No one mentioned that part of the hard work might be making connections with other people in my chosen profession. It shouldn't have been hard for me to figure out. My father was an architect, and the weekly Rotary meetings he attended helped him connect with other professionals and land jobs. But I was just a kid, an aspiring singer/songwriter who seemed to have no trouble getting local gigs. It didn't occur to me that what my father was doing was an important part of his job, or that it had anything to do with me.

Then I grew up and moved to Boston. Suddenly, I found myself competing with thousands of aspiring musicians. My performing partner tried to tell me I needed to get out of my apartment and make connections. But I hated the idea of hanging out in smoky rock clubs, trading phone numbers with rowdy musicians, unscrupulous club owners and horny record label underlings.

Not surprisingly, my music career stalled after the first refrain. So I got out of the music business, became a children's librarian, and eventually tried my hand at writing children's books. Now this was a career I could understand! You wrote a fabulous manuscript, you sent it out. An editor liked it, she bought it. No networking required.

Or so I thought. In reality, it was networking that helped me make my first sale. I was reviewing young adult books for a magazine called *Kliatt*. The office was in a Boston suburb, so I went there every month to pick up my books. One day I mentioned to the *Kliatt* editors that I was writing children's books. They suggested I call their friend Cyrisse Jaffe, a former librarian who was now working as an editor at Addison-Wesley. I did and she agreed to read my manuscripts. A few weeks later, she made an offer on my young adult novel, *Good Rockin' Tonight*.

Fifteen years have passed since I sold *Good Rockin' Tonight*, and the business of publishing has changed. Most publishing houses are now run by international entertainment conglomerates. Editors are no longer allowed to buy manuscripts just because they believe in them. At acquisitions meetings, they must answer questions like, "What are the author's past sales figures? How can we market this book? What's the potential for merchandising tie-ins?"

Once again, I've been slow to catch on. While the publishing industry has been talking bottom line, I've been sitting at home writing books. Nothing wrong with that, of course—that's what writers do. But gradually, I've come to realize it's only part of the equation. After you write a book and sell it, you have to sell it again—not to your publisher, but to the public. How do you do that? By making yourself known to the people who promote, review, sell, buy and honor books. In other words, networking.

So I've made a conscious effort to get out of my chair and start meeting people. It hasn't

FRANCESS LANTZ *has written 26 books for young people, including novels, nonfiction and series fiction. Her young adult novel* Someone to Love *was honored as an American Library Association Best Book for Young Adults. Her latest titles are* Stepsister from the Planet Weird *(Random House) and* Fade Far Away *(Avon). Lantz can be contacted through her website: http://www.silcom.com/~writer.*

always been easy. It's taken time, money and plenty of chutzpah. I've had to learn how to walk into a cocktail party full of bookstore owners and publishers' reps and make entertaining small talk. I've gotten sore feet and a sore throat from six hours of telling school librarians why I love to do school visits. I've even stood at the counter during a poorly advertised book signing and hawked my novels like a used car salesman.

But it's starting to pay off. Bookstore owners who had never heard of me are now hand-selling my books. My publisher selected my middle grade novel, *Stepsister from the Planet Weird*, to be the "Hot Pick of the Month" on their website. I'm getting school visits, which not only add to my meager author's salary but also put my books in front of thousands of eager readers. And as a side benefit, I'm making dozens of new friends who care about the same things I care about—children and books.

If I did it, you can do it, too. All you need is desire, a sensible pair of shoes, and a few ideas to get you started.

MEET AN AUTHOR, MAKE A FRIEND

If you're an aspiring children's book writer or illustrator, the first group of people to connect with are published authors. They've been where you are and they've gone where you want to go. As a result, they can give you encouragement, understanding and plenty of useful advice.

Is there a published children's book author or illustrator in your town? Go to one of her bookstore signings or school visits and introduce yourself. Don't be pushy and don't thrust your manuscript in her face. Be friendly and polite—and be sure you've read the author's work so you can say something intelligent. Explain that you're writing children's books and you'd like to ask one or two questions. Then listen—and learn.

Even after you're published, attending a bookstore signing can be inspiring, and a whole lot more. Wendelin Van Draanen, author of the Sammy Keyes mystery novels (Knopf), drove two hours to meet popular mystery writer Sue Grafton and have her autograph a book. While she was there, she also asked Grafton if she'd be willing to read the first Sammy Keyes manuscript.

"The Sue Grafton connection was something that happened because of my editor's encouragement," Van Draanen explains. "It's not in my nature to push myself on people, so asking her to look at the manuscript was an uncomfortable thing for me to do." It paid off, though. Grafton read her manuscript, and liked it so much she faxed in a positive quote, which Knopf put on the book jacket.

If meeting a professional author or illustrator in a more relaxed setting sounds more appealing—and less stressful—try taking a class. Many authors teach university or adult education classes. Look for a class in which the author will critique your work. You'll learn a lot, and if you teacher is impressed, she might be able to recommend you to an editor or agent.

That's what happened to April Wayland, author of the Knopf picture book *It's Not My Turn to Look for Grandma!* A few years ago, she took a class on writing and illustrating picture books with Barbara Bottner. "She read my manuscript, which had been on an editor's desk for over a year," Wayland says, "and told me, 'Get it off that other editor's desk and send it to my editor at Scholastic.' " The result was her first sale, the picture book *To Rabbittown*.

Another way to meet authors and illustrators is to attend a writing conference. Sherry Shahan, author of the novel *Frozen Stiff* (Delacorte Press), made her first sale that way. While attending the Cuesta College Writers' Conference, she took a workshop with children's book author Elizabeth Van Steenwyk. "At the end of the class, I asked if she would critique my middle-grade novel," Shahan says. "Of course, I offered to pay for her time." The result? "The teacher was so enthusiastic about my writing she introduced me to her editor at Willowisp Press. Not only did I sell them my first novel, but I signed contracts for another seven!"

UNITED WE STAND

Once you've gotten to know some published authors and illustrators, you can keep up your connections by joining a writing group. (For more on the topic, see Writing Groups: Succeeding Together on page 58.) I met aspiring children's book author Lou Lynda Richards when she took a creative writing class I was teaching. I was so impressed with her writing that I asked her to join my writing group. When her first novel was completed, I recommended her to my agent, who is now her agent too.

After you sell your first book, your friendships with other authors will continue to be important. You can share information, commiserate about the market, complain about contracts, and generally offer each other moral support. Author friendships can even lead to work. When my friend Michael Petracca sold a proposal for a creative writing college textbook to Simon & Schuster, he asked me to write the chapter on young adult fiction. The textbook, *The Graceful Lie: A Method for Making Fiction*, was published this year.

CONNECT WITH THE EXPERTS: LIBRARIANS AND RETAILERS

The next group you should make a point of meeting are your local children's librarians, school librarians and bookstore employees. They know what's being published, what kids are reading, and which books are winning awards. They can tell you if your brilliant idea for a tooth fairy picture book has already been done, and they know what subjects kids like which haven't yet been done to death.

Librarians and bookstore owners often know other people in the book community. Evelyn Mott, author of *The Dancing Rainbow: A Pueblo Boy's Story* (Penguin), sold her first book with the help of a librarian. She created the dummy for a picture book entitled *Steam Train Ride* and wondered, "What do I do now?" She showed it to the library coordinator for her county, who suggested Evelyn write to her friend Barbara Bates, a retired children's book editor. Evelyn called instead and discovered that Bates was not retired, but was working part-time for Walker & Company. Even better, she had once written a popular children's book about trains. Evelyn sent her *Steam Train Ride* and she bought it.

Once you have a published book to promote, bookstore owners and librarians can become an even greater resource. Mary K. Whittington, whose stories have been anthologized in *The Haunted House* (HarperCollins) and *Bruce Coville's Book of Ghosts* (Scholastic), has been hired to do dozens of school visits because her name is on a list of recommended authors complied by The Secret Garden Children's Bookshop in Seattle. Booksellers and librarians can also personally recommend your books to readers, and even nominate them for awards.

After you've connected with your local bookstore employees and librarians, it's time to promote yourself to the larger world of bookseller and librarian associations. The purpose is to get your name known in the children's book world, increase sales of your books, get invited to bookstore events and land school visits.

Many local booksellers' associations hold monthly meetings. Ask if you can attend. Usually, you will be given a few minutes to stand up and promote your books. As a result, booksellers will be encouraged to order your books, invite you to local book fairs, and possibly recommend you for school visits.

Ask bookstore owners about local trade shows and conventions. Sometimes you need to be sponsored by your publisher. Last year, Random House, publisher of my middle-grade novel *Stepsister from the Planet Weird*, sent me and 50 free copies of my novel (give-aways to bookstore owners) to the Southern California Children's Bookseller Association trade show. Some conferences, like those held by state chapters of the International Reading Association and the American Library Association, schedule authors as guest speakers. If you are selected to speak, your books will be featured at the conference and you will have a chance to meet a number of influential people in the book community. Competition is fierce, however; only authors who propose unique, relevant, well-researched talks are chosen.

Another way to make an impact at a conference is to rent a table in the exhibitor's hall. Although you can't sell your books without a vendor's license, you can display them, introduce yourself to conference attendees, promote yourself as a speaker, and hand out business cards, flyers and bookmarks. The cost can be high ($300 and up), so consider renting a table with one or more other authors or illustrators.

THOSE ELUSIVE EDITORS AND AGENTS

To an unpublished children's book writer, editors and agents appear all-powerful, mysterious and reclusive. It seems hard enough to convince one of them to look at your manuscript—forget trying to rope an editor or agent into actually talking to you face-to-face!

In fact, it is possible to meet editors and agents in person—just attend a writing conference, workshop or retreat which features an editor or agent as the guest speaker. The Society of Children's Book Writers and Illustrators (SCBWI) holds dozens of local conferences each year, as well as a national conference in August. Many colleges and universities sponsor writing conferences as well.

Another way to meet editors and agents—not to mention other writers—is to do volunteer work with a writer's association. Joanne Rocklin, author of *Strudel Stories* (Bantam), put in many hours volunteering for her local SCBWI chapter, and was the editor of their newsletter for four years. "All this work kept me in touch with the market and exposed my own stories as well," she says. Eventually, Rocklin began speaking at SCBWI conferences herself. "I met the editor of my forthcoming novel at a conference I spoke at," she explains. "After meeting her I really wanted to work with her, and I had the confidence to send her an easy reader, which she bought. And then she bought my novel!"

After you're published, maintaining a good relationship with your editor—and everyone else at your publishing house—is essential. Let them know you're out there working to promote your book. Publicity departments are more eager to get behind an author who is pulling her own weight, rather than one who is complaining that not enough is being done for her.

And remember, publishing houses know how to network too. Ruth Katcher, senior editor at Avon Books, calls it "quietly planting seeds." When she attends conferences and conventions, she networks with people who are influential in the world of children's literature, talking about authors and their books. "I don't expect immediate results," she says. "It pays off down the road, although sometimes not for years."

NETWORKING ON THE NET

Not everybody can travel across the country to attend conferences and trade shows. If financial concerns or family responsibilities keep you at home, you can still network with authors, editors and librarians on the Internet. Live chat sessions and bulletin boards pertaining to children's literature are easy to find, as are authors' websites (which always include some way to contact them). Library and teacher organizations have their own websites, as do booksellers' associations and many bookstores. You can even take writing courses on the Web.

Kristine O'Connell George, author of *Old Elm Speaks: Tree Poems* and *Little Dog Poems*, found that creating her own website put her in touch with hundreds of children and educators. The website promotes her books, and also serves as a resource site for children's poetry. "I'm building a mailing list of people who have expressed an interest in learning about my upcoming titles," she says. "And I'm developing an online poetry workshop with a group of second graders in Massachusetts."

EVERYONE IS A RESOURCE

You never know what contact will pay off, so don't confine your networking solely to the world of children's books. Jamie Callan, author of the young adult novel *Just Too Cool*, met writer/actress Mary Garipoli at a writers' workshop. Garipoli was looking for a book that could

TEN WEBSITES YOU SHOULD KNOW

1. Inkspot (www.inkspot.com) offers writing info, live chats, Internet relay chats and bulletin boards.

2. The Writer's Club (www.writersclub.com) offers writing courses via email, live chats and message boards.

3. The Sandbaggers (www.utahlinx.com/users/kcummings) offers information on starting your own email critique group, joining a private discussion group for children's writers, plus email addresses of Sandbagger authors.

4. The Children's Writing Resource Center (www.write4kids.com) offers writing info and a live chat group for children's book writers.

5. Listserv Discussion Groups (www.title.net/tile/listserv/index.html) offers an index of Listserv discussion groups, including ones on libraries, children's literature and writing for children.

6. America Online (www.aol.com) hosts a members' only weekly chat group on writing for children.

7. The Society of Children's Book Writers and Illustrators (www.scbwi.org) offers information on forming a critique group, conferences and retreats, plus links to members' websites.

8. The American Library Association (www.ala.org) includes information on conferences and conventions of the ALA.

9. The International Reading Association (www.ira.org) includes information on conferences and conventions of the IRA.

10. The American Booksellers Association (www.ambook.org/aba) includes addresses of bookstores across the country.

---

be turned into a musical for teens. Callan mentioned *Just Too Cool*. "Before I knew it," Callas says, "it was up and running at Theater West in Los Angeles to rave reviews."

Judith Harlan, author of the nonfiction book *Girl Talk: Staying Strong, Feeling Good, Sticking Together* (Walker & Company), met Mary Kalifon, coordinator of the Parent-Child Resource Center at Cedar-Sinai Medical Center, at a booksellers' conference. "We hit it off," Harlan says. "And soon afterwards she hired me to do a lunch-hour talk at Cedar-Sinai on Take Our Daughters To Work Day."

Don't give up on a contact just because it doesn't pay off immediately. Bruce Balan, author of *Buoy, Home at Sea* (Delacorte), was once put in touch with an editor in England. The editor liked one of Balan's manuscripts but never bought it. Balan stayed in touch, however, and the connection eventually paid off—the editor left the company, but recommended Balan's manuscript to the new editor who bought it.

NETWORKING ETIQUETTE

Networking makes some people uncomfortable. That's because they hate the idea of "using" people to get ahead. It's a legitimate concern, but one that can be put to rest if you think of networking as a two-way street—you ask for help, and you also give help to others.

Enjoy the contacts you're making. If you're getting close to people simply because they can help your career, you aren't going to feel good about yourself. Besides, it won't take long for your new "friends" to realize you're not sincere. If, on the other hand, you enjoy meeting authors, editors, booksellers and librarians because they share your love of children's books, you're probably on the right track. Friendships will blossom, and soon your colleagues will be sharing information and doing you favors—and you'll be doing the same for them.

Go on, put yourself out there. You've got nothing to lose, and a world of connections to gain.

Writing Groups: Succeeding Together

BY SARA MURRAY-PLUMER

Three years ago I formed a writing group with three women I met at a writers' conference. Since then, we have met once a month and shared moments of insight and aggravation. When we started, none of us had been published in the children's market. Within a year we each had received an acceptance letter, amid a pile of rejections. I credit this success, in part, to our writing group.

Together we motivate each other and provide support for what can be a lonely and confusing endeavor. Is your story really good, or are you just delusional after spending hours staring at a computer screen? Is your main character believable, or is she just the cardboard cut-out that you move through your plot? Is your plot interesting? Are you targeting the right editors? Writing groups give you the opportunity to struggle and succeed together.

BENEFITS OF A GROUP

In *Writing Together*, authors Dawn Denham Haines, Susan Newcomer and Jacqueline Raphael note that according to Anne Ruggles Gere in her book *Writing Groups: History, Theory, and Implications*, writing groups are not a new phenomenon. Benjamin Franklin formed one of the first "mutual improvement" groups in 1728. His group met weekly to share their essays and discuss current events. They, perhaps, were some of the first individuals to discover the power of writers joining together.

Writing groups can simply offer an opportunity to share a mutual love for writing, or they can provide much more tangible results through manuscript critiques and resource sharing. Here are some of the many benefits of belonging to a writing group:

An audience for your work. Many writers create stories, poems and essays years before they share them with anyone. A writing group provides a safe place to share your work.

Objective viewpoint. Your family and friends offer kudos for your effort, but the accolades are often hollow, because those close to you do not understand the children's market and cannot offer an objective review. A writing group's sole mission is to help you become the best writer possible, not become best friends.

Constructive criticism. My family rarely feels comfortable critiquing my writing efforts. However, the members of my writing group have invested many hours helping me improve my writing. They are no longer shy about asking where the plot is or pointing out where the story is confusing.

Sharing resources. In a practical sense, writing groups can save you money. Ordering catalogs and writers guidelines or buying reference books can be expensive. The writers in my

SARA MURRAY-PLUMER *is the regional advisor for the Indiana Society of Children's Book Writers and Illustrators. Her stories have appeared in* Spider *and* Pockets *and she's written a series of nonfiction articles for* U*S* Kids. *Her book,* A Hero and a Halo, *sold more than 600 copies in Indianapolis during the 1997 holiday season and raised money for the local Humane Society. She works full time as a public relations professional for USA Group, Inc. in Indianapolis and is active in two local writing groups.*

group bring copies of publishers' guidelines to each meeting and share other information or publications.

Problem solving/brainstorming. Oliver Wendell Holmes said, "Many ideas grow better when they are transplanted into another mind than the one where they sprang up." Writing colleagues can help you overcome plot obstacles by brainstorming possible solutions.

Conference companion. Again, from a practical viewpoint, you now know a group of people who can share traveling and lodging expenses while attending writing conferences.

Dedication. Joining a group and agreeing to meet on a regular basis certainly increases your commitment to writing. It demonstrates to you and others that you are serious about writing.

Motivation. As a member of a writing group, you are accountable to someone else. You feel obligated to each other to revise manuscripts and produce new material. You will find you go the extra mile to keep from showing up empty-handed.

Encouragement. It is easy to get discouraged when your favorite manuscript gets rejected for the fourth or fourteenth time.. Your writing pals understand your artistic miseries. Fellow writers can keep you motivated and offer advice on how to revise your story, as well as provide encouragement to send it out again. In addition, your group can push you to try new styles or move out of your comfort zone.

Celebration. I find I am almost more excited to share my successes with my writing group than my friends and family. My fellow writers have struggled through several drafts and appreciate what each success—big and small—means.

GETTING STARTED

Before you can reap the rewards of a writing clique, you must first determine what type of group will enrich your writing goals. Do you want a structured group that will critique your work and offer marketing suggestions? Or, do you want, what I call, a writers' support group— writers who meet to share their love of the written word and develop their craft together? Perhaps you want a combination of both? Before you join or form a group, set your expectations, then you are more likely to find a group that meets your needs.

I belong to two writing groups. My critique group specifically focuses on marketing stories to the children's market. Our goal is to prepare each piece for publication. We critique each other's work in detail and offer suggestions as to which publishers or magazines to target. Each month we set goals for ourselves and are accountable to each other for meeting these goals.

My other writing group is less structured. We share a love of writing in all forms—poetry, drama, songwriting, fiction and nonfiction. Typically we do a timed writing that may focus on character development, dialogue or another aspect of fiction writing. We share stories, trade books, and leave refreshed and energized for the weeks of writing ahead.

Once you have decided what you want from a writing group, your search begins for like-minded writers. Finding a group of authors to share and grow with represents a significant challenge. Odds are you will not have trouble finding writers. It is surprising how many people have manuscripts tucked in a drawer or books already outlined in their heads. The trick is to find a group that meets your needs.

I have found that local workshops and conferences are the best places to collect a roster of interested writers. Other groups have formed by placing advertisements in small local newspapers or special interest magazines, such as regional magazines written for women, children or teachers. You may want to consider creating a simple flier to post in your local library, bookstores, colleges or coffee shops.

The advisor for your local chapter of the Society of Children's Book Writers and Illustrators (SCBWI) has a roster of members. If you are a SCBWI member, the SCBWI advisor may be able to connect you with other writers in the area. The World Wide Web is another option for writers who are isolated in rural communities. This high-tech option will be covered later.

IRONING OUT THE DETAILS

You have decided what you want from a writing group, and, now you have a list of potential candidates. Next, you need to set your first meeting. This is a time for some tough decisions. Your group will need to agree on certain ground rules immediately. Other decisions can wait or will be sorted out as time goes by. Below is a list of questions to pose at your first meeting.

1. Who will lead the group? The group leader should be responsible for maintaining the group. The leader does not, and probably should not, facilitate every meeting. But without an identified leader, the group may quickly fade. The leader should organize the meeting schedule, call members if meeting dates are changed, and make sure each meeting runs smoothly.

2. How often will we meet? There is no magic cycle for writing groups. Some successful groups gather twice a week; others meet only once a month. Again, decide what you want from your group, then outline an intense or relaxed schedule that meets your needs.

3. When and where should we meet? I recommend that you immediately select several meeting dates. Although the dates may change later, you will at least have the time blocked on your calendar. This minimizes absences and reduces excuses. You may want to find out where your group members live and select a central meeting location.

Also, consider what activities you want to do together. If you plan to read aloud or do timed writing, you may want to select a quiet spot, such as a member's house or the library. However, if you will discuss writing and review each other's manuscripts, a restaurant or bookstore may work fine.

4. How long should each meeting last? Set aside two or three hours initially. If your group meets weekly, you may reduce the time of each meeting. Overall, let the activities you choose determine how long each meeting runs.

5. What will the group do together? At your first meeting, you may want to ask each member what he/she expects from the writing group. The responses should give you a good feel for the group's expectations. If the group's goal is to get published, your meetings should be structured to share information on writers' markets and to prepare each other's manuscripts for submission. Alternatively, if your group members have diverse writing interests, you may want to plan writing exercises and discussions about general writing principles.

6. How many writers should you invite? SCBWI recommends starting with 3 to 5 members, with a maximum of 10 to 12. For initial planning purposes, having five to six members is ideal. Six is enough to expect a manageable group at each meeting. Because some writers immediately drop out and others will loose interest, you may want to make a list of alternates. Ask group members up front how they want to add new members. Never invite someone to the meeting without asking the group first. Each new member will add something unique to the group, so be prepared. Remember to explain the group's objectives and meeting format to the new members.

CRITIQUING TIPS

If your group decides to critique each other's work, you should set expectations for the way critiques will be conducted. When you have spent hours creating your literary masterpiece, it is difficult to hear that your characters are not believable or your plot is rough. The following list of questions drawn from the book *Writing Together* may help you establish some ground rules to make sure the critique process runs smoothly.

- Will you read the work aloud at the meeting or hand out manuscripts to review before your next meeting?
- How many manuscripts will you critique at each meeting?
- How will you decide whose manuscript is critiqued?
- What type of feedback does the author want—grammar, flow, character, plot, etc.?
- Will the author remain silent through the critique or lead the discussion?

Giving and receiving feedback on each other's stories should be a positive experience. When reviewing someone else's work, you should start by telling the author what you liked most. No manuscript is without merit. When pointing out both the positive and negative aspects of someone's work, be specific. Do not say, "Your main character is weak." Offer specific examples from the story that have led to your conclusion. If points in the story are unclear or confusing, ask questions of the author. Everyone in the group needs to recognize that you are offering an opinion. Offer your suggestion to the author, allow him or her to consider your comment, and then either accept, reject or absorb your criticism. Although it may be difficult, be honest. You joined the group to help each other improve. Do not hold back or remain silent if you think a manuscript needs work. The quality of the entire group will increase with open, honest and specific feedback.

WEB OPTIONS

If your location or schedule will not accommodate a writing group, the World Wide Web offers another option for you to share your work. Beyond offering a number of wonderful resources—from publishers' writing guidelines to help from grammar experts—the Web can also provide interaction with writers around the world. By surfing the Web, you will discover bulletin boards where writers post questions and other writers provide answers. Many of these same websites offer listservs. These are basically e-mail newsletters that are primarily made up of messages from listserv members. If you want to start an online critique group, you can post your want ad on bulletin boards and in some listservs.

Although the Web has become a great tool for writers, it also has many limitations. How comfortable are you with posting your story on an e-zine (a Web magazine) or sending it to people you do not know well? If you are looking for a writing group to share insight and inspiration, a Web group probably will not meet your needs. If you want to exchange manuscript critiques and get feedback from a variety of writers, the Web could be your answer. The tough part will be finding a critique partner or group. One Web service matches writing partners for a minimal fee. Some writing groups have formed from meetings in chat rooms or after meeting someone at a writers' conference. The web can offer isolated writers another avenue for interaction, but it should not replace the multiple benefits of actually meeting face-to-face with writers.

PATIENCE AND COMMITMENT

Every writing group will have its ups and downs. Each member should commit up front to attending the meetings regularly and taking this commitment seriously. Your group may not gel right away. Periodically each group should take a pulse check and discuss what's working and what's not. If you stick with it and remain flexible, open and honest with your writing colleagues, you will eventually settle with a productive and supportive core of writers. Whether you're a published author or a novice, the right writing group can elevate your writing to new heights.

WRITING EXERCISES

Writing groups can also grow from writing together. *Writing Together—How to Transform Your Writing in a Writing Group* calls it freewriting. Natalie Goldberg, a teacher and author of several books for writers, calls it writing practice. By setting aside time during your meetings for directed writing, you give group members the freedom to create together and learn from each other. Too often writers focus on one type of writing—fiction or nonfiction, romance or mystery. Writing practice gives each writer the chance to playfully experiment with all types of writing. Many of my story ideas have evolved from these simple timed writings.

The members of my group have been amazed at what flows from our collective brains to the page when we write together. Typically, one member of the group either leads the group in a discussion or provides a prompt to write from. Next, we establish how long we will write— usually 15 to 40 minutes. Decide before hand if you will share your work when the time is up.

ILLUSTRATORS ONLINE

My illustration and writing critique group meets frequently, offers support, advice, constructive criticism and a shoulder to cry on for those days when nothing goes right in an illustration or story, yet the members are separated by many miles and time zones. How does this happen? The group meets online through the Internet.

Our group grew as a result of meeting each other through online classes and e-mail listservs. The group consists of Joy Allen (see Insider Report on page 172), Kevan Atteberry, Janie Bynum (see page 16), Katie Davis (See How to Make a Smart Dummy on page 18), Laura Jacobsen, John Kanzler, Phyllis Pollema-Cahill (see page 234) and myself—all with different styles, interests, experience levels and mediums ranging from colored pencil, watercolor and acrylic to digital art. Many of the members both write and illustrate their own work. (There are links to most of the members sites through the illustrator links page at http://members.aol.com/thebrandon.)

We exchange ideas and images through e-mail attachments or we post our images on websites. We share sketches, works-in-progress, and finished artwork as well as rough drafts and final drafts of stories as we look for constructive criticism and support. Our varied backgrounds and interests provide an assortment of different viewpoints and opinions, each meriting thoughtful consideration.

We e-mail one another daily, and occasionally "meet" in a chat room for a interesting evening of good news, bad puns and camaraderie. We also share market tips, advice on publicity, industry gossip and information on techniques and media. Our critique group has been meeting for over a year online. (Many of us got to meet in person at SCBWI National Conference in Los Angeles in 1998.)

In some ways, this online group is more convenient than an in-person group, as we can read and answer our e-mail at our leisure, and take time to come up with well thought-out suggestions on each other's work. We've become stronger illustrators and writers through this supportive safety net of respected peers.

If you would like to form your own online critique group, start looking for illustrators and authors by surfing websites, check the SCBWI members website (http://www.scbwi.org/member.htm) or join a listserv. (To join the illustration listserv, e-mail the command "subscribe" to illustration-request@world.std.com. To join the SCBWI member listserv, send e-mail to listadmin@scbwi.org. In the subject line, write SCBWI E-MAIL LIST. Put nothing else in the body of the note—leave it blank.)

You can keep your group focused on children's book illustration and/or writing, or aim for a wider range of styles and interests. Remember the rules of a successful critique: make constructive suggestions layered with praise and keep your comments focused on media, technique and composition, even if the subject matter isn't something you empathize with.

A group may grow and change over the years as people drop in and out, but an online group can keep members even if they move far away. Any critique group is a valuable resource, and an online group is just one more way to share experiences with people you respect and admire.

—Theresa Brandon

At first, my fellow writers were self-conscious and resisted sharing our mini-creations. Someone might say, "This isn't very good, but here goes," before sharing with the group. After two meetings, we no longer felt the need to protect our feelings and our work with such caveats. We look forward to seeing the variety of directions one writing prompt will create.

Finding interesting writing exercises for your group is easy. Natalie Goldberg's book, *Wild Mind*, offers several good writing exercises. *Writing Together*, by Dawn Denham Haines, Susan Newcomer and Jacqueline Raphael dedicates an entire chapter to writing prompts. These exercises can be as simple as selecting a photo from a magazine and writing for 20 minutes. Your group could write about different pictures or about the same one. You could pull a sentence from your favorite book or a magazine article and have the group start their story from there. You could do a quick timed writing and then pass your creation to the left and let that person finish your story. The possibilities are limitless. Be creative in your writing activities.

Reaching the Youngest Audience: Writing for Babies & Toddlers

BY KELLY MILNER HALLS

"The minds of infants are active from the time they are born and are shaped by their early experiences." So said Yale child development expert Dale Cohen in *Newsweek* magazine (April 1997).

Dozens of other high-profile publications, from *Time* to *Parents*, have echoed the declaration, telling parents, educators, editors and writers that children three and under need good, age-appropriate stimulation if they are to live up to their intellectual potential.

The good news is, writers are listening. The bad news is, they seem confused about how to successfully proceed. "What exactly *is* good and age-appropriate stimulation for babies?" they wonder. "How can we best create it? And how will we know when we have?"

"It isn't easy," says Donna Johnson, editor for the National Wildlife Federation's *Your Big Backyard*. "But a lot of people think it is. No one would ever say, 'Oh I can go write novels, I can be the next Tom Clancy.' But because it's for kids, everyone thinks they can do it."

Some of the best children's writers find it difficult to craft books for babies and toddlers, according to HarperCollins Growing Tree vice president Mary Alice Moore. "Even seasoned authors sometimes focus too much on the parameters of writing for this market," she says. "If they get stuck on the idea that a children's book should teach a lesson or tell kids what to think, how to feel or what to do, the work becomes pedantic."

"Someone wanting to write for young children really needs to be familiar with living breathing human children of the age group," says Paula Morrow, editor of *Babybug*. "Many of the submissions I receive seem to be looking over the child's head. They're talking to the parent standing behind, instead of speaking directly to the child."

"Exactly," says editor Donna Johnson. "Too many writers don't take time to know who they're writing for. At least 25% of what I see cross my desk is unusable because the age range or subject matter is inappropriate."

Even a passing glance at a single issue of *Your Big Backyard* would make it clear submissions on self-help or quantum physics don't fit Johnson's editorial needs. And yet she receives dozens of similar queries every month.

Johnson also senses a lack of respect for young readers among would-be authors. "They underestimate the kids," she says. "Even very young children deserve a story with a plot, a beginning, a middle and an end, and characters they can care about. Most of what I get— I'd say 70%—doesn't fill the bill."

Mary Alice Moore set out to study, and more importantly, fill the needs of this very important but vulnerable age group. "We gathered all the books we could find in the marketplace intended

KELLY MILNER HALLS *has been a full-time professional writer for almost a decade. Her work has been featured in the* Chicago Tribune, FamilyFun, Guideposts for Kids, Highlights for Children, Teen People, U*S*Kids *and* Writer's Digest. *She writes a monthly newsletter on writing for children for America Online's* Writer's Club, *and has been a contributing editor at* Dinosaurus Magazine, the Dino Times. *Her first book* Dino Trekking *was a 1996 American Booksellers Pick of the List science book. (See her interview with Jon Scieszka and Lane Smith on page 78.)*

My First SONGS

pictures by Jane Manning

Mary Alice Moore, vice president of HarperCollins and founder of the company's new Harper Growing Tree program, studied books for babies and toddlers, and found that rhythm and rhyme were the heart and soul of the best in child-centered literature. "We latched onto the idea of a strong rhythmic quality," she says. "We realized, before babies understand words, they understand rhyme and rhythm." Growing Tree titles like *My First Songs* (for ages 1 1/2 and up), featuring ditties like "Pop! Goes the Weasel," "Take Me Out to the Ballgame" and "Row, Row, Row Your Boat," couple rhyme and rhythm with colorful illustrations to spark the minds of young "readers."

to land in the hands of babies," Moore says. "A lot of the books published for babies had dreadful text, poor quality art or a format inconsistent with what babies could actually do." Conclusion: No wonder writers are so confused.

"Then someone came to me and said, 'You're Harper, and Harper has always been about quality literature. Why not extend that same tradition to babies?' So we drew from books beloved by kids, books like *Goodnight Moon* and *Jamberry*, as a jumping off point for creating something fresh and new."

Moore found that rhythm and rhyme were the heart and soul of the best in child-centered literature. "We latched onto the idea of a strong rhythmic quality," she says. "And we asked, 'how do babies acquire language?' We realized, before babies understand words, they understand rhyme and rhythm."

"Poetry is good," says Paula Morrow. "But writers don't always use it to their full advantage. People try to sneak through with half a rhyme or an almost rhyme. I probably receive a dozen submissions a month about leaves falling 'down' and rhyming with 'ground.' Very young children are just developing an ear and a sensibility. If you give them mediocre things early on, they're going to settle for mediocre things all their lives."

"Read what's already out there as a guide," says Donna Johnson. "If you write poetry, don't work too hard on the rhymes. Good nature poetry sounds like it flows naturally."

After months of editorial planning, "in-the-trenches" market research, and extensive analysis from experts in early education, Moore proudly unveiled Harper Growing Tree in spring of 1998—a new line of quality books expressly created for babies from birth to three years of age.

With it, she introduced a whole new philosophy on reading to and writing for very young children. "My experience coming into this was that I'd run a children's book store for a few years," Moore admits. "The people least comfortable with buying books were shopping for books for their babies. Time and again they said, 'How do I know what to read to my baby, when my baby can't tell me what she likes?' "

While Moore concedes that most publishing houses have a wealth of fascinating titles for very young readers, she believes Harper Growing Tree is the first comprehensive, extensively researched reading program aimed at babies and toddlers. "We set out to identify and deliver precisely what toddlers want and need," she says.

One important guideline towards that end, according to Donna Johnson, is a story's basic mechanics. "I look for simple sentences—no compounds, a single thought. And I avoid blatant word play. Kids just don't get it." But the rebus, says Johnson, can be an ideal vehicle for very young children. "It empowers them," she says. "It helps them say, 'This is *my* magazine.' "

"I like to be surprised," says Paula Morrow. "If you can take an old topic—and in fact, most topics are old—and give it a twist of joy, a sense of wonder, or an unexpected last line, that makes it new.

"You need to be out in the world," says Morrow. "You have to be interested in the topic yourself, to make it exciting for very young readers. That's one reason we never make assignments at *Babybug*. We want the author to come up with the idea herself, so she'll give it her own, unique twist."

Mary Alice Moore believes the secret to good baby and toddler reading material lies in defining and identifying the relationship parents have with their babies. "It's not about just picking the right theme or topic. Reading to a baby is physical. It's about closeness."

"That's where the read-to-me story comes in," says Johnson. "And those tend to have an even broader appeal, age-wise, because the parent is so actively involved. But frankly, I don't get that much usable read-to-me material, so I generally draw from existing children's books." Using pick-ups, according to Johnson, guarantees not only well written text, but engaging art work as well.

"*Your Big Backyard* is very visually centered," Johnson says. "Everything, from our fiction to our nonfiction, focuses on the artwork."

"Strong illustration is essential," says Moore. "Growing Tree illustrations focus on the use of color. Books for the youngest readers are slightly simpler. But we still try to make the art part of the narrative. Our illustrations are so clear, the child can follow along based on visuals alone."

Bottom line, according to Moore and most experts, "reading to your baby should be fun. If it's not, you're going to get discouraged and give up. The idea is to help parents relax and have fun with it." Harper Growing Tree books and magazines like *Babybug* and *Your Big Backyard* are designed to make that goal easier to attain.

from the publishers of Ladybug

Carus Publishing introduced *Babybug* in 1994 to reach children ages 6 to 24 months. "Someone wanting to write for young children really needs to be familiar with living breathing human children of the age group. Many of the submissions I receive seem to be looking over the child's head. They're talking to the parent standing behind, instead of speaking directly to the child," says Paula Morrow, *Babybug*'s editor. "I like to be surprised. If you can take an old topic and give it a twist of joy, a sense of wonder, or an unexpected last line, that makes it new."

If the idea of shifting a baby's already enthusiastic imagination into overdrive appeals to you, consider these ten tips. They'll help you stay on track when it comes to early childhood development.

1. Know your prospective audience. Don't expect to write well for very young children if you have no interaction with very young children. Sit in on preschool classes. Volunteer at the local daycare facility. Babysit with the very young children of friends and family. Take the time to study your readers—before you sit down to write.

Your Big Backyard is a monthly wildlife magazine written for 3- to 6-year- olds. One important guideline for writing for this age group, says editor Donna Johnson, is paying attention to a story's basic mechanics. "I look for simple sentences—no compounds, a single thought. And I avoid blatant word play. Kids just don't get it." But the rebus, says Johnson, can be an ideal vehicle for very young children. "It empowers them," she says. "It helps them say, 'This is *my* magazine.' "

2. Read successful existing books for babies and toddlers. If you feel the burning desire to create top-notch fiction and nonfiction for babies and toddlers, study what's already doing well. Only by making yourself familiar with the best in the genre can you hope to join its ranks. Draw the finest points from these books, and add your own distinctive touch. Look to books like Bruce Degen's tender *Jamberry*, Jean Marzollo's inventive I Spy books or Eric Hill's delightful Spot series for top-quality direction.

3. Do you connect with the baby and toddler books you've read? As you read a cross section of books for very young readers, ask yourself: Do I feel a core connection to this book? If so, how and why? Use your personal insights to help develop your own baby and toddler book ideas. Look for that same connection in your own work.

4. Consider the minimum and maximum baby and toddler attention span. Never forget how quickly a baby's imagination is captured, or how soon that spark of interest can fade away. When writing for babies and toddlers, tight and bright should be your ultimate goals. Baby and toddler manuscripts vary depending on the format, but seem to come in at under 100 words, on average. Vocabulary, according to Mary Alice Moore, has a little more room for play. "We're careful in our selection of words," she admits. "But our books sometimes celebrate the way a word sounds—how it rolls off the tongue—as much as what it means."

5. Consider the physical abilities of babies and toddlers. Never introduce a concept or activity your readers can't grasp themselves. Babies and toddlers will have little cause to cherish books about jumping rope or folding paper airplanes if they can't at least imagine doing it themselves (even with a little help from their favorite grown-ups).

6. Never underestimate cuddle appeal. Reading with babies and toddlers is very often a laptime endeavor. Never underestimate the power of genuine heart. If the grown-ups reading your book aloud to their babies are touched by the text and artwork, that warmth and enthusiasm will flow through their bodies and voices into the little readers they hold.

7. Respect your audience. Never talk down to or patronize babies or toddlers with the work

TIPS ON WRITING POETRY FOR TOTS

Picture a toddler's pull toy. Push it, it rolls away from you. Pull the string, it rolls toward you. Very simple. Very age-appropriate. Bob Morrow described it for *Babybug* in the poem "Push-Pull."

I push my truck. Away it goes. I pull my truck. Look out, toes!

Four short lines young children will quickly memorize. Poetry they can recite as they play with their own toys.

First, be aware of the rhythm. The first three lines are iambic—perhaps the most natural cadence in English. The last line contains three single-stressed beats, giving a natural emphasis to the surprise ending.

What would happen if we play around with the meter? Maybe the toy is a bright red wooden fire truck.

I push my red truck . . .

Nope. the stress just shifted from the noun to the adjective.

I push my fire truck . . .

The stress is more logical because fire truck is a compound noun with emphasis on the first word. Now the line ends with a trochee (one long syllable followed by one short syllable), which in itself is fine. But line two still starts with an iamb (one short syllable followed by one long syllable), so we've lost the forward momentum by having two consecutive unstressed syllables. We could change the second line, too.

I push my fire truck. Off it goes!

Now the meter is better and the poem moves forward naturally. But line two steals the effectiveness of line four by using the three consecutive stressed beats too early. This spoils the surprise ending.

Next let's look at the rhyme. "Goes . . . toes" is true rhyme, accurate in vowel sounds and in final consonants. The toddler has to be barefoot, because we couldn't end with "Look out, shoes!" The spelling may be the same, but the spoken words are what we call "almost-rhyme." For a young child, this confuses the concept of rhyme. Use true rhyme, or don't rhyme at all.

A student writer might be tempted to avoid rhyming "truck" with "truck," perhaps by changing line three to "I pull it back." No, that's another almost-rhyme. The general writer's caveat against using a word more than once in close succession is flexible. Here, the strength of the parallel lines justifies rhyming a word with itself. Deliberate, controlled repetition is good for young children. The key is to use it for a clear reason.

Finally, consider the reader. A toddler will ask to hear a poem over and over again. "Push-Pull" is one an adult will be able to stand through dozens of repetitions. Its very simplicity—coupled with its genuine delight—make it a poem that will last.

Note: The best explanations I've seen for understanding how a poem works are by David McCord: "Write Me a Verse" in *Take Sky* (Little, Brown, 1962) and "Write Me Another Verse" in *One At a Time* (Little, Brown, 1974). Both are out of print, but check at your favorite library.

—*Paula Morrow, editor,* Babybug

you create. If you can't believe in the beauty of a cloud or the magic of a soap bubble, your reader won't believe it either.

8. Think visuals. When you write your books for babies and toddlers, remember the important, in fact crucial, role illustrations will play in that book's ultimate success. If you can't imagine age-appropriate illustrations, neither can an artist. Try to visualize each important element of your manuscript. Consider making side notes based on those visualizations to submit with your manuscript. Those comments sometimes make it easier for the artist to successfully illustrate your book and keep you visually on track as a writer.

9. Read it out loud. Read your own manuscripts out loud—alone and for the children in your world—to be sure your work is easy to share with young readers. Read it without ego or fear of self-edits or improvements. If you don't enjoy reading your own book, others won't either. Ask yourself these basic questions: Does my text flow when I read it aloud, or do I verbally stumble on certain passages? Can I easily navigate my selection of words, or must I second-guess their meanings? Are sentence-structures simple enough to keep the pacing brisk?

10. Use rhyme and rhythm with flair! Be sure your rhythms are natural and yet distinctive. Realize babies and toddlers appreciate the sound of the text as much as or more than the meaning in their earliest weeks of life.

Nonfiction: Can Informational Books Be Sexy?

BY KATHLEEN KRULL

Is it possible to esteem informational books, otherwise known as nonfiction, as a sexy genre? This article will answer in the affirmative, bolstering its case with ten tips, a list of known voids, a bibliography of role models, and even a little aerobic exercise for desk-bound minds.

(At this point, *Children's Writer's & Illustrator's Market* was to supply a line of dancing boys. If they are missing from your copy, the burden is on me to start off with an explanation of "sexy" and how in the world this could apply to books for children.)

Webster's dictionary to the rescue—"Stimulating (see erotic)," it says. If we skip the "(see erotic)" part and leave it at "stimulating," we're talking about books that turn people on. Books that grab you and can grab readers. For synonyms, see cool, gripping, suspenseful, innovative, fascinating, flashy, flamboyant . . . We may be children's book writers, but I think we just know the difference between sexy and unsexy.

My theory is that informational books are way more stimulating than the average writer, especially the one starting out, gives them credit for. Floating about is a snobbish prejudice toward them that it's time to dispel. This genre can be terribly attractive, and that is what I mean by "sexy."

A quick disclaimer: I don't label myself an "informational books author" and rarely even use the term "nonfiction"—one of the world's great ugly words. I do all kinds of writing—chapter books, picture books, mysteries—and hope to continue shaping words that reflect my passions into formats that seem to match. But I'm convinced that books containing information are the best way to get one's writing "foot" into the publishing "door," and that they can actually support the working writer. Paying bills may not sound too sexy, but isn't the sound of money worth paying attention to?

I believe that kids don't distinguish as much as we think they do between fiction and informational books. Not being snobs or literary critics, they aren't into labels. Their attitude toward a book is pretty simple: "Do I want to read this?" They have high standards for getting a "yes" to this question, and those standards don't automatically exclude genres. Most kids—especially boys, especially reluctant readers—are and will always be hungry for books that present information in an attractive way.

By now you might be wondering: Isn't this genre only for those of us who are left-brained— the organized, clear, logical ones? If I'm right-brained—creative, wild—can I stop reading now? Wait. First do this little aerobic exercise. Lace the fingers of both your hands together as if you're going to recite, "Here is the church, here is the steeple . . ." Now, which of your thumbs rests naturally on top? According to my acupuncturist (I live in California), if your left thumb

KATHLEEN KRULL, *a member of the SCBWI National Board of Directors, is a full-time writer of children's books. Her newest books are* Lives of the Presidents: Fame, Shame (and What the Neighbors Thought) *(Harcourt);* Alex Fitzgerald's Cure for Nightmares *and* Alex Fitzgerald, TV Star *(chapter books from Troll); and* They Saw the Future: Psychics, Oracles, Scientists, Inventors, and Pretty Good Guessers *(Atheneum, 1999). She has also written* 12 Keys to Writing Books That Sell, *from Writer's Digest.*

In *Wish You Were Here: Emily's Guide to the 50 States*, Kathleen Krull uses a fictional character, Emily, to teach young readers about real interesting sights in America. The book chronicles Emily's jaunt across the states with her grandma during summer vacation. The young traveler "describes the breathtaking sights, scrumptious food, funny stories, and fascinating history that make each state unique."

Illustration © 1997 Amy Schwartz. Reprinted with permission of Bantam Doubleday Dell Publishing.

comes out on top, then you are dominated by your left brain. The ideal brain for informational books—you really should give this field a try. Conversely, right thumb on top means you're right-brained. Continue reading, because this too is ideal. Informational books can be one cool way to express creativity—and this genre needs you.

This genre is perfect for anyone intrigued by the idea of transforming her areas of expertise into books. It's just right for the person who believes that life is a continuing process of self-education, a web of learning—and that getting paid at the same time is a nice bonus.

So, the first thing to deal with, when contemplating your informational writing, is the Eyewitness series. Published by Dorling Kindersley, these are mainly illustrated family reference books, with many photos and a trademark use of white space. Familiarize yourself with them, as they occupy a large corner in this territory. In the lesser bookstores, Eyewitnesses are the only books on the "nonfiction" shelf. The point here is to make your book differ from an Eyewitness. For example, instead of having an anonymous, assembled-by-committee feeling, you will want to turn your book in a more personal direction. Instead of focusing more on the pictures than the text, you may want to polish your words into the real grabbers. In any case, this shelf is your first stop in seeing what's out there (more later).

As you might guess, informational books are published for two basic age groups: picture books for approximately ages 5 to 8, and middle-grade books for approximately 8 to 12. The topics, writing style, and approach should be appropriate to each. There is such a thing as young adult (YA) nonfiction, for ages 12 and up, and it's a hungry audience. But there is so little agreement on how to bridge the gap in the marketplace between books and teens that for now this area can be a dead end for a writer.

There are also two markets for informational books. Books for the retail or trade market need to have wide appeal, to catch your eye in a bookstore. The school and library market favors

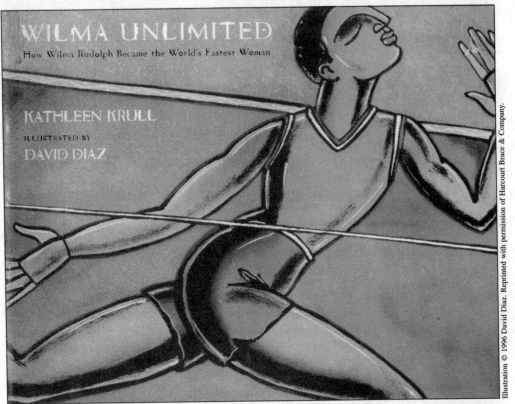

Kathleen Krull's *Wilma Unlimited: How Wilma Rudolph Became the World's Fastest Woman* tells the inspiring story (in a picture book format) of runner Wilma Rudolph, who triumphed over childhood polio and eventually became the first woman to win three gold medals at a single Olympics. Krull urges writers to "choose nonfiction topics of great meaning to you. An element of passion is in all of my books. With *Wilma Unlimited*, I was fascinated by strong women (because I know many) and polio (because I might have had it)."

books tied to the curriculum, the topics kids have to do reports on. (This genre is perfect for ex-teachers, by the way, as familiarity with the curriculum is a major plus.) Hitting both markets is an ambitious goal, but either one is worth your while. There are now more children under 18 than at any time in American history (and that includes the baby boom years). In this respect, the market has never been healthier.

Now, on with the tips:

1. Ignore this genre at your peril! Sorry to sound alarming, but this is the biggest tip: According to statistics compiled by *School Library Journal*, some 2,500 of the 5,000 books published for children each year are nonfiction. That is 50% of the market for your writing. Can you afford to think of nonfiction as not sexy, boring, just for drones, too pedestrian to bother with? Everyone wants to do picture books or novels, and editors' desks are glutted with them— the good, the bad, the very bad. A well-written, well-thought-out informational book proposal really stands out. This is the best way to get your foot in the door, and beginning writers seldom think of it. A few years ago I was asked to teach a class at the University of California at San Diego. With people always hounding me for how to break into this field, and out of a sincere desire to help, I decided to focus on writing nonfiction for kids. To my disappointment, only two people showed up the first night, and the class had to be canceled. Most disappointing of all, just two weeks earlier I had plugged the class to a local Society of Children's Book Writers and Illustrators conference—an audience of 100 struggling writers, not one of whom came to the class. (Now you see why I'm resorting to "sexy" to stress my point.)

2. Know thy competition. The usual tip in any genre, but essential here. Get on intimate terms with the current year's Subject Guide to *Books in Print*, a reference book available in most libraries. A convenient substitute, for those with Internet access, is searching by subject at Amazon.com (http://www.amazon.com), the online bookstore. As soon as you get an idea, dash to find out if it's been done, and if it has, how you can do it differently. This is the exact thought process the editor uses, and you need to get there first. With almost all of my books, I know I'm on to something when there is no competition—this is a moment of real excitement, when the blood starts flowing (sounds sexy, doesn't it?). For example, when I got the idea for *Gonna Sing My Head Off!: American Folk Songs for Children* (Knopf, 1992), I discovered in short order that my nearest competition was *The Fireside Book of Folk Songs*. This collection, illustrated by Alice and Martin Provensen, was lovely—but it had come out in 1948, and it was time for a new one. And that was the hook I used to sell the book.

3. Invest time in focusing your material. Facts are everywhere, less than a dime a dozen, really. But kids love facts presented in new ways, and you need to come up with an approach that will make your material fresh. You must take a point of view on your facts—this is the only thing people will pay you money for. So think "big," think "small," think "weird." Try not to think "neighbors," as I have already used this approach in *Lives of the Musicians: Good Times, Bad Times (and What the Neighbors Thought)* (Harcourt, 1993), and its companion books. Think "one child," as in Jim Murphy's book subtitled *The American Revolution as Experienced by One Boy* (see sidebar). Or invent a fictional character to experience your facts. *Linnea in Monet's Garden* (see sidebar) brilliantly uses a compelling voice to "process" information in totally kid-like language. I borrowed this very technique in my own *Wish You Were Here: Emily's Guide to the 50 States* (Doubleday, 1997), which combines fiction with nonfiction.

4. Think visual. In fact, this is one way of testing your idea: Does it have strong graphic appeal? True, the words are primary. But these days, the writer is responsible to varying degrees for the graphics in an informational book. You may have to do some photo research, or hire a researcher, or tell the publisher how to proceed. At the very least, you should have some tentative ideas for how you visualize the book, to prove that it is in fact illustrate-able. With my books, visuals have always factored in early on. In my Lives of series, the graphics are so crucial that they technically came first: Ever since the day I saw Kathryn Hewitt's gorgeous caricatures, I wanted to do books to match. With *V Is for Victory: America Remembers World War II* (Knopf, 1995), the text weaves inextricably around memorabilia, old letters and photos from the era.

5. Have passion! (Sexiness again.) This means choosing topics of great meaning to you. *School Library Journal* recently did a survey of nonfiction writers and was surprised to report that "personal interest" was not the main reason writers chose their topics—40% chose on the basis of "outside influence or commission request." We all have to eat, but save part of your brain for what grabs you. An element of passion is in all of my books. With *Wilma Unlimited: How Wilma Rudolph Became the World's Fastest Woman* (Harcourt, 1996), I was fascinated by strong women (because I know many) and polio (because I might have had it). *V Is for Victory* started with an interest in my own family's history. *Lives of the Musicians* was inspired by my love of music and—of nearly equal importance—love of gossip. *They Saw the Future* (Atheneum, 1999) came about because as a teen I was obsessed with Alvin Toffler's *Future Shock* and as an adult have been rumored to visit psychics. Psychics are relevant here, actually, as they could very well help you define your passions; inspiring messages from fortune cookies give clues, too . . . Anyway, the point here, as in life, is to know yourself.

6. Good writing is just as urgent here as in any other genre. Love of language will always triumph. It is always the key factor in getting an editor to say "yes." Maintain your sense of humor, indulge your sense of play, but be concise, boil things down. Hone those research skills—there are many books on this, plus librarians love to assist. In essence, do a ton of it (research), but present only the tip of its iceberg. Sometimes writers have told me that this whole

Lives of the Presidents: Fame, Shame (and What the Neighbors Thought) is the fourth book in a series written by Kathleen Krull for Harcourt Brace, in which Krull takes a gossipy approach to imparting information on historical figures, offering what *Publishers Weekly* called "living, breathing anecdotes—the stuff of which the best biography is made." "Kids love facts presented in new ways, and you need to come up with an approach that will make your material fresh," says Krull. "You must take a point of view on your facts. So think 'big,' think 'small,' think 'weird.' Try not to think 'neighbors,' as I have already used this approach in my series."

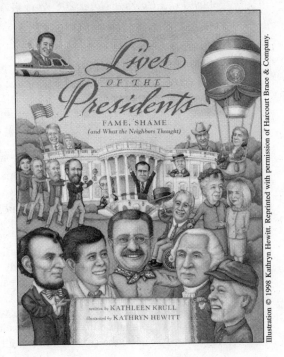

idea of research puts them off of trying nonfiction— "ugh, too much work." If you think of it this way, all writing is work, particularly sweating a picture book text down to those precious few well-chosen words, agonizing over the umpteenth draft of your novel—and suffering through the rejection process when editors are deluged with picture books and novels.

7. This is cool: You can sometimes make the sale on the basis of an outline and sample chapter, or occasionally even just the idea. Fiction can't be sold this way; editors generally won't commit until they know you can pull off the whole thing. Nonfiction is different—editors will either respond to the basic idea or they won't—and the decisions are quicker. Also, with nonfiction, you can multiply submit (send to more than one publisher at a time, letting them know what you're doing), something I ordinarily counsel strongly against.

8. Another cool thing in this genre is something called back matter. Back matter is a bunch of factual material at the back of the book that ties in to your topic, or extends it in weird and wonderful ways. This means you can choose a topic and treat it in a light, offbeat, fresh way—and then beef it up with solid info that will thrill teachers and librarians. What was just a fun idea becomes, with development, suddenly worth spending $15 on. Many of the books on my suggested reading list (see sidebar) make delightful use of back matter; the premier example is Debra Frasier's *On the Day You Were Born.*

9. Cultivate the company of librarians, who will tell you the many subject areas where they can't fill requests. Certain librarians love doing this and can be fanatic. Here are a few voids I've been told about:

- most subjects for the 5-8 age group, with the exception of animals
- current topics, current political figures, current news stories
- serious problems, like child abuse, spousal abuse, addictions, handicaps, stepfamilies (a huge gap), ADD and ADHD
- gross topics done tastefully (this is not my particular forte, but my husband, Paul Brewer, is starting his illustration career in just this way, with *The Grossest Joke Book Ever* and

French Fries Up Your Nose: 208 Ways to Annoy People, both from Avon)

- any topic that touches Latinos (perhaps the biggest void of all: by 2050, 40% of the U.S. population will be Latino, and in no way does the percentage of books for them come close)
- general immigration issues (according to the Census Bureau, the children of immigrants will account for 88% of the increase in the under-18 population in the next 50 years)
- gay and lesbian themes
- the topic of sex itself! (kids are asking the embarrassing questions at a younger and younger age)
- spiritual and religious topics

Actually, once you start thinking in terms of informational books, ideas are literally everywhere. Getting them will be the least of your problems. Deciding which ones to invest your valuable energy in will be the dilemma.

10. It's crucial to pay attention to informational books getting published. The children's books of 1999 are not the books we remember from childhood. Subscribe to *Publishers Weekly*, *Booklist*, *The Horn Book*; become a pest at your nearest bookstore; do whatever you have to do to keep up. The reading list accompanying this article (see sidebar) has some of the recent books I've loved. Most are by authors who have a body of work, so you can look for other books by the same names. These are just some of the creative people who use both their right and left brains in informational writing. I did have a tip 11—how to sleep your way to publication—but *Children's Writer's & Illustrator's Market* has a very rigid word count. . . . So I must wrap up by saying that informational books can be an exciting, exhilarating way to make a living—and the sound of money can be the sexiest thing of all.

READING LIST OF NONFICTION INNOVATORS

Younger nonfiction (approximately ages 5-8):

Communication, by Aliki, Greenwillow, 1993.

A Is for Asia, by Chin-Lee, Orchard, 1997.

The Magic School Bus Exploring the Five Senses, by Joanna Cole, Scholastic, 1999.

Hands, by Lois Ehlert, Harcourt, 1997.

My Map Book, by Sara Fanelli, HarperCollins, 1995.

On the Day You Were Born, by Debra Frasier, Harcourt, 1991.

Roman Numerals I to MM: Numerabilia Romana Uno ad Duo Mila, by Arthur Geisert, Houghton Mifflin, 1996.

My First Book of Proverbs: Mi Primer Libro de Dichos, by Ralfka Gonzalez, Children's Book Press, 1995.

Cactus Hotel, by Brenda Z. Guiberson, Holt, 1991.

Seven Brave Women, by Betsy Hearne, Greenwillow, 1997.

I Wonder What's Under There?: A Brief History of Underwear, by Deborah Nourse Lattimore, Harcourt, 1998.

Messages in the Mailbox: How to Write a Letter, by Loreen Leedy, Holiday House, 1991.

Contemplating Your Bellybutton, by Jun Nunao, Kane/Miller, 1995.

The Seasons Sewn: A Year in Patchwork, by Ann Whitford Paul, Harcourt, 1996.

How to Make an Apple Pie and See the World, by Marjorie Priceman, Knopf, 1994.

The Buck Stops Here: The Presidents of the United States, by Alice Provensen, Harcourt, 1997.

Diego, by Jeanette Winter, Knopf, 1991.

Older Nonfiction (approximately ages 8-12):

Linnea in Monet's Garden, by Christina Bjork, R & S Books, 1987.

Victoria and Her Times, by Jean-Loup Chiflet and Alain Beaulet, Holt, 1996.

Why Can't I Live Forever?: And Other Not Such Dumb Questions About Life, by Vicki Cobb, Dutton, 1997.

How to Read Your Mother's Mind, by James M. Deem, Houghton Mifflin, 1994.

Kids at Work: Lewis Hine and the Crusade Against Child Labor, by Russell Freedman, Clarion, 1994.

George Washington's Mother, by Jean Fritz, Putnam, 1992.

Period, by JoAnn Gardner-Loulan, et al, Volcano, 1991.

When Plague Strikes: The Black Death, Smallpox, AIDS, by James Cross Giblin, HarperCollins, 1995.

It's Perfectly Normal: Changing Bodies, Growing Up, Sex & Sexual Health, by Robie H. Harris, Candlewick, 1994.

Mistakes That Worked and *Accidents May Happen*, by Charlotte Foltz Jones, Doubleday, 1991 and 1996.

She's Wearing a Dead Bird on Her Head!, by Kathryn Lasky, Hyperion, 1995.

Christmas in the Big House, Christmas in the Quarters, by Patricia and Fredrick McKissack, Scholastic, 1994.

A Young Patriot: The American Revolution as Experienced by One Boy, by Jim Murphy, Clarion, 1996.

One World, Many Religions: The Ways We Worship, by Mary Pope Osborne, Knopf, 1996.

Alvin Ailey, by Andrea Davis Pinkney, Hyperion, 1993.

It's Disgusting and We Ate It!: True Food Facts from Around the World and Throughout History, by James Solheim, Simon & Schuster, 1998.

The Book of Goddesses, by Kris Waldherr, Beyond Words, 1995.

Gladiator, by Richard Watkins, Houghton Mifflin, 1997.

A Drop of Water, by Walter Wick, Scholastic, 1997.

Jon Scieszka & Lane Smith: A Perfect Partnership Leads to Stinky Sweet Success

BY KELLY MILNER HALLS

Author Jon Scieszka and illustrator Lane Smith were worlds apart before their wives narrowed the gap. Scieszka was a teacher, shaping the hearts and minds of New York second graders. Smith was doing freelance editorial illustrations for heavy hitters like *Time*, *Newsweek* and *Ms.*

Working together at *Sport Magazine*, Scieszka's wife Jeri and Smith's girlfriend (now wife) Molly Leech must have seen the writing on the wall. They knew these two brilliant, quirky guys should meet. "Yeah," Smith says, "they got us together because we were goofing off too much."

Once introduced, Scieszka and Smith were unstoppable. "I showed Lane the text for *The True Story of the 3 Little Pigs*," Scieszka says, "and I told him I didn't have a real clear idea of what I wanted them to look like." But that wasn't a problem. Smith's vision picked up where Scieszka's left off.

Photo: Brian Smale

Lane Smith and Jon Scieszka

Smith and Scieszka submitted *3 Little Pigs* to Viking as a team—something rarely done in the world of children's publishing. And as a team, they were awarded a contract. Almost as soon as the book was on bookstores shelves (in October of 1989) it was a hit.

"Our editor kept warning us, 'Guys, not every book is like this,' " Scieszka remembers. But their follow-up, *The Stinky Cheese Man and Other Fairly Stupid Tales* (1993), did even better. *Math Curse* (1995), a concept Smith wasn't sure could *be* funny, shot to the top of the bestseller list. And their latest, *Squids Will Be Squids: A Modern Book of Fables* (1998) has also risen to the top. "She's given up on warning us now," Scieszka says with a smile.

You have often submitted work as a team. Isn't it unusual for an author and illustrator to work together so closely?

KELLY MILNER HALLS *has been a full-time professional writer for almost a decade. Her work has been featured in* FamilyFun, Guideposts for Kids, Highlights for Children, Teen People, U*S*Kids *and* Writer's Digest. *Her first book* Dino Trekking *was a 1996 American Booksellers Pick of the List science book. (See her article* Reaching the Youngest Audience: Writing for Babies & Toddlers *on page 64)*

In *Squids Will Be Squids: Fresh Morals, Beastly Fables*, the latest from Jon Scieszka and Lane Smith, the author/illustrator dynamic duo do for the fable what they did in for the fairy tale in *The Stinky Cheese Man*. In a starred review, *Publishers Weekly* says of *Squids*, "Foxes and grapes are too pedestrian for these veteran absurdists, who tackle boastfulness in 'Duckbilled Platypus vs. BeefSnakStik®' and vanity in the story of a skateboarding frog . . .beneath this duo's playful eccentricity readers will discover some powerful insights into human nature."

Scieszka: Yes, I think it's very unusual.

Smith: A lot of times the author and the illustrator never even meet. The text is approved, and assigned to an illustrator the publisher picks. But I think it's crucial for Jon and I to know each other in order to work together. If I didn't know Jon and talk to him, I might misinterpret something he's written.

Jon, do you imagine Lane's illustrations as you write?

Scieszka: No, not really. My imagination is much more aural in that I hear the words and see the text. And I think that's why Lane and I are such a good combination, because I don't imagine stuff. Illustrators appreciate writers that don't overburden them with expectations. I appreciate who Lane is, what he does, so I just let him work.

Smith: That's why it's worked out so well with us. We have a great creative rapport in our work. We each completely support and admire what the other does. I couldn't write like Jon and he can't draw, that's for sure.

Do you ever make suggestions about one another's work?

Scieszka: We have great relationship in that we can change things. There was a story in Squids called "Little Llama Lips." Lane thought a walrus would be funnier, so we changed it to "Little Walrus Lips."

Smith: Anyone else would be grossly offended. But I told Jon the only way I could paint a llama and make it funny would be to over exaggerate . . . to give it big eyelashes and things like that. A walrus was a no brainer.

Working together is really fun for you two, isn't it? Does that help keep your books fresh and fun?

Scieszka: Yeah, it's fun to work with Lane. We end up cracking each other up so much. And yes, I think kids definitely pick up on that—it translates into the work.

Smith: Absolutely, yes. We get these comments—people who clump us in with some sophisticated group of adult books under the guise of a children's book. But we fight that. These are kids books—books that appeal to goofy kids.

Was it always your goal to create books for children?

Scieszka: No. I started out more interested in science. In college, I was officially pre-med—studying to be a doctor, along with writing. Eventually, I got accepted to Columbia writing school and got a masters in fiction. But I was thinking I'd write adult novels.

Smith: I studied illustration at a school called Art Center College of Design in Pasadena. When I was there, they didn't have a kids' book department. Michael Hague was the only one I know of who studied there before I did, and went on to make children's books.

Did you have any idea when you started you'd enjoy such enormous success?

Scieszka: We were never really looking at it from a sales angle. I think when a writer thinks in those terms, it's a tremendous mistake.

Smith: No. In fact, I warned Jon, do this because you love it, but keep your day job. Even after *3 Little Pigs* came out, we were having fun with it, but as far as selling hundreds and thousands of copies, we had no idea. I don't think we even realized it was a success until we went to the

RE-DEFINING DESIGN

After years of designing graphics for publications like *Sport Magazine*, Molly Leach knew how to make words visually pleasing. She knew how to add impact and dramatic flare to the body of a story and illustrations. By manipulating fonts, layouts and color, she could turn up the heat, even on a lukewarm project.

When Leach turned that expertise on her husband illustrator Lane Smith and author Jon Scieszka's hot and sassy picture books, it was a marriage made in heaven. It proved to be a union that would change the complexion and stretch the boundaries of children's book design forever.

"I had no background in kids' books at all when we started *The True Story of the 3 Little Pigs*," she says. "And traditionally, children's books are designed in house, by the publisher. But from the beginning, Lane and Jon wanted a different look. Most art directors at most publishing houses are too over worked to experiment so I took it on."

First on Leach's creative agenda? To get in on the ground floor. "For most designers, the art comes in, then the text comes in and they put it together—they are detached," according to Lane Smith. "But with Molly, she's here from the beginning. It's a collaborative three way from the very start." How closely does Leach work with Lane Smith and Jon Scieszka? "Well, she sleeps with me," says her husband Smith. "How much closer can it get?"

"I also build some walls so we don't look at each other all the time," Leach counters playfully. "But it's true, I get in on it as soon as they start talking about a book. If Lane is working on an illustration, he'll ask me what size he should make it. And Jon is fabulous. He truly understands the value of design. If I ask him to lose a word, he's very flexible. He knows it can be better for the work."

Next, Leach makes the break from primary colors. "I look at a lot of those kids' books and magazines and think, 'Oiey, the colors. Why do they always pick bright primary colors? I broke from that. I used the same pallet I would use for *Business Week*. I think children can and do appreciate the whole spectrum of color."

"A lot of those subtle choices people attribute to me," says illustrator Lane Smith. "Things like the background tints in *Hooray for Diffendoofer Day!* that lend themselves so well to Seuss, are really Molly's doing."

Next, Leach invades the gutters. She challenges the frame of emptiness that traditionally surrounds the meat and potatoes of children's books. "That was really hard at first for Viking," she admits. "On *Stinky*, when I first did that, they hated it. It was my first book, and the wildest thing they'd ever seen. They kept saying, 'this is a book not a magazine. It's gonna get trimmed.' But I didn't care if it got trimmed. I wanted all that type to go right to the edge."

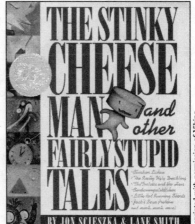

Designer Molly Leach pushes the boundaries of traditional picture book design on Scieszka/Smith titles. When Viking first saw the design for *The Stinky Cheese Man* "they hated it," says Leach. "It was my first book, and the wildest thing they'd ever seen."

Lastly, Leach uses font selections not only to spell out the words, but to accentuate content. "I'll vary the size, layout, even the color to emphasize key points within the text."

The end result is a swirl of vibrant activity, a sophistication new to children's books, that readers eagerly embrace. "Kids can handle sophistication," Leach insists. "And if they can handle it, why not give them what they want?"

—*Kelly Milner Halls*

ALA convention and all these people came up to us saying how much they loved the book.

Was making your books distinctive a conscious choice?

Scieszka: When we started, I thought the business was missing some alternative choices. There were plenty of warm fuzzy stories out there, and there is a place for that. But it was as if all books had to live up to some moral standard, as if kids had to learn a lesson from everything they read. And that's just not true. Books can be entertaining, too.

Do you think the wacky nature of your books ever works against you?

Scieszka: Well, I suppose it works against us in the world of big awards and acclaim. But I don't think kids care one way or another. And hey, Lane got a Caldecott Honor for *Stinky*. It's promising that the committee would honor any book with the words "stinky" and "stupid" both in the title.

Smith: Yeah, I apologize for that. I don't know what they were thinking. No, it was such a pleasant surprise to receive that honor. But that's not really what our books are about. When we were kids, the only wacky books were books by Dr. Seuss. It's great to have that choice now—to make books that kids actually want to read.

How do you stay tuned in to the kids within your target audience?

Scieszka: I go out and read to kids. I love editing and honing my stuff that way. To me, children's books are a continuation of the old oral traditions. People who write stuff and don't read aloud are missing the point. Something that looks good on paper might be too clunky to wrap your tongue around.

Smith: We had our own little focus group with *Squids*. Jon really tapped into the humor of those kids. I think Jon misses teaching so he's great that way. I like meeting the kids too, but I'm a little more reclusive. I'm an illustrator. I like to be alone with my thoughts and my paint brushes. Jon's a social guy.

Did you run into any stumbling blocks as a beginner? And how did you overcome them?

Scieszka: Overcoming that dread of getting rejected is important. I think it's best to just accept that rejection will happen, then get out there and get it over with. It's really not personal. Publishers are a great group of people who are looking for good stuff. So persistence is the key. People come up to me and say, I was thinking of sending something in. But no one is going to give you a contract based on a thought. You've got to write the thing and get it out there.

And a second common problem is submitting things in the wrong format. That's like shooting yourself in the foot before you even get started. Most people don't realize that picture books are 32 pages long, just 28 printed pages. That's small. At least start by working in that format.

Smith: Stinky Cheese Man was rejected by a lot of publishers. In fact, while we were promoting *The True Story of the 3 Little Pigs*, Jon would tell kids not everything he wrote was so great, and read from *Stinky*. As soon as he did, the kids would die laughing. So we started thinking maybe we should go back and do these stories. Eventually, the publisher gave the *Stinky* stories a green light. But they were originally goofy rejects.

Your books are all so unique. Was it ever tempting to play it safe? Follow a formula?

Scieszka: Lane and I go to great lengths to avoid being predictable. After *3 Little Pigs*, we did something stranger. Then, after *Stinky*, people expected more fairy tales, so we ran for the hills and did *Math Curse*. Then everyone expected *Science Curse* because of the joke at the end. The

STEPPING INTO SEUSSIAN SHOES

By the time Random House offered him the chance to create original art for the last manuscript by Dr. Seuss, Lane Smith was already an established professional. He had illustrated a string of critically acclaimed titles with author Jon Scieszka (including *The True Story of the 3 Little Pigs*, *The Stinky Cheese Man and Other Fairly Stupid Tales*, *Math Curse*, and *Squids Will Be Squids: Fresh Morals, Beastly Fables*) as well as a number of his own book projects.

Smith admits his personal sense of achievement was essential to making *Hooray for Diffendoofer Day!* a vibrant new children's book.

"It was an intimidating project." he says. "Because I was such a big fan of Theodore Geisel's, I really wanted to do justice to his legacy. I didn't want to shy away from the Dr. Seuss look and do just my own thing. But at the same time I didn't want to copy. I knew I had to find that middle ground. I had to do it in my own style—flowing bursts of radiating lines—while acknowledging Geisel's touch."

To accomplish his goal, Smith had only one choice—to jump in with both feet. "I have all his books, so I went back and read them, along with his biography by Neil and Judith Morgan. I watched some of his films, including his live action stuff from the '50s. Then Ted's long timeeditor Janet Schulmann gave me her blessing and told me not to damage Seuss' original art, which was one of the greatest things about doing this book. There I was, surrounded by his notes and sketches, his art." Was Smith also visited by the spirit of Dr. Seuss? "I won't even go there," he says. "But yeah, you do think about that. I also thought about Roald Dahl when I was doing the film and books for *James and the Giant Peach*. These men are icons. Of course you're aware of their presence and want to do right by them."

According to Theodore Geisel's widow Audry, Smith successfully met the challenge. "I was a little worried," Smith admits. "I didn't know what she would think. I was afraid she'd want to change the artwork or have restrictions, but there weren't any. I

Reprinted with permission of Alfred A. Knopf, Inc.

Lane Smith felt honored to illustrate the last manuscript by the late Dr. Seuss, *Hooray for Diffendoofer Day*. "It was an intimidating project." he says. "Because I was such a big fan of Theodore Geisel's, I really wanted to do justice to his legacy."

think she could tell I was sincere in my regard for her husband's work. I think she was pleased I incorporated his images in my illustrations. In fact, I think it really surprised her."

Smith's one regret is "only that I never met Theodore Geisel himself. When I started *Diffendoofer*, I went to his house and met Audry, saw his art collection and how he worked. So I really got a sense of him. But that's a true regret, not meeting Dr. Seuss. I think of all the authors and illustrators in our business, he would be the one I'd most like to meet."

In a very real sense, Lane Smith considers *Hooray for Diffendoofer Day!* more than a feather in his professional cap. He sees it as a tribute to an American icon. "People will know it's my work, but there are definite Seuss things going on, a deliberate homage. I hope putting pieces of his work into mine bring up fond memories. I hope it works on that level."

—*Kelly Milner Halls*

JON SCIESZKA + LANE SMITH

"I know, I know. A math book, doesn't sound very funny. Lane said the same thing. But it worked," says Jon Scieszka. *Math Curse* was the follow-up to Scieszka and partner Lane Smith's wildly successful *The Stinky Cheese Man and Other Fairly Stupid Tales. Math Curse* begins, "On Monday in math class Mrs. Fibonacci says, 'You know, you can think of almost everything as a math problem./ On Tuesday I start having problems," sending the young narrator through 20-plus pages of equation hell and number nightmares.

point is, we have respect for the kids. We're not just cranking out some product.

Speaking of *Math Curse* . . .

Scieszka: I know, I know. A math book doesn't sound very funny. Lane said the same thing. But it worked.

Smith: I was surprised that *Math Curse* did so well 'cause it was a book about math.

Tell us a little about *Squids*. How did it come about?

Scieszka: I was working on a bunch of different things when my editor said, "You probably should be thinking of putting a new book out." I was thinking *Math Curse* just came out. But it had been like two years. So I just started writing these fables—rewriting stories my daughter or my son told me. I discovered if you change peoples names into animals, you can write about anything.

Smith: Squids goes back to our core audience. *Stinky* fans will not be disappointed. And this one is even more *out there*. Jon even did one story about beef snack.

Is it fun to bring unusual characters like a beef snack to life?
Scieszka: Sure, it's fun to stretch the boundaries.

Smith: They're challenges, but really fun challenges. For years I told Jon, "Don't do stories with people so much," and he really out did himself in *Squids*. There are insects, animals, objects. One story we took out was about a question mark, an exclamation mark and a comma. That would have been a fun one to illustrate.

Will we ever see your books cross over into other mediums?
Scieszka: We're working on a couple of things. We'd like to bring the Time Warp books (a middle series they write and illustrate) to TV. And we'd like to do a *Stinky* movie. But the nice thing is we're under no pressure. So we're not all crazy just because a studio calls.

Smith: We would like to do *Stinky* as a movie and we're always negotiating, but it may not go anywhere. We are very particular with how we do the books and the same with the film. It's a lot harder to make movies. Everyone wants to water down your product. We'll give it a shot, but if in the end they try to make it what it's not, we'll walk away.

KEY TO SYMBOLS & ABBREVIATIONS

N Indicates a listing new in this edition.

⚐ Indicates a Canadian listing.

◻ Indicates a publisher produces educational material.

⊞ Indicates a book packager/producer.

✓ Indicates a company's contact information has changed since the 1998 edition.

A Indicates a publisher accepts agented submissions only.

⚑ Indicates an award-winning publisher.

● Indicates a comment from the editor of *Children's Writer's & Illustrator's Market.*

ms or **mss** Stands for manuscript or manuscripts.

SASE Refers to a self-addressed stamped envelope.

SAE Refers to a self-addressed envelope.

IRC Stands for International Reply Coupon. These are required with SAEs sent to markets in countries other than your own.

b&w Stands for black and white.

IMPORTANT LISTING INFORMATION

• Listings are based on questionnaires, phone calls and updated copy. They are not advertisements nor are markets reported here necessarily endorsed by the editor of this book.

• Information in the listings comes directly from the companies and is as accurate as possible, but situations may change and needs may fluctuate between the publication of this directory and the time you use it.

• *Children's Writer's & Illustrator's Market* reserves the right to exclude any listing that does not meet its requirements.

COMPLAINT PROCEDURE

If you feel you have not been treated fairly by a listing in *Children's Writer's & Illustrator's Market*, we advise you to take the following steps:

• First try to contact the listing. Sometimes one phone call or a letter can quickly clear up the matter.

• Document all your correspondence with the listing. When you write to us with a complaint, provide the details of your submission, the date of your first contact with the listing and the nature of your subsequent correspondence.

• We will enter your letter into our files and attempt to contact the listing.

• The number and severity of complaints will be considered in our decision whether or not to delete the listing from the next edition.

Book Publishers

Getting published can seem like a crap shoot—you must get the right manuscript on the right editor's desk at the right time. Doing research before you submit, however, can better your odds. It's important to learn publishers' needs, see what kind of books they're producing and decide which publishers your work is best suited for. *Children's Writer's & Illustrator's Market* is but one tool in this process. To help you narrow down the list of possible publishers for your work, we've included several indexes at the back of this book. **The Subject Index** lists book and magazine publishers according to their fiction and nonfiction needs or interests. **The Age-Level Index** indicates which age groups publishers cater to. **The Photography Index** indicates which markets buy photography for children's publications. **The Poetry Index** lists publishers accepting poetry.

If you write contemporary fiction for young adults, for example, and you're trying to place a book manuscript, go first to the Subject Index. Locate the fiction categories under Book Publishers and copy the list under Contemporary. Then go to the Age-Level Index and highlight the publishers on the Contemporary list that are included under the Young Adults heading. Read the listings for the highlighted publishers to see if your work matches their needs.

Remember, *Children's Writer's & Illustrator's Market* should not be your only source for researching publishers. Here are a few other sources of information:

- SCBWI offers members an annual market survey of children's book publishers. (Members send a SASE with $3 postage.)
- The Children's Book Council website (http://www.cbcbooks.org) gives information on member publishers.
- If a publisher interests you, send a SASE for submission guidelines *before* submitting. For a searchable database of more than 1,000 publishers' guidelines, visit http://www.writersdi gest.com.
- Check publishers' websites. Many include their complete catalogs which you can browse.
- Spend time at your local bookstore to see who's publishing what. While you're there, browse through *Publishers Weekly*, *The Horn Book* and *Riverbank Review*.

SUBSIDY AND SELF-PUBLISHING

Some determined writers who receive rejections from royalty publishers may look to subsidy and co-op publishers as an option for getting their work into print. These publishers ask writers to pay all or part of the costs of producing a book. We strongly advise writers and illustrators to work only with publishers who pay them. For this reason, we've adopted a policy not to include any subsidy or co-op publishers in *Children's Writer's & Illustrator's Market* (or any other Writer's Digest Books market books).

If you're interested in publishing your book just to share it with friends and relatives, self-publishing is a viable option, but it involves a lot of time and energy. You oversee all book production details. Check with a local printer for advice and information on cost.

Whatever path you choose, keep in mind that the market is flooded with submissions, so it's important for you to hone your craft and submit the best work possible. Competition from thousands of other writers and illustrators makes it more important than ever to research publishers before submitting—read their guidelines, look at their catalogs, check out a few of their titles and visit their websites.

BOOK PUBLISHERS

ADVICE FROM INSIDERS

For insight and advice on getting published from a variety of perspectives, be sure to read the Insider Reports in this section. Subjects include young adult novelist **Nancy Garden** (page 112); literary agent and editor **Ann Tobias** (page 122); Meadowbrook editor and author **Bruce Lansky** (page 146); Morehouse Publishing editor **Debra Farrington** (page 152); Caldecott medal-winning author/illustrator **Peggy Rathmann** (page 166); prolific electronic illustrator **Joy Allen** (page 172); renowned picture book artist **Barry Moser** (page 178); Newbery winner **Karen Hesse** (page 184); and Pulitzer Prize winner **Anna Quindlen** (page 196).

ACROPOLIS BOOKS, 747 Sheridan Blvd., #1-A, Lakewood CO 80214. (303)231-9923. Fax: (303)235-0492. E-mail: acropolisbooks@worldnet.att.net. Website: http://www.acropolisbooks.com. Imprints: I Level, Awakening, Flashlight. Book publisher. **Manuscript/Art Acquisitions:** Constance J. Wilson, editor in chief. Publishes 2 picture books/year; 2 young readers/year; and 2 middle readers/year. 50% of books by first-time authors.
Fiction: Picture books, young readers: animal, folktales, poetry, religion. Middle readers, young adults/teens: folktales, poetry, religion. "No fantasy—please understand our focus. We are just bringing up our children's imprint—the books scheduled all have a gentle theme of wisdom and help a child understand his/her true identity."
Nonfiction: Picture books, young readers, middle readers: animal, religion, self help. Young adults/teens: religion, self help. Recently published *Closer Walk with God*, written by Jim Rosemergy (young adult); *Living Joyfully with Children*, written by Win Sweet (adult); and *Oxford Books of English Mystical Verse* (adult).
How to Contact/Writers: Fiction: Submit complete ms. Reports on queries in 1 month; mss in 2 months. Publishes a book 18-24 months after acceptance. Will consider simultaneous submissions.
Illustration: Works with 3 illustrators/year. Reviews ms/illustration packages from artists. Illustrations only: Query first. Reports back in 2 months. Samples returned with SASE; samples filed for 6 months.
Photography: Buys stock and assigns work. Model/property releases required. Uses color prints. Submit cover letter, résumé, published samples, promo piece.
Terms: Pays authors royalty of 7-12.5% based on wholesale price. Offers advances (varies) based on wholesale price. Pays illustrators by the project or royalty (varies) based on wholesale price. Pays photographers by the project (varies). Sends galleys to authors; dummies to illustrators. Book catalog available for $3; ms guidelines for SASE.
Tips: "Understand our publishing focus on consciousness (wisdom through spiritual understanding) in expression today. We are interested in eternal, timeless truth, not specific religious/religions."

N □ ACTION PUBLISHING, P.O. Box 391, Glendale CA 91209. (213)478-1667. Fax: (213)478-1767. Website: http://actionpub.com. Book publisher. Estab. 1996. Publishes rapid learning and values oriented material featuring the Kuekumber Kids and other series by Scott E. Sutton. **Publisher:** Michael Metzler. **Art Acquisitions:** Art Director. Publishes 4 young readers/year; 2 middle readers/year; and 2 young adult titles/year.
Nonfiction: Young readers: arts/crafts, geography, health, how-to, nature/environment, reference, science, sports, textbooks. Middle readers, young adults: arts/crafts, careers, cooking geography, health, history, how-to, reference, science, sports, textbooks. Recently published *Kuekumber Kids Meet the Monster of Manners* and *The Secret of Gorbee Grotto!*, both written and illustrated by Scott Sutton (ages 7-11).
How to Contact/Writers: Query. Reports on queries in 1 week; mss in 5 weeks. Publishes a book 16 months after acceptance. Will consider simultaneous submissions and previously published work.
Illustration: Works with 2 illustrators/year. Reviews ms/illustration packages from artists. Query. Contact: Publisher. Send promotional literature. Contact: Art Director. Reports on submissions in 1 week. Samples returned with SASE or kept on file if interested and OK with illustrator.
Photography: Buys stock and assigns work. Contact: Art Director. "We use photos on as-needed basis.

**FOR EXPLANATIONS OF THESE SYMBOLS,
SEE THE INSIDE FRONT AND BACK COVERS OF THIS BOOK**

Mainly publicity, advertising and copy work." Uses 35mm or 4×5 transparencies. Submit cover letter and promo piece.

Terms: Pays authors royalty based on wholesale price. Offers advances against royalties. Pays illustrators by the project or royalty. Pays photographers by the project or per photo Sends galleys to authors. Original art returned as negotiated depending on project. Book catalog available for #10 SAE and 1 first-class stamp.

Tips: "Many of our projects are originated in-house but we are always interested in new work. Send us a query along with a brief sample allowing fast evaluation. We will respond quickly."

✓ **ADVOCACY PRESS**, P.O. Box 236, Santa Barbara CA 93102. (805)962-2728. Fax: (805)963-3580. Division of The Girls Incorporated of Greater Santa Barbara. Book publisher. Editorial Contact: Fred Klein. Publishes 2-4 children's books/year.

Fiction: Picture books, young readers, middle readers: adventure, animal, concepts in self-esteem, contemporary, fantasy, folktales, gender equity, multicultural, nature/environment, poetry. "Illustrated children's stories incorporate self-esteem, gender equity, self-awareness concepts." Published *Nature's Wonderful World in Rhyme* (birth-age 12, collection of poems); *Shadow and the Ready Time* (32-page picture book). "Most publications are 32-48 page picture stories for readers 4-11 years. Most feature adventures of animals in interesting/educational locales."

Nonfiction: Middle readers, young adults: careers, multicultural, self-help, social issues, textbooks.

How to Contact/Writers: "Because of the required focus of our publications, most have been written inhouse." Reports on queries/mss in 1-2 months. Include SASE.

Illustration: "Require intimate integration of art with story. Therefore, almost always use local illustrators." Average about 30 illustrations per story. Reviews ms/illustration packages from artists. Submit ms with dummy. Contact: Fred Klein. Reports in 1-2 months. Samples returned with SASE.

Terms: Authors paid by royalty or outright purchase. Pays illustrators by project or royalty. Book catalog and ms guidelines for SASE.

Tips: "We are not presently looking for new titles."

AFRICA WORLD PRESS, P.O. Box 1892, Trenton NJ 08607. (609)844-9583. Fax: (609)844-0198. Book publisher. **Manuscript Acquisitions:** Kassahun Checole. **Art Acquisitions:** Kassahun Checole, editor. Publishes 5 picture books/year; 15 young reader and young adult titles/year; 8 middle readers/year. Books concentrate on African-American life.

Fiction: Picture books, young readers: adventure, concept, contemporary, folktales, history, multicultural. Middle readers, young adults: adventure, contemporary, folktales, history, multicultural.

Nonfiction: Picture books, young readers, middle readers, young adults: concept, history, multicultural. Does not want to see self-help, gender or health books.

How to Contact/Writers: Query; submit outline/synopsis and 2 sample chapters. Reports on queries in 30-45 days; mss in 3 months. Will consider previously published work.

Illustration: Works with 10-20 illustrators/year. Reviews ms/illustration packages from artists. Query. Illustrations only: Query with samples. Reports in 3 months.

Terms: Pays authors royalty based on retail price. Pays illustrators by the project or royalty based on retail price. Book catalog available for SAE; ms and art guidelines available for SASE.

✓ **ALADDIN PAPERBACKS**, 1230 Avenue of the Americas, 4th Floor, New York NY 10020. Paperback imprint of Simon & Schuster Children's Publishing Children's Division. Vice President/Editorial Director: Ellen Krieger. **Manuscript Acquisitions:** Stephen Fraser, executive editor. **Art Acquisitions:** Steve Scott, art director. Publishes 130 titles/year.

● Aladdin publishes primarily reprints of successful hardcovers from other Simon & Schuster imprints. They accept query letters with proposals for middle grade and young adult series, beginning readers and commercial nonfiction.

✓ **ALYSON PUBLICATIONS, INC.**, P.O. 4371, Los Angeles CA 90078. (323)860-6065. Fax: (323)467-0173. Book publisher. **Acquisitions:** Editorial Department. Publishes 1 (projected) picture book/year and 3 (projected) young adult titles/year. "Alyson Wonderland is the line of illustrated children's books. We are looking for diverse depictions of family life for children of gay and lesbian parents."

Fiction: All levels: adventure, animal, contemporary, fantasy, history, humor, multicultural, nature/environment, science fiction. Young readers and middle readers: suspense, mystery. Teens: anthology.

Nonfiction: Teens: concept, social issues. "We like books that incorporate all racial, religious and body types, as well as dealing with children with gay and lesbian parents—which all our books must deal with. Our YA books should deal with issues faced by kids growing up gay or lesbian." Published *Heather Has Two Mommies*, by Lesléa Newman; and *Daddy's Wedding*, by Michael Willhoite.

How to Contact/Writers: Submit outline/synopsis and sample chapters (young adults); submit complete ms (picture books/young readers). Reports on queries/mss within 3 months. Include SASE.
Illustration: Works with 2 illustrators/year. Reviews mss/illustration packages from artists. Illustrations only: Submit "representative art that can be *kept on file*. Good quality photocopies are OK." Reports only if interested. Samples returned with SASE; samples kept on file.
Terms: Pays authors royalty of 8-12% based on retail price. "We *do* offer advances." Pays illustrators by the project (range: $25-100). Pays photographers per photo (range: $50-100). Book catalog and/or ms guidelines free for SASE.
Tips: "We only publish kids' books aimed at the children of gay or lesbian parents."

☑ **AMERICAN BIBLE SOCIETY**, 1865 Broadway, New York NY 10023. Fax: (212)408-1305. Website: http://www.americanbible.org. Book publisher. Estab. 1816. **Manuscript Acquisitions:** Barbara Bernstengel. **Art Acquisitions:** Christina Murphy, assistant director. Publishes 1-2 picture books/year; 1 young reader/year; 1 youth activity/year; and 1 young adult/year. Publishes books with spiritual/religious themes based on the Bible. "The purpose of the American Bible Society is to provide the Holy Scriptures to every man, woman and child in a language and form each can easily understand, and at a price each can easily afford. This purpose is undertaken without doctrinal note or comment." Please do not call. Submit all sample submissions, résumés, etc. for review via mail.
Nonfiction: All levels: activity books, multicultural, religion, self-help, nature/environment, reference, social issues and special needs. Multicultural needs include innercity lifestyle; African-American, Hispanic/Latino, Native American, Asian; mixed groups (such as choirs, classrooms, church events). "Unsolicited manuscripts will be returned unread! We prefer published writing samples with résumés so we can contact copywriters when an appropriate project comes up." Recently published *Jesus Loves You*, a children's activity booklet (ages 5-9, 48 full color pages and cover) and accompanying 8-panel activity leaflet (16 b&w interior illustrations and activities).
How to Contact/Writers: All mss developed inhouse. Query with résumé and writing samples. Contact: Barbara Bernstengel. Unsolicited mss rejected. No credit lines given.
Illustration: Works with 2-3 illustrators/year. Reviews ms/illustration packages from artists. Contact: Christina Murphy via mail. Illustrations only: Query with samples; if interested, a personal interview will be arranged to see portfolio; send "résumés, tearsheets and promotional literature to keep; slides will be returned promptly." Reports on queries within 1 month. Samples returned; samples sometimes filed. Book catalog free on written request.
Photography: Contact: Christina Murphy via mail. Buys stock and assigns work. Looking for "nature, scenic, multicultural, intergenerational people shots." Model/property releases required. Uses any size b&w prints; 35mm, 2¼×2¼ and 4×5 transparencies. Photographers should query with samples first. If interested, a personal interview will be set up to see portfolio; provide résumé, promotional literature or tearsheets.
Terms: Photographers paid by the project (range: $800-5,000); per photo (range $100-400). Credit line given on most projects. Most photos purchased for one-time use. Factors used to determine payment for ms/illustration package include "nature and scope of project; complexity of illustration and continuity of work; number of illustrations." Pays illustrators $200-1,000/illustration; based on fair market value. Sends 2 complimentary copies of published work to illustrators. ABS owns all publication rights to illustrations and mss.
Tips: Illustrators and photographers: "Submit in a form that we can keep on file if we like such as tearsheets, postcards, photocopies, etc."

ATHENEUM BOOKS FOR YOUNG READERS, 1230 Avenue of the Americas, New York NY 10020. (212)698-7200. Website: http://www.simonsays.com/kidzone. Imprint of Simon & Schuster Children's Publishing Division. Book publisher. Vice President/Associate Publisher and Editorial Director: Jonathan Lanman. Estab. 1960. **Manuscript Acquisitions:** Anne Schwartz, editorial director of Anne Schwartz Books; Jean Karl, editor of Jean Karl Books. Marcia Marshall, executive editor; Caitlyn Dlouhy, senior editor. **Art Acquisitions:** Ann Bobco. Publishes 15-20 picture books/year; 4-5 young readers/year; 20-25 middle readers/year; and 10-15 young adults/year. 10% of books by first-time authors; 50% of books from agented writers. "Atheneum publishes original hardcover trade books for children from pre-school age through young adult. The style and subject matter of the books we publish is almost unlimited. We do not, however, publish textbooks, coloring or activity books, greeting cards, magazines or pamphlets or religious publications. Anne Schwartz Books is a highly selective line of books within the Atheneum imprint. The lists of Charles Scribner's Sons Books for Young Readers have been folded into the Atheneum program."
Fiction: Picture books and middle readers: animal, contemporary, fantasy. Young readers and young adults: contemporary, fantasy.
Nonfiction: All levels: animal, biography, history, nature/environment, science.

How to Contact/Writers: Fiction/Nonfiction: Query only for all projects. Reports on queries in 3 months. Publishes a book 18-24 months after acceptance. Will consider simultaneous submissions from previously unpublished authors; "we request that the author let us know it is a simultaneous submission." **Illustration:** Works with 40-50 illustrators/year. Editorial reviews ms/illustration packages from artists. Query first. Illustrations only: Submit résumé, tearsheets. Samples returned with SASE; samples filed. Reports on art samples only if interested. **Terms:** Pays authors in royalties of 8-10% based on retail price. Pays illustrators royalty of 5-6¼% or by the project. Pays photographers by the project. Sends galleys to authors; proofs to illustrators. Original artwork returned at job's completion. Ms guidelines for #10 SAE and 1 first-class stamp.

▢ A/V CONCEPTS CORP., 30 Montauk Blvd., Oakdale NY 11769. (516)567-7227. Fax: (516)567-8745. Educational book publisher. **Manuscript Acquisitions:** Laura Solimene, editor. **Art Acquisitions:** President: Phil Solimene, president. Publishes 6 young readers/year; 6 middle readers/year; 6 young adult titles/year. 20% of books by first-time authors. Primary theme of books and multimedia is classic literature, math, science, language arts, self esteem.
Fiction: Middle readers: hi-lo. Young adults: hi-lo, multicultural, special needs. "We hire writers to adapt classic literature."
Nonfiction: All levels: activity books. Young adults: hi-lo, multicultural, science, self help, textbooks. Average word length: middle readers—300-400; young adults—500-950.
How to Contact/Writers: Fiction: Submit outline/synopsis and 1 sample chapter. Reports on queries in 1 month.
Illustration: Works with 4-6 illustrators/year. Reviews ms/illustration packages from artists. Submit ms with 3-4 pieces of final art. Illustrations only: Query with samples. Reports in 1 month. Samples returned with SASE; samples filed.
Photography: Submit samples.
Terms: Work purchased outright from authors (range $50-1,000). Pays illustrators by the project (range: $50-1,000). Pays photographers per photo (range: $25-250). Ms and art guidelines available for 9×12 SASE.

☑ AVON BOOKS/BOOKS FOR YOUNG READERS (Avon Flare, Avon Camelot and Avon hardcover), 1350 Avenue of the Americas, New York NY 10019. (212)261-6800. Website: http://www.av onbooks.com. A division of The Hearst Corporation. Book publisher. Elise Howard, executive editor. **Acquisitions:** Ruth Katcher, senior editor and Abigail McAden, assistant editor. Publishes 12 hardcovers, 25-30 middle readers/year, 20-25 young adults/year. 10% of books by first-time authors; 80% of books from agented writers.
Fiction: Middle readers: comedy, contemporary, problem novels, sports, spy/mystery/adventure. Young adults: contemporary, problem novels, romance. Average length: middle readers—100-150 pages; young adults—150-250 pages. Avon does not publish preschool picture books.
Nonfiction: Middle readers: hobbies, music/dance, sports. Young adults: "growing up." Average length: middle readers—100-150 pages; young adults—150-250 pages.
How to Contact/Writers: "Please send for guidelines before submitting." Fiction/nonfiction: Submit outline/synopsis and 3 sample chapters. Reports on mss in 1-2 months. Publishes a book 18-24 months after acceptance. Will consider simultaneous submissions.
Illustration: Will not review ms/illustration packages.
Terms: Pays authors in royalties of 6% based on retail price. Average advance payment is "very open." Book catalog available for 9×12 SAE and 4 first-class stamps; ms guidelines for #10 SASE.
Tips: "We have three young readers imprints: Avon Camelot, books for the middle grades; Avon Flare, young adults; and Avon hardcover. Our list includes both individual titles and series, with the emphasis on high quality recreational reading—a fresh and original writing style; identifiable, three-dimensional characters; a strong, well-paced story that pulls readers in and keeps them interested." Writers: "Make sure you really know what a company's list looks like before you submit work. Is your work in line with what they usually do? Is your work appropriate for the age group that this company publishes for? Keep aware of what's in your bookstore (but not what's in there for too long!)" Illustrators: "Submit work to art directors and people who are in charge of illustration at publishers. This is usually not handled entirely by the editorial department. Do *not* expect a response if no SASE is included with your material."

THE SUBJECT INDEX, located in the back of this book, lists book publishers and magazines according to the fiction and nonfiction subjects they seek.

⬛ BANTAM DOUBLEDAY DELL, Books for Young Readers, 1540 Broadway, New York NY 10036. (212)354-6500. Website: http://www.bdd.com. Book publisher Vice President/Publisher: Craig Virden. Deputy Publisher/Editor-in-Chief: Beverly Horowitz. **Manuscript Acquisitions:** Michelle Poploff, editorial director, paperbacks; Françoise Bui, executive editor, series; Wendy Lamb, executive editor, hardcovers. **Art Acquisitions:** Patrice Sheridan, art director. Publishes 16 picture books/year; new line of first choice chapter yearling; 60 middle reader books/year; 60 young adult titles/year. 10% of books by first-time authors; 70% of books from agented writers. "Bantam Doubleday Dell Books for Young Readers publishes award-winning books by distinguished authors and the most promising new writers."

Fiction: Picture books: adventure, animal, contemporary, easy-to-read, fantasy, humor. Young readers: animal, contemporary, humor, easy-to-read, fantasy, sports, suspense/mystery. Middle readers: adventure, animal, contemporary, humor, easy-to-read, fantasy, sports, suspense/mystery. Young adults: adventure, contemporary issues, humor, coming-of-age, suspense/mystery. Published *Brian's Winter*, by Gary Paulsen; *Expecting The Unexpected*, by Mavis Jukes; and *Shadowmaker*, by Joan Lowery Nixon.

Nonfiction: "Bantam Doubleday Dell Books for Young Readers publishes a very limited number of nonfiction titles."

How to Contact/Writers: Submit through agent; accepts queries from published authors. "All unsolicited manuscripts returned unopened with the following exceptions: Unsolicited manuscripts are accepted for the Delacorte Press Prize for a First Young Adult Novel contest (see Contests & Awards section) and the Marguerite de Angeli Prize for a First Middle Grade Novel contest (see Contests & Awards section)." Reports on queries in 6-8 weeks; mss in 3 months.

Illustration: Number of illustrations used per fiction title varies considerably. Reviews ms/illustration packages from artists. Query first. Do not send originals. "If you submit a dummy, please submit the text separately." Reports on ms/art samples only if interested. Cannot return samples; samples filed. Illustrations only: Submit tearsheets, résumé, samples that do not need to be returned. Original artwork returned at job's completion.

Terms: Pays authors advance and royalty. Pays illustrators advance and royalty or flat fee.

⬛ BARRONS EDUCATIONAL SERIES, 250 Wireless Blvd., Hauppauge NY 11788. (516)434-3311. Fax: (516)434-3723. Book publisher. Estab. 1945. "Barrons tends to publish series of books, both for adults and children." **Acquisitions:** Grace Freedson, managing editor/director of acquisitions. Publishes 20 picture books/year; 20 young readers/year; 20 middle reader titles/year; 10 young adult titles/year. 25% of books by first-time authors; 25% of books from agented writers.

Fiction: Picture books: animal, concept, multicultural, nature/environment. Young readers: Adventure, multicultural, nature/environment, suspense/mystery. Middle readers: adventure, horror, multicultural, nature/environment, problem novels, suspense/mystery. Young adults: horror, problem novels. Recently published *One Dollar: My First Book About Money*, by Lynette Long; *Painless Research Projects* by R&J Elliot.

Nonfiction: Picture books: concept, reference. Young readers: how-to, reference, self help, social issues. Middle readers: hi-lo, how-to, reference, self help, social issues. Young adults: how-to, self help, social issues.

How to Contact/Writers: Fiction: Query. Nonfiction: Submit outline/synopsis and sample chapters. "Submissions must be accompanied by SASE for response." Reports on queries in 1 month; mss in 6-8 months. Publishes a book 1 year after acceptance. Will consider simultaneous submissions.

Illustration: Works with 10 illustrators/year. Reviews ms/illustration packages from artists. Query first; 3 chapters of ms with 1 piece of final art, remainder roughs. Illustrations only: Submit tearsheets or slides plus résumé. Reports in 3-8 weeks.

Terms: Pays authors in royalties of 10-16% based on wholesale price or buys ms outright for $2,000 minimum. Pays illustrators by the project based on retail price. Sends galleys to authors; dummies to illustrators. Book catalog, ms/artist's guidelines for 9×12 SAE.

Tips: Writers: "We are predominately on the lookout for preschool storybooks and concept books. No YA fiction/romance or novels." Illustrators: "We are happy to receive a sample illustration to keep on file for future consideration. Periodic notes reminding us of your work are acceptable." Children's book themes "are becoming much more contemporary and relevant to a child's day-to-day activities."

⬛ BEACH HOLME PUBLISHERS, 2040 W. 12th Ave., Suite 226, Vancouver, British Columbia V6J 2G2 Canada. (604)733-4868. E-mail: bhp@beachholme.bc.ca. Website: http://www.beachholme.bc.ca. Book publisher. **Manuscript Acquisitions:** Joy Gugeler, managing editor. **Art Acquisitions:** Joy Gugeler and Teresa Bubela. Publishes 4 young adult titles/year and 4 adult literary titles/year. 20% of books by first-time authors. "We publish primarily regional historical fiction. We publish young adult novels for children aged 8-12. We are particularly interested in works that have a historical basis and are set in the

Pacific Northwest, or northern Canada. Include ideas for teachers guides or resources and appropriate topics for a classroom situation if applicable."

• Beach Holme *only* accepts work from Canadian writers.

Fiction: Young adults: contemporary, folktales, history, multicultural, nature/environment, poetry. Multicultural needs include themes reflecting cultural heritage of the Pacific Northwest, i.e., first nations, Asian, East Indian, etc. Does not want to see generic adventure or mystery with no sense of place. Average word length: middle readers—15-20,000; young adults/teens—30,000-40,000. Recently published *Shabash!*, by Ann Walsh (ages 8-12, young adult fiction); *White Jade Tiger*, by Julie Lawson (ages 10 +, young adult fiction); and *Finders Keepers*, by Andrea Spalding (ages 8-12, young adult fiction).

How to Contact/Writers: Fiction: Submit outline/synopsis and 3 sample chapters. Reports on queries in 4-8 weeks; mss in 2 months. Publishes a book 6 months-1 year after acceptance. Will consider simultaneous submissions (if specified).

Illustration: Works with 3 illustrators/year. Reports on submissions in 4 weeks in interested. Samples returned with SASE; samples filed.

Terms: Pays authors 10-12% royalty based on retail price. Offers advances (average amount: $500). Pays illustrators by the project (range: $500-1,000). Pays photographers by the project (range: $100-300). Sends galleys to authors. Book catalog available for 9 × 12 SAE and 3 first-class Canadian stamps; ms guidelines available with SASE.

Tips: "Research what we have previously published to familiarize yourself with what we are looking for. Please, be informed."

BEECH TREE BOOKS, 1350 Avenue of the Americas, New York NY 10019. (212)261-6500. Website: http://www.williammorrow.com. Editor-in-Chief/Vice President: Paulette Clark Kaufman. A division of William Morrow & Co. Paperback book publisher. Publishes 40 titles/year.

Fiction: Middle readers, young adult: activity books, adventure, contemporary, family, history.

Nonfiction: Middle readers, young adult: biography.

How to Contact/Writers: Query.

☑ BEHRMAN HOUSE INC., 235 Watchung Ave., West Orange NJ 07052. (973)669-0447. Fax: (973)669-9769. Book publisher. Estab. 1921. Managing Editor: Bob Tinkham. **Acquisitions:** Editorial Department. Publishes 3 young reader titles/year; 3 middle reader titles/year; and 3 young adult titles/year. 12% of books by first-time authors; 2% of books from agented writers. Publishes books on all aspects of Judaism: history, cultural, textbooks, holidays. "Behrman House publishes quality books of Jewish content—history, Bible, philosophy, holidays, ethics—for children and adults."

Fiction: All levels: Judaism.

Nonfiction: All levels: Judaism, Jewish educational textbooks. Average word length: young reader—1,200; middle reader—2,000; young adult—4,000. Published *My Jewish Year*, by Adam Fisher (ages 8-9); *Partners with God*, by Gila Gevirtz (ages 8-9); and *It's a Mitzvah!*, by Bradley Artson (adult).

How to Contact/Writers: Fiction/Nonfiction: Submit outline/synopsis and sample chapters. Reports on queries in 1 month; mss in 2 months. Publishes a book 2½ years after acceptance. Will consider simultaneous submissions.

Illustration: Works with 6 children's illustrators/year. Reviews ms/illustration packages from artists. "Query first." Illustrations only: Query with samples; send unsolicited art samples by mail. Reports on queries in 1 month; mss in 2 months.

Photography: Purchases photos from freelancers. Buys stock and assigns work. Uses photos of families involved in Jewish activities. Uses color and b&w prints. Photographers should query with samples. Send unsolicited photos by mail. Submit portfolio for review.

Terms: Pays authors in royalties of 3-10% based on retail price or buys ms outright for $1,000-5,000. Offers advance. Pays illustrators by the project (range: $500-5,000). Sends galleys to authors; dummies to illustrators. Book catalog free on request.

Tips: Looking for "religious school texts" with Judaic themes or general trade Judaica.

Ⓝ BENCHMARK BOOKS, Imprint of Marshall Cavendish, 99 White Plains Rd., Tarrytown NY 10591. (914)332-8888. Fax: (914)332-1888. **Manuscript Acquisitions:** Joyce Stanton and Kate Nunn. Publishes 90 young reader, middle reader and young adult books/year. "We look for interesting treatments of primarily nonfiction subjects related to elementary, middle school and high school curriculum."

Nonfiction: Most nonfiction topics are appropriate but ms should be curriculum related. Average word length for all books: 8,000-12,000.

How to Contact/Writers: Nonfiction: submit complete ms or submit outline/synopsis and 1 or more sample chapters. Reports on queries and mss in 3 months. Publishes a book 2 years after acceptance. Will consider simultaneous submissions.

Photography: Buys stock and assigns work.

Terms: Pays authors royalty based on retail price or buys work outright. Offers advances. Sends galleys to authors. Book catalog available. All imprints included in a single catalog.

THE BENEFACTORY, One Post Rd., Fairfield CT 06430. (203)255-7744. Fax: (203)255-6200. Book publisher. Estab. 1990. **Manuscript/Art Acquisitions:** Cindy Germain, production manager. Publishes 6-12 picture books/year with the Humane Society of the United States; 6-12 picture books/year with The National Wildlife Federation. 50% of books by first-time authors. The Benefactory publishes "classic" true stories about real animals, through licenses with the Humane Society of the United States and National Wildlife Federation. Each title is accompanied by a read-along audiocassette and a plush animal. A percentage of revenues benefits the HSUS or NWF. Target age for NWF titles: 4-7; for HSUS titles: 5-10.

Nonfiction: Picture books: nature/environment; young readers: animal, nature/environment. Average word length: HSUS titles: 1,200-1,500; NWF titles: 700-800. Recently published *Chessie, the Travelin' Man*, written by Randy Houk, illustrated by Paula Bartlett (ages 5-10, picture book); *Condor Magic*, written by Lyn Littlefield Hoopes, illustrated by Peter C. Stone (ages 5-10, picture book); and *Caesar: On Deaf Ears*, written by Loren Spiotta-DiMare, illustrated by Kara Lee (ages 5-10, picture book).

How to Contact/Writers: Reports on queries in 3 weeks; ms in 6 months. Publishes a book 1 year after acceptance. Will consider simultaneous submissions. Send SASE for writer's guidelines.

Illustration: Works with 6-8 illustrators/year. Uses color artwork only. Reviews ms/illustration packages from artists. Query or send ms with dummy. Illustrations only: Send résumé, promo sheet and tearsheets to be kept on file. Reports in 6 months. Samples returned with SASE; samples filed. Send SASE for artist guidelines.

Terms: Pays authors royalty of 3-5% based on wholesale price. Offers advances (Average amount: $5,000). Pays illustrators royalty of 3-5% based on wholesale price. Sends galleys to authors; dummies to illustrators. Originals returned to artist at job's completion. Book catalog available for 8 1/2 × 11 SASE; ms and art guidelines available for SASE.

◘ BESS PRESS, 3565 Harding Ave., Honolulu HI 96816. (808)734-7159. Fax: (808)732-3627. E-mail: publisher@besspress.com. Website: http://www.besspress.com. **Manuscript Acquisitions:** Benjamin Bess. **Art Acquisitions:** Carol Colbath. Publishes 1-2 picture books/year; 1-2 young readers/year; 0-1 middle readers/year. 60% of books by first-time authors. "Bess Press specializes in trade and educational titles about Hawaiian life and culture and educational titles about the Pacific islands."

Fiction: Picture books, young readers, middle readers: adventure, animal, anthology, concept, folktales, hi-lo, history, humor, multicultural, nature/environment, sports. Multicultural material must be specific to Hawaii. Published *Sumorella*, by Sandi Takayama, illustrated by Esther Szegedy (ages 3-8); and *Angel and Tutu*, by Helen M. Swanson (middle reader).

Nonfiction: Picture books: concept. Young readers: activity books. Picture books, middle readers, young readers: animal, hi-lo, history, multicultural, nature/environment, sports, textbooks. Published *State of Hawaii Coloring Book*, by Wren (ages 3-8, coloring book); and *Hawaiian Wildlife Coloring and Activity Book*, by Tammy Yee (ages 5-8, activity book).

How to Contact/Writers: Fiction/Nonfiction: Submit complete ms. Reports on queries in 4-6 weeks; on mss in 3-4 weeks. Publishes a book 6-12 months after acceptance. Will consider simultaneous submissions and previously published work.

Illustration: Works with 3 illustrators/year. Reviews ms/illustration packages from artists. Submit ms with dummy. Illustrations only: Query with samples. Reports only if interested. Samples returned with SASE; samples filed.

Terms: Pays authors royalty of 2½-10% based on wholesale price or work purchased outright. Pays illustrators by the project, royalty of 2½-5% based on wholesale price. Sends galleys to authors; dummies to illustrators. Original artwork returned at job's completion. Book catalog available for SASE. Ms guidelines available for SASE.

Tips: Looks for "books with commercial or educational appeal in our primary markets—Hawaii, the Western United States and libraries. Primarily interested in books about Hawaiian life and culture."

BETHANY HOUSE PUBLISHERS, 11300 Hampshire Ave. S., Minneapolis MN 55438-2455. (612)829-2500. Website: http://www.bethanyhouse.com. Book publisher. **Manuscript Acquisitions:** Rochelle Glöege, Natasha Sperling. **Art Acquisitions:** Cathy Engstrom. Publishes 2 young readers/year; 18 middle-grade readers/year; and 16 young adults/year. Bethany House Publishers is a non-profit publisher seeking to publish imaginative, excellent books that reflect an evangelical worldview without being preachy. Publishes picture books under Bethany Backyard imprint.

Fiction: Series for early readers, middle readers, young adults: historical and contemporary adventure, history, humor, multicultural, suspense/mystery, religion, sports and current issues. Young adult: romance. Does not want to see poetry or science fiction. Average word length: early readers—6,000; young readers—20,000; young adults—40,000. Published *Too Many Secrets*, by Patricia H. Rushford (young adult/teens, mystery series); *The Ghost of KRZY*, by Bill Myers (middle-graders, mystery/humor series); and *The Mystery of the Dancing Angels*, by Elspeth Campbell Murphy (young readers, mystery series).

Nonfiction: Young readers, middle readers, young adults: religion/devotional, self-help, social issues. Published *Can I Be a Christian Without Being Weird?*, by Kevin Johnson (early teens, devotional book); and *Hot Topics, Tough Questions*, by Bill Myers (young adult/teen, Biblically based advice).

How to Contact/Writers: Fiction/Nonfiction: Query. Reports on queries in 2 months; mss in 4 months. Picture Books: does not accept unsolicited mss, query only. Publishes a book 12-18 months after acceptance. Will consider simultaneous submissions.

Illustration: Works with 12 illustrators/year. Reviews illustration samples from artists. Illustrations only: Query with samples. Reports in 2 months. Samples returned with SASE.

Terms: Pays authors royalty based on net sales. Pays illustrators by the project. Pays photographers by the project. Sends galleys to authors. Book catalog available for 11 × 14 SAE and 5 first-class stamps.

Tips: "Research the market, know what is already out there. Study our catalog before submitting material. We look for an evangelical message woven delicately into a strong plot and topics that seek to broaden the reader's experience and perspective."

BEYOND WORDS PUBLISHING, INC., 20827 N.W. Cornell Rd., Hillsboro OR 97124. (503)531-8700. Fax: (503)531-8773. E-mail: beyondword@beyondword.com. Book publisher. Director, Children's Division: Michelle Roehm. Publishes 6-10 picture books/year. 40% of books by first-time authors. "Our company mision statement is 'Inspire to Integrity,' so it's crucial that your story inspires children in some way."

Fiction: Picture books: adventure, animal, contemporary, fantasy, folktales, history, multicultural, nature/environment. "We are looking for Native American, African-American, Asian-American, etc. authors/illustrators; stories that will appeal to girls and women." Average length: picture books—32 pages. Recently published *Frog Girl*, written and illustrated by Paul Owen Lewis (ages 5-10, Native American myth).

Nonfiction: Picture books, young readers: biography, geography, health, history, multicultural, nature/environment, reference, science, self-help. *The Book of Goddesses*, by Kris Waldherr (all ages, multicultural historic reference); and *Girls Know Best* (compilation of 38 girls' writing—ages 7-15).

How to Contact/Writers: Fiction: Submit complete ms. Nonfiction: Submit outline/synopsis. Reports on queries/mss in 6 months. Will consider simultaneous submissions and previously published work.

Illustration: Works with 4-6 illustrators/year. Reviews ms/illustration packages from artists. Submit ms with 2-3 pieces of final art. "No originals please!" Illustrations only: Send résumé, promo sheet, "samples—no originals!" Reports in 6 months only if interested. Samples returned with SASE; samples filed.

Photography: Works on assignment only.

Terms: Sends galleys to authors; dummies to illustrators. Book catalog for SAE; ms and artist's guidelines for SASE.

Tips: "Please research the books we have previously published. This will give you a good idea if your proposal fits with our company."

☑ **BLACKBIRCH PRESS, INC.**, P.O. Box 3573, Woodbridge CT 06525. E-mail: staff@blackbirch.com. Website: http://www.blackbirch.com. Book publisher. Senior Editor: Deborah Kops. **Manuscript Acquisitions:** Bruce Glassman. **Art Acquisitions:** Sonja Kalter. Publishes 20 middle readers, and 70 young adult titles/year. 15% of books by first-time authors.

Nonfiction: Picture books: animal, concept, geography, history, nature/environment, science. Young readers: animal, biography, geography, multicultural, nature/environment, special needs. Middle readers and young adults: geography, nature/environment, reference, special needs. Does not want to see dogs, spiritual, medical themes. Average word length: young adult readers—8,000-10,000; middle readers—5,000-7,000. Recently published *Alaska Pipeline* (ages 8-10); and *Notorious Americans* (biography series).

How to Contact/Writers: Nonfiction: Query. Materials will not be returned. Publishes a book 1 year after acceptance. Will consider simultaneous submissions.

Illustration: Works with 10 illustrators/year. Uses color artwork only. Reviews ms/illustration packages from artists. Submit query. Illustrations only: Query with samples; send résumé, promo sheet. Samples not returned; samples filed.

Photography: Buys photos from freelancers. Buys stock and assigns work. Uses animal, human culture, geography. Captions required. Uses 35mm, 2¼×2¼, 4×5 transparencies. Submit cover letter, published samples and promo piece.

Terms: Pays authors royalty or work purchased outright from author. Offers advances. Pays illustrators by the project or royalty. Pays photographers by the project, per photo or royalty. Original artwork returned at job's completion. Book catalog available for 8×10 SAE and 3 first-class stamps. Ms guidelines available for SASE.

BLUE SKY PRESS, 555 Broadway, New York NY 10012. (212)343-6100. Website: http://www.scholastic .com. Book publisher. Imprint of Scholastic Inc. **Acquisitions:** Bonnie Verberg. Publishes 8 picture books/ year; 2 young adult titles/year. 1% of books by first-time authors. Publishes hardcover children's fiction and nonfiction including high-quality novels and picture books by new and established authors.

● Blue Sky is currently not accepting unsolicited submissions.

Fiction: Picture books: adventure, animal, concept, contemporary, fantasy, folktales, history, humor, multicultural, nature/environment, poetry. Young readers: adventure, anthology, contemporary, fantasy, folktales, history, humor, multicultural, nature/environment, poetry. Young adults: adventure, anthology, contemporary, fantasy, history, humor, multicultural, poetry. Multicultural needs include "strong fictional or nonfictional themes featuring non-white characters and cultures." Does not want to see mainstream religious, bibliotherapeutic, adult. Average length: picture books—varies; young adults—150 pages. Recently published *To Every Thing There Is a Season*, illustrated by Leo and Diane Dillon (all ages, picture book); *Freak the Mighty*, by Rodman Philbrick (ages 8 and up, young adult, middle readers); and *A Bad Case of Stripes*, by David Shannon (ages 5 and up, picture book).

Nonfiction: Picture books: animal, biography, concept, history, multicultural, nature/environment. Young readers: biography, history, multicultural, nature/environment. Young adults: history, multicultural. Average length: picture books—varies; young adults 150 pages. "Often there is a nonfiction element to Blue Sky Press fiction picture books; otherwise we have not yet published nonfiction."

How to Contact/Writers: "Due to large numbers of submissions, we are discouraging unsolicited submissions—send query (don't call!) only if you feel certain we publish the type of book you have written." Fiction: Query (novels, picture books). Reports on queries in 6 months. Publishes a book 1-3 years after acceptance; depending on chosen illustrator's schedule. Will not consider simultaneous submissions.

Illustration: Works with 10 illustrators/year. Uses both b&w and color artwork. Reviews illustration packages "only if illustrator is the author." Submit ms with dummy. Illustrations only: Query with samples, tearsheets. Reports only if interested. Samples returned with SASE. Original artwork returned at job's completion.

Photography: Buys photos from freelancers. Contact: Photo Research Department. Buys stock and assigns work. Uses photos to accompany nonfiction. Model/property releases required. Captions required. Submit cover letter, résumé, client list, stock photo list.

Terms: Author's royalty varies by project—usually standard trade rates. Offers variable advance. Pays illustrators by the project or standard royalty based on retail price. Pays photographers by the project or royalty.

Tips: "Read currently published children's books. Revise—never send a first draft. Find your own voice, style, and subject. With material from new people we look for a theme or style strong enough to overcome the fact that the author/illustrator is unknown in the market. Children's book publishers are becoming more selective, looking for irresistible talent and fairly broad appeal; yet most are still willing to take risks, just to keep the game interesting."

□ BOINGO BOOKS, INC., 12720 Yardley Dr., Boca Raton FL 33428. **Acquisitions:** Lisa McCourt, creative director. Packages trade picture books for major children's book publishers. Averages 30 titles/ year.

Fiction/Nonfiction: Recently published *I Love You, Stinky Face,* by Lisa McCourt, illustrated by Cyd Moore; *The West Texas Chili Monster*, by Judy Cox, illustrated by John O'Brien; *Chocolatina*, by Erik Kraft, illustrated by Denise Brunkus.

How to Contact/Writers: Not accepting unsolicited mss. "To check for a change in our submission status, send a #10 SASE to the above address."

Illustration: Works with 30 illustrators/year. Uses color artwork only. Send samples, résumé, promo sheet,

---

THE AGE-LEVEL INDEX, located in the back of this book, lists book publishers and magazines according to the age-groups for which they need material.

client list. Samples are filed unless illustrator has included a SASE and "requested the return of the materials." Contact: Lisa McCourt.

Photography: Buys photos from freelancers. Contact: Lisa McCourt. Works on assignment only. Submit résumé, client list, samples or promo pieces.

Terms: All contracts negotiated separately; offers variable advance.

BOYDS MILLS PRESS, 815 Church St., Honesdale PA 18431. (800)490-5111. Fax: (717)253-0179. Imprint: Wordsong (poetry). Book publisher. **Manuscript Acquisitions:** Beth Troop. **Art Acquisitions:** Tim Gillner. 5% of books from agented writers. Estab. 1990. "We publish a wide range of quality children's books of literary merit, from preschool to young adult."

Fiction: All levels: adventure, contemporary, history, humor, multicultural, poetry. Picture books: animal. Young readers, middle readers, young adult: problem novels, sports. Middle readers, young adults: problem novels, sports. Multicultural themes include any story showing a child as an integral part of a culture and which provides children with insight into a culture they otherwise might be unfamiliar with. "Please query us on the appropriateness of suggested topics for middle grade and young adult. For all other submissions send entire manuscript." Does not want to see talking animals, coming-of-age novels, romance and fantasy/ science fiction. Recently published *My Freedom Trip*, by Frances Park and Ginger Parker, illustrated by Debra Reid Jenkins (ages 5-8, multicultural picture book); and *Haircuts at Sleepy Sam's* by Michael R. Strickland, illustrated by Keaf Holliday (ages 4-8, contemporary picture book).

Nonfiction: All levels: nature/environment, science. Picture books, young readers, middle readers: animal, multicultural. Does not want to see reference/curricular text. Recently published *Everybody Has a Bellybutton*, by Laurence Pringle (ages 4-8, science); and *Lots and Lots of Zebra Stripes*, by Stephen R. Swinburne (ages 3-7, science).

How to Contact/Writers: Fiction/Nonfiction: Submit complete ms or submit through agent. Query on middle reader, young adult and nonfiction. Reports on queries/mss in 1 month.

Illustration: Works with 25 illustrators/year. Reviews ms/illustration packages from artists. Submit complete ms with 1 or 2 pieces of art. Illustrations only: Query with samples; send résumé and slides. Reports back only if interested. Samples returned with SASE. Samples filed. Originals returned at job's completion.

Photography: Assigns work.

Terms: Authors paid royalty or work purchased outright. Offers advances. Illustrators paid by the project or royalties; varies. Photographers paid by the project per photo, or royalties; varies. Mss/artist's guidelines available for #10 SASE.

Tips: "Picture books—with fresh approaches, not work themes—are our strongest need at this time. Check to see what's already on the market before submitting your story. An increasing number of publishers seem to be closing their doors to unsolicited submissions, but at the same time, many new publishing houses are starting. Sometimes a new author can get a foot in the door with a new or small house, then develop credentials for approaching bigger houses. Authors should keep this in mind when looking for a publisher."

BRIGHT LAMB PUBLISHERS, P.O. Box 844, Evans GA 30809. (706)863-2237. Fax: (706)651-9589. E-mail: brightlamb@aol.com. Website: http://www.brightlamb.com. Book publisher. Estab. 1995. **Contact:** Acquisitions Editor. "We publish books with product concepts or gift items to coincide with the storyline." Publishes 3 picture books/year; 3 young readers/year. 50% of books by first-time authors.

● Bright Lamb is not currently accepting mss.

Illustration: Works with 3 illustrators/year. Reviews ms/illustration packages from artists. Send ms with dummy. Illustrations only: Query with samples; send résumé, client list and tear sheets to be kept on file. Reports back only if interested.

Terms: Pays authors royalty based on wholesale price. Pays illustrators royalty based on wholesale price. Book catalog available for 4×7 SASE and 2 first-class stamps; ms guidelines available for SASE.

Tips: "Study our catalog before submitting."

BRIGHT RING PUBLISHING, INC, P.O. Box 31338, Bellingham WA 98228-3338. (360)734-1601 or (800)480-4278. Fax: (360)676-1271. E-mail: brightring@aol.com. Estab. 1985. **Acquisitions:** MaryAnn Kohl. Publishes 1 young reader title/year. 50% of books by first-time authors. "Bright Ring Publishing is *not* looking for picture books, juvenile fiction, poetry, manuals or coloring books. We are highly interested in creative activity/resource books for adults to use with children, or for children to use independently. We prefer books that match our own successful style for pre-school through elementary school (ages 3-12), and must work equally well for a parent and child at home or a teacher and children at school."

Nonfiction: Young readers and middle readers: activity books involving art ideas, hobbies, cooking, how-to, multicultural, music/dance, nature/environment, science. "No picture books, no poetry, no stories of any kind and no coloring books." Average length: "about 125 ideas/book. We are moving into only recipe-style resource books in any variety of subject areas—useful with children 2-12. Interested in integrated art with other subjects." Recently published SCRIBBLE ART: *Independent Creative Art Experiences for Children*; MUDWORKS: *Creative Clay, Dough, and Modeling Experiences*; and SCIENCE ARTS: *Discovering Science Through Art Experiences* (all by Mary Ann Kohl); and *Discovering Great Artists: Hands-on Art for Children in the Styles of the Great Masters* (1997).

How to Contact/Writers: Nonfiction: write for guidelines; submit complete ms. Reports on queries in 2 weeks; mss in 6 weeks. Publishes a book 1 year after acceptance. Will consider simultaneous submissions.

Illustration: Works with 2 illustrators. Prefers to review "black line (drawings) for text." Reviews ms/illustration packages from artists. "Query first." Write for guidelines. Illustrations only: Query with samples; send tearsheets and "sample of ideas I request after query." Reports in 1 month.

Terms: Pays authors in royalties of 3-5% based on net sales. Work purchased outright (range: $500-2,000). Pays illustrators $500-2,000. Also offers "free books and discounts for future books." Book catalog, ms/artist's guidelines for business-size SAE and 32¢ postage.

Tips: "We cannot accept book ideas which require unusual packaging such as attached toys or unique binding or paper."

BROWNDEER PRESS, 9 Monroe Pkwy., Suite 240, Lake Oswego OR 97035-1487. (503)697-1017. Imprint of Harcourt Brace & Co. **Manuscript Acquisitions:** Linda Zuckerman, editorial director. Publishes 12 titles/year.

• Browndeer only accepts mss from agents, previously published authors, and SCBWI members.

Fiction: Picture books, young readers: adventure, animal, contemporary, fantasy, folktales, humor, multi-cultural, nature/environment, poetry.

Nonfiction: Picture books: music/dance, nature/environment. Young readers: nature/environment.

How to Contact/Writers: For picture books send complete ms with cover letter listing publishing credits or résumé; for longer fiction and nonfiction send cover letter, outline/synopsis and 3 sample chapters. Include SASE with all submissions. Reports on queries/mss in 3 months.

Illustration: Works with 9 illustrators/year. Send samples with SASE. Reports on artist's queries/submissions in 3 months. Originals returned at job's completion.

Terms: Pay authors royalty. Pay illustrators royalty for books; flat fee for book jackets. Send SASE for writer's and artist's guidelines.

CANDLEWICK PRESS, 2067 Massachusetts Ave., Cambridge MA 02140. (617)661-3330. Fax: (617)661-0565. E-mail: bigbear@candlewick.com. Children's book publisher. Estab. 1991. **Manuscript Acquisitions:** Liz Bickenll, editor-in-chief; Amy Ehrlich, editor-at-large; Mary Lee Donovan, senior editor; Gale Pryor, editor; Liz Gavril, assistant editor. **Art Acquisitions:** Ann Stott, senior designer; Anne Moore, senior designer; Anne Ghory-Goodman, art director; and Julie Bushway, designer. Publishes 175 picture books/year; 5 middle readers/year; and 5 young adult titles/year. 5% of books by first-time authors. "Our books are truly for children, and we strive for the very highest standards in the writing, illustrating, designing and production of all of our books. And we are not averse to risk."

• Candlewick Press is not accepting queries or unsolicited mss at this time.

Fiction: Picture books, young readers: animal, concept, contemporary, fantasy, folktales, history, humor, multicultural, nature/environment, poetry. Middle readers, young adults: animal, anthology, contemporary, fantasy, history, humor, multicultural, poetry, science fiction, sports, suspense/mystery.

Nonfiction: Picture books: activity books, concept, biography, geography, nature/environment. Young readers: activity books, biography, geography, nature/environment.

Illustration: Works with 20 illustrators/year. "We prefer to see a variety of the artist's style." Reviews ms/illustration packages from artists. "General samples only please." Illustrations only: Submit résumé and portfolio to the attention of Design Dept. Reports on samples in 4-6 weeks. Samples returned with SASE; samples filed.

Terms: Pays authors royalty of 2.5-10% based on retail price. Offers advances. Pays illustrators 2.5-10% royalty based on retail price. Sends galleys to authors; dummies to illustrators. Photographers paid 2.5-10% royalty. Original artwork returned at job's completion.

ⓝ CAPSTONE PRESS INC., P.O. Box 669, Mankato MN 56002. (507)388-6650. Fax: (507)388-1227. Book publisher. Acquisitons: Helen Moore. Imprints: Capstone Press, Bridgestone Books (both Helen Moore, acquisitions).

   SPECIAL COMMENTS by the editor of *Children's Writer's & Illustrator's Market* are set off by a bullet.

Nonfiction: Publishes only nonfiction books for emergent, early, challenged and reluctant readers. Currently looking for experienced authors to write on vehicle and sport topics and the science, social studies, and pleasure reading areas. All levels: careers, animals, arts/crafts, biography, geography, health, history, hobbies, special needs. Young adults only: Hi-lo, cooking, self help.

How to Contact/Writers: Does not accept submissions. Do not send mss. Instead, send query letter, résumé and samples of nonfiction writing to be considered for assignment.

Photographers: Buys stock and assigns work. Contact: Sheri Gosewisch, photo researcher. Model/property release required. Uses 35mm slides, 4×5, 8×10 transparencies. Submit slides, stock photo list.

Terms: Photographers paid by the project or per photo. Originals returned to artist at job's completion. Book catalog available for large format SAE; ms guidelines available for large format SASE.

Tips: "See catalog prior to submitting."

CAROLRHODA BOOKS, INC., 241 First Ave. N., Minneapolis MN 55401. (612)332-3344. Website: http://www.lernerbooks.com. Imprint of Lerner. Book publisher. Estab. 1969. **Acquisitions:** Rebecca Poole. Publishes 1-2 picture books/year; 25 young reader titles/year; and 30 middle reader titles/year. 20% of books by first-time authors; 10% of books from agented writers. "Carolrhoda Books is a children's publisher focused on producing high-quality, socially conscious nonfiction and fiction books for young readers that help them learn about and explore the world around them."

Fiction: Picture books: folktales, multicultural, nature/environment. Young readers, middle readers: historical, special needs. Average word length: picture books—1,000-1,500; young readers—2,000. Recently published historical fiction: *The Flight of the Union*, by Tekla White (grades 1-3); *Between the Dragon & the Eagle*, by Mical Schneider (grades 4-7).

Nonfiction: Picture books: activity books, biography, science. Young readers, middle readers: animal, biography, history, hobbies, multicultural, nature/environment, photo books, art and craft, science, social issues, special needs. Multicultural needs include biographies. Average word length: young readers—2,000; middle readers—6,000. Recently published *Wildlife Watching with Charles*, by Michael Elsohn Ross (grades 3-6); *Vacuum Cleaners*, by Elaine Marie Alphin (grades-3-6, household history series); *Roller Coasts, or I Had So Much Fun I Almost Puked*, by Nick Cook (grades 1-5).

How to Contact/Writers: Fiction/Nonfiction: Submit complete ms. Reports on queries in 3-4 weeks; mss in 3-5 months. Publishes a book 18 months after acceptance. Will consider simultaneous submissions. Must enclose SASE.

Illustration: Works with 20-30 illustrators/year. "Do not send originals. We like illustrators to send samples we can keep on file." Reviews ms/illustration packages from artists. Submit at least 1 sample illustration (in form of photocopy, slide, duplicate photo) with full ms. Illustrations only: Query with samples; send résumé/slides. Reports on art samples only if interested. Samples kept on file.

Photography: Purchases photos from freelancers. Buys stock and assigns work.

Terms: Pays authors royalty based on wholesale price or work purchased outright. Factors used to determine final payment for illustrations: color vs. b&w, number of illustrations, quality of work. Sends galleys to authors; dummies to illustrators. Book catalog available for 9×12 SAE and 3 first-class stamps; ms guidelines for #10 SAE and 1 first-class stamp.

Tips: Writers: "Research the publishing company to be sure it is in the market for the type of book you're interested in writing. Familiarize yourself with the company's list. We specialize in nonfiction beginning readers, photo essays and books published in series. We do very few single-title picture books and some historical fiction. For more detailed information about our publishing program, consult our catalog. We do not publish any of the following: textbooks, workbooks, songbooks, puzzles, plays and religious material. In general, we suggest that you steer clear of alphabet books; preachy stories with a moral to convey; stories featuring anthropomorphic protagonists ('Amanda the Amoeba,' 'Frankie the Fire Engine,' 'Tonie the Tornado'); and stories that revolve around trite, unoriginal plots. Be sure to avoid racial and sexual stereotypes in your writing, as well as sexist language." (See also Lerner Publications.)

CARTWHEEL BOOKS, Imprint of Scholastic Inc., 555 Broadway, New York NY 10012. (212)343-6100. Fax: (212)343-4437. Website: http://www.scholastic.com. Book publisher. **Manuscript Acquisitions:** Bernette G. Ford, vice president/editorial director. **Art Acquisitions:** Edie Weinberg, art director. Publishes 25-30 picture books/year; 30-35 easy readers/year; 15-20 novelty/concept books/year. "With each Cartwheel list, we strive for a pleasing balance among board books and novelty books, hardcover picture books and gift books, nonfiction, paperback storybooks and easy readers. Cartwheel seeks to acquire 'novelties' that are books first; play objects second. Even without its gimmick, a Cartwheel novelty book should stand along as a valid piece of children's literature. We want all our books to be inviting and appealing, and to have inherent educational and social value. We believe that small children who develop personal 'relationships' with books and grow up with a love for reading, become book consumers, and ultimately better human beings."

Fiction: Picture books: adventure, animal, anthology, concept, contemporary, fantasy, folktales, history, humor, multicultural, nature/environment, poetry, science fiction, sports, suspense/mystery. Young readers: adventure, animal, concept, contemporary, fantasy, folktales, history, humor, multicultural, nature/environment, poetry, science fiction. Does not want to see too much of picture books; fantasy; folktales; history; nature. Average work length: picture books—1-3,000; young readers—100-3,000.

Nonfiction: Picture books, young readers: animal, biography, concept, history, multicultural, nature/environment, sports. "Most of our nonfiction is either written on assignment or is within a series. We do not want to see any arts/crafts or cooking." Average word length: picture books—100-3,000; young readers—100-3,000.

How to Contact/Writers: Cartwheel Books is no longer accepting unsolicited mss. All unsolicited materials will be returned unread. Fiction/nonfiction: For previously published or agented authors, submit complete ms. Reports on queries in 1-2 months; mss in 3-6 months. Publishes a book 18-24 months after acceptance. Will consider simultaneous submissions; electronic submissions via disk or modem; previously published work.

Illustration: Works with 100 illustrators/year. Reviews ms/illustration packages from artists. Send ms with dummy. Illustrations only: Query with samples; arrange personal portfolio review; send promo sheet, tearsheets to be kept on file. Reports in 2 months. Samples returned with SASE; samples filed.

Photography: Buys stock and assigns work. Uses photos of kids, families, vehicles, toys, animals. Submit published samples, color promo piece.

Terms: Pays authors royalty of 2-8% based on retail price or work purchased outright for $600-5,000. Offers advances (Average amount: $3,000). Pays illustrators by the project (range: $2,000-10,000); royalty of 1-3% based on retail price; flat fee; or advance against royalties. Photographers paid by the project (range: $250-10,000); per photo (range: $250-500); or royalty of 1-3% of wholesale price. Sends galley to authors; dummy to illustrators. Originals returned to artist at job's completion. Book catalog available for 9×12 SAE and 2 first-class stamps; ms guidelines for SASE.

Tips: "Know what types of books we do. Check out bookstores or catalogs to see where your work would 'fit' best."

✓ CHARIOT VICTOR PUBLISHING, (formerly Chariot Books), 4050 Lee Vance View, Colorado Springs CO 80918. A division of Cook Communications. Book publisher. **Acquisitions:** Kathy Davis or Jeannie Harmon, senior editors. Publishes 15-20 picture books/year; 6-8 young readers/year; and 6-12 middle readers/year. Less than 5% of books by first-time authors; 15% of books from agented authors. "All books have overt Christian values, but there is no primary theme."
   • Chariot does not read unsolicited mss. Writers must query.

Illustration: Works with 15 illustrators/year. "Send color material I can keep." Query with samples; send résumé, promo sheet, portfolio, tearsheets. Reports only if interested. Samples returned with SASE; samples filed.

Terms: Pays illustrators by the project, royalty or work purchased outright. Sends dummies to illustrators. Original artwork returned at job's completion. Ms guidelines available for SASE.

CHARLESBRIDGE, 85 Main St., Watertown MA 02172. (617)926-0329. Fax: (617)926-5720. Website: http://www.charlesbridge.com. Book publisher. Estab. 1980. Publishes 80% nonfiction, 20% fiction titles. books and board books. Publishes nature, science, multicultural and fiction picture books and board books. Charlesbridge also has an educational division. **Manuscript Acquisitions:** Harold Underdown, senior editor.

Fiction: Picture books: "Strong, realistic stories with enduring themes." Considers the following categories: adventure, animal, concept, contemporary, fantasy, folktales, health, history, humor, multicultural, nataure/environment, special needs, sports, suspense/mystery. Recently published: *Mr. Belinsky's Bagels*, by Ellen Schwartz, illustrated by Stefan Czernecki.

Nonfiction: Picture books: animal, biography, careers, concept, geography, health, history, multicultural, music/dance, nature/environment, religion, science, social issues, special neeeds, sports. Average word length: picture books—1,500. Recently published: *Turn of the Century*, by Ellen Jackson, illustrated by Jan Derey Ellis; and *COW*, by Jules Older, illustrated by Lyn Severance; and *Domino Addition*, by Lynette Long, Ph.D.

How to Contact/Writers: Send ms and SASE. Exclusive submissions only. Reports on mss in 2 months.

Illustration: Works with 2 illustrators/year. Uses color artwork only. Illustrations only: Query with samples; provide résumé, tearsheets to be kept on file. "Send no original artwork, please." Reports back only if interested.

Terms: Pays authors in royalties or work purchased outright. Pays illustrators by the project. Ms/art guidelines available for SASE. Exclusive submissions only.

Tips: Wants "books that have humor and are factually correct. Concerning educational material, we want to integrate the reading of good stories with instructional material."

CHICAGO REVIEW PRESS, 814 N. Franklin St., Chicago IL 60610. (312)337-0747. Fax: (312)337-5985. E-mail: ipgbook@mcs.com. Website: http://www.ipgbook.com. Book publisher. Estab. 1973. **Manuscript Acquisitions:** Cynthia Sherry, editorial director. **Art Acquisitions:** Joan Sommers, art director. Publishes 1 middle reader/year and "about 4" young adult titles/year. 50% of books by first-time authors; 30% of books from agented authors. "We publish activity books for young children. We do not publish fiction."
Nonfiction: Young readers, middle readers and young adults: activity books, arts/crafts. "We're interested in hands-on, educational books; anything else probably will be rejected." Average length: young readers and young adults—175 pages. Recently published *Colonial Kids*, by Laurie Carlson (ages 5-12); *The Wind at Work*, by Gretchen Woelfle (ages 8-13); and *On Stage! Theater Games and Activities for Kids*, by Lisa Bany-Winters (ages 6-12).
How to Contact/Writers: Reports on queries/mss in 3 weeks. Publishes a book 1-2 years after acceptance. Will consider simultaneous submissions and previously published work.
Illustration: Works with 4 illustrators/year. Uses primarily b&w artwork. Reviews ms/illustration packages from artists. Submit 1-2 chapters of ms with corresponding pieces of final art. Illustrations only: Query with samples, résumé. Reports back only if interested. Samples returned with SASE.
Photography: Buys photos from freelancers ("but not often"). Buys stock and assigns work. Wants "instructive photos. We consult our files when we know what we're looking for on a book-by-book basis." Uses b&w prints.
Terms: Pays authors royalty of 7½-12½% based on retail price. Offers advances ("but not always") of $500-1,500. Pays illustrators by the project (range varies considerably). Pays photographers by the project (range varies considerably). Sends galleys to authors. Original artwork "usually" returned at job's completion. Book catalog/ms guidelines available for $3.
Tips: "We're looking for original activity books for small children and the adults caring for them—new themes and enticing projects to occupy kids' imaginations and promote their sense of personal creativity. We like activity books that are as much fun as they are constructive. Please write for guidelines so you'll know what we're looking for."

CHILDREN'S BOOK PRESS, 246 First St. #101, San Francisco CA 94105. (415)995-2200. Fax: (415)995-2222. E-mail: cbookpress@igc.org. **Acquisitions:** Submissions Editor. Publishes 6-8 picture books/year. 50% of books by first-time authors. "Children's Book Press is a nonprofit publisher of multicultural and bilingual children's literature. We publish folktales and contemporary stories reflecting the traditions and culture of the emerging majority in the U.S. and from countries around the world. Our goal is to help broaden the base of children's literature in this country to include more stories from the African-American, Asian-American, Hispanic and Native American communities as well as the diverse Spanish-speaking communities throughout the Americas."
Fiction: Picture books, middle readers: contemporary, folktales, history, multicultural, poetry. Average word length: picture books—800-1,600.
Nonfiction: Picture books, middle readers: history, multicultural, music/dance, social issues.
How to Contact/Writers: Submit complete ms to Submissions Editor. Reports on queries in 2-4 months, mss in 2-4 months. Publishes a book 1 year after acceptance. Will consider simultaneous submissions.
Illustration: Works with 6-8 illustrators/year. Uses color artwork only. Reviews ms/illustration packages from artists. Send ms with 3 or 4 color photocopies. Illustrations only: Send slides. Reports in 1-4 months. Samples returned with SASE.
Terms: Pays royalties to authors and illustrators. Original artwork returned at job's completion. Book catalog available; ms guidelines available for SASE.
Tips: "Vocabulary level should be approximately third grade (eight years old) or below. Keep in mind, however, that many of the young people who read our books may be nine, ten, or eleven years old or older. Their life experiences are often more advanced than their reading level, so try to write a story that will appeal to a fairly wide age range. We are especially interested in humorous stories and original stories about contemporary life from the multicultural communities mentioned above by writers *from* those communities."

CHILDREN'S LIBRARY PRESS, P.O. Box 1919, Joshua Tree CA 92252. Book Publisher. Editor-in-Chief: Teresa Bjornson. Publishes 4-5 picture books/year. 80% of books by first-time authors.
Fiction: Picture books: adventure, animal, anthology, concept, contemporary, fantasy, folktales, history, humor, multicultural, nature/environment, science fiction, suspense/mystery.
Nonfiction: Picture books: animal, cooking, geography, history, hobbies, nature/environment, science.
How to Contact/Writers: Fiction/Nonfiction: Submit complete ms. Reports on queries/mss in 6 months.

Publishes a book 2 years after acceptance. Will consider simultaneous submissions.

How to Contact/Illustrators: Only interested in agented material.

Terms: Pays authors royalty based on wholesale price (amount determined on a per-book basis). Offers advances (amount varies). Sends galleys to authors.

Tips: Looking for "simple, well-written texts."

CHILDREN'S WRITER'S & ILLUSTRATOR'S MARKET, 1507 Dana Ave., Cincinnati OH 45207. (513)531-2690, ext. 546. E-mail: cwim@fwpubs.com. Publication of Writer's Digest Books. Editor: Alice Pope.

    ● *CWIM* needs examples of art sold to listings in this book which we can reproduce as well as good query letters.

Nonfiction: "We'd love to see copies of query letters that resulted in sales to publishers or magazines listed in the book. See Before Your First Sale for examples. Also open to queries for articles on issues of interest to children's writers and illustrators—feel free to e-mail.

Illustration: Send samples—photographs, tearsheets or good quality photocopies of artwork. Continuous tone b&w artwork reproduces best. Since *Children's Writer's & Illustrator's Market* is published only once a year, submissions are kept on file for the upcoming edition until selections are made in the summer. Material is then returned by SASE if requested.

Terms: Buys one-time rights. Pays $50 to holder of reproduction rights for artwork and $50 to reproduce query letters and free copy of *CWIM* when published.

Tips: "I need examples of art that have been sold to one of the listings in *CWIM*. Thumb through the book for examples. The art must have been freelanced; it cannot have been done as staff work. Include the name of the publisher that purchased the work and what the art was used for."

CHINA BOOKS & PERIODICALS, 2929 24th St., San Francisco CA 94110. (415)282-2994. Fax: (415)282-0994. E-mail: info@chinabooks.com. Website: http://www.chinabooks.com. Book publisher, distributor, wholesaler. Estab. 1960. **Acquisitions:** Wendy Lee, editor. Publishes 1 picture book/year; 1 middle readers/year; and 1 young adult title/year. 100% of books by first-time authors. Publishes books about China and Chinese culture. "China Books is the main importer and distributor of books and magazines from China, providing an ever-changing variety of useful tooks for travelers, scholars and others interested in China and Chinese culture."

Fiction: All levels: animal, anthology, folktales, history, multicultural, nature/environment. Recently published *Sing Chinese! Popular Children's Songs & Lullabies*, by Ma Baolin and Cindy Ma (children—adults/song book); and *The Moon Maiden and Other Asian Folktales*, by Hua Long (children to age 12/folktales).

Nonfiction: All levels: activity books, animal, arts/crafts, cooking, how-to, multicultural, music/dance, reference, textbooks. Recently published *West to East: A Young Girl's Journey to China*, by Qian Gao (young adult nonfiction travel journal).

How to Contact/Writers: Fiction/Nonfiction: Query. Reports on queries and mss in 2 months. Publishes a book 1 year after acceptance. Will consider simultaneous submissions, electronic submissions via disk or modem, previously published work.

Illustration: Works with 4-5 illustrators/year. Reviews ms/illustration packages from artists. Query. Illustrations only: Query with samples. Send résumé, promo sheet, tearsheets. Reports in 1 month only if interested. Samples returned with SASE; samples filed.

Photography: Buys stock and assigns work. Submit cover letter, résumé, promo piece. "Include SASE always."

Terms: Pays authors 4-10% royalty based on wholesale price or work purchased outright. Pays illustrators and photographers by the project (range $400-1,500) or royalty based on wholesale price. Sends galleys to authors; dummies to illustrators. Originals returned to artist at job's completion. Book catalog for $1; ms and art guidelines available for SASE.

CHRISTIAN ED. PUBLISHERS, P.O. Box 26639, San Diego CA 92196. (619)578-4700. Book publisher. Managing Editor: Carol Rogers. Publishes 64 curriculum titles/year. "We publish curriculum for

---

TO RECEIVE REGULAR TIPS AND UPDATES about writing and Writer's Digest publications via e-mail, send an e-mail with "SUBSCRIBE NEWSLETTER" in the body of the message to newsletter-request@writersdigest.com

children and youth, including program and student books (for youth) and take-home papers (for children)—all handled by our assigned freelance writers only."

Fiction: Young readers: contemporary. Middle readers: adventure, contemporary, suspense/mystery. "We publish fiction for Bible club take-home papers. All fiction is on assignment only."

Nonfiction: Publishes Bible curriculum and take-home papers for all ages. Recently published *Jet Flight Take-Home Papers*, by Treena Herrington and Letitia Zook, illustrated by Beverly Warren (Bible club curriculum for grades 4-6); and *Honeybees Classroom Activity Sheets*, by Janet Miller and Wanda Pelfrey, illustrated by Aiko Gilson and Terry Walderhaug (Bible club curriculum for ages 2-3).

How to Contact/Writers: Fiction/Nonfiction: Query. Reports on queries in 4-5 weeks. Publishes a book 1 year after acceptance. Send SASE for guidelines.

Illustration: Works with 6-7 illustrators/year. Uses primarily b&w artwork. Query; include a SASE; we'll send an application form. Contact: Carol Rogers, managing editor. Reports in 3-4 weeks. Samples returned with SASE.

Terms: Work purchased outright from authors for 3¢/word. Pays illustrators by the project (range: $300-400/book). Book catalog available for 9 × 12 SAE and 5 first-class stamps; ms and art guidelines available for SASE.

Tips: "Read our guidelines carefully before sending us a manuscript or illustrations. All writing and illustrating is done on assignment only, and must be age-appropriate (preschool-6th grade)."

CHRISTIAN PUBLICATIONS, INC., 3825 Hartzdale Dr., Camp Hill PA 17011. (717)761-7044. Fax: (717)761-7273. E-mail: editors@cpi-horizon.com. Website: http://cpi-horizon.com. Managing Editor: David Fessenden. **Manuscript Acquisitions:** George McPeek. **Art Acquisitions:** Marilynne Foster. Imprints: Christian Publications, Horizon Books. Publishes 1-2 young readers/year; and 1-2 young adult titles/year. 50% of books by first-time authors. The missions of this press are promoting participation in spreading the gospel worldwide and promoting Christian growth.

Fiction: "Not accepting unsolicited fiction."

Nonfiction: Young adults: religion. Does not want to see evangelistic/new Christian material. "Children and teens are too often assumed to have a shallow faith. We want to encourage a deeper walk with God." Average word length: young adults—25,000-40,000 words. Recently published *Grace and Guts to Live for God*, by Les Morgan (Bible study on Hebrews, 1 and 2 Peter); and *Holy Moses! And other Adventures in Vertical Living*, by Bob Hostetler. (Both are teen books which encourage a deeper commitment to God. Both illustrated by Ron Wheeler.) "Not accepting unsolicited material for age levels lower than teenage."

How to Contact/Writers: Nonfiction: Submit outline/synopsis and 2 sample chapters (including chapter one). Reports on queries in 6 weeks; mss in 2 months. Publishes a book 8-16 months after acceptance. Will consider simultaneous submissions, electronic submissions via disk or modem ("a one page, please").

Illustration: Works with 1-3 illustrators/year. Query with samples. Contact: Marilynne Foster, promotions coordinator. Reports back only if interested. Samples returned with SASE; samples filed.

Terms: Pays authors royalty of 5-10% based on retail price. Offers advances. Pays illustrators by the project. Sends galleys to authors; dummies to illustrators (sometimes). Originals returned to artist at job's completion (if requested). Ms guidelines available for SASE.

Tips: "Writers: Only opportunity is in teen market, especially if you have experience working with and speaking to teens. Illustrators: Show us a few samples."

CHRONICLE BOOKS, 85 Second St., San Francisco CA 94105. (415)537-3730. Fax: (415)537-4420. Book publisher. **Acquisitions:** Victoria Rock, associate publisher, children's books; Amy Novesky, assistant managing editor. Publishes 25-50 (both fiction and nonfiction) picture books/year; 2-4 middle readers nonfiction titles/year; 2-4 beginning readers or middle readers fiction/year. 10-50% of books by first-time authors; 10-50% of books from agented writers.

Fiction: Picture books: animal, folktales, history, multicultural, nature/environment. Young readers: animal, folktales, history, multicultural, nature/environment, poetry. Middle readers: animal, history, multicultural, nature/environment, poetry, problem novels. Young adults: multicultural needs include "projects that feature diverse children in everyday situations." Recently published *I Love You the Purplest*, by Barbara M. Joosse; and *Hush Little Baby*, by Sylvia Long.

Nonfiction: Picture books: animal, history, multicultural, nature/environment, science. Young readers: animal, arts/crafts, cooking, geography, history, multicultural and science. Middle readers: animal, arts/crafts, biography, cooking, geography, history, multicultural and nature/environment. Young adults: biography and multicultural. Recently published *A Rainbow at Night*, by Bruce Hucko; and *Artist in Overalls: The Life of Grant Wood*, by John Duggleby.

How to Contact/Writers: Fiction/Nonfiction: Submit complete ms (picture books); submit outline/synopsis and 3 sample chapters (for older readers). Reports on queries/mss in 2-18 weeks. Publishes a book 1-3 years after acceptance. Will consider simultaneous submissions, as long as they are marked "multiple submission." Will not consider submissions by fax. Must include SASE.

Illustration: Works with 15-20 illustrators/year. Wants "unusual art, graphically strong, something that will stand out on the shelves. Either bright and modern or very traditional. Fine art, not mass market." Reviews ms/illustration packages from artists. "Indicate if project *must* be considered jointly, or if editor may consider text and art separately." Illustrations only: Submit samples of artist's work (not necessarily from book, but in the envisioned style). Slides, tearsheets and color photocopies OK. (No original art.) Dummies helpful. Résumé helpful. "If samples sent for files, generally no response—unless samples are not suited to list, in which case samples are returned. Queries and project proposals responded to in same time frame as author query/proposals."

Photography: Purchases photos from freelancers. Works on assignment only. Wants nature/natural history photos.

Terms: Generally pays authors in royalties based on retail price "though we do occasionally work on a flat fee basis." Advance varies. Illustrators paid royalty based on retail price or flat fee. Sends proofs to authors and illustrators. Book catalog for 9×12 SAE and 8 first-class stamps; ms guidelines for #10 SASE.

Tips: "Chronicle Books publishes an eclectic mixture of traditional and innovative children's books. We are interested in taking on projects that have a unique bent to them—be it in subject matter, writing style, or illustrative technique. As a small list, we are looking for books that will lend our list a distinctive flavor. Primarily we are interested in fiction and nonfiction picture books for children ages infant-8 years, and nonfiction books for children ages 8-12 years. We are also interested in developing a middle grade/YA fiction program, and are looking for literary fiction that deals with relevant issues. Our sales reps are witnessing a resistance to alphabet books. And the market has become increasingly competitive. The '80s boom in children's publishing has passed, and the market is demanding high-quality books that work on many different levels."

☑ CLARION BOOKS, 215 Park Ave. S., New York NY 10003. (212)420-5889.Fax: (212)420-5855, Website: http://www.hmco.com/trade/. Imprint of Houghton Mifflin Company. Book publisher. Estab. 1965. **Manuscript Acquisitions:** Dinah Stevenson, editorial director; Nina Ignatowicz, senior editor; Virginia Buckley, contributing editor. **Art Acquisitions:** Joann Hill.
  ● Clarion's list is full through 2000. Do not send timely material.
How to Contact/Writers: Fiction: Send complete mss. Nonfiction: query. Must include SASE. Will accept simultaneous submission if informed.
Illustration: Send samples (no originals).
Terms: Pays illustrators royalty; flat fee for jacket illustration.

CLEAR LIGHT PUBLISHERS, 823 Don Diego, Santa Fe NM 87501. (505)989-9590. Fax: (505)989-9519. Book publisher. **Acquisitions:** Harmon Houghton, publisher. Publishes 3 middle readers/year; and 3 young adult titles/year.
Nonfiction: Middle readers and young adults: multicultural, American Indian only.
How to Contact/Writers: Fiction/Nonfiction: Submit complete ms. Will consider simultaneous submissions. Reports in 3 months.
Illustration: Reviews ms/illustration packages from artists. Submit ms with dummy.
Terms: Pays authors royalty of 10% based on wholesale price. Offers advances (average amount: up to 50% of expected net sales). Sends galleys to authors.
Tips: "We're looking for authentic American Indian art and folklore."

COMPASS PRODUCTIONS, 211 E. Ocean Blvd., #360, Long Beach CA 90802. (562)432-7613. Fax: (562)495-0445. **Acquisitions:** Dick Dudley, vice president. Book packager/producer.
Fiction: Pop-up and novelty books: adventure, fantasy, humor, juvenile, mystery, religious. Recently published *Counting On Angels*, by Ward (pop-up).
Nonfiction: "All our books are pop-up and novelty books". Subjects: animals, concept, education, recreation, regional, religion. Recently published *Busy Beaver Pond*, by Silver (pop-up).
How to Contact/Writers: Fiction/Nonfiction: Query with SASE. Reports in 6 weeks.
Terms: Produces hardcover originals. Pays 2-8% royalty on wholesale price for total amount of books sold to publisher. Offers $2,000 advance for idea/text.

MARKET CONDITIONS are constantly changing! If you're still using this book and it is 2000 or later, buy the newest edition of *Children's Writer's & Illustrator's Market* at your favorite bookstore or order directly from Writer's Digest Books.

Tips: "Keep in mind our books are *pop-up*, *dimensional*, or novelty *only*! Short verse, couplets or short nonfiction text for 6-7 spreads per book."

☑ **CONCORDIA PUBLISHING HOUSE**, 3558 S. Jefferson Ave., St. Louis MO 63118. (314)268-1000. Fax: (314)268-1329. Book publisher. **Manuscript Acquisitions:** Dawn Weinstock, Rachel Hoyer, Jane Wilke. **Art Acquisitions:** Ed Luhmann, art director. "Concordia Publishing House produces quality resources which communicate and nurture the Christian faith and ministry of people of all ages, lay and professional. These resources include curriculum, worship aids, books, multimedia products and religious supplies. We publish approximately 60 quality children's books each year. Most are fiction, with some nonfiction, based on a religious subject. We boldly provide Gospel resources that are Christ-centered, Bible-based, and faithful to our heritage."
Fiction: Picture books: concept, religion. Young readers, middle readers, young adults: concept, contemporary, humor, religion, suspense/mystery. "All books must contain explicit Christian content." Recently published *Toddler's Action Bible*, by Robin Curne (devotional, ages 4-7); *Smelly Tales*, by Mora Hodgien (beginning reader series); and *Invasion from Planet X*, by Buchanan and Randall (juvenile fiction).
Nonfiction: Picture books, young readers, middle readers: activity books, arts/crafts, religion. Young adults: religion.
How to Contact/Writers: Fiction: Submit complete ms (picture books); submit outline/synopsis and sample chapters (novel-length). May also query. Reports on queries in 1 month; mss in 2 months. Publishes a book 18 months after acceptance. Will consider simultaneous submissions. "No phone queries."
Illustration: Illustrations only: Query with samples. Contact: Ed Luhmann, art director.
Terms: Pays authors in royalties based on retail price or work purchased outright (minimum $500). Sends galleys to author. Ms guidelines for 1 first-class stamp and a #10 envelope.
Tips: "Do not send finished artwork with the manuscript. If sketches will help in the presentation of the manuscript, they may be sent. If stories are taken from the Bible, they should follow the Biblical account closely. Liberties should not be taken in fantasizing Biblical stories."

🍁 **COTEAU BOOKS LTD.**, 401-2206 Dewdney Ave., Regina, Sasketchewan S4R 1H3 Canada. (306)777-0170. E-mail: coteau@coteau.unibase.com. Thunder Creek Publishing Co-op Ltd. Book publisher. Estab. 1975. **Acquisitions:** Barbara Sapergia, acquisitions editor; Geoffrey Ursell, publisher. Publishes 3-4 juvenile and/or young adult books/year, 12-14 books/year. 10% of books by first-time authors. "Coteau Books publishes the finest Canadian fiction, poetry, drama and children's literature, with an emphasis on western writers."
● Coteau Books publishes Canadian writers and illustrators only; mss from the U.S. are returned unopened.
Fiction: Young readers, middle readers, young adults: adventure, contemporary, fantasy, history, humor, multicultural, nature/environment, science fiction, suspense/mystery. "No didactic, message pieces, nothing religious. No picture books. Material should reflect the diversity of culture, race, religion, creed of humankind—we're looking for fairness and balance." Recently published *Angels in the Snow*, by Wenda Young (ages 11-14); *Bay Girl*, by Betty Dorion (ages 8-11); and *The Intrepid Polly McDoodle*, by Mary Woodbury (ages 8-12).
Nonfiction: Young readers, middle readers, young adult: biography, history, multicultural, nature/environment, social issues.
How to Contact/Writers: Fiction: Submit complete ms to acquisitions editor Barbara Sapergia. Include SASE or send up to 20-page sample by e-mail, as an attached file, in the Mime protocol. Reports on queries in 3-4 months; mss in 3-4 months. Publishes a book 1-2 years after acceptance. Send for guidelines.
Illustration: Works with 1-4 illustrators/year. Illustrations only: Submit nonreturnable samples. Reports only if interested. Samples returned with SASE; samples filed.
Photography: "Very occasionally buys photos from freelancers." Buys stock and assigns work.
Terms: Pays authors in royalties based on retail price. Pays illustrators and photographers by the project. Sends galleys to authors; dummies to illustrators. Original artwork returned at job's completion. Book catalog free on request with 9×12 SASE.
Tips: "Truthfully, the work speaks for itself! Be bold. Be creative. Be persistent! There is room, at least in the Canadian market, for quality novels for children, and at Coteau, this is a direction we will continue to take."

Ⓝ **COUNCIL OAK BOOKS**, 1350 E. 15th St., Tulsa OK 74120. (918)587-6454. Fax: (918)583-4995. E-mail: oakie@ionet.net. Estab. 1984. Publishes fiction, trade books, educational material, multicultural material. 50% of books by first-time authors. "Council Oak Books publishes high quality books for readers of all ages. Our children's books generally have a Native American theme."
Fiction: Picture books, young readers: animal, folktales, history, nature/environment, Native American.

Recently published *Green Snake Ceremony*, by Sherrin Watkins, illustrated by Kim Doner (ages 3-8); *White Bead Ceremony*, by Sherrin Watkins, illustrated by Kim Doner (ages 3-8); and *Cherokee Animal Tales*, by George Scheer, illustrated by Robert Frankenberg (ages 6-10).

Nonfiction: Picture books: activity books, nature/environment, teacher's guide. Recently published *Earth Child 2000*, by Kathryn Sheehan and Mary Waidner, Ph.D. (preschool-10).

How to Contact/Writers: Fiction/nonfiction: query. Reports on queries in 3 weeks; mss in 3 months. Publishes a book 1 year after acceptance. Will consider simultaneous submissions and previously published work.

Illustration: Works with 1 illustrator/year. Reviews ms/illustration packages from artists. Query editorial department. Illustrations only: query with samples. Contact editorial department. Reports in 3 months. Samples returned with SASE; samples not filed.

Photography: Buys stock and assigns work. Contact editorial department. Uses images with Native American themes. Model/property release required. Submit cover letter, resume, published samples and client list.

Terms: Terms vary by project. Book catalog available for free. All imprints included in a single catalog. Writer's guidelines available for SASE.

Tips: "We are a small, independent publishing house with limited publishing focus. Council Oak Books publishes approximately one children's book per year. All queries should be made by mail and should fall within the Native American theme for ages three to ten."

☑ **CROCODILE BOOKS**, 46 Crosby St., Northampton MA 01060. (413)582-7054. Fax: (413)582-7057. E-mail: interpg@aol.com. Imprint of Interlink Publishing Group, Inc. Book publisher. **Acquisitions:** Pam Thompson, associate publisher. Publishes 4 picture books/year. 25% of books by first-time authors.
   ● Crocodile does not accept unsolicited mss.

Fiction: Picture books: animal, contemporary, history, spy/mystery/adventure.

Nonfiction: Picture book: history, nature/environment.

Terms: Pays authors in royalties. Sends galleys to author; dummies to illustrator.

CROSSWAY BOOKS, Good News Publishers, 1300 Crescent, Wheaton IL 60187. (630)682-4300. Fax: (630)682-4785. Book Publisher. Estab. 1938. Editorial Director: Marvin Padgett. **Acquisitions:** Jill Carter. Publishes 1-2 picture books/year; and 1-2 young adult titles/year. "Crossway Books is committed to publishing books that bring Biblical reality to readers and that examine crucial issues through a Christian world view."

Fiction: Picture books: religion. Middle readers: adventure, contemporary, history, humor, religion, suspense/mystery, Christian realism. Young adults: contemporary, history, humor, religion, suspense/mystery, Christian realism. Does not want to see horror novels, romance or prophecy novels. Not looking for picture book submissions at present time. Recently published *Lewis & Clark Squad Series*, by Stephen Bly (middle reader, mystery suspense); *Noah*, by Mary Rice Hopkins, illustrated by Wendy Francisce (preschool-8, picture book); and *I'll Be with You Always*, by Jane Eareckson Tada, illustrated by Craig Nelson (young reader, fiction).

How to Contact/Writers: Fiction: Query with outline/synopsis and up to 2 sample chapters. Reports on queries/mss in 6-8 weeks. Publishes a book 12-18 months after acceptance. Will consider simultaneous submissions.

Illustration: Works with 3-4 illustrators/year. Reviews ms/illustration packages from artists. Query. Illustrations only: Query with samples; provide résumé, promo sheet and client list. Reports on artists' queries/submissions in 6-8 weeks. Samples returned with SASE; samples filed.

Terms: Pays authors royalty based on wholesale price. Pays illustrators by the project. Sends galleys to authors; dummies to illustrators. Book catalog available; ms guidelines available for SASE.

CROWN PUBLISHERS (CROWN BOOKS FOR CHILDREN), 201 E. 50th St., New York NY 10022. (212)940-7742. Website: http://www.randomhouse.com/kids. Imprint of Random House, Inc. See Random House listing. Book publisher. Publisher: Simon Boughton. **Manuscript Acquisitions:** Tracy Gates, senior editor; Nancy Siscoe, editor. **Art Acquisitions:** Isabel Warren-Lynch, art director. Publishes 20 picture books/year; 10 nonfiction titles/year. 5% of books by first-time authors; 70% of books from agented writers.

Fiction: Picture books: animal, humor, nature/environment. Young readers: history, nature/environment. Does not want to see fantasy, science fiction, poetry. Average word length: picture books—750. Recently published: *My Little Sister Ate One Hare*, by Bill Grossman; and *Me on the Map*, by Joan Sweeney.

Nonfiction: Picture books, young readers and middle readers: activity books, animal, biography, careers, health, history, hobbies, music/dance, nature/environment, religion, science, sports. Average word length: picture books—750-1,000; young readers—20,000; middle readers—50,000. Does not want to see ABCs.

Recently published: *Rosie the Riviter*, by Penny Coleman (ages 9-14); and *Children of the Dust Bowl*, by Jerry Stanley (9-14 years, middle reader).

How to Contact/Writers: Fiction/nonfiction: Submit query letter. Reports on queries/mss in 3-4 months if SASE is included. Publishes book approximately 2 years after acceptance. Will consider simultaneous submissions.

Illustration: Works with 20 illustrators/year. Reviews ms/illustration packages from artists. "Submit double-spaced, continuous manuscripts; do not supply page-by-page breaks. One or two photocopies of art are fine. *Do not send original art*. Dummies are acceptable." Reports in 2 months. Illustrations only: Submit photocopies, portfolio or slides with SASE; provide business card and tearsheets. Contact: Isabel Warren-Lynch, Art Director. Original artwork returned at job's completion.

Terms: Pays authors royalty based on retail price. Advance "varies greatly." Pays illustrators by the project or royalty. Sends galleys to authors; proofs to illustrators. Book catalog for 9×12 SAE and 4 first-class stamps. Ms guidelines for $4\frac{1}{2} \times 9\frac{1}{2}$ SASE; art guidelines not available.

CSS PUBLISHING, 517 S. Main St., P.O. Box 4503, Lima OH 45802-4503. (419)227-1818. Fax: (419)222-4647. E-mail: acquisitions@csspub.com. Website: http://www.csspub.com. Book publisher. Imprints include Fairway Press and Express Press. **Manuscript Acquisitions:** Thomas Lentz. **Art Acquisitions:** Scott Swiebel. Publishes books with religious themes. "We are seeking material for use by clergy, Christian education directors and Sunday school teachers for mainline Protestant churches. Our market is mainline Protestant clergy."

Fiction: Picture books, young readers, middle readers, young adults: religion, religious poetry and humor. Needs children's sermons (object lesson) for Sunday morning worship services; dramas for Advent, Christmas or Epiphany involving children for church services; activity and craft ideas for Sunday school or mid-week services for children (particularly pre-school and first and second grade). Does not want to see secular picture books. Published *That Seeing, They May Believe*, by Kenneth Mortonson (lessons for adults to present during worship services to pre-schoolers-third graders); *What Shall We Do With This Baby?*, by Jan Spence (Christmas Eve worship service involving youngsters from newborn babies-high school youth); and *Miracle in the Bethlehem Inn*, by Mary Lou Warstler (Advent or Christmas drama involving pre-schoolers-high school youth and adult.)

Nonfiction: Picture books, young readers, middle readers, young adults: religion. Young adults only: social issues and self help. Needs children's sermons (object lesson) for Sunday morning workship services; dramas for Advent, Christmas or Epiphany involving children for church services; activity and craft ideas for Sunday school or mid-week services for children (particularly pre-school and first and second grade). Does not want to see secular picture books. Published *Mustard Seeds*, by Ellen Humbert (activity/bulletins for pre-schoolers-first graders to use during church); and *This Is The King*, by Cynthia Cowen.

How to Contact/Writers: Reports on queries in 2 weeks; mss in 1-3 months. Publishes a book 9 months after acceptance. Will consider simultaneous submissions.

Terms: Work purchased outright from authors. Ms guidelines and book catalog available for SASE.

MAY DAVENPORT, PUBLISHERS, 26313 Purissima Rd., Los Altos Hills CA 94022-4539. (415)948-6499. Fax: (650)947-1373. Independent book producer/packager. Estab. 1976. **Acquisitions:** May Davenport, editor/publisher. Publishes 1-2 picture books/year; and 2-3 young adult titles/year. 99% of books by first-time authors. Seeks books with literary merit. "We like to think that we are selecting talented writers who have something humorous to write about today's unglued generation in 30,000-50,000 words for teens and young adults in junior/senior high school before they become tomorrow's 'functional illiterates.'" This publisher is overstocked with picture book/elementary reading material.

Fiction: Young adults (15-18): contemporary, humorous fictional literature for use in English courses in junior-senior high schools in US. Average word length: 40,000-60,000. Recently published *The Ghost, The Gold and The Whippoorwill*, by Frank Nuckols, illustrated by Alec Nuckols (adventure/mystery for middle grades); *The Newman Assignment*, by Kurt Haberl, illustrated by Keith Neely (ages 12 and up, novel with teachers' lesson plans to read/discuss/write); and *Drivers' Ed is Dead*, by Pat Delgado, illustrated by Keith Neely (ages 12 and up, novel with teachers' lesson plans to read/discuss/write).

Nonfiction: Teens: humorous. Published *Just a Little off the Top*, by Linda Ropes (essays for teens).

How to Contact/Writers: Fiction: Query. Reports on queries/mss in 2-3 weeks. "We do not answer queries or manuscripts which do not have SASE attached." Publishes a book 6-12 months after acceptance.

Illustration: Works with 1-2 illustrators/year. "Have enough on file for future reference."

Terms: Pays authors royalties of 15% based on retail price. Pays "by mutual agreement, no advances." Pays illustrators by the project (range: $175-300). Book catalog, ms guidelines free on request with SASE.

Tips: "Create stories to enrich the non-reading 12-and-up readers. They might not appreciate your similies and metaphors and may find fault with your alliterations with the letters of the alphabet, but show them how you do it with memorable characters in today's society. Just project your humorous talent and entertain with more than two sentences in a paragraph."

☑ **DIAL BOOKS FOR YOUNG READERS**, Penguin Putnam Inc., 345 Hudson St., New York NY 10014. Website: http://www.penguinputnam.com. President/Publisher: Phyllis J. Fogelman. **Acquisitions:** Submissions Coordinator. Publishes 70 picture books/year; 10 young reader titles/year; 5 middle reader titles/year; and 10 young adult titles/year.

• Dial prefers submissions from agents and previously published authors.

Fiction: Picture books: adventure, animal, contemporary, folktales, history, nature/environment, poetry, religion, science fiction, sports, suspense/mystery. Young readers: animal, contemporary, easy-to-read, fantasy, folktales, history, nature/environment, poetry, science fiction, sports, mystery/adventure. Middle readers, young adults: animal, contemporary, folktales, history, nature/environment, poetry, problem novels, religion, science fiction, sports, spy/mystery/adventure. Published *Brother Eagle, Sister Sky,* illustrated by Susan Jeffers (all ages, picture book); *Amazing Grace,* by Mary Hoffman (ages 4-8, picture book); and *Soul Looks Back in Wonder,* by Tom Feelings, Maya Angelou, et al (ages 7 and up, poetry picture book.)

Nonfiction: Will consider query letters for submissions of outstanding literary merit. Picture books: animals, biography, history, nature/environment, sports. Young readers: animals, biography, history, nature/environment, sports. Middle readers: biography, history. Young adults: biography, contemporary. Recently published *Thanks to My Mother,* by Schoschana Rabinovici (ages 12 and up, YA) and *Handmade Counting Book,* by Laura Rankin (ages 3-8, picture book).

How to Contact/Writers: Prefers agented material (but will accept queries with a SASE). Send a SASE for submission guidelines. "We do not supply specific guidelines, but we will send you a recent catalog if you send us a 9×12 envelope SASE with four 32¢ stamps attached. Questions and queries should only be made in writing. We will not reply to anything without a SASE."

Illustration: To arrange a personal interview to show portfolio, send samples and a letter requesting an interview. Art samples should be sent to Ms. Toby Sherry and will not be returned without a SASE.

Photography: Prefers agented material.

Terms: Pays authors and illustrators in royalties based on retail price. Average advance payment "varies."

DK INK, 95 Madision Ave., New York NY 10016. (212)213-4800. Fax: (212)213-5240. Imprint of DK Publishing, Inc. Website: http://www.dk.com. Book publisher. Estab. 1997. Will publishes 50-60 titles/year; first list included 20 titles. **Acquisitions:** Neal Porter, publisher; Richard Jackson, senior editor; Melanie Kroupa, senior editor. "DK Ink is a distinctive imprint consisting primarily of picture books and fiction for children and adults, created by authors and illustrators you know and respect as well as exciting new talents. The main goal of these books is to edify, entertain and encourage kids to think about the human condition."

Fiction: Looking for picture books, middle readers and young adult material. Recently published: *Jack and the Beanstalk,* told by Rosemary Wells, illustrated by Norman Messenger (retelling of classic story for ages 2-5); *Hob and the Peddler,* by William Mayne (fantasy for ages 8-11); and *Chills in the Night,* by Jackie Vivelo (collection of ghost stories for ages 9-14).

Nonfiction: Nonfiction titles under DK Ink will have a distinctively different look from DK Publishing nonfiction titles.

How to Contact/Writers: Fiction: Submit complete ms. Nonfiction: Submit outline/sysnopsis and sample chapters. Reports in 8-10 weeks.

Illustration: Submit samples to Art Director.

Terms: Pays authors royalty; offers advance. Pays illustrators royalty or flat fee, depending on assignment.

☑ Ⓐ **DK PUBLISHING, INC.**, 95 Madison Ave., New York NY 10016. (212)213-4800. Fax: (212)689-1799. Website: http://www.dk.com. U.S. division of Dorling Kindersley. **Acquisitions:** Beth Sutinis, submissions editor. Imprint: DK Ink. Publishes 30 picture books/year; 30 young readers/year; 30 middle readers/year; and 2 young adult titles/year.

• DK works with previously published authors or agented authors only.

Fiction: Picture books: animal, contemporary, folktales, nature/environment. Young readers: adventure, anthology, contemporary, folktales. Middle readers: adventure, anthology, contemporary, fantasy, folktales, history, humor, sports, suspense/mystery. Young adult: adventure, contemporary, fantasy, problem novels. Average page count: picture books, middle readers: 32 pages; young readers: 128 pages. Recently published: *Eyewitness Classics: Black Beauty,* by Anna Sewell, illustrated by Victo Ambrus (for young readers); and *Cybermama,* by Alexandre Jardin (for middle readers).

Nonfiction: Picture books: animal, concept, nature/environment. Young readers: activity books, animal, arts/craft, nature/environment. Middle readers: activity books, gepgraphy, history, nature/environment, reference, science, sports. Young adults: biography, careers, history, reference, science, social issues, sports.

Average page count: picture books, middle readers: 32 pages; young readers: 128 pages. Recently published *Children Just Like Me: Our Favorite Stories*, by Jamila Gavin (for all ages); and *Stephen Biesty's Cross-Sections Castle* (for ages 8 and up).

How to Contact/Writers: Only interested in agented material. Query with outline/synopsis. Reports in 10-12 weeks. Publishes a book 9 months after acceptance. Will consider simultaneous submissions.

Illustration: Only interested in agented material. Uses color artwork only. Reviews ms/illustration packages from artists. Query with printed samples. Illustrations only: Query with samples. Send résumé and promo sheet. Reports back only if interested. Samples filed.

Photography: Buys stock and assigns work. Uses color prints. Submit cover letter, résumé, published samples, color promo piece.

Terms: Pays authors royalty. Offers advances. Book catalog available for 10×13 SASE and $3 first-class postage. All imprints except DK Ink included in a single catalog. Ms/artist's guidelines available for SASE.

Tips: "Most of our projects are generated in London where authors and illustrators are solicited."

DOWN EAST BOOKS, P.O. Box 679, Camden, ME 04843-0679. (207)594-9544. Fax: (207)594-7215. Website: http://www.mainebooks.com. Book publisher. Senior Editor: Karin Womer. **Acquisitions:** Alice Devine, associate editor. Publishes 1-2 young middle readers/year. 70% of books by first-time authors. "As a small regional publisher Down East Books specializes in non-fiction books with a Maine or New England theme."

Fiction: Picture books, middle readers: animal, history, nature/environment. Published *Cats in the Dark*, by Kate Rowinski, illustrated by Bonnie Bishop (young-middle readers, animal); and *Captain's Castaway*, by Angeli Perrow, illustrated by Emily Harris (young-middle readers, animal).

Nonfiction: Picture books, middle readers: animal, history, nature/environment. Published *Do Whales Ever . . .? What you Really Want to Know About Whales, Porpoises and Dolphins*, by Nathalie Ward, illustrated by Tessa Morgan (young-middle readers, animal).

How to Contact/Writers: Fiction/Nonfiction: Query. Reports on queries/mss in 1-2 months. Publishes a book 6-18 months after acceptance. Will consider simultaneous and previously published submissions.

Illustration: Works with 1-2 illustrators/year. Reviews ms/illustration packages from artists. Query. Illustrations only: Query with samples. Reports in 2-4 weeks. Samples returned with SASE; samples filed sometimes.

Terms: Pays authors royalty (varies widely). Pays illustrators by the project or by royalty (varies widely). Sends galleys to authors; dummies to illustrators. Original artwork returned at job's completion. Book catalog available. Ms guidelines available for SASE.

☑ ☑ **DUTTON CHILDREN'S BOOKS**, Penguin Putnam Inc., 345 Hudson St., New York NY 10014. (212)366-2600. Fax: (212)414-3397. Website: http://www.penguinputnam.com. Book publisher. **Acquisitions:** Lucia Monfried, editor-in-chief. **Art Acquisitions:** Sara Reynolds, art director. Publishes approximately 60 picture books/year; 4 young reader titles/year; 10 middle reader titles/year; and 8 young adult titles/year. 10% of books by first-time authors. "We publish high-quality trade books and are interested in well-written manuscripts with fresh ideas and child appeal. We have a complete publishing program. Though we publish mostly picture books, we are very interested in acquiring more novels for middle and young adult readers. We are also expanding our list to include more books for preschool-aged children."

● Dutton's title *Rapunzel*, by Paul O. Zelinsky, won the Caldecott Medal in 1998.

Fiction: Picture books: adventure, animal, folktales, history, multicultural, nature/environment, poetry. Young readers: adventure, animal, contemporary, easy-to-read, fantasy, pop-up, suspense/mystery. Middle readers: adventure, animal, contemporary, fantasy, history, multicultural, nature/environment, suspense/mystery. Young adults: adventure, animal, anthology, contemporary, fantasy, history, multicultural, nature/environment, poetry, science fiction, suspense/mystery. Recently published *A Monster in the House*, by Elisa Kleven (picture book); and *The Shakespeare Stealer*, by Gary Blackwood (novel).

Nonfiction: Picture books: animal, history, multicultural, nature/environment. Young readers: animal, history, multicultural, nature/environment. Middle readers: animal, biography, history, multicultural, nature/environment. Young adults: animal, biography, history, multicultural, nature/environment, social issues. Recently published *Quinceañera: Celebrating Fifteen*, by Elizabeth King (ages 10-15, photo essay); and *Ten Queens: Portraits of Women of Power*, by Milton Meltzer illustrated by Bethanne Anderson (ages 12 and up).

How to Contact/Writers: Query (for longer books), or submit complete ms (if picture book). Publishes a book 12-18 months after acceptance. Will consider simultaneous submissions.

Illustration: Works with 40-60 illustrators/year. Reviews ms/illustration packages from artists. Query first. Illustrations only: Query with samples; send résumé, portfolio, slides—no original art please. Reports on art samples in 2 months. Original artwork returned at job's completion.

Photography: Will look at photography samples and photo-essay proposals.
Terms: Pays authors royalties of 4-10% based on retail price. Book catalog, ms guidelines for SASE with 8 first-class stamps. Pays illustrators royalties of 2-10% based on retail price unless jacket illustration—then pays by flat fee.
Tips: "Avoid topics that appear frequently. In nonfiction, we are looking for history, general biography, science and photo essays for all age groups." Illustrators: "We would like to see samples and portfolios from potential illustrators of picture books (full color), young novels (b&w) and jacket artists (full color)."

E.M. PRESS, INC., P.O. Box 4057, Manassas VA 20108. (540)439-0304. Book publisher. **Acquisitions:** Beth Miller, publisher/editor. "E.M. Press has narrowed its focus to manuscripts of local interest (Virginia, Maryland, D.C.); manuscripts by local authors; nonfiction manuscripts; and children's books. We're now publishing illustrated children's books." 50% of books by first-time authors.
Fiction: Recently published *How Will They Get That Heart Down Your Throat? A Child's View of Transplants*, by Karen Walton (educates children regarding "recycling" life); and *The Relationship*, by John H. Hyman (story of a summer in the lives of two young boys—one white, one "colored"—in rural, 1940s North Carolina).
Nonfiction: Young adults: religion, children. Recently published *Santa's New Reindeer*, by Judie Schrecker; *Virginia's Country Stores: A Quiet Passing*, by Joseph E. Morse (illustrated history of the origins of the old community store).
How to Contact/Writers: Query with outline/synopsis and SASE for novel-length work and complete ms for shorter work. Reports on ms/queries in 3 months. Publishes a book 18 months after acceptance. Will consider simultaneous submissions.
Illustration: Works with 3 children's illustrators/year. Illustration packages should be submitted to Beth Miller, publisher. Reports back in 3 months. Samples returned with SASE; samples kept on file.
Terms: "We've used all means of payment from outright purchase to royalty." Offers varied advances. Sends galleys to authors. Original artwork returned at job's completion. Book catalog for SASE.
Tips: "Present the most professional package possible. The market is glutted, so you must find a new approach."

☑ WM. B. EERDMANS PUBLISHING COMPANY, 255 Jefferson Ave. SE, Grand Rapids MI 49503. (616)459-4591. Book publisher. **Manuscript Acquisitions:** Judy Zylstra, children's book editor. **Art Acquisitions:** Gayle Brown. Publishes 8 picture books/year; 4 young readers/year; and 4 middle readers/year.
Fiction: All levels: parables, religion, retold Bible stories from a Christian perspective. Picture books: animal, poetry.
Nonfiction: All levels: biography, religion.
How to Contact/Writers: Fiction/Nonfiction: Query (novels) or submit complete ms (picture books). Reports on queries in 3-6 weeks; mss in 8 weeks.
Illustration: Works with 10-12 illustrators/year. Reviews ms/illustration packages from artists. Reports on ms/art samples in 1 month. Illustrations only: Submit résumé, slides or color photocopies. Samples returned with SASE; samples filed.
Terms: Pays authors and illustrators royalties of 5-7% based on retail price. Sends galleys to authors; dummies to illustrators. Original artwork returned at job's completion. Book catalog free on request; ms and/or artist's guidelines free on request.
Tips: "We are looking for material that will help children build their faith in God and explore God's world. We accept all genres."

ENSLOW PUBLISHERS INC., 44 Fadem Rd., Box 699, Springfield NJ 07081. Website: http://www.enslow.com. Estab. 1978. **Acquisitions:** Brian D. Enslow, vice president. Publishes 50 middle reader titles/year; and 75 young adult titles/year. 30% of books by first-time authors.
Nonfiction: Young readers, middle readers, young adults: animal, biography, careers, health, history, hobbies, nature/environment, social issues, sports. Average word length: middle readers—5,000; young adult—18,000. Published *Louis Armstrong*, by Patricia and Fredrick McKissack (grades 2-3, biography); and *Lotteries: Who Wins, Who Loses?*, by Ann E. Weiss (grades 6-12, issues book).

A SELF-ADDRESSED, STAMPED ENVELOPE (SASE) should always be included with submissions within your own country. When sending material to other countries, include a self-addressed envelope (SAE) and International Reply Coupons (IRCs).

How to Contact/Writers: Nonfiction: Query. Reports on queries/mss in 2 weeks. Publishes a book 18 months after acceptance. Will not consider simultaneous submissions.
Illustration: Submit résumé, business card or tearsheets to be kept on file.
Terms: Pays authors royalties or work purchased outright. Sends galleys to authors. Book catalog/ms guidelines available for $2.

EVAN-MOOR EDUCATIONAL PUBLISHERS, 18 Lower Ragsdale Dr., Monterey CA 93940-5746. (408)649-5901. Fax: (408)649-6256. E-mail: editorial@evan-moor.com. Website: http://www.evan-moor.com. Book publisher. **Manuscript Acquisitions:** Marilyn Evans, editor. **Art Acquisitions:** Joy Evans, production director. Publishes 30-50 books/year. Less than 10% of books by first-time authors. " 'Helping Children Learn' is our motto. Evan-Moor is known for high-quality educational materials written by teachers for use in the classroom and at home. We publish teacher resource and reproducible materials in most all curriculum areas and activity books (language arts, math, science, social studies). No fiction or nonfiction literature books."
Nonfiction: Nonfiction: Published in 1998: series of 10 Early Learning Resources for Grades PreK-1, including *Circle Time Activities*, by Martha Cheney and Brenda Austin, illustrated by Jo Larsen; 5-book series—*Daily Language Review for grades 1-5*, by Laura B. Williams, Jo Ellen Moore and Jill Norris; 3-book series—*Building Spelling Skills, grades 1-2, 3-4, 5-6*, by Jo Ellen Moore. Activity books are 32 pages; teacher resource books are 64-160 pages. Audience: children age 5-11; grades PreK-6.
How to Contact/Writers: Query or submit complete ms. Reports on queries in 2 months; mss in 3-4 months. Publishes a book 12-18 months after acceptance. Will consider simultaneous submissions if so noted. Send SASE for submission guidelines.
Illustration: Works with 6-8 illustrators/year. Uses b&w artwork primarily. Illustrations only: Query with samples; send résumé, tearsheets. Contact: Joy Evans, production director. Reports only if interested. Samples returned with SASE; samples filed.
Terms: Work purchased outright from authors, "dependent solely on size of project and 'track record' of author." Pays illustrators by the project (range: varies). Sends galleys to authors. Artwork is not returned. Book catalog available for 9×12 SAE; ms guidelines available for SASE.
Tips: "Writers—know the supplemental education or parent market. (These materials are *not* children's literature.) Tell us how your project is unique and what consumer needs it meets. Illustrators—you need to be able to produce quickly, and be able to render realistic and charming children and animals." A number of subject areas are of ongoing interest. They include: interdisciplinary/cross-curricular units; science and math materials which emphasize "real-world," hands-on; learning and critical thinking/problem solving skills; materials related to cultural diversity, global awareness; geography materials; assessment materials; and materials for parents to use with their children at home.

EXCELSIOR CEE PUBLISHING, P.O. Box 5861, Norman OK 73070-5861. (405)329-3909. Fax: (405)329-6886. Book publisher. Estab. 1989. **Manuscript Acquisitions:** J.C. Marshall.
How to Contact/Writers: Nonfiction: Query or submit outline/synopsis. Reports on queries in 1 month. Publishes a book 1 year after acceptance. Will consider simultaneous submission.

FACTS ON FILE, 11 Penn Plaza, New York NY 10001. (212)967-8800. Book publisher. Editorial Director: Laurie Likoff. **Acquisitions:** Eleanora VonDehsen, science and technology/nature; Nicole Bowen, American history and studies; Anne Savarese, language and literature; Mary Kay Linge, world studies; Jim Chambers, arts and entertainment. Estab. 1941. "We produce high-quality reference materials for the school library market and the general nonfiction trade." Publishes 25-30 young adult titles/year. 5% of books by first-time authors; 25% of books from agented writers; additional titles through book packagers, co-publishers and unagented writers.
Nonfiction: Middle readers, young adults: animal, biography, careers, geography, health, history, multicultural, nature/environment, reference, religion, science, social issues and sports. Recently published *Great Women Writers 1900-1950*, by Christina Gombar; *African American Explorers*, by Catherine Reef; and *Modern Mathematics*, by Harry Henderson; and *Children's Atlas*, by Jill and David Wright.
How to Contact/Writers: Nonfiction: Submit outline/synopsis and sample chapters. Reports on queries in 8-10 weeks. Publishes a book 10-12 months after acceptance. Will consider simultaneous submissions. Sends galleys to authors. Book catalog free on request. Send SASE for submission guidelines.
Tips: "Most projects have high reference value and fit into a series format."

FARRAR, STRAUS & GIROUX INC., 19 Union Square W., New York NY 10003. (212)741-6900. Fax: (212)633-2427. Book publisher. Imprint: Frances Foster Books. Children's Books Editorial Director: Margaret Ferguson. **Acquisitions:** Frances Foster, publisher, Frances Foster Books; Beverly Reingold, executive editor; Wesley Adams, senior editor; Elizabeth Mikesell, associate editor. Estab. 1946. Publishes

Facing the challenge of tackling tough issues for teens

photo: Midge Eliassen

Nancy Garden

Some people reflect fondly on their teenage years as a carefree age, but most of us remember the reality of life on the verge of adulthood—it's confusing and sometimes just plain hard. Experiencing relationships for the first time is especially challenging, and many adolescents look to novels for guidance during this turbulent period. As a writer who suspected she was a lesbian at an early age, Nancy Garden understands the necessity of having books where teens can read about peers who have experienced—and survived—issues like prejudice or isolation. "I grew up reading and enjoying books about straight people," says Garden, "but as a kid I also longed for books about my own people; both are necessary."

Unsettled by the lack of literature for teenagers with sexual orientations different from those portrayed in mainstream young adult novels, Garden took action through her own writing. "Novels that feature homosexual characters are important reflections of the world as it really is," she says. "It's important for all adolescents to grow up acquainted with the rich diversity of the human race, and that diversity includes gay, lesbian, bisexual and transgendered people." Through books like *Annie on My Mind* and *Good Moon Rising* (both Farrar, Straus & Giroux), Garden shows the hardships associated with "coming out, or acknowledging one's sexual orientation to oneself and to others," but also reveals how happy characters are once they are allowed to be true to themselves. More importantly, her books demonstrate that most issues concerning teenagers are universal.

"There are issues common to most gay and lesbian kids, just as there are issues common to most kids from other minorities," Garden says. "For example, coming out is an important ongoing process for all gay and lesbian (and bisexual and transgendered) people.

"On the other hand, I don't think there should be any 'essential' issues in a young adult novel centering on lesbian characters; a novel about young lesbian characters is first and foremost a story about individuals. In many YAs featuring straight teens, the girl has a boyfriend or the boy has a girlfriend; that is background, but the novel itself is about something else. I think we need similar books featuring gay and lesbian teens. Being gay, contrary to what some people believe, is not just 'gay' sex. Sex is fundamental in the lives of both gay and straight people, but it's hardly the sole focus of one's life. I wrote a book called *Lark in the Morning* (Farrar, Straus & Giroux). It has a lesbian protagonist, Gillian, who is comfortable with her sexual orientation, but the book is only peripherally about her relationship. It is actually about how Gillian helps two young (straight) runaways." Nevertheless, *Lark in the Morning* has not sold as well as her books dealing directly with coming out, which perhaps affirms just how significant this topic is to homosexual youth.

INSIDER REPORT, *Garden*

Nancy Garden's novel *Annie on My Mind* (Farrar, Straus & Giroux) tells the story of a relationship between Liza and Annie, two teenagers coming to terms with their homosexuality. Eleven years after its initial printing, *Annie* was banned and burned in Kansas City, but a judge finally declared the banning unconstitutional. "The important issue was the First Amendment, not the book itself or even the fact that the book is about lesbian characters," says Garden.

Illustration © 1992 Elaine Norman. Reprinted with permission.

Garden's devotion to exploring the broad range of issues homosexuals deal with daily has garnered a tremendous response from her readers. "Over the years I've gotten many wonderful, moving letters from readers that say *Annie on My Mind* or *Good Moon Rising* is the first book they've read that makes them feel good about themselves, and that reflects their feelings and their lives. One teacher even told me that he thought *Annie* had been instrumental in keeping a young woman from suicide."

Regardless of the positive effects following the publication of Garden's books, some people believe there is no room in young adult literature for works dealing with controversial material. "I think anti-gay censors are louder now than they were back in 1982 when *Annie* was published," says Garden. "But we—gays and lesbians—are more visible now and more open politically than we were back then. I also think publishers are more willing than before to publish gay and lesbian YAs. My publisher, Farrar, Straus & Giroux, has always been supportive and never shied away from controversy."

And controversy is exactly what Garden faced in 1993 when *Annie* was banned in school libraries in Kansas and burned in front of school district offices in Kansas City, Missouri—11 years after its initial printing. "I felt numb," describes Garden. "I kept thinking, 'Only Nazis burn books.' I'd been told the book had been doused with gasoline, dropped into a metal bucket, and set on fire, and I kept picturing that in my mind.

The book had just been reprinted with a new cover—the best it had ever had—and I could see that cover curling in the heat, blackening, and probably smelling horrible. Gradually, with that image, the burning became more real to me."

A victory transpired when Judge G.T. Van Bebber ruled the banning unconstitutional. "I don't really think of *Annie* as 'my' case," says Garden. "The important issue was the First Amendment, not the book itself or even the fact that the book is about lesbian characters. Yes, it was wonderful that a gay book was vindicated, but the First Amendment victory transcends that, especially in this era of increasing attempts to erode freedom of speech. And I'd also like to stress that prime credit for the victory goes to the courageous librarians in Olathe, Kansas who supported the book when it was ordered off the shelves, the equally courageous plaintiffs—high school and junior high kids and their parents— and the friendly, hardworking team of lawyers from the firm of Shook, Hardy and Bacon who took on the case *pro bono*. All of those extraordinarily dedicated people were the real heroes, and it's they who saved *Annie* and selflessly defended the First Amendment." And she received immeasurable support from her partner, Sandy Scott; her publisher, Farrar, Straus & Giroux; and the American Library Association.

Having such loyal fans is due in part to Garden's keen ability to target the precise details young adults can relate to in their own lives. "Unlike some other children's writers, I consciously write for kids as well as, of course, for myself," she says. And learning the needs of different audiences is one way Garden tests her own writing skills. "Lately I've found myself thinking of stories that would work better for younger kids. It's a challenge for me to write for younger kids—and a huge one to write for much younger kids—but I like challenges. I also like to write more than one kind of thing; I don't enjoy the literary equivalent of being typecast."

An examination of Garden's many titles proves that she refuses to fit any single mold. Her 20-plus novels range from the Monster Hunters series to *Dove and Sword* (Farrar, Straus & Giroux), a historical novel exploring the life of Joan of Arc. "I've written lots of books, some mysteries, some fantasies, one historical novel and several realistic contemporary novels that don't touch on homosexuality. I haven't written about 'witchy' creatures for a while, and several times I've vowed to stop, for serious fiction is my real love. But one can't be serious all the time, and those books are fun to write! They also tend to sell better than serious fiction, and like most people, I need to worry about money."

Learning to cross genres also meant understanding the ever-changing publishing industry. "The most important thing I've had to figure out along the way is that success is fickle," says Garden. "One has never really 'made it' in any permanent sense. One book may be a critical and/or commercial success, but the next book may flop. Things change in publishing, too; what publishers bought eagerly ten years ago isn't necessarily what they want to buy now or can buy in this very bottom-line-conscious age."

Nevertheless, Garden has sound advice for writers who want to get their controversial manuscripts published. "The best thing to do is study publishers' lists and see which ones have done controversial novels in the past. You can also find that out by reading reviews and articles in magazines like *The Horn Book*, *School Library Journal*, *Voya*, *Booklist*, *The Bulletin of the Center for Children's Books* and *Publishers Weekly*."

When it comes to the craft of writing controversial novels, Garden shares a significant lesson she had to master in her own writing. "In many of my more serious books, I've had to be careful not to stand on my soapbox and preach; those books usually deal with issues about which I feel passionately. I think the greatest dangers when writing about

INSIDER REPORT, *Garden*

Dove & Sword (Farrar, Straus & Giroux) is a novel centered on the life of Joan of Arc. Nancy Garden tells Joan's story from the perspective of her fictional friend Gabrielle. Garden spent a great deal of time doing library research for the novel, and even traveled to France to trace Joan's path, visiting churches, libraries and museums there. "Doing research for *Dove & Sword* was so exciting it was almost hard for me to stop and write the book!" says Garden.

Illustration © 1995 Alexa Rutherford. Reprinted with permission.

controversial subjects are preaching, being didactic, and manipulating characters and plot in order to serve one's purpose. In any novel, the important thing is to tell a story about real-seeming people.

"Another important thing," continues Garden, "is to write from your heart. Not all writers agree, but I feel it's more important to do that and to worry later about selling your book than it is to study the market and write what you think publishers want. Don't expect instant success, and don't be resistant to honest constructive criticism. If you're just beginning to publish, keep in mind that most editors have the same goal you do—to produce the best possible book. A good editor can be a tremendous help to any willing writer."

—Donya Dickerson

21 picture books/year; 6 middle reader titles/year; and 15 young adult titles/year. 10% of books by first-time authors; 20% of books from agented writers.

Fiction: All levels: all categories. "Original and well-written material for all ages." Published *Belle Prater's Boy*, by Ruth White (ages 10 up).

Nonfiction: All levels: all categories. "We publish only literary nonfiction."

How to Contact/Writers: Fiction/Nonfiction: Query with outline/synopsis and sample chapters. Do not fax submissions or queries. Reports on queries in 6-8 weeks; mss in 1-3 months. Publishes a book 18 months after acceptance. Will consider simultaneous submissions.

Illustration: Works with 30-60 illustrators/year. Reviews ms/illustration packages from artists. Submit ms with 1 example of final art, remainder roughs. Illustrations only: Query with tearsheets. Reports back in 1-2 months. Samples returned with SASE; samples sometimes filed.

Terms: "We offer an advance against royalties for both authors and illustrators." Sends galleys to authors; dummies to illustrators. Original artwork returned at job's completion. Book catalog available for 9×12 SAE and 96¢ postage; ms guidelines for 1 first-class stamp.
Tips: "Study our catalog before submitting. We will see illustrator's portfolios by appointment. Don't ask for criticism and/or advice—it's just not possible. Never send originals. Always enclose SASE."

N THE FEMINIST PRESS, Wingate Hall/City College, Convent Ave. at 138th St., New York NY 10031. (212)650-8890. Fax: (212)650-8869. Website: http://www.web.gsuc.cuny.edu/feministpress. Estab. 1970. Acquisitions Editor: Denise Maynard. Publishes 1 picture book/year; 4 middle readers/year; 1 young adult title/year. "We are a nonprofit, tax-exempt, education publishing organization interested in changing the curriculum, the classroom and consciousness."
Fiction: Picture books, middle readers, young adult: multicultural. Average word length: 20,000-30,000. Recently published *Families*, by Meredith Tax, illustrated by Maryln Hafner (ages 4-8); *Carly*, by Annegert Fuchshuber (ages 5 and up); and *The Lilith Summer*, by Hadley Irwin (ages 10 and up).
Nonfiction: Picture books: multicultural and social issues. Middle readers and young adults: biography, multicultural and social issues. Average word length: middle readers—20,000; young adult—30,000. Recently published *Aung San Su Kyi: Standing Up for Democracy in Burma*, by Bettina Ling (ages 10 and up); *Rigoberta Menchui: Defending Human Rights in Guatemala*, by Michael Silverstone (ages 10 and up); and *Mairead Corrigan and Betty Williams: Making Peace in Northern Ireland*, by Sarah Busher and Bettina Ling (ages 10 and up).
How to Contact/Writers: Fiction: query. Nonfiction: submit complete ms. Reports on queries in 1 months; mss in 3 months. Publishes a book 18 months after acceptance. Will consider simultaneous submissions and previously published work.
Illustration: Reviews ms/illustration packages from artists. Send ms with dummy. Contact: Denise Maynard, assistant editor. Illustration only: query with samples. Contact: Denise Mayanrd, assistant editor. Reports back only if interested. Samples returned with SASE.
Photography: Buys stock and assigns work. Contact: Dayna Navaro, production/design manager. Model/property releases required. Uses color and b&w prints. Submit published samples.
Terms: Pays authors royalty of 10% based on wholesale price. Offers advances (average amount $250). Pays illustrators and photographers by the project. Originals returned to artist at job's completion. Book catalog available for $8\frac{1}{2} \times 11$ SAE and 4 first-class stamps. All imprints included in single catalog. Catalog available on website. Writer's guidelines available for SASE.

N FIESTA CITY PUBLISHERS, Box 5861, Santa Barbara CA 93150-5861. (805)733-1984. E-mail: fcooke3924@aol.com. Book publisher. **Manuscript Acquisitions:** Frank E. Cooke. **Art Acquisitions:** Ann Cooke, president. Publishes 1 middle reader/year; 1 young adult/year. 25% of books by first-time authors. Publishes books about cooking and music or a combination of the two.
Fiction: Young adults: contemporary, humor, musical plays.
Nonfiction: Young adult: cooking, how-to, music/dance, reference, self-help. Average word length: 30,000. Does not want to see "cookbooks about healthy diets or books on rap music." Published *Kids Can Write Songs, Too!* (revised second printing), by Eddie Franck; *Bent-Twig*, by Frank E. Cooke, with some musical arrangements by Johnny Harris (a 3-act musical for young adolescents).
How to Contact/Writers: Query. Reports on queries in 2 weeks; on mss in 1 month. Publishes a book 1 year after acceptance. Will consider simultaneous submissions.
Illustration: Works with 1 illustrator/year. Will review ms/illustrations packages (query first). Illustrations only: Send résumé. Samples returned with SASE; samples filed.
Terms: Pays authors 5-10% royalty based on wholesale price.
Tips: "Write clearly and simply. Do not write 'down' to young adults (or children). Looking for self-help books on current subjects, original and unusual cookbooks, and books about music, or a combination of cooking and music." Always include SASE.

N FIREFLY BOOKS LTD., 3680 Victoria Park Ave., Willowdale, Ontario M2H 3K1 Canada. (416)499-8412. Fax: (416)499-8313. Book publisher and distributor.
  ● Firefly Books Ltd. does not accept unsolicited mss.

☑ FIRST STORY PRESS, Imprint of Rose Book Group, 1800 Business Park Dr., Suite 205, Clarksville TN 37040. (931)572-0806. Fax: (931)552-3200. Publisher/Editor in Chief: Judith Pierson. Publishes 4 books/year. 50% of books by first-time authors. Publishes books on multicultural and grandparent themes.
Fiction: Picture books, young readers: animal, contemporary, folktales, humor, multicultural. Average word length: picture books—700-1,500; young readers—1,500. Recently published *Together on the Mountain*, by Bredda M. Moore (picture book).

How to Contact/Writers: Fiction: Submit complete ms. Reports on queries/mss in 3 months. Publishes a book 18-36 months after acceptance. Will consider simultaneous submissions.
Illustration: Works with 4-6 illustrators/year. Reviews ms/illustration packages from artists. Send ms with dummy. Contact: Editor. Illustrations only: Send résumé, promo sheet and tearsheets to be kept on file. Contact: Editor. Reports in 3 months. Samples returned with SASE; samples filed.
Terms: Pays authors royalty of 4-5% based on retail price or work purchased outright. Offers advances. Pays illustrators royalty of 4-5% based on retail price. Originals returned to artist. Ms guidelines available for SASE.
Tips: "SASE is always required. Do not send original artwork. Guidelines available—send SASE. Take a look at our books."

FITZHENRY & WHITESIDE LTD., 195 Allstate Pkwy., Markham, Ontario L3R 4T8 Canada. (905)477-9700. Fax: (905)477-9179. Book publisher. President: Sharon Fitzhenry. **Children's Publisher:** Gail Winskill. Publishes 6 picture books/year; 8 young readers/year; 5 middle readers/year; 7 young adult titles/year. 10% of books by first-time authors. Publishes fiction and nonfiction—social studies, visual arts, biography, environment. Prefers Canadian subject or perspective.
Fiction: Picture books: contemporary, folktales, history, multicultural, nature/environment and sports. Young readers: contemporary, health, history, multicultural, nature/environment and sports. Middle readers: adventure, contemporary, history, humor, multicultural, nature/environment, mystery and sports. Young adults: adventure, contemporary, history, multicultural, nature/environment, sports and suspense/mystery. Average word length: young readers—less than 1,500; middle readers—2,000-5,000; young adults—10,000-20,000.
Nonfiction: Picture books: arts/crafts, biography, history, multicultural, nature/environment, reference and sports. Young readers: arts/crafts, biography, geography, history, hobbies, multicultural, nature/environment, reference, religion and sports. Middle readers: arts/crafts, biography, careers, geography, history, hobbies, multicultural, nature/environment, reference, social issues and sports. Young adults: arts/crafts, biography, careers, geography, health, hi-lo, history, multicultural, music/dance, nature/environment, reference, social issues and sports. Average word length: young readers—500-1,000; middle readers—2,000-5,000; young adults—10,000-20,000. Recently published *Sea Otter Inlet*, by Celia Godkin; *Surfers of Snow*, by Kim Askew; and *Just Imagine*, by Deanne Lee Bingham.
How to Contact/Writers: Fiction: Submit outline/synopsis and 1 sample chapter. Nonfiction: Submit outline/synopsis. Reports in 4 months. Publishes a book 12-18 months after acceptance. Will consider simultaneous submissions.
Illustration: Works with 15 illustrators/year. Reviews ms/illustration packages from artist. Submit outline and sample illustration (copy). Illustrations only: Query with samples and promo sheet. Reports in 3 months. Samples returned with SASE; samples filed if no SASE.
Photography: Buys photos from freelancers. Buys stock and assigns work. Captions required. Uses b&w 8×10 prints; 35mm and 4×5 transparencies. Submit stock photo list and promo piece.
Terms: Pays authors royalty of 10%. Offers "respectable" advances. For picture books, 5% to author, 5% to illustrator. Pays illustrators by the project and royalty. Pays photographers per photo. Sends galleys to authors; dummies to illustrators.
Tips: "We respond to quality."

FORWARD MOVEMENT PUBLICATIONS, 412 Sycamore St., Cincinnati OH 45202. (513)721-6659. Fax: (513)721-0729. E-mail: forwardmovement@msn.com. Website: http://www.forwardmovement. org.
Fiction: Middle readers and young adults: religion and religious problem novels, fantasy and science fiction.
Nonfiction: Religion.
How to Contact/Writers: Fiction/Nonfiction: Query. Reports in 1 month.
Illustration: Query with samples. Samples returned with SASE.
Terms: Pays authors honorarium. Pays illustrators by the project.
Tips: "Forward Movement is now exploring publishing books for children and does not know its niche. We are an agency of the Episcopal Church and most of our market is to mainstream Protestants."

FRANKLIN WATTS, Sherman Turnpike, Danbury CT 06816. (203)797-3500. Subsidiary of Grolier Inc. Book publisher.
• See listing for Grolier Publishing (Children's Press and Franklin Watts).

FREE SPIRIT PUBLISHING, 400 First Ave. N., Suite 616, Dept. CWI, Minneapolis MN 55401-1730. (612)338-2068. Fax: (612)337-5050. E-mail: help4kids@freespirit.com. Website: http://www.freespi

rit.com. Book publisher. **Acquisitions:** Caryn Pernu. Publishes 15-20 titles/year for children and teens, teachers and parents. "We believe passionately in empowering kids to learn to think for themselves and make their own good choices."

● Free Spirit no longer accepts fiction or picture book submissions.

Nonfiction: "Free Spirit Publishing specializes in SELF-HELP FOR KIDS®, with an emphasis on self-esteem and self awareness, stress management, school success, creativity, friends and family, social action, and special needs (i.e., gifted and talented, children with learning differences). We prefer books written in a natural, friendly style, with little education/psychology jargon. Need books in our areas of emphasis, and prefer titles written by specialists such as teachers, counselors, and other professionals who work with youth." Recently published *What Do You Stand For: A Kid's Guide to Building Character*, by Barbara A. Lewis; *When Nothing Matters Anymore: A Survival Guide for Depressed Teens*, by Bev Cobain, RN; and *The Reading Tutor's Handbook: A Commonsense Guide to Helping Students Read and Write*, by Jeanne Shay Schumm, Ph.D. and Gerald E. Schumm Jr., D.Min.

How to Contact/Writers: Send query letter, or outline with sample chapters. Reports on queries/mss in 2 months. "If you'd like materials returned, enclose a SASE with sufficient postage." Write or call for catalog and submission guidelines before sending submission. Accepts queries only by e-mail. Submission guidelines available online.

Illustration: Submit samples to acquisitions editor for consideration. If appropriate, samples will be kept on file and artist will be contacted if a suitable project comes up. Enclose SASE if you'd like materials returned.

Photography: Submit samples to acquisitions editor for consideration. If appropriate, samples will be kept on file and photographer will be contacted if a suitable project comes up. Enclose SASE if you'd like materials returned.

Terms: Pays authors in royalties of 7-12% based on wholesale price. Offers advance. Pays illustrators by the project. Pays photographers by the project or per photo.

Tips: "Prefer books that help kids help themselves, or that help adults help kids help themselves; that complement our list without duplicating current titles; and that are written in a direct, straightforward manner."

FREESTONE, Peachtree Publishers, 494 Armour Circle NE, Atlanta GA 30324. (404)876-8761. Estab. 1997. Publishes 3-4 young adult titles/year. "We look for very good stories that are well-written, and written from the author's experience and heart with a clear application to today's young adults. We feel teens need to read about issues that are relevant to them, rather than reading adult books."

● Freestone is an imprint of Peachtree Publishers. See the listing for Peachtree for submission information.

FRONT STREET BOOKS, 20 Battery Park Ave., #403, Ashville NC 28801. (704)681-0811. Fax: (828)236-3098. E-mail: roxburgh@frontstreetbooks.com. Website: http://www.frontstreetbooks.com. Book publisher. Estab. 1995. **Acquisitions:** Stephen Roxburgh, publisher. Publishes 10-15 titles/year. "We are a small independent publisher and have chosen to be out of the corporate loop in the belief that as long as our books are of the highest quality, they will find an audience. We believe that each of the books on our list represents the best of its kind."

● Front Street accepts submissions via e-mail. See their website for details and instructions, as well submission guidelines and their complete catalog. Front Street focuses on fiction, but will publish poetry, anthologies, nonfiction and high-end picture books. They are not currently accepting unsolicited picture book mss.

Fiction: Recently published: *Piggy's Birthday Dream*, by Anke de Vries, illustrated by Jung-Hee Spetter (picture book about a shy pig's first surprise birthday party for ages 2-5); *Apple Island, or The Truth About Teachers*, by Douglas Evans, illustrated by Larry di Fiori (a comic fable about the origins of teachers for ages 8-12); and *Don't Read This! And Other Tales of the Unnatural* (a collection of spooky stories from authors around the world published in a dozen languages for ages 10-14).

How to Contact/Writers: Fiction: Submit cover letter and complete ms if under 30 pages; submit cover letter, one or two sample chapters and plot summary if over 30 pages. Nonfiction: Submit detailed proposal and sample chapters. Poetry: Submit no more than 25 poems. Include SASE with submissions if you want them returned. "It is our policy to consider submissions in the order in which they are received. This is a time-consuming practice and we ask you to be patient in awaiting our response."

Illustration "If you are the artist or are working with an artist, we will ba happy to consider your project." Submit ms, dummy and a sample piece of art "rendered in the manner and style representative of the final artwork."

Terms: Pays royalites.

N **FRONT STREET/CRICKET BOOKS**, Imprint of Carus Publishing Company, 332 S. Michigan, Suite 1100, Chicago IL 60604. Imprint estab. 1999; company estab. 1973. **Manuscript Acquisitions:** Laura Tillotson. **Art Acquisitions:** John Grandits. Publishes 3 young readers/year; 3 middle readers/year. 33% of books by first time authors. "We have published high-quality fiction for children in our magazines for 25 years and will apply that expertise in our new book imprint."
Fiction: Young readers, middle readers: adventure, animal, contemporary, fantasy, humor, sports, suspense/ mystery. Recently published *Casebook of a Private (Cat's) Eye*, by Mary Stolz, illustrated by Pam Levy (middle grade).
How to Contact/Writers: Fiction: submit complete ms. Reports on queries in 6-8 weeks; mss in 10-12 weeks. Publishes a book 18 months after acceptance. Will consider simultaneous submissions.
Illustration: Works with 3 illustrators/year. Illustration only: query with samples. Contact: John Grandits, art director. Reports back only if interested. Samples returned with SASE; samples filed.
Terms: Authors paid royalty of 7% based on retail price. Offers advances. Illustrators paid royalty of 3% based on retail price. Sends galleys to authors. Originals returned to artist at job's completion. Writer's and artist's guidelines available for SASE.
Tips: "At this time we are only considering chapter book and middle-grade submissions. No nonfiction or picture books. Study *Cricket* and *Spider* magazines to learn more of what we're looking for."

N **FULCRUM KIDS**, Imprint of Fulcrum Publishing, 350 Indiana St., Suite 350, Golden CO 80401-5093. (303)277-1623. Fax: (303)279-7111. E-mail: fulcrum@fulcrum-resources.com. Website: http://www. fulcrum-resources.com. Estab. 1984. Specializes in nonfiction and educational material. **Manuscript Acquisitions:** Suzanne I. Barchers, editorial director. Publishes 4 middle readers/year. 25% of books by first-time authors.
Nonfiction: Middle readers: activity books, multicultural, nature/environment. Recently published *Big Stuff in the Ocean*, by John Christopher Fine (nature ages 8-12); *Why the Leopard Has Spots: Dan Stories from Liberia*, written by Won-Ldy Paye and Met Lipper, illustrated by Ashley Bryan (multicultural, ages 8-12 yrs.); and *Exploring the Oceans*, by Anthony Fredericks (nature/activity, ages 8 and up).
How to Contact/Writers: Submit complete ms or submit outline/synopsis and 2 sample chapters. Reports on queries in 2-3 weeks; mss in 1-2 months. Publishes a book 12-18 months after acceptance. Will consider simultaneous submissions.
Illustration: Works with 4 illustrators/year. Reviews ms/illustration packages from artists. Send ms with dummy or submit ms with 3 pieces of final art. Send résumé, promotional literature and tearsheets. Contact: Suzanne Barchers, acquisitions editor. Reports back only if interested. Samples not returned; samples filed.
Photography: Works on assignment only.
Terms: Pays authors royalty based on wholesale price. Offers advances (Average amount: $1,500). Pays illustrators by the project (range: $300-2,000) or royalty of 2-5% based on wholesale price. Sends galleys to authors; dummies to illustrators. Originals returned to artist at job's completion. Book catalog available for 9 × 12 SAE and 3 first-class stamps ms guidelines available for SASE. Catalog available on website.
Tips: "Research our line first. We are emphasizing science and nature nonfiction. We look for books that appeal to the school market and trade. Be sure to include SASE."

GIBBS SMITH, PUBLISHER, P.O. Box 667, Layton UT 84041. (801)544-9800. Fax: (801)544-5582. Imprint: Gibbs Smith Junior. Book publisher. Editorial Director: Madge Baird. **Acquisitions:** Suzanne Taylor, children's book editor. Publishes 6-8 books/year. 10% of books by first-time authors. 50% of books from agented authors.
Fiction: Picture books: adventure, contemporary, humor, multicultural, nature/environment, suspense/mystery, western. Average word length: picture books—1,000. Recently published *Why the Banana Split*, by Rick Walton, illustrated by Jimmy Holder (ages 4-8); and *The Magic Boots*, by Scott Emerson, illustrated by Howard Post (ages 4-8).
Nonfiction: Middle readers: activity, arts/crafts, cooking, how-to, nature/environment, science. Average word length: up to 10,000. Recently published *Dinner From Dirt*, by Emily Scott and Catherine Duffy, illustrated by Denise Kirby (ages 7-12); and *Sleeping in a Sack: Camping Activities for Kids*, by Linda White, illustrated by Fran Lee (ages 7-12).

"PICTURE BOOKS" are for preschoolers to 8-year-olds; "Young readers" are for 5- to 8-year-olds; "Middle readers" are for 9- to 11-year-olds; and "Young adults" are for ages 12 and up.

KEEPERS OF THE EARTH

Native American Stories and Environmental Activities for Children

Michael J. Caduto and Joseph Bruchac

Foreword by N. Scott Momaday
Illustrations by John Kahionhes Fadden and Carol Wood

The bold colors and unique style of New Mexico artist Sam English's cover illustration for *Keepers of the Earth* gets lots of attention from parents, teachers and children. This educational workbook, written by Michael J. Caduto and Joseph Bruchac, features Native American stories and environmental activities for children. Suzanne I. Barchers, editorial director for Fulcrum Kids, likes English's "fresh, bright use of colors" and has worked with him on the covers of several Native American titles and calendars.

How to Contact/Writers: Fiction/Nonfiction: Submit several chapters or complete ms. Reports on queries and mss in 8-10 weeks. Publishes a book 1-2 years after acceptance. Will consider simultaneous submissions. Ms returned with SASE.

Illustration: Works with 6-8 illustrators/year. Reviews ms/illustration packages from artists. Query. Submit ms with 3-5 pieces of final art. Illustrations only: Query with samples; provide résumé, promo sheet, slides (duplicate slides, not originals). Reports back only if interested. Samples returned with SASE; samples filed.

Terms: Pays authors royalty of 4-7½% based on wholesale price or work purchased outright ($500 minimum). Offers advances (average amount: $2,000). Pays illustrators by the project or royalty of 4-5% based on wholesale price. Sends galleys to authors; color proofs to illustrators. Original artwork returned at job's completion. Book catalog available for 9 × 12 SAE and postage. Ms guidelines available.

Tips: "We target ages 5-11."

☑ **DAVID R. GODINE, PUBLISHER**, 9 Hamilton Place, Boston MA 02108. (617)451-9600. Fax: (617)350-0250. Book publisher. Estab. 1970. **Acquisitions:** Mark Polizzotti, editorial director. Publishes 1 picture book/year; 1 young reader title/year; 1 middle reader title/year. 10% of books by first-time authors; 75% of books from agented writers. "We publish books that matter for people who care."

● This publisher is no longer considering unsolicited mss of any type.

Fiction: Picture books: adventure, animal, contemporary, folktales, nature/environment. Young readers: adventure, animal, contemporary, folk or fairy tales, history, nature/environment, poetry. Middle readers: adventure, animal, contemporary, folk or fairy tales, history, mystery, nature/environment, poetry. Young adults/teens: adventure, animal, contemporary, history, mystery, nature/environment, poetry. Recently published *The Empty Creel*, by Geraldine Pope (Paterson Prize winning book with vinyl-cut illustrations).

Nonfiction: Picture books: alphabet, animal, nature/environment. Young readers: activity books, animal, history, music/dance, nature/environment. Middle readers: activity books, animal, biography, history, music/dance, nature/environment. Young adults: biography, history, music/dance, nature/environment.

How to Contact/Writers: Query. Reports on queries in 2 weeks. Reports on solicited ms in 2 weeks (if not agented) or 2 months (if agented). Publishes a book 2 years after acceptance.

Illustration: Only interested in agented material. Works with 4-6 illustrators/year. Reviews ms/illustration packages from artists. "Submit roughs and one piece of finished art plus either sample chapters for very long works or whole ms for short works." Illustrations only: "After query, submit slides, with one full-size blow-up of art." Reports on art samples in 2 weeks. Original artwork returned at job's completion. "Almost all of the children's books we accept for publication come to us with the author and illustrator already paired up. Therefore, we rarely use freelance illustrators." Samples returned with SASE; samples filed (if interested).

Terms: Pays authors in royalties based on retail price. Number of illustrations used determines final payment for illustrators. Pay for separate authors and illustrators "differs with each collaboration." Illustrators paid by the project. Sends galleys to authors; dummies to illustrators. Originals returned at job's completion. Book catalog available for SASE.

Tips: "Always enclose a SASE. Keep in mind that we do not accept unsolicited manuscripts and that we rarely use freelance illustrators."

GOLDEN BOOKS, 850 Third Ave., New York NY 10022. (212)583-6700. Fax: (212)371-1091. Imprint of Golden Books Family Entertainment Inc.

● Golden Books does not accept unsolicited submissions.

GREENE BARK PRESS, P.O. Box 1108, Bridgeport CT 06601-1108. (203)372-4861. Fax: (203)371-5856. E-mail: greenebark@aol.com. Website: http://www.bookworld.com/greenebark. Book publisher. **Acquisitions:** Michele Hofbauer; associate publisher. Thomas J. Greene, publisher. Publishes 4-6 picture books/year. 40% of books by first-time authors. "We publish quality hardcover picture books for children."

Fiction: Picture books, young readers: adventure, fantasy. Average word length: picture books—650; young readers—1,400. Recently published *Bug & Slug in the Rug*, by Steve Allen, illustrated by Michele Hofbauer (ages 5-9, young reader); *Cookie for the President*, by Anita Bott, illustrated by Pat Collins (ages 5-9, young reader); and *Molly Meets Mona & Friends*, by Gladys Walker, illustrated by Denise Minnerly Bennett (ages 5-9, young reader).

How to Contact/Writers: Reports on queries in 1 month; ms in 2-4 months. Publishes a book 18 months after acceptance. Will consider simultaneous submissions. Prefer to review complete mss with illustrations.

Illustrations: Works with 2-3 illustrators/year. Uses color artwork only. Reviews ms/illustration packages from artists. Submit ms with 3 pieces of final art (copies only). Illustrations only: Query with samples. Reports in 2 months only if interested. Samples returned with SASE; samples filed.

Agent and author—partners in publishing

Ann Tobias started out as an editor at Harper and Row under the legendary Ursula Nordstrom. She later freelance edited for Harper, Morrow, Crown and Dial; spent some years working full-time for Greenwillow Books and a year for Scholastic; and ultimately moved to Washington, D.C., where she founded A Literary Agency for Children's Books, although she continues to edit special projects for Dial and Hyperion. Tobias candidly reveals her agenting philosophy, discusses editors moving, and comments on the climate of children's publishing today.

How do you define your job as an agent?
My job is to help my clients grow a career. I am not a one-book agent. If a brilliant manuscript comes my way, I want to see others the author has written. I want to talk to the author and see where she is going and how she feels about children's books. It's a slow growth in children's books. First it takes talent, then it takes patience and discipline. I don't tell people to give up their day jobs in the beginning.

How savvy do you expect authors to be about publishing?
If they want to work with me, I need them to do their homework. I will guide them editorially, but I don't want to be in a position to educate people about the children's book scene, nor do I want people to say, "Here's my manuscript, take it and do something with it." For most of my clients, next to their families, this is the most important thing in their lives. They have to take some responsibility for it. I can tell them where their book fits in. I can say this is the kind of publisher that would be interested. I can do all that, but I need their participation. I consider my clients and me to have a partnership.

What impresses you about a piece of writing?
Themes impress me. Everything else—plot, characterization, setting, pacing, language—emanates from the theme. So, one of my first questions when I get a manuscript is, "What does this author want kids to think about?"

What do you want from the writing itself?
I'm looking for writing that is honest, where the author has paid attention to the language and the rhythm. I'm not talking about poetry, but good prose that has internal rhythm. I'm looking for writing that moves me, that makes me think, that shows me something funny even. It doesn't have to be serious writing. If the theme is strong and the writing makes it all work, then that is what I'm looking for.

INSIDER REPORT, *Tobias*

Are first novels a hard sell?

A first novel is easy if it's great. And it has to be great or I'm not going to take it. I don't send around my manuscripts a lot. They get taken the first few times out. I will tell you what is a hard sell, and that's when a writer calls me and says, "I would like to send you a picture book." I never know what to say because a picture book text these days probably runs between one and three pages, double-spaced. And, I want to make a lifetime commitment to this author. I want this author to make a lifetime commitment to me. Even if I love the picture book, even if it is brilliant, how do I know it wasn't a mistake, a monkey at the typewriter kind of thing? So I don't know what to do with people who have written one picture book, except to tell them to write several more.

Do you send out multiple submissions?

I believe very strongly in submitting exclusively to one editor at a time. I will send a manuscript out to an editor and give them two months. At that point, I will call and say, "Have you any sense of this? If you don't, when will you?" But I can do that. I don't submit to people I don't know. Most of the people I submit to, I worked with for years. I know them well, I know their children. It's not just business and I'm never going to see them again. I want these people to trust my client and to trust me.

Do you submit to an editor, or to a publishing house?

I definitely submit to editors, but I look at the house. I pay attention to whether they are asking someone to buy them, any little gossip I can pick up.

How would the sale of a publishing house affect you as an agent?

Let's take one that has already happened. When Simon & Schuster acquired Macmillan, the number of imprints available to me as an agent was sharply reduced. The editors I liked and submitted to were out of work. I can tell you that when I sat down to become an agent, I made a list of the publishers I respected and would like to see clients published at. I felt there were three dozen very good publishers that I would be proud to have my clients published by. The last time I sat down and counted, the list was half.

So when an editor moves to a new publishing house, you want the manuscript to go with her?

If the manuscript were contractually free, absolutely. Even if the editor didn't want to take it, I would like to see her take it. The editor is the one who sees what kind of book the manuscript is going to be. Until recently, editors were encouraged to be subjective. I have a theory. We were all paid so badly back in the old days, one of the reasons we became children's book editors was because we were given a fair amount of autonomy and allowed to use our heads. A residue of that lingers, I'm glad to say, even though editors are being downgraded in favor of marketers. So the person who contracted for the book, who made the offer, who had the vision for the book, is the person the book belongs with. Since a new editor will not have the same vision, writers can lose valuable time. My job is to know what my clients should do when the bottom drops out and an editor leaves.

How would you characterize today's children's book scene?

I'm depressed by it. Don't forget, I was active in the "golden years" of children's publishing, when we would have been fired for even thinking of publishing a Goosebumps.

INSIDER REPORT, *continued*

In those days, if some editor had published a series like that, the librarians would have organized a strike on Fifth Avenue. I think the children's book departments flourished because of the benign neglect on the part of publishers. We were called "the girls." We were put in the darkest offices at the end of the hall with no air conditioning. We were not valued, and we were allowed to go ahead and do whatever we wanted as long as we didn't lose money. And we didn't. We worked closely with librarians who worked closely with children. The books were child-oriented. Nowadays, librarians don't have the clout they once had. The chain booksellers have taken over. They don't work with children. They don't know the obscure midlist writers who are very good.

How do you maintain your insider's eye?
My worry is that as publishing changes so rapidly, my insider's eye is getting worn out. That's one of the reasons I do editing still, because it keeps me on top of what's going on in publishing companies. It's useful for my clients.
  —Anna Olswanger

Terms: Pays authors royalty of 10-15% based on wholesale price. Pays illustrators by the project (range: $1,500-3,000) or 5-7½% royalty based on wholesale price. No advances. Send galleys to authors; dummies to illustrators. Originals returned to artist at job's completion. Book catalog available for 8½×11 SAE. All imprints included in a single catalog. Ms and art guidelines available for SASE.
Tips: "As a guide for future publications do not look to our older backlist. Please no telephone, e-mail or fax queries."

[N] THE GREENWICH WORKSHOP PRESS, One Greenwich Place, P.O. Box 875, Shelton CT 06484-0875. (203)925-0131. Fax: (203)925-0262. E-mail: gwsbooks@ix.netcom.com. Website: http://www.greenwichworkshop.com. Estab. 1972. **Manuscript and Art Acquisitions:** Wendy Wentworth. Publishes 3 picture books/year; 1 young adult title/year. "As a fine art limited edition print publisher, our books are all visual with beautiful art. Our middle reader/young adult books are 'family classics,' illustrated lavishly."
Fiction: Picture books: adventure, animal, contemporary, fantasy, folktales, multicultural, nature/environment. Young adult: adventure, fantasy. Recently published *Across the River*, by Michael Price (ages 4-8); and *Forest Has Eyes*, by Elise Maclay, illustrated by Bev Doolittle (ages 4-8).
How to Contact/Writers: Fiction/nonfiction: query. Reports on queries immediately; mss in 4 months. Publishes a book 18-24 months after acceptance.
Illustration: Works with 3-6 illustrators/year. Uses color artwork only. Reviews ms/illustration packages from artists. Submit ms with 3 pieces of final art. Contact: Wendy Wentworth, director. Illustration only: arrange personal portfolio review or send slides. Contact: Wendy Wentworth, director. Reports in 3 months. Samples returned with SASE; samples kept on file if possible.
Terms: Pays authors royalty of 1-4% based on retail price or purchases work outright for $2,000-10,000. Offers advances. Pays illustrators by the project or royalty of 4-5% based on retail price. Sends galleys to authors; dummies to illustrators. Originals returned to artist at job's completion. Book catalog available for 9×12 SAE and 4 first-class stamps. All imprints included in single catalog.
Tips: "We are an illustrated book publisher for children, family and adults, both fiction and nonfiction. Study our catalog to judge appropriateness of your submission."

GREENWILLOW BOOKS, 1350 Avenue of the Americas, New York NY 10019. (212)261-6500. Imprint of William Morrow & Co. Book publisher. Editor-in-Chief: Susan Hirschman. **Manuscript Acquisitions:** Submit to Editorial Department. **Art Acquisitions:** Ava Weiss, art director. Publishes 50 picture books/year; 5 middle readers books/year; and 5 young adult books/year. "Greenwillow Books publishes picture books, fiction for young readers of all ages, and nonfiction primarily for children under seven years of age. We hope you will read many children's books (especially those on our list), decide what you like or don't like about them, then write the story *you* want to tell (not what you think we want to read), and send it to us!"

Fiction: Will consider all levels of fiction; various categories.

Nonfiction: Will consider nonfiction for children under seven.

How to Contact/Writers: Submit complete ms. "If your work is illustrated, we ask to see a typed text, rough dummy, and a *copy* of a finished picture. Please do not send original artwork with your submission." Do not call. Reports on mss in 10-12 weeks. Publishes a book 18-24 months after acceptance. Will consider simultaneous submissions.

Illustration: Reviews ms/illustration packages from artists. Illustrations only: Query with samples, résumé.

Terms: Pays authors royalty. Offers advances. Pays illustrators royalty or by the project. Sends galleys to authors. Book catalog available for 9 × 12 SAE with $2.20 postage; ms guidelines available for SASE.

Tips: "You need not have a literary agent to submit to us. We accept—and encourage—simultaneous submissions to other publishers and ask only that you so inform us. Because we receive thousands of submissions, we do not keep a record of the manuscripts we receive and cannot check the status of your manuscript. We do try to respond within ten weeks' time."

☑ **GROLIER PUBLISHING, (Children's Press and Franklin Watts)**, 90 Sherman Turnpike, Danbury CT 06816. (203)797-3500. Book publisher. Vice President/Publisher: John Selfridge. **Manuscript Acquisitions:** Mark Friedman, executive editor. **Art Acquisitions:** Marie Greco, art director. Publishes more than 200 titles/year. 5% of books by first-time authors; very few titles from agented authors. Publishes informational (nonfiction) for K-12; picture books for young readers, grades 1-3.

Fiction: Publishes 1 picture book series, Rookie Readers, for grades 1-2. Does not accept unsolicited mss.

Nonfiction: Photo-illustrated books for all levels: animal, arts/crafts, biography, careers, concept, geography, health, history, hobbies, how-to, multicultural, nature/environment, science, social issues, special needs, sports. Average word length: young readers—2,000; middle readers—8,000; young adult—15,000.

How to Contact/Writers: Fiction: Does not accept fiction proposals. Nonfiction: Query; submit outline/synopsis, résumé and/or list of publications, and writing sample. SASE required for response. Reports in 2-3 months. Will consider simultaneous submissions. Contact: Mark Friedman, executive editor. No phone or e-mail queries; will not respond to phone inquiries about submitted material.

Illustration: Works with 15-20 illustrators/year. Uses color artwork and line drawings. Illustrations only: Query with samples or arrange personal portfolio review. Contact: Marie Greco, art director. Reports back only if interested. Samples returned with SASE. Samples filed. Do not send originals. No phone or e-mail inquiries; contact only by mail.

Photography: Purchases photos from freelancers. Contact: Caroline Anderson, Photo Manager. Buys stock and assigns work. Model/property releases and captions required. Uses color and b&w prints; 2¼ × 2¼, 35mm transparencies, images on CD-ROM. Photographers should send cover letter and stock photo list.

Terms: Pays authors royalty based on net or work purchased outright. Pays illustrators at competitive rates. Photographers paid per photo. Sends galleys to authors; dummies to illustrators.

GROSSET & DUNLAP, INC./PRICE STERN SLOAN. (212)951-8700. Imprint of The Putnam & Grosset Group.
 • Grosset & Dunlap/Price Stern Sloan does not accept unsolicited submissions.

◪ **GRYPHON HOUSE**, P.O. Box 207, Beltsville MD 20704-0207. (301)595-9500. Fax: (301)595-0051. E-mail: kathyc@ghbooks.com. Book publisher. **Acquisitions:** Kathy Charner, editor-in-chief.

Nonfiction: Parent and teacher resource books—activity books, textbooks. Recently published *500 Five Minute Games*, by Jackie Silberg; *Global Art*, by MaryAnn Kohl and Jean Potter; *Count on Math*, by Pam Schiller; and *The Complete Resource Book*, by Pam Schiller.

How to Contact/Writers: Query. Submit outline/synopsis and 2 sample chapters. Reports on queries/mss in 3 months. Publishes a book 18 months after acceptance. Will consider simultaneous submissions, electronic submissions via disk or modem.

Illustration: Works with 3-4 illustrators/year. Uses b&w artwork only. Reviews ms/illustration packages from artists. Submit query letter with table of contents, introduction and sample chapters. Illustrations only: Query with samples, promo sheet. Reports back in 2 months. Samples returned with SASE; samples filed.

Photography: Buys photos from freelancers. Buys stock and assigns work. Submit cover letter, published samples, stock photo list.

Terms: Pays authors royalty based on wholesale price. Offers advances. Pays illustrators by the project. Pay photographers by the project or per photo. Sends galleys to authors. Original artwork returned at job's completion. Book catalog and ms guidelines available for SASE.

Tips: "Send a SASE for our catalog and manuscript guidelines. Look at our books, then submit proposals that complement the books we already publish or supplement our existing books. We are looking for books of creative, participatory learning experiences that have a common conceptual theme to tie them together."

The books should be on subjects that parents or teachers want to do on a daily basis."

GULLIVER BOOKS, 15 E. 26th St., New York NY 10010. (212)592-1000. Imprint of Harcourt Brace & Co. **Acquisitions:** Elizabeth Van Doren, editorial director, Anne Dover, editor. Publishes 25 titles/year.
● Gulliver only accepts mss submitted by agents, previously published authors, or SCBWI members.
Fiction: Emphasis on picture books. Also publishes middle grade and young adult.
Nonfiction: Publishes nonfiction.
How to Contact/Writers: Fiction/Nonfiction: Query or send ms for picture book.

HACHAI PUBLISHING, 156 Chester Ave., Brooklyn NY 11218. (718)633-0100. Fax: (718)633-0103. E-mail: info@hachai.com. Website: http://www.hachai.com. Book publisher. **Manuscript Acquisitions:** Devorah Leah Rosenfeld, submissions editor. Publishes 3 picture books/year; 3 young readers/year; 1 middle reader/year. 75% of books published by first-time authors. "All books have spiritual/religious themes, specifically traditional Jewish content. We're seeking books about morals and values; the Jewish experience in current and Biblical times; and Jewish observance, Sabbath and holidays."
Fiction: Picture books and young readers: contemporary, history, religion. Middle readers: adventure, contemporary, problem novels, religion. Does not want to see animal stories, romance, problem novels depicting drug use or violence. Recently published *As Big As An Egg*, by Rachel Sandman, illustrated by Chana Zakashanskaya (ages 3-6, picture book); and *Red, Blue, and Yellow Yarn*, by Miriam Kosman, illustrated by Valeri Gorbachev (ages 3-6, picture book).
Nonfiction: Published *My Jewish ABC's*, by Draizy Zelcer, illustrated by Patti Nemeroff (ages 3-6, picture book).
How to Contact/Wrtiers: Fiction/Nonfiction: Submit complete ms.
Illustration: Works with 4 illustrators/year. Uses primary color artwork, some b&w illustration. Reviews ms/illustration packages from authors. Submit ms with 1 piece of final art. Contact: Devorah Leah Rosenfeld, submissions editor. Illustrations only: Query with samples; arrange personal portfolio review. Reports in 6 weeks. Samples returned with SASE.
Terms: Work purchased outright from authors for $1,000. Pays illustrators by the project (range: 2,000). Book catalog, ms/artist's guidelines available for SASE.
Tips: "Write a story that incorporates a moral . . . not a preachy morality tale. Originality is the key. We feel Hachai is going to appeal to a wider readership as parents become more interested in positive values for their children."

N HAMPTON ROADS PUBLISHING COMPANY, INC., 134 Burgess Lane, Charlottesville VA 22902. (804)296-2772. Fax: (804)296-5096. E-mail: hrpc@hrpub.com. Website: http://www.hrpub.com. Estab. 1989. **Manuscript Acquisitions:** Robert Friedman. **Art Acquisitions:** Jane Hagaman. Publishes 3 picture books/year. 60% of books by first-time authors. "Mission Statement: to work as a team to seek, create, refine and produce the best books we are capable of producing, which will impact, uplift and contribute to positive change in the world; to promote the physical, mental, emotional and financial well-being of all its staff and associates; to build the company into a powerful, respected and prosperous force in publishing in the region, the nation and the world in which we live."
Fiction: Picture books, young readers, middle readers, young adult titles: metaphysical and spiritual. Average word length: picture books—100-200; young readers—1,000-5,000; middle readers—500-4,000. Recently published *Star Babies*, by Mary Summer Rain (preschool-age 8); *Little Souls*, by Neale Donald Walsch (ages 7-12); *OBO*, by Robert Anderson (preschool-age 8).
Nonfiction: Picture books, young readers, middle readers, young adult titles: metaphysical and spiritual. Average word length: picture books—100-200; young readers—1,000-5,000; middle readers—500-4,000. Recently published *Mountain, Meadows and Moonbeams*, by Mary Summer Rain (ages 5-8).
How to Contact/Writers: Fiction/nonfiction: submit complete ms. Reports on queries in 1-2 months; mss in 3-4 months. Publishes a book 6-12 months after acceptance. Will consider simultaneous submissions.
Illustration: Works with 2-3 illustrators/year. Reviews ms/illustration packages from artists. Submit ms with 2-3 pieces of final art. Contact: Robert Friedman, president. Illustration only: query with samples. Contact: Jane Hagaman, art director. Reports in 2 months. Samples returned with SASE.
Terms: Pays authors royalty of 10-20% based on retail price. Offers advances (average amount: $1,000). Pays illustrators by the project (range: $250-1,000). Occasionally pays by royalty. Sends galleys to authors. Original returned to artist at job's completion. Book catalog available for SASE. Writer's guidelines available for SASE.
Tips: "Please familiarize yourself with our mission statement and/or the books we publish. Preferably send manuscripts that can by recycled rather than returned. If there is no SASE, they will be recycled."

A **HARCOURT BRACE & CO.**, 525 B St., Suite 1900, San Diego CA 92101-4495. (619)231-6616. Children's Books Division includes: Harcourt Brace Children's Books (Allyn Johnston, editorial director), Gulliver Books (Elizabeth Van Doren, editorial director), Browndeer Press (Linda Zuckerman, editorial director), Silver Whistle Books (Paula Wiseman, editorial director), Voyager Paperbacks, Odyssey Paperbacks, and Red Wagon Books. Book publisher. **Manuscript Acquisitions:** Manuscript Submissions. **Art Acquisitions:** Art Director. Publishes 50-75 picture books/year; 5-10 middle reader titles/year; 10 young adult titles/year. 20% of books by first-time authors; 50% of books from agented writers. "Harcourt Brace & Company owns some of the world's most prestigious publishing imprints—which distinguish quality products for the juvenile, educational and trade markets worldwide."
- The staff of Harcourt Brace's children's book department is no longer accepting unsolicited manuscripts. Only query letters from previously published authors and mss submitted by agents will be considered.

Fiction: All levels: Considers all categories. Average word length: picture books—"varies greatly"; middle readers—20,000-50,000; young adults—35,000-65,000. Recently published *Home Run*, by Robert Burleigh, illustrated by Mike Wimmer (ages 6-10, picture book/biography); *Cast Two Shadows*, by Ann Rinaldi (ages 12 and up; young adult historical fiction); *Tell Me Something Happy Before I Go to Sleep*, by Joyce Dunbar, illustrated by Debi Gliori (ages 4-8, picture book).
Nonfiction: All levels: animal, biography, concept, history, multicultural, music/dance, nature/environment, science, sports. Average word length: picture books—"varies greatly"; middle readers—20,000-50,000; young adults—35,000-65,000. Recently published *Lives of the Presidents*, by Kathleen Krull; illustrated by Kathryn Hewitt (ages 8-12, illustrated nonfiction).
How to Contact/Writers: Only interested in agented material. Fiction: Query or submit outline/synopsis. Nonfiction: Submit outline/synopsis. Reports on queries/mss in 6-8 weeks.
Illustration: Works with 150 illustrators/year. Reviews ms/illustration packages from artists. "For picture books ms—complete ms acceptable. Longer books—outline and 2-4 sample chapters." Send one sample of art; no original art with dummy. Illustrations only: Submit résumé, tearsheets, color photocopies, color stats all accepted. "Please DO NOT send original artwork or transparencies." Samples are not returned; samples filed. Reports on art samples only if interested.
Photography: Works on assignment only.
Terms: Pays authors and illustrators in royalty based on retail price. Pays photographers by the project. Sends galleys to authors; dummies to illustrators. Original artwork returned at job's completion. Book catalog available for 8×10 SAE and 4 first-class stamps; ms/artist's guidelines for business-size SASE. All imprints included in a single catalog.
Tips: "Become acquainted with Harcourt Brace's books in particular if you are interested in submitting proposals to us."

HARPERCOLLINS CHILDREN'S BOOKS, 10 E. 53rd St., New York NY 10022-5299. (212)207-7044. Fax: (212)207-7192. Website: http://www.harpercollins.com. Book publisher. Editor-in-Chief: Kate Morgan Jackson. **Art Acquisitions:** Harriett Barton, art director. Imprints: Laura Geringer Books, Michael diCapua Books, Joanna Cotler Books.
- HarperCollins is not accepting unsolicited mss not addressed to a specific editor.

Fiction: Picture books: adventure, animal, anthology, concept, contemporary, fantasy, folktales, hi-lo, history, multicultural, nature/environment, poetry, religion. Middle readers: adventure, hi-lo, history, poetry, suspense/mystery. Young adults/teens: fantasy, science fiction, suspense/mystery. All levels: multicultural. "Artists with diverse backgrounds and settings shown in their work."
Nonfiction: Picture books: animal, arts/crafts, biography, geography, multicultural, nature/environment. Middle readers: how-to.
Illustration: Works with 100 illustrators/year. Reports only if interested. Samples returned with SASE; samples filed only if interested.
How to Contact/Writers: Nonfiction: Query.
Terms: Ms and art guidelines available for SASE.

HARVEST HOUSE PUBLISHERS, 1075 Arrowsmith, Eugene OR 97402-9197. (541)343-0123. Fax: (541)342-6410. Book publisher. Manuscript Coordinator: Teresa Burke. Publishes 1-2 picture books/year and 2 young reader titles/year. 2-5% of books by first-time authors. Books follow a Christian theme.
- Harvest House no longer accepts unsolicited children's mss.

Illustration: Works with 2-3 illustrators/year. Reviews ms/illustration packages from artists. Submit copies (do not send originals) of art and any approximate rough sketches. Send résumé, tearsheets. Submit to color design coordinator. Reports on art samples in 6-8 weeks. Samples returned with SASE; samples filed.
Terms: Pays authors in royalties of 10-15%. Average advance payment: "negotiable." Pays illustrator:

"Sometimes by project." Sends galleys to authors; sometimes sends dummies to illustrators. SASE for book catalog.

HAYES SCHOOL PUBLISHING CO. INC., 321 Pennwood Ave., Wilkinsburg PA 15221. (412)371-2373. Fax: (412)371-6408. **Acquisitions:** Mr. Clair N. Hayes. Estab. 1940. Produces folders, workbooks, stickers, certificates. Wants to see supplementary teaching aids for grades K-12. Interested in all subject areas. Will consider simultaneous and electronic submissions.
How to Contact/Writers: Query with description or complete ms. Reports in 3-4 weeks. SASE for return of submissions.
Terms: Work purchased outright. Purchases all rights.

HEALTH PRESS, P.O. 1388, Santa Fe NM 87504. (505)982-9373 or (800)643-2665. Fax: (505)983-1733. E-mail: hlthprs@trail.com. Website: http://www.healthpress.com. Book publisher. **Acquisitions:** Contact Editor. Publishes 4 young readers/year; 4 middle readers/year. 100% of books by first-time authors.
Fiction: Young readers, middle readers: health, special needs. Average word length: young readers—1,000-1,500; middle readers—1,000-1,500. Recently published *Blueberry Eyes*, by Monica Driscoll Beatty, illustratrated by Peg Michel (ages 3-8); *My Sister Rose Has Diabetes*, by Monica Driscoll Beatty, illustrated by Kathy Parkinson (ages 8-12); *The Paper Chair*, by Clair Blake and Eliza Blanchard, illustrated by Kathy Parkinson (ages 3-8).
Nonfiction: Young readers, middle readers: health, special needs.
How to Contact/Writers: Submit complete ms. Reports in 1 month. Publishes a book 9 months after acceptance. Will consider simultaneous submissions.
Terms: Pays authors royalty. Sends galleys to authors. Book catalog available.

HENDRICK-LONG PUBLISHING COMPANY, P.O. Box 25123, Dallas TX 75225. Fax: (214)352-4768. E-mail: hendrick-long@worldnet.att.net. Book publisher. Estab. 1969. **Acquisitions:** Joann Long, vice president. Publishes 1 picture book/year; 4 young reader titles/year; 4 middle reader titles/year. 20% of books by first-time authors. Publishes fiction/nonfiction about Texas of interest to young readers through young adults/teens.
Fiction: Middle readers: history books on Texas and the Southwest. No fantasy or poetry. Recently published *Molasses Cookies*, by Janet Kaderli, illustrated by Patricia Arnold (K-5); and *Terror from the Sea*, by Martha Tannery Jones (grades 3-5).
Nonfiction: Middle, young adults: history books on Texas and the Southwest, biography, multicultural. Recently published *Lone Star Justice: A Biography of Justice Tom C. Clark* (grades 9-12).
How to Contact/Writers: Fiction/Nonfiction: Query with outline/synopsis and sample chapter. Reports on queries in 1-4 weeks; mss in 2 months. Publishes a book 18 months after acceptance. No simultaneous submissions. Include SASE.
Illustration: Works with 2-3 illustrators/year. Uses primarily b&w interior artwork; color covers only. Illustrations only: Query first. Submit résumé or promotional literature or photocopies or tearsheets—no original work sent unsolicited. Reports back only if interested.
Terms: Pays authors in royalty based on selling price. Advances vary. Pays illustrators by the project or royalty. Sends galleys to authors; dummies to illustrators. Ms guidelines for 1 first-class stamp and #10 SAE.
Tips "Material **must** pertain to Texas or the Southwest. Check all facts about historical firgures and events in both fiction and nonfiction. Be accurate."

HIGHSMITH PRESS, P.O. Box 800, Ft. Atkinson WI 53538-0800. (920)563-9571. (920)563-4801. E-mail: hpress@highsmith.com. Website: http://www.hpress.highsmith.com. Imprints: Highsmith Press, Alleyside Press. Book publisher. **Acquisitions:** Donald J. Sager, publisher. Highsmith Press publishes library reference and professional books. Alleyside Press publishes reading activity materials, storytelling aids, and library/study skills instructional resources for youth PreK-12 grade.
Nonfiction: All levels: reading activity books, library skills, reference, study skills. Multicultural needs include storytelling resources. Average length: 48-120 pages. Published *Research to Write*, by Maity Schrecengost (ages 8-11, study skills); *An Alphabet of Books, Literature Based Activities for Schools and Libraries*, by Robin Davis (ages 3-7, activity book); and *World Guide to Historical Fiction for Young Adults*, by Lee Gordon (ages 11-17, reference).
How to Contact/Writers: Query or submit complete ms or submit outline/synopsis. Reports on queries in 1 month; mss in 6-8 weeks. Publishes a book 6 months after acceptance. Will consider simultaneous submissions.
Illustration: Works with 6-12 illustrators/year. Reports in 1 month. Samples returned with SASE; samples filed.

Terms: Pays authors royalty of 10-12% based on wholesale price. Pays illustrators by the project; varies considerably. Offers advances. Sends galleys to authors. Book catalog available for 9 × 12 SAE and 2 first-class stamps; ms guidelines available for SASE.

Tips: "Review our catalog and ms guidelines to see what we publish. Our complete catalog and current guidelines can be found at our website on the Internet (address above), as well as a list of projects for which we are seeking authors. We are seeking ms which help librarians and teachers to stimulate reading and how to use the Internet for instructional purposes."

HINTERLAND PUBLISHERS, Box 198, Sandy Hook, Manitoba R0C 2W0 Canada. (204)389-3842. Fax: (204)339-3635. E-mail: hinterland@gatewest.net. Website: http://www.hinterland.mb.ca. Book publisher. **Manuscript/Art Acquisitions:** Norma Norton, managing director. Publishes 4 picture books/year. 100% of books by first-time authors.

Fiction: Picture books: adventure, contemporary, multicultural. For multicultural fiction, needs First Nation's contemporary (realistic) fiction. Does not want to see material on legends. Average word length: picture books—1,000-2,000. Recently published *The Moons of Goose Island*, written by Don K. Philpot, illustrated by Margaret Hessian (ages 6-12, contemporary realistic fiction).

How to Contact/Writers: Fiction: Query only.

Illustration: Query or send ms with dummy. Illustrations only: Query with samples; send résumé and portfolio to be kept on file. Reports in 6 weeks. Samples returned with SASE. Must have proper postage for Canada (International Coupon).

Terms: Pays authors royalty of 10-25% based on retail price. Pays illustrators royalty of 10-25% based on retail price. Sends galleys to authors; dummies to illustrators. Originals returned to artist at job's completion.

Tips: "Quality is a top consideration at Hinterland Publishers. Stories must be fresh, thoughtful and imaginative. Stylistically, a writer must demonstrate an excellent command on the English language. Stories told in a literary style will receive special attention."

N: HODDER CHILDREN'S BOOKS, Hodder Headline PLC, 338 Euston Rd., London NW1 3BH England. (0171)873-6000. Fax: (0171)873-6229. Book publisher. **Manuscript Acquisitions:** Margaret Conroy (nonfiction, audio), Kate Burns (picture books), Isabel Boissier (fiction). **Art Acquisitions:** Claire Bond. Publishes 12 picture books/year; 24 young readers/year; 50 middle readers; 6 young adult titles/year.

Fiction: Young readers and middle readers: adventure, animal, contemporary, fantasy, humor, science fiction and suspense/mystery. Young adults: adventure, contemporary, fantasy, science fiction, sports, suspense/mystery, horror. Average word length: picture books—1,000; read alones (6-8 years) 2,000-4,000; story books (7-9 years) 8,000-12,000; novels (8 and up) 20,000-50,000.

Nonfiction: Picture books: animal. Young readers: activity books, humor. Middle readers: activity books. Young adults: activity books, animal, health, history, hobbies, how-to, reference, science. self-help, social issues. Average word length: picture books—1,000; young readers—5,000; middle readers—15,000; young adults—20,000. Recently published *Skellig*, by David Almond; *Bear*, by Mick Inkpen; and *Saving the Animals*, by Kate Petty.

How to Contact/Writers: Fiction: Submit outline/synopsis and 3 sample chapters. Reports on queries in 1 month if SAE enclosed; mss in 6-8 weeks if SAE enclosed. Publishes a book 12-18 months after acceptance. Will consider simultaneous submissions.

Illustration: Works with 80 illustrators/year. Uses both b&w and color artwork. Reviews ms/illustration packages from authors. Submit ms with dummy. Contact: Children's Editor. Illustrations only: query with photocopied samples. Reports in 1 month only if interested. Samples returned with SASE; samples filed.

Photography: Buys photos from freelancers. Contact: Children's Art Dept. Buys stock and assigns work. Submit cover letter.

Terms: Pays authors 4-10% royalty based on retail price or work purchased outright. Pays illustrators by the project or royalty. Pays photographers by the project. Original artwork returned at job's completion. Sends galleys to authors. Ms guidelines available.

Tips: "Write from the heart. Don't patronize your reader. Do your research—read the finest writers around, see where the market is. We're looking for something original with a clear sense of the first reader."

✓ HOLIDAY HOUSE INC., 425 Madison Ave., New York NY 10017. (212)688-0085. Fax: (212)421-6134. Book publisher. Estab. 1935. Vice President/Editor-in-Chief: Regina Griffin. **Acquisitions:** Lisa Hopp, associate editor. Publishes 35 picture books/year; 3 young reader titles/year; 10 middle reader titles/year; and 3 young adult titles/year. 20% of books by first-time authors; 10% from agented writers.

Fiction: All levels: adventure, contemporary, ghost, historical, humor, school. Picture books, middle readers, young adults: animal, humor. Recently published *The Magic Dreidels*, by Eric A. Kimmel, illustrated by Katya Krenina; *The Golem*, by Barbara Rogasky, illustrated by Trina Schart Hyman; and *The Life and*

Death of Crazy Horse, by Russell Freedman, photos by Amos Bad Heart Bull.

Nonfiction: All levels: animal, biography, concept, contemporary, geography, historical, math, nature/environment, science, social studies.

How to Contact/Writers: Send queries and mss to Lisa Hopp. Reports on queries in 3 weeks; mss in 8-10 weeks. Mss returned only with SASE.

Illustration: Works with 35 illustrators/year. Reviews ms illustration packages from artists. Send ms with dummy. Reports back only if interested. Samples returned with SASE or filed.

Terms: Pays authors and illustrators an advance against royalties. Originals returned at job's completion. Book catalog, ms/artist's guidelines available for a SASE.

Tips: "Fewer books are being published. It will get even harder for first timers to break in."

HENRY HOLT & CO., INC., 115 W. 18th St., New York NY 10011. (212)886-9200. Book publisher. **Manuscript Acquisitions:** Laura Godwin, editor-in-chief/associate publisher of Books for Young Readers dept.; Marc Aronson, senior editor, Christy Ottaviano, senior editor. **Art Acquisitions:** Martha Rago, art director. Publishes 20-40 picture books/year; 4-6 chapter books/year; 10-15 middle grade titles/year; 8-10 young adult titles/year. 8% of books by first-time authors; 40% of books from agented writers. "Henry Holt and Company Books for Young Readers is known for publishing quality books that feature imaginative authors and illustrators. We tend to publish many new authors and illustrators each year in our effort to develop and foster new talent."

Fiction: Picture books: animal, anthology, concept, folktales, history, humor, multicultural, nature/environment, poetry, special needs, sports. Middle readers: adventure, contemporary, history, humor, multicultural, special needs, sports, suspense/mystery. Young adults: contemporary, multicultural, problem novel, sports.

Nonfiction: Picture books: animal, arts/crafts, biography, concept, geography, history, hobbies, multicultural, music dance, nature/environment, sports. Middle readers, young readers, young adult: biography, history, multicultural, sports.

How to Contact/Writers: Fiction/Nonfiction: Submit complete ms. Reports on queries in 6 weeks; mss in 3-4 months. Will not consider simultaneous submissions.

Illustration: Works with 50-60 illustrators/year. Reviews ms/illustration packages from artists. Random samples OK. Illustrations only: Submit tearsheets, slides. Do *not* send originals. Reports on art samples in 1 month. Samples returned with SASE; samples filed. If accepted, original artwork returned at job's completion.

Terms: Pays authors/illustrators royalty based on retail price. Sends galleys to authors; proofs to illustrators.

HOUGHTON MIFFLIN CO., Children's Trade Books, 222 Berkeley St., Boston MA 02116. (617)351-5000. Fax: (617)351-1111. Website: http://www.hmco.com. Book publisher. Vice President and Publisher: Anita Silvey. **Manuscript Aquisitions:** Sarah Hines-Stephens, assistant editor; Kim Keller, assistant managing editor; Ann Rider, Margaret Raymo, senior editors; Amy Thrall, associate editor; Eden Edwards, Sandpiper Paperback editor; Matilda Welber, contributing editor; Walter Lorraine, Walter Lorraine Books, editor. **Art Acquisitions:** Bob Kosturko, art director. Averages 60 titles/year. Publishes hardcover originals and trade paperback reprints and originals. Imprints include Clarion Books. "Houghton Mifflin gives shape to ideas that educate, inform, and above all, delight."

Fiction: All levels: all categories except religion. "We do not rule out any theme, though we do not publish specifically religious material." *Burnt Toast on Davenport Street*, by Tim Egan (ages 4-8, picture book); *Woman in the Wall*, by Patrice Kindl (ages 10-14, novel); and *Three Stories You Can Read to Your Cat*, by Sara Swan Miller, illustrated by True Kelley (ages 7-10, early readers).

Nonfiction: All levels: all categories except religion. Recently published *Animal Dads*, by Sneed B. Collard III, illustrated by Steve Jenkins (ages 4-8, picture book); *Secrets of Animal Flight*, by Nic Bishop (ages 4-8, photo); *Life and Times of the Peanut*, by Charles Micucci (ages 5-8, illustrated).

How to Contact/Writers: Fiction: Submit complete ms. Nonfiction: Submit outline/synopsis and sample chapters. Always include SASE. Response within 3 months.

Illustration: Works with 60 illustrators/year. Reviews ms/illustration packages from artists. Ms/illustration packages or illustrations only: Query with samples (colored photocopies are fine); provide tearsheets. Reports in 6-8 weeks. Samples returned with SASE; samples filed if of interest.

Terms: Pays standard royalty based on retail price; offers advance. Illustrators paid by the project and royalty. Ms and artist's guidelines available for SASE.

☑ **HUNTER HOUSE PUBLISHERS**, P.O.Box 2914, Alameda CA 94501-0914. Fax: (510)865-4295. E-mail: editorial@hunterhouse.com. Book publisher. **Manuscript Acquisitions:** Kiram Rane. **Art Acquisitions:** Wendy Low, art director. Publishes 0-1 titles for teenage women/year. 50% of books by first-time authors; 5% of books from agented writers.

Nonfiction: Picture books: activity books, social issues, music/dance, self-help. Middle readers: music/dance. Young adults: health, multicultural, self help (self esteem), social issues. "We emphasize that all our books try to take multicultural experiences and concerns into account. We would be interested in a social issues or self-help book on multicultural issues." Books are therapy/personal growth-oriented. Does *not* want to see books for young children; fiction; illustrated picture books; autobiography. Published *Turning Yourself Around: Self-Help Strategies for Troubled Teens*, by Kendall Johnson, Ph.D.; *Safe Dieting for Teens*, by Linda Ojeda, Ph.D.

How to Contact/Writers: Query; submit overview and chapter-by-chapter synopsis, sample chapters and statistics on your subject area, support organizations or networks and marketing ideas. "Testimonials from professionals or well-known authors are crucial." Reports on queries in 1 month; mss in 3 months. Publishes a book 18 months after acceptance. Will consider simultaneous submissions.

Illustration: Works with 1 illustrator/year. Reports back only if interested. Samples returned with SASE; samples filed.

Photography: Purchases photos from freelancers. Buys stock images.

Terms: Payment varies. Sends galleys to authors. Book catalog available for 9 × 12 SAE and 79¢ postage; ms guidelines for standard SAE and 1 first-class stamp.

Tips: Wants therapy/personal growth workbooks; teen books with solid, informative material. "We do few children's books. The ones we do are for a select, therapeutic audience. No fiction! Please, no fiction."

HUNTINGTON HOUSE PUBLISHERS, P.O. Box 53788, Lafayette LA 70505. (318)237-7049. Fax: (318)237-7060. Book publisher. **Acquisitions:** Mark Anthony, publisher. Publishes 6 young readers/year. 30% of books by first-time authors. "Most books have spiritual/religious themes."

Fiction: Picture books, young readers, middle readers, young adults: all subjects. Does not want to see romance or multicultural. Average word length: picture books—12-50; young readers—100-300; middle readers—4,000-15,000; young adults/teens—10,000-40,000. Published *Greatest Star of All*, by Greg Gulley and David Watts (ages 9-11, adventure/religion).

Nonfiction: Picture books: animal, religion. Young readers, middle readers, young adults/teens: biography, history, religion. No nature/environment, multicultural. Average word length: picture books—12-50; young readers—100-300; middle readers—4,000-15,000; young adult/teens—10,000-40,000. Published *To Grow By Storybook Readers*, by Marie Le Doux and Janet Friend (preschool to age 8, textbook) *High on Adventure*, by Steve Arrington (young adult).

How to Contact/Writers: Fiction/Nonfiction: Query. Submit outline/synopsis, table of contents and proposal letter. One or two sample chapters are optional. Send SASE. Reports on queries/mss in 2-3 months. Publishes a book 8 months after acceptance. Will consider simultaneous submissions.

Illustration: Works with 2 illustrators/year. Reviews ms/illustration packages from artists. Query; submit ms with dummy. Contact: Mark Anthony, editor-in-chief. Reports in 1 month. Illustrations only: Query with samples; send résumé and client list. Reports in 2-3 months. Samples returned with SASE; samples filed. Original artwork returned at job's completion.

Photography: Buys photos from freelancers. Contact: Managing Editor. Buys stock images. Model/property releases required. Submit cover letter and résumé to be kept on file.

Terms: Contracts negotiable. Pays authors royalty of 10% based on wholesale price. Pays illustrators by the project (range: $50-250) or royalty of 10% based on wholesale price. Sends galleys to authors; dummies to illustrators. Book catalog available for #10 SAE and 2 first-class stamps; ms guidelines for SASE.

☑ **HYPERION BOOKS FOR CHILDREN**, 114 Fifth Ave., New York NY 10011. (212)633-4400. Fax: (212)633-4833. Website: http://www.disney.com/DisneyBooks/. An operating unit of Walt Disney Publishing Group, Inc. Book publisher. **Manuscript Acquisitions:** Katherine Tegen, editorial director. **Art Acquisitions:** Ellen Friedman, creative director. 30% of books by first-time authors. Publishes various categories.

Fiction: Picture books, young readers, middle readers, young adults: adventure, animal, anthology (short stories), contemporary, fantasy, folktales, history, humor, multicultural, poetry, science fiction, sports, suspense/mystery. Middle readers, young adults: problem novels, romance. Recently published *Sons of Liberty*, by Adele Griffin (ages 10 and up); and *Zoom Broom*, by Margie Palatini (ages 5-9).

Nonfiction: All trade subjects for all levels.

How to Contact/Writers: Only interested in agented material. ·

Illustration: Works with 100 illustrators/year. "Picture books are fully illustrated throughout. All others depend on individual project." Reviews ms/illustration packages from artists. Submit complete package. Illustrations only: Submit résumé, business card, promotional literature or tearsheets to be kept on file. Reports back only if interested. Original artwork returned at job's completion.

Photography: Works on assignment only. Publishes photo essays and photo concept books. Provide résumé, business card, promotional literature or tearsheets to be kept on file.

Terms: Pays authors royalty based on retail price. Offers advances. Pays illustrators and photographers royalty based on retail price or a flat fee. Sends galleys to authors; dummies to illustrators. Book catalog available for 9×12 SAE and 3 first-class stamps; ms guidelines available for SASE.

☑ IDEALS CHILDREN'S BOOKS, an imprint of Hambleton-Hill Publishing, Inc., 1501 County Hospital Rd., Nashville TN 37218-2501. Book publisher. **Manuscript and Art Acquisitions:** Bethany Snyder. Publishes 30-35 picture books/year. 10-15% of books by first-time authors; 5-10% of books from agented writers.

● Ideals Children's Books only accepts mss from members of the Society of Children's Book Writers and Illustrators (SCBWI), agented authors, and/or previously published book authors (submit with a list of writing credits) All others will be returned unread provided a SASE has been enclosed.

Fiction: Picture books: adventure, concept, contemporary, folktales, history, humor, multicultural, nature/environment, religion, sports, suspense/mystery. Average word length: picture books—200-1,200. Recently published *Molly*, by Joseph Bonsall, illustrated by Erin M. Mauterer (ages 5-8); *The Littlest Tree*, by Charles Tazewell, illustrated by Karen A. Jerome (all ages); and *Arianna and the Strawberry Tea*, by Maria Fasal Faulconer, illustrated by Katy Keek Arnsteen (ages 5-9).

How to Contact/Writers: Prefers to see complete ms rather than queries. Reports in 3-6 months. Publishes a book 18-24 months after acceptance. Must include SASE for response.

Illustration: Works with 15-20 illustrators/year. Uses color artwork only. Editorial reviews ms/illustration packages from artists. Submit ms with 1 color photocopy of final art and remainder roughs. Illustrations only: Submit résumé and tearsheets showing variety of styles. Reports on art samples only if interested. "No original artwork, please." Samples returned with SASE, but prefers to keep them on file.

Terms: "All terms vary according to individual projects and authors/artists." Ms guidelines/artist guidelines for business envelope and 1 first-class stamp.

Tips: "Searching for strong storylines with realistic characters as well as 'fun for all kids' kinds of stories. We are not interested in young adult romances. We do not publish chapter books. We are not interested in alphabet books or anthropomorphism." Illustrators: "Be flexible in contract terms—and be able to show as much final artwork as possible."

Ⓝ ILLUMINATION ARTS, P.O. Box 1865, Bellevue WA 98009. (425)646-3670. Fax: (425)646-4144. Book publisher. Estab. 1987. "All of our books are inspirational/spiritual. We specialize in children's picture books, but our books are designed to appeal to all readers, including adults." **Acquisitions:** Ruth Thompson, editorial director.

Fiction: Average word length: picture books—1,500-3,000. Recently published *The Right Touch*, by Sandy Kleven, illustratrated by Jody Bergsma; and *Sky Castle*, by Sandra Hanken, illustrated by Jody Bergsma.

How to Contact/Writers: Fiction: Submit complete ms. Reports on queries in 1 month. Publishes a book 2 years after acceptance. Will consider simultaneous submissions.

Illustration: Works with 2 illustrators/year. Uses color artwork only. Reviews ms/illustration packages from artists. Query or send ms with dummy. Illustrations only: Query with samples; send résumé and promotional literature to be kept on file. Contact: Ruth Thompson, editorial director. Reports back in 1 week. Samples returned with SASE or filed.

Terms: Pays authors royalty based on wholesale price. Sends galleys to authors; dummies to illustrators. Originals returned to artist at job's completion. Book fliers available for SASE.

Tips: "Follow our guidelines. Expect considerable editing. Be patient. The market is tough. We receive 10-15 submissions a week and publish two books a year."

Ⓝ IMPACT PUBLISHERS, INC., P.O. Box 910, San Luis Obispo CA 93406-0910. (805)543-5911. Fax: (805)543-4093. E-mail: info@impactpublishers.com. Estab. 1970. Nonfiction publisher. **Manuscript Acquisitions:** Children's Editor. **Art Acquisitions:** Sharon Skinner, production manager. Imprints: Little Imp Books, The Working Caregiver Series, The Practical Therapist Series. Publishes 1 young reader/year;

FOR EXPLANATIONS OF THESE SYMBOLS,
SEE THE INSIDE FRONT AND BACK COVERS OF THIS BOOK

1 middle reader/year; and 1 young adult title/year. 50% of books by first-time authors. "Our purpose is to make the best human services expertise available to the widest possible audience."

Fiction: Young readers: teaching stories. Recently published *The Way of the Circle*, by James Vollbracht, illustratrated by Chris Foleen (ages 8-13, teaching story, principles of harmony, love, kindness).

Nonfiction: Young readers, middle readers, young adults: self-help. Recently published *Cool Cats, Calm Kids*, by Mary Williams, illustrated by Dianne O'Quinn Burke (ages 7-12, relaxation and stress management).

How to Contact/Writers: Fiction/Nonfiction: Query or submit complete ms. Reports on queries in 8-10 weeks; mss in 10-12 weeks. Will consider simultaneous submissions or previously published work.

Illustration: Works with 1 or less illustrator/year. Uses b&w artwork only. Reviews ms/illustration packages from artists. Query. Contact: Children's Editor. Illustrations only: query with samples. Contact: Sharon Skinner, production manager. Reports back only if interested. Samples not returned; samples filed.

Terms: Pays authors royalty of 10-12%. Offers advances. Pays illustrators by the project. Sends galleys

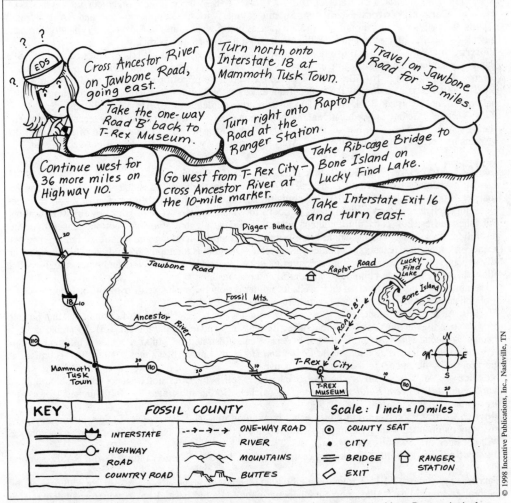

Kathleen Bullock's Bone Island map illustration is representative of the work art director Marta Drayton looks for at educational publisher Incentive Publications, Inc. Drayton likes Bullock's spontaneous style yet accurate rendering. "This is a good combination of fun and realism, which is what we look for in educational products." When hiring freelance artists, Drayton looks for artists who can illustrate an entire project. "We pay for the entire project. Some pages have a small spot, some pages have more elaborate illustrations. An artist who can work swiftly, maintaining a style throughout and is age-level appropriate, will do very well."

to authors. Originals returned to artist at job's completion. Book catalog available for #10 SAE with 2 first-class stamps; ms guidelines available for SASE. All imprints included in a single catalog.

INCENTIVE PUBLICATIONS, INC., 3835 Cleghorn Ave., Nashville TN 37215-2532. (615)385-2934. Fax: (615)385-2967. E-mail: incentiv@nashville.net. Website: http://www.nashville.net/~incentiv. Estab. 1970. "Incentive publishes developmentally appropriate instructional aids for tots to teens." **Manuscript Acquisitions:** Contact Editor. **Art Acquisitions:** Marta Drayton, art director. Approximately 20% of books by first-time authors. "We publish only educational resource materials (for teachers and parents of children from pre-school age through the middle grades). We publish *no fiction*. Incentive endeavors to produce developmentally appropriate research-based educational materials to meet the changing needs of students, teachers and parents. Books are written by teachers for teachers for the most part."
Nonfiction: Black & white line illustrated books, young reader, middle reader: activity books, arts/craft, multicultural, science, special needs, social issues, supplemental educational materials. "Any manuscripts related to child development or with content-based activities and innovative strategies (K-8) will be reviewed for possible publication." Recently published Basic/Not Boring series, by Imogene Forte and Marjorie Frank, illustrated by Kathleen Bullock (grades K-8+, basic skills enrichment activity books).
How to Contact/Writers: Nonfiction: Submit outline/synopsis, sample chapters and SASE. Usually reports on queries/mss in 1 month. Reports on queries in 4-6 weeks; mss in 6-8 weeks. Typically publishes a book 18 months after acceptance. Will consider simultaneous submissions.
Illustration: Works with 2-6 illustrators/year. Reports back in 2-4 weeks if reply requested (send SASE). Samples returned with SASE; samples filed. Need 4-color cover art; b&w line illustration for content.
Terms: Pays authors in royalties (5-10% based on wholesale price) or work purchased outright (range: $500-1,000). Pays illustrators by the project (range: $200-1,500). Pays photographers by the project. Original artwork not returned. Book catalog and ms and artist guidelines for SAE and $1.78 postage.
Tips: Writers: "We buy only educational teacher resource material that can be used by teachers and parents (home schoolers). Please do not submit fiction! We look for a whimsical, warm style of illustration that respects the integrity and age of the child. We work primarily with local artists, but not exclusively."

JALMAR PRESS, P.O. Box 1185, Torrance CA 90505. (310)816-3085. Fax: (310)816-3092. E-mail: blwjalmar@worldnet.att. Website: http://www.ierc.com/jalmar/. Subsidiary of B.L. Winch and Associates. Book publisher. Estab. 1971. **Acquisitions:** Bradley Winch, publisher; Cathy Zippi, manager. Does not publish children's picture books or books for young readers. 10% of books by first-time authors. Publishes self-esteem (curriculum content related), drug and alcohol abuse prevention, peaceful conflict resolution, stress management, whole-brain learning, accelerated learning and emotional intelligence materials for counselors, teachers, and other care givers. "Our goal is to empower children to become personally and socially responsible through activities presented by teachers, counselors and other caregivers that allow them to experience being both successful and responsible."
● Jalmar's catalog is found on their website. Jalmar is now the exclusive distributor for Innerchoice Publishing's entire line of school counselor-oriented material (K-12).
Fiction: All levels: self-concept, self-esteem. Does not want to see "children's fiction books that have to do with cognitive learning (as opposed to affective learning) and autobiographical work." Published *Hilde Knows: Someone Cries for the Children*, by Lisa Kent, illustrated by Mikki Macklen (child abuse); and *Scooter's Tail of Terror: A Fable of Addiction and Hope*, by Larry Shles (ages 5-105). "All submissions must teach (by metaphor) in the areas listed above."
Nonfiction: All levels: activity books, social issues, self-help. Does not want to see autobiographical work. Published *Esteem Builders Program*, by Michele Borba, illustrated by Bob Burchett (for school use—6 books, tapes, posters).
How to Contact/Writers: Only interested in agented material. Fiction/Nonfiction: Submit complete ms. Reports on queries in 1 month; mss in 6 months. Publishes a book 12-18 months after acceptance. Will consider simultaneous submissions.
Illustration: Works with 2 illustrators/year. Reports in 1 week. Samples returned with SASE; samples filed.
Terms: Pays authors 7½-15% royalty based on net receipts. Average advance varies. Pays illustrators by the project on a bid basis. Pays photographers per photo on a bid basis. Book catalog/ms guidelines free on request.
Tips: Wants "thoroughly researched, tested, practical, activity-oriented, curriculum content and grade/level correlated books on self-esteem, peaceful conflict resolution, stress management, emotional intelligence, and whole brain learning and books bridging self-esteem to various 'trouble' areas, such as 'at risk,' 'dropout prevention,' etc. Illustrators—make artwork that can be reproduced. Emotional intelligence is becoming a 'hot' category."

JEWISH PUBLICATION SOCIETY, 1930 Chestnut St., Philadelphia PA 19103. (215)564-5925. Fax: (215)564-6640. Editor-in-Chief: Dr. Ellen Frankel. Children's Editor: Bruce Black. Book publisher. All work must have Jewish content.

Fiction: Picture books, young readers, middle readers and young adults: adventure, contemporary, folktales, history, mystery, problem novels, religion, romance, sports. Recently published *The Violin Players*, by Eileen Bluestone Sherman (ages 10 and up); and *Agnon's Alef Bet*, poems by S.Y. Agnon, illustrated by Arien Zeldich (all ages).

Nonfiction: Picture books: biography, history, religion. Young readers, middle readers, young adults: biography, history, religion, sports. Recently published *Hannah Szenes: A Song of Light*, by Maxine Rose Schur (ages 9 and up).

How to Contact/Writers: Fiction/Nonfiction: Query or submit outline/synopsis and sample chapters. Will consider simultaneous submissions (please advise). Reports on queries/mss in 6-8 weeks.

Illustration: Works with 3-4 illustrators/year. Will review ms/illustration packages. Query first or send 3 chapters of ms with 1 piece of final art, remainder roughs. Illustrations only: Query with photocopies; arrange a personal interview to show portfolio.

Terms: Pays authors and illustrators flat fees or royalties based on net. Reports back only if interested. Samples returned with SASE. Orginals returned at job's completion.

Tips: "Don't worry about the market. Write what you feel most passionately about, the subject which stirs your soul. Most of all, keep writing!"

KAEDEN BOOKS, P.O. Box 16190, Rocky River OH 44116. (216)356-0030. Fax: (216)356-5081. Book publisher. **Acquisitions:** Dennis Graves, vice president. Publishes 40 young readers/year. 50% of books by first-time authors.

Fiction: Young readers: adventure, animal, concept, contemporary, health, history, humor, multicultural, nature/environment, science fiction, sports, suspense/mystery. Average word length: picture books—20-150 words; young readers—20-150 words. Recently published *The Big Fish*, by Joe Yukish, illustated by Kate Salley Palmer; *Sammy Gets A Ride*, by Karen Evans and Kathleen Urmston, illustrated by Gloria Gedeon; and *Time for a Bath*, by Jan Mader, illustrated by Karen Maizel.

Nonfiction: Young readers: activity books, animal, biography, careers, geography, health, history, hobbies, how-to, multicultural, music/dance, nature/environment, religion, science, sports. Multicultural needs include group and character diversity in stories and settings. Average word length: picture books—20-150 words; young readers—20-150 words.

How to Contact/Writers: Fiction/nonfiction: Query or submit complete ms. Reports on queries in 2-4 weeks; mss in 6-9 months. Will consider simultaneous submissions, electronic submissions via disk or modem.

Illustration: Works with 30 illustrators/year. Reviews ms/illustration packages from artists. Query. Submit art samples in color. Can be photocopies or tearsheets. Illustrations only: Query with samples. Send résumé, promo sheet, tearsheets, photocopies of work, preferably in color. Reports only if interested. Samples are filed.

Terms: Work purchased outright from authors. "Royalties to our previous authors." Offers negotiable advances. Pays illustrators by the project (range: $50-150/page). Book catalog available for 8½ × 11 SAE and 2 first-class stamps.

Tips: "Our books are written for emergent and fluent readers to be used in the educational teaching environment. A strong correlation between text and visual is necessary along with creative and colorful juvenile designs."

N **KAMEHAMEHA SCHOOLS PRESS**, 1887 Makuakane St., Honolulu HI 96817. (808)842-8880. Fax: (808)842-8875. E-mail: kspress@ksbe.edu. Website: http://www.ksbe.edu/pubs/KSPress/catalo g.html. Estab. 1933. Specializes in educational and multicultural material. **Manuscript Acquisitions:** Henry Bennett. "Kamehameha Schools Press publishes in the areas of Hawaiian history, culture, language and studies."

Nonfiction: Middle readers, young adults: biography, history, multicultural, Hawaiian folklore. Recently published *Voyage from the Past*, by Julie Stewart Williams, illustrated by Robin Yoko Burningham (Polynesian explorers and canoe voyaging).

How to Contact/Writers: Query. Reports on queries in 6-8 weeks; mss in 2-3 months. Publishes a book 12-18 months after acceptance.

Illustration: Uses b&w artwork only. Illustrations only: Query with samples. Reports back only if interested. Samples not returned.

Terms: Work purchased outright from authors. Pays illustrators by the project. Sends galleys to authors. Book catalog available for #10 SASE and 1 first-class stamp. All imprints included in a single catalog. Catalog available on website.

Tips: "Writers and illustrators *must* be knowledgeable in Hawaiian history/culture and be able to show credentials to validate their proficiency. Greatly prefer to work with writers/illustrators available in the Honolulu area."

KAR-BEN COPIES, INC., 6800 Tildenwood Lane, Rockville MD 20852-4371. (301)984-8733. Fax: (301)881-9195. E-mail: karben@aol.com. Website: http://www.karben.com. Book publisher. Estab. 1975. **Manuscript Acquisitions:** Madeline Wikler, vice president. Publishes 5-10 picture books/year; 20% of books by first-time authors. All of Kar-Ben Copies' books are on *Jewish themes for young children* and families.
Fiction: Picture books, young readers: adventures, concept, contemporary, fantasy, folktales, history, humor, multicultural, religion, special needs, suspense/mystery; *must be* on a Jewish theme. Average word length: picture books—2,000. Published *Northern Lights*, by Diana Cohen Conway; *Sammy Spider's First Hanukkah*, by Sylvia Rouss; *Matzah Ball, A Passover Story*, by Mindy Avra Portnoy; and *Terrible, Terrible!*, by Robin Bernstein.
Nonfiction: Picture books, young readers: activity books, arts/crafts, biography, careers, concept, cooking, history, how-to, multicultural, religion, social issues, special needs; must be of Jewish interest. Average word length: picture books—2,000. Published *Jewish Holiday Games for Little Hands*, by Ruth Brinn; *Tell Me a Mitzvah*, by Danny Siegel; and *My First Jewish Word Book*, by Roz Schanzer.
How to Contact/Writers: Fiction/nonfiction: Submit complete ms. Reports on queries in 1 week; ms in 2 weeks. Publishes a book 1 year after acceptance. Will consider simultaneous submissions.
Illustration: Works with 6-10 illustrators/year. Prefers "four-color art in any medium that is scannable." Reviews ms/illustration packages from artists. Submit whole ms and sample of art (no originals). Illustrations only: Submit tearsheets, photocopies, promo sheet or anything representative that does *not* need to be returned. Enclose SASE for response. Reports on art samples in 1 week.
Terms: Pays authors in royalties of 6-8% based on net sales or work purchased outright (range: $500-2,000). Offers advance (average amount: $1,000). Pays illustrators royalty of 6-8% based on net sales or by the project (range: $500-3,000). Sends galleys to authors. Original artwork returned at job's completion. Book catalog free on request. Ms guidelines for 9×12 SAE and 2 first-class stamps.
Tips: Looks for "books for young children with Jewish interest and content, modern, non-sexist, not didactic. Fiction or nonfiction with a *Jewish* theme—can be serious or humorous, life cycle, Bible story, or holiday-related."

KEY PORTER BOOKS, 70 The Esplanade, Toronto, Ontario M5E 1R2 Canada. (416)862-7777. Fax: (416)862-2304. Book publisher. **Manuscript Acquisitions:** Susan Renouf, editor-in-chief. Publishes 4 picture books/year; and 4 young readers/year. 30% of books by first-time authors.
Fiction: Young readers, middle readers, young adult: animal, anthology, concept, health, multicultural, nature/environment, science fiction, special needs, sports, suspense/mystery. Does not want to see religious material. Average word length: picture books—1,500; young readers—5,000.
Nonfiction: Picture books: animal, history, nature/environment, reference, science. Middle readers: animal, careers, history, nature/environment, reference, science and sports. Average word length: picture books—1,500; middle readers—15,000. Recently published *How on Earth: A Question and Answer Book About How Animals & Plants Live*, by Ron Orenstein (ages 8-10, nature/environment); *Super Skaters: World Figure Skating Stars*, by Steve Milton (ages 8 and up, sports); and *The Seven Chairs*, by Helen Lanteigne (ages 4-8).
How to Contact/Writers: Only interested in agented material from Canadian writers; *no unsolicited mss.*
Photography: Buys photos from freelancers. Buys stock and assigns work. Captions required. Uses 35mm transparencies. Submit cover letter, résumé, duplicate slides, stock photo list.
Terms: Pays authors royalty of 4-10% based on retail price. Offers advances (average amount: $4,000-20,000, Canadian). Pays illustrators by the project (range: $4,000-20,000, Canadian). Pays photographers by the project (range: $4,000-10,000, Canadian); per photo (range: $50-250, Canadian); royalty (range: 4-10% of retail price). Sends galleys to authors; dummies to illustrators. Book catalog available for 8½×11 SAE and 2 first-class stamps.

KINGFISHER, Imprint of Larousse Kingfisher Chabers, 95 Madison Ave., New York NY 10016. (212)686-1060. Fax: (212)686-1082.
● Kingfisher Books is not currently accepting unsolicited mss.

ALFRED A. KNOPF BOOKS FOR YOUNG READERS, 29th Floor, 201 E. 50th St., New York NY 10022. (212)751-2600. Website: http://www.randomhouse.com/kids. Imprint of Random House, Inc. Book publisher. Estab. 1915. Publishing Director: Simon Boughton. **Acquisitions:** send mss to Knopf

Editorial Department. 90% of books published through agents. "Knopf is known for high quality literary fiction, and is willing to take risks with writing styles. It publishes for children ages 5 and up."

Fiction: All levels: considers all categories.

Nonfiction: All levels: animal, arts/crafts, biography, history, how to, multicultural, music/dance, nature/environment, science, self help, sports.

How to Contact/Writers: Fiction/nonfiction: "We read agented material immediately. We will read queries from nonagented authors and then, possibly, request ms." Publishes a book 12-18 months after acceptance. Will consider simultaneous submissions. All mss must be accompanied by a SASE. Reports on queries/mss in 6 months.

Illustration: Reviews ms/illustration packages from artists through agent only. Illustration only: Contact: Art Director. Reports back only if interested. Samples returned with SASE; samples filed.

Terms: Pays authors in royalties. Pays illustrators and photographers by the project or royalties. Original artwork returned at job's completion. Book catalog and ms guidelines free on request with SASE.

LEE & LOW BOOKS, INC., 95 Madison Ave., New York NY 10016-7801. (212)779-4400. Website: http://www.leeandlow.com. Book publisher. Estab. 1991. **Acquisitions:** Philip Lee, publisher. Publishes 8-10 picture books/year. 50% of books by first-time authors. Lee & Low publishes only picture books with multicultural themes.

• Lee & Low Books is dedicated to publishing culturally authentic literature. The company makes a special effort to work with writers and artists of color and encourages new voices. Two Lee & Low titles received the Coretta Scott King Award in 1998—the author award for *Forged by Fire*, by Sharon M. Draper and the illustrator award for *In Daddy's Arms I Am Tall*, illustrated by Javaka Steptoe.

Fiction: Picture books: Concept. Picture books, young readers: anthology, contemporary, history, multicultural, poetry. "We are not considering folktales, animal stories and chapter books." Average word length: picture books—1,000-1,500 words. Recently published *Sam and the Lucky Money*, by Karen Chinn, illustrated by Cornelius Van Wright and Ying-Hwa Hu (ages 3-9, picture book); and *In Daddy's Arms I Am Tall: African Americans Celebrating Fathers*, illustrated by Javaka Steptoe (ages 4 and up, picture book).

Nonfiction: Picture books: biography, history and multicultural. Average word length: picture books—1,500. Recently published *Dia's Story Cloth: The Hmong People's Journey of Freedom*, by Dia Cha, illustrated by Chue and Nhia Thao Cha (ages 6 and up, picture book).

How to Contact/Writers: Fiction/Nonfiction: Submit complete ms. Reports in 1-4 months. Publishes a book 12-24 months after acceptance. Will consider simultaneous submissions.

Illustration: Works with 8-10 illustrators/year. Uses color artwork only. Reviews ms/illustration packages from artists. Submit ms with dummy. Illustrations only: Query with samples, résumé, promo sheet and tearsheets. Samples returned with SASE; samples filed. Original artwork returned at job's completion.

Photography: Buys photos from freelancers. Works on assignment only. Model/property releases required. Submit cover letter, résumé, promo piece and book dummy.

Terms: Pays authors royalty. Offers advances. Pays illustrators royalty plus advance against royalty. Photographers paid royalty plus advance against royalty. Sends galleys to authors; proofs to illustrators. Book catalog available for 9 × 12 SAE and $1.01 postage; ms and art guidelines available for SASE.

Tips: "We strongly urge writers to familiarize themselves with our list before submitting. Materials will only be returned with SASE."

LEGACY PRESS, Imprint of Rainbow Publishers, P.O. Box 261129, San Diego CA 92196. (619)271-7600. Book publisher. Estab. 1997. **Manuscript/Art Acquisitions:** Christy Allen, editor. Publishes 3 young readers/year; 3 middle readers/year; 3 young adult titles/year. Published nonfiction, Bible-teaching books.

Nonfiction: Young readers, middle readers, young adults: reference, religion. Recently published *My Prayer Journal*, by Mary Davis (ages 10-12, journal); and *The Dickens Family Gospel*, by Robert Hanna (all ages, devotional).

How to Contact/Writers: Nonfiction: Submit outline/synopsis and 3-5 sample chapters. Reports on queries in 6 weeks; on ms in 3 months. Publishes a book 18 months after acceptance. Will consider simultaneous submissions; electronic submissions via disk or modem; previously published work.

Illustration: Works with 5 illustrators/year. Reviews ms/illustration packages from artists. Submit ms with 5-10 pieces of final art. Illustrations only: Query with samples to be kept on file. Reports in 6 weeks. Samples returned with SASE.

Terms: Pays authors royalty or work purchased outright. Offers advances. Pays illustrators by the project. Sends galley to authors. Book catalog available for business size SASE; ms guidelines for SASE.

Tips: "Get to know the Christian bookstore market. We are looking for innovative ways to teach and encourage children about the Christian life. No fiction, please."

Baby Born

by ANASTASIA SUEN • *illustrated by* CHIH-WEI CHANG

© 1998 Lee & Low Books

The charming multicultural cover of *Baby Born*, published by Lee & Low Books, is the first picture book for Taiwan-based illustrator Chih-Wei Chang. Written by Anastasia Suen, the book pairs her poetic verse with Chang's whimsical watercolor illustrations following new babies through their first year. Known for their dedication to publishing multicultural picture books, Lee & Low makes a special effort to work with writers and artists of color and encourages new voices. Their goal is to meet the growing need for books that address children of color, and to present literature that all children can identify with.

LERNER PUBLICATIONS CO., 241 First Ave. N., Minneapolis MN 55401. (612)332-3344. Fax: (612)332-7615. Website: http://www.lernerbooks.com. Book publisher. Estab. 1959. **Manuscript Acquisitions:** Jennifer Martin, editor and Tamara Blake (geography projects only). **Art Acquisitions:** Art Director. Publishes 10-15 young readers/year; 50-70 middle readers/year; and 5 young adults/year. 20% of books by first-time authors; 5% of books from agented writers. Most books are nonfiction for children, grades 3-9. "Our goal is to publish books that educate, stimulate and stretch the imagination, foster global awareness, encourage critical thinking and inform, inspire and entertain."
Fiction: Middle readers, young adults: multicultural, problem novels, sports, suspense/mystery. "Especially interested in books with ethnic characters." Published the *Vivi Hartman Adventure Series*, by Harriet K. Feder and *Nick's Mission*, by Claire H. Blatchferd (grades 4-7, mystery).

Nonfiction: Middle readers, young adults: animal, arts/crafts, biography, careers, cooking, geography, health, history, hobbies, how-to, multicultural, music/dance, nature/environment, sports, science/math, social issues. Multicultural material must contain authentic details. Does not want to see textbooks, workbooks, song books, audiotapes, puzzles, plays, religious material, books for teachers or parents, picture or alphabet books. Average word length: young readers—3,000; middle readers—7,000; young adults—12,000. Published *Emily Dickinson: Singular Poet*, by Carol Dommermuth-Costa (grades 5 and up, Lerner Biographies series); and *Eric Lindras: High-Flying Center*, by Jeff Savage (grades 4-9, Sports Achievers series); and *Arthur Ashe*, by Caroline Lazo (grades 5 and up, A&E Biography series).

How to Contact/Writers: Fiction: Submit outline/synopsis and sample chapters. Nonfiction: Query with outline/synopsis and sample chapters. Reports on queries/mss in 2-3 months. Publishes a book 12-18 months after acceptance. Will consider simultaneous submissions.

Illustration: Works with 1-2 illustrators/year. "We tend to work mostly with local talent." Reviews ms/illustration packages from artists. Ms/illustration packages and illustrations only: Query with samples and résumé. Samples kept on file or returned with SASE. Reports back only if interested.

Photography: Contact: Photo Research Department. Buys stock and assigns work. Model/property releases required. Publishes photo essays. Photographers should query with samples.

Terms: Pays authors royalty or work purchased outright. Pays illustrators by the project. Sends galleys to authors. Book catalog available for 9 × 12 SAE and $3 postage; ms guidelines for 4 × 9 SAE and 1 first-class stamp.

Tips: Wants "straightforward, well-written nonfiction for children in grades 3-9 backed by solid current research or scholarship. Before you send your manuscript to us, you might first take a look at the kinds of books that our company publishes. We specialize in publishing high-quality educational books for children from second grade through high school. Avoid sex stereotypes (e.g., strong, aggressive, unemotional males/weak, submissive, emotional females) in your writing, as well as sexist language." (See also Carolrhoda Books, Inc.)

ARTHUR LEVINE BOOKS, 555 Broadway, New York NY 10012. (212)343-6100. Imprint of Scholastic Inc. Book publisher. Estab. 1997. **Acquisitions:** Arthur Levine, publisher. Publishes 8-10 titles/year. "Arthur Levine Books is looking for distinctive literature, for whatever's extraordinary. We plan to focus on fiction. We are willing to work with first-time authors, with or without agent."

Fiction: Recently published *When She Was Good*, by Norma Fox Mazer (young adult novel), *Beautiful Warrior: The Legend of the Nun's Kung Fu*, by Emily Arnold McCully (picture book); and *Jonah, the Whale*, by Susan Shreve (middle-grade novel).

How to Contact/Writers: Query only. Include SASE.

Terms: Pays royalty on retail price. Advance varies. Book catalog for 9 × 12 SASE.

N ☐ LINNET BOOKS, Imprint of The Shoe String Press Inc., 2 Linsley St., North Haven CT 06473-2517. (203)239-2702. Fax: (203)239-2568. E-mail: sspbooks@aol.com. Estab. 1952. Specializes in nonfiction, educational material, multicultural material. **Manuscript Acquisitions:** Diantha C. Thorpe. **Art Acquisitions:** Sanna Stanley, production manager. Imprints: Linnet Books, Linnet Professional Publications, Archon Books—Diantha C. Thorpe, acquisitions for all. Publishes 8-10 middle readers/year.

Nonfiction: Young readers: activity books, animal. Middle readers: animal, biography, geography, history, multicultural, music/dance, nature/environment, reference, science. Young adults: animal, biography, geography, history, multicultural, nature/environment, reference. Recently published *On the Home Front: Growing Up in Wartime England*, by Ann Stalcup (grade 3-6); *The Seventeenth Child*, by Dorothy Marie Rice and Lucille Mabel Walthall Payne (grade 5 and up); and *Why Goats Smell Bad and Other Stories from Benin*, translated and retold by Raouf Mama, illustrated by Imna Arroyo (all ages).

How to Contact/Writers: Nonfiction: Query or submit outline/synopsis and 3 sample chapters. Reports on queries in 3-4 weeks; mss in 3-4 months. Publishes a book 9-12 months after acceptance. Will consider simultaneous submissions "only if, when we indicate serious interest, the author withdraws from other publishers."

Illustration: Works with 2 illustrators/year. Uses b&w artwork only. Illustrations only: Query with samples. "We keep on file—send only disposable ones."

Photography: Buys stock. "We keep work on file but generally our authors are responsible for photo illustrations." Uses 5 × 7 glossy b&w prints. Send "anything that tells us what you specialize in."

Terms: Pays authors variable royalty. Offers advances. Sends galleys to authors; dummies to illustrators. Book catalog available for 9 × 12 SASE.

✓ Ⓐ LITTLE, BROWN AND COMPANY, Three Center Plaza, Boston MA 02108. (617)227-0730. Website: http://www.LittleBrown.com. Book publisher. Estab. 1873. Editor-in-Chief: Maria Modugno. Editors: Megan Tingley, Stephanie Peters. Art Director. **Art Acquisitions:** Dana Guthrie, art assistant. Estab.

Children's Writer's & Illustrator's Market '99

1837. Publishes 50% picture books/year; 5% young reader titles/year; 30% middle reader titles/year; 15% young adult titles/year.

● Little, Brown does not accept unsolicited mss.

Fiction: Picture books: adventure, animal, contemporary, fantasy, folktales, history, humor, multicultural, nature/environment. Young adults: contemporary, health, humor, multicultural, nature/environment, suspense/mystery. Multicultural needs include "any material by, for and about minorities." No "rhyming texts, anthropomorphic animals that learn a lesson, alphabet and counting books, and stories based on an event rather than a character." Average word length: picture books—1,000; young readers—6,000; middle readers—15,000-25,000; young adults—20,000-40,000. Recently published *Tinker and Tom and the Star Baby*, by David McPhail (ages 4-8, picture book); *Miss Mary Mack*, by Mary Ann Hoberman (ages 4-8, picture book); and *Cheat the Moon*, by Patricia Hermes (ages 10 and up, young adult fiction).

Nonfiction: Picture books: nature/environment, sciences. Middle readers: arts/crafts, biography, history, multicultural, nature, self help, social issues, sports. Young adults: multicultural, self-help, social issues. Average word length: picture books—2,000; young readers—4,000-6,000; middle readers—15,000-25,000; young adults—20,000-40,000. Recently published *The Tiger's Eye, The Bird's Fist*, by Louise Rafkin (ages 8 and up, middle reader); and *The Girls Guide to Life*, by Catherine Dee (ages 10 and up, middle reader).

How to Contact/Writers: Only interested in agented material. Fiction: Submit complete ms. Nonfiction: Submit a proposal, outline and 3 sample chapters. Reports on queries in 2 weeks. Reports on mss in 2 months.

Illustration: Works with 40 illustrators/year. Illustrations only: Query art director with samples; provide résumé, promo sheet or tearsheets to be kept on file. Reports on art samples in 6-8 weeks. Original artwork returned at job's completion.

Photography: Works on assignment only. Model/property releases required; captions required. Publishes photo essays and photo concept books. Uses 35mm transparencies. Photographers should provide résumé, promo sheets or tearsheets to be kept on file.

Terms: Pays authors royalties based on retail price. Pays illustrators and photographers by the project or royalty based on retail price. Sends galleys to authors; dummies to illustrators. Artist's and writer's guidelines for SASE.

Tips: "Publishers are cutting back their lists in response to a shrinking market and relying more on big names and known commodities. In order to break into the field these days, authors and illustrators research their competition and try to come up with something outstandingly different."

[N] LITTLE FRIEND PRESS, 28 New Driftway, Scituate MA 02066. (781)545-1025. Estab. 1994. **Manuscript Acquisitions:** Lynne Finnegan. Publishes 2-3 picture books/year. 50% of books by first-time authors. "Several years ago a grandmother knit her grandson a special sweater that had a secret pocket knit inside. In that pocket she placed a Little Friend that stimulated the imagination of her grandson and established Little Friend Press. We are committed to providing a variety of merchandise and books to enhance the enjoyment and imagination that inspired the original Little Friend concept."

Fiction: Average word length: picture books—24-32 pages. Recently published *The Wishing Star*, by Diane R. Houghton (ages 3-7, rewards of friendship, picture book); *Aliens Took My Child*, by Mr. Hendersen (ages 3-7, humorous account of a toddler's busy day, picture book); and *What's Behind The Bump?*, by Mr. Hendersen (ages 3-7, a child's perception of a mother's pregnancy).

Nonfiction: Average word length: picture books—24-32 pages. Recently published *My Little Friend Goes to School*, by Evelyn M. Finnegan (ages 3-7, account of first day nursery/kindergarten).

How to Contact/Writers: Fiction/Nonfiction: Submit complete ms. Reports on queries in 2-4 weeks; mss in 3-6 months. Publishes a book 1 year after acceptance. Will consider simultaneous submissions.

Illustration: Works with 2-3 illustrators/year. Uses color artwork only. Reviews ms/illustration packages from artists. Send résumé, promotional literature and tearsheets. Contact: Lynne Finnegan. Reports back only if interested. Samples kept on file.

Terms: Pays authors royalty. Pays illustrators by the project or royalty. Sends galleys to authors; dummies to illustrators. Originals returned to artist at job's completion. Book catalog available. Writer's guidelines for SASE. All imprints included in a single catalog.

☑ LITTLE TIGER PRESS, XYZ Group, N16 W23390 Stoneridge Dr., Waukesha WI 53188. (414)544-2001. E-mail: jody@xyzgroup.com. **Acquisitions:** Jody Linn. Publishes hardcover originals. Publishes 20-25 titles/year. 75% of books from first-time authors; 85% from unagented writers.

Fiction: Picture books: animals, anthology, fantasy, folktales, humor, poetry. "Humorous stories, stories about animals, children's imagination, or realistic fiction are especially sought." Send ms with SASE. Recently published *Beware of the Bears!*, by Alan MacDonald, illustrated by Gwyneth Williamson; *It Could Have Been Worse*, by A.H. Benjamin, illustrated by Tim Warnes; and *Counting Leopard Spots*, by Hiawyn Oran, illustrated by Tim Warnes.

How to Contact/Writers: Reports in 1 month on queries and proposals, 2 months on mss. Publishes book 1 year after acceptance. Will consider simultaneous submissions.

Illustration: "Send 2 or 3 samples, photocopies, computer printouts, b&w and color prints and transparencies, line art and drawing are all fine." Do not send originals! Reports back on artists' queries/submissions only if interested. Samples returned with SASE only; samples filed.

Terms: Pays 7½-10% royalty on retail price or for first-time authors, $800-2,500. Offers $2,000 minimum advance.

Tips: "Audience is children 3-8 years old. We are looking for simple, basic picture books, preferably humorous, that children will enjoy again and again. We do not have a multicultural or social agenda."

N ☑ LOBSTER PRESS, 1250 René-Lévesque Blvd. W., Suite 2200, Montréal, Quebec H3B 4W8 Canada. (514)989-3121. Fax: (514)989-3168. E-mail: fripp@lobsterpress.com. Website: http://www.lobster press.com. Estab. 1997. **Manuscript and Art Acquisitions:** Alison Fripp. Publishes 4 picture books/year; 1 young reader/year. 100% of books by first-time authors. "We publish quality books for children in English and French."

Fiction: Picture books: adventure, animal, contemporary, fantasy, history, humor, suspense/mystery. Young readers, middle readers: adventure, contemporary, fantasy, history, humor, suspense/mystery. Average word length: picture books—200-1,000.

Nonfiction: Picture books, young readers, middle readers: activity books, arts/crafts, geography, history, hobbies, how-to, nature/environment, sports, travel. Average word length: middle readers—40,000. Recently published *The Lobster Kids' Guide to Exploring Montréal*, by John Symon, illustrated by Christine Battuz.

How to Contact/Writers: Fiction: submit complete ms. Nonfiction: submit complete ms or submit outline/synopsis and 2 sample chapters. Reports on queries in 2-3 weeks; mss in 3-6 months. Publishes a book 18 months after acceptance.

Illustration: Works with 5 illustrators/year. Uses color artwork only. Reviews ms/illustration packages from artists. Query with samples. Contact: Alison Fripp, acquisitions editor. Illustrations only: query with samples. Contact: Alison Fripp, acquisitions editor. Reports only if interested. Samples not returned; samples kept on file.

Terms: Pays authors 5-10% royalty based on retail price. Offers advances (average amount: $600-750). Pays illustrators by the project (range: $500-1,500) or 2-7% royalty based on retail price. Sends galleys to authors; dummies to illustrators. Originals returned to artist at job's completion. Writer's and artist's guidelines available for SASE.

Tips: "Do not send manuscripts or samples registered mail or with fancy envelopes or bows and ribbons—everything is received and treated equally. Please do not call and ask for an appointment. We do not meet with anyone unless we are going to use their work."

LOTHROP, LEE & SHEPARD BOOKS, 1350 Avenue of the Americas, New York NY 10019. (212)261-6500. Fax: (212)261-6648. Website: http://www.williammorrow.com. An imprint of William Morrow Co. Inc., Children's Fiction and Nonfiction. **Manuscript Acquisitions:** Susan Pearson, editor-in-chief; Melanie Donovan, senior editor. **Art Acquisitions:** Art Director. Publishes 30 total titles/year. "Lothrop publishes almost solely picture books, with an emphasis on multicultural titles. No licensed products or merchandising."

• Lothrop, Lee & Shepard only accepts mss from agents and previously published authors.

Fiction: Picture books, young readers, middle readers: animal, history, poetry. Middle readers, young adults: folktales. All levels: multicultural. Recently published *The Secret Knowledge of Grown-Ups*, written and illustated by David Wisniewski (full-color picture book for ages 7 and up); *So Many Bunnies: A Bedtime ABC & Counting Book*, by Rick Walton, illustrated by Paige Miglio Blair (full-color picture book for ages 2 and up).

Nonfiction: All levels: biography, history, multicultural, nature/environment. Recently published *African Beginnings*, by James Haskins and Kathleen Benson, illustrated by Floyd Cooper (full-color picture book for all ages); *A World of Words: An ABC of Quotations*, by Tobi Tobias, illustrated by Peter Malone (full-color picture book for all ages).

How to Contact/Writers: Fiction/nonfiction: Prefers agented material, but will accept picture book mss and queries for novels and older nonfiction; "no unsolicited mss." Reports on queries in 1 month (longer for novels). Reports on mss in 2 months. Enclose SASE with submissions.

Illustration: Works with 25-30 illustrators/year. Editorial reviews ms/illustration packages from artists. Illustrations only: Query with samples; submit portfolio for review. Reports back only if interested. Samples returned with SASE; samples kept on file.

Photography: Purchases photos from freelancers. Buys stock and assigns work.

Terms: Payment terms vary with project. Royalties/advances negotiated.

Tips: Currently seeking unique picture books and imaginative nonfiction. "Multicultural books of all types" are popular right now. Does not want books written to fill a special need instead of from the writer's experience and personal conviction. Also does not want film scripts, cartoon merchandising ideas or pedantic books. Work should come from the heart.

LOWELL HOUSE JUVENILE/ROXBURY PARK JUVENILE, 2020 Avenue of the Stars, Suite 300, Los Angeles CA 90067. (310)552-7555. Fax: (310)552-7573. Book publisher, independent book producer/packager. **Manuscript Acquisitions:** Michael Artenstein, editor-in-chief, Roxbury Park Juvenile; Amy Downing, editor-in-chief, Lowell House Juvenile. **Art Acquisitions:** Shelly Pomeroy, Treesha Runnells and Bret Perry. Publishes 1-2 picture books/year; 30 young readers/year; 60 middle readers/year; 5 young adult titles/year. 25% of books by first-time authors. Lowell House Juvenile is best known for its trade workbooks, especially The Gifted & Talented series. Roxbury Park Juvenile specializes in middle grade fiction, and sports, science, and classics for midgraders and young adults.
- Lowell House does not accept mss. Instead they generate ideas inhouse then find writers to work on projects.

Fiction: Middle readers, young adults: adventure, anthology, contemporary, nature/environment, problem novels, multicultural, sports. Recently published *Qwan: the Showdown*, by A.L. Kim, cover art by Richard Kirk (ages 13 and up action novel); *Rafters*, by Nilsson Honnelly (ages 7-10, an adventure novel); *Classic Ghost Stories*; illustrated by Barbara Kiwak (ages 13 and up, collection of short scary stories); and *Shadows*, by Jonathan Schmidt (ages 10-14).

Nonfiction: Picture books, young readers: activity books, educational, arts/crafts. Middle readers: activity books, arts/crafts, social issues, multicultural, concept, cooking, geography, health, history, hobbies, reference, religion, science, sports. Young adult/teen: multicultural, reference, science social issues, sports. Recently published *The Ultimate Soccer Almanac*, by Dan Woog (ages 10 and up); *Gifted & Talented Counting Workbook for Preschoolers*, by Martha Cheney, illustrated by Treesha Runnells (ages 3-5); *Tutor Book: Letter Recognitioin*, by Melissa Del'Homme, illustrated by Kelly McMahon (ages 5-8).

How to Contact/Writers: Reports on queries/mss in 1 month.

Illustration: Works with 75 illustrators/year. Send samples to give a feel for style. Include sample drawings with kids in them. Illustrations only: arrange personal portfolio review; send promo sheet, portfolio, tearsheets. Reports back only if interested. Samples returned with SASE; files samples.

Photography: Buys stock and assigns work. "We're not looking for more photographers at this time."

Terms: Payment decided on project-by-project basis. Authors are paid $1,000-5,000 for outright purchase. Illustrators paid by the project ($100-1,000). Photographers paid by the project ($50-1,000).

Tips: "Send art: lots of drawings of kids, samples to keep on file. Don't be afraid to send b&w art—never see enough junior-high aged kids! Editorial: We are interested in writing samples to lead to future jobs, but we do not accept manuscripts, preferring to generate ideas ourselves."

THE LUTTERWORTH PRESS, Imprint of James Clarke & Co. Ltd., P.O. Box 60, Cambridge England CB1 2NT. (01223)3350865. Fax: (01223)366951. Book publisher. **Acquisitions:** Adrian Brink, managing director.

Fiction: Picture books, young readers, middle readers and young adults: adventure, animal, folktales, health, history, nature/environment, religion.

Nonfiction: Picture books, young readers, middle readers and young adults: activity books, animal, arts/crafts, history, nature/environment, religion, science.

How to Contact/Writers: Fiction/Nonfiction: Submit outline/synopsis and 1 or 2 sample chapters. Reports on queries in 2 weeks; ms in 6 months.

Illustration: Reviews ms illustration packages from authors. Submit ms with color or b&w copies of illustration. Illustration only: Query with samples. Reports in 2-3 weeks. Samples returned with SASE; samples filed.

Photography: "Occasionally" buys photos from freelancers. Send résumé and samples. Works on assignment only.

Terms: Royalty negotiable. Book catalog available for SAE.

MAGINATION PRESS, 750 First Street NE, Washington DC 20002. Book publisher. **Acquisitions:** Darcie Conner Johnston, managing editor. Publishes up to 15 picture books and young reader titles/year.

MARKET CONDITIONS are constantly changing! If you're still using this book and it is 2000 or later, buy the newest edition of *Children's Writer's & Illustrator's Market* at your favorite bookstore or order directly from Writer's Digest Books.

"We publish books dealing with the psycho/therapeutic treatment or resolution of children's serious problems and psychological issues, most written by mental health professionals."

- Magination Press was acquired by the American Psychological Association; it is now an imprint of the Educational Publishing Foundation of the APA.

Fiction: Picture books, young readers: concept, mental health, multicultural, special needs. Recently published *I Don't Have an Uncle Phil Anymore*, by Marjorie Pellegrino (ages 4-11); *Tibby Tried It*, by Sharon and Ernie Useman (ages 3-7); and *Sam and Gram and Their First Day of School*, by Dianne Blomberg (ages 4-6).

Nonfiction: Picture books, young readers: concept, mental health, how-to, multicultural, psychotherapy, special needs. Recently published *Help Is on The Way: A Book About ADD*, by Marc Nemiroff, illustrated by Margaret Scott (ages 5-9); and *My Parents Are Divorced Too*, by M., A. and S. Ford (ages 8-13).

How to Contact/Writers: Fiction/nonfiction: Submit complete ms. Reports on queries/mss: "up to four months (may be only days)." Publishes a book 1 year after acceptance.

Illustration: Works with 10-15 illustrators/year. Reviews ms/illustration packages. Will review artwork for future assignments.

How to Contact/Illustrators: Illustrations only: Query with samples. Original artwork returned at job's completion.

Terms: Pays authors 5-15% in royalties based on selling price. Pays illustrators by the project. Book catalog and ms guidelines on request with SASE.

☑ **McCLANAHAN BOOK COMPANY INC.**, 23 W. 26th St., New York NY 10010. (212)725-1515. Fax—editorial: (212)684-2785; art: (212)684-2785. E-mail: highq@mcclanahanbook.com. Book publisher. CEO: Susan McClanahan. **Manuscript Acquisitions:** Kenn Goin, editorial director. **Art Acquisitions:** Dave Werner, creative director. Publishes 90 picture books/year. Publishes "affordable, high quality mass market, with educational value, including activity books, concept storybooks, workbooks, nonfiction, baby/toddler concept books and novelty books.

Fiction: Mainly baby and toddler concept books, also nature, animal, history and sports. Generally no single-title fiction. Recently published *Goodnight, Baby*, by Elizabeth Hathon.

Nonfiction: Activity, concept, novelty, interactive. Picture books: career, arts/crafts, biography, history, nature, reference, science and sports. Recently published: *High Q™ Wipe off Books World Sticker Book*.

How to Contact/Writers: Query only. Reports on queries in 1 months. Ms guidelines available with SASE. Assignments to writers for projects originated inhouse.

Illustration: Works with up to 15 illustrators/photographers a year. Send samples, which will be returned with SASE and/or filed. Reports in 1 month.

Terms: Usually pays writers and illustrators/photographers on work-for-hire basis (flat fee by project). May pay small royalty for certain project originated by writer or artist. Artists' originals returned after job's completion.

MARGARET K. McELDERRY BOOKS, 1230 Sixth Ave., New York NY 10020. (212)698-2761. Fax: (212)698-2796. Website: http://www.simonsays.com/kidzone. Imprint of Simon & Schuster Children's Publishing Division. Editor at Large: Margaret K. McElderry. **Manuscript Acquisitions:** Emma Dryden, senior editor. **Art Acquisitions:** Ann Bobco, art director. Publishes 10-12 picture books/year; 2-4 young reader titles/year; 8-10 middle reader titles/year; and 5-7 young adult titles/year. 10% of books by first-time authors; 33% of books from agented writers. "Margaret K. McElderry Books publishes original hardcover trade books for children from pre-school age through young adult. This list includes picture books, easy-to-read books, fiction and non-fiction for eight to twelve-year-olds, poetry, fantasy and young adult fiction and non-fiction. The style and subject matter of the books we publish is almost unlimited. We do not publish textbooks, coloring and activity books, greeting cards, magazines and pamphlets or religious publications."

- Margaret K. McElderry Books not currently accepting unsolicited mss. Send queries only for picture books. Send queries and sample chapters for middle grade and young adult projects; also looking for strong poetry.

Fiction: Young readers: adventure, contemporary, fantasy, history. Middle readers: adventure, contemporary, fantasy, mystery. Young adults: contemporary, fantasy, mystery, poetry. "Always interested in publishing humorous picture books and original beginning reader stories. We see too many rhymed picture book manuscripts which are not terribly original or special." Average word length: picture books—500; young readers—2,000; middle readers—10,000-20,000; young adults—45,000-50,000. Recently published *Wow! It's Great Being a Duck*, by Joan Rankin; *The Old Cotton Blues*, by Linda England and Teresa Flavin; *The Exiles in Love*, by Hilary McKay.

Nonfiction: Young readers, young adult teens, biography, history. Average word length: picture books—500-1,000; young readers—1,500-3,000; middle readers—10,000-20,000; young adults—30,000-45,000.

Never Were Men So Brave: The Irish Brigade During the Civil War, by Susan Beller.

How to Contact/Writers: Fiction/nonfiction: Submit query and sample chapters with SASE; may also include brief résumé of previous publishing credits. Reports on queries in 2-3 weeks; mss in 3-4 months. Publishes a book 18 months after contract signing. Will consider simultaneous submissions (only if indicated as such).

Illustration: Works with 20-30 illustrators/year. Query with samples; provide promo sheet or tearsheets; arrange personal portfolio review. Contact: Ann Bobco, art director. Reports on art samples in 2-3 months. Samples returned with SASE or samples filed.

Terms: Pays authors royalty based on retail price. Pay illustrators royalty based on retail price. Pays photographers by the project. Sends galleys to authors; dummies to illustrators. Original artwork returned at job's completion. Ms guidelines free on request with SASE.

Tips: "We're looking for strong, original fiction. We are always interested in picture books for the youngest age reader."

☑ Ⓐ MEADOWBROOK PRESS, 5451 Smetana Dr., Minnetonka MN 55343. (612)930-1100. Fax: (612)930-1940. E-mail: meadowpr@bitsream.net. Book publisher. **Manuscript Acquisitions:** Heather Hooper, submissions editor. **Art Acquisitions:** Joe Gagne, art director. Publishes 1-2 middle readers/year; and 2-4 young readers/year. 20% of books by first-time authors; 10% of books from agented writers. Publishes children's activity books, gift books, humorous poetry anthologies and story anthologies.

- Meadowbrook does not accept unsolicited children's picture books or novels. They are primarily a nonfiction press. The publisher offers specific guidelines for various types of submissions (such as Newfangled Fairy Tales, poetry and Girls to the Rescue anthologies). Be sure to specify the type of project you have in mind when requesting guidelines.

Fiction: Young readers and middle readers: anthology, folktales, humor, multicultural, poetry. "Poems and short stories representing people of color encouraged." Published *The New Adventures of Mother Goose*; *Girls to the Rescue* (short stories featuring strong girls, for ages 8-12); and *A Bad Case of the Giggles* (children's poetry anthology).

Nonfiction: Young readers, middle readers: activity books, arts/crafts, cooking, hobbies, how-to, multicultural, self help. Multicultural needs include activity books representing traditions/cultures from all over the world, and especially fairy tale/folk tale stories with strong, multicultural heroines and diverse settings. "Books which include multicultural activities are encouraged." Average word length: varies. Recently published *Pick-a-Party Cookbook*, by Penny Warner; *Free Stuff for Kids* (activity book); and *Kids' Holiday Fun* (activity book).

How to Contact/Writers: Fiction/Nonfiction: Query or submit outline/synopsis or submit complete ms with SASE. Reports on queries/mss in 2-3 months. Publishes a book 1-2 years after acceptance. Send a business-sized SASE and 2 first-class stamps for free writer's guidelines and book catalog before submitting ideas. Will consider simultaneous submissions.

Illustration: Only interested in agented material. Works with 2-3 illustrators/year. Reviews ms/illustration packages from artists. Submit ms with 2-3 pieces of final art. Illustrations only: Submit résumé, promo sheet and tearsheets. Reports back only if interested. Samples not returned; samples filed.

Photography: Buys photos from freelancers. Buys stock and assigns work. Model/property releases required. Submit cover letter.

Terms: Pays authors in royalties of 5-7½% based on retail price. Offers average advance payment of $2,000-4,000. Pays for illustrators: $100-25,000; ¼-¾% of total royalties. Pays photographers per photo ($250). Originals returned at job's completion. Book catalog available for 5×11 SASE and 2 first-class stamps; ms guidelines and artists guidelines available for SASE.

Tips: "Illustrators and writers should send away for our free catalog and guidelines before submitting their work to us. Also, illustrators should take a look at the books we publish to determine whether their style is consistent with what we are looking for. Writers should also note the style and content patterns of our books. For instance, our children's poetry anthologies contain primarily humorous, rhyming poems with a strong rhythm; therefore, we would not likely publish a free-verse and/or serious poem. I also recommend that writers, especially poets, have their work read by a critical, objective person before they submit anywhere. Also, please correspond with us by mail before telephoning with questions about your submission. We work with the printed word and will respond more effectively to your questions if we have something in front of us."

☑ ▥ ❖ MEGA-BOOKS, INC., 240 E. 60th St., New York NY 10022. (212)355-6200. Fax: (212)355-6303. President: John Craddock. **Acquisitions:** John Krieger. Book packager/producer. Produces trade paperback and mass market paperback originals and fiction and nonfiction for the educational market. Works with first-time authors, established authors and unagented writers.

- Mega-Books does not accept unsolicited mss.

Fiction: Young adult: mystery. Recently published Nancy Drew and Hardy Boys series; Pocahontas and The Lion King books (Disney).
How to Contact/Writers: Submit résumé, publishing history and clips.
Terms: Work purchased outright for $3,000 and up. Offers average 50% advance.
Tips: "Please be sure to obtain a current copy of our writers' guidelines before writing."

MERIWETHER PUBLISHING LTD., 885 Elkton Dr., Colorado Springs CO 80907-3557. Fax: (719)594-9916. E-mail: meriwthpub@aol.com. Book publisher. Estab. 1969. Executive Editor: Arthur L. Zapel. **Manuscript Acquisitions:** Ted Zapel, educational drama; Rhonda Wray, religious drama. "We do most of our artwork in-house; we do not publish for the children's elementary market." 75% of books by first-time authors; 5% of books from agented writers. "Our niche is drama. Our books cover a wide variety of theatre subjects from play anthologies to theatrecraft. We publish books of monologs, duologs, short one-act plays, scenes for students, acting textbooks, how-to speech and theatre textbooks, improvisation and theatre games. We also publish some general humor trade books. Our Christian books cover worship on such topics as clown ministry, storytelling, banner-making, drama ministry, children's worship and more. We also publish anthologies of Christian sketches. We do not publish works of fiction or devotionals."
Fiction: Middle readers, young adults: anthology, contemporary, humor, religion. "We publish plays, not prose-fiction."
Nonfiction: Middle readers: activity books, how-to, religion, textbooks. Young adults: activity books, drama/theater arts, how-to church activities, religion. Average length: 250 pages. Recently published *Perspectives*, by Mary Krell-Oishi (a book of scenes for teenage actors); and *Fool of the Kingdom*, by Philip Noble (a book on clown ministry).
How to Contact/Writers: Nonfiction: Query or submit outline/synopsis and sample chapters. Reports on queries in 2 weeks; mss in 6-8 weeks. Publishes a book 6-12 months after acceptance. Will consider simultaneous submissions.
Illustration: Works with 2 illustrators/year. Reviews ms/illustration packages from artists. Query first. Illustrations only: Query with samples; send résumé, promo sheet or tearsheets. Reports on art samples in 6-8 weeks. Samples returned with SASE. Samples kept on file. Originals returned at job's completion.
Terms: Pays authors in royalties of 10% based on retail or wholesale price. Outright purchase $200-1,000. Pays for illustrators by the project (range: $50-2,000); royalties based on retail or wholesale price. Sends galleys to authors. Book catalog for SAE and $2 postage; ms guidelines for SAE and 1 first-class stamp.
Tips: "We are currently interested in finding unique treatments for theater arts subjects: scene books, how-to books, monologs and short plays for teens."

MILKWEED EDITIONS, 430 First Ave. North, Suite 400, Minneapolis MN 55401-1743. (612)332-3192. Fax: (612)332-6248. Book Publisher. Estab. 1980. **Manuscript Acquisitions:** Emilie Buchwald, publisher; Elizabeth Fitz, manuscript coordinator. **Art Acquisitions:** Beth Olson. Publishes 3-4 middle readers/year. 25% of books by first-time authors. "Milkweed Editions publishes with the intention of making a humane impact on society, in the belief that literature is a transformative art uniquely able to convey the essential experiences of the human heart and spirit. To that end, Milkweed Editions publishes distinctive voices of literary merit in handsomely designed, visually dynamic books, exploring the ethical, cultural, and esthetic issues that free societies need continually to address."
Fiction: Middle readers: adventure, animal, contemporary, fantasy, humor, multicultural, nature/environment, suspense/mystery. Does not want to see anthologies, folktales, health, hi-lo, picture books, poetry, religion, romance, sports. Average length: middle readers—90-200 pages. Recently published *The Dog with Golden Eye*, by Frances Wilbur (middle reader, adventure/nature, comtemporary); and *The Treasures of Pawther Peak*, by Aileen Kilgore Henderson (middle reader, adventure/contemporary, nature).
How to Contact/Writers: Fiction: Submit complete ms. Reports on mss in 2-6 months. Publishes a book 1 year after acceptance. Will consider simultaneous submissions.
Illustration: Works with 2-4 illustrators/year. Reviews ms/illustration packages from artists. Query; submit ms with dummy. Illustrations only: Query with samples; provide résumé, promo sheet, slides, tearsheets and client list. Samples filed or returned with SASE; samples filed. Originals returned at job's completion.
Terms: Pays authors royalty of 7½% based on retail price. Offers advance against royalties. Illustrators contracts are decided on an individual basis. Sends galleys to authors. Book catalog available for $1.50 to cover postage; ms guidelines available for SASE. Must include SASE with ms submission for its return.

☑ **THE MILLBROOK PRESS**, 2 Old New Milford Rd., Brookfield CT 06804. (203)740-2220. Fax: (203)775-5643. Book publisher. Estab. 1989. **Manuscript Acquisitions:** Meghann French, manuscript coordinator. **Art Acquisitions:** Judie Mills, art director. Publishes 20 picture books/year; 40 young readers/year; 50 middle readers/year; and 10 young adult titles/year. 10% of books by first-time authors; 20% of

INSIDER REPORT

Ta-da! Publisher-magician's secrets revealed!

Bruce Lansky has four books that have sold over a million copies, a TV series in the works and an upcoming, sure-to-be-mega-hit poetry book. Plus, he's editor and publisher of Meadowbrook Press, whose book list has one bestseller after another. How does he create such success? Magic!

Lansky identifies magic as a great book read by a child comfy in his pajamas and so swept away in the story the toothpaste still dangles from his chin and mom's cries of "Lights out!" fall upon deaf ears. "Most writers don't think of themselves as magicians, but that's the deal," says Lansky.

Bruce Lansky

"There are two key concepts in developing a big seller," Lansky says. "One, you need a big idea or concept; and two, you need to execute it better than anyone else."

So, what is this big idea and how do you find it? The big idea is the trick no one has pulled off—yet. Finding it could be as easy as a trip to a library or bookstore. See what's hot and brainstorm. While browsing, Lansky urges writers to figure out what's missing on the shelves and then go home and make it appear. "Look at what's out there and figure out how to do it better. Can you make a book that's funnier, scarier or more reader-friendly?"

Once you've got a show-stopper idea, it's time to write and rewrite. Lansky has perfected what he terms the write-feedback-rewrite model. "We set up a fairly elaborate testing process," he says. His model includes teachers reading and students critiquing and grading his work. This has made his poetry book, *A Bad Case of The Giggles*, flawless. "If a poem has a faulty rhythm, the reader will stumble and the poem will die."

This feedback enables Lansky to ditch what's not working and perfect what is. Because of this testing on kids, Lansky says, "I've gone from the world's worst poet to the world's most consistent poet."

Lansky is consistently funny because of his fine-tuning and only keeping the cream of the crop. Through this sifting process he ends up trashing 90% of his work and, according to the readers' grades, leaving 10% of pure magic. "Ultimately, I'm in the business of pleasing kids."

Beginning writers can find themselves pleasing kids and editors with three other tricks Lansky has up his sleeve:

• Trick 1: Beginning writers can create their own feedback system. "As a beginner, simply go to your child's class and read your stuff and get responses." No kids? Lansky suggests volunteering as storyteller at any bookstore, daycare or church. There is a word of caution with this method. "If a writer is performing her own work, half of the success comes from her performance. Try to test in a way that's neutral."

INSIDER REPORT, *Lansky*

• Trick 2: Copy off your story. "Select five to ten kids who can distinguish between good and bad and act as critics. Ask what they do and don't like. That's how you learn."

• Trick 3: Test your story, poem, or essay against the best that is out there and make sure yours wins.

Once the tricks have been performed and the responses are in, act on them. Lansky says "tweaking" your manuscript will have editors responding. "The only way you can get attention to your book is if every single element is great—every word, every comma. Make everything better than it's ever been done before.

"A good editor is just waiting for a great book. There are never enough great books. If you're providing the great stuff, then your career is made in the shade! If you're providing what kids want—you win!

"Even though it's just a manuscript you want the reader magically wafted away to your fictional image," Lansky says. So don't settle for mediocrity. "Have amazingly high sights. Keep writing and testing and asking, 'Is this the stuff that resonates magic?'"

It's this quest that keeps Lansky successfully directed. Receiving teachers' comments like, "My kids love your books," and "My kids fight over your books," is the trick that Lansky feels is most rewarding. "I'm not yet the best-selling children's poet, but I like knowing I knock kids out. I magically turn nonreaders into readers."

—*Tricia Branson*

Illustrations © Joy Allen. Reprinted with permission of Meadowbrook Press.

Successful Meadowbrook series like *Newfangled Fairy Tales* and *Girls to the Rescue* are the result of editor/author/ publisher Bruce Lansky's research into what's missing in the market. "The vast majority of fairy tales and folk tales present boys as heroes and girls as wimps," he says. "Girls need to read stories presenting positive female role models, too." Lansky urges writers to look for voids in children's publishing—and fill them.

books from agented authors. Publishes nonfiction, concept-oriented/educational books. Publishes under Twenty-First Century Books imprint also.

Fiction: Picture books: concept. Young adults: history.

Nonfiction: All levels: animal, arts/craft, biography, cooking, geography, how-to, multicultural, music/dance, nature/environment, reference, science. Picture books: activity books, concept, hi-lo. Middle readers: hi-lo, social issues, sports. Young adults: careers, social issues. No poetry. Average word length: picture books—minimal; young readers—5,000; middle readers—10,000; young adult/teens—20,000. Published *Dandelion Adventures*, by Patricia L. Kite (grades PreK-1, picture book); *Love and Marriage Around the World*, by Carol Gelber (grades 4-6, history); and *Our Changing Constitution*, by Isobel V. Morin (grades 7 and up, history).

How to Contact/Writers: Query with outline/synopsis and 1 sample chapter. Reports on queries/mss in 1 month.

Illustration: Work with 75 illustrators/year. Reviews ms/illustration packages from artists. Query; submit 1 chapter of ms with 1 piece of final art. Illustrations only: Query with samples; provide résumé, business card, promotional literature or tearsheets to be kept on file. Samples returned with SASE; samples filed. Reports back only if interested.

Photography: Buys photos from freelancers. Buys stock and assigns work.

Terms: Pays author royalty of 5-7½% based on wholesale price or work purchased outright. Offers advances. Pays illustrators by the project, royalty of 3-7% based on wholesale price. Sends galleys to authors. Book catalog, ms and artist's guidelines for SASE.

MIRACLE SOUND PRODUCTIONS, INC., 1560 W. Bay Area Blvd., Suite 110, Friendswood TX 77546-2668. (281)286-4575. Fax: (281)286-0009. E-mail: cdsimsw@ghg.net. Book publisher. **Acquisitions:** Trey Boring, director of special projects. Estab. 1997. Publishes 2 young readers/year. 100% of books by first-time authors. Miracle Sound Productions is best known for "positive family values in multimedia products."

Fiction: Young readers. Average word length: young readers—500. Recently published *CoCo's Luck*, by Warren Chaney and Don Boyer (ages 3-8, Read-A-Long book and tape).

Illustration: Only interested in agented material. Works with 1 illustrator/year. Uses color artwork only. Reviews ms/illustration packages from artists. Submit ms with dummy. Contact: Trey W. Boring, director, special projects. Illustrations only: Send résumé and portfolio to be kept on file.

Photography: Works on assignment only. Contact: Trey W. Boring, director, special projects.

Terms: Payment negotiable for authors, illustrators and photographers.

MITCHELL LANE PUBLISHERS, INC., 17 Matthew Bathon Court, Elkton MD 21921-3669. (410)392-5036. Fax: (410)392-4781. E-mail: mitchelllane@dpnet.net. Website: http://www.angelfire.com/biz/mitchelllane/index.html. Book publisher. **Acquisitons:** Barbara Mitchell, president. Publishes 6-12 young adult titles/year. "We publish authorized multicultural biographies of role models for children and young adults."

Nonfiction: Young readers, middle readers, young adults: biography, multicultural. Average word length: 4,000-50,000 words. Recently published *Selena*, by Barbara Marvis; *Robert Rodriguez*; and *Mariah Carey* (grades K-4, all real-life reader biographies for grades K-4); and *Rafael Palmeiro: At Home with the Baltimore Orioles*, by Ed Brandt (ages 11 and up).

How to Contact/Writers: Nonfiction: Query or submit outline/synopsis and 3 sample chapters. Reports on queries only if interested. Publishes a book 18 months after acceptance.

Illustration: Works with 2-3 illustrators/year. Reviews ms/illustration packages from artists. Query; arrange portfolio review, including color copies of work. Illustration only: query with samples; arrange personal portfolio review; send résumé, portfolio, slides, tearsheets. Reports back only if interested. Samples not returned; samples filed.

Photography: Buys stock images. Needs photos of famous and prominent minority figures. Captions required. Uses b&w prints. Submit cover letter, résumé, published samples, stock photo list.

Terms: Pays authors 5-10% royalty based on wholesale price or work purchased outright for $250-2,000. Pays illustrators by the project (range: $40-250). Sends galleys to authors.

Tips: "Most of our assignments are work-for-hire. Submit résumé and samples of work to be considered for future assignments."

MONDO PUBLISHING, One Plaza Rd., Greenvale NY 11548. (516)484-7812. Fax: (516)484-7813. Website: http://www.mondopub.com. Book publisher. **Acquisitions:** Louise May, senior editor. Publishes 60 picture and chapter books/year. 10% of books by first-time authors. Publishes various categories. "Our motto is 'creative minds creating ways to create lifelong readers.' We publish for both educational and trade markets, aiming for the highest quality books for both."

Fiction: Picture books, young readers, middle readers: adventure, animal, contemporary, fantasy, folktales, history, humor, multicultural, nature/environment, poetry, sports. Multicultural needs include: stories about children in different cultures or about children of different backgrounds in a U.S. setting. Recently published *Lucy Takes a Holiday*, by Salvatore Murdocca (ages 5-10); and *Twiddle Twins* series by Howard Goldsmith (ages 6-10, adventure chapter books).

Nonfiction: Picture books, young readers, middle readers: animal, biography, geography, how-to, multicultural, nature/environment, science, sports. Recently published *Up and Away!*, by Meredith Davis (ages 6-10, technology); and *Thinking About Ants*, by Barbara Brenner (ages 5-10, animals).

How to Contact/Writers: Fiction/Nonfiction: Query or submit complete ms. Reports on queries in 1 month; mss in 6 months. Will consider simultaneous submissions. Mss returned with SASE. Queries must also have SASE.

Illustration: Works with 40 illustrators/year. Reviews ms/illustration packages from illustrators. Illustration only: Query with samples, résumé, portfolio. Reports only if interested. Samples returned with SASE; samples filed.

Photography: Occasionally uses freelance photographers. Buys stock images. Uses mostly nature photos. Uses color prints, transparencies.

Terms: Pays authors royalty of 2-5% based on wholesale/retail price. Offers advance based on project. Pays illustrators by the project (range: 3,000-9,000), royalty of 2-4% based on retail price. Pays photographers by the project or per photo. Sends galleys to authors depending on project. Originals returned to artists at job's completion. Book catalogs available for 9 × 12 SASE with $3 postage.

Tips: "Prefer illustrators with book experience or a good deal of experience in illustration projects requiring consistency of characters and/or setting over several illustrations. Prefer manuscripts targeted to trade market plus crossover to educational market."

MOREHOUSE PUBLISHING CO., 4775 Linglestown Rd., Harrisburg PA 17112. (717)541-8130. Fax: (717)541-8136. Book publisher. Estab. 1884. Publisher: Harold Rast. **Manuscript Acquisitions:** Debra Farrington, editorial director. **Art Acquisitions:** Valerie Gittings, managing editor. Publishes 4 picture books/year. 25% of books by first-time authors. "Morehouse is a publisher and provider of books, church curricula, church resources materials and communications services for the Episcopal Church and other mainline church groups and organizations."

Fiction: Picture Books: spirituality, religion. Wants to see new and creative approaches to theology for children. Recently published *Elizabeth's Beauty*, by Nancy Markham Alberts, illustrated by Pat Skiles.

Nonfiction: Picture Books: religion, craft-related. Recently published *Make Five Bible Models*, by Gordon and Charlotte Stowell.

How to Contact/Writers: Fiction/nonfiction: Submit outline/synopsis and sample chapters. Reports on queries in 2 weeks; mss in 2-4 weeks. Publishes a book 2 years after acceptance.

Illustration: Works with 2-3 illustrators/year. Reviews ms/illustration packages from artists. Submit 3 chapters of ms with 1 piece of final art. Illustrations only: Submit résumé, tearsheets. Reports on art samples in 2 weeks. Samples returned with SASE; samples filed.

Terms: Pays authors royalty based on net price. Offers modest advance payment. Pays illustrators royalty based on net price. Sends galleys to authors. Original artwork returned at job's completion. Book catalog free on request if SASE ($2 postage) is supplied.

Tips: "Morehouse Publishing seeks books that wrestle with important theological questions in words and story that children can understand."

MORGAN REYNOLDS PUBLISHING, 620 S. Elm St., Suite 384, Greensboro NC 27406. (910)275-1311. Fax: (910)274-3705. E-mail: anita@morganreynolds.com. Website: http://www.morganreynolds.com. **Acquisitions:** John Riley, editor. Book publisher. Publishes 12 young adult titles/year. 50% of books by first-time authors.

• Morgan Reynolds has added two new series: Makers of the Media and Women in Sciences, directed toward the YA reader.

Fiction: Middle readers, young adults/teens: history, religion, sports.

Nonfiction: Middle readers, young adults/teens: biography, history, multicultural, social issues, sports. Multicultural needs include Native American, African-American and Latino subjects. Average word length: 12,000-20,000. Recently published *Tiger Woods*, by Aaron Boyd; *Myra Bradwell: First Woman Lawyer*, by Nancy Whitelaw; and *The Ordeal of Olive Oatman: A True Story of the American West*, by Margaret Rau.

How to Contact/Writers: Prefers to see entire ms. Query; submit outline/synopsis with 3 sample chapters. Reports on queries in 1 month; mss in 1-2 months. Publishes a book 9 months after acceptance. Will consider simultaneous submissions.

Terms: Pays authors royalty of 8-12% based on wholesale price. Offers advances. Sends galleys to authors.

"Quirky and fun, with great humor in the details" is how senior editor Louise May at Mondo Publishing describes the work of children's illustrator and author Salvatore Murdocca. This illustration was taken from the book *Lucy Takes a Holiday*, which was written and illustrated by Murdocca. May had known Murdocca's work for many years before she met him. "The manuscript originally came through an agent, but then I met Sal at a conference, and we continued to refine the project over the course of many months. Eventually, the project became a reality."

Book catalog available for business-size SAE with 1 first-class stamp; ms guidelines available for SASE. **Tips:** "We are open to suggestions—if you have an idea that excites you send it along. Recent trends suggest that the field is open for younger, smaller companies. Writers, especially ones starting out, should search us out."

WILLIAM MORROW AND CO., 1350 Avenue of the Americas, New York NY 10019. (212)261-6500. See listings for Beech Tree Books, Greenwillow Books, Lothrop, Lee & Shepard Books and Morrow Junior Books.

☑ **MORROW JUNIOR BOOKS**, 1350 Avenue of the Americas, New York NY 10019. Website: http://www.williammorrow.com. "Morrow is one of the nation's leading publishers of books for children, including bestselling fiction and nonfiction." **Acquisitions**: Barbara Lalicki, editor-in-chief; Meredith Carpenter, executive editor; Andrea Curley, senior editor. Publishes 50 titles/year.
   • Morrow Junior accepts only mss from agents or previously published authors.
Fiction: Recently published *Rumpelstiltskin's Daughter*, by Diane Stanley; *Engelbert Joins the Circus*, by Tom Paxton, illustrated by Roberta Wilson; and *Flood*, by Mary Calhoun, illustrated by Erick Ingraham.
Nonfiction: Recently published *I'm a Big Brother, I'm a Big Sister*, by Joanna Cole, illustrated by Maxie Chambliss; and The honey Makers, by Gail Gibbons (nature).
How to Contact/Writers: Query.
Terms: Offers variable advance. All contracts negotiated individually. Book catalog and guidelines available for 9×12 SAE with 3 first-class stamps.

Ⓝ **MOUNT OLIVE COLLEGE PRESS**, 634 Henderson St., Mount Olive NC 28365. (919)658-2502. Book publisher. Estab. 1990. **Acquisitions:** Pepper Worthington, editor. Publishes 1 middle reader/year. 85% of books by first-time authors.
Fiction: Middle readers: animal, humor, poetry. Average word length: middle readers—3,000 words.
Nonfiction: Middle readers: nature/environment, religion, self help. Average word length: middle readers—3,000 words.
How to Contact/Writers: Submit complete ms or outline/synopsis and 3 sample chapters. Reports on queries in 6-12 months. Publishes a book 1 year after acceptance.
Illustration: Uses b&w artwork only. Submit ms with 50% of final art. Contact: Pepper Worthington, editor. Reports in 6-12 months if interested. Samples not returned.
Terms: Payment negotiated individually. Book catalog available for SAE and 1 first-class stamp.

☑ **TOMMY NELSON**, Imprint of Thomas Nelson, Inc., 404 BNA Dr., Bldg. 200, Suite 508, Nashville TN 37217. (615)889-9000. Fax: (615)902-2415. Book publisher. **Acquisitions Editor:** Laura Minchew. Publishes 15 picture books/year; 20 young readers/year; and 25 middle readers/year. Evangelical Christian publisher.
Fiction: Picture books: concept, humor, religion. Young readers: adventure, concept, humor, religion. Middle readers: adventure, humor, religion, sports, suspense/mystery. Young adults: adventure, problem novels, religion, sports, suspense/mystery. Recently published *Mountain Magic*, by Alice Boggs Lentz, illustrated by David Griffin (picture book for ages 3-7); The Sports Mystery Series, by Sigmund Brouwer (ages 10-14); and The Winning Edge Series, by Lynn Kirby (ages 10-14).
Nonfiction: Picture books, young readers: activity books, religion, self help. Middle readers, young adults: reference, religion, self help. Recently published *My Faith Journal*, by Karen Hill, illustrated by Bobby Gombert (ages 6-12); *Genesis For Kids*, by Rick Osbourne (ages 8-14); and *The Children's Bible Story Book*, retold by Anne Degraff (ages 3-11).
How to Contact/Writers: Does not accept unsolicited mss, queries or proposals.
Illustration: Reviews ms/illustration packages from artists. Query with samples. Reports back only if interested. Samples filed. Contact: Karen Phillips, art director.
Terms: Pays authors royalty of 5% based on wholesale price or work purchased outright. Offers advances of $1,000 and up. Pays illustrators by the project or royalty.
Tips: "Know the CBA market—and avoid preachiness."

☑ **NEW HOPE**, Imprint of Women's Missionary Union, P.O. Box 12065, Birmingham AL 35202-2065. (205)991-8100. Website: http://www.newhopepubl.com. Book publisher. **Acquisitions:** Leslie Caldwell,

---

VISIT THE WRITER'S DIGEST WEBSITE at http://www.writersdigest.com for hot new markets, daily market updates, writers' guidelines and much more.

INSIDER REPORT

Teaching children spirituality through picture books

From the time Debra Farrington was getting her first skinned knees and sporting front-toothless grins, she knew books ruled her world. "I read constantly as a child," says Farrington, who won a creative writing award in high school. She found a perfect fit when she got a job in college at her college bookstore. "I stayed in bookstores for the next 20 years."

Farrington concluded her two-decade stint managing The Graduate Theological Union Bookstore, the largest theological bookstore in the West, when Morehouse Publishing snatched her away. Given the position as Editorial Director, Farrington enacted change. "We've gone from publishing one or two children's books to four or five picture books a year," she says.

Debra Farrington

One of Farrington's first jobs when she entered her position at Morehouse was to determine what was working and what wasn't. "I discovered that we did very well with the overtly religious books, and other books (based on good values, but not specifically religious) did much less well," so knowing what direction to go was an easy decision. "I decided to pursue the kind of book that was meeting the needs of our primary market, which is religious." Farrington also chose to focus on picture books for children ages three to seven, which had always sold best for Morehouse.

With the focus in place, Farrington encourages writers to submit books "of solid theology written in language children can understand, embedded in a really good story that engages children and adults alike. After all the adults buy the children's books, so you have to capture them first.

"We are looking for stories that teach children about prayer and spirituality, about God's work in the world, about our traditions and heritage. The books must be innovative and creative. We would rather publish two really wonderful children's books a year than five or six mediocre ones," says Farrington. "So many children's books are simply moralistic and pedagogical and that doesn't hold the interest of a child for very long. The message of the book cannot overwhelm the story itself."

Farrington also advises writers not to be afraid to really deal with children's questions and take them seriously. "Children want good solid engagement with their concerns. And an honest, 'We don't know the answer to that' is better than a trumped-up sweet response that tells them nothing."

Remember the old adage "show, don't tell," she says. "Make sure the story brings pictures into the head of the reader—in other words, it has to be 'illustrate-able.' There need to be scene changes, and action and such that an illustrator can work with."

Farrington encourages writers to research before submitting. "Spend time reading

INSIDER REPORT, *Farrington*

what's already out there in the children's market. A great deal of what I receive has already been written many times. I must get one or two manuscripts on death a week, but unless they are better than the books already doing very well in this field, I'm not going to look at them for more than a few moments. Make your manuscript unique and compelling, rather than something that has been done many times already.

"Think through your theology very clearly. Theology is a tricky thing, and it is hard to convey it clearly and helpfully to children. Make sure you think through the implications of your story and don't inadvertently teach something that may be very harmful to children." For instance, if you want to teach that God answers prayers, what will happen to the child who prays and "nothing happens?" Does that mean God doesn't like that particular child? Or that the child prayed incorrectly?

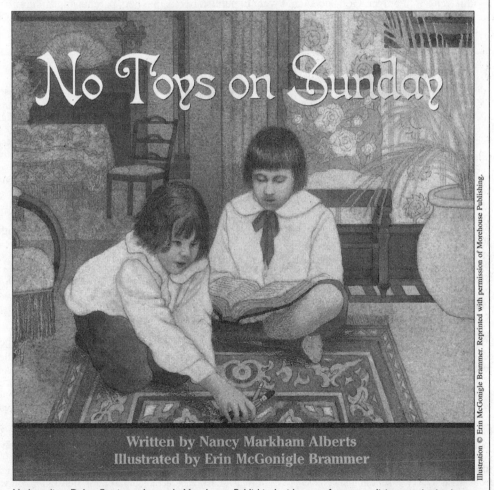

No Toys on Sunday

Written by Nancy Markham Alberts
Illustrated by Erin McGonigle Brammer

Illustration © Erin McGonigle Brammer. Reprinted with permission of Morehouse Publishing.

Under editor Debra Farrington's watch, Morehouse Publishing's titles now focus on religious stories in picture book form, the two areas that have been most successful for the company. "We are looking for stories that teach children about prayer and spirituality, about God's work in the world, about our traditions and heritage," she says. *No Toys on Sunday*, the story of two boys whose strict parents forbid then to play with toys on Sunday (and how they solved the problem), typifies the type of books in their line.

INSIDER REPORT, *continued*

"I think [books on] prayer and spirituality have lots of space for growth at the moment," says Farrington. "There are lots of books of prayers, but not many good books that actually help children learn to pray. We are dealing with the children of baby boomers right now, and it's important to keep in mind that the boomers are the ones who are buying spirituality books by the handful. They want books that help them explain their own searching and questions to their children. I want to see more books that really explore prayer—how to do it, how we understand it—and even books on prayer and healing and the other things that are capturing the adult market."

Most important to Farrington is the family closeness that her picture books can create. "I think parents want to talk with their children about religion and spirituality, but many of them have been away from church for decades and they don't know how to talk to children about prayer, God and such. I want to publish books that help parents and children have those conversations."

—Tricia Branson

editorial specialist. Publishes 2-3 picture books/year; 1-2 young readers/year; and 1-2 middle readers/year. 75% of books by first-time authors. "Our goal is to provide missions-related programs, information, resources and training to motivate and enable churches and believers to meet spiritual, physical and social needs, locally and globally."

Fiction: All levels: multicultural, religion. Multicultural fiction must be related to Christian concepts, particularly Christian missions. Recently published *The Elephant Path*, by Judy Langley, illustrated by Wendy Kikugawa (picture book, preschool).

Nonfiction: All levels: multicultural, religion. Multicultural nonfiction must be related to Christian concepts, particularly Christian missions.

How to Contact/Writers: Submit complete ms. Reports on queries in 1 month; mss in 1-3 months. Publishes a book 2 years after acceptance. Will consider simultaneous submissions.

Illustration: Works with 2-3 illustrators/year. Reviews ms/illustration packages from artists. Send ms with dummy. Illustrations only: query with samples (color copies). Reports back only if interested. Samples not returned; samples filed.

Photography: Buy stock already on file. Model/property releases required.

Terms: Pays authors royalty of 7-10% based on retail price or work purchased outright (depends on length). Pays illustrators by the project. Sends galleys to author. Originals returned to artist at job's completion. Book catalog available for 10 × 12 SAE and 3 first-class stamps; ms guidelines for SASE.

Tips: "Obtain the catalog first to see the kinds of material we publish."

NORTH WORD PRESS, Creative Publishing International, 5900 Green Oak Dr., Minnetonka MN 55343. (612)936-4700. Fax: (612)932-0380. Estab. 1985. Publishes 2-3 picture books/year; 4-6 middle readers/year. 60% of books by first time authors.

Nonfiction: Picture books, middle readers: animal, nature/environment. Average word length: picture books—900; middle readers—3,000. Recently published *Foxes for Kids*, by Shuler (ages 8-12); *Children of the Earth . . . Remember*, by Schimmel (all ages); and *Wildflowers, Blooms & Blossoms*, by Burns (ages 8-12).

How to Contact/Writers: Nonfiction: query or submit complete ms. Reports on queries and ms in 3 months. Publishes a book 1 year after acceptance. Will consider simultaneous submissions and previously published work.

Illustration: Works with 2-3 illustrators/year. Uses color artwork only. Reviews ms/illustration packages from artists. Query or submit ms with 4-5 pieces of final art. Contact: acquisitions editor. Illustrations only: query with samples. Contact: acquisitions editor. Reports in 3 months. Samples returned with SASE; samples kept on file.

Photography: Buys stock. Contact: photo researcher. Uses nature and wildlife images. Model/property releases required; captions required. Uses 35mm, 2¼ × 2¼ and 4 × 5 color transparencies. Submit cover letter, resume, slides and stock photo list.

Terms: Pays authors royalty based on wholesale price. Offers advances. Pays illustrators by the project.

Pays photographer by the project or by the photo. Send galleys to authors; dummies to illustrators. Originals returned to artist at job's completion. Book catalog available for 9 × 12 SAE and 7 first-class stamps; ms and art guidelines available for SASE. All imprints included in a single catalog.

NORTHLAND PUBLISHING, P.O. Box 1389, Flagstaff AZ 86002-1389. (520)774-5251. Fax: (520)774-0592. E-mail: editorial@northlandpub.com. Website: http://www.northlandpub.com. Book publisher. **Manuscript Acquisitions:** Aimee Jackson, children's associate editor. **Art Acquisitions:** Jennifer Schaber, art director. Publishes 10-12 picture books/year; 4-6 middle-reader novels. 50% of books by first-time authors. "Our goal for Rising Moon is to expand into new genres with titles that have mainstream and national appeal."
Fiction: Picture books, young readers: folktales, humor, contemporary. Middle readers: adventure, contemporary, suspense/mystery. All levels: history, nature/environment, multicultural. "Multicultural needs include stories with characters/plots that have to do with multicultural aspects of Hispanic and Native Americans. No religion, science fiction, anthology. Average word length: picture books—800; young readers—1,500; middle readers—20,000. Recently published *A Campfire for Cowboy Billy*, by Wendy K. Ulmer, illustrated by Kenneth S. Spengler (picture book, (ages 5-8); *Jack and the Giant: A Story Full of Beans*, by Jim Harris (picture book, ages 5-8).
Nonfiction: Picture books, young readers: activity books, concept, animal, multicultural. Middle readers: arts/crafts, biography, cooking, history. Average word length: picture books—800; young readers—1,500; middle readers—20,000.
How to Contact/Writers: Reports on queries/mss in 3-6 months. "Acknowledgment sent immediately upon receipt." If ms and art are complete at time of acceptance, publication usually takes 2-3 years. Will consider simultaneous submissions if labelled as such. "We accept all unsolicited picture book submissions, but only agented submissions for juvenile novels."
Illustration: Works with 10-12 illustrators/year. Uses color artwork only. Reviews ms/illustration packages from artists. Submit ms with samples; slides or color photocopies. Illustrations only: Query art director with samples, promo sheet, slides, tearsheets. Samples returned with SASE; samples filed.
Terms: Pays authors advance and royalty. Pays illustrators advance and royalty, or flat fee.
Tips: "No phone, fax or e-mail queries or submissions. Follow standard submission guidelines carefully (check SCBWI if unsure how to submit manuscripts). Accepts unsolicited picture books, but will only accept juvenile novels from previous, or agented authors. Especially looking for contemporary stories with humor and message."

Ⓐ **NORTH-SOUTH BOOKS**, 1123 Broadway, Suite 800, New York NY 10010. (212)463-9736. Website: http://www.northsouth.com. **Acquisitions:** Marc Cheshire, president, publisher and art director. U.S. office of Nord-Siid Verlag, Switzerland. Publishes 75 titles/year; 25 acquired through U.S. office.
Fiction: Picture books.
Nonfiction: Publishes nonfiction occasionally.
How to Contact/Writers: Only interested in agented material.
Illustration: Uses artists for picture book illustration.
Terms: Pays authors and illustrators advance and royalties.

THE OLIVER PRESS, INC., Charlotte Square, 5707 W. 36th St., Minneapolis MN 55416. Phone: (612)926-8981. Fax: (612)926-8965. E-mail: theoliverpress@mindspring.com. Website: http://www.mindspring.com/~theoliverpress. Book publisher. **Acquisitions:** Denise Sterling, Teresa Faden, Pete Pawelski. Publishes 8 young adult titles/year. 10% of books by first-time authors. "We publish collective biographies of people who made an impact in one area of history, including science, government, archaeology, business and crime. Titles from The Oliver Press can connect young adult readers with their history to give them the confidence that only knowledge can provide. Such confidence will prepare them for the lifelong responsibilities of citizenship. Our books will introduce students to people who made important discoveries and great decisions."
Nonfiction: Middle reader, young adults: biography, history, multicultural, science, history of science and technology. "Authors should only suggest ideas that fit into one of our existing series. We would like to add to our Innovators series on the history of technology." Average word length: young adult—20,000 words. Recently published *Legendary Labor Leaders*, by Nathan Aaseng (ages 10 and up, collective biography); *Women in Medicine*, by Jacqueline C. Kent (ages 10 and up, collective biography); *Communications: Sending the Message*, by Thomas Streissgath (ages 10 and up, collective biography); and *Aviation: Reaching for the Sky*, by Don Berliner (ages 10 and up, collective biography).
How to Contact/Writers: Nonfiction: Query with outline/synopsis. Reports in 6 months. Publishes a book approximately 1 year after acceptance.
Photography: Buys photos from freelancers. Buys stock images. Looks primarily for photos of people

in the news. Captions required. Uses 8 × 10 b&w prints. Submit cover letter, résumé and stock photo list.
Terms: Work purchased outright from authors (fee negotiable). Sends galleys to authors upon request. Book catalog and ms guidelines available for SASE.
Tips: "Authors should read some of the books we have already published before sending a query to The Oliver Press. Authors should propose collective biographies for one of our existing series."

ORCHARD BOOKS, 95 Madison Ave., New York NY 10016. (212)951-2600. Website: http://www.groli er.com. Imprint of Grolier, Inc. Book publisher. President and Publisher: Judy V. Wilson. **Manuscript Acquisitions:** Sarah Caguiat, editor; Ana Cero, editor. **Art Acquisitionis:** Art Director. "We publish between 60 and 70 books yearly including fiction, poetry, picture books, and some non-fiction." 10-25% of books by first-time authors.
● Orchard is not accepting unsolicited mss; query letters only.
Fiction: All levels: animal, anthology, contemporary, fantasy, folktales, history, humor, multicultural, nature/environment, poetry, science fiction, sports, suspense/mystery.
Nonfiction: Picture books, young readers: animal, history, multicultural, nature/environment, science, social issues. "We publish nonfiction on a very selective basis."
How to Contact/Writers: Query only with SASE.
Illustration: Works with 40 illustrators/year. Art director reviews ms/illustration portfolios. Submit "tear-sheets or photocopies or photostats of the work." Reports on art samples in 1 month. Samples returned with SASE. No disks or slides, please.
Terms: Most commonly an advance against list royalties. Sends galleys to authors; dummies to illustrators. Original artwork returned at job's completion. Book catalog free on request with 8½ × 11 SASE with 4 oz. postage.
Tips: "Read some of our books to determine first whether your manuscript is suited to our list."

OTTENHEIMER PUBLISHERS, 5 Park Center Court, Suite 300, Owings Mills MD 21117-5001. (410)902-9100. Fax: (410)902-7210. Imprints: Dream House, Halo Press. Independent book producer/packager. Estab. 1896. **Manuscript Acquisitions:** Laura J. Wallace, editorial director. **Art Acquisitions:** Lauren Loran, art director. Publishes 2 picture books/year; 30 early readers/year. 20% of books by first-time authors. "We publish series; rarely single-tile ideas. Early learning, religious, Beatrix Potter, activity books. We do lots of novelty formats and always want more ideas for inexpensive and creative packaging concepts. We are sticker book and pop-up book experts."
Nonfiction: Picture books: activity books, animal, concept, early learning novelty formats, geography, nature/environment, reference, religion. Recently published *My Bible Alphabet Block Pop-Up Book* (ages 3-6); *Wonders of Nature* (ages 3-6); and *Christmas Stocking Stuffer Activity Books* (ages 3-6).
How to Contact/Writers: Fiction (very rarely): Query. Nonfiction: Submit complete ms. Reports on queries/mss in 6-8 weeks. Publishes a book 6 months to 1 year after acceptance. Will consider simultaneous submissions; previously published work.
Illustration: Works with 8 illustrators/year. Reviews ms/illustration packages from artists. Query. Illustrations only: Send promo sheet and tearsheets to be kept on file. Reports back only if interested. Samples returned with SASE; samples kept on file.
Photography: Buys stock images.
Terms: Pays authors royalty of 5-10% based on wholesale price or work purchased outright for $200-1,000. Offers advances. Pays illustrators by the project (range: $200-16,000). Sends galleys to authors. Originals returned to artist at job's completion. Ms guidelines for SASE.
Tips: "Don't submit single stories; we want series concepts for early learners, ages three to seven."

OTTER CREEK PUBLISHING, P.O. Box 126, Mulvane KS 67110-0126. (316)777-9099. Fax: (316)777-0139. Estab. 1994. **Manuscript and Art Acquisitions:** Brad Steventon. Publishes 1 picture book/year; 2 young readers/year; 2 middle readers/year. 20% of books by first-time authors.
Fiction: Picture books, young readers, middle readers: adventure, animal, contemporary, fantasy, folktales, humor, nature/environment, science fiction, sports, suspense/mystery. Average word length: picture books—500; young readers—1,000; middle readers—10,000. Recently published *Secret Jealousy*, by Misty Henson (ages 9-11); *Jack Rabbit Jack*, by John Loeb (ages 5-8); *Messy Tessie Has a Tea Party*, by Julie Brown (preschool-8).
How to Contact/Writers: Fiction: submit complete ms. Reports on mss in 1 month. Publishes a book 1 year after acceptance. Will consider simultaneous submissions.
Illustration: Works with 3 illustrators/year. Reviews ms/illustration packages from artists. Send ms with dummy. Contact: Brad Steventon, editor/art director. Illustrations only: query with samples or send resume, promo sheet and portfolio. Contact: Brad Steventon, editor/art director. Reports back only if interested. Samples returned with SASE; samples kept on file.

Terms: Pays authors a 5-10% royalty. Pays illustrators by the project (range: $20-1,500). Sends galleys to authors; dummies to illustrators. Book catalog available for #10 SAE with 1 first-class stamp. Writer's and artist's guidelines available for SASE.
Tips: "We are not accepting new manuscripts until the year 2000."

OUR CHILD PRESS, P.O. Box 74, Wayne PA 19087-0074. (610)964-0606. Fax: (610)964-0938. Book publisher. **Acquisitions:** Carol Hallenbeck, president. 90% of books by first-time authors.
Fiction/Nonfiction: All levels: adoption, multicultural, special needs. Published *Don't Call Me Marda*, written and illustrated by Sheila Kelly Welch; *Is That Your Sister?* by Catherine and Sherry Burin; and *Oliver: A Story About Adoption*, by Lois Wichstrom.
How to Contact/Writers: Fiction/Nonfiction: Query or submit complete ms. Reports on queries/mss in 6 months. Publishes a book 6-12 months after acceptance.
Illustration: Works with 1 illustrator/year. Uses primarily b&w artwork. Reviews ms/illustration packages from artists. Ms/illustration packages and illustration only: Query first. Submit résumé, tearsheets and photocopies. Contact: Carol Hallenbeck, president. Reports on art samples in 2 months. Samples returned with SASE; samples kept on file.
Terms: Pays authors in royalties of 5-10% based on wholesale price. Pays illustrators royalties of 5-10% based on wholesale price. Original artwork returned at job's completion. Book catalog for business-size SAE and 52¢ postage.
Tips: Won't consider anything not related to adoption.

OUR SUNDAY VISITOR, INC., 200 Noll Plaza, Huntington IN 46750. (219)356-8400. Fax: (219)356-8472. Book publisher. **Acquisitions:** Jacquelyn M. Lindsey, James Manney. Publishes primarily religious, educational, parenting, reference and biographies.
 • Our Sunday Visitor, Inc., is publishing only those children's books that tie in to sacramental preparation. Contact the acquisitions editor for ms guidelines and a book catalog.
How to Contact/Writers: Nonfiction: Query, submit complete ms, or submit outline/synopsis, and 2-3 sample chapters. Reports on queries in 2 months. Publishes a book 18-24 months after acceptance. Will consider simultaneous submissions, electronic submissions via disk or modem, previously published work.
Illustration: Reviews ms/illustration packages from artists. Contact: Jacquelyn Lindsey or James Manney, acquisitions editors. Illustration only: Query with samples. Contact: Aquisitions Editor. Reports in 2 months. Original artwork returned at job's completion.
Photography: Buys photos from freelancers. Contact: Jacquelyn Lindsey, acquisitions editor.
Terms: Pays authors based on net receipts. Offers royalty. Sends galleys to authors; dummies to illustrators. Book catalog available for SAE; ms guidelines available for SASE.
Tips: "Stay in accordance with our guidelines."

RICHARD C. OWEN PUBLISHERS, INC., P.O. Box 585, Katonah NY 10536. (914)232-3903. Fax: (914)232-3977. Website: http://www.rcowen.com. Book publisher. **Acquisitions:** Janice Boland, children's books editor/art director. Publishes 20 picture story books/year. 90% of books by first-time authors. We publish "child-focused books about characters and situations with which five-, six-, and seven-year-old children can identify—books that can be read for meaning, entertainment, enjoyment and information. We include multicultural stories that present minorities in a positive and natural way. Our stories show the diversity in America."
Fiction: Picture books for young readers: adventure, animal, anthology, contemporary, folktales, humor, multicultural, nature/environment, poetry, science fiction, sports, suspense/mystery. Does not want to see holiday, religious themes, moral teaching stories. "No talking animals with personified human characteristics, jingles and rhymes, holiday stories, alphabet books, stories without plots, stories with nostalgic views of childhood, soft or sugar-coated tales. No stereotyping." Average word length: 40-100 words. Recently published *Spiders Everywhere*, by Betty Baker, illustrated by Judith Pfeiffer; and *Jump the Broom*, by Candy Grant Helmso, illustrated by Joanne Friar.
Nonfiction: Picture books for young readers: animals, careers, how-to, music/dance, geography, multicultural, nature/environment, science, sports. Multicultural needs include: "Good stories respectful of all heritages, races, cultural—African-American, Hispanic, American Indian." Wants lively stories. No "encyclopedic" type of information stories. Average word length: 40-100 words. Recently published *New York City Buildings*, by Ann Mace, photos by Tim Holmstron.
How to Contact/Writers: Fiction/nonfiction: Submit complete ms. "*Must* request guidelines first with #10 SASE." Reports on mss in 1-8 months. Publishes a book 2-3 years after acceptance. Will consider simultaneous submissions.
Illustration: Works with 20 illustrators/year. Uses color artwork only. Illustration only: Send color copies/

reproductions or photos of art or provide tearsheets; do not send slides. Must request guidelines first. Reports only if a project comes up; samples filed.

Photography: Buys photos from freelancers. Contact: Janice Boland, art director. Wants photos that are child-oriented; candid shots; not interested in portraits. "Natural, bright, crisp and colorful—of children and of interesting subjects and compositions attractive to children. If photos are assigned, we buy outright—retain ownership and all rights to photos taken in the project." Sometimes interested in stock photos for special projects. Uses 35mm, 2¼×2¼, color transparencies.

Terms: Pays authors royalties of 5% based on net price. Offers no advances. Pays illustrators by the project (range: $800-2,500). Pays photographers by the project (range: $500-1,500) or per photo ($100-150). Original artwork returned 12-18 months after job's completion. Book brochure, ms/artists guidelines available for SASE.

Tips: Seeking "stories (both fiction and nonfiction) that have charm, magic, impact and appeal; that children living in today's society will want to read and reread; books with strong storylines, child-appealing language, action and interesting, vivid characters. Write for the ears and eyes and heart of your readers—use an economy of words. Visit the children's room at public library and immerse yourself in the best children's literature."

PACIFIC VIEW PRESS, P.O. Box 2657, Berkeley CA 94702. (510)849-4213. Fax: (510)843-5835. E-mail: PVP@sirius.com. Book publisher. **Acquisitions:** Pam Zumwalt, president. Publishes 1-2 picture books/year. 50% of books by first-time authors. "We publish unique, high-quality introductions to Asian cultures and history for children 8-12, for schools, libraries and families. Our children's books focus on hardcover illustrated nonfiction. We look for titles on aspects of the history and culture of the countries and peoples of the Pacific Rim, especially China, presented in an engaging, informative and respectful manner. We are interested in books that all children will enjoy reading and using, and that parents and teachers will want to buy."

Nonfiction: Young readers, middle readers: Asia-related multicultural only. Recently published *Kneeling Carabao and Dancing Giants: Celebrating Filipino Festivals*, by Rena Krasno, illustrated by Ileana C. Lee (ages 8-12, nonfiction on festivals and history of Philippines); and *Made in China: Ideas and Inventions from Ancient China*, by Suzanne Williams, illustrated by Andrea Fong (ages 10-12, nonfiction on history of China and Chinese inventions).

How to Contact/Writers: Query with outline and sample chapter. Reports in 3 months.

Illustration: Works with 2 illustrators/year. Reports back only if interested. Samples returned with SASE.

Terms: Pays authors royalty of 8-12% based on wholesale price. Pays illustrators by the project (range: $2,000-5,000).

Tips: "We welcome proposals from persons with expertise, either academic or personal, in their area of interest. While we do accept proposals from previously unpublished authors, we would expect submitters to have considerable experience presenting their interests to children in classroom or other public settings, and to have skill in writing for children."

☑ **PAPERSTAR BOOKS**, Imprint of Penguin Putnam Books for Young Readers, 345 Hudson St., New York NY 10014. Book publisher. **Manuscript Acquisitions:** Susan Kochan, editor. **Art Acquisitions:** Cecilia Yung, art director. Publishes 50 picture books/year; 20 middle readers/year.

● PaperStar does not publish original fiction in paperback, only reprint picture books that were first hardcovers and middle grade novels from Putnam, Philomel and other publishers.

Fiction: Middle readers: adventure, contemporary, humor, multicultural, sports, suspense/mystery. Recently published *The Cat Ate My Gymsuit*, by Paul Danziger; *My Life Among the Aliens*, by Gail Gauthier; and *A Season of Comebacks*, by Kathy Mackel.

How to Contact/Writers: Reports on mss in 2 months. Publishes a book 18 months after acceptance. Previously published work only. Please include copies of reviews and award information.

Illustration: Works with 20 illustrators/year. Send samples of cover art (tearsheets). Reports back only if interested. Samples returned with SASE.

Terms: Pays authors royalty of 6%. Offers advances (average amount: $4,000-5,000). Pays illustrators by

---

"PICTURE BOOKS" are for preschoolers to 8-year-olds; "Young readers" are for 5- to 8-year-olds; "Middle readers" are for 9- to 11-year-olds; and "Young adults" are for ages 12 and up.

the project. Originals returned to artist at job's completion. Book catalog available for 9×11 SAE and 2 first-class stamps.

PARENTING PRESS, INC., P.O. Box 75267, Seattle WA 98125. (206)364-2900. Fax: (206)364-0702. E-mail: office@parentingpress.com. Website: http://www.parentingpress.com. Book publisher. Estab. 1979. Publisher: Carolyn Threadgill. Publishes 4-5 books/year for parents or/and children and those who work with them. 40% of books by first-time authors. "Parenting Press publishes educational books for children in story format—no straight fiction. We publish books that help build competence in parents and children. We are interested in books that help people feel good about themselves because they gain skills needed in dealing with others. We are particularly interested in material that provides 'options' rather than 'shoulds.' "
• Parenting Press's guidelines are available on their website.
Fiction: Publishes social skills books, problem-solving books, safety books, dealing-with-feelings books that use a "fictional" vehicle for the information. "We rarely publish straight fiction." Recently published *I Can't Wait, I Want It, My Name Is Not Dummy*, by Elizabeth Crary, illustrations by Marina Megale (ages 3-8, social skill building); *Telling Isn't Tattling*, by Kathryn Hammerseng, illustrations by Dave Garbot (ages 4-12, personal safety); and 4 toddler board books on expressing feelings.
Nonfiction: Picture books: health, social skills building. Young readers: health, social skills building books. Middle readers: health, social skills building. No books on "new baby; coping with a new sibling; cookbooks; manners; books about disabilities (which we don't publish at present); animal characters in anything; books that tell children what they should do, instead of giving options." Average word length: picture books—500-800; young readers—1,000-2,000; middle readers—up to 10,000. Published *Kids to the Rescue*, by Maribeth and Darwin Boelts (ages 4-12).
How to Contact/Writers: Query. Reports on queries/mss in 3 months, "after requested." Publishes a book 18 months after acceptance. Will consider simultaneous submissions.
Illustrations: Works with 3 illustrators/year. Reviews ms/illustration packages from artists. "We do reserve the right to find our own illustrator, however." Query. Illustrations only: Submit "résumé, samples of art/drawings (no original art); photocopies or color photocopies okay." Reports in 3 weeks. Samples returned with SASE; samples filed.
Terms: Pays authors royalties of 3-8% based on wholesale price. Outright purchase of ms, "negotiated on a case-by-case basis. Not common for us." Offers average advance of $150. Pays illustrators (for text) by the project; 3-4% royalty based on wholesale price. Pays illustrators (for covers) by the project ($300-800). Pays photographers royalty of 3-4%. Sends galleys to authors; dummies to illustrators. Book catalog/ms/artist's guidelines for #10 SAE and 1 first-class stamp.
Tips: "Make sure you are familiar with unique nature of our books. All are aimed at building certain 'people' skills in adults or children. Our publishing for children follows no trend that we find appropriate. Children need nonfiction social skill-building books that help them think through problems and make their own informed decisions."

PAULIST PRESS, 997 Macarthur Blvd., Mahwah NJ 07430. (201)825-7300. Fax: (201)825-8345. Website: http://.paulistpress.com. Book publisher. Estab. 1865. **Acquisitions:** Karen Scialabba, editor. Publishes 9-11 picture books/year; 8-10 young reader titles/year; and 3-4 middle reader titles/year. 80% of books by first-time authors; 30% of books from agented writers. "Our goal is to produce books that 'heal with kid-appeal,' 'share the goodness,' and delight in diversity."
Fiction: Picture books, young readers, middle readers and young adults: interested mainly in books providing an accessible introduction to basic religious and family values, but not preachy. Recently published *I Hate Goodbyes*, by Kathleen Szaj, illustrated by Mark A. Hicks; Walking With God series: *Spirit!, Yes, I Can!, Imagine!* and *Where Is God?*, by Heidi Bratton; *Elizabeth, Who is NOT a Saint*, by Kathleen Szaj, illustrated by Mark A. Hicks; and *Little Blessings*, by Sally Ann Conan, illustrated by Kathy Rogers.
Nonfiction: All levels: biography, concept, multicultural, religion, self help, social issues.
How to Contact/Writers: Fiction/nonfiction: Submit complete ms. Reports on queries/mss in 6-8 months. Publishes a book 12-16 months after acceptance.
Illustration: Works with 10-12 illustrators/year. Editorial reviews all varieties of ms/illustration packages from artists. Submit complete ms with 1 piece of final art (photocopy only) remainder roughs. Illustrations only: Submit résumé, tearsheets. Reports on art samples in 6-8 months.
Photography: Buys photos from freelancers. Works on assignment only. Uses inspirational photos.
Terms: Pays authors royalty of 6-8% based on retail price. Offers average advance payment of $500. Pays illustrators by the project (range: $50-100) or royalty of 2-6% based on retail price. Pays photographers by the project (range: $25-150; negotiable). Factors used to determine final payment: color art, b&w, number of illustrations, complexity of work. Pay for separate authors and illustrators: Author paid by royalty rate; illustrator paid by flat fee, sometimes by royalty. Sends galleys to authors; dummies to illustrators. Original artwork returned at job's completion, "if requested by illustrator."

Tips: "We cannot be responsible for unsolicited manuscripts. Please send copies, not originals. We try to respond to all manuscripts we receive—please understand if you have not received a response within six months the manuscript does not fit our current publishing plan. We look for authors who diligently promote their work."

PEACHTREE PUBLISHERS, LTD., 494 Armour Circle NE, Atlanta GA 30324. (404)876-8761. Fax: (404)875-2578. Website: http://www.peachtree-online.com. Book publisher. Imprints: Peachtree Jr. and Freestone. Estab. 1977. **Acquisitions:** Helen Harriss. Publishes 20 titles/year.
Fiction: Picture books: adventure, animal, concept, history, nature/environment. Young readers: adventure, animal, concept, history, nature/environment, poetry. Middle readers: adventure, animal, history, nature/environment, sports. Young adults: history, humor, nature/environment. Does not want to see science fiction, romance.
Nonfiction: Picture books: animal, history, nature/environment. Young readers, middle readers, young adults: animal, biography, history, nature/environment. Does not want to see sports, religion.
How to Contact/Writers: Fiction/Nonfiction: Submit complete ms. Reports on queries in 2-3 months; mss in 4 months. Publishes a book 1-1½ years after acceptance. Will consider simultaneous and previously published submissions.
Illustration: Works with 8 illustrators/year. Illustrations only: Query with samples, résumé, slides, color copies to keep on file. Reports back only if interested. Samples returned with SASE; samples filed.
Terms: Ms guidelines for SASE, or call for a recorded message.

PEEL PRODUCTIONS, P.O. Box 546, Columbus NC 28722. (704)894-8838. Fax: (704)894-8839. E-mail: peelbks@aol.com. Book publisher. **Acquisitions:** Susan Dubosque, editor. Publishes 1 picture book/year; and 5 how-to-draw books/year.
Fiction: Peel Productions will not publish fiction for children until 1999.
Nonfiction: Young readers, middle readers: activity books (how to draw).
How to Contact/Writers: Fiction/Nonfiction: Submit outline/synopsis and 2 sample chapters. Reports on queries in 2-3 weeks; mss in 6 weeks. Publishes a book 1 year after acceptance. Will consider simultaneous submissions.
Terms: Pays authors royalty. Offers advances. Sends galleys to authors. Book catalog available for SAE and 2 first-class stamps. Ms guidelines available for SASE.

PELICAN PUBLISHING CO. INC., P.O. Box 3110, Gretna LA 70054-3110. (504)368-1175. E-mail: office@pelicanpub.com. Website: http://www.pelicanpub.com. Book publisher. Estab. 1926. **Manuscript Acquisitions:** Nina Kooij, editor-in-chief. **Art Acquisitions:** Tracey Clements, production manager. Publishes 20 young readers/year and 2 middle reader titles/year. 5% of books from agented writers. "Pelican publishes hardcover and trade paperback originals and reprints. Our children's books (illustrated and otherwise) include history, bilingual, sports, folklore and textbooks."
Fiction: Young readers: folktales, history, multicultural. Middle readers: history, multicultural, sports. Multicultural needs include stories about African-Americans, Irish-Americans, Jews, Asian-Americans, Cajuns and Hispanics. Does not want animal stories, general Christmas stories, "day at school" or "accept yourself" stories. Average word length: 1,100 young readers; middle readers—40,000. Recently published *Tuesday in Arizona*, by Marian Harris.
Nonfiction: Young readers: biography, history. Middle readers: biography, history. Published *Jim Thorpe, the Legend Remembered*, by Rosemary K. Updyke (ages 8-12, biography).
How to Contact/Writers: Fiction/Nonfiction: Query. Reports on queries in 1 month; mss in 3 months. Publishes a book 12-18 months after acceptance.
Illustration: Works with 10 illustrators/year. Reviews ms/illustration packages from artists. Query first. Illustrations only: Query with samples (no originals). Reports only if interested. Samples returned with SASE; samples kept on file.
Terms: Pays authors in royalties; buys ms outright "rarely." Sends galleys to authors. Illustrators paid by "various arrangements." Book catalog and ms guidelines available for SASE.
Tips: "No anthropomorphic stories, pet stories (fiction or nonfiction), fantasy, poetry, science fiction or romance. Writers: Be as original as possible. Develop characters that lend themselves to series and always be thinking of new and interesting situations for those series. Give your story a strong hook—something that will appeal to a well-defined audience. There is a lot of competition out there for general themes. We look for stories with specific 'hooks' and audiences, and writers who actively promote their work."

PENGUIN PUTNAM INC., 345 Hudson St., New York NY 10014. See listings for Dial Books for Young Readers, Dutton Children's Books, Philomel Books, Puffin Books, G.P. Putnam's Sons and Viking Children's Books.

⊞ PERFECTION LEARNING CORPORATION, Cover to Cover, 10520 New York, Des Moines IA 50322. (515)278-0133. Fax: (515)278-2980. E-mail: perflern@netins.net. Book publisher, independent book producer/packager. **Manuscript Acquisitions:** S. Thies (K-12). **Art Acquisitions:** Randy Messer, art director. Publishes 20 early chapter books/year; 40-50 middle readers/year; 25 young adult titles/year.
● Perfection Learning Corp. publishes *all* hi-lo children's books on a variety of subjects.
Fiction: All levels: adventure, animal, contemporary, fantasy, folktales, history, humor, multicultural, nature/environment, poetry, problem novels, science fiction, special needs, sports, suspense/mystery. Average word length: early chapter books—4,000; middle readers—10,000-14,000; young adults: 10,000-30,000. Recently published *Holding the Yellow Rabbit*; and *Prairie Meeting*.
Nonfiction: All levels: activity, animal, biography, careers, geography, health, history, hobbies, multicultural, nature/environment, science, self-help, social issues, special needs, sports. Multicultural needs include stories, legends and other oral tradition narratives by authors who are of the culture. Does not want to see ABC books. Average word length: early chapter books—4,000; middle readers—10,000-14,000; young adults—10,000-14,000.
How to Contact/Writers: Fiction/Nonfiction: Submit complete ms. Reports on queries in 1 month; mss in 4 months. Publishes a book 18 months after acceptance.
Illustration: Works with 10-15 illustrators/year. Illustration only: Query with samples; send résumé, promo sheet, client list, tearsheets. Contact: Randy Messer, art director. Reports only if interested. Samples returned with SASE; samples filed.
Photography: Buys photos from freelancers. Contact: Randy Messer, art director. Buys stock and assigns work. Uses children. Uses color or up to 8× b&w glossy prints; 2¼×2¼, 4×5 transparencies. Submit cover letter, client list, stock photo list, promo piece (color or b&w).
Terms: Pays authors "depending on going rate for industry." Offers advances, Pays illustrators by the project. Pays photographers by the project. Original artwork returned on a "case by case basis."
Tips: "Our materials are sold through schools for use in the classroom. Talk to a teacher about his/her needs."

☑ PHILOMEL BOOKS, Penguin Putnam Inc., 345 Hudson St., New York NY 10014. (212)414-3610. Website: http://www.penguinputnam.com. Putnam Books. Book publisher. Estab. 1980. **Manuscript Acquisitions:** Patricia Gauch, editorial director; Alison Keehn, editorial assistant. **Art Acquisitions:** Ben Caldwell, design assistant. Publishes 18 picture books/year; 2 middle-grade/year; 2 young readers/year; 4 young adult/year. 5% of books by first-time authors; 80% of books from agented writers. "We look for beautifully written, engaging manuscripts for children and young adults."
Fiction: All levels: adventure, animal, anthology, contemporary, fantasy, folktales, hi-lo, history, humor, poetry, sports, multicultural. Middle readers, young adults: problem novels, science fiction, suspense/mystery. No concept picture books, mass-market "character" books, or series. Average word length: 1,000 for picture books; 1,500 young readers; 14,000 middle readers; 20,000 young adult.
Nonfiction: Picture books, young readers, middle readers: hi-lo. "Creative nonfiction on any subject." Average word length: 2,000 for picture books; 3,000 young readers; 10,000 middle readers.
How to Contact/Writers: Fiction: Submit outline/synopsis and first two chapters. Nonfiction: Query. Reports on queries in 3 months; mss in 4 months.
Illustration: Works with 20-25 illustrators/year. Reviews ms/illustration packages from artists. Query with art sample first. Illustrations only: Query with samples. Send résumé and tearsheets. Reports on art samples in 1 month. Original artwork returned at job's completion. Samples returned with SASE, or kept on file.
Terms: Pays authors in royalties. Average advance payment "varies." Illustrators paid by advance and in royalties. Sends galleys to authors; dummies to illustrators. Book catalog, ms guidelines free on request with SASE (9×12 envelope for catalog).
Tips: Wants "unique fiction or nonfiction with a strong voice and lasting quality. Discover your own voice and own story—and persevere." Looks for "something unusual, original, well-written. Fine art. The genre (fantasy, contemporary, or historical fiction) is not so important as the story itself, and the spirited life the story allows its main character. We are also interested in receiving adolescent novels that contain regional spirit, such as a story about a young boy or girl written from a Southern, Southwestern or Northwestern perspective."

◘ PHOENIX LEARNING RESOURCES, 12 W. 31st St., New York NY 10001. (212)629-3887. (212)629-5648. Book publisher. Executive Vice President: John A. Rothermich. Publishes 20 textbooks/year.
Nonfiction: All levels: textbooks. Recently published *Reading for Concepts*, Third Edition.
How to Contact/Writers: Nonfiction: Submit outline/synopsis. Reports on queries in 2 weeks; mss in 1 month. Will consider simultaneous submissions and previously published work.
Photography: Buys stock. Contact: John A. Rothermich, executive vice president. Uses color prints and

35mm, 2¼×2¼, 4×5 transparencies. Submit cover letter.

Terms: Pays authors royalty based on wholesale price or work purchased outright. Pays illustrators and photographers by the project. Sends galleys to authors. Book catalog available for SASE.

Tips: "We look for classroom tested and proven materials."

THE PLACE IN THE WOODS, "Different" Books, 3900 Glenwood Ave., Golden Valley MN 55422-5302. (612)374-2120. Book publisher. **Acquisitions:** Roger Hammer, publisher/editor; Kathryn Smitley, special editor. Publishes 4 elementary-age titles/year and 2 middle readers/year; 2 young adult titles/year. 100% of books by first-time authors. Books feature primarily diversity/multicultural storyline and illustration.

Fiction: All levels: adventure, animal, contemporary, fantasy, folktales, hi-lo, history, humor, poetry, multicultural, special needs, suspense/mystery.

Nonfiction: All levels: activity books, hi-lo, history, multicultural, special needs. Multicultural themes must avoid negative stereotypes. "Generally, we don't publish nonfiction, but we would look at these."

How to Contact/Writers: Fiction/Nonfiction: Submit complete ms. Reports on queries/mss in 1 month with SASE. "No multiple or simultaneous submissions. Please indicate a time frame for response."

Illustration: Works with 2 illustrators/year. Uses primarily b&w artwork only. Reviews ms/illustration packages from authors. Query; submit ms with dummy. Contact: Roger Hammer, editor. Illustration only: Query with samples. Reports in 1 week. Include SASE. "We buy all rights."

Photography: Buys photos from freelancers. Works on assignment only. Uses photos that appeal to children. Model/property releases required; captions required. Uses any b&w prints. Submit cover letter and samples with SASE.

Terms: Work purchased outright from authors ($50-250). Pays illustrators by the project (range: $10-500). Pays photographers per photo. For all contracts, "initial payment repeated with each printing." Original artwork not returned at job's completion. Guidelines available for SASE.

PLAYERS PRESS, INC., P.O. Box 1132, Studio City CA 91614-0132. (818)789-4980. Book publisher. Estab. 1965. Vice President/Editorial: Robert W. Gordon. **Manuscript Acquisitions:** Attention: Editor. **Art Acquisitions:** Attention: Art Director. Publishes 7-25 young readers dramatic plays and musicals/year; 2-10 middle readers dramatic plays and musicals/year; and 4-20 young adults dramatic plays and musicals/year. 35% of books by first-time authors; 1% of books from agented writers.

Fiction: "We use all categories (young readers, middle readers, young adults) but only for dramatic plays and/or musicals. No novels or storybooks." Multicultural needs include plays and musicals. Recently published *Tower of London*, a play by William Hezlep; *Punch and Judy*, a play by William-Alan Landes; and *Silly Soup!*, by Carol Kerty (a collection of short plays with music and dance).

Nonfiction: "Any children's nonfiction pertaining to the entertainment industry, performing arts and how-to for the theatrical arts only." Needs include and activity, arts/crafts, careers, history, how-to, multicultural, music/dance, reference and textbook. Published *Stagecrafter's Handbook*, by I.E. Clark; and *New Monologues for Readers Theatre*, by Steven Porter. Recently published *Assignments in Musical Theatre Acting & Directing*, by Jacque Wheeler and Halle Laughlin (how-to on teaching or learning to a musical theater actor or director); and *Theatre for Children in the United States: A History*, by nellie McCaslin (complete history of children's theater from the turn of the century through 1996).

How to Contact/Writers: Fiction/nonfiction: Submit plays or outline/synopsis and sample chapters of entertainment books. Reports on queries in 1 week; mss in 1-12 months. Publishes a book 10 months after acceptance. No simultaneous submissions.

Illustration: Works with 1-5 illustrators/year. Use primarily b&w artwork. Illustrations only: Submit résumé, tearsheets. Reports on art samples in 1-6 weeks only if interested. Samples returned with SASE; samples filed.

Terms: Pays authors in royalties of 6-12% based on wholesale price or by outright purchase. Pay illustrators by the project; royalties range from 2-5%. Sends galleys to authors; dummies to illustrators. Book catalog and ms guidelines available for SASE.

Tips: Looks for "plays/musicals and books pertaining to the performing arts only. Illustrators: send samples that can be kept for our files."

✓ **PLAYSKOOL BOOKS**, 345 Hudson St., New York NY 10014. (212)414-3700. Fax: (212)414-3397. Website: http://www.penguin.com. Book publisher. Division of Dutton Children's Books. **Manuscript Acquisitions:** Lucia Monfried, editor-in-chief. **Manuscript/illustration packages:** Lucia Monfried. **Art acquisitions:** Rick Farely, art director.Published 20 picture books/year. 5% by first-time authors. "We publish books for preschoolers that emphasize play and learning."

Fiction: Picture books: animal, concept, contemporary, humor, multicultural, novelty. Does not want to see folktales. Recently published: *My First Toolbox*; *My Photo Book About Me*, illustrated by Angie Sage;

and *Mr. Potato Head's Costume Party: A Mix and Match Book* (all novelty books for ages 2-5).
Nonfiction: Picture Books: activity books, animal, concept. Recently published: *Seeing Shapes*, photographed by Sandra Lousada (concept board book for ages 2-5).
How to Contact/Writers: Submit complete ms. Reports in 2 months. Published a book 1 year after acceptance. Will consider simultaneous submissions.
Illustration: Works with 12-20 illustrators/year. Uses color artwork only. Reviews ms/illustration packages from artists. Send ms with dummy. Illustrations only: send tearsheets. Reports in 1 month. Samples returned with SASE; samples filed.
Photography: Buys stock images. Contact: Rick Farley, art director or Susan Van Metre, editor. Looking for photos of animals and children. Uses color prints and 35mm transparencies. Send color promo piece.
Terms: Work purchased outright from authors; fee negotiable. Pays illustrators and photographers by the project; negotiable. Sends galleys to authors; dummies to illustrators. Original artwork returned at job's completion. Book catalog availab e for 9×12 SAE with 3 first-class stamps. All imprints included in a single catalog. Ms guidelines available for SASE.
Tips: "We are only interested in manuscripts and art appropriate for preschool age children."

PLEASANT COMPANY PUBLICATIONS, 8400 Fairway Place, Middleton WI 53562-0998. (608)836-4848. Fax: (608)836-1999. Website: http://www.americangirl.com. Book publisher. Editorial Director: Judi Woodburn. **Manuscript Acquisitions:** Jennifer Hirsch, submissions editor; Jodi Evert, senior editor, The American Girls Collection; Michelle Watkins, senior editor, American Girl Library. **Art Acquisitions:** Jane Varda, art director. Imprints: The American Girls Collection, American Girl Library, Bitty Baby Collection. Publishes 8-10 middle readers/year. 10% of books by first-time authors. Publishes fiction and nonfiction for girls 7 and up. "Pleasant Company's mission is to educate and entertain girls with high-quality products and experiences that build self-esteem and reinforce positive social and moral values."
  ● Pleasant Company publishes *American Girl* magazine. Pleasant Company also sponsors a contest for writers—see listing in Contests & Awards section for Pleasant T. Rowland Prize for Fiction for Girls.
Fiction: Middle readers: adventure, animal, contemporary, history, suspense/mystery. Recently published *Changes for Josefina*, by Valerie Tripp, illustrated by Jean-Paul Tibbles (ages 7-12, historical fiction); *Meet Addy*, by Connie Porter, illustrated by Melodye Rosales (ages 7-12, historical fiction).
Nonfiction: Middle readers: activity books, arts/crafts, cooking, history, hobbies, how-to, self help, sports. Recently published *Ooops! The Manners Guide for Girls*, by Nancy Holyoke, illustrated by Debbie Tilley (ages 8 and up, self help); *Super Slumber Parties*, by Brooks Whitney, illustrated by Nadine Westcott (ages 8 and up, how-to); and *Josefina's Cookbook, Pleasant Company* (ages 7-12, cooking).
How to Contact/Writers: Fiction/nonfiction: Query or submit entire ms. Reports on queries/mss in 2 months. Will consider simultaneous submissions.
Illustration: Works with 8 illustrators/year. Reviews ms/illustration packages from artists. Illustrations only: Query with samples. Reports back only if interested. Samples returned with SASE; copies of samples filed.
Photography: Buys stock and assigns work. Submit cover letter, published samples, promo piece.
Terms: Pays authors royalty or work purchased outright. Pays illustrators by the project. Pays photographers by the project. Sends galleys to authors; dummies to illustrators. Originals returned to artist at job's completion. Book catalog available for 8½×11 SAE and 4 first-class stamps. All imprints included in a single catalog.

☒ PONTALBA PRESS, 4417 Dryades St., New Orleans LA 70115. (888)436-3724. Fax: (504)822-6028. E-mail: winter@comm.net. Website: http://www.comm.net.pontalba. Estab. 1996. **Manuscript and Art Acquisitions:** Christian Allman. Publishes 1 picture book/year; 2 young readers/year. 50% of books by first-time authors. "We publish work by both established and new authors and focus on titles and subjects that have mainstream appeal but are often overlooked or ignored by mainstream publishers."
Fiction: Picture books: adventure, concept, contemporary, fantasy, folktales, health, history, humor, science fiction, sports, suspense/mystery. Young readers: adventure, animal, concept, fantasy, folktales, health, history, humor, science fiction, sports, suspense/mystery. Middle readers: adventure, animal, fantasy, folktales, multicultural, nature/environment, science fiction, sports, suspense/mystery. Young adult: adventure, animal, fantasy, health, history, humor, nature/environment, science fiction, sports, suspense/mystery. Recently published *Where the Womblies Are*, by Steve Allen (ages 8-12); and *Clark and His Alien Food*, by Janet Densmore (ages 8-12).
Nonfiction: Young readers: activity books, animal, careers, cooking, health, music/dance, reference, social issues, sports. Middle readers: activity books, history, music/dance. Young adults: arts/crafts, biography, health. Recently published *Wake Up, Wise Up, Win*, by L.F. Zimerman (teens-adult); *Unlock Your Possibilities*, by Rita Losee (teens-adult).

How to Contact/Writers: Fiction: query, submit outline/synopsis or submit outline/synopsis and 3 sample chapters. Nonfiction: submit outline/synopsis and 3 sample chapters. Reports on queries in 6-8 weeks; mss in 2-3 months. Publishes a book 6 months after acceptance. Will consider electronic submissions via disk or modem and previously published work.

Illustration: Works with 2 illustrators/year. Reviews ms/illustration packages from artists. Submit ms with 3 pieces of final art. Contact: Christian Allman, marketing/editorial director. Illustrations only: query with samples or send portfolio, client list and tearsheets. Contact: Christian Allman. Reports in 2-3 months. Samples returned with SASE.

Photography: Works on assignment only. Contact: Christian Allman. Uses all types of photos, but especially dramatic people photos. Captions required. Uses color prints and 4×5 transparencies. Submit cover letter, client list and published samples.

Terms: Pays authors negotiated royalty. Pays illustrators by the project (range: $1,000-3,000). Sends galleys to authors. Originals returned to artist at job's completion. Book catalog available for SAE with 4 first-class stamps; ms and art guidelines available for SASE. All imprints included in a single catalog. Catalog available on website.

Tips: "Be specific and complete with your queries. We give preference to brief synopses and full manuscripts and authors who have at least a basic understanding about how and to whom to market their work."

PRICE STERN SLOAN, INC.. See listing for Grosset & Dunlap, Inc./Price Stern Sloan.

☑ **PRIDE & IMPRINTS,** (formerly Pride Publications), 7419 Ebbert Dr. SE, Port Orchard WA 98367. Phone/fax: (360)769-7174 (DO NOT call with queries). E-mail: PridePblsh@aol.com. (e-mail queries OK, do not attach files). Website: http://www.pride-imprints.com. **Acquisitions:** Ms. Cris Newport, senior editor. Publishes trade paperback originals and reprints. Publishes 10 titles/year. 50% of books from first-time authors; 50% from unagented writers. Pride & Imprints consists of the following imprints: Little Blue Works—Children's titles and young adult novels released in paper and on multimedia CD-ROM; Pride—Cutting-edge fiction. Publishes genre fiction and poetry primarily in paper and on multimedia CD-ROM; Keystone—General audience titles in paper, on multimedia CD-ROM, as audiobooks and on video; RAMPANT Gaming—Role-playing and other games for ages 14 and up; and Arts Ex Machine—Theatre, film and other arts. "Pride & Imprints publishes work that is revolutionary in content. In order to understand what we mean by this, please read several of our books from the different imprints. We do not publish work that is racist, homophobic, sexist or graphically violent in content. All of our authors and artists should expect to be proactive in marketing their work. If you do not wish to read from and/or sign your books and/or artwork, you should not submit work to us."

Fiction: All levels and categories. Published *Caruso the Mouse*, by Landis Emond, illustrated by Susie Lester; *The Garden Stories*, by Carmen Alexander, illustrated by Stacey Roswell (Multimedia CD-ROM); and *Tonight I Heard the Ghost Cat*, by Jennifer Anna, illustrated by Patric Dengate.

Nonfiction: All levels and categories.

How to Contact/Writers: Accepts work from agented and unagented authors. Reports on queries within 1 month, partial mss within 1 month and full mss within 3 months.

Illustration: Works with 10 illustrators/year. "We will send a letter to an artist telling her or him we have received a portfolio within 2 weeks of receipt. Then we will contact him or her when we have an appropriate project. Because we do so many different kinds of work, we usually can offer work to artists working in a wide range of styles. We keep all samples on file. Do not send originals. Artists may update portfolios whenever they wish. All work that is contracted for a specific project is returned to the artist after we have sent the book to the printer. The artist is then free to sell the originals or keep them.".

Photography: Buys photos from freelancers. Query first.

Terms: Pays 10-15% royalty based on wholesale price. Will consider simultaneous submissions. Artists and photographers are paid up to $1,000 for covers only. All other work is paid on royalty basis. Royalty payment is 10% of gross monies received." For a copy of our catalog, send $2 and a 6×9 envelope with 78¢ in postage. For submission guidelines, send SASE.

PROMETHEUS BOOKS, 59 John Glenn Dr., Amherst NY 14228-2197. Fax: (716)564-2711. E-mail: slmpbbooks@aol.com. Website: http://www.PrometheusBooks.com. Book publisher. Estab. 1969. **Acquisitions:** Steven L. Mitchell, editor-in-chief. **Art Acquisitions:** Jacqueline Cook. Publishes 1-2 titles/year. 40% of books by first-time authors; 50% of books from agented writers. "Our primary focus is to publish children's books with alternative viewpoints: humanism, free thought, skepticism toward the paranormal, moral values, critical reasoning, human sexuality, and independent thinking based upon science and reasoning. Areas include education, current events, young readers, health, gerontology, social science and more. Prometheus publishes both trade and academic titles. We are dedicated to offering its customers the highest-quality books. We are also committed to the development of new markets both in North America and throughout the world."

Nonfiction: All levels: sex education, moral education, critical thinking, nature/environment, science, self help, skepticism, social issues. Average word length: picture books—2,000; young readers—10,000; middle readers—20,000; young adult/teens—60,000. Recently published *It's Up to You, What Do You Do*, by S.M. Humphrey (decision making, ages 6 and up); *Bringing UFOs Down to Earth*, by P. Klass (skepticism, ages 9 and up); and *Little Feelings*, by J.S. Bartan (self-help, ages 3-8).

How to Contact/Writers: Submit complete ms with sample illustrations (b&w). Reports on queries in 1-2 months; mss in 2-3 months. Publishes a book 12-18 months after acceptance. SASE required for return of ms/proposal.

Illustration: Works with 1-2 illustrators/year. "We will keep samples in a freelance file, but freelancers are rarely used." Reviews ms/illustration packages from artists. "Prefer to have full work (manuscript and illustrations); will consider any proposal." Include résumé, photocopies.

Terms: Pays authors royalty of 5-15% based on wholesale price. "Author hires illustrator; we do not contract with illustrators." Pays photographers per photo (range: $50-100). Sends galleys to author. Book catalog is free on request.

Tips: "Book should reflect secular humanist values, stressing nonreligious moral education, critical thinking, logic, and skepticism. Authors should examine our book catalog to learn what sort of manuscripts we're looking for."

☑ **PUFFIN BOOKS**, Penguin Putnam Inc., 345 Hudson St., New York NY 10014-3657. (212)366-2000. Website: http://www.penguinputnam.com. Imprint of Penguin Putnam Inc. **Acquisitions:** Sharyn November, senior editor; Joy Peskin, assistant editor. Publishes trade paperback originals (very few) and reprints. Publishes 175-200 titles/year. Receives 300 queries and mss/year. 1% of books by first-time authors; 5% from unagented writers. "Puffin Books publishes high-end trade paperbacks and paperback originals and reprints for preschool children, beginning and middle readers, and young adults."

Fiction: Picture books, young adult novels, middle grade and easy-to-read grades 1-3. "We publish mostly paperback reprints. We publish few original titles." Recently published *The Ear, the Eye, and the Arm*, by Nancy Farmer (Puffin novel).

Nonfiction: Biography, children's/juvenile, illustrated book, young children's concept books (counting, shapes, colors). Subjects include education (for teaching concepts and colors, not academic), women in history. " 'Women in history' books interest us." Reviews artwork/photos. Send color photocopies. Recently published *Rachel Carson: Pioneer of Ecology*, by "Fadlinski" (history); *Grandma Moses*, by O'Neill Ruff (history).

How to Contact/Writers: Fiction: Submit complete picture book ms or 3 sample chapters with SASE. Nonfiction: Submit 5 pages of ms with SASE. "It could take up to 5 months to get response." Publishes book 1 year after acceptance. Will consider simultaneous submissions, if so noted.

Terms: Pays royalty. Offers advance (varies). Book catalog for 9×12 SASE with 7 first-class stamps; send request to Marketing Department.

☑ **G.P. PUTNAM'S SONS**, Penguin Putnam Inc., 345 Hudson St., New York NY 10014. (212)366-2000. Website: http://www.penguinputnam.com. Book publisher. **Manuscript Acquisitions:** Kathy Dawson, senior editor; Susan Kochan, editor. **Art Acquisitions:** Cecilia Yung, art director, Putnam and Philomel. Publishes 20 picture books/year; 10 middle readers/year; and 4 young adult titles/year. 5% of books by first-time authors; 50% of books from agented authors.

Fiction: Picture books: animal, concept, contemporary, humor, multicultural, special needs. Young readers: adventure, contemporary, history, humor, multicultural, special needs, suspense/mystery. Middle readers: adventure, contemporary, history, humor, multicultural, problem novels, special needs, sports, suspense/mystery. Young adults: contemporary, history, problem novels, special needs. "Multicultural books should reflect different cultures accurately but unobtrusively." Regarding special needs, "stories about physically or mentally challenged children should portray them accurately and without condescension." Does not want to see series, romances. Very little fantasy. Average word length: picture books—200-1,500; middle readers—10,000-30,000; young adults—40,000-50,000. Recently published *Saving Sweetness*, by Diane Stanley, illustrated by Brian Karas (ages 4-8); and *Amber Brown Sees Red*, by Paula Danziger (ages 7-10).

Nonfiction: Picture books: animal, concept, nature/environment. Young readers: biography, history, multicultural, nature/environment, social issues, special needs. Middle readers: biography, history, social issues, special needs. Young adults: history, social issues, special needs. No hard science, series. Average word length: picture books—200-1,500; middle readers: 10,000-30,000; young adults: 30,000-50,000. Recently published *Irresistible Spirit*, by Susan Kuklin (ages 11 up); and *The Case of Roe vs. Wade*, by Leonard Stevens (ages 11 up).

How to Contact/Writers: Fiction/nonfiction: Query with outline/synopsis and 3 sample chapters. Unso-

INSIDER REPORT

Hamsters, ants, deadlines and big-headed baldies—how a great picture book comes to life

If you discovered hundreds of ants treating your new house as the latest hot spot for lunch, how would you react? Call an exterminator? Buy a bug bomb? Poison the little freeloaders? Author/illustrator Peggy Rathmann set out buffets for her uninvited insect invaders.

The ants were first attracted to a pear Rathmann left on a windowsill to ripen. "There were enough of them to carry the pear away. It was as though the ants were on tour and found a new tourist attraction. I could see tour buses full of ants, and tour directors. But when they ran out of food, they all disappeared. So I put out another pear and they were back in an instant. It was as though they were calling to each other on cell phones."

This genuine fascination with the world around her, with something as seemingly mundane as a line of ants, is what

Peggy Rathmann

makes Rathmann great at creating picture books. Instead of saying, "Damn!" she said, "Wow!" Instead of pests, the ants became characters.

Rathmann's latest picture book masterpiece, *10 Minutes till Bedtime* (her first since the 1996 Caldecott Medal winner *Officer Buckle and Gloria*), features touring *hamsters*. The adorable rodents feast their eyes on a child's getting-ready-for bed ritual, as his father counts down the minutes.

The first version of *10 Minutes* was created about ten years ago, an idea Rathmann came up with in a class. Her original vision was a pop-up, count-down book featuring "Ten little big-headed baldies preparing for bed," she says. "But this version gave my family the heebie-jeebies" and she didn't pick up the project again until *Officer Buckle* was finished.

Even for a Caldecott winner, "nothing's obvious when you start a new book. You've got all the choices in the world, and all you want to do is make the one that's the best, but there are no real guidelines." As her work on *10 Minutes* progressed, Rathmann's characters went through many incarnations. First she changed the big-headed baldies to salamanders. "Over the months that followed, I changed the salamanders into beavers, the beavers into armadillos, and the armadillos into multi-colored wiener dogs. There was even a brief period in which the boy in the story was cohabiting with flamingos," says Rathmann. "It wasn't until I tried putting the boy into a bathtub with ten manatees that I knew I was in trouble."

Through her revision process, Rathmann talked regularly with her editor at Putnam.

INSIDER REPORT, *Rathmann*

10 Minutes till Bedtime (Putnam), the latest picture book from Caldecott-winning author/illustrator Peggy Rathmann, is a countdown bedtime story complete with a host of hamsters hanging out at One Hoppin' Place. Two hamster parents with ten hamster kids wearing numbered jerseys join dozens of hamster "tourists" as they observe a boy's getting-ready-for-bed ritual led by a hamster tour guide. The hamsters are alerted that the tour is beginning through www.hamstertours.com. The site exists in real life, too, as a fun, interactive enhancement to the book.

"I'd blown through 20 deadlines and was hiding out. I considered faking my own death. I needed professional help," jokes Rathmann. "I broke down and called my editor. She said, 'Would this be a good time to take a few minutes and just talk about what you're trying to say in this book?' "

Rathmann thought, "Yeah. I've just blown a year auditioning animal acts, and now if I want to put this book to bed this century, I'll have to finish the whole thing in about ten minutes." That's when it finally clicked—her book was about deadlines. Deadlines and distractions. "Knowing my book was about deadlines, however, didn't keep me from changing the manatees into gerbils. And then, when someone asked me what ten gerbils were doing watching a boy go to bed, I decided it was because the gerbils were *gerbil-tourists* who thought the boy's bedtime ritual was an interesting *tourist attraction.*"

With the focus of the book clear, how did the gerbils become hamsters? "I was congratulating myself for having solved all the book's problems when an author friend told me that gerbils were illegal in California because they were considered an agricultural threat," explains Rathmann. "If the book became popular little children might attempt to smuggle gerbils into California and the gerbils would wipe out the agricultural industry there. Furthermore, my author friend said, 'It will be all your fault, Peggy.' "

So Rathmann turned the gerbils into hamsters. And the ten hamsters became dozens of hamsters. And one hamster alerted the others of the bedtime tour through a hamster website. A beginning page of the book features the hamster tour guide with his mouse clicking on www.hamstertours.com, homepage of "The 10-Minute Bedtime Tour—Free snacks! Clean restroom! Families welcome!"

The book's hamstertours.com led to a real-life website with the same address. "Once I decided the hamster tour guide needed the Internet in order to get the word out fast enough, I knew I had to make his homepage be real. I could've used a bogus site, but I thought, what if somebody tries to call it up—won't that be disappointing?

INSIDER REPORT, *continued*

With one minute to go on Peggy Rathmann's *10 Minutes till Bedtime* hamster tour, the tub is one of the last stops. Like this bathroom scene, Rathmann packed her new book with tons of wonderful Where's Waldo-like details. "Kids are extremely loyal as a readership. They want to hear a story over and over," says Rathmann. "Enriching the background with details allows the book to unfold in surprising ways over time" and keeps a story fresh for younger readers, older readers and parents.

"When I started the book idea, I hoped it would be satisfying to the very young. I wondered, how many one- and two-year-olds know about computers? It turns out, quite a few of them. I had never been on the Internet. I found it slightly threatening. But there was a buzz about Jan Brett's website, and I knew Dav Pilkey had a really fun site. It's a great way of getting out information."

In addition to creating a website as a fun, interactive enhancement to the book, Rathmann is touring (just as her hamsters are) to promote *10 Minutes till Bedtime*. "Touring is fun, but there's a lot of preparation involved. I try to adapt my presentation to each place I visit." Her tour is limited to California (Rathmann doesn't fly) and her publisher is solidly behind promoting *10 Minutes* on the heels of its successful predecessor, *Officer Buckle and Gloria*.

"With every successful book you bring out, your publisher will allocate more resources for your next book's promotion. Promoted books reach people more quickly, which is good, but people still have to decide if they like them. A marketing person once told me that over the long haul, it's word-of-mouth that sells books, which is why even a new author can have a book that sells a million copies."

—Alice Pope

licited picture book mss only. Reports on queries in 2-3 weeks; mss in 4-10 weeks. Publishes a book 2 years after acceptance. Will consider simultaneous submissions on queries only.

Illustration: Works with 40 illustrators/year. Reviews ms/illustration packages from artists. Ms/illustration packages and illustration only: Query. Reports back only if interested. Samples returned with SASE; samples filed.

Terms: Pays authors royalty based on retail price. Pays illustrators by the project or royalty based on retail price. Sends galleys to authors. Original artwork returned at job's completion. Books catalog and ms and artist's guidelines available for SASE.

Tips: "Study our catalogs and get a sense of the kind of books we publish, so that you know whether your project is likely to be right for us. Putnam publishes high-quality books with child appeal as well as outstanding design and text. We have published two Caldecott Medal winners, *Mirette on the High Wire*, by Emily Arnold McCully and *Officer Buckle and Gloria*, by Peggy Rathmann. Our books are frequently nominated for state awards, and we have also won several awards such as the Christopher Award, the Carter G. Woodwon Award and the Jane Addams Peace Award, for our nonfiction books on social issues."

N **RAGWEED PRESS**, P.O. Box 2023, Charlottetown, Prince Edward Island C1A 7N7 Canada. (902)566-5750. Fax: (902)566-4473. E-mail: editor@ragweed.com. Book publisher. **Contact:** Managing Editor. Publishes 1 picture book/year; 2 young adult titles/year. 20% of books by first-time authors.
   ● Ragweed accepts work from Canadian authors only.

Fiction: Young readers: adventure, multicultural, suspense/mystery. Middle readers, young adults: adventure, anthology, contemporary, history, multicultural. Average word length: picture books—1,000-24 pages (full color illustration); middle readers: 96 pages; young adults: 256 pages. Recently published *Ghostwise: A Book of Midnight Stories*, collected by Dan Yashinsky (for ages 12 and up).

How to Contact/Writers: Fiction: Submit complete ms. Reports on queries/mss in 5-6 months. Publishes a book 6 months from final ms, "up to 2 years before editorial process is completed." Will consider simultaneous submissions.

Illustration: Works with 1-2 illustrators/year. Uses color artwork only. Reviews illustration packages from artists. Query with samples. Contact: Managing Editor. Samples returned with SASE if requested; samples filed.

Terms: Pays authors/illustrators royalty of 5-10% based on retail price. Sends galleys to authors. Original artwork returned at job's completion. Book catalog available for 9 × 12 SAE and 2 first-class stamps; ms and art guidelines available for SASE.

Tips: "Submit in writing—phone calls won't get results. We do look at everything we receive and make our decision based on our needs. Be patient."

RAINBOW PUBLISHERS, P.O. Box 261129, San Diego CA 92196. (619)271-7600. Fax: (619)578-4795. Book publisher. Estab. 1979. Imprints: Rainbow Books; Legacy Press. **Acquisitions:** Christy Allen, editor. Publishes 5 young readers/year; 5 middle readers/year; and 5 young adult titles/year. 50% of books by first-time authors. "Our mission is to publish Bible-based, Christ-centered materials that contribute to and inspire spiritual growth and development."

Nonfiction: Young readers, middle readers, young adult/teens: activity books, arts/crafts, how-to, reference, religion. Does not want to see traditional puzzles. Recently published (Rainbow): *Instant Bible Lessons*, by Pamela Kuhn, illustrated by Joel Ryan and Roger Johnson (series of 4; Christian lessons and activities for ages 5-10); and *Make & Learn Bible Toys*, by Linda Adams, illustrated by Joel Ryan (4 craft books for age 2-grade 4). (Legacy): *The Dickens Family Gospel*, by Robert C. Hanna, illustrated by Terry J. Walderhaug (all ages; family devotions); and *My Prayer Journal*, by Mary Davis, illustrated by Joel Ryan (upper elementary; journal).

How to Contact/Writers: Nonfiction: Submit outline/synopsis and 3-5 sample chapters. Reports on queries in 6 weeks; mss in 3 months. Publishes a book 18 months after acceptance. Will consider simultaneous submissions, electronic submissions via disk and previously published work.

Illustration: Works with 2-5 illustrators/year. Reviews ms/illustration packages from artists. Submit ms with 2-5 pieces of final art. Illustrations only: Query with samples. Reports in 6 weeks. Samples returned with SASE; samples filed.

Terms: Pays authors royalty of 4% and up based on wholesale price or work purchased outright (range: $500 and up). Pays illustrators by the project (range: $300 and up). Sends galleys to authors. Book catalog

THE SUBJECT INDEX, located in the back of this book, lists book publishers and magazines according to the fiction and nonfiction subjects they seek.

available for 10×13 SAE and 2 first-class stamps; ms guidelines available for SASE.

Tips: "Our Rainbow imprint carries reproducible books for teachers of children in Christian ministries, including crafts, activities, games and puzzles. Our Legacy imprint (new in '97) handles nonfiction titles for children and adults in the Christian realm, such as Bible story books, devotional books, and so on. Please write for guidelines and study the market before submitting material."

☑ **RAINTREE STECK-VAUGHN**, Imprint of Steck-Vaughn, 466 Southern Blvd., Chatham NJ 07928. (973)514-1525. Fax: (973)514-1612. Book publisher. Publishing Directors: Frank Sloan and Walter Kossmann. Art Director Joyce Spicer (Steck-Vaughn, 4515 Seton Center Pkwy., Suite 30, Austin TX 78759.) Publishes 30 young readers/year; 30 middle readers/year; 20 young adults/year.
● Raintree Steck-Vaughn publishes strictly nonfiction titles.
Nonfiction: Picture books, young readers, middle readers: animal, biography, geography, health, history, multicultural, nature/environment, science, sports. Young adults: biography, careers, geography, health, history, sports. Average page length: young readers—32; middle readers—48; young adults: 64-78. Recently published: Innovative Mind series (about famous scientists); World's Top Ten series (about famous geographical sites); and *Who's That in the White House?* (a U.S. Presidents series).
How to Contact/Writers: Nonfiction: query. Reports on queries/mss in 3-4 months.
Illustration: Contact Joyce Spicer at above Texas address.
Photography: Contact Joyce Spicer at above Texas address.
Terms: Pays authors royalty or flat fee. Offers advance. Sends galleys to authors. Book catalog available for 9×12 SAE and $3 first-class postage. Ms guidelines available for SASE.
Tips: "Request a catalog so you're not proposing books similar to those we've already done. Always include SASE."

☑ Ⓐ **RANDOM HOUSE BOOKS FOR YOUNG READERS**, 201 E. 50th St., New York NY 10022. (212)572-2600. Random House, Inc. Book publisher. Estab. 1935. "Random House Books aims to create books that nurture the hearts and minds of children, providing and promoting quality books and a rich variety of media that entertain and educate readers from 6 months to 12 years." Vice President/Publishing Director: Kate Klimo. Vice President/Associate Publishing Director: Cathy Goldsmith. **Acquisitions:** Easy-to-Read Books (step-into-reading): Heidi Kilgras, editor. Nonfiction: Alice Jonaihs, editor. Picture Books: Mallory Loehr, assistant publishing director. First Stepping Stones: Ruth Koeppel. Middle Grade Fiction: Lisa Banim, creative director. Fantasy & Science Fiction: Alice Alfonsi, senior editor. Young Adult: Ruth Koeppel, senior editor. Baby & Toddler Books: Shana Corey. 100% of books published through agents; 2% of books by first-time authors.
● Random House accepts only agented material.
Fiction: Picture books: animal, easy-to-read, history, sports. Young readers: adventure, animal, easy-to-read, history, sports, suspense/mystery. Middle readers: adventure, history, science, sports, suspense/mystery.
Nonfiction: Picture books: animal. Young readers: animal, biography, hobbies. Middle readers: biography, history, hobbies, sports.
How to Contact/Writers: Fiction/Nonfiction: Submit through agent only. Publishes a book 12-18 months after acceptance. Will consider simultaneous submissions.
Illustration: Reviews ms/illustration packages from artists through agent only.
Terms: Pays authors in royalties; sometimes buys mss outright. Sends galleys to authors. Book catalog free on request.

RED DEER COLLEGE PRESS, 56th Ave. and 32nd St., Box 5005, Red Deer, Alberta T4N 5H5 Canada. (403)342-3321. Fax: (403)357-3639. E-mail: vmix@admin.rdc.ab.ca. Imprints: Northern Lights Books for Children, Northern Lights Young Novels. Book publisher. Estab. 1975. **Manuscript/Art Acquisitions:** Peter Carver, children's editor. Publishes 4 picture books/year; 4 young adult titles/year. 50% of books by first-time authors. Red Deer College Press is known for their "high-quality international children's program that tackles risky and/or serious issues for kids."
Fiction: Picture books, young readers: adventure, animal, contemporary, fantasy, folktales, history, humor, multicultural, nature/environment, poetry; middle readers, young adult/teens: adventure, anima, contemporary, fantasy, folktales, hi-lo, history, humor, multicultural, nature/environment, problem novels, suspense/mystery. Recently published *Hope Springs a Leak*, by Ted Staunton (novel for ages 9 and up); and *Spider's Web*, by Sharon Stewart (novel for ages 9 and up).
How to Contact/Writers: Fiction/Nonfiction: Query or submit outline/synopsis. Reports on queries in 6 months; ms in 6-8 months. Publishes a book 18 months after acceptance. Will consider simultaneous submissions.
Illustration: Works with 3-5 illustrators/year. Illustrations only: Query with samples. Reports back only

if interested. Samples not returned; samples filed.

Photography: Buys stock and assigns work. Model/property releases required. Submit cover letter, résumé and color promo piece.

Terms: Pays authors royalty (negotiated). Offers advances (negotiated). Pays illustrators and photographers by the project or royalty (depends on the project). Sends galleys to authors. Originals returned to artist at job's completion. Guidelines not available.

Tips: "Red Deer College Press is currently not accepting children's manuscripts unless the writer is an established Canadian children's writer with an original project that fits its publishing program. Writers, illustrators and photographers should familiarize themselves with RDC Press's children's publishing program."

N **RED WHEELBARROW PRESS, INC.**, P.O. Box 33143, Austin TX 78764. (512)441-4191. E-mail: publisher@rwpress.com. Website: http://www.rwpress.com. Estab. 1997. Trade book publisher specializing in fiction (with slant) and educational material. **Manuscript Acquisitions:** L.C. Sajbel, publisher. Publishes 1-2 young readers/year. 100% of books by first-time authors. "Red Wheelbarrow Press is in business to publish distinctive literature for a niche market composed of readers interested in new authors and in sophisticated, enjoyable fiction, nonfiction and poetry."

Fiction: Young readers: concept. Young readers, middle readers: adventure, contemporary, folktales, history, humor, multicultural, poetry, suspense/mystery. Recently published *The Ambitious Baker's Batter*, written/illustrated by Wendy Seese (ages 5-11 humorous poetry picture book).

Nonfiction: "We have not yet published nonfiction yet, but we're open to it."

How to Contact/Writers: Fiction: Query, submit complete ms or submit outline/synopsis and 3 sample chapters. Nonfiction: Query. Reports on queries in 4-6 weeks; mss in 6-8 weeks. Publishes a book 1 year after acceptance.

Illustration: Works with 1-2 illustrators/year. Send ms with dummy. Contact: L.C. Sajbel, publisher. Samples returned with SASE; samples filed if requested by artist.

Terms: Pays authors royalty of 8-12% based on retail price. Pays illustrators royalty of 5-10%. Sends galleys to authors; dummies to illustrators. Originals returned to artist at job's completion. Ms guidelines available for SASE.

Tips: "We are looking for a fresh approach and for stories or works that appeal to ages 5-12. Work that teaches a concept or a moral without appearing didactic is of interest to us; we want our books to teach children to think and to imagine. The more 'layers' a story has, the more it appeals to our editor and to our readers. We want literature to be exciting for young audiences."

REIDMORE BOOKS INC., 18228-102 Ave., Edmonton, Alberta T5S 1S7 Canada. (780)444-0912. Fax: (780)444-0933. E-mail: reidmore@compusmart.ab.ca. Website: http://www.reidmore. com. Book publisher. **Acquisitions:** Leah-Ann Lymer, editorial director. Publishes 4 textbooks/year (grades 2-12). 25% of books by first-time authors.

● Reidmore Books is not looking at fiction titles this year. See their listing in the Multimedia Section.

Nonfiction: Young readers: history. Middle readers, young adults/teens: geography, history, multicultural, textbooks. Does not want to see "material that is not directly tied to social studies curricula. No picture books, please." Recently published: *Finding Your Voice: You and Your Government*, by Flaig and Galvin (grades 5-6, social studies textbook).

How to Contact/Writers: Nonfiction: Query, submit complete ms, submit outline/synopsis. Reports on queries in 1 month, mss in 2 months. Publishes a book 18 months after acceptance. Will consider simultaneous submissions.

Illustration: Works with 1 illustrator/year. Uses color artwork and b&w outlines. Illustration only: Query with samples. Contact: Leah-Ann Lymer, editorial director. Samples returned with SASE; samples filed.

Photography: Buys photos from freelancers. Buys stock images. Uses "content-rich photos, often geography-related." Photo captions required. Uses color prints and 35mm transparencies. Submit cover letter.

Terms: Pays authors royalty. Pays illustrators by the project. Pays photographers by the project or per photo. Sends galleys to authors. Book catalog available for 9×12 SAE and 2 first-class stamps.

Tips: "There are fewer titles being published in Canada. Call before submitting—it tends to speed up the process and saves everyone time, money and effort."

RONSDALE PRESS, 3350 W. 21st Ave., Vancouver, British Columbia V6S 1G7 Canada. (604)738-4688. Fax: (604)731-4548. E-mail: ronhatch@pinc.com. Website: http://ronsdalepress.com. Book publisher. Estab. 1988. **Manuscript/Art Acquisitions:** Veronica Hatch, children's editor. Publishes 1 young reader/year. 100% of titles by first-time authors. Publishes children's novels with b&w illustrations. "Ronsdale Press is a literary publishing house dedicated to publishing books from across Canada. Ronsdale feels

INSIDER REPORT

Electronic art—a perfect medium for children's books

Joy Allen

After working 15 years as an art director and graphic designer, Joy Allen decided to switch paths and do what she always wanted—illustrate books for children. Working in graphics, Allen says, gave her special knowledge which helps her in illustrating children's books and magazines. "Customers would come in and bring me a screw and say, 'We make these screws. We need a beautiful, exciting brochure about our screws.' We'd have to make something for these clients that didn't have any text, only their product. Soon you learn how to get into the psyche of each customer, understand each person's needs." When she started illustrating books, this empathy was valuable. "I can relate to a book and understand (hopefully) what the author is trying to convey and expand on it."

Her background also gave Allen a strong knowledge of computers. In fact, much of her artwork is created on computer. "I went into electronic art because I was in graphics and had seen the programs, and I knew the printing industry. I knew in the long run using a computer would be a great asset to anybody who printed. You don't have to go through three or four color separations—you know you'll end up with the color you want. You don't have to worry about registration—it's going to come out crisp. I knew those were things that would make a book look great."

Allen began pursuing computer illustration work for children's publications against most advice. "I had no knowledge. I got all the no's back. There's definitely a prejudice against electronic art because it can look too 'slick.' But it's the perfect medium for children's books, if the work keeps the integrity of style and uniqueness. Some electronic art can look so 'techy.' I still never say, 'This is electronic art' when I send out a package—I wait for them to ask me. They usually don't realize it is. I don't want my work to look electronic."

Her style does not look "techy" or cookie-cutter. It's soft and loose, full of characters with expression and personality. "I think that's my strength," she says. "When I draw, I want the viewer to feel the pain or laughter or joy of the characters—faces say so much, they are the essence of the character. Everything else is just complimentary."

As she begins an illustration project, Allen does "what any illustrator would do—I create some thumbnails, get my ideas down about what I want to do in the book. Then I make sketches of my piece on a regular board—a pencil sketch. This sketch is scanned into my computer." The initial sketch is "super rough." Once it's scanned in Allen refines it. "After I get the sketch where I want it, I create a layer in Photoshop—I call that my color layer. I put my pencil layer on top of my color layer and multiply it through the other layers. Then I choose my paintbrush, my color . . . and I paint. This way, I can keep the looseness of my original sketch undisturbed. The constant sketching and resketching required in traditional art that can create a 'tighter' sometimes less-lifelike painting is not a problem.

"I love working this way because if I decide to change the color of the sky, for instance, I'll test it. I'll make a new layer and try it out. If I like it, great; if not, I just dump it into the computer trash and continue. I don't always like sitting in front of a screen. I'd like to give more time to doing traditional work. But then I get spoiled. Using the computer, I can change colors, change backgrounds; I don't have to start all over again."

During Allen's career shift from graphic design to children's publishing, promoting her artwork to prospective publishers became a big part of her job. But before she dived in and contacted publishers, she decided to learn as much as she could about how things worked, something she can't recommend highly enough to those shifting careers or just delving into children's publishing.

She took a class with illustrator Marla Frazee (*The Seven Silly Eaters*), learned about the Society of Children's Book Writers and Illustrators (SCBWI) and joined it, and began attending conferences sponsored by SCBWI. She also researched the publishing market—going to libraries and bookstores to browse and get an idea of which publishers might appreciate her style.

Through classes, memberships and conference contacts, Allen was able to amass a network of illustrators throughout the country via the Internet. She interacts with one group of over 100 illustrators who regularly share information and advice; and a group of 5 other illustrators who actually critique each other's works-in-progress. (For more on how this illustrators' critique group works, see sidebar on page 62.)

Joy Allen's adorable electronic illustration featuring a little girl and her lemonade stand appears on the cover of *A Dollar for Penny* (Random House). Allen consulted with her online illustrators' critique group as she worked on the piece. "I originally had her little dress in yellow, and the tabletop in white," she says. "But I felt there wasn't enough spark to it, so I sent it to my group. Because of their input, I decided to make it a checkered tablecloth, and I made her dress red and added circles—like pennies."

INSIDER REPORT, *continued*

Joy Allen's illustration "Fantastic Flying Machines" appeared on the back cover of a *Guideposts for Kids* magazine "which had a fun story on the migration of birds. The article was rather fact-based, and they wanted me to come up with a 'Seussy' style to give a little twist," Allen says. "If you look closely, you'll see a few chicks reading *Guideposts for Chicks*. I am now selling Giclée prints of this piece in galleries."

Allen got her first assignment from *Guideposts for Kids* magazine, and her illustrations appeared in all but one edition of *Guideposts* in 1997. After her first year she had enough work to fill ten hours a day, six days a week. In addition to *Guideposts*, she's had illustrations published in *Spider*, *Highlights for Children*, *Your Big Back Yard*, *Clubhouse*, *Trails-N-Treasures* and *U*S* Kids*. She is currently illustrating a picture book, *Hold the Boat!*, for Bethany House and a combination picture book and color book, *Prayer for a Child's Day*, for Standard Publishing. She illustrated *A Dollar for Penny*, an early reader for Random House and eight picture books for Harcourt Brace, Stech-Vaughn and Creative Teaching Press (all educational publishers).

She has a contract with Price, Stern, Sloan, and has done several covers for Meadowbrook Press (books in their successful Girls to the Rescue and Newfangled Fairy Tales series—for examples see the Insider Report on page 146). Allen acquired a rep at an SCBWI conference and she's had Giclée prints of her work (digital prints on watercolor stock) displayed in several galleries in the U.S. She's also developed and written several book dummies.

But with all this success as an illustrator, "the critique group is one of the best things that's happened to me this year," says Allen. "Not only for the constructive comments, but for the support. We have a deep respect of each other's work. I love the kinship—I feel we all help each other. The people in the children's industry are so different than in the commercial end. If there's something I can do for somebody, I want to do it for them. You don't have that feeling of, 'We're competing.' Instead you have this feeling of, 'I think you're really great, maybe I can help you.' "

—*Alice Pope*

it particularly important not to neglect the work of multicultural writers. Of special interest are 'parallel text' books in two languages."

Fiction: Young readers, middle readers, young adults: adventure, animal, contemporary, fantasy, folktales, history, humor, multicultural, nature/environment, poetry, problem novels. Average word length: young readers—90; middle readers—90. Recently published *Willobe of Wuzz*, written by Sandra Glaze, illustrated by Pamela Breeze Currie (ages 3-12); *Long Long Ago*, written by Robin Skelton, illustrated by Pamela Breeze Currie (ages 3-12); and *Molly Brown is Not a Clown*, written by Linda Rogers, illustrated by Rick Van Krugel (ages 5-11).

Nonfiction: Young readers, middle readers, young adults: animal, concept, history, multicultural, nature/environment, social issues. Average word length: young readers—90; middle readers—90.

How to Contact/Writers: Fiction/Nonfiction: Submit complete ms. Reports on queries in 2 weeks; ms in 2 months. Publishes a book 1 year after acceptance. Will consider simultaneous submissions.

Illustrations: Works with 1-2 illustrators/year. Reviews ms/illustration packages from artists. Submit ms with dummy. Reports back in 2 weeks. Samples returned with SASE.

Terms: Pays authors royalty or 10% based on retail price. Pays illustrators royalty of 10% based on retail price. Sends galleys to authors; dummies to illustrators. Originals returned to artist at job's completion. Book catalog available for 8½×11 SAE and $1 postage; ms and art guidelines available for SASE.

Tips: "We publish at present only Canadian authors. We prefer authors to approach us with illustrators already chosen."

✅ **THE ROSEN PUBLISHING GROUP**, 29 E. 21st St., New York NY 10010. (212)777-3017. Fax: (212)253-6915. E-mail: rosened@erols.com. Book publisher. Estab. 1950. Publisher: Roger Rosen. **Manuscript Acquisitions:** Michele Drohan, young adult; Kristin Ward, juvenile. Publishes 144 juvenile readers/year; 75 middle readers/year; and 100 young adults/year. 35% of books by first-time authors; 1% of books from agented writers. "We publish quality self-help/guidance books for children, young adults and at-risk youth."

Nonfiction: Young readers: animal, concept, cooking, history, how-to, nature/environment, religion, science, sports. Middle readers: hi-lo. Young adult: careers, hi-lo, religion. All levels: biography, health, multicultural, self-help, social issues, special needs. No fiction. Average word length: juvenile—800; middle readers—8,000; young adults—40,000. Published *Anorexia: When Food Is the Enemy*, by Erica Smith (13-18 years); *Coping with Discrimination and Prejudice*, by Mary-Bowman-Kruhm (13-18 years); and *Learning About Courage through the Life of Christopher Reeve*, by Jane Kelly Kosek (4-8 years).

How to Contact/Writers: Submit outline/synopsis and sample chapters. Reports on queries in 2-4 months; mss in 4-6 months. Publishes a book 9 months after acceptance.

Photography: Buys photos from freelancers. Contact: Olga Vega. Works on assignment only.

Terms: Pays authors in royalties of 6-10% based on wholesale price or work purchased outright for $1,000-1,500. Pays illustrators and photographers by the project. Book catalog free on request.

Tips: "Target your manuscript to a specific age group and reading level and write for established series published by the house you are approaching."

✅ **ST. ANTHONY MESSENGER PRESS**, 1615 Republic St., Cincinnati OH 45210-1298. (513)241-5615. Fax: (513)241-0399. E-mail: stanthony@americancatholic.org. Website: http://www.AmericanCatholic.org. Book publisher. Managing Editor: Lisa Biedenbach. **Manuscript Acquisitions:** Katie Carroll. 25% of books by first-time authors. Imprints include Franciscan Communication (print and video) and Ikonographics (video). "Through print and electronic media marketed in North America and worldwide, we endeavor to evangelize, inspire and inform those who search for God and seek a richer Catholic, Christian, human life. We also look for books for parents and religious educators."

● St. Anthony Messenger Press book *Can You Find Jesus?*, by Philip Gallery and Janet Harlow was named best children's book by the 1997 Catholic Book Awards.

Nonfiction: Young readers, middle readers, young adults: religion. "We like all our resources to include anecdotes, examples, etc., that appeal to a wide audience. All of our products try to reflect cultural and racial diversity." Does not want to see fiction, story books, picture books for preschoolers. Recently published *The Wind Harp and Other Angel Tales*, by Ethel Pochocki (middle to adult readers); *Can You Find Jesus? Introducing Your Child to the Gospel*, by Philip Gallery and Janet Harlow (ages 5-10) and *God Is Calling* (family based catechetical program for ages 11-14 and under 10).

How to Contact/Writers: Query or submit outline/synopsis and sample chapters. Reports on queries in 1 month; mss in 2 months. Publishes a book 12-18 months after acceptance.

Illustration: Works with 1-2 illustrators/year. "We design all covers and do most illustrations in-house, unless illustrations are submitted with text." Uses primarily b&w artwork. Reviews ms/illustration packages from artists. Query with samples, résumé. Contact: Mary Alfieri, art director. Reports on queries in 2-4 weeks. Samples returned with SASE; or samples filed.

Photography: Purchases photos from freelancers. Contact: Mary Alfieri, art director. Buys stock and assigns work.

Terms: Pays authors royalties of 10-12% based on net receipts. Offers average advance payment of $1,000. Pays illustrators by the project. Pays photographers by the project. Sends galleys to authors. Book catalog and ms guidelines free on request.

Tips: "Know our audience—Catholic. We seek popularly written manuscripts that include the best of current Catholic scholarship. Parents, especially baby boomers, want resources for teaching children about the Catholic faith for passing on values. We try to publish items that reflect strong Catholic Christian values."

ST. MARY'S PRESS, Christian Brothers Publications, 702 Terrace Heights, Winona MN 55987-1320. (507)457-7900 or (800)533-8095. Fax: (507)457-7990. Book publisher. "Our mission is to significantly advance the ministry of sharing the Good News among youth . . . employing all appropriate settings, means, and media." **Contact:** Steve Nagel.

Fiction: Young adults: history, mystery, science fiction, all topics that "both give insight into the struggle of teens to become healthy, hopeful adults and also shed light on Catholic experience, history or cultures."

How to Contact/Writers: Query with cover letter and sample chapter. Cover letter should include personal bio including background and experience; a tentative title; table of contents; date of availability for final ms; estimated word count; author's address, phone numbers and Social Security number. SASE. Simultaneous submissions are okay with notification.

Terms: Payment varies.

Tips: "Here are key questions to ask yourself before submitting: does my work further SMP's publishing program and mission? Am I clearly in touch with the needs of my audience? Has my book been critiqued by those who are qualified to do so? If you wish to learn more about us, call our toll free number and ask for a free catalog."

SCHOLASTIC CANADA LTD., 175 Hillmount Rd., Markham, Ontario L6C 1Z7 Canada. (905)887-READ. Fax: (905)887-1131. Imprints: North Winds Press (contact Joanne Richter); Les Éditions Scholastic (contact Sylvie Andrews, French editor). **Acquisitions**: Diane Kerner, Sandra Bogart Johnston, editors, children's books. Publishes hardcover and trade paperback originals. Publishes 30 titles/year; imprint publishes 4 titles/year. 3% of books from first-time authors; 50% from unagented writers. Strongly prefers Canadian authors.

Fiction: Children's/juvenile, young adult. Recently published *After the War*, by Carol Matas (novel).

Nonfiction: Animals, history, hobbies, nature, recreation, science, sports. Reviews artwork/photos as part of ms package. Send photocopies. Recently published *Whose Bright Idea Was It?*, by Larry Verstraete (about amazing inventions).

How to Contact/Writers: Query with synopsis, 3 sample chapters and SASE. Nonfiction: Query with outline, 1-2 sample chapters and SASE. Reports on queries in 1 month; on proposals in 3 months. Publishes book 1 year after acceptance.

Terms: Pays 5-10% royalty on retail price. Offers advance: $1,000-5,000 (Canadian). Book catalog for 8½×11 SAE with 2 first-class stamps (IRC or Canadian stamps only).

SCHOLASTIC INC., 555 Broadway, New York NY 10012. (212)343-6100. Website: http://www.scholastic.com. Estab. 1920. Vice President, Editor-in-Chief: Jean Feiwel. **Manuscript Acquisitions:** Scholastic Press: Elizabeth Szabla, editorial director; Blue Sky Press: Bernette Ford, editorial director; Trade Paperback: Craig Walker, editorial director; Scholastic trade: Ann Reit, executive editor; Cartwheel Books: Bernette Ford, editorial director; Arthur A. Levine Books: Arthur Levine; Scholastic Reference: Wendy Barrish, editorial director. **Art Acquisitions:** David Saylor, creative director. "We are proud of the many fine, innovative materials we have created—such as classroom magazines, book clubs, book fairs, and our new literacy and technology programs. But we are most proud of our reputation as 'The Most Trusted Name in Learning.' "

● Scholastic is not interested in receiving ideas for more fiction paperback series. They do not accept unsolicited mss.

Illustration: Works with 60 illustrators/year. Does not review ms/illustration packages. Illustrations only:

● **SPECIAL COMMENTS** by the editor of *Children's Writer's & Illustrator's Market* are set off by a bullet.

send promo sheet and tearsheets.Reports back only if interested. Samples not returned. Original artwork returned at job's completion.

Terms: All contracts negotiated individually; pays royalty. Sends galleys to author; dummies to illustrators.

SCHOLASTIC PRESS, 555 Broadway, New York NY 10012. (212)343-6100. Book publisher. Imprint of Scholastic Inc. **Manuscript Acquisitions:** Diane Hess, executive director (picture book fiction/nonfiction); Anne Dunn, senior editor (middle grade and YA fiction); Lauren Thompson, senior editor (picture book fiction/nonfiction); Tracy Mack, editor (picture book, middle grade, YA). **Art Acquisitions:** David Saylor, Scholastic Press, Reference, Paperback; Edie Weinberg, Cartwheel Books. Publishes 37 picture books/year; 28 young adult titles/year. 1% of books by first-time authors.

- Scholastic's title *Out of the Dust*, by Karen Hesse, won the Newbery Medal in 1998.

Fiction: All levels: adventure, animal, anthology, concept, contemporary, fantasy, health, history, humor, multicultural, nature/environment, poetry, religion, science fiction, sports, suspense/mystery. Picture books: concept, folktales. Middle readers: folktales, problem novels, romance. Young adults: problem novels, romance. Multicultural themes include: strong fictional or nonfictional themes featuring non-white characters and cultures. Does not want to see mainstream religious, bibliotherapeutic, adult. Average word length: picture books—varies; young adults—150 pages. Recently published *Out of the Dust*, by Karen Hesse; *Rocking Horse Christmas*, by Mary Pope Osborne, illustrated by Ned Bittinger.

Nonfiction: All levels: animal, biography, history, multicultural, music/dance, nature/environment, science, social issues, sports. Picture books: concept. Multicultural needs "usually best handled on biography format." Average word length: picture book—varies; young adults—150 pages. Recently published *Women of Hope*, by Joyce Hansen.

How to Contact/Writers: Fiction: "Due to large numbers of submissions, we are discouraging unsolicited submissions—send query (don't call!) only if you feel certain we publish the type of book you have written." Nonfiction: young adult titles: query. Picture books: submit complete ms. Reports in 1-3 months.

Illustrations: Works with 30 illustrators/year. Uses both b&w and color artwork. Contact: Editorial Submissions. Illustration only: Query with samples; send tearsheets. Reports only if interested. Samples returned with SASE. Original artwork returned at job's completion.

Photography: Buys photos from freelancers. Contact: Photo Research Dept. Buys stock and assigns work. Uses photos to accompany nonfiction. Model/property releases required; captions required. Submit cover letter, résumé, client list, stock photo list.

Terms: Pays authors by varying royalty (usually standard trade roles) or outright purchase (rarely). Offers variable advance. Pays illustrators by the project (range: varies) or standard royalty based on retail price. Pays photographers by the project or royalty. Sends galleys to authors.

Tips: "Read *currently* published children's books. Revise, rewrite, rework and find your own voice, style and subject. We are looking for authors with a strong and unique voice who can tell a great story and have the ability to evoke genuine emotion. Children's publishers are becoming more selective, looking for irresistable talent and fairly broad appeal, yet still very willing to take risks, just to keep the game interesting."

SEEDLING PUBLICATIONS, INC., 4522 Indianola Ave., Columbus OH 43214-2246. (614)267-7333. Fax (614)267-4205. E-mail: Sales@SeedlingPub.com. Website: http://www.SeedlingPub.com. **Manuscript Acquisitions:** Josie Stewart, vice president. **Art Acquisitions:** Lynn Salem. Publishes 5-10 young readers/year. 20% of books by first-time authors. Publishes books for the beginning reader in English and Spanish. "Natural language and predictable text are requisite to our publications. Patterened text acceptable, but must have a unique storyline. Poetry, books in rhyme, full-length picture books or chapter books are not being accepted at this time. Illustrations are not necessary."

Fiction: Beginning reader books: adventure, animal, fantasy, hi-lo, humor, multicultural, nature/environment, special needs. Multicultural needs include stories which include children from many cultures and Hispanic centered storylines. All mss to be published in Spanish must be submitted in both English and Spanish. Does not want to see texts longer than 16 pages or over 150-200 words or stories in rhyme. Averge word length: young readers—100. Recently published *All Over the World*, by Deirdre Jones and *Boxes, Boxes, Boxes*, by L. Salem and J. Stewart (ages 3-7, paperback early reader).

Nonfiction: Beginning reader books: animal, concept, hi-lo, multicultural, music/dance, nature/environment, science, special needs, sports. Does not want to see texts longer than 16 pages or over 150-200 words. Average word length: young readers—100. Recently published *Use Your Beak*, by Betty Erickson (ages 3-7, early reader).

How to Contact/Writers: Fiction/Nonfiction: Submit complete ms. Reports in 6 months. Publishes a book 1-2 years after acceptance. Will consider simultaneous submissions.

Illustration: Works with 4-5 illustrators/year. Uses color artwork only. Reviews ms/illustration packages

INSIDER REPORT

On implication, ambiguity and issues for illustrators

As for my illustrations, or "pictures" as I prefer to call them, they are rarely based on fantasy or flights of imagination. I base my images on facts and on things observed. I find that nature and the world around me create and suggest things stranger and more wonderful than things my mind and eye invent.

Barry Moser
Children's Books and Their Creators

Barry Moser

photo: Reassurance Wunder

Since 1969, Barry Moser has illustrated more than 120 books. In 1987 *The New York Times* named Moser's *Jump, Again! The Further Adventures of Brer Rabbit* one of the "Ten Best Illustrated Children's Books." The same year *Redbook* named it a "Best Book for Children." More awards followed, including the Boston Globe-Horn Book Award in 1991 for *Appalachia, the Voice of Sleeping Birds*; an International Board of Books for Young People's "Best Book" the same year for *Big Double the Bear Meets Little Tricker the Squirrel*; a *Parents Magazine* "Best of the Year" in 1994 for *My Dog Rosie*; an ALA Notable Book in 1995 for *Whistling Dixie* and again in 1997 for *When Birds Could Talk and Bats Could Sing*. But Moser values study and hard work above awards. For beginning children's book illustrators, here are Moser's thoughts . . .

. . . On History
I think a puritan suspicion of intellect runs through our society. I find it among my students, and among beginning children's book illustrators. They don't seem to be concerned with the intellectual life. They seem to be concerned only with making cute pictures. *Cute, corny,* and *obvious* are the three things I have a battle with. That's not original with me, by the way. John Gardner in *The Art of Fiction* says the writer should avoid those three things.

I don't see beginning illustrators interested in the intellectual history of what they are doing and how they fit into it. I tell my students, "If you want to do what you're doing well, you've got to be aware of what came before you, and you've got to be aware of what effect you will have on the future. You've got to stand with a foot in both places. You owe to the past, and you owe to the future."

. . . On Literature
I have started requiring my students at Rhode Island School of Design to write. I tell them, "You have to understand that you're in the business of words as much as you are in pictures. You have to understand how those words are put together. You have to understand

INSIDER REPORT, *Moser*

the art and craft of literature and writing, at least moderately well, before you can hope to intelligently put pictures to words."

. . . On Self-Expression
I don't hold much with this "expressing one's self" business. I believe that what I do is a craft. It's something I manufacture, in the original meaning of the word, which is to say "to make by hand." Mozart and Bach were more concerned with form than expression. I have tried to learn from them.

. . . On Art School
Art school can cut down your participatory time in the early stages, but it's not a prerequisite. I have never had a course in watercolor. I have never had a course in engraving, calligraphy, typography, book design, or any of the things I do. I don't think a children's illustrator has to be anything except alert and willing to learn. And it doesn't matter where you learn.

. . . On Keeping a Journal
Every morning I enter in a journal the things I did the day before. It's a road map for me, except it's a backwards road map. It's like the dodo bird flying backwards—he doesn't care where he's going, he just wants to see where he's been. I'm inspired by Jean Cocteau's

© 1995 Barry Moser. Reprinted with permission of Scholastic, Inc.

Award-winning illustrator Barry Moser wrote *My Cats Nick & Nora* (Blue Sky Press) with the help of his oldest granddaughter, Isabelle Harper, who stars in the book with her cousin Emmie, and their beloved feline friends. Moser also collaborated with his granddaughter on two books featuring canine characters—*My Dog Rosie* and *Our New Puppy.*

INSIDER REPORT, *continued*

diary of making *The Beauty and the Beast*, which I have my students read because it's the best literary example of what an artist's life is like. It's nothing about self-expression.

It's about the carbuncles that one of the actresses got and couldn't sit on the saddle. It's about the Luftwaffe flying overhead. It's about setting up the scene, but the sun is in the wrong place—all of these practical, day-to-day things that are what the artist's life is about. That's what I deal with in my journal.

. . . On Failure

Faulkner said, "The only thing worthwhile is failing," and in another place he said, "But failing in the quest for perfection." You're always looking to do something perfectly but if you did, you might as well cut your throat and die, get out of here, bye-bye. Failure is where growth comes from. If you started out doing something well, you wouldn't have room to grow.

. . . On Work-for-Hire

If somebody comes to me and says, "We want you to illustrate this, but we're going to retain ownership of your painting," I say, "Are you kidding? Call me back when you have something interesting to say." Now, I can tell beginning illustrators what the pitfalls are, but you go out there and you've got to make the rent payment this month. You've got to take the job given to you. You're going to end up doing work-for-hire and signing your work away because you don't have any kind of a reputation. You have no bargaining power. Those come with determination and hard work.

. . . On Agents

I was walking down the street in San Francisco, and I saw Michael Hague's illustrated edition of Tolkien's *The Hobbit*. I stood there and said, "How come he got that job? How come I didn't know about it?" I thought, if I had somebody who had his ear to the ground in the industry, maybe I would get a job like that, and so that's primarily what led me to getting an agent, that and getting exploited a couple of times by publishers and needing somebody to read a contract. I did that for a long time, but then after looking at so many contracts, I realized that they're all pretty much the same. Why should I give an agent 15 percent of everything I make to read a contract? I have pet things in a contract that I look for, and if they're not there, I raise a ruckus.

. . . On Working with Authors' Texts

Sometimes an author expects an illustrator to be able to do something that's impractical. It's easy enough to write a line that says, "There were 150 people on the street." How long does it take you to write that sentence? To make a painting of 150 people on the street is a different issue. And it's not so much that the writer shouldn't write those things, but it's the editor who shouldn't expect the illustrator to do them, unless they are absolutely essential to telling the story. Even at that, a good illustrator is going to sidestep them. He's going to find a way to imply them. Implication and ambiguity are two of the greatest tools an illustrator has in his bag. Benedetto Croce wrote in the 17th century, "The greater the degree of ambiguity, the greater the degree of expression." That's an old idea, but it's true.

The more ambiguous your images are, the more expressive they are, the more they suggest. You don't tell everything, just like good writers don't tell everything. One of the

INSIDER REPORT, *Moser*

Barry Moser's beautiful paintings give life to *On Call Back Mountain* (Blue Sky Press), Eve Bunting's story of two boys, their connection with the wilderness and their love of a mountain forest. This book is just one of the 100-plus children's titles Moser has illustrated in his career spanning 3 decades.

problems with beginning children's book illustrators is they want to paint every pine needle on a pine tree. I know one fairly well-known illustrator who was proud of that fact that he had done his illustrations with a double-ought brush. A double-ought brush has like six hairs in it. Who cares? The fact is that the illustrations look labored. They don't look easy. You go in and look at some of the great paintings of Rembrandt and Diego Velazquez. They take your breath away with their simplicity, the way they look like they were done effortlessly. And yet, a lot of these children's book illustrators sit around and do these scratchy, scratchy, scratchy . . . oh, God save me!

. . . On Awards

I couldn't care less whether I have another award or not. It doesn't do anything for my work. It doesn't make me a better artist. I've had my awards framed and hung in a room in the farthest corner of my house where no one goes except me. God only knows where they all came from, the American Book Award, and so forth, and right in the middle of them is a little engraved motto that says, "God will not examine our medals and our diplomas, but our scars."

—*Anna Olswanger*

from artists. Submit ms with dummy. Illustrations only: Send color copies. Reports back only if interested. Samples returned with SASE only; samples filed if interested.

Photography: Buys photos from freelancers. Works on assignment only. Model/property releases required. Uses color prints and 35mm transparencies. Submit cover letter and color promo piece.

Terms: Pays authors royalty of 5% based on retail price or work purchased outright. Pays illustrators and photographers by the project. Original artwork is not returned at job's completion. Book catalog available for 2 first-class stamps.

Tips: "Follow our guidelines carefully and test your story with children and educators."

SILVER MOON PRESS, 160 Fifth Ave., New York NY 10010. (212)242-6499. E-mail: mail@silvermoon press.com. Website: http://www.silvermoonpress.com. Publisher: David Katz. Book publisher. Publishes 2 books for grades 4-6. 25% of books by first-time authors; 10% books from agented authors. "We publish books of entertainment and educational value and develop books which fit neatly into curriculum for grades 4-6."

Fiction: Middle readers: historical, multicultural and mystery. Average word length: 14,000. Recently published *A Message for General Washington*, by Vivian Schurfranz; and *A Secret Party in Boston Harbor*, by Kris Hemphill (both historical fiction, ages 8-12).

How to Contact/Writers: Fiction/Nonfiction: Query. Reports on queries in 2-4 weeks; mss in 1-2 months. Publishes a book 1-2 years after acceptance. Will consider simultaneous submissions, electronic submissions via disk or modem, previously published work.

Illustration: Works with 2 illustrators/year. Reviews ms/illustration packages from artists. Query. Illustrations only: Query with samples, résumé, client list. Reports only if interested. Samples returned with SASE. Original artwork returned at job's completion.

Photography: Buys photos from freelancers. Buys stock and assigns work. Uses archival, historical, sports photos. Captions required. Uses color, b&w prints; 35mm, 2¼×2¼, 4×5, 8×10 transparencies. Submit cover letter, résumé, published samples, client list, promo piece.

Terms: Pays authors royalty or work purchased outright. Pays illustrators by the project, royalty. Pays photographers by the project, per photo, royalty. Sends galleys to authors; dummies to illustrators. Book catalog available for SAE.

SIMON & SCHUSTER BOOKS FOR YOUNG READERS, 1230 Avenue of the Americas, New York NY 10022. (212)698-7200. Website: http://www.simonsays.com/kidzone. Imprint of Simon & Schuster Children's Publishing Division. Vice President/Editorial Director: Stephanie Owens Lurie. **Manuscript Acquisitions:** David Gale, executive editor (middle grade and YA fiction); Rebecca Davis, editor (picture books, poetry, fiction); Kevin Lewis, editor (young picture books); Sarah Thomson, associate editor (picture books, middle grade and YA fiction); John Ranolph, editorial assistant (picture books and fiction). **Art Acquisitions:** Paul Zakris, art director. Publishes 80 books/year. "We publish high-quality fiction and nonfiction for a variety of age groups and a variety of markets. Above all we strive to publish books that will offer kids a fresh perspective on their world."

Fiction: Picture books: animal, concept. Middle readers, young adult: adventure, suspense/mystery. All levels: anthology, contemporary, history, humor, poetry, nature/environment. Recently published *When Mama Comes Home Tonight*, by Eileen Spinelli, illustrated by Jane Dyer; *The Year of the Sawdust Man*, by A. LaFaye; and *Heaven*, by Angela Johnson.

Nonfiction: All levels: biography, history, nature/environment. Picture books: concept. "We're looking for innovative and accessible nonfiction for all age levels." Recently published *It's Disgusting and We Ate It*, by James Solheim, illustrated by Eric Brace; *I Have Lived a Thousand Years*, by Livia Bitton-Jackson.

How to Contact/Writers: Accepting query letters only. Reports in 1-2 months. Publishes a book 2-4 years after acceptance. Will consider simultaneous submissions.

Illustration: Works with 70 illustrators/year. Do not submit original artwork. Editorial reviews ms/illustration packages from artists. Submit query letter to Submissions Editor. Illustrations only: Query with samples; provide promo sheet, tearsheets. Reports only if interested.

Terms: Pays authors royalty (varies) based on retail price. Pays illustrators or photographers by the project or royalty (varies) based on retail price. Original artwork returned at job's completion. Ms/artist's guidelines free on request.

Tips: "We're looking for picture books centered on a strong, fully-developed protagonist who grows or changes during the course of the story; YA novels that are challenging and psychologically complex; also imaginative and humorous middle-grade fiction. And we want nonfiction that is as engaging as fiction. Send a query letter only. Take a look at what we're publishing to see if your work would fit in. The hardcover market is shrinking and so it is more difficult than ever to break in for the first time. Your work must sparkle with humor, imagination, wit and creativity."

🍁 ☑️ Ⓐ **SOMERVILLE HOUSE BOOKS LIMITED**, (formerly Somerville House, Inc.), 3080 Yonge St., Suite 5000, Toronto, Ontario M4N 3N1 Canada. (416)488-5938. Fax: (416)488-5506. E-mail: sombooks@goodmedia.com. Website: http://www.sombooks.com. Somerville publishes books and develops products. **Acquisitions:** Linda Pruessen, editor, acquisitions and development. Produces 20-30 titles/year in nonfiction and novelty formats.

● Somerville is currently accepting unsolicited mss in the areas of natural science, activities, sports and novelty formats.

Nonfiction: Young readers and middle readers: activity books, animal, arts/crafts, cooking, geography, history, hobbies, music/dance, nature/environment, science, sports. Recently published *Ice Age Mammals Books and Bones: Mammoth*, by Barbara Hehner (ages 6-12); *Time Capsule For The 21st Century*, by Sharon McKay (ages 6-12).

How to Contact/Writers: Only interested in agented material. Reports on queries/mss in 2-3 months.

Illustration: Works with 20-30 illustrators/year. Reports back only if interested. Samples not returned; samples filed.

SOUNDPRINTS, 353 Main Ave., Norwalk CT 06851-1552. (203)846-2274. Fax: (203)846-1776. E-mail: sndprnts@ix.netcom.com. Website: http://www.soundprints.com. Book publisher. Lines: Smithsonian's Backyard, Smithsonian Oceanic Collection, Smithsonian Odyssey and The Nature Conservancy series. **Manuscript Acquisitions:** Attn: Editorial Assistant. **Art Acquisitions:** Diane Hinze Kanzler, graphic designer. Publishes 16-20 picture books/year. "Soundprints publishes books about wildlife (including oceanic and backyard wildlife and habitats) and history created to educate while entertaining. Each book communicates information about its subject through an exciting storyline. At the same time, each book is based solidly in fact and all aspects must be supported by careful research. All titles are published with an audio and toy component. Each book is illustrated in full-color and contains a glossary and 'about the subject' paragraph to further explain to young children information in the text. All materials in Soundprints' books require the approval of curators and reviewers at the Smithsonian Institution and The Nature Conservancy. This curatorial review is a careful scrutiny that frequently necessitates changes in the text or art before approval will be granted."

Fiction: Picture books: animal, nature/environment. *No* fantasy or anthropomorphic animals. Young readers, middle readers: history, nature/environment. Average word length: picture books (grades PS-2)—800-1,000; (grades 2-5)—1,800-2,200. Recently published *Deer Mouse of Old Farm Road*, by Laura Gates Garvin, illustrated by Katy Bratun (grades PS-2, picture book); *Humpback Goes North*, by Darile Bailer, illustrated by Stephen Marches (grades PS-2, picture book); *Handshake in Space*, by Sheri Tan, illustrated by Higgins Bond (grades 2-5, picture book); and *Through TSQVD*, by Schuyler Bull , illustrated by Paul Kraner (grades 1-4, picture book).

Nonfiction: Picture books, young readers: animal, history. "Soundprints books are fiction, but based in research, with an intent to teach."

How to Contact/Writers: Query. Reports on queries 2-3 weeks, mss in 4-6 weeks. Publishing time approximately 2 years. Will consider simultaneous submissions. "Do not send manuscripts without reading our guidelines first."

Illustration: Works with 8-10 illustrators/year. Uses color artwork only. Illustrations are usually full bleed 2-page spreads. Reviews ms/illustration packages from artists "if subject matter is appropriate." Query. Illustrations only: Query with samples; provide résumé, portfolio, promo sheet, slides. "If interest is generated, additional material will be requested." Reports back only if interested. Samples returned with SASE or filed.

Terms: Authors are paid $1,500-2,500 for outright purchase of work. Illustrators paid by the project ($5,000-8,000). Original artwork returned at job's completion. Book catalog for 8½×11 SAE and $1.05 postage; ms guidelines and artist guidelines for #10 SASE. "It's best to request both guidelines and catalog. Both can be sent in self-addressed envelope at least 8½×11 with $1.05 postage."

Tips: "We want books that educate children about the subject while capturing the interest of the reader/listener through an entertaining storyline. As of Spring 1998, Soundprints offers 14 titles in the Smithsonian Wild heritage collection, 15 titles in the Smithsonian's Backyard series, 15 titles in the Smithsonian Oceanic Collection 8 titles in the Smithsonian Odyssey series and 8 titles in The Nature Conservancy Series. Authors should read a few of the titles in the relevant series before submitting a manuscript. Soundprints has very specific guidelines for each line and it is unlikely that a manuscript written by an author who is not familiar with our books will be acceptable. It is also a good idea to verify in advance that Soundprints has not already published, or is not currently working on, a book on your chosen topic."

SOUTHWEST PARKS & MONUMENTS ASSOCIATION, 221 N. Court St., Tucson AZ 85701. (520)622-1999. Fax: (520)623-9519. E-mail: dgallagher@spma.org. Nonprofit association. Publishes 10 young adult and picture books/year; and 2 middle readers/year. 50% of books by first-time authors. Pub-

INSIDER REPORT

Passion and perseverence pay off for Newbery winner

Karen Hesse, winner of the 1998 Newbery Award for *Out of the Dust*, has an undeniable passion for writing. "Write remembering your intial joy in language and story," she advises new writers, "and if you are certain writing is your passion, is your path, don't give up." While the myth of the overnight sensation is entrenched in our consciousness, Hesse, the author of ten children's books, was rejected for nine years before she sold her first book. But she didn't let the rejection letters bury her desire to be a writer. "Portray life as honestly, as convincingly, as compellingly as you are able," says Hesse, "and publishers will take notice."

photo: Cheryl Liston

Karen Hesse

Her award-winning young adult novel *Out of the Dust* proves that Hesse takes her own advice. Set in the Dust Bowl of Oklahoma, *Out of the Dust* tells the story of 14-year-old Billy Jo, a fierce heroine coming of age during the Depression. Hesse, who began her writing career as a poet, wrote the narrative in free-verse poetry, expressively depicting what she describes as the "spare and unvarnished elegance" of her hard-working characters. This unrelentingly bleak portrait of an era and powerful account of a family's trials is told in diary format providing the narrative with a palpable immediacy and intimacy. With each page, you can feel the dry dust in your mouth, the longing for rain and healing, and the hope that fights to persevere in Billy Jo's brutally honest voice: "Daddy came in,/ he sat across from Ma and blew his nose./ Mud streamed out./ He coughed and spit out mud./ If he had cried,/ his tears would have been mud too,/ but he didn't cry./ And neither did Ma."

Hesse does extensive research for her historical fiction, and *Out of the Dust*, her third historical novel, was no exception. "I threw myself into research, first using library materials, then moving on to the newspapers from the time and geographical setting. I read books written during the period, listened to music written during the period, lingered over photographs documenting the period." During her research process, she found a 1936 Walker Evans photograph of a young girl named Lucille Burroughs and kept it at her writing desk. The photograph eventually ended up on the book cover. "I often write with the image of my narrator visible somewhere on my desk," explains Hesse. "I will look into the eyes of the person in the photograph and know immediately whether they would say certain things or not, and how they would say them. The photographic image helps me keep my focus and consistency in character throughout the writing of the book."

Hesse has written children's books that cross the age spectrum, from picture books such as *Come on Rain!* and *Poppy's Chair*, to early chapter books for young readers such as *Sable* and *Just Juice*, to critically acclaimed YA novels such as *Letters from Rifka*, *The Music of Dolphins* and *Out of the Dust*. For Hesse, each age group presents its own unique challenges and rewards in writing. "Picture books are the hardest to write well," she

The striking cover photo appearing on Karen Hesse's Newbery-winning *Out of the Dust* inspired the writer as she worked. "I often write with the image of my narrator visible somewhere on my desk. I will look into the eyes of the person in the photograph and know immediately whether they would say certain things or not, and how they would say them." Hesse discovered the 1936 Walker Evans portrait of Lucille Burroughs as she researched her historical novel.

says. "Every word counts. Early chapter books are a joy to write. You have more room to explore character, plot and setting than you have in a picture book, but not so much room that you stand in danger of getting lost the way you might in a novel. I seem to have the greatest empathy, though, for my middle and older readers. I tackle topics that have the potential for disturbing them because those same topics disturb me. These are the most exhausting books to write, but also the most rewarding, the most healing." Hesse admits that she is never sure when she begins a new book what age group it will ultimately be for. "It is the narrative voice which determines the age and subject material of each book. I simply try to define the voice and follow where it leads."

Influenced by her experience as a hospice volunteer, Hesse's YA novels have explored challenging themes such as death, illness and loss. While many adults view the "grim" themes in Hesse's work as too much for children to handle, Hesse believes children will put down a book that is beyond their grasp. "A child will close a book she is not ready to read and turn to the TV or play with the dog or head outside. A child will keep reading a book if there is some resonance that transfers from the book to her heart." In fact, Hesse receives a great deal of fan mail from her audience that shows how strongly her books resonate with the thoughts and emotions of young readers. "Children, touched by something in my books, often write moving testaments to me of their own courage. I answer every letter I receive, often working on weekends to keep up with the mail. But each letter is an affirmation that what I'm doing has meaning, has an impact."

For other YA authors interested in writing about challenging issues, Hesse believes honesty is the key to getting your work published. "Publishers are open to solid, compelling writing. If YA writers are drawn to challenging issues they must be conscientious in their research and keep a keen eye to honesty, integrity and humanity in their portrayals. These difficult issues must not be sugar-coated, nor should they be portrayed with the pounding fist of pessimism. In this life, we are asked, young and old alike, to survive certain trials, tests, to confront certain painful issues. But usually these issues do not overwhelm the everyday details of life . . . perhaps now and then they do, but usually when life punches you in the stomach, you still have to go to school the next day, keep on eating, sleeping, reading to your little brother on the weekend, starting dinner for your mother on Tuesday night, etc. Put the issues you are exploring into perspective. The issue is just one aspect of a full life."

A full life is exactly what Hesse lives, too, as she continues to deal with the ongoing struggle to maintain a writing career and a family. Beginning her writing career as a poet, Hesse says she doesn't know if she would have found her way into children's literature if she hadn't had children. However, the demands of carrying and caring for her two daughters, while ultimately rewarding, pushed her to her absolute limits as a writer. "Because I was late coming to parenthood, I had already defined myself as a writer. Being unable to write because of this new role, having to steal moments to develop a new approach to the writing craft between parental chores, drove me at times to despair. When the children were small I often wrote during their naps. In the evening, while they slept, I'd catch five hours of sleep for myself, retiring as soon as I'd put them down at seven or eight. Then I'd set the alarm for one or two in the morning in order to write for several hours before my day began again. It wasn't easy, but it did discipline me. When I sit down at the keyboard, I work. No dawdling. My creative spirit is conditioned to kick in as soon as I place my hands on the keys."

Hesse credits her writing group as being a major source of support and indispensable

INSIDER REPORT, *Hesse*

feedback and encouragement. "My writing group has encouraged me when I felt the despair of rejection . . . and they have challenged me to go beyond good enough. I have no doubt that I would not be read by a single soul if I hadn't received the assistance and nurturing of my writing group."

No one can argue that Hesse's passion and perseverance hasn't paid off in a rewarding writing career, but she reminds new writers that it also takes single-minded focus and commitment to get published. "Anyone who wishes to publish must be well-read in the field. Write everyday and do not be discouraged by rejection. Form a writing group or join an existing writing group and no matter how painful you find critique, listen to it, learn from it. Network with other writers at conferences, in your state, through the mail, online. Prepare an itinerary for your finished work. When a manuscript comes back rejected from one house, put it into an envelope addressed to the next publisher on the list and send it right out again. Try to maintain your own unique voice in all your work. Write what you know in your gut."

—Tricia Waddell

---

lishes books to help children understand and appreciate national parks in the Southwest.

Nonfiction: Middle readers: animal, geography, history, nature/environment. Average word length: middle readers—2,000. Recently published *101 Questions About Desert Life*; and *101 Questions About Ancient Southwest Cultures.*

How to Contact/Writers: Nonfiction: Query. Reports on queries in 6 weeks; mss in 3 months. Publishes a book 1 year after acceptance. Will consider simultaneous submissions and electronic submissions via disk or modem.

Illustration: Works with 2 illustrators/year. Reviews ms/illustration packages from artists. Query. Contact: Derek Gallagher, director of publishing. Illustrations only: Query with samples. Contact: Derek Gallagher, director of publishing. Reports in 6 weeks. Samples returned with SASE; samples filed.

Photography: Buys stock and assigns work. Contact: Kim Beth-Poe, production editor. Uses photographs of sites in national parks and monuments in the Southwest. General natural history photographs (for example, animals). Model/property releases required; captions required. Uses 2¼×2¼, 4×5 or 8×10 transparencies. Submit published samples, promo piece or other nonreturnable samples.

Terms: Work purchased outright from authors ($1,000-2,500). Pays illustrators by the project (range: $500-2,500). Pays photographers by the project (range: $1,000-5,000) or per photo (range: $50-250). Sends galleys to authors. Book catalog available for SAE and 55¢ postage. All imprints included in a single catalog.

Tips: "We are a nonprofit association (private) working with 53 national parks in the Southwest. Any work submitted to us should advance the understanding of visitors to the parks as to the resources the parks preserve and protect."

THE SPEECH BIN, INC., 1965 25th Ave., Vero Beach FL 32960. (561)770-0007. Fax: (561)770-0006. Book publisher. Estab. 1984. **Acquisitions:** Jan J. Binney, senior editor. Publishes 10-12 books/year. 50% of books by first-time authors; less than 15% of books from agented writers. "Nearly all our books deal with treatment of children (as well as adults) who have communication disorders of speech or hearing or children who deal with family members who have such disorders (e.g., a grandparent with Alzheimer's disease or stroke)."

● The Speech Bin is currently overstocked with fiction.

Fiction: Picture books: animal, easy-to-read, fantasy, health, special needs. Young readers, middle readers, young adult: health, special needs.

Nonfiction: Picture books, young readers, middle readers, young adults: activity books, health, textbooks, special needs. Published *Chatty Hats and Other Props*, by Denise Mantione; *Holiday Hoopla: Holiday Games for Language & Speech*, by Michele Rost; and *Speech Sports*, by Janet M. Shaw.

How to Contact/Writers: Fiction/Nonfiction: Query. Reports on queries in 4-6 weeks; mss in 2-3 months. Publishes a book 10-12 months after acceptance. "Will consider simultaneous submissions *only* if notified; too many authors fail to let us know if manuscript is simultaneously submitted to other publishers! We *strongly* prefer sole submissions."

Illustration: Works with 4-5 illustrators/year ("usually inhouse"). Reviews ms/illustration packages from artists. Ms/illustration packages and illustration only: "Query first!" Submit tearsheets (no original art). SASE required for reply or return of material.

Photography: Buys stock and assigns work. Looking for scenic shots. Model/property releases required. Uses glossy b&w prints, 35mm or 2¼×2¼ transparencies. Submit résumé, business card, promotional literature or tearsheets to be kept on file.

Terms: Pays authors in royalties based on selling price. Pay illustrators by the project. Photographers paid by the project or per photo. Sends galleys to authors. Original artwork returned at job's completion. Book catalog for 5 first-class stamps and 9×12 SAE; ms guidelines for #10 SASE.

Tips: "No calls, please."

Ⓝ SRI RAMA PUBLISHING, Box 2550, Santa Cruz CA 95063. (408)426-5098. Book publisher. Estab. 1975. Secretary/Manager: Anthony Budding. Publishes 1 or fewer young reader titles/year.
   ● Sri Rama is not accepting mss for the 1998-99 book year.

Illustration: Illustrations used for fiction. Will review artwork for possible future assignments. Contact: James McElheron, graphic design director. Not reviewing at this time, however.

Terms: "We are a nonprofit organization. Proceeds from our sales support an orphanage in India, so we encourage donated labor, but each case is worked out individually." Pays illustrators $200-1,000. Sends galleys to authors; dummies to illustrators. Book catalog free on request.

STANDARD PUBLISHING, 8121 Hamilton Ave., Cincinnati OH 45231. (513)931-4050. Fax: (513)931-0950. Book publisher. Estab. 1866. Director, New Products: Diane Stortz. **Manuscript Acquisitions:** Greg Holder, children's editor. **Art Acquisitions:** Coleen Davis, creative director. Number and type of books varies yearly. Many projects are written inhouse. No juvenile or young adult novels. 25-40% of books by first-time authors; 1% of books from agented writers. "We publish well-written, upbeat books with a Christian perspective. Books are fun with relevancy in Christian education."
   ● Standard publishes *LiveWire, Kidz Chat* and *Straight*. Also see listing for Standard Publishing in the Greeting Cards, Puzzles & Games section. Standard is currently not accepting unsolicited mss due to backlog.

Fiction: Adventure, animal, contemporary, Bible stories. Average word length: board/picture books—400-1,000.

Nonfiction: Bible background, nature/environment, sports devotions. Average word length: 400-1,000. Recently published *The Bible Time Travelers On the Scene With Jesus*, by Mikal Keefer, illustrated by Carl Moore (picture book); and *Some Kind of Journey: On the Road With Audio/Adrenaline* (teens).

Illustration: Works with 15-20 new illustrators/year. Illustrations only: Submit cover letter and photocopies. Reports on art samples only if interested. Samples returned with SASE; samples filed.

Terms: Pays authors royalties based on net price or work purchased outright (range varies by project). Pays illustrators (mostly) by project. Pays photographers by the photo. Sends galleys to authors on most projects. Book catalog available for $2 and 8½×11 SAE; ms guidelines for letter-size SASE.

Tips: "We look for manuscripts that help draw children into a relationship with Jesus Christ; help children develop insights about what the Bible teaches; make reading an appealing and pleasurable activity."

STEMMER HOUSE PUBLISHERS, INC., 2627 Caves Rd., Owings Mills MD 21117-9919. (410)363-3690. Fax: (410)363-8459. E-mail: stemmerhousepublishers@erols.com. Website: http://www.stemmer.c om. Book publisher. Estab. 1975. **Acquisitions:** Barbara Holdridge, president. Publishes 1-3 picture books/year. "Sporadic" numbers of young reader, middle reader and young adult titles/year. 60% of books by first-time authors. "Stemmer House is best known for its commitment to fine illustrated books, excellently produced."

Fiction: Picture books: animal, folktales, multicultural, nature/environment. Middle readers: folktales, nature/environment. Does not want to see anthropomorphic characters. Published *How Pleasant to Know Mr. Lear: Poems by Edward Lear*, illustrated by Bohdan Butenko; and *The Marvelous Maze*, by Maxine Rose Schur, illustrated by Robin DeWitt and Patricia DeWitt-Grush.

Nonfiction: Picture books: animal, multicultural, nature. All level: animals, nature/environment. Multicul-

---

THE AGE-LEVEL INDEX, located in the back of this book, lists book publishers and magazines according to the age-groups for which they need material.

tural needs include Native American, African. Recently published *A Duck in a Tree*, by Jennifer A. Loomis, photographs by the author; *The Bird Alphabet Encyclopedia Coloring Book*, by Julia Pinkham; *Ask Me If I'm a Frog*, by Ann Milton, illustrated by Jill Chambers.

How to Contact/Writers: Fiction/Nonfiction: Query or submit outline/synopsis and sample chapters. Reports on queries/mss in 2 weeks. Publishes a book 18 months after acceptance. Will consider simultaneous submissions.

Illustration: Works with 2-3 illustrators/year. Uses color artwork only. Reviews ms/illustration packages from artists. Query first with several photocopied illustrations. Illustrations only: Submit tearsheets and/or slides (with SASE for return). Reports in 2 weeks. Samples returned with SASE; samples filed "if noteworthy."

Terms: Pays authors royalties of 4-10% based on wholesale price. Offers average advance payment of $300. Pays illustrators royalty of 4-10% based on wholesale price. Pays photographers 4-10% royalty based on wholesale price. Sends galleys to authors. Original artwork returned at job's completion. Book catalog and ms guidelines for 9×12 SASE.

Tips: Writers: "Simplicity, literary quality and originality are the keys." Illustrators: "We want to see ms/illustration packages—don't forget the SASE!"

STODDART KIDS, A Division of Stoddart Publishing Co. Ltd., 34 Lesmill Rd., Toronto, Ontario M3B 2T6 Canada. (416)445-3333. Fax: (416)445-5967. E-mail: kelly.jones@ccmailgw.genpub.com. Book publisher. **Acquisitions:** Kathryn Cole, publisher. Publishes 15 picture books/year; 6 young readers/year; 6 young adults/year. 20% of books by first-time authors.

Fiction: Picture books: adventure, animal, contemporary, folktales, history, humor, multicultural. Young readers: contemporary, folktales, history. Young adult: contemporary, history, multicultural, suspense/mystery. Does not want to see science fiction. Average word length: picture books—800; young readers—38,000; young adult/teens—70,000. Recently published *Maple Moon*, by Connie Crook and Scott Cameron (ages 4-7, picture book); *Biscuits in the Cupboard*, by Barbara Nichol and Phillipe Beha (all ages, picture book); *Turns on a Dime*, by Julie Lawson (ages 10-14, young reader); and *Moonkid and Prometheus*, by Paul Kropp (ages 12-16, young adult book).

How to Contact/Writers: Fiction: submit outline/synopsis and 2 sample chapters. Reports on queries in 3 weeks; mss in 4 months. Publishes a book 18 months after acceptance. Will consider simultaneous submissions.

Illustration: Works with 18 illustrators/year. Reviews ms/illustration packages from artists. Submit ms and photocopied artwork (no originals) and SASE. Illustrations only: Send photocopied artwork, SASE and query. Reports in 2 months. Samples returned with SASE; samples filed "if desirable."

Terms: Author and illustrator payments vary with project size and type. Sends galleys to authors. Originals returned to artist at job's completion. Book catalog available for large SASE and 2 first-class stamps. Ms guidelines available to SASE.

Tips: "Stoddart Kids is interested in developing a strong Canadian publishing program and therefore encourages the submission of Canadian materials. However, topics that cover both American and Canadian markets are also welcome."

SUMMERHOUSE PRESS, P.O. Box 1492, Columbia SC 29202. (803)779-0870. Fax: (803)779-9336. E-mail: robin@summerhousepress.com. Website: http://www.summerhousepress.com. Estab. 1995. **Manuscript and Art Acquisitions:** Robin Sumner Asbury. Publishes 3 picture books/year; 2 young readers/year; 1 middle reader/year; 1 young adult title/year. 80% of books by first-time authors.

Fiction: Picture books, young readers, middle readers, young adult: adventure, animal, anthology, contemporary, fantasy, folktales, health, hi-lo, history, humor, multicultural, nature/environment, poetry, problem novels, religion, science fiction, special needs, sports, suspense/mystery. Recently published *Moonlight & Mill Whistles*, by Terry Wark Tucker (young adult); *Hungry Ants*, by Pam McGrath (pre-school-3 years); and *Sheldon the Selfish Shellfish*, by Philip Moore (middle reader).

Nonfiction: Picture books, young readers, middle readers, young adults: activity books, animal, arts/crafts, biography, careers, concept, cooking, geography, health, hi-lo, history, hobbies, how-to, multicultural, music/dance, nature/environment, reference, religion, science, self-help, social issues, special needs, sports, textbooks. Recently published *All the Mamas*, by Carol Gandee Shough (middle reader).

How to Contact/Writers: Fiction/nonfiction: query or submit complete ms. Reports on queries in 1 month; mss in 10 weeks. Publishes a book 12-18 months after acceptance. Will consider simultaneous submissions, electronic submissions via disk or modem and previously published work.

Illustration: Works with 5 illustrators/year. Reviews ms/illustration packages from artists. Query or send ms with dummy. Contact: Robin Asbury, publisher. Illustrations only: send resume and portfolio. Contact: Robin Asbury, publisher. Samples returned with SASE.

Terms: Pays authors and illustrators negotiated royalty. Send galleys to authors; dummies to illustrators.

Originals returned to artist at job's completion. Book catalog available for 10×13 SAE with 3 first-class stamps. All imprints included in a single catalog. Catalog available on website.

 **SUNBELT MEDIA, INC./EAKIN PRESS**, P.O. Box 90159, Austin TX 78709. (512)288-1771. Fax: (512)288-1813. Book publisher. Estab. 1978. President: Ed Eakin. Publishes 1-2 picture books/year; 2-3 young readers/year; 9 middle readers/year; 2 young adult titles/year. 50% of books by first-time authors; 5% of books from agented writers.

Fiction: Picture books: animal. Middle readers, young adults: history, sports. Average word length: picture books—3,000; young readers—10,000; middle readers—15,000-20,000; young adults—20,000-30,000. "90% of our books relate to Texas and the Southwest."

Nonfiction: Picture books: animal. Middle readers and young adults: history, sports. Recently published *Sam and the Speaker's Chair.*

How to Contact/Writers: Fiction/Nonfiction: Query. Reports on queries in 2 weeks; mss in 6 weeks. Publishes a book 18 months after acceptance. Will consider simultaneous submissions.

Illustration: Reviews ms/illustration packages from artists. Query. Illustrations only: Submit tearsheets. Reports on art samples in 2 weeks.

Terms: Pays authors royalties of 10-15% based on net to publisher. Pays for separate authors and illustrators: "Usually share royalty." Pays illustrators royalty of 10-15% based on wholesale price. Sends galleys to authors. Book catalog, ms/artist's guidelines for $1.25 postage and SASE.

Tips: Writers: "Be sure all elements of manuscript are included—include bio of author or illustrator." Submit books relating to Texas only.

TIDEWATER PUBLISHERS, Imprint of Cornell Maritime Press, Inc., P.O. Box 456, Centreville MD 21617-0456. (410)758-1075. Fax: (410)758-6849. **Acquisitions:** Charlotte Kurst, managing editor. Estab. 1938. "Tidewater Publishers handles juvenile fiction and with a regional focus." Publishes hardcover and paperback originals. Publishes 7-9 titles/year. Receives 150 submissions/year. 41% of books from first-time authors; 99% from unagented writers.

Nonfiction: Regional subjects only. Recently published *Twilight on the Bay: The Excursion Boat Empire of B.B. Wills*, by Brian Cudahy

Fiction: Regional juvenile fiction only. Query or submit outline/synopsis and sample chapters. Recently published *Sam, The Tale of a Chesapeake Bay Rockfish*, by Kristina Henry, illustrated by Jeff Dombek.

How to Contact/Writers: Query or submit outline and sample chapters. Reviews artwork/photos as part of ms package.

Terms: Pays 7½-15% royalty on retail price. Publishes book 1 year after acceptance. Reports in 2 months. Book catalog for 10×13 SAE with 5 first-class stamps.

Tips: "Our audience is made up of readers interested in works that are specific to the Chesapeake Bay and Delmarva Peninsula area."

TILBURY HOUSE, PUBLISHERS, 132 Water St., Gardiner ME 04345. (207)582-1899. Fax: (207)582-8227. Book publisher. Publisher: Jennifer Elliott. Publishes 1-3 young readers/year.

Fiction: Young readers and middle readers: multicultural, nature/environment. Special needs include books that teach children about tolerance and honoring diversity.

Nonfiction: Young readers and middle readers: multicultural, nature/environment. Recently published *Talking Walls* and *Who Belongs Here?* both by Margy Burns Knight, illustrated by Anne Sibley O'Brien (grades 3-8).

How to Contact/Writers: Fiction/Nonfiction: Submit outline/synopsis. Reports on queries/mss in 1 month. Publishes a book 1-2 years after acceptance. Will consider simultaneous submissions "with notification."

Illustration: Works with 1-2 illustrators/year. Illustrations only: Query with samples. Contact: J. Elliott, associate publisher. Reports in 1 month Samples returned with SASE. Original artwork returned at job's completion.

Photography: Buys photos from freelancers. Contact: J. Elliott, publisher. Works on assignment only.

Terms: Pays authors royalty. Pays illustrators/photographers by the project; royalty. Sends galleys to authors. Book catalog available for 9×12 SAE and 78¢ postage.

Tips: "We are primarily interested in children's books that teach children about tolerance in a multicultural society and honoring diversity. We are also interested in books that teach children about environmental issues."

N: TOR BOOKS, Forge, Orb, 175 Fifth Ave., New York NY 10010. E-mail: caseykait@tor.com. Website: http://www.tor.com. Publisher, Middle Grade and Young Adult Division: Kathleen Doherty. Children's, Young Adult Editor: Jonathan Schmidt. Educational Sales Coordinator: Casey Kait. Publishes 5-10 middle readers/year; 5-10 young adults/year.

Fiction: Middle readers, young adult: adventure, animal, anthology, concept, contemporary, fantasy, folktales, health, history, humor, multicultural, nature/environment, poetry, problem novel, science fiction, special needs, sports, suspense/mystery. "We are interested and open to books which tell stories from a wide range of perspectives. We are interested in materials that deal with a wide range of issues." Average word length: middle readers—10,000; young adults—30,000-60,000. Published *Mind Quakes: Stories to Shatter Your Brain* and *Scorpions Shards*, by Neal Shusterman (ages 8 and up); and *From One Experience to Another*, edited by Helen and Jerry Weiss (ages 10 and up).

Nonfiction: Middle readers and young adult: activity books, geography, history, how-to, multicultural, nature/environment, science, social issues. Does not want to see religion, cooking. Average word length: middle readers—10,000-15,000; young adults—40,000. Published *Strange Unsolved Mysteries*, by Phyllis Rabin Emert; *Stargazer's Guide* (to the Galaxy), by Q.L. Pearce (ages 8-12, guide to constellations, illustrated).

How to Contact/Writers: Fiction/Nonfiction: Submit outline/synopsis and 3 sample chapters or complete ms. Reports on queries in 3 weeks; mss in 4-6 months.

Illustration: Works with 40 illustrators/year. Reviews ms/illustration packages from artists. Query with samples. Contact: Nichole Rajana or Jonathan Schmidt. Reports only if interested. Samples returned with SASE; samples kept on file.

Terms: Pays authors royalty. Offers advances. Pays illustrators by the project. Book catalog available for 9×12 SAE and 3 first-class stamps. Submission guidelines available with SASE.

Tips: "Know the house your are submitting to, familiarize yourself with the types of books they are publishing. Get an agent. Allow him/her to direct you to publishers who are most appropriate. It saves time and effort."

N: TRADEWIND BOOKS, 2216 Stephens St., Vancouver, British Columbia V6K 3W6 Canada.(604)730-0153. Fax: (604)730-0154. E-mail: tradewindbooks@yahoo.com. Website: http://tradewindbooks.com. Estab. 1994. Trade book publisher. **Manuscript Acquisitions:** Michael Katz, publisher. **Art Acquisitions:** Carol Frank, art director. Publishes 3 picture books/year. 25% of books by first-time authors.

Fiction: Picture books: adventure, animal, multicultural, special needs. Average word length: 900 words. Recently published *Lucy and the Pirates*; *The Zoo at Night*; and *Mr. Belinsky's Bagels*.

How to Contact/Writers: Fiction: Submit complete ms. Will consider simultaneous submissions.

Illustration: Works with 3 illustrators/year. Uses color artwork only. Reviews ms/illustration packages from artists. Send ms with dummy. Illustrations only: Query with samples. Samples returned with SASE, or filed.

Photography: Works on assignment only. Uses color prints.

Terms: Pays authors royalty of 7½-10% based on wholesale price. Offers advances against royalties. Pays illustrators by the project or royalty of 7½% based on wholesale price. Sends galleys to authors; dummies to illustrators. Originals returned to artist at job's completion. Book catalog available for 8×10 SAE and 3 first-class stamps. Catalog available on website.

☑ TREASURE LEARNING SYSTEMS, (formerly Treasure Publishing), 1133 Riverside, Suite B, Fort Collins CO 80524-3216. (970)484-8483. Fax: (970)495-6700. E-mail: mark@treasurelearning.com. Website: http://www.treasurelearning.com. Book publisher. **Acquisitions:** Mark Steiner, editor. "Treasure Learning Systems exists to assist the Church of Jesus Christ in fulfilling the Great Commission. We create, market and distribute Christian education resouces which feature excellence in biblical content, educational methodology and product presentation. Our primary responsibility is to serve the local and international Church. We began in 1935 as *Through the Bible Publishers* and developed into an established publishing ministry with a reputation for solid, biblical curriculum. The company was later renamed Roper Press. In 1995, after proclaiming God's Word for 60 years, Roper Press changed ownership and moved from Texas to Colorado. Our new name, Treasure!, reflects the central value we shall continue to place on the Scriptures. With the Lord's guidance, our team anticipates creating many new resources and making many new friends in the coming months and years."

Nonfiction: Bible study resources for children ages 6-12. Recently published DiscipleLand curriculum.
How to Contact/Writers: Submit complete ms with SASE. Reports in 1 month. Publishes a book 1 year after acceptance.
Illustration: Works with 6 illustrators/year. Uses color artwork only. Reviews ms/illustration packages from artists. Send ms with dummy. Illustrations only: Send résumé, promo sheet. Reports back only if interested. Samples returned with SASE; samples filed.
Terms: Work purchased outright from authors (average: $1,000). Illustrators paid by the project. Original artwork returned at job's completion. Book catalog for 9×12 SAE and 2 first-class stamps. Ms guidelines for SASE.
Tips: "Our present interests include: children's material; topical and exegetical Bible study resources; freelance editors—to revise children's Bible curriculum. No fiction, please."

TRICYCLE PRESS, Imprint of Ten Speed Press, P.O. Box 7123, Berkeley CA 94707. Website: http://www.tenspeed.com. **Acquisitions:** Nicole Geiger, editor. Publishes 7 picture books/year; and 4 activity books/year. 30% of books by first-time authors. "Tricycle Press looks for something outside the mainstream; books that encourage children to look at the world from a possibly different angle."
Fiction: Picture books: concept, health, nature/environment. Average word length: picture books—1,200. Recently published *Amelia Takes Command*, by Marissa Moss (ages 7-12, picture book); *Arm in Arm*, by Remy Charlip (ages 7 and up, picture book); *Hey, Little Ant*, by Phillip and Hannah Hoose (ages 4-8, picture book).
Nonfiction: Picture books: activity books, arts/crafts, concept, geography, health, how-to, nature/environment, science, self help, social issues. Young readers: activity books, arts/crafts, health, how-to, nature/environment, science, self help, social issues. Recently published *G is for Googol: A Math Alphabet Book*, by David M. Schwartz (ages 9 and up, picture book); *Gold Rush! The Young Prospector's Guide to Striking It Rich*, by James Klein (activity book, ages 8-12); and *Divorce is Not the End of the World: Zoe's and Evan's Coping Guide for Kids*, by Zoe, Evan and Ellen Sue Stern (self help, ages 9-14).
How to Contact/Writers: Fiction: Submit complete ms for picture books. "No queries!" Nonfiction: Submit complete ms. Reports on mss in 2-5 months. Publishes a book 1-2 years after acceptance. Welcomes simultaneous submissions. Do not send original artwork; copies only, please.
Illustration: Works with 10 illustrators/year. Reviews ms/illustration package from artists. Submit ms with dummy. Illustrations only: Query with samples, promo sheet, tearsheets. Reports back only if interested. Samples returned with SASE; samples filed. Original artwork returned at job's completion unless work for hire.
Terms: Pays authors royalty. Offers advances. Pays illustrators by the project or royalty. Sends galleys to authors. Book catalog for 9×12 SASE ($1.01). Ms guidelines for SASE.
Tips: "We are looking for something a bit outside the mainstream and with lasting appeal (no one-shot-wonders). Lately we've noticed a sacrifice of quality writing for the sake of illustration."

Ⓐ TROLL COMMUNICATIONS, 100 Corporate Dr., Mahwah NJ 07430. (201)529-4000. Book publisher. **Acquisitions:** Marian Frances, editor.
  ● Troll Communications only accepts agented mss; they are open to receiving samples from illustrators.
Fiction: Picture books: animal, contemporary, folktales, history, nature/environment, poetry, sports, suspense/mystery. Young readers: adventure, animal, contemporary, folktales, history, nature/environment, poetry, science fiction, sports, suspense/mystery. Middle readers: adventure, anthology, animal, contemporary, fantasy, folktales, health-related, history, nature/environment, poetry, problem novels, romance, science fiction, sports, suspense/mystery. Young adults: problem novels, romance and suspense/mystery.
Nonfiction: Picture books: activity books, animal, biography, careers, history, hobbies, nature/environment, sports. Young readers: activity books, animal, biography, careers, health, history, hobbies, music/dance, nature/environment, sports. Middle readers: activity books, animal, biography, careers, health, history, hobbies, music/dance, nature/environment, sports. Young adults: health, music/dance.
How to Contact/Writers: Fiction: Query or submit outline/synopsis and 3 sample chapters. Nonfiction: Query. Reports in 4 weeks.
Illustration: Reviews ms/illustration packages from artists. Contact: Marian Frances, editor. Illustrations only: Query with samples; provide résumé, promotional literature or tearsheets to be kept on file. Reports in 4 weeks.
Photography: Interested in stock photos. Model/property releases required.
Terms: Pays authors royalty or work purchased outright. Pays illustrators by the project or royalty. Photographers paid by the project.

Joan Holub wrote and illustrated *Ivy Green, Cootie Queen*, an early chapter book for ages seven to nine for Troll. While she had previously illustrated three other books for Troll, this was the first manuscript she sold to them. To market her work, Holub has an artist's rep and promotes herself through her website, http://www.joanholub.com. "If you are unpublished," says Holub, "consider starting with magazines and educational publishers to develop your style and gain confidence. With tearsheets from this work, you'll be able to show book publishers you are able to complete assignments in a professional way."

TROPHY BOOKS, 10 E. 53rd St., New York NY 10022. Fax: (212)207-7915. Subsidiary of HarperCollins Children's Books Group. Book publisher. Publishes 6-9 chapter books/year, 25-30 middle grade titles/year, 20 reprint picture books/year, 10-15 young adult titles/year.
  ● Trophy is primarily a paperback reprint imprint. They publish a limited number of chapter book, middle grade and young adult manuscripts each year.

TURTLE BOOKS, 866 United Nations Plaza, Suite 525, New York NY 10017. (212)644-2020. Website: http://www.turtlebooks.com. Book Publisher. Estab. 1997. **Acquisitions:** John Whitman. "Turtle Books publishes only picture books for very young readers. We plan to bring most of our titles out in hardcover, in both English and Spanish at the same time."
Fiction: Picture books: adventure, animal, concept, contemporary, fantasy, folktales, hi-lo, history, humor, multicultural, nature/environment, religion, sports, suspense/mystery. Recently published: *Caribbean*; *The Legend of Mexicatl*, by Jo Harper, illustrated by Robert Casilla (the story of Mexicatl and the origin of the Mexican people); *Vroom, Chugga, Vroom-Vroom*, by Anne Miranda, illustrated by David Murphy (a number identification book in the form of a race car story); *The Crab Man*, by Patricia VanWest, illustrated by Cedric Lucas (the story of a young Jamaican boy who must make the difficult decision between making an income and the ethical treatment of animals); and *Prairie Dog Pioneers*, by Jo and Josephine Harper, illustrated by Craig Spearing (the story of a young girl who doesn't want to move, set in 1870s Texas).
How to Contact/Writers: Send complete ms. "Queries are a waste of time." Response time varies.
Illustrators: Works with 6 illustrators/year. Reports on artist's queries/submissions only if interested. Samples returned with SASE only.
Terms: Pays royalty. Offers advances.

N̲ TURTLE PRESS, P.O. Box 290206, Wethersfield CT 06129-0206. (860)529-7770. Fax: (860)529-7775. E-mail: editorial@turtlepress.com. Website: http://www.turtlepress.com. Estab. 1990. Publishes trade books. Specializes in nonfiction, multicultural material. **Manuscript Acquisitions:** Cynthia Kim. Publishes 1 young reader/year; 1 middle reader/year. 40% of books by first-time authors.

Fiction: Young readers, middle readers, young adults: multicultural, sports. Recently published *A Part of the Ribbon: A Time Travel Adventure Through the History of Korea.*

Nonfiction: Young readers, middle readers, young adults: multicultural, sports. Recently published *Martial Arts Training Diary for Kids* and *Everyday Warriors.*

How to Contact/Writers: Fiction/Nonfiction: Query. Nonfiction: Query. Reports on queries in 1 month; 2 months on mss. Publishes a book 12-18 months after acceptance. Will consider simultaneous submissions.

Illustration: Works with 1-2 illustrators/year. Reviews ms/illustration packages from artists. Query. Reports in 1 month. Samples returned with SASE.

Photography: Buys stock.

Terms: Pays authors royalty of 8-12%. Offers advances against royalties of $1,000. Pays illustrators by the project. Sends galleys to authors. Book catalog available for 6×9 SAE and 3 first-class stamps; ms guidelines for SASE. All imprints included in a single catalog. Catalog available on website.

Tips: "We focus on martial arts and related cultures."

Ⓐ TYNDALE HOUSE PUBLISHERS, INC., 351 Executive Dr., P.O. Box 80, Wheaton IL 60189. (630)668-8300. Book publisher. Estab. 1962. **Manuscript Acquisitions:** Karen Watson. **Art Acquisitions:** Beth Sparkman. Publishes approximately 20 Christian children's titles/year.

• Tyndale House no longer reviews unsolicited mss. Only accepts agented material.

Fiction: Middle readers: adventure, religion, suspense/mystery.

Nonfiction: Picture books: religion. Young readers: Christian living, Bible.

How to Contact/Writers: Only interested in agented material. "Request children's writer guidelines from (630)668-8310 ext. 836 for more information."

Illustration: Uses full-color for book covers, b&w or color spot illustrations for some nonfiction. Illustrations only: Query with photocopies (color or b&w) of samples, résumé. Contact: Talinda Ziehr.

Photography: Buys photos from freelancers. Works on assignment only.

Terms: Pay rates for authors and illustrators vary.

Tips: "All accepted manuscripts will appeal to Evangelical Christian children and parents."

☑ UAHC PRESS, 633 Third Ave., New York NY 10017. (212)650-4120. Fax: (212)650-4119. E-mail: press@uahc.org. Website: http://www.uahc.press.org. Book publisher. Estab. 1876. **Manuscript/Art Acquisitions:** Rabbi Hard Person, managing editor. Publishes 4 picture books/year; 4 young readers/year; 4 middle readers/year; 2 young adult titles/year. "The Union of American Hebrew Congregations Press publishes textbooks for the religious classroom, children's tradebooks and scholarly work of Jewish education import—no adult fiction."

Fiction: Picture books, young readers, middle readers, young adult/teens: religion. Average word length: picture books—150; young readers—500; middle readers—3,000; young adult/teens—20,000. Recently published *A Thousand and One Chickens*, written by Seymour Rosser, illustrated by Vlad Guzner (ages 10 and up, Jewish folktales); *The Mystery of the Coins*, written and illustrated by Chara Burnstein (ages 10 and up, juvenile Jewish fiction); and *Rooftop Secrets*, by Lawrence Bush (ya, stories of anti-semitism).

Nonfiction: Picture books, young readers, middle readers, young adult/teens: religion. Average word length: picture books—150; young readers—500; middle readers—3,000; young adult/teens—20,000. Recently published *Tot Shabbat*, illustrated by Camille Kress (toddlers' board book); *Book of the Jewish Year*, by Stephen Wylen (ages 12 and up, Jewish holidays); and *The Number on My Grandfather's Arm*, by David Adler (ages 6 and up, Holocaust survival).

How to Contact/Writers: Fiction: Submit outline/synopsis and 2 sample chapters. Nonfiction: Submit complete ms. Reports of queries/ms in 1-2 months. Publishes a book 18 months after acceptance. Will consider simultaneous submissions.

Illustration: Works with 10 illustrators/year. Reviews ms/illustration packages from artists. Send ms with dummy. Illustrations only: Send portfolio to be kept on file. reports in 2 months. Samples returned with SASE.

Photography: Buys stock and assigns work. Uses photos with Jewish content. Prefer modern settings. Submit cover letter and promo piece.

Terms: Offers advances. Pays photographers by the project (range: $200-3,000) or per photo (range:$20-100). Book catalog free; ms guidelines for SASE.

Tips: "Look at some of our books. Have an understanding of the Reform Jewish community. We sell mostly to Jewish congregations and day schools.' "

Ⓝ UNITY BOOKS, 1901 NW Blue Pkwy., Unity Village MO 64065-0001. (816)524-3550, ext. 3190. Fax: (816)251-3552. Website: http://www.unityworldhq.org. Book publisher. Estab. 1896. Publishes "spiritual, metaphysical, new thought publications." **Manuscript Acquisitions:** Raymond Teague. Other imprints: Wee Wisdom. Publishes 1 picture book/year.

Mr. Belinsky's Bagels

Ellen Schwartz · Illustrated by Stefan Czernecki

Canadian illustrator Stefan Czernecki first realized he wanted to write and illustrate picture books after seeing the movie *Turtle Diary* with Glenda Jackson. "The next morning I woke up and started writing. I haven't stopped." Czernecki completed seven books for Hyperion Books for Children before illustrating *Mr. Belinsky's Bagels*, by Ellen Schwartz for Charlesbridge (U.S.) and Tradewind Books (Canada). "In my next book, *Mama God, Papa God*, by Richard Keens-Douglass, I take my illustration in a new direction. I am always exploring ways to make children's book art more exciting."

INSIDER REPORT

'A good book should make you more human'

Pulitzer Prize-winning columnist and bestselling author Anna Quindlen took a roundabout route to writing children's books. "My first children's book was an assignment, pure and simple," she says. "An editor at *The New York Times* asked me to do a short story for the Christmas Eve issue of the magazine. Afterward, a number of editors approached my agent about finding an illustrator and turning it into a book for children." *The Tree That Came to Stay* (Crown, 1992), the story of a New England family that devises an ingenious way to hold on to the magic of Christmas, was written with "grace and a good sense of childhood pleasures," wrote a reviewer for *Kirkus Reviews*.

Anna Quindlen

Storytelling comes naturally to Quindlen, who was raised in a large, Irish Catholic family in Philadelphia. "I come from a rich tradition of storytellers who embroider the truth almost as a matter of honor," she says. "I like to think I learned about revision by listening to my father and his brothers telling the same stories over and over, making them richer, fuller, and more exciting each time. 'Never let the truth stand in the way of a good story,' they sometimes say in the newspaper business. I first learned that dictum in my grandparents' living room."

Although storytelling is in her blood, fiction writing had to wait. After graduating from Barnard College with a degree in English Literature, Quindlen began looking for work as a journalist. "I wanted to make money," she says with characteristic candor. "I had read that you couldn't make money as a fiction writer. There certainly wasn't a steady paycheck in it." Dogged persistence won her a job on the copy desk of a small newspaper, which eventually led to her work as a general assignment reporter for *The New York Times*. After the birth of her first child, Quindlen began freelancing a column targeted at women for *The Times'* Home section. There she settled into the subject matter that would form the center of her novels, and indirectly, her children's books—family relations.

"I can't think of anything to write about except families," Quindlen told an interviewer for *Publishers Weekly*. "They are a metaphor for every other part of society." Family formed the center of her three bestselling novels, and family politics was the indirect subject of her 1997 children's book *Happily Ever After* (Viking), a feminist take on the traditional princess-meets-handsome-prince fairy tale. Featuring the cartoon-like illustrations of James Stevenson, *Happily Ever After* stars an eight-year-old, baseball-playing heroine named Kate who owns a magical Eddie Bestelli mitt. The mitt transports her to a land of dragons, towers and a prince who "looked as if someone had drawn him with colored pencils," where she learns her own resources are enough to save her from a witch, troll and dragon, thank you very much.

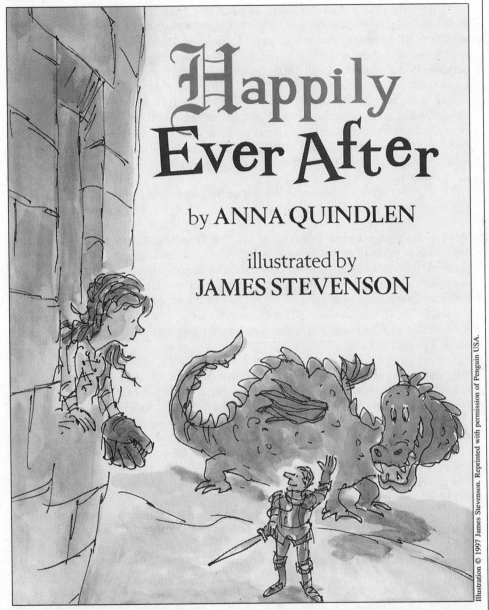

Pulitzer Prize-winning author Anna Quindlen wrote *Happily Every After* (Viking) as a feminist take on the traditional princess-meets-handsome-prince fairy tale. Her story stars Kate, an eight-year-old, baseball-playing heroine, whose magical Eddie Bestelli mitt transports her to a land of dragons, towers and a prince. But instead of being rescued, Kate learns her own resources are enough to save her from a witch, troll and dragon.

INSIDER REPORT, *continued*

"Personally, I like a story that leaves a listener limp from laughter, draped over the edge of the bed. . . . *Happily Ever After* suits those criteria perfectly, especially the gross bits unsuitable for grownups," wrote Margaret Moorman in *The New York Times Book Review*.

'Unsuitable for grownups' is a description Quindlen might approve of as a seal of authenticity for good children's literature. In an introduction she contributed to Ludwig Bemelmans' *Mad About Madeline: The Complete Tales*, Quindlen writes: "There are certain books written with a grown-up's idea of children, of who they are and what they should be like, of what we like to think absorbs and amuses them. And then there are the books that are written for real children by people who manage, however they do it, to maintain an utterly childlike part of their minds. They understand that children prize both security and adventure, both bad behavior and conformity, both connections and independence."

Here Quindlen talks about where she gets her inspiration for children's books, and what she looks for in the classics.

Where did you get your inspiration for *The Tree That Came to Stay?*
That book is the only thing I've ever written that is almost entirely autobiographical. It pretty closely mirrors Christmas in our household, although the baby in the story is now nine years old. It also occasions the most consistent mocking of my work within our household, since each year great hilarity surrounds the notion of The Wreath That Came to Stay, or The Christmas Cookie That Came to Stay. I'm sure my children will appreciate it more once they've managed to snarl their way through adolescence and once again see me as a living saint.

You've put together a Western Canon for children, which includes Madeleine L'Engle's *A Wrinkle in Time*, Norman Juster's *The Phantom Tollbooth*, Louisa May Alcott's *Little Women*, Roald Dahl's *The BFG*, J.D. Salinger's *The Catcher in the Rye* and *The Diary of Anne Frank*. Are there other contemporary children's authors whose work you admire?
I like Kevin Henkes' *Julius, the Baby of the World*, which is a terrific book about sibling rivalry. I love just about everything Maurice Sendak does, but especially *Where the Wild Things Are*. Jerry Spinelli's young adult books are very good, as are Katherine Paterson's and Lois Lowry's.

I don't believe in a canon, really, because books are happening all around us that we don't even know about, even if we're very well read. For instance, all three of my children read on their own, and the youngest is nine. So I might not know about a marvelous picture book being published right now.

In your opinion, what is the best children's literature can set out to do?
The goal is no different than it is for adult literature. A good book should make you more human. It does this in several ways—by making you think about your own emotions and beliefs, by introducing you to situations which are unfamiliar and engrossing, and by absorbing you in a world either different enough or similar enough to your own to make you understand yourself in new ways.

Did you find it difficult to adjust your voice for a younger audience?
I never feel that I'm doing that. Exposition in my books quite often consists of detailed

descriptions of place and character. One of the reasons I've turned down opportunities to write plays is because I desperately need that exposition to feel that I've truly created a world. Dialogue alone doesn't do it for me.

Where did you get your inspiration for *Happily Ever After*?
I think subconsciously I'd always felt that the central characters in most fairy tales led a rather dull life, particularly the women. I was a very outspoken, nervy child who never shut up; in some odd, freefloating way I was intensely ambitious when I was only eight or nine years old. But at that time—this was in the late '50s-early '60s, there wasn't anything much for a girl to be ambitious for. So I was both sucked into the princess thing and bored to tears by it. And that's the genesis of *Happily Ever After*. I wanted to subtitle it 'A Feminist Fairy Tale,' but the 'F' word was not that popular among editors and publishers.

My kids helped on that book. They read drafts and made suggestions. I think Maria was the one who suggested I have Kate, the main character, teach the troll and witch how to do the hokey pokey. And my editor didn't care for it when I compared the color of the dragon to the color of boogers. There was a revolt in the back of the minivan when I told the kids that. The boogers stayed.

Are you planning any future projects for children?
I will write another book for children as soon as I'm well-launched on my new novel. I had a rather hectic time in 1998, with a 15-city book tour for *Black and Blue*, and delivery of the manuscript for the Library of Contemporary Thought book I did, *How Reading Changed My Life*. The end result was that I had no time to work on the book I'd started once *Black and Blue* was done. Once I've broken the back of that new book, I'll start to think about another project for children.
—*Anne Bowling*

Fiction: All levels: religion. Published *I Turn to the Light*, by Connie Bowen (picture book); and *Adventures of the Little Green Dragon*, by Mari Prirette Ulmer, illustrated by Mary Maass (picture book anthology).
Nonfiction: All levels: religion.
How to Contact/Writers: Fiction/Nonfiction: Submit outline/synopsis and 1-3 sample chapters. Reports on queries/mss in up to 2 months. Publishes a book approximately 1 year after acceptance. Will consider simultaneous submission, electronic submissions via disk or modem or previously self-published work.
Illustration: Reviews ms/illustration packages from artists. Query. Contact: Raymond Teague, associate editor.
Terms: Pays authors royalty of 10-15% based on retail price or work purchased outright. Offers advances (Average amount: $1,500). Book catalog available.
Tips: "Read our Writer's Guidelines and study our catalog before submitting. All of our publications reflect Unity's spiritual teachings, but the presentations and applications of those teachings are wide open."

VIKING CHILDREN'S BOOKS, Penguin Putnam Inc., 345 Hudson St., New York NY 10014-3657. (212)366-2000. E-mail: jcarey@penguinputnam.com. Website: http://www.penguinputnam.com. **Acquisitions:** Judy Carey, assistant editor (picture books); Cathy Hennessy, middle-grade fiction; Jill Davis, nonfiction; Melanie Cecka, easy-to-read. **Art Acquisitions:** Denise Cronin. Publishes hardcover originals. Publishes 80 books/year. Receives 7500 queries/year. 25% of books from first-time authors; 33% from unagented writers. "Viking Children's Books publishes the highest quality trade books for children including fiction, nonfiction, and novelty books for pre-schoolers through young adults." Publishes book 1 year after acceptance of ms. Accepts simultaneous submissions. Reports in 2 months on queries.
Fiction: All levels: adventure, animal, anthology, contemporary, hi-lo, humor, multicultural, problem nov-

els, suspense/mystery, easy-to-read. Recently published *The Awful Aardvarks Go to School*, by Reeve Lindbergh (picture book); *Virtual World*, by Chris Westwood (young adult novel).
Nonfiction: Picture books: activity books, biography, concept. Young readers, middle readers, young adult: biography, history, reference, religion, science, sports.
Illustration: Works with 30 illustrators/year. Reports on artist's queries/submissions only if interested. Samples returned with SASE or samples filed. Originals returned at job's completion.
How to Contact/Writers: Picture books: submit entire ms and SASE. Novels: submit outline with 3 sample chapters and SASE. Nonfiction: query with outline, one sample chapter and SASE. Reports on queries/mss in 2-3 months.
Terms: Pays 4-10% royalty on retail price or flat fee. Advance negotiable.
Tips: Mistake often made is that "authors disguise nonfiction in a fictional format."

VOLCANO PRESS, Box 270, Volcano CA 95689. (209)296-3345. Fax: (209)296-4515. Website: http://www.volcanopress.com. Book publisher. **Acquisitions:** Ruth Gottstein, president/publisher. "We believe that the books we are producing today are of even greater value than the gold of yesteryear, and that the symbolism of the term 'Mother Lode' is still relevant to our work."
Fiction: All levels: animals, folktales, multicultural, nature/environment, history.
Nonfiction: Young readers, middle readers, young adult: self help, social issues, special needs. Sees too much "fiction, trite fantasy, didactic and moralistic material, bad fairy tales, anthropomorphic male animal heroes."
How to Contact/Writers: Nonfiction: Submit outline/synopsis and sample chapters. Reports on queries in 2-3 weeks; mss in 4-6 weeks. Publishes a book 1 year after acceptance. "Please always enclose SASE."
Terms: Pays authors royalty. Book catalog for #10 SASE.
Tips: Considers "non-racist, non-sexist types of books that are empowering to women and girls."

WALKER AND CO., 435 Hudson St., New York NY 10014. (212)727-8300. Fax: (212)727-0894. Division of Walker Publishing Co. Inc. Book publisher. Estab. 1959. **Manuscript Acquisitions:** Emily Easton, publisher; Soyung Pak, editor. **Art Acquisitions:** Marlene Tungseth, art director. Publishes 16 picture books/year; 4-6 middle readers/year; 2-4 young adult titles/year. 5% of books by first-time authors; 65% of books from agented writers.
Fiction: Picture books: animal, history, multicultural. Young readers: contemporary, history, humor, multicultural. Middle readers: animal, contemporary, history, multicultural, humor. Young adults: contemporary and historical fiction. Recently published *Milkman's Boy*, by D. Hall; *Ethan Between Us*, by A. Myers (young adult); *Devil's Den*, by S. Pfeffer (middle grade).
Nonfiction: Young readers: animals. Middle readers: animal, biography, health, history, multicultural, reference, social issues. Young adults: biography, health, history, multicultural, reference, social issues, sports. Published *Bold and Bright Black and White Animals*, by D. Patent (picture book history); and *What's Going on Down There*, by K. Graville (young adult health). Multicultural needs include "contemporary, literary fiction and historical fiction written in an authentic voice. Also high interest nonfiction with trade appeal."
How to Contact/Writers: Fiction/nonfiction: Submit outline/synopsis and sample chapters. Reports on queries/mss in 2-3 months. Send SASE for writer's guidelines.
Illustration: Works with 10-12 illustrators/year. Uses color artwork only. Editorial reviews ms/illustration packages from artists. Query or submit ms with 4-8 samples. Illustrations only: Tearsheets. "Please do not send original artwork." Reports on art samples only if interested. Samples returned with SASE.
Terms: Pays authors and illustrators in royalties of 5-10%. Offers advance payment against royalties. Original artwork returned at job's completion. Sends galleys to authors. Book catalog available for 9×12 SASE; ms guidelines for SASE.
Tips: Writers: "Make sure you study our catalog before submitting. We are a small house with a tightly focused list. Illustrators: "Have a well-rounded portfolio with different styles." Does not want to see folktales, ABC books, genre fiction (mysteries, science fiction, fantasy). "Walker and Company is committed to introducing talented new authors and illustrators to the children's book field."

✔️ 🔲 **DANIEL WEISS ASSOCIATES, INC.**, 11th Floor, 33 W. 17th St., New York NY 10011. (212)645-3865. Fax: (212)633-1236. Independent book producer/packager. Estab. 1987. **Manuscript Acquisitions:** Jennifer Klein, editorial assistant; Kieran Scott, YA romance/friendship; Laura Burns, middle grade horse books; and Lisa Papendemetrios, middle grade. **Art Acquisitions:** Paul Matarazzo, art director (illustrations); Mike Rivilis, assistant art director (ms/illustration packages). Publishes 30 young readers/year; 40 middle readers/year; and 70 young adults/year. 25% of books by first-time authors. "We do mostly series! We mainly publish middle grade and YA series and hire writers for books in these series. As a book packager, we work with the larger publishing houses."

Illustrations © Kendahl Jan Jubb, published by Walker and Company

Kendahl Jan Jubb successfully made the jump from fine artist to children's book illustrator. In her second book for Walker and Company, *Bold and Bright Black-and-White Animals*, her watercolor illustrations perfectly complement the words of author Dorothy Patent. It was actually Patent who saw Jubb's artwork in their hometown of Missoula, Montana and recommended her to illustrate their prior book for Walker, *Flashy Fantastic Rain Forest Frogs*. Since they worked together so successfully the first time, they decided to team up again for equally exciting results.

Fiction: Middle readers: sports. Young adults: fantasy, romance. Recently published Love Stories #27, *Trust Me*; Sweet Valley High #139, *Elizabeth is Mine*.

Nonfiction: Young adults. Recently published *Ultimate Cheerleading Handbook Scene* series.

How to Contact/Writers: Send SASE for guidelines to write for series currently in production. No unsolicited mss.

Illustration: Works with 20 illustrators/year. Reviews ms/illustration packages from artists. Submit query. Illustrations only: Provide promo sheet. Reports in 2 months. Samples returned with SASE. Original artwork returned at job's completion.

Terms: Pays authors royalty on work purchased outright from authors. Offers advances. Pays illustrators by the project.

WHITECAP BOOKS, 351 Lynn Ave., North Vancouver, British Columbia V7J 2C4 Canada. (604)980-9852. E-mail: whitecap@pinc.com. Book publisher. **Acquisitions:** Robin Rivers, editorial director. Publishes 4 young readers/year; and 2 middle readers/year.

● Whitecap is publishing 2 children's picture books this year.

Fiction: Picture books for children 3-7.

Nonfiction: Young readers, middle readers: animal, nature/environment. Does not want to see text that writes down to children. Recently published *Welcome to the World of Wolves*, by Diane Swanson (ages 5-

7); *Buffalo Sunrise*, by Diane Swanson (ages 9-11); and *The Day of the Twelve-Story Wave*, illustrated by Laura Cook (ages 9-11).

How to Contact/Writers: Nonfiction: Query. Reports on queries in 1 month; ms in 3 months. Publishes a book 6 months after acceptance. Will consider simultaneous submissions. Please send international postal voucher if submission is from US.

Illustration: Works with 1-2 illustrators/year. Reviews ms/illustration packages from artists. Query. Illustrations only: Query with samples—"never send original art." Contact: Robin Rivers. Samples returned with SASE with international postal voucher for Canada if requested.

Photography: Buys stock. "We are always looking for outstanding wildlife photographs." Uses 35mm transparencies. Submit cover letter, client list, stock photo list.

Terms: Pays authors a negotiated royalty or purchases work outright. Offers advances. Pays illustrators by the project or royalty (depends on project). Pays photographers per photo (depends on project). Originals returned to artist at job's completion unless discussed in advance. Ms guidelines available for SASE with international postal voucher for Canada.

Tips: "Writers and illustrators should spend time researching what's already available on the market. Whitecap specializes in nonfiction for children and adults."

☑ **ALBERT WHITMAN & COMPANY**, 6340 Oakton St., Morton Grove IL 60053-2723. (847)581-0033. Fax: (847)581-0039. Website: http://www.awhitmanco.com. Book publisher. Estab. 1919. **Manuscript Acquisitions:** Kathleen Tucker, editor-in-chief. **Art Acquisitions:** Scott Piehl, designer. Publishes 30 books/year. 15% of books by first-time authors; 15% of books from agented authors.

Fiction: Picture books, young readers, middle readers: adventure, animal, concept, contemporary, folktales, health, history, humor, multicultural, nature/environment, special needs. Middle readers: problem novels, suspense/mystery. "We are mostly interested in contemporary multicultural stories, set both in the U.S. and in other countries. We publish a wide variety of topics, and are interested in stories that will help children deal with their problems and concerns. Does not want to see "religion-oriented, ABCs, pop-up, romance, counting or any book that is supposed to be written in." Published *Missing: One Stuffed Rabbit*, by Maryann Cocca-Leffler; *Grandmother's Dreamcatcher*, by Becky Ray McCain, illustrated by Stacey Schuett; and *The Borrowed Hanukkah Latkes*, by Linda Glaser, illustrated by Nancy Cote.

Nonfiction: Picture books, young readers, middle readers: animal, biography, concept, geography, health, history, hobbies, multicultural, music/dance, nature/environment, special needs. Middle readers: careers. Middle readers, young adults: biography, social issues. Does not want to see "religion, any books that have to be written in, biographies of living people." Recently published *The Fragile Frog*, by William P. Mara, illustrated by John R. Quinn; *Small Steps: The Year I Got Polio*, by Peg Kehret; and *Sugar Was My Best Food: Diabetes and Me*, by Carol Peacock, Adair Gregory and Kyle Gregory.

How to Contact/Writers: Fiction/Nonfiction: Submit complete ms. Reports on queries in 4-6 weeks; mss in 3-4 months. Publishes a book 18 months after acceptance. Will consider simultaneous submissions "but let us know if it is one."

Illustration: Works with 30 illustrators/year. Uses more color art than b&w. Reviews ms/illustration packages from artists. Illustrations only: Query with samples. Send slides or tearsheets. Reports back in 2 months.

Photography: Publishes books illustrated with photos but not stock photos—desires photos all taken for project. "Our books are for children and cover many topics; photos must be taken to match text. Books often show a child in a particular situation (e.g., kids being home-schooled, a sister whose brother is born prematurely)." Photographers should query with samples; send unsolicited photos by mail.

Terms: Pays authors royalty. Offers advances. Pays illustrators and photographers royalty. Sends galleys to authors; dummies to illustrators. Original artwork returned at job's completion. Ms/artist's guidelines available for SASE, or on website. Book catalogs available with 9 × 12 SASE and $1.47 in postage.

Tips: "In both picture books and nonfiction, we are seeking stories showing life in other cultures and the variety of multicultural life in the U.S. We also want fiction and nonfiction about mentally or physically challenged children—some recent topics have been AIDS, asthma, diabetes. Look up some of our books first, to be sure your submission is appropriate for Albert Whitman & Co."

JOHN WILEY & SONS, INC., 605 Third Ave., New York NY 10158. (212)850-6206. Fax: (212)850-6095. Website: http://www.wiley.com. Book publisher. **Acquisitions:** Kate Bradford, editor. Publishes 18 middle readers/year; 2 young adult titles/year. 10% of books by first-time authors. Publishes educational, nonfiction primarily history, science, and other activities.

Nonfiction: Middle readers: activity books, animal, arts/crafts, biography, cooking, geography, health, history, hobbies, how-to, nature/environment, reference, science, self help. Young adults: activity books, arts/crafts, health, hobbies, how-to, nature/environment, reference, science, self help. Average word length middle readers—20,000-40,000. Recently published: *Outrageous Women of the Middle Ages*, by Vicki

León (ages 10-14, history); and *The New York Public Library Amazing African American History* (ages 12 and up, history).
How to Contact/Writers: Query. Submit outline/synopsis, 2 sample chapters and an author bio. Reports on queries in 1 month; mss in 3 months. Publishes a book 1 year after acceptance. Will consider simultaneous and previously published submissions.
Illustration: Works with 6 illustrators/year. Uses primarily black & white artwork. Reviews ms/illustration packages from artists. Query. Illustrations only: Query with samples, résumé, client list. Reports back only if interested. Samples filed. Original artwork returned at job's completion. No portfolio reviews.
Photography: Buys photos from freelancers.
Terms: Pays authors royalty of 4-10% based on wholesale price, or by outright purchase. Offers advances. Pays illustrators by the project. Photographers pay negotiable. Sends galleys to authors. Book catalog available for SAE.
Tips: "We're looking for topics and writers that can really engage kids' interest—plus we're always interested in a new twist on time-tested subjects."

WILLIAMSON PUBLISHING CO., Box 185, Charlotte VT 05445. (802)425-2102. Fax: (802)425-2199. Website: http://www.williamsonbooks.com. Book publisher. Estab. 1983. **Manuscript Acquisitions:** Susan Williamson, editorial director. **Art Acquisitions:** Jack Williamson, publisher. Publishes 12-15 young readers titles/year. 50% of books by first-time authors; 10% of books from agented authors. Publishes "very successful nonfiction series (Kids Can!® Series—2,000,000 sold) on subjects such as nature, creative play, arts/crafts, geography. Successfully launched *Little Hands*® series for ages 2-6 and *Tales Alive*® series (tales plus activities) and recently introduced the new *Kaleidoscope Kids*™ series. Our mission is to help every child fulfill his/her potential and experience personal growth.
  • Williamson won Benjamin Franklin Awards for Best Nonfiction, juvenile; Best Fiction, juvenile; Best Multicultural. Also winner of Oppenheim Toy Award, Parents' Choice Awards.
Nonfiction: Young readers: hands-on activity books, animal, arts/crafts, folktales with activities, cooking, health, history, how-to, math, multicultural, music/dance, nature/environment, science, self-help, social issues. Does not want to see textbooks, picture books, poetry, fiction. "We are looking for books in which learning and doing are inseparable." Published *Super Science Concoctions*, by Jill Hauser, illustrated by Michael Kline (ages 6-12, exploring science); *Shapes, Sizes and More Surprises*, by Mary Tomczyk, illustrated by Loretta Trezzo Braren (ages 2-6, early learning skills); and *Bird Tales from Near & Far*, retold by Susan Milord, illustrated by Linda Wingerter (ages 4 and up, multicultural tales with activities).
How to Contact/Writers: Query with outline/synopsis and 2 sample chapters. Reports on queries in 4 months; mss in 6 months. Publishes book, "depending on graphics, about 1 year" after acceptance. Writers may send a SASE for guidelines.
Illustration: Works with 6 illustrator and 6 designers/year. "We're interested in expanding our illustrator and design freelancers." Uses primarily b&w artwork; some 2-color and 4-color.
Photography: Buys photos from freelancers
Terms: Pays authors royalty based on wholesale price. Offers advances. Pays illustrators by the project. Pays photographers by the project or per photo. Sends galleys to authors. Book catalog available for 8½×11 SAE and 4 first-class stamps; ms guidelines available for SASE.
Tips: "We're interested in interactive learning books with a creative approach packed with interesting information, written for young readers ages 2-6 and 4-10. In nonfiction children's publishing, we are looking for authors with a depth of knowledge shared with children through a warm, embracing style. Our publishing philosophy is based on the idea that all children can succeed and have positive learning experiences. Children's lasting learning experiences involve participation."

☑ WOMAN'S MISSIONARY UNION, P.O. Box 830010, Birmingham AL 35283-0010. (205)991-8100. Fax: (205)995-4841. Website: http://www.wmu.com/wmu. Imprint: New Hope. **Acquisitions:** Coy Batson. Publishes 2 picture books/year; 5 young readers/year; 10 middle readers/year; and 20 young adult titles/year. 25% of books by first-time authors.
Fiction: All levels: multicultural, religion. Multicultural fiction must be related to mission/ministry.
Nonfiction: All levels: multicultural, religion. Multicultural nonfiction must be related to Christian concepts, particularly Christian missions.
How to Contact/Writers: Fiction/nonfiction: Submit complete ms. Reports on queries in 3 months; mss in 3-6 months. Publishes a book 2 years after acceptance. Will consider simultaneous submissions.
Illustration: Works with 2-3 illustrators/year. Reviews ms/illustration packages from artists. Send ms with dummy. Illustrations only: Query with samples (color copies). Reports back only if interested. Samples filed.
Photography: Buys stock already on file. Model/property releases required.
Terms: Pays authors royalty of 7-10% (depends on length). Pays illustrators by the project. Sends galleys

to authors. Originals returned to artist at job's completion. Book catalog available for 10×12 SAE and 3 first-class stamps. Ms guidelines available for SASE.

Tips: "Obtain the catalog first to see the kinds of material we publish."

N: WORLD BIBLE PUBLISHERS, 2976 Ivanrest Ave., Grandville MI 49418. (616)531-9110. Fax: (616)531-9120. E-mail: worldpub@aol.com. Bible and devotion publisher. Estab. 1928. **Acquisitions:** Carol A. Ochs, publishing assistant.

Nonfiction: All levels: religion.

How to Contact/Writers: Reports on queries/mss in 2 months. Publishes a book 1 year after acceptance.

Illustration: Query with samples. Contact: Carol Ochs, publishing assistant. Reports back in 2 months. Samples returned with SASE; or filed.

Terms: Pays authors royalty. Pays illustrators by the project.

Tips: "World mainly publishes Bibles and devotional books. Any children's product must be closely tied to scripture. No calls, please."

WORLD BOOK, INC., 525 W. Monroe St., Chicago IL 60661. (312)258-3700. Fax: (312)258-3950. Website: http://www.worldbook.com. Book publisher. **Manuscript Acquisitions:** Paul A. Kobasa, product development director. **Art Acquisitions:** Roberta Dimmer, executive art director. Publishes 6-10 picture books/year; 6-10 young readers/year; 6-10 middle readers/year; and 15-20 young adult titles/year. 20% of books by first-time authors. "World Book, Inc. (publisher of *The World Book Encyclopedia*) publishes reference sources and nonfiction series for children in the areas of science, mathematics, English-language skills, basic academic and social skills, social studies, history, and health and fitness. We publish print and nonprint material appropriate for children ages 3 to 14. WBT does not publish fiction, poetry, or wordless picture books."

Nonfiction: Picture books: animal, concept, reference. Young readers: activity books, animal, arts/crafts, careers, concept, geography, health, reference. Middle readers: activity books, animal, arts/crafts, careers, geography, health, history, hobbies, how-to, nature/environment, reference, science. Young adult: arts/crafts, careers, geography, health, history, hobbies, how-to, nature/environment, reference, science. Average word length: picture books—10-20 words; young readers—20-100 words; middle readers—100-400 words; young adults—500-2,000 words. Recently published *Ancient Egypt* (ages 7-11); *Interfact: Aztecs* (ages 7-12); *Stand Up for Your Rights* (ages 11 and up).

How to Contact/Writers: Nonfiction: Submit outline/synopsis only; no mss. Reports on queries/mss in 1-2 months. Unsolicited mss will not be returned. Publishes a book 18 months after acceptance. Will consider simultaneous submissions.

Illustration: Works with 10-30 illustrators/year. Illustrations only: Query with samples. Contact: Roberta Dimmer, executive art director. Reports only if interested. Samples returned with SASE; samples filed "if extra copies and if interested."

Photography: Buys stock and assigns work. Needs broad spectrum; editorial concept, specific natural, physical and social science spectrum. Model/property releases and captions required. Uses color 8×10 gloss and matte prints, 35mm, 2¼×2¼, 4×5, 8×10 transparencies. Submit cover letter, résumé, promo piece (color and b&w).

Terms: Payment negotiated on project-by-project basis. Sends galleys to authors. Book catalog available for 9×12 SAE. Ms and art guidelines for SASE.

WRITERS PRESS, 2309 Mt. View Dr., Suite 190, Boise ID 83706. (208)327-0566. Fax: (208)327-3477. E-mail: writers@cyberhighway.net. Website: www.writerspress.com. **Acquisitions:** Kaylin Cherry, editor. Publishes hardcover and trade paperback originals. Publishes 6 titles/year. Receives 50 queries and 30 mss/year. 60% of books from first-time authors; 100% from unagented writers. "Our philosophy is to publish educational literature that equally represents all children, including children with disabilities, as a natural part of our environment."

Fiction: Picture books, young adult: Adventure, historical, inclusion, special education. Recently published *Eagle Feather*, by Sonia Gardner, illustrated by James Spurlock (picture book).

Nonfiction: Education, history, inclusion, special education. Reviews artwork/photos as part of ms package. Send photocopies.

How to Contact/Writers: Fiction/Nonfiction: Query.

Terms: Pays 4-12% royalty or work purchased outright for up to $1,500. Catalog and guidelines free.

Magazines

Children's magazines are a great place for unpublished writers and illustrators to break into the market. Illustrators, photographers and writers alike may find it easier to get book assignments if they have tearsheets from magazines. Having magazine work under your belt shows you're professional and have experience working with editors and art directors and meeting deadlines.

But magazines aren't merely a breaking-in point. Writing, illustration and photo assignments for magazines let you see your work in print quickly, and the magazine market can offer steady work and regular paychecks (a number of them pay on acceptance). Book authors, illustrators and photographers may have to wait a year or two before receiving royalties from a project. The magazine market is also a good place to use research material that didn't make it into a book project you're working on. You may even work on a magazine idea that blossoms into a book project.

TARGETING YOUR SUBMISSIONS

It's important to know the topics typically covered by different children's magazines. To help you match your work with the right publications, we've included several indexes in the back of this book. The **Subject Index** lists both book and magazine publishers by the fiction and nonfiction subjects they're seeking. **If you're a photographer**, the **Photography Index** lists children's magazines that use photos from freelancers. Using these two indexes in combination, you can quickly narrow your search of markets that suit your work. For instance, if you photograph sports, compare the Magazine list in the Photography Index with the list under Sports in the Subject Index. Highlight the markets that appear on both lists, then read those listings to decide which magazines might be best for your work.

If you're a writer, use the Subject Index in conjunction with the **Age-Level Index** to narrow your list of markets. Targeting the correct age group with your submission is an important consideration. Most rejection slips are sent because a writer has not targeted a manuscript to the correct age. Few magazines are aimed at children of all ages, so you must be certain your manuscript is written for the audience level of the particular magazine you're submitting to.

If you're a poet, refer to the new **Poetry Index** to find which magazine publish poems.

Each magazine has a different editorial philosophy. Language usage also varies between periodicals, as does the length of feature articles and the use of artwork and photographs. Reading magazines *before* submitting is the best way to determine if your material is appropriate. Also, because magazines targeted to specific age groups have a natural turnover in readership every few years, old topics (with a new slant) can be recycled.

Since many kids' magazines sell subscriptions through direct mail or schools, you may not be able to find a particular publication at bookstores or newsstands. Check your local library, or send for copies of the magazines you're interested in. Most magazines in this section have sample copies available and will send them for a SASE or small fee.

Also, many magazines have submission guidelines and theme lists available for a SASE. (Visit http://www.writersdigest.com for a searchable database of more than 1,000 writers guidelines.) Check magazines' websites, too. Many offer excerpts of articles, submission information and the editorial philosophy of the publication.

For advice straight from magazine editors, read the Insider Reports in this section with **Kelly White**, senior editor of *Girls' Life* (page 226); **Lori Berger**, editor of *Jump* (page 236); and **Kate Allen**, editor of *Kids' Wall Street News* (page 242).

☑ **ADVOCATE, PKA'S PUBLICATION**, PKA Publication, 301A Rolling Hills Park, Prattsville NY 12468. (518)299-3103. **Publisher**: Patricia Keller. Bimonthly tabloid. Estab. 1987. Circ. 12,000. "*Advocate* advocates good writers and quality writings. We publish art, fiction, photos and poetry. *Advocate*'s submitters are talented people of all ages who do not earn their livings as writers. We wish to promote the arts and to give those we publish the opportunity to be published through a for-profit means rather than in a not-for-profit way. We do this by selling advertising and offering reading entertainment."

• Gaited Horse Association newsletter is now included in our publication. Horse oriented stories, poetry, art and photos are currently needed.

Fiction: Middle readers and young adults/teens: adventure, animal, contemporary, fantasy, folktales, health, humorous, nature/environment, problem-solving, romance, science fiction, sports, suspense/mystery. Looks for "well written, entertaining work, whether fiction or nonfiction." Buys approximately 42 mss/year. Average word length: 1,500. Byline given. Wants to see more humorous material, nature/environment and romantic comedy.

Nonfiction: Middle readers and young adults/teens: animal, arts/crafts, biography, careers, concept, cooking, fashion, games/puzzles, geography, history, hobbies, how-to, humorous, interview/profile, nature/environment, problem-solving, science, social issues, sports, travel. Buys 10 mss/year. Average word length: 1,500. Byline given.

Poetry: Reviews poetry any length.

How to Contact/Writers: Fiction/nonfiction: send complete ms. Reports on queries in 4-6 weeks/mss in 6-8 weeks. Publishes ms 2-18 months after acceptance.

Illustration: Uses b&w artwork only. Uses cartoons. Reviews ms/illustration packages from artists. Submit a photo print (b&w or color), an excellent copy of work (no larger than 8 × 10) or original. Illustrations only: "Send previous unpublished art with SASE, please." Reports in 2 months. Samples returned with SASE; samples not filed. Credit line given.

Photography: Buys photos from freelancers. Model/property releases required. Uses color and b&w prints. Send unsolicited photos by mail with SASE. Reports in 2 months. Wants nature, artistic and humorous photos.

Terms: Pays on publication. Acquires first rights for mss, artwork and photographs. Pays in copies. Original work returned upon job's completion. Sample copies for $4. Writer's/illustrator/photo guidelines for SASE.

Tips: "Artists and photographers should keep in mind that we are a b&w paper."

☑ **AIM MAGAZINE, America's Intercultural Magazine**, P.O. Box 1174, Maywood IL 60153-8174. **Contact:** Ruth Apilado (nonfiction), Mark Boone (fiction). **Photo Editor:** Betty Lewis. Quarterly magazine. Circ. 8,000. Readers are high school and college students, teachers, adults interested in helping, through the written word, to create a more equitable world. 15% of material aimed at juvenile audience.

Fiction: Young adults/teens: adventure, folktales, humorous, history, multicultural, "stories with social significance." Wants stories that teach children that people are more alike than they are different. Does not want to see religious fiction. Buys 20 mss/year. Average word length: 1,000-4,000. Byline given.

Nonfiction: Young adults/teens: biography, interview/profile, multicultural, "stuff with social significance." Does not want to see religious nonfiction. Buys 20 mss/year. Average word length: 500-2,000. Byline given.

How to Contact/Writers: Fiction: Send complete ms. Nonfiction: Query with published clips. Reports on queries in 2 weeks; mss in 6 weeks. Will consider simultaneous submissions.

Illustration: Buys 6 illustrations/issue. Preferred theme: Overcoming social injustices through nonviolent means. Reviews ms/illustration packages from artists. Query first. Illustrations only: Query with tearsheets. Reports on art samples only if interested. Samples returned with SASE or filed. Original artwork returned at job's completion "if desired." Credit line given.

Photography: Wants "photos of activists who are trying to contribute to social improvement."

Terms: Pays on acceptance. Buys first North American serial rights. Pays $15-25 for stories/articles. Pays in contributor copies if copies are requested. Pays $25 for b&w cover illustration. Photographers paid by the project. Sample copies for $5.

Tips: "We need material of social significance, stuff that will help promote racial harmony and peace and illustrate the stupidity of racism."

ALL ABOUT YOU, Petersen Publishing Co., L.L.C., 6420 Wilshire Blvd., 15th Floor, Los Angeles CA 90048. (213)782-2950. Fax: (213)782-2660. **Editor:** Beth Mayall. **Art Director:** Philip Pirolo. Magazine published 10 times/year. Estab. 1994. "Teen fashion and beauty magazine with a focus on self-esteem. Quizzes and self-help pieces. Fun, hip voice, Informative yet entertaining."

Nonfiction: Young adults/teens: health, humorous, interview/profile, problem-solving. Does not want to see anything sex related; or anything written in a voice/language that a teen wouldn't relate to. Buys 100 mss/year. Average word length: 1,700-4,000. Byline given.

How to Contact/Writers: Nonfiction: Query with published clips. Reports on queries/mss in 1 month. Publishes ms 4 months after acceptance. Will consider electronic submissions via disk or modem.

Illustration: Buys 4 illustrations/issue; 32 illustrations/year. Uses color artwork only. Works on assignment only. Reviews ms/illustration packages from artists. Contact: Philip Pirolo, art director. Illustrations only: Send promo sheet, tearsheets. Contact: Dianna Quarry, art director. Reports back only if interested. Samples are not returned. Credit line given.

Photography: Query with samples. Reports back only if interested.

Terms: Pays on publication. Buys all rights. Buys all rights for artwork. Pays $150-600 for articles. Pays illustrators $150-500 for color (inside). Writer's guidelines for SASE.

Tips: "Talk to readers in a voice they'll listen to—honest, young, not preachy or condescending. Keep it fun but informational."

☑ **AMERICAN CHEERLEADER**, Lifestyle Publications LLC, 250 W. 57th St., Suite 420, New York NY 10107. (212)265-8890. Fax: (212)265-8908. **Editor:** Julie Davis. Bimonthly magazine. Estab. 1995. Circ. 200,000. Special interest teen magazine for kids who cheer.

Nonfiction: Young adults: careers, fashion, health, how-to, problem-solving, sports, cheerleading specific material. "We're looking for authors who know cheerleading." Buys 50 mss/year. Average word length: 200-1,000. Byline given.

How to Contact/Writers: Query with published clips. Reports on queries/mss in 3 months. Publishes ms 3 months after acceptance. Will consider electronic submission via disk or modem.

Illustration: Buys 6 illustrations/issue; 30-50 illustrations/year. Works on assignment only. Reviews ms/illustration packages from artists. Illustrations only: Query with samples; arrange portfolio review. Reports only if interested. Samples filed. Originals not returned at job's completion. Credit line given.

Photography: Buys photos from freelancers. Looking for cheerleading at different sports games, events, etc. Uses 35mm, 2¼×2¼ transparencies. Query with samples; provide résumé, business card, tearsheets to be kept on file. "After sending query, we'll set up an interview." Reports only if interested.

Terms: Pays on publication. Buy all rights for mss, artwork and photographs. Pays $100-1,000 for stories. Pays illustrators $50-200 for b&w inside, $100-300 for color inside. Pays photographers by the project $300-750; per photo (range: $25-100). Sample copies for $5.

Tips: "Authors: Absolutely must have cheerleading background. Photographers and illustrators must have teen magazine experience or high profile experience."

☑ **AMERICAN GIRL**, Pleasant Company, 8400 Fairway Place, P.O. Box 620986, Middleton WI 53562-0984. (608)836-4848. **Editor:** Sarah Jane Brian. **Managing Editor:** Julie Finlay. **Contact:** Editorial Dept. Assistant. Bimonthly magazine. Estab. 1992. Circ. 750,000. "For girls ages 8-12. We run fiction and nonfiction, historical and contemporary."

Fiction: Middle readers: contemporary, historical, multicultural, suspense/mystery, good fiction about anything. No preachy, moralistic tales or stories with animals as protagonists. Only a girl or girls as characters—no boys. Buys approximately 6 mss/year. Average word length: 1,000-2,300. Byline given.

Nonfiction: Any articles aimed at girls ages 8-12. Buys 3-10 mss/year. Average word length: 600. Byline sometimes given.

How to Contact/Writers: Fiction: Send complete ms. Nonfiction: Query with published clips. Reports on queries/mss in 6-12 weeks. Will consider simultaneous submissions.

Illustration: Works on assignment only.

Terms: Pays on acceptance. Buys first North American serial rights. Pays $500 minimum for stories; $300 minimum for articles. Sample copies for $3.95 and 9×12 SAE with $1.93 in postage (send to Editorial Department Assistant). Writer's guidelines free for SASE.

Tips: "Keep (stories and articles) simple but interesting. Kids are discriminating readers, too. They won't read a boring or pretentious story. We're looking for shor (maximum 175 words) how-to stories and short profiles of girls for 'Girls Express' section, as well as word games, puzzles and mazes."

🆕 **APPLESEEDS**, Cobblestone Publishing, 30 Grove St., Suite C, Peterborough NH 03458. (603)924-7209. **Co-Editors:** Susan Buckley and Barbara Burt. Magazine published monthly except June, July and August.

• *Appleseeds* is a new publication from Cobblestone Publishing. Contact them for submission guidelines and theme list.

ASPCA ANIMAL WATCH, ASPCA, 424 E. 92nd St., New York NY 10128. (212)876-7700, ext. 4441. Fax: (212)410-0087. Website: http://www.aspca.org. **Art Director:** Sibylle von Fischer. Quarterly magazine. Estab. 1951. Circ. 210,000. "The American Society for the Prevention of Cruelty to Animals publishes *Animal Watch*, a four-color magazine for its members. We cover many different topics related to animals, including companion and domestic animals, endangered species, animal abuse, lab animals and animal testing, animals in entertainment and environmental issues related to animals."

• Also see listing for *ASCPA Animaland* in this section.

Fiction: Young readers, middle readers: adventure, folktales, multicultural, animal, nature/environment, history, problem-solving.

Nonfiction: Young readers, middle readers: animal, geography, how-to, multicultural, science, arts/crafts, nature/environment, social issues, history, interview/profile, problem-solving, careers, games/puzzles, hobbies.

How to Contact/Writers: Reports on queries in 1-2 weeks; on mss in 3-4 weeks.

Illustration: Buys 5 illustrations/issue; 12 illustrations/year. Works on assignment only. Reviews ms/illustration packages from artists. Send ms with dummy. Illustrations only: "Please send a photocopy or tearsheet sample that we can hold on file for reference. We need dynamic, endearing, descriptive and imaginative images which communicate ideas or emotions. Off-beat, alternative techniques are always welcome. We are always in need of heart-warming portraits of cats (and kittens), dogs (and puppies). We have plenty of 'realistic wildlife' as well as single-cell pen and ink cartoons and do not need any of these." Samples returned with SASE or kept on file. Originals returned upon job's completion. Credit line given.

Photography: Looking for animal care and animal protection. Model/property releases required. Uses 8×10, glossy color/b&w prints; 35mm, $2\frac{1}{4} \times 2\frac{1}{4}$ and 4×5 transparencies. Please send originals or dupes (35mm slides or any larger format transparency) of your work, a brief statement of the kind of photography you do or a résumé as well as a properly posted SASE. You may submit anywhere from 10 to 100 slides of various images or all of the same subject."

Terms: Pays on publication. Buys one-time rights for artwork/photographs. Original artwork returned at job's completion. Pays illustrators $200-400 for color cover; $50-150 for b&w inside, $50-250 for color inside. Pays photographer per photo (range: $75-200). Sample copies for 9×12 SASE with $2 postage. Writer's guidelines not available. Illustrator's/photo guidelines for SASE.

Tips: Trends include "more educational, more interactive" material.

Ⓝ ASPCA ANIMALAND, 424 E. 92nd St., New York NY 10128. (212)876-7700, ext. 4441. Fax: (212)410-0087. Website: http://www.aspca.org. **Articles Editor:** Allen Salzberg. . **Art Director:** Sibylle von Fischer. Bimonthly magazine. For the young members of the ASPCA (ages 7-12). All topics related to animals.

• Also see listing for *ASPCA Animal Watch* in this section.

Fiction: Young readers, middle readers: animal, history, problem-solving.

Nonfiction: Young readers, middle readers: careers, hobbies, nature/environment.

Illustration: Buys 5 illustrations/issue; 12 illustrations/year. Works on assignment only. Reviews ms/illustration packages from artists. Send ms with dummy. Illustrations only: "Please send a photocopy or tearsheet sample that we can hold on file for reference. We need dynamic, endearing, descriptive and imaginative images which communicate ideas or emotions. Off-beat, alternative techniques are always welcome. We are always in need of heart-warming portraits of cats (and kittens), dogs (and puppies). We have plenty of 'realistic wildlife' as well as single-cell pen and ink cartoons and do not need any of these." Samples returned with SASE or kept on file. Originals returned upon job's completion. Credit line given.

Photography: Looking for animal care and animal protection. Model/property releases required. Uses 8×10, glossy color/b&w prints; 35mm, $2\frac{1}{4} \times 2\frac{1}{4}$ and 4×5 transparencies. Please send originals or dupes (35mm slides or any larger format transparency) of your work, a brief statement of the kind of photography you do or a résumé as well as a properly posted SASE. You may submit anywhere from 10 to 100 slides of various images or all of the same subject."

BABYBUG, Carus Publishing Company, P.O. Box 300, Peru IL 61354. (815)224-6656. **Editor**: Paula Morrow. **Art Director:** Suzanne Beck. Published 9 times/year (every 6 weeks). Estab. 1994. "A listening and looking magazine for infants and toddlers ages 6 to 24 months, *Babybug* is 6 $\frac{1}{4} \times 7$, 24 pages long,

**FOR EXPLANATIONS OF THESE SYMBOLS,
SEE THE INSIDE FRONT AND BACK COVERS OF THIS BOOK**

printed in large type (26-point) on high-quality cardboard stock with rounded corners and no staples."
  • See Reaching the Youngest Audience: Writing for Babies and Toddlers on page 64 for more from *Babybug* editor Paula Morrow.
Fiction: Looking for very simple and concrete stories, 4-6 short sentences maximum.
Nonfiction: Must use very basic words and concepts, 10 words maximum.
Poetry: Maximum length 8 lines. Looking for rhythmic, rhyming poems.
How to Contact/Writers: "Please do not query first." Send complete ms with SASE. "Submissions without SASE will be discarded." Reports in 3 months.
Illustration: Uses color artwork only. Works on assignment only. Reviews ms/illustration packages from artists. "The manuscripts will be evaluated for quality of concept and text before the art is considered." Contact: Paula Morrow, editor. Illustrations only: Send tearsheets or photo prints/photocopies with SASE. "Submissions without SASE will be discarded." Reports in 12 weeks. Samples filed.
Terms: Pays on publication for mss; after delivery of completed assignment for illustrators. Buys first rights with reprint option or (in some cases) all rights. Original artwork returned at job's completion. Rates vary ($25 minimum for mss; $250 minimum for art). Sample copy for $5. Guidelines free for SASE.
Tips: "*Babybug* would like to reach as many children's authors and artists as possible for original contributions, but our standards are very high, and we will accept only top-quality material. Before attempting to write for *Babybug*, be sure to familiarize yourself with this age child." (See listings for *Cricket, Cicada, Ladybug, Muse* and *Spider*.)

☑ **BLACK BELT FOR KIDS**, Rainbow Publications, P.O. Box 918, Santa Clarita CA 91380. (805)257-4066. Fax: (805)257-3028. **Articles Editor:** Douglas Jeffrey. Bimonthly. Special insert in *Karate/Kung Fu Illustrated* magazine. Estab. 1995. Circ. 35,000. "We publish instructional, inspirational and philosophical pieces written for children who study martial arts."
Nonfiction: Picture-oriented material: health, history, humorous, sports, travel. Young readers: health, history, humorous, interview/profile, sports, travel. Middle readers, young adults/teens: health, history, how-to, humorous, interview/profile, sports, travel. Does not want to see profiles written by parents about their own kid. Buys 10-15 mss/year. Average word length: 800-1,500. Byline given.
How to Contact/Writers: Nonfiction: Query. Reports on queries/mss in 1 month. Publishes ms 6 months after acceptance. Will consider electronic submissions via disk or modem.
Terms: Pays on publication. Buys all rights for mss. Pays $100-200 for articles. Sample copies free for 9×12 SAE and 6 first-class stamps. Writer's guidelines free for SASE.
Tips: "Make it fun."

☑ **BLUE JEAN MAGAZINE**, Blue Jean Magazine Inc., P.O. Box 507, Rochester NY 14564. (716)924-4080. Fax: (716)654-6785. E-mail: editors@bluejeanmag.com. Website: http://www.bluejeanmag.com. **Articles Editor:** Sherry Handel, publisher. Bimonthly magazine. Estab. 1996. "*blue jean magazine* is the only magazine written and produced by young women from around the world. *blue jean* publishes teen-produced artwork, poetry, fiction and nonfiction. *blue jean* provides young women (ages 12-19) with the opportunity to gain international recognition for their work." 90% of publication is written by teen girls. Considers all types of fiction. "We love multicultural fiction—fiction that's written in the voice of a woman of color about her experiences interacting with society." Byline given.
Fiction: Young adults/teens: Considers all types of fiction.
Nonfiction: Young adults/teens: Considers all categories of nonfiction, especially arts/crafts, careers, health, journalistic reporting by teens, interviews/profiles, how-to, multicultural and social issues. Multicultural needs include: "Any writings by young women of color!" Buys 6-10 mss/year. Average word length: 700 (1 page) to 1,400 (2 pages). Byline given.
Poetry: Reviews poetry by teen girls.
How to Contact/Writers: Fiction/nonfiction: Send complete ms. Reports on queries in 2 months; mss in 2 months. Publishes ms 3 months or more after acceptance. Will consider simultaneous submissions, electronic submissions via disk or modem (no attached files).
Terms: Pays on publication. Buys one-time rights. Pays $75 flat rate. Writer's guidelines for SASE. Sample magazine copies available fro $8.
Tips: "Request submission guidelines! *blue jean magazine* is an alternative to the fashion and beauty magazines targeting young women. *blue jean* is advertising-free, so you will find no beauty tips, fashion spreads or super models on our pages. Our diverse coalition of teen editors and correspondents is dedicated to publishing what young women are thinking, saying and doing. *blue jean* profiles girls and women who are changing the world!"

BOYS' LIFE, Boy Scouts of America, 1325 W. Walnut Hill Lane, P.O. Box 152079, Irving TX 75015-2079. (214)580-2000. Website: http://www.bsa.scouting.org. **Editor-in-Chief:** J.D. Owen. **Managing Edi-**

tor: W.E. Butterworth, IV. **Articles Editor:** Michael Goldman. **Fiction Editor:** Shannon Lowry. **Director of Design:** Joseph P. Connolly. **Art Director:** Elizabeth Hardaway Morgan. Monthly magazine. Estab. 1911. Circ. 1,300,000. *Boys' Life* is "a general interest magazine for boys 8 to 18 who are members of the Cub Scouts, Boy Scouts or Explorers; a general interest magazine for all boys."

• *Boys' Life* ranked number 3 on *Writer's Digest's* 1998 Fiction 50, the magazine's annual list of the most writer-friendly publications.

Fiction: Middle readers: adventure, animal, contemporary, fantasy, history, humor, problem-solving, science fiction, sports, spy/mystery. Does not want to see "talking animals and adult reminiscence." Buys 12 mss/year. Average word length: 1,000-1,500. Byline given.

Nonfiction: "Subject matter is broad. We cover everything from professional sports to American history to how to pack a canoe. A look at a current list of the BSA's more than 100 merit badge pamphlets gives an idea of the wide range of subjects possible. Even better, look at a year's worth of recent issues. Column headings are science, nature, earth, health, sports, space and aviation, cars, computers, entertainment, pets, history, music and others." Average word length: 500-1,500. Columns 300-750 words. Byline given.

How to Contact/Writers: Fiction: Send complete ms with SASE. Nonfiction: query with SASE for response. Reports on queries/mss in 6-8 weeks.

Illustration: Buys 5-7 illustrations/issue; 23-50 illustrations/year. Works on assignment only. Reviews ms/illustration packages from artists. "Query first." Illustrations only: Send tearsheets. Reports on art samples only if interested. Original artwork returned at job's completion.

Terms: Buys first rights. Pays $750 and up for fiction; $400-1,500 for major articles; $150-400 for columns; $250-300 for how-to features. Sample copies for $3 plus 9×12 SASE. Writer's/illustrator's/photo guidelines available for SASE.

Tips: "I strongly urge you to study at least a year's issues to better understand type of material published. Articles for *Boys' Life* must interest and entertain boys ages 8 to 18. Write for a boy you know who is 12. Our readers demand crisp, punchy writing in relatively short, straightforward sentences. The editors demand well-reported articles that demonstrate high standards of journalism. We follow *The New York Times* manual of style and usage. All submissions must be accompanied by SASE with adequate postage."

BOYS' QUEST, The Bluffton News Publishing and Printing Co., 103 N. Main St., Bluffton OH 45817. (419)358-4610. Fax: (419)358-5027. **Articles Editor:** Marilyn Edwards. **Art Submissions:** Becky Jackman. Bimonthly magazine. Estab. 1995. "*Boys' Quest* is a magazine created for boys from 6 to 13 years, with youngsters 8, 9 and 10 the specific target age. Our point of view is that every young boy deserves the right to be a young boy for a number of years before he becomes a young adult. As a result, *Boys' Quest* looks for articles, fiction, nonfiction, and poetry that deal with timeless topics, such as pets, nature, hobbies, science, games, sports, careers, simple cooking, and anything else likely to interest a young boy."

Fiction: Young readers, middle readers: adventure, animal, history, humorous, nature/environment, problem-solving, sports, jokes, building, cooking, cartoons, riddles. Does not want to see violence, teenage themes. Buys 30 mss/year. Average word length: 200-500. Byline given.

Nonfiction: Young readers, middle readers: animal, arts/crafts, biography, cooking, games/puzzles, history, how-to, humorous, math, problem-solving, science. Prefer photo support with nonfiction. Buys 30 mss/year. Average word length: 200-500. Byline given.

Poetry: Reviews poetry. Maximum length: 21 lines. Limit submissions to 6 poems.

How to Contact/Writers: Fiction/Nonfiction: Query or send complete ms (preferred). Send SASE with correct postage. No faxed material. Reports on queries in 1-2 weeks; mss in 3 weeks (if rejected); 3-4 months (if scheduled). Publishes ms 3 months-3 years after acceptance. Will consider simultaneous submissions and previously published work.

Illustration: Buys 6 illustrations/issue; 36-45 illustrations/year. Uses b&w artwork only. Works on assignment only. Reviews ms/illustration packages from artists. Send ms with dummy. Illustrations only: Query with samples, arrange portfolio review. Send portfolio, tearsheets. Reports in 2 weeks. Samples returned with SASE; samples filed. Credit line given.

Photography: Photos used for support of nonfiction. "Excellent photographs included with a nonfiction story is considered very seriously." Model/property releases required. Uses b&w, 5×7 or 3×5 prints. Query with samples; send unsolicited photos by mail. Reports in 2-3 weeks.

Terms: Pays on publication. Buys first North American serial rights for mss. Buys first rights for artwork. Pays 5¢/word for stories and articles. Additional payment for ms/illustration packages and for photos accompanying articles. Pays $150-200 for color cover. Pays photographers per photo (range: $5-10). "*Boys' Quest*, as a new publication, is aware that its rates of payment are modest at this time. But we pledge to increase those rewards in direct proportion to our success. Meanwhile, we will strive to treat our contributors and their work with respect and fairness. That treatment, incidentally, will include quick decision on all submissions." Originals returned to artist at job's completion. Sample copies for $3. Writer's/illustrator's/photo guidelines free for SASE.

Tips: "We are looking for lively writing, most of it from a young boy's point of view—with the boy or boys directly involved in an activity that is both wholesome and unusual. We need nonfiction with photos and fiction stories—around 500 words—puzzle, poems, cooking, carpentry projects, jokes and riddles. Nonfiction pieces that are accompanied by black and white photos are far more likely to be accepted than those that need illustrations. We will entertain simultaneous submissions as long as that fact is noted on the manuscript."

BREAD FOR GOD'S CHILDREN, Bread Ministries, Inc., P.O. Box 1017, Arcadia FL 34265-1017. (941)494-6214. Fax: (941)993-0154. E-mail: bread@desoto.net. Website: http://www.peacerivervalley. com/Bread. **Editor:** Judith M. Gibbs. Monthly magazine. Estab. 1972. Circ. 10,000 (US and Canada). "*Bread* is designed as a teaching tool for Christian families." 85% of publication aimed at juvenile market.
Fiction: Young readers, middle readers, young adult/teen: adventure, religious, problem-solving, sports. Looks for "teaching stories that portray Christian lifestyles without preaching." Buys approximately 20 mss/year. Average word length: 900-1,500 (for teens); 600-900 (for young children). Byline given.
Nonfiction: Young readers, middle readers: animal. All levels: how-to. "We do not want anything detrimental of solid family values. Most topics would fit if they are slanted to our basic needs." Buys 3-4 mss/ year. Average word length: 500-800. Byline given.
Illustration: "The only illustrations we purchase are those occasional good ones coming with a story we accept."
How to Contact/Writers: Fiction/nonfiction: Send complete ms. Reports on mss in 3 weeks-6 months "if considered for use." Will consider simultaneous submissions and previously published work.
Terms: Pays on publication. Pays $10-50 for stories; $25 for articles. Sample copies free for 9×12 SAE and 5 first-class stamps (for 2 copies).
Tips: "We want stories or articles that illustrate overcoming by faith and living solid, Christian lives. Know our publication and what we have used in the past . . . know the readership . . . know the publisher's guidelines. Stories should teach the value of morality and honesty without preaching. Edit carefully for content and grammar."

CALLIOPE, World History for Kids, Cobblestone Publishing, Inc., 7 School St., Peterborough NH 03458. (603)924-7209. **Managing Editor:** Denise L. Babcock. **Art Director:** Ann Dillon. Magazine published 9 times/year. "*Calliope* covers world history (East/West) and lively, original approaches to the subject are the primary concerns of the editors in choosing material."
Fiction: Middle readers and young adults: adventure, folktales, plays, history, biographical fiction. Material must relate to forthcoming themes. Word length: up to 800.
Nonfiction: Middle readers and young adults: arts/crafts, biography, cooking, games/puzzles, history. Material must relate to forthcoming themes. Word length: 300-800.
Poetry: Maximum line length: 100. Wants "clear, objective imagery. Serious and light verse considered."
How to Contact/Writers: "A query must consist of the following to be considered (please use nonerasable paper): a brief cover letter stating subject and word length of the proposed article; a detailed one-page outline explaining the information to be presented in the article; an extensive bibliography of materials the author intends to use in preparing the article; a self-addressed stamped envelope. Writers new to *Calliope* should send a writing sample with query. If you would like to know if your query has been received, please also include a stamped postcard that requests acknowledgment of receipt. In all correspondence, please include your complete address as well as a telephone number where you can be reached. A writer may send as many queries for one issue as he or she wishes, but each query must have a separate cover letter, outline, bibliography and SASE. Telephone queries are not accepted. Handwritten queries will not be considered. Queries may be submitted at any time, but queries sent well in advance of deadline *may not be answered for several months*. Go-aheads requesting material proposed in queries are usually sent five months prior to publication date. Unused queries will be returned approximately three to four months prior to publication date."
Illustration: Illustrations only: Send tearsheets, photocopies. Original work returned upon job's completion (upon written request).
Photography: Buys photos from freelancers. Wants photos pertaining to any forthcoming themes. Uses b&w/color prints, 35mm transparencies. Send unsolicited photos by mail (on speculation).
Terms: Buys all rights for mss and artwork. Pays 20-25¢/word for stories/articles. Pays on an individual basis for poetry, activities, games/puzzles. "Covers are assigned and paid on an individual basis." Pays photographers per photo ($15-100 for b&w; $25-100 for color). Sample copy for $3.95 and SAE with $1.05 postage. Writer's/illustrator's/photo guidelines for SASE. (See listings for *Cobblestone, Faces* and *Odyssey*.)

N CAMPUS LIFE, Christianity Today, Inc., 465 Gundersen Dr., Carol Stream IL 60188. (630)260-6200. Fax: (630)260-0114. E-mail: cledit@aol.com. Website: http://www.campuslife.net. **Articles and Fiction Editor:** Chris Lutes. **Art Director:** Doug Johnson. Bimonthly magazine. Estab. 1944. Circ. 100,000. "Our purpose if to help Christian high school students navigate adolescence with their faith intact."
Fiction: Young adults: humorous, problem-solving. Buys 5-6 mss/year. Byline given.
Poetry: Reviews poetry.
How to Contact/Writers: Fiction/nonfiction: Query.
Illustration: Works on assignment only. Reviews illustration packages from artists. Contact: Doug Johnson, design director. Illustrations only: Query; send promo sheet. Contact: Doug Johnson, design director. Reports back only if interested. Credit line given.
Photography: Looking for photos depicting lifestyle/authentic teen experience. Model/property release required. Uses 8×10 glossy prints and 35mm, $2\frac{1}{4} \times 2\frac{1}{4}$, 4×5 transparencies. Query with samples. Reports only if interested.
Terms: Pays on acceptance. Original artwork returned at job's completion. Writer's/illustrator's/photo guidelines for SASE.

✓ CAREER WORLD, Curriculum Innovations Group, 900 Skokie Blvd., Suite 200, Northbrook IL 60062-4028. (847)205-3000. Fax: (847)564-8197. **Articles Editor:** Carole Rubenstein. **Art Director:** Carl Krach. Monthly (school year) magazine. Estab. 1972. A guide to careers, for students grades 7-12.
Nonfiction: Young adults/teens: education, how-to, interview/profile, career information. Byline given.
How to Contact/Writers: Nonfiction: Query with published clips and résumé. "We do not want any unsolicited manuscripts." Reports on queries in 2 weeks.
Illustration: Buys 5-10 illustrations/year. Works on assignment only. Reviews ms/illustration packages from artists. Ms/illustration packages and illustration only: Query; send promo sheet and tearsheets. Credit line given.
Photography: Purchases photos from freelancers.
Terms: Pays on publication. Buys all rights. Pays $100-400 for articles. Pays illustrators $100-250 for color cover; $25-35 for b&w inside; $50-75 for color inside. Writer's guidelines free, but only on assignment.

CARUS PUBLISHING COMPANY, P.O. Box 300, Peru IL 61354. See listing for *Babybug*, *Cicada*, *Cricket*, *Ladybug*, *Muse* and *Spider*.

✓ CAT FANCY, The Magazine for Responsible Cat Owners, Fancy Publications, P.O. Box 6050, Mission Viejo CA 92690. (949)855-8822. Fax: (949)855-3045. Website: http://www.catfancy.com. Monthly magazine. Estab. 1965. Circ. 300,000. "Our magazine is for cat owners who want to know more about how to care for their pets in a responsible manner. We want to see 500-750-word articles showing children relating to or learning about cats in a positive, responsible way. We'd love to see more craft projects for children." 3% of material aimed at juvenile audience.
Fiction: Middle readers, young adults/teens: animal (all cat-related). Does not want to see stories in which cats talk. Buys 2 mss/year. Average word length: 750-1,000. Byline given. Never wants to see work showing cats being treated abusively or irresponsibly or work that puts cats in a negative light. Never use mss written from cats' point of view. Query first.
Nonfiction: Middle readers, young adults/teens: careers, arts/crafts, puzzles, profiles of children who help cats (all cat-related). Buys 3-9 mss/year. Average word length: 450-1,000. Byline given. Would like to see more crafts and how-to pieces for children.
Poetry: Reviews short poems only. "No more than five poems per submission please."
How To Contact/Writers: Fiction/nonfiction: Send query only. Reports on queries in 1-2 months. Publishes ms (juvenile) 4-12 months after acceptance. Send SASE for writer's guidelines.
Illustration: Buys 2-10 illustrations/year. "Most of our illustrations are assigned or submitted with a story. We look for realistic images of cats done with pen and ink (no pencil)." Illustration only: "Submit photocopies of work; samples of spot art possibilities." Samples returned with SASE. Reports in 1-2 months. Credit line given.
Photography: "Cats only, in excellent focus and properly lit. Send SASE for photo needs and submit according to them."

"PICTURE-ORIENTED MATERIAL" are for preschoolers to 8-year-olds; "Young readers" are for 5- to 8-year-olds; "Middle readers" are for 9- to 11-year-olds; and "Young adults" are for ages 12 and up.

Terms: Pays on publication. Buys first North American serial rights. Buys one-time rights for artwork and photos. Originals returned to artist at job's completion. Pays $50-200 for stories; $75-400 for articles; $35-50 for crafts or puzzles; $20 for poems. Pays illustrators $50-200 for color inside. Photographers paid per photo (range: $35-200). Writer's/artist's/photo guidelines free for #10 SAE and 1 first-class stamp.

Tips: "Perhaps the most important tip we can give is: Consider what 9- to 14-year-olds want to know about cats and what they enjoy most about cats, and address that topic in a style appropriate for them. Writers, keep your writing concise, and don't be afraid to try again after a rejection. Illustrators, we use illustrations mainly as spot art; occasionally we make assignments to illustrators whose spot art we've used before."

CHICKADEE, 179 John St., Suite 500, Toronto, Ontario M5T 3G5 Canada.
- *Chickadee* editors prefer not to receive submissions. See listings for *Chirp* and *OWL*.

CHILD LIFE, Children's Better Health Institute, 1100 Waterway Blvd., P.O. Box 567, Indianapolis IN 46206. Parcels and packages: please send to 1100 Waterway Blvd., 46202. (317)636-8881. **Editor:** Lise Hoffman. **Art Director:** Phyllis Lybarger. Magazine published 8 times/year. Estab. 1921. Circ. 80,000. Targeted toward kids ages 9-11. Focuses on health, sports, fitness, nutrition, safety, general interests, and the nostalgia of *Child Life's* early days.
- *Child Life* is no longer accepting manuscripts for publication. See listings for *Children's Digest, Children's Playmate, Humpty Dumpty's Magazine, Jack and Jill, Turtle Magazine* and *U*S*Kids*.

CHILDREN'S BETTER HEALTH INSTITUTE, 1100 Waterway Blvd., P.O. Box 567, Indianapolis IN 46206. See listings for *Child Life, Children's Digest, Children's Playmate, Humpty Dumpty's Magazine, Jack and Jill, Turtle* and *U*S* Kids*.

CHILDREN'S DIGEST, Children's Better Health Institute, 1100 Waterway Blvd., Box 567, Indianapolis IN 46206. (317)636-8881. **Editors:** Danny Lee and Jeff Ayers. **Art Director:** Mary Stropoli. Magazine published 8 times/year. Estab. 1950. Circ. 125,000. For preteens; approximately 33% of content is health-related.
- *Children's Digest* would like to see more photo stories about current events and topical matters and more nonfiction in general.

Fiction: Adventure, humorous, mainstream, mystery. Stories should appeal to both boys and girls. "We need some stories that incorporate a health theme. However, we don't want stories that preach, preferring instead stories with implied morals. We like a light or humorous approach."

Nonfiction: Historical, craft ideas, health, nutrition, fitness and sports. "We're especially interested in factual features that teach readers about fitness and sports or encourage them to develop better health habits. We are *not* interested in material that is simply rewritten from encyclopedias. We try to present our health material in a way that instructs *and* entertains the reader."

Poetry: Accepts poetry.

How to Contact/Writers: Reports in 2 months. Send complete ms.

Photography: State availability of full color or b&w photos. Model releases and identification of subjects required.

Terms: Pays on publication. Buys all rights. Pays up to 12¢/word for articles/stories. Pays $20 minimum for poetry.

CHILDREN'S PLAYMATE, Children's Better Health Institute, 1100 Waterway Blvd., Box 567, Indianapolis IN 46206. (317)636-8881. **Editor:** Terry Harshman. **Art Director:** Chuck Horsman. Magazine published 8 times/year. Estab. 1929. Circ. 135,000. For children ages 6-8 years; approximately 50% of content is health-related.

Fiction: Young readers: animal, contemporary, fantasy, folktales, history, humorous, science fiction, sports, suspense/mystery/adventure. Buys 25 mss/year. Average word length: 300-700. Byline given.

Nonfiction: Young readers: animal, arts/crafts, biography, cooking, games/puzzles, health, history, how-to, humorous, sports, travel. Buys 16-20 mss/year. Average word length: 300-700. Byline given.

Poetry: Maximum length: 20-25 lines.

How to Contact/Writers: Fiction/nonfiction: Send complete ms. Reports on mss in 8-10 weeks.

Illustration: Works on assignment only. Reviews ms/illustration packages from artists. Query first.

Photography: Buys photos with accompanying ms only. Model/property releases required; captions required. Uses 35mm transparencies. Send completed ms with transparencies.

Terms: Pays on publication for illustrators and writers. Buys all rights for mss and artwork; one-time rights for photos. Pays 17¢/word for assigned articles. Pays $275 for color cover illustration; $35-90 for b&w inside; $70-155 for color inside. Pays photographers per photo (range: $10-75). Sample copy $1.25.

Writer's/illustrator's guidelines for SASE. (See listings for *Child Life, Children's Digest, Humpty Dumpty's Magazine, Jack And Jill Turtle Magazine* and *U*S* Kids*.)
Tips: See listings for *Child Life, Children's Playmate, Humpty Dmpty's Magazine, Jack and Jill, Turtle* and *U*S* Kids*.

✓ **CHIRP**, 179 John St., Suite 500, Toronto, Ontario M5T 3G5 Canada. E-mail: owl@owl.on.ca. Website: http://www.owl.on.ca. **Editor-in-chief:** Marybeth Leatherdale. **Creative Director:** Tim Davin. Published monthly during school year. Nature magazine for children ages 2-6. "*Chirp* aims to introduce preschool non-readers to reading for pleasure about the world around them."
Fiction: Picture-oriented material: nature/environment, adventure, animal, multicultural, problem-solving, sports. Word length: 250 maximum.
Nonfiction: Picture-oriented material: fun, easy craft ideas, animal, games/puzzles, how-to, multicultural, nature/environment, problem-solving.
Poetry: Wants rhymes and poetry. Maximum length: 8 lines.
How to Contact/Writers: Query. Reports on queries/mss in 1 month.
Illustration: Pays approximately 15 illustrations/issue; 135 illustrations/year. Samples returned with SASE. Originals returned at job's completion. Credit line given.
Terms: Pays on acceptance. Buys all rights. Pays on publication. Pays writers $250 (Canadian); illustrators $450 (Canadian); photographers paid per photo ($150-375 Canadian). Sample copies available for $4 (Canadian).
Tips: "Chirp editors prefer to read completed manuscripts of stories and articles, accompanied by photographs or suggestions of visual references where they are appropriate. All craft ideas should be based on materials that are found around the average household." See listings for *Chickadee* and *OWL*.

N: CICADA, Carus Publishing Company, P.O. Box 300, 315 Fifth St., Peru IL 61354. (815)224-6656. Fax: (815)224-6615. E-mail: cicada@caruspub.com. Website: http://www.cicadamag.com. **Editor:** Deborah Vetter. **Associate Editor:** John D. Allen. **Senior Art Director:** Ron McCutchan. Bimonthly magazine. Estab. 1998. *CICADA* publishes fiction and poetry with a genuine teen sensibility, aimed at the high school and college-age market. The editors are looking for stories and poems that are thought-provoking but entertaining.
Fiction: Young adults: adventure, animal, contemporary, fantasy, history, humorous, multicultural, nature/environment, romance, science fiction, sports, suspense/mystery, stories that will adapt themselves to a sophisticated cartoon, or graphic novel format. Buys up to 60 mss/year. Average word length: about 5,000 words for short stories; up to 15,000 for novellas only—we run one novella per issue.
Nonfiction: Young adults: first-person, coming-of-age experiences that are relevant to teens and young adults (example-life in the Peace Corps). Buys 6 mss/year. Average word length: about 5,000 words. Byline given.
Poetry: Reviews serious, humorous, free verse, rhyming (if done well) poetry. Maximum length: up to 25 lines. Limit submissions to 5 poems.
How to Contact/Writers: Fiction/nonfiction: send complete ms. Reports on mss in 8-10 weeks. Publishes ms 1-2 years after acceptance. Will consider simultaneous submissions if author lets us know.
Illustration: Buys 20 illustrations/issue; 120 illustrations/year. Uses color artwork for cover; b&w for interior. Works on assignment only. Reviews ms/illustration packages from artists. Send ms with 1-2 sketches and samples of other finished art. Contact: Ron McCutchan, senior art director. Illustrations only: Query with samples. Contact: Ron McCutchan, senior art director. Reports in 6 weeks. Samples returned with SASE; samples filed. Credit line given.
Photography: Wants documentary photos (clear shots that illustrate specific artifacts, persons, locations, phenomena, etc., cited in the text) and "art" shots of teens in photo montage/lighting effects etc. Uses b&w 4×5 glossy prints. Submit portfolio for review. Reports in 6 weeks.
Terms: Pays on publication. Buys first rights for mss. Buys one-time, first publication rights for artwork and photographs. Pays up to 25¢/word. Pays illustrators $750 for color cover; $50-150 for b&w inside. Pays photographers per photo (range: $50-150). Sample copies for $8.50. Writer's/illustrator's/photo guidelines for SASE.
Tips: "Please don't write for a junior high audience. We're looking for good character development, strong plots, and thought-provoking themes for young people in high school and collge. Don't forget humor!" (See listings for *Babybug, Cricket, Ladybug, Muse* and *Spider*.)

✓ **CLASS ACT**, Class Act, Inc., P.O. Box 802, Henderson KY 42419-0802. E-mail: classact@henderson .net. Website: http://www.henderson.net/~classact. **Articles Editor:** Susan Thurman. Monthly, September-May. Newsletter. Estab. 1993. Circ. 300. "We are looking for practical, ready-to-use ideas for the English/ language arts classroom (grades 6-12)."

Nonfiction: Middle readers and young adults/teens: games/puzzles, how-to. Does not want to see esoteric material; no master's theses; no poetry (except articles about how to write poetry). Buys 20 mss/year. Average word length: 200-4,000. Byline given.

How to Contact/Writers: Send complete ms. Reports in 6 weeks. Usually publishes ms 3-12 months after acceptance. Will consider simultaneous submissions. Must send SASE.

Terms: Pays on acceptance. Pays $10-30 per article. Buys all rights. Sample copy for $3 and SASE.

Tips: "We're only interested in language arts-related articles for teachers and students. Writers need to realize teens often need humor in classroom assignments. In addition, we are looking for teacher-tested ideas that have already worked in the classroom. If sending puzzles, we usually need at least 20 entries per puzzle to fit our format. Be clever. We've already seen a zillion articles on homonyms and haikus. If a SASE isn't sent, we'll assume you don't want a response."

☑ **COBBLESTONE: Discover American History**, Cobblestone Publishing Co., 30 Grove St., Suite C, Peterborough NH 03458. (603)924-7209. Fax: (603)924-7380. **Editor:** Meg Chorlian. **Art Director:** Ann Dillon. **Managing Editor:** Denise L. Babcock. Magazine published 9 times/year. Circ. 36,000. "*Cobblestone* is theme-related. Writers should request editorial guidelines which explain procedure and list upcoming themes. Queries must relate to an upcoming theme. It is recommended that writers become familiar with the magazine (sample copies available)."

Nonfiction: Middle readers (school ages 8-14): activities, biography, games/puzzles (no word finds), history (world and American), interview/profile, science, travel. All articles must relate to the issue's theme. Buys 120 mss/year. Average word length: 600-800. Byline given.

Poetry: Up to 100 lines. "Clear, objective imagery. Serious and light verse considered." Pays on an individual basis. Must relate to theme.

How to Contact/Writers: Fiction/nonfiction: Query. "A query must consist of all of the following to be considered: a brief cover letter stating the subject and word length of the proposed article, a detailed one-page outline explaining the information to be presented in the article, an extensive bibliography of materials the author intends to use in preparing the article, a self-addressed stamped envelope. Writers new to *Cobblestone* should send a writing sample with query. If you would like to know if your query has been received, please also include a stamped postcard that requests acknowledgment of receipt. In all correspondence, please include your complete address as well as a telephone number where you can be reached. A writer may send as many queries for one issue as he or she wishes, but each query must have a separate cover letter, outline, bibliography and SASE. Telephone queries are not accepted. Handwritten queries will not be considered. Queries may be submitted at any time, but queries sent well in advance of deadline *may not be answered for several months*. Go-aheads requesting material proposed in queries are usually sent five months prior to publication date. Unused queries will be returned approximately three to four months prior to publication date."

Illustration: Buys 4 color illustrations/issue; 36 illustrations/year. Preferred theme or style: Material that is simple, clear and accurate but not too juvenile. Sophisticated sources are a must. Works on assignment only. Reviews ms/illustration packages from artists. Query. CIllustrations only: Send photocopies, tearsheets, or other nonreturnable samples. "Illustrators should consult issues of *Cobblestone* to familiarize themselves with our needs." Reports on art samples in 2 weeks. Samples returned with SASE; samples not filed. Original artwork returned at job's completion (upon written request). Credit line given.

Photography: Photos must relate to upcoming themes. Send transparencies and/or color prints. Submit on speculation.

Terms: Pays on publication. Buys all rights to articles and artwork. Pays 20-25¢/word for articles/stories. Pays on an individual basis for poetry, activities, games/puzzles. Pays photographers per photo ($15-100 for b&w; $25-100 for color). Sample copy $4.95 with 7½ × 10½ SAE and 5 first-class stamps; writer's/illustrator's/photo guidelines free with SAE and 1 first-class stamp.

Tips: Writers: "Submit detailed queries which show attention to historical accuracy and which offer interesting and entertaining information. Study past issues to know what we look for. All feature articles, recipes, activities, fiction and supplemental nonfiction are freelance contributions." Illustrators: "Submit color samples, not too juvenile. Study past issues to know what we look for. The illustration we use is generally for stories, recipes and activities." (See listings for *Calliope, Faces,* and *Odyssey.*)

COBBLESTONE PUBLISHING, INC., 7 School St., Peterborough NH 03458. See listings for *Appleseeds, Calliope, Cobblestone, Faces* and *Odyssey.*

🎨 **COLLEGE BOUND MAGAZINE**, Ramholtz Publishing, Inc., 2071 Clove Rd., Suite 206, Staten Island NY 10304. (718)273-5700. Fax: (718)273-2539. E-mail: editorial@cbnet.com. Website: http://www.cbnet.com. **Articles Editor:** Gina LaGuardia. **Art Director:** Giulio Rammiarone. Monthly magazine and website. Estab. 1987. Circ. 75,000 (regional); 750,000 (national). *College Bound Magazine* is written by college students for high school juniors and seniors. It is designed to provide an inside view of college life, with college students from around the country serving as correspondents. The magazine's editorial content offers its teen readership personal accounts on all aspects of college, from living with a roommate, choosing a major, and joining a fraternity or soroity, to college dating, interesting courses, beating the financial aid fuss, and other college-bound concerns. *College Bound Magazine* is published six times regionally throughout the tri-state area. Special issues include the Annual National Edition (published each February) and Fall and Spring California issues. The magazine also has an award-winning website, *CollegeBound.NET*, at http://www.cbnet.com.

Nonfiction: Young adults: careers, concept, fashion, health, how-to, interview/profile, math, problem-solving, social issues, college life. Buys 70 mss/year. Average word length: 400-1,100 words. Byline given.

How to Contact/Writers: Nonfiction: Query with published clips. Reports on queries in 5 weeks; mss in 5-6 weeks. Publishes ms 2-3 months after acceptance. Will consider electronic submission via disk or modem, previously published work (as long as not a competitor title).

Illustration: Buys 2-3 illustrations/issue. Uses color artwork only. Works on assignment only. Reviews ms/illustration packages from artists. Query. Contact: Giulio Rammiarone, art director. Illustrations only: Query with samples. Reports in 2 months. Samples kept on file. Credit line given.

Terms: Pays on publication. Buys first North American serial rights, all rights or reprint rights for mss. Buys first rights for artwork. Originals returned if requested, with SASE. Pays $25-100 for articles 30 days upon publication. All contributors receive 3 issues with payment. Pays illustrators $25-125 for color inside. Sample copies free for #10 SAE and $3 postage. Writer's guidelines for SASE.

Tips: "Review the sample issue and get a good feel for the types of articles we accept and our tone and purpose."

COUNSELOR, Cook Communications Ministries, P.O. Box 36640, Colorado Springs CO 80936. (719)536-0100 or (800)708-5550. Fax: (719)536-3243. E-mail: burtonj@cookministries.org. **Editor:** Janice K. Burton. **Art Director:** Randy Maid. Newspaper distributed weekly; published quarterly. Estab. 1940. "Audience: children 8-10 years. Papers designed to present everyday living stories showing the difference Christ can make in a child's life. Must have a true Christian slant, not just a moral implication. Correlated with Scripture Press Sunday School curriculum."

Fiction: Middle readers: adventure, animal, contemporary, folktales, history, humorous, multicultural, nature/environment, problem-solving, religious, sports (all with a strong Christian context). "Appreciate well-written fiction that shows knowledge of our product. Suggest people write for samples." Buys approximately 12 mss/year. Average word length: 850. Byline given.

Nonfiction: Middle readers: animals, arts/crafts, biography, games/puzzles, geography, health, history, hobbies, how-to, humorous, interview/profile, multicultural, nature/environment, problem-solving, religion, science, social issues, sports (all with Christian context). Buys approximately 12 mss/year. Average word length: 300-800. Byline given.

How to Contact/Writers: Fiction/nonfiction: Send complete ms. Reports on queries in 6 weeks; mss in 6-8 weeks. Publishes ms 1-2 years after acceptance ("we work a year in advance"). Will consider previously published work.

Illustrations: Buys approximately 1-2 illustrations/issue; 12-20 illustrations/year. Reports back on artists submissions only if interested. Samples kept on file. Credit line given.

Terms: Pays on acceptance. Buys second (reprint) rights, one-time rights, or all rights for mss. Pays 7-10¢/word for stories or articles, depending on amount of editing required. Pays illustrators $450-700 for color cover. Sample copies for #10 SAE and 1 first-class stamp. Writers guidelines for SASE.

Tips: "Send copy that is as polished as possible. Indicate if story is true. Indicate rights offered. Stick to required word lengths. Include Social Security number on manuscript. Write for tips for writers, sample copies and theme lists."

✓ **CRAYOLA KIDS: Family Time Fun**, Meredith Corporation, 1716 Locust St., Des Moines IA 50309-3023. (515)284-2170. Fax: (515)284-2064. **Articles Editor:** Mary Heaton. **Art Director:** Bob Riley. Bimonthly magazine. Estab. 1994. Circ. 500,000. "The mission of *Crayola Kids: Family Time Fun*, is to enrich the lives of families with young children (ages 3-8) by encouraging creative fun and the joy of discovery through reading. Each bimonthly issue focuses on a single theme and features a full-length reprint of a previously published picture book (trade book) and related puzzles, crafts and activities."

Nonfiction: Picture-oriented material, young readers: animal, arts/crafts, games/puzzles, how-to, multicultural, nature/environment, science, travel. "Seasonal tie-ins are a plus." Does not want to see biographies. Buys 20-30 mss/year. Average word length: 250. Byline given.

How to Contact/Writers: Nonfiction: Query. Reports on queries in 6-8 weeks. Reports on mss in 2-3 months.

Illustration: Only interested in agented material.

Terms: Pays on acceptance. Buys all rights for mss. Pays $15-200 for articles. "Depends on subject, length, complexity, originality." Sample copies for $3.50 plus SASE (large enough to hold a magazine).

Tips: "We are interested in highly creative multicultural, nonsexist activities, visual puzzles, games and craft ideas related to the theme or seasonality of an issue. Submit a sample of a craft or a Polaroid shot of it. Tell us your story or activity idea and what's unique and fun about it. Convince us that kids will love reading it, doing it, or making it. Study the magazine. Query for theme list."

CRICKET MAGAZINE, Carus Publishing, Company, P.O. Box 300, Peru IL 61354. (815)224-6656. **Articles/Fiction Editor-in-Chief:** Marianne Carus. **Editor:** Deborah Vetter. **Art Director:** Ron McCutchan. Monthly magazine. Estab. 1973. Circ. 83,000. Children's literary magazine for ages 9-14.

● *Cricket* ranked number 11 on *Writer's Digest*'s 1998 Fiction 50, the magazine's annual list of the most writer-friendly publications.

Fiction: Middle readers, young adults/teens: adventure, animal, contemporary, fantasy, folk and fairy tales, history, humorous, multicultural, nature/environment, science fiction, sports, suspense/mystery. Buys 180 mss/year. Maximum word length: 2,000. Byline given.

Nonfiction: Middle readers, young adults/teens: animal, arts/crafts, biography, environment, experiments, games/puzzles, history, how-to, interview/profile, natural science, problem-solving, science and technology, space, sports, travel. Multicultural needs include articles on customs and cultures. Requests bibliography with submissions. Buys 180 mss/year. Average word length: 1,200. Byline given.

Poetry: Reviews poems, 1-page maximum length. Limit submissions to 5 poems or less.

How to Contact/Writers: Send complete ms. Do not query first. Reports on mss in 2-3 months. Does not like but will consider simultaneous submissions. SASE required for response.

Illustration: Buys 35 illustrations (14 separate commissions)/issue; 425 illustrations/year. Uses b&w and full-color work. Preferred theme or style: "strong realism; strong people, especially kids; good action illustration; no cartoons. All media, but prefer other than pencil." Reviews ms/illustration packages from artists "but reserves option to re-illustrate." Send complete ms with sample and query. Illustrations only: Provide tearsheets or good quality photocopies to be kept on file. SASE required for response/return of samples. Reports on art samples in 2 months.

Photography: Purchases photos with accompanying ms only. Model/property releases required. Uses color transparencies, b&w glossy prints.

Terms: Pays on publication. Buys first publication rights in the English language. Buys first publication rights plus promotional rights for artwork. Original artwork returned at job's completion. Pays up to 25¢/word for unsolicited articles; up to $3/line for poetry. Pays $750 for color cover; $75-150 for b&w, $150-250 for color inside. Pays $750 for color cover; $75-150 for b&w, $150-250 for color inside. Writer's/illustrator's guidelines for SASE.

Tips: Writers: "Read copies of back issues and current issues. Adhere to specified word limits. *Please* do not query." Illustrators: "Edit your samples. Send only your best work and be able to reproduce that quality in assignments. Put name and address on *all* samples. Know a publication before you submit—is your style appropriate?" (See listings for *Babybug*, *Cicada*, *Ladybug*, *Muse* and *Spider*.)

CRUSADER, Calvinist Cadet Corps, P.O. Box 7259, Grand Rapids MI 49510. (616)241-5616. Fax: (616)241-5558. **Editor:** G. Richard Broene. **Art Director:** Robert DeJonge. Magazine published 7 times/year. Circ. 13,000. "Our magazine is for members of the Calvinist Cadet Corps—boys aged 9-14. Our purpose is to show how God is at work in their lives and in the world around them. Our magazine offers nonfiction articles and fast-moving fiction—everything to appeal to interests and concerns of boys, teaching Christian values subtly."

● *Crusader*'s 1998-1999 theme list includes issues on courage, integrity and rich/poor. Send SASE for current list of themes before submitting. New theme list available in January 1999.

Fiction: Middle readers, young adults/teens: adventure, humorous, multicultural, problem-solving, religious, sports. Buys 12 mss/year. Average word length: 900-1,500.

Nonfiction: Middle readers, young adults/teens: arts/crafts, games/puzzles, hobbies, how-to, humorous, interview/profile, problem-solving, science, sports. Buys 6 mss/year. Average word length: 400-900.

How to Contact/Writers: Fiction/nonfiction: Send complete ms. Reports on queries in 2-4 weeks; on mss in 1-2 months. Will consider simultaneous submissions.

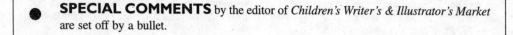

● **SPECIAL COMMENTS** by the editor of *Children's Writer's & Illustrator's Market* are set off by a bullet.

Illustration: Buys 1 illustration/issue; buys 6 illustrations/year. Works on assignment only. Reviews ms/ illustration packages from artists. Reports in 3-5 weeks. Samples returned with SASE. Originals returned to artist at job's completion. Credit line given.

Photography: Buys photos from freelancers. Wants nature photos and photos of boys.

Terms: Pays on acceptance. Buys first North American serial rights; reprint rights. Pays 4-5¢/word for stories/articles. Pays illustrators $50-200 for b&w/color cover or b&w inside. Sample copy free with 9×12 SAE and 4 first-class stamps.

Tips: "We are most open to fiction; write for a list of themes (available yearly in January). We use mostly fast-moving fiction that appeals to a boy's sense of adventure or sense of humor. Avoid preachiness; avoid simplistic answers to complicated problems; avoid long dialogue with little action. Articles on sports, outdoor activities, bike riding, science, crafts, etc. should emphasize a Christian perspective, but avoid simplistic moralisms."

N: THE CRYSTAL BALL, The Starwind Press, P.O. Box 98, Ripley OH 45167. (937)392-4549. **Articles/Fiction Editor:** Marlene Powell. Quarterly magazine. Estab. 1997. Circ. 1,000. Publishes science fiction and fantasy for young adults.

Fiction: Young adults: fantasy, folktale, science fiction. Buys 8-12 mss/year. Average word length: 1,500-5,000. Byline given.

Nonfiction: Young adults: biography, how-to, interview/profile, science. Buys 8-12 mss/year. Average word length: 1,000-3,000.

Poetry: Only publishes poetry by kids.

How to Contact/Writers: Fiction: send complete ms. Nonfiction: query. Reports on queries and mss in 2-3 months. Publishes ms 6-12 months after acceptance. Will consider previously published work if published in noncompeting market.

Illustration: Buys 6-10 illustrations/issue; 12-15 illustrations/year. Uses b&w camera ready artwork only. Works on assignment only. Reviews ms/illustration packages from artists. Send ms with dummy. Contact: Marlene Powell, editor. Illustrations only: query with samples. Contact: Marlene Powell, editor. Reports in 2-3 months if SASE enclosed. Samples kept on file. Credit line given.

Photography: Looking for photos to illustrate nonfiction pieces. Uses b&w, line shots or already screened. Reports in 2-3 months.

Terms: Pays on acceptance. Buys first North American serial rights for mss, artwork and photos. Original artwork returned at job's completion if requested. Pays $5-20 for stories and articles. Additional payment for photos accompanying article. Pays illustrators $5-20 for b&w inside and cover. Pays photographers per photo (range: $5-20). Sample copies for $3. Writer's/illustrator's guidelines for SASE.

CURIOCITY FOR KIDS, Thomson Target Media, 730 N. Franklin St., #706, Chicago IL 60610. (312)573-3800. Fax: (312)573-3810. Website: http://freezone.com. **Articles Acquisitions:** Andrew Scott. **Art Acquisitions:** Art Director. Monthly magazine. Estab. 1994. Circ. 250,000. "*Curiocity* takes a light-hearted approach to inform and entertain kids 8-12."

Fiction: No fiction accepted currently.

Nonfiction: Middle readers, young adult/teens: biography, geography, interview/profile, nature/environment, science, social issues, sports. Buys 10 mss/year. Average word length: 300-800. Byline given.

How to Contact/Writers: Fiction/nonfiction: Query with published clips. "We do not review unsolicited manuscripts." Reports on queries in 6 weeks. Publishes ms 10 weeks after acceptance.

Illustration: Buys 20 illustrations/year. Works on assignment only. Reviews ms/illustration packages from artists. Query. Contact: Design Director, Thomson Target Media. Query with samples. Send promo sheet and tearsheets. Contact: Design Director, Thompson Target Media. Reports back only if interested. Samples filed. Credit line given.

Photography: Looks for color-peak action, emotions—fun angles. Model/property release required; captions required. Uses color, b&w up to 11×17 prints and 35mm, 2½×2½, 4×5, 8×10 transparencies. Query with samples, provide promotional literature; tearsheets to be kept on file. Reports back only if interested.

Terms: Pays on acceptance. Buys all rights. Buys first time print and Web rights for artwork/photos. Original artwork returned at job's completion. Pays $100-450. Additional payment for ms/illustration packages and for photos accompanying articles. Pays illustrators $700-1,000 for color cover; $125-500 for b&w inside, $350-750 for color inside. Pays photographers by the project (range: $500-1,200). Sample copies for $5. Writer's guidelines for SASE.

Tips: "Our freelance needs are low, so make sure your ideas are on target for our interests."

Cartoonist Ron Wheeler's mission is "to use cartoons as a communications vehicle for spreading God's truth." This humorous illustration was featured on the cover of *Discoveries* (August 2, 1998), a Sunday school reader from the Church of the Nazarene Children's Ministries. Assistant editor Kathleen Johnson chose Wheeler's work because his art is very appealing to children. "Children seem to be more interested in the story if they like the art," she says. Wheeler has built his freelance career on creating cartoon designs for various religious publishing markets. Check out more of his cartoon creations at http://www.cartoonworks.com.

DINOSAURUS, Made For Kids, Dinosaurus, Inc., 826 Broadway, New York NY 10003. (212)979-1333. Fax: (212)979-6555. **Managing Editor:** Vanessa Etherington. **Art Director:** Wendy Palitz. Bi-monthly magazine. Estab. 1994. Circ. 100,000.

Fiction: Young readers, middle readers: dinosaurs.

Nonfiction: Young readers, middle readers: arts/crafts, games/puzzles, geography, how-to, nature/environment, science. Buys 80 mss/year. Average word length: 250-1,000 words. Byline given.

How to Contact/Writers: Fiction/nonfiction: Query with published clips. Reports on queries/mss in 1 month. Publishes ms 2-6 months after acceptance. Will consider electronic submission via disk or modem.

Illustration: Buys 12 illustrations/issue; 72 illustrations/year. Uses color artwork only. Works on assignment only. Reviews ms/illustration packages from artists. Query. Contact: Vanessa Etherington, managing editor. Illustrations only: arrange portfolio review; send résumé, promo sheet, portfolio, slides client list and tearsheets. Contact: Wendy Palitz, art director. Reports in 3 weeks. Samples not returned. Samples filed. Credit line given.

Photography: Photos purchased separately. Wants dinosaur-related photos. Uses 35mm, 2⅓×2⅓, 4×5 or 8×10 transparencies. Submit portfolio for review. Provide business card or tearsheets. Reports in 3 weeks.

Terms: Pays on acceptance. Buys one-time rights. Original artwork returned at job's completion. Pays $200-800 for stories; $250-1,250 for articles. Additional payment for ms/illustration packages and for photos accompanying articles. Pays photographers by the project. Sample copies for SASE. Writer's/illustrator's/photo guidelines for SASE.

DISCOVERIES, Children's Ministries, 6401 The Paseo, Kansas City MO 64131. (816)333-7000. Fax: (816)333-4439. E-mail: rraleigh@nazarene.org. **Editor**: Rebecca Raleigh. **Executive Editor**: Mark York. **Assistant Editor:** Kathleen M. Johnson. Weekly tabloid. *"Discoveries* is a leisure-reading piece for third and fourth graders. It is published weekly by WordAction Publishing. The major purpose of the magazine is to provide a leisure-reading piece which will build Christian behavior and values and provide reinforcement for Biblical concepts taught in the Sunday School curriculum. The focus of the reinforcement will be life-related, with some historical appreciation. *Discoveries'* target audience is children ages eight to ten in grades three and four. The readability goal is third to fourth grade."

Fiction: Middle readers: adventure, contemporary, humorous, religious. "Fiction—stories should vividly portray definite Christian emphasis or character-building values, without being preachy. The setting, plot and action should be realistic." 500 word maximum. Byline given.

Nonfiction: Game/puzzles, history (all Bible-related) and Bible "trivia."

How to Contact/Writers: Fiction: Send complete ms. Reports on mss in 6-8 weeks.

Illustration: Buys 1 illustration/issue; 53 illustrations/year. *"Discoveries* publishes a wide variety of artistic styles, i.e., cartoon, realistic, montage, etc., but whatever the style, artwork must appeal to eight-to ten-year-old children. It should not simply be child-related from an adult viewpoint. All artwork for *Discoveries* is assigned on a work-for-hire basis. Samples of art may be sent for review. Illustrations only: send résumé, portfolio, client list, tearsheets. Reports back only if interested. Samples returned with SASE. Credit line given.

Terms: Pays "approximately one year before the date of issue." Buys multi-use rights. For illustration, buys all rights. Pays 5¢/word. Pays illustrators $75 for color cover; $40 for b&w cover. Contributor receives 4 complimentary copies of publication. Sample copy free for #10 SASE with 1 first-class stamp. Writer's/artist's guidelines free with #10 SAE.

Tips: *"Discoveries* is committed to reinforcement of the Biblical concepts taught in the Sunday School curriculum. Because of this, the themes needed are mainly as follows: faith in God, obedience to God, putting God first, choosing to please God, accepting Jesus as Savior, finding God's will, choosing to do right, trusting God in hard times, prayer, trusting God to answer, importance of Bible memorization, appreciation of Bible as God's Word to man, Christians working together, showing kindness to others, witnessing." (See listing for *Power and Light.*)

DISCOVERY, The John Milton Society for the Blind, 475 Riverside Dr., Room 455, New York NY 10115. (212)870-3335. Fax: (212)870-3229. E-mail: dquigley@jmsblind.org. Website: http://www.jmsblind.org. **Assistant Editor**: Ingrid Peck. **Executive Director & Editor**: Darcy Quigley. Quarterly braille magazine. Estab. 1935. Circ. 2,000. *"Discovery* is a free braille magazine for blind and visually impaired youth ages 8-18. 95% of material is stories, poems, quizzes and educational articles, reprinted from 20 Christian and other magazines for youth. Original pieces from individual authors must be ready to print with little or no editing involved. We cannot offer reprint fees. Christian focus."

Fiction: Middle readers, young adults/teens: all categories and issues pertaining to blind. Does not want stories in which blindness is described as a novelty. It should be part of a story with a larger focus. Buys less than 10 mss/year. Average word length: 1,500 words (maximum). Byline given.

Nonfiction: Middle readers, young adults/teens: all categories. Also want inspirational stories involving visually impaired. Buys less than 10 mss/year. Average word length: 1,500 words (maximum). Byline given.

Poetry: Reviews poetry. Maximum length: 500 words.

How to Contact/Writers: Fiction/nonfiction: Send complete ms. Reports on queries/mss in 6-8 weeks. Publishes ms 3-12 months after acceptance. Will consider simultaneous submissions, previously published work.

Terms: Acquires reprint rights. Authors do not receive payment, only sample copy.

Tips: "95% of the material in *Discovery* is reprinted from Christian and other periodicals for youth. Previously unpublished material must therefore be ready to print with little or no editing involved. Please send complete manuscripts or request our 'Writers' Guidelines' which includes a list of periodicals we reprint from."

N DISCOVERY TRAILS, Gospel Publishing House, 1445 Boonville Ave., Springfield MO 65802-1894. (417)862-2781. E-mail: uelemcurr@ag.org. **Articles Editor:** Sinda S. Zinn. **Art Director:** Dale Gehris. Quarterly take-home paper. Circ. 40,000.

Fiction: Middle readers: adventure, animal, contemporary, humorous, problem-solving, religious, suspense/mystery. Buys 100 or less mss/year.

Nonfiction: Middle readers: arts/crafts, games/puzzles, how-to, humorous, problem-solving, religion. Buys 50-100 mss/year. Average word length: 200-500. Byline given.

Poetry: Reviews poetry. Limit submissions to 2 poems.

How to Contact/Writers: Fiction/nonfiction: Send complete ms. Reports on queries in 2-4 weeks. Publishes ms 15-24 months after acceptance. Will consider simultaneous submissions or previously published work.
Illustration: Buys 100 illustrations/year. Uses color artwork only. Works on assignment only. Send promo sheet, portfolio. Contact: Dale Gehris, art coordinator. Reports back only if interested. Samples returned with SASE; samples filed.
Terms: Pays on acceptance. Buys first rights or reprint rights for mss. Buys all rights for artwork. Sample copies for 6×9 SAE and 2 first-class stamps. Writer's guidelines for SASE.

☑ DOLPHIN LOG, The Cousteau Society, 61 E. Eighth St., Box 112, New York NY 10003. (212)673-9097. Fax: (212)673-9183. **Editor:** Lisa Rao. Bimonthly magazine for children ages 7-13. Circ. 80,000. Entirely nonfiction subject matter encompasses all areas of science, natural history, marine biology, ecology and the environment as they relate to our global water system. The philosophy of the magazine is to delight, instruct and instill an environmental ethic and understanding of the interconnectedness of living organisms, including people. Of special interest are articles on ocean- or water-related themes which develop reading and comprehension skills.
Nonfiction: Middle readers, young adult: animal, games/puzzles, geography, interview/profile, nature/environment, science, ocean. Multicultural needs include indigenous peoples, lifestyles of ancient people, etc. Does not want to see talking animals. No dark or religious themes. Buys 10 mss/year. Average word length: 500-700. Byline given.
How to Contact/Writers: Nonfiction: Query first. Reports on queries in 3 months; mss in 6 months.
Illustration: Buys 1 illustration/issue; buys 6 illustrations/year. Preferred theme: Biological illustration. Reviews ms/illustration packages from artists. Illustrations only: Query; send résumé, promo sheet, slides. Reports on art samples in 8 weeks only if interested. Credit line given to illustrators.
Photography: Wants "sharp, colorful pictures of sea creatures. The more unusual the creature, the better." Submit duplicate slides only.
Terms: Pays on publication. Buys first North American serial rights; reprint rights. Pays $75-250 for articles. Pays $100-400 for illustrations. Pays $75-200/color photos. Sample copy $2.50 with 9×12 SAE and 3 first-class stamps. Writer's/illustrator's guidelines free with #10 SASE.
Tips: Writers: "Write simply and clearly and don't anthropomorphize." Illustrators: "Be scientifically accurate and don't anthropomorphize. Some background in biology is helpful, as our needs range from simple line drawings to scientific illustrations which must be researched for biological and technical accuracy."

DRAMATICS, Educational Theatre Association, 3368 Central Pkwy., Cincinnati OH 45225. (513)559-1996. (513)559-0012. E-mail: pubs@one.net. Website: http://www.etassoc.org. **Articles Editor:** Don Corathers. **Art Director:** William Johnston. Published monthly September-May. Estab. 1929. Circ. 40,000. "Dramatics is for students (mainly high school age) and teachers of theater. Mix includes how-to (tech theater, acting, directing, etc.), informational, interview, photo feature, humorous, profile, technical, We want our student readers to become a more discerning and appreciative audience. Material is directed to both theater students and their teachers, with strong student slant."
Fiction: Young adults: drama (one-act and full-length plays.) Does not want to see plays that show no understanding of the conventions of the theater. No plays for children, no Christmas or didactic "message" plays. "We prefer unpublished scripts that have been produced at least once." Buys 5-9 plays/year. Emerging playwrights have better chances with short plays, 10 minute or one-act.
Nonfiction: Young adults: arts/crafts, careers, how-to, interview/profile, multicultural (all theater-related). "We try to portray the theater community in all its diversity." Does not want to see academic treatises. Buys 50 mss/year. Average word length: 750-3,000. Byline given.
How to Contact/Writers: Send complete ms. Reports in 2-3 months (longer for plays). Published ms 3 months after acceptance. Will consider simultaneous submissions and previously published work occasionally.
Illustration: Buys 0-2 illustrations/year. Works on assignment only. Arrange portfolio review; send résumé, promo sheets and tearsheets. Reports back only if interested. Samples returned with SASE; sample not filed. Credit line given.
Photography: Buys photos with accompanying ms only. Looking for "good-quality production or candid photography to accompany article. We very occasionally publish photo essays." Model/property release and captions required. Uses 5×7 or 8×10 b&w glossy prints and 35mm transparencies. Query with résumé of credits. Reports back only if interested.
Terms: Pays on acceptance. Buys one-time rights, occasionally reprint rights. Buys one-time rights for artwork and photos. Original artwork returned at job's completion. Pays $100-400 for plays; $50-300 for articles; up to $100 for illustrations. Pays photographers by the project or per photo. Sometimes offers

additional payment for ms/illustration packages and photos accompanying a ms. Sample copy available for $2.50 and 9×12 SAE. Writer's and photo guidelines available for SASE.

Tips: "Obtain our writer's guidelines and look at recent back issues. The best way to break in is to know our audience—drama students, teachers and others interested in theater—and write for them. Writers who have some practical experience in theater, especially in technical areas, have an advantage, but we'll work with anybody who has a good idea. Some freelancers have become regular contributors."

✔ **DYNAMATH**, Scholastic Inc., 555 Broadway, New York NY 10012-3999. (212)343-6458. **Editor:** Matt Friedman. **Art Director:** Joan Michael. Monthly magazine. Estab. 1981. Circ. 225,000. Purpose is "to make learning math fun, challenging and uncomplicated for young minds in a very complex world."

Nonfiction: Middle readers: animal, arts/crafts, cooking, fashion, games/puzzles, health, history, hobbies, how-to, humorous, math, multicultural, nature/environment, problem-solving, science, social issues, sports—all must relate to math and science topics.

How to Contact/Writers: Nonfiction: Query with published clips, send ms. Reports on queries in 1 month; mss in 6 weeks. Publishes ms 4 months after acceptance. Will consider simultaneous submissions.

Illustration: Buys 4 illustrations/issue. Illustration only: Query first; send résumé and tearsheets. Reports back on submissions only if interested. Credit line given.

Terms: Pays on acceptance. Buys all rights for mss, artwork, photographs. Originals returned to artist at job's completion. Pays $50-350 for stories. Pays artists $800-1,000 for color cover illustration; $100-800 for color inside illustration. Pays photographers $300-1,000 per project.

Tips: See listings for *Junior Scholastic, Scholastic Math Magazine, Science World* and *Superscience*.

✔ **FACES, People, Places & Cultures**, Cobblestone Publishing, Inc., 30 Grove St., Peterborough NH 03458. (603)924-7209. Fax: (603)924-7380. E-mail: faces@cobblestonepub.com. Website: http://www.cob blestonepub.com. **Editor**: Elizabeth Crooker. **Managing Editor**: Denise L. Babcock. **Art Director**: Ann Dillon. Magazine published 9 times/year (September-May). Circ. 15,000. *Faces* is a theme-related magazine; writers should send for theme list before submitting ideas/queries. Each month a different world culture is featured through the use of feature articles, activities and photographs and illustrations.

Fiction: Middle readers, young adults/teens: adventure, folktales, history, multicultural, plays, religious, travel. Does not want to see material that does not relate to a specific upcoming theme. Buys 9 mss/year. Maximum word length: 800. Byline given.

Nonfiction: Middle readers and young adults/teens: animal, anthropology, arts/crafts, biography, cooking, fashion, games/puzzles, geography, history, how-to, humorous, interview/profile, nature/environment, religious, social issues, sports, travel. Does not want to see material not related to a specific upcoming theme. Buys 63 mss/year. Average word length: 300-800. Byline given.

Poetry: Clear, objective imagery; up to 100 lines. Must relate to theme.

How to Contact/Writers: Fiction/nonfiction: Query with published clips and 2-3 line biographical sketch. "Ideas should be submitted six to nine months prior to the publication date. Responses to ideas are usually sent approximately four months before the publication date."

Illustration: Buys 3 illustrations/issue; buys 27 illustrations/year. Preferred theme or style: Material that is meticulously researched (most articles are written by professional anthropologists); simple, direct style preferred, but not too juvenile. Works on assignment only. Roughs required. Reviews ms/illustration packages from artists. Illustrations only: Send samples of b&w work. "Illustrators should consult issues of *Faces* to familiarize themselves with our needs." Reports on art samples only if interested. Samples returned with SASE. Original artwork returned at job's completion (upon written request). Credit line given.

Photography: Wants photos relating to forthcoming themes.

Terms: Pays on publication. Buys all rights for mss and artwork. Pays 20-25¢/word for articles/stories. Pays on an individual basis for poetry. Covers are assigned and paid on an individual basis. Pays illustrators $50-300 for color inside. Pays photographers per photo ($25-100 for color). Sample copy $4.95 with 7½×10½ SAE and 5 first-class stamps. Writer's/illustrator's/photo guidelines free with SAE and 1 first-class stamp.

Tips: "Writers are encouraged to study past issues of the magazine to become familiar with our style and content. Writers with anthropological and/or travel experience are particularly encouraged; *Faces* is about world cultures. All feature articles, recipes and activities are freelance contributions." Illustrators: "Submit

---

A SELF-ADDRESSED, STAMPED ENVELOPE (SASE) should always be included with submissions within your own country. When sending material to other countries, include a self-addressed envelope (SAE) and International Reply Coupons (IRCs).

b&w samples, not too juvenile. Study past issues to know what we look for. The illustration we use is generally for retold legends, recipes and activities." (See listing for *Calliope, Cobblestone* and *Odyssey*.)

☑ **THE FLICKER MAGAZINE**, Hillview Lake Publishing Co., P.O. Box 660544, Birmingham AL 35266-0544. (205)824-3311. Fax: (205)824-0151. E-mail: yellowhamr@aol.com. Website: http://www.flic kermag.com. **Editor:** Ann Dorer. **Art Director:** Jimmy Bass. Bimonthly magazine. Estab. 1994. Circ. 7,000. *"The Flicker Magazine* is a publication that promotes balanced growth in all areas of life—physical, spiritual, social, mental and emotional. It includes nonfiction, fiction, poetry, interviews, etc." Target audience is 10- to 12-year olds.

Fiction: Middle readers: adventure, animal, contemporary, folktale, health, history, humorous, multicul-tural, nature/environment, problem-solving, religious, sports, travel. Does not want to see science fiction, fantasy or romance. Sees too much fantasy and didactic materials. Wants more humorous submissions. Buys 75-80 mss/year. Word length: 800-850. Byline given.

Nonfiction: Middle readers: arts/crafts, biography, concept, cooking, games/puzzles, geography, health, history, hobbies, how-to, humorous, multicultural, nature/environment, problem-solving, religion, science, social issues, sports, travel. Need how-to's. Buys 15-25 mss/year. Word length: 500 words or fewer. Byline given.

Poetry: Reviews poetry. Maximum length: 4-24 lines. Humorous preferred.

How to Contact/Writers: Fiction/Nonfiction: Send complete ms. Reports on queries/mss in 2-3 months. Will consider simultaneous submissions. Buys all rights.

Illustration: Buys 5 illustrations/issue; 30 illustrations/year. Uses color artwork only. Works on assignment only. Reviews illustrations from artists. Contact: Jimmy Bass, art director. Send promo sheet and tearsheets. Reports back only if interested. Samples returned with SASE; samples filed. Credit line given.

Terms: Pays on publication. Buys all rights for mss, artwork and photos. Pays 10¢/word for stories; 10¢/word for articles; $25 for poems; $10 for jokes. Pays illustrators $50-250 for color inside. Pays photogra-phers by the project (range: $50-200). Sample copies for $2.95. Writer's/illustrator guidelines and theme list free for SASE.

Tips: "If you are submitting illustrations, please do not send originals unless otherwise specified. The magazine usually has a central theme. Send SASE for guidelines. Remember our target audience is 10- to 12-year of age. Work needs to have kid appeal."

☑ **FOCUS ON THE FAMILY CLUBHOUSE; FOCUS ON THE FAMILY CLUBHOUSE JR.**, Focus on the Family, 8605 Explorer Dr., Colorado Springs CO 80920. (719)531-3400. Fax: (719)531-3499. **Editor:** Jesse Florea. **Art Director:** Timothy Jones. Monthly magazine. Estab. 1987. Combined circulation is 200,000. *"Focus on the Family Clubhouse* is a 24-page Christian magazine, published monthly, for children ages 8-12. Similarly, *Focus on the Family Clubhouse Jr.* is published for children ages 4-8. We want fresh, exciting literature that promotes biblical thinking, values and behavior in every area of life."

Fiction: Young readers, middle readers: adventure, contemporary, multicultural, nature/environment, reli-gious, science fiction. Middle readers: history, sports. Multicultural needs include: "interesting, informa-tive, accurate information about other cultures to teach children appreciation for the world around them." Buys approximately 6-10 mss/year. Average word length: *Clubhouse*, 500-1,400; *Clubhouse Jr.*, 250-1,100. Byline given on all fiction; not on puzzles.

Nonfiction: Young readers, middle readers: arts/crafts, cooking, games/puzzles, how-to, multicultural, nature/environment, religion, science. Young readers: animal. Middle readers, young adult/teen: interview/profile. Middle readers: sports. Buys 3-5 mss/year. Average word length: 200-1,000. Byline given.

Poetry: Wants to see "humorous or biblical" poetry. Maximum length: 250 words.

How to Contact/Writers: Fiction/nonfiction: send complete ms. Reports on queries/mss in 4-6 weeks.

Illustration: Buys 8 illustrations/issue. Uses color artwork only. Works on assignment only. Reviews ms/illustration packages from artists. Submit ms with rough sketches. Contact: Tim Jones, art director. Illustra-tions only: Query with samples, arrange portfolio review or send tearsheets. Contact: Tim Jones, art director. Reports in 2-3 months. Samples returned with SASE; samples kept on file. Credit line given.

Photography: Buys photos from freelancers. Uses 35mm transparencies. Photographers should query with samples; provide résumé and promotional literature or tearsheets. Reports in 2 months.

Terms: Pays on acceptance. Buys first North American serial rights for mss. Buys first rights or reprint rights for artwork and photographs. Original artwork returned at job's completion. Additional payment for ms/illustration packages. Pays writers $100-300 for stories; $50-150 for articles. Pays illustrators $300-700 for color cover; $200-700 for color inside. Pays photographers by the project or per photo. Sample copies for 9×12 SAE and 3 first-class stamps. Writer's/illustrators/photo guidelines for SASE.

Tips: "Test your writing on children. The best stories avoid moralizing or preachiness and are not written *down* to children. They are the products of writers who share in the adventure with their readers, exploring the characters they have created without knowing for certain where the story will lead. And they are not always explicitly Christian, but are built upon a Christian foundation (and, at the very least, do not contradict biblical views or values)."

N: FOR SENIORS ONLY, Campus Communications, Inc., 339 N. Main St., New York NY 10956. (914)638-0333. **Publisher:** Darryl Elberg. **Articles/Fiction Editor:** Judi Oliff. **Art Director:** David Miller. Semiannual magazine. Estab. 1971. Circ. 350,000. Publishes career-oriented articles for high school students, college-related articles, and feature articles on travel, etc.

Fiction: Young adults: health, humorous, sports, travel. Byline given.

Nonfiction: Young adults: careers, games/puzzles, health, how-to, humorous, interview/profile, social issues, sports, travel. Buys 4-6 mss/year. Average word length: 1,000-2,500. Byline given.

How to Contact/Writers: Fiction/nonfiction: Send complete ms. Publishes ms 2-4 months after acceptance. Will consider simultaneous submissions, electronic submissions via disk or modem and previously published work.

Illustration: Reviews ms/illustration packages from artists. Query; submit complete package with final art; submit ms with rough sketches. Illustrations only: Query; send slides. Reports back only if interested. Samples not returned; samples kept on file. Original work returned upon job's completion. Credit line given.

Photography: Model/property release required. Uses $5\frac{1}{2} \times 8\frac{1}{2}$ and $4\frac{7}{8} \times 7\frac{3}{8}$ color prints; 35mm and 8×10 transparencies. Query with samples; send unsolicited photos by mail. Reports back only if interested.

Terms: Pays on publication. Buys exclusive magazine rights. Payment is byline credit. Writer's/illustrator's/photo guidelines for SASE.

THE FRIEND MAGAZINE, The Church of Jesus Christ of Latter-day Saints, 50 E. North Temple, 23rd Floor, Salt Lake City UT 84150. (801)240-2210. **Editor:** Vivian Paulsen. **Art Director:** Richard Brown. Monthly magazine for 3-11 year olds. Estab. 1971. Circ. 350,000.

Fiction: Picture material, young readers, middle readers: adventure, animal, contemporary, folktales, history, humorous, problem-solving, religious, ethnic, sports, suspense/mystery. Does not want to see controversial issues, political, horror, fantasy. Average word length: 400-1,000. Byline given.

Nonfiction: Picture material, young readers, middle readers: animal, arts/crafts, biography, cooking, games/puzzles, history, how-to, humorous, problem-solving, religious, sports. Does not want to see controversial issues, political, horror, fantasy. Average word length: 400-1,000. Byline given.

Poetry: Reviews poetry. Maximum length: 20 lines.

How to Contact/Writers: Fiction/nonfiction: Send complete ms. Reports on mss in 2 months.

Illustration: Illustrations only: Query with samples; arrange personal interview to show portfolio; provide résumé and tearsheets for files.

Terms: Pays on acceptance. Buys all rights for mss. Pays 9-11¢/word for unsolicited fiction articles; $25 and up for poems; $10 for recipes, activities and games. Contributors are encouraged to send for sample copy for $1.50, 9×11 envelope and 4 32¢ stamps. Free writer's guidelines.

Tips: "*The Friend* is published by The Church of Jesus Christ of Latter-day Saints for boys and girls up to twelve years of age. All submissions are carefully read by the *Friend* staff, and those not accepted are returned within two months when a self-addressed, stamped envelope is enclosed. Submit seasonal material at least eight months in advance. Query letters and simultaneous submissions are not encouraged. Authors may request rights to have their work reprinted after their manuscript is published."

GIRLS' LIFE, Monarch Avalon, 4517 Harford Rd., Baltimore MD 21214. (410)254-9200. Fax: (410)254-0991. Website: http://www.girlslife.com. **Articles Editor:** Kelly White. **Art Director:** Chun Kim. Bimonthly magazine. Estab. 1994. General interest magazine for girls, ages 8-15.

Nonfiction: Cooking, crafts, health, hobbies, humorous, interview/profile, multicultural, nature/environment, new products, party ideas, skin care, social issues, sports, travel. Buys approximately 25 mss/year. Word length varies. Byline given. "No fiction!"

How to Contact/Writers: Nonfiction: Query with published clips or send complete ms on spec only. Reports in 2 weeks. Publishes ms 3 months after acceptance. Will consider simultaneous submissions.

Illustration: Buys 4 illustrations/issue. Uses color artwork only. Works on assignment only. Reviews ms/illustration packages from artists. Send ms with dummy. Contact: Kelly White, senior editor. Illustration only: Query with samples; send tearsheets. Contact: Chun Kim, art director. Reports back only if interested. Samples returned with SASE; samples filed. Credit line given.

Photography: Buys photos from freelancers. Uses 35mm transparencies. Provide samples. Reports back only if interested.

Terry Julien used watercolor, pastel dust and pencil to create this illustration for *Focus on the Family Clubhouse Jr.*, a religious magazine for children ages four to eight. Five years ago, Julien saw the magazine in the library, added it to his mailing list and has been receiving monthly assignments ever since. He was paid $600 for this cover illustration. Julien admits marketing his work is his "big weakness. It's easy to become overwhelmed by the business aspects of freelancing and forget the simple joy of creating a picture. Try to find the right balance between 'job' and 'fun.'"

Talking girl talk to smart young readers

"Our girls are intelligent, they're savvy. We don't talk down to our readers."

Kelly White, senior editor of *Girls' Life*, a magazine for girls 8-14, not only generates story ideas, but also assigns stories to freelancers and regular contributors, researches and writes feature stories and department columns, conducts celebrity interviews, edits all copy, oversees professional photo shoots, and tests recipes at home in her kitchen. She also makes time to test "Surf Frogs" (a live frog habitat with tiki club and a surfboard) and whip up toothbrush-handle bracelets. White calls herself a "middle-aged cool chick." Here she shares her advice on keeping up with what interests her readers, talks about where she goes for article ideas, and reveals her style as an editor.

Kelly White

What makes *Girls' Life* different from other magazines?

Other magazines have a tea party mentality. *American Girl*, for example, has a lot of historical fiction, while we're more contemporary. We're "teen" in the sense that we're hip and trendy, but we don't talk about issues, like sex, that are too old for girls in our 8-14 age group. Our readers are smart and opinionated. Yes, they like boys and, yes, they like things that are pretty, but they still have thoughts and opinions. They like sports; they like music; they're consumers.

What's your mission at *Girls' Life*?

Our mission is to boost girls' self-esteem, and make them feel powerful and good about themselves. For example, we don't set up a prototype of what little girls are supposed to look like. We give them the message that they are all cute, no matter what their height, shape, hair color, eye color. And we challenge their minds. Just because girls like things that are pretty doesn't mean they're not smart.

Where do you get article ideas?

We listen to our readers through letters and e-mail. Occasionally we send out written questionnaires and ask girls what's cool and what's not, if they've ever cheated on school work, that sort of thing. Plus, we always post a "Question of the Week" on our website (http://www.girlslife.com). Recently we asked how girls feel about single-sex classrooms, so we're doing a feature on it. And because we listen to our readers, we do a lot more boy and crush stuff than we used to.

We also look at other magazines and see what they're writing about. That's not to say we steal their ideas, but we keep on top of what's out there. We watch Nickelodeon and The Disney Channel. And we talk to kids. I have kids, so I know what the trends are.

All of our issues scream a certain season or holiday: December/January is a holiday

INSIDER REPORT, *White*

Senior editor Kelly White is looking for short, punchy queries for articles of interest to girls ages 8-14, the audience of *Girls' Life* magazine. "Our mission is to boost girls' self-esteem, and make them feel powerful and good about themselves," White says. "We challenge their minds. Just because girls like things that are pretty doesn't mean they're not smart."

You asked for it! **Jonathan Taylor Thomas** plus new movies, books, videos and music!

The New Magazine for Girls $2.95

Girls' Life

June/July 1997
Vol. 3, Issue 6

Are you ready for summer?
Our guide to cool hair and great skin

Wedding Bell Blues
When a parent remarries

Quiz: Are you ready to date? Surprising answers

Wish you had someone else's body? You won't after you read this

The **BEST** new swimsuits

Are girls getting an equal chance to play sports?
Throw an ice cream party • The legend of Misty

Reprinted with permission of Girls' Life.

issue; February/March is a big crush issue because of Valentine's Day; April/May is spring; June/July is summer; August/September is back-to-school; October/November is fall.

What do you need most?
It's been four years now, and we have done most of the party articles ourselves, and we're dry. Our "Party" department appears in nearly every issue. Writers should send queries with ideas for invitations, decorations, games, activities and recipes. We just did a "bon voyage" party for a girl who was moving, and we gave it a nautical theme with origami sailboat invitations, nautical flag banners, buckets filled with Old Bay fried chicken and seashell pasta salad, tug-of-war over a wading pool . . . you get the drift (no pun intended). We could also use feature ideas and quizzes. We found that girls like to have quizzes in each issue—they're hot!

What do you not need?
We have a department called "One Girl/One Solution." We feature a girl who has done something cool, some community service—for example, we once we had a girl who wrote her own book and had it published. We love charity, and we like to tell girls they should get out and volunteer. We get a lot of queries about "this girl did a food drive," or "a clothes drive" or "a neighborhood trash pickup," but we see too much of those particular things.

We don't print original fiction. We only do reprints, and there is a reason for that. It's cheaper for us to buy the reprint rights because then we get the art. Otherwise we would have to buy the piece from the writer and assign art and pay double or more than what we pay to get reprint rights and scan in the existing art.

INSIDER REPORT, *continued*

What's your advice to writers for querying?

I hate to see somebody go to the trouble of completing a manuscript that's going to be rejected, so I like to see a query wrapped up in a couple sentences. If it doesn't grab me in the first couple of sentences, it's going in the reject pile. I don't have time to read a two-page letter. The query should be fun and punchy, and if I like the idea, I will assign it to that person whether or not I have seen the writing. I can fix the article if I have to.

I prefer clips with a query. But some people don't have clips if they're just breaking into writing. I will give anybody a chance if their idea rocks.

Some writers may be used to writing for a younger audience, and they send me articles that read like they're talking to a dog. It's insulting. Our readers are intelligent, they're savvy. Just judging from their letters, they're not dummies. So we don't ever talk down to our readers. Even if they're not at a certain reading level, the more they read, the more they will get to that level. Sometimes we say, "Maybe we shouldn't put this word in," but then we say, "No, they can look it up. That's how they learn."

Are you a harsh editor?

I do the red pen. I take the hard copy and mark it. I go to town on this stuff, let me tell you. But sometimes I just send the article back. For example, we had someone do an article on jump-roping for our "Try It" department. The writer interviewed a jump-roping team in Indianapolis, and the whole article came out as a profile of the team. I sent it back and asked her to put it in a "hands on" perspective. You know: "give us some moves."

It sounds as though beginning writers might have a tough time breaking in at *Girls' Life*.

No. If they send me a query with a great idea, I'll assign it. I think as long as the pertinent information is there, I can fix it if it's not well written. I can make it readable. That is not to say they shouldn't try to make the article great, but I'm not going to say, "Oh, I like this query, but I don't like her clips so we're going to do it in house." I don't steal people's ideas, ever.

What do you do to fix an article?

That depends. If an article comes in and it's a snore, and just needs to be "funned up" a little, I fun it up. I inject it with cool words, like "awesome" and "rad." (I say this tongue-in-cheek.)

How can writers learn cool words?

This has a lot to do with personality. You can hang out and listen to how kids in that age group talk, you can read the magazines they read, watch the television shows they watch. But many writers try to weave trendy language into their pieces, and it comes out sounding contrived. Our magazine has an overall voice that is laid-back and not uptight.

So are you editing mainly for voice?

Sometimes I'm working out sentence structure. For example, a lot of sentences start with "there"—it's unnecessary. One of the most overused words in the world is "that," and I take it out. A lot of times I turn a sentence around so you don't have so many sentences starting with the same word. Sometimes articles are choppy. They don't flow very well, and I make them flow, or if there's not good transition from one paragraph to the next,

INSIDER REPORT, *White*

that kind of thing. Other times, the lead needs to be rewritten, or the whole thing needs to be restructured—something at the end is more important and should be pulled to beginning.

One thing I see a lot of is generalizing: I just got an article about mothers and daughters that said something like, "Maybe you and your mother should try to do more things together." Instead of being general, I want the writer to be specific and say, "Maybe you and your mother should go out and buy roller blades and go rollerblading together."

What's your final advice to writers?
They should read the magazine, that's my main advice. Then they get a feel for what our voice is. We are, like I said, not condescending. Still, we try to speak our readers' language.
—*Anna Olswanger*

Terms: Pays on publication. Original artwork returned at job's completion. Pays $500-800 for features; $150-350 for departments. Sample copies available for $5. Writer's guidelines for SASE.
Tips: "Don't call with queries. Make query short and punchy."

☑ **THE GOLDFINCH, Iowa History for Young People**, State Historical Society of Iowa, 402 Iowa Ave., Iowa City IA 52240. (319)335-3916. Fax: (319)335-3935. **Interim Editor**: Millie K. Frese. Quarterly magazine. Estab. 1975. Circ. 2,500. "The award-winning *Goldfinch* consists of 10-12 nonfiction articles, short fiction, poetry and activities per issue. Each magazine focuses on an aspect or theme of history that occurred in or affected Iowa."
Fiction: Middle readers: historical fiction only. "Study past issues for structure and content. Most manuscripts written inhouse." Average word length: 500-1,500. Byline given.
Nonfiction: Middle readers: arts/crafts, biography, games/puzzles, history, interview/profile, "all tied to an Iowa theme." Uses about 10 freelance mss/year. Average word length: 500-800. Byline given.
Poetry: Reviews poetry. No minimum or maximum word length; no maximum number of submissions. "All poetry must reflect an Iowa theme."
How to Contact/Writers: Fiction/nonfiction: Query with published clips. Reports on queries/mss in up to 2 months. Publishes ms 1 month-1 year after acceptance. Will consider electronic submissions via disk or modem.
Illustration: Buys 8 illustrations/issue; 32 illustrations/year. Works on assignment only. Prefers cartoon, line drawing. Illustrations only: Query with samples. Reports in up to 2 months. Samples returned with SASE.
Photography: Types of photos used vary with subject. Model/property releases required with submissions. Uses b&w prints; 35mm transparencies. Query with samples. Reports in 2-4 weeks.
Terms: Pays on publication. Buys all rights. Payment begins at $25 per article. Pays illustrators $10-150. Sample copy for $4. Writer's/illustrator's guidelines free for SASE.
Tips: "The editor researches the topics and determines the articles. Writers, most of whom live in Iowa, work from primary and secondary research materials to write pieces. The presentation is aimed at children 8-14. All submissions must relate to an upcoming Iowa theme. Please send SASE for our writer's guidelines and theme lists before submitting manuscripts."

☑ **GUIDE MAGAZINE**, Review and Herald Publishing Association, 55 W. Oak Ridge Dr., Hagerstown MD 21740. (301)791-7000. **Articles Editor**: Tim Lale. **Art Director**: Bill Kirstein. Weekly magazine. Estab. 1953. Circ. 32,000. "Ours is a weekly Christian journal written for middle readers and young adults, presenting true stories relevant to the needs of today's young person, emphasizing positive aspects of Christian living."
Nonfiction: Middle readers, young adults/teens: adventure, animal, character-building, contemporary, games/puzzles, humorous, multicultural, problem-solving, religious. "We need true, or based on true, happenings, not merely true-to-life. Our stories and puzzles must have a spiritual emphasis." No violence. No articles. "We always need humorous adventure stories." Buys 150 mss/year. Average word length: 500-600 minimum, 1,000-1,200 maximum. Byline given.
How to Contact/Writers: Nonfiction: Send complete ms. Reports in 3-4 weeks. Will consider simulta-

neous submissions. "We can only pay half of the regular amount for simultaneous submissions." Reports on queries/mss in 4-6 weeks. Credit line given.

Terms: Pays on acceptance. Buys first North American serial rights; first rights; one-time rights; second serial (reprint rights); simultaneous rights. Pays 6-12¢/word for stories and articles. "Writer receives several complimentary copies of issue in which work appears." Sample copy free with 5×9 SAE and 2 first-class stamps. Writer's guidelines for SASE.

Tips: "Children's magazines want mystery, action, discovery, suspense and humor—no matter what the topic. For us, truth is stronger than fiction."

☑ GUIDEPOSTS FOR KIDS, P.O. Box 638, Chesterton IN 46304. **Editor**: Mary Lou Carney. **Assistant Fiction Editor:** Tracey Dils. **Art Director**: Mike Lyons. **Photo Editor**: Julie Brown. Bimonthly magazine. Estab. 1990. Circ. 200,000. "*Guideposts for Kids* is published bimonthly by Guideposts for kids 7-12 years old (emphasis on upper end of that age bracket). It is a value-centered, direct mail magazine that is *fun* to read. It is *not* a Sunday school take-home paper or a miniature *Guideposts*."

Fiction: Middle readers: adventure, animal, contemporary, fantasy, folktales, health, historical, humorous, multicultural, nature/environment, problem-solving, religious, romance, science fiction, sports, suspense/mystery, travel. Multicultural needs include: Kids in other cultures—school, sports, families. Does not want to see preachy fiction. "We want real stories about real kids doing real things—conflicts our readers will respect; resolutions our readers will accept. Problematic. Tight. Filled with realistic dialogue and sharp imagery. No stories about 'good' children always making the right decision. If present at all, adults are minor characters and *do not* solve kids' problems for them." Buys approximately 10 mss/year. Average word length: 500-1,400. Byline given.

Nonfiction: Middle readers: animal, biography, careers, concept, cooking, current events, fashion, games/puzzles, geography, health, history, how-to, humorous, interview/profile, math, multicultural, nature/environment, problem-solving, profiles of kids, religious, science, seasonal, social issues, sports, travel. "Make nonfiction issue-oriented, controversial, thought-provoking. Something kids not only *need* to know, but *want* to know as well." Buys 20 mss/year. Average word length: 200-1,300. Byline usually given.

How to Contact/Writers: Fiction: Send complete ms. Nonfiction: Query or send ms. Reports on queries/mss in 6 weeks.

Illustration: Buys 10 illustrations/issue; 60 illustrations/year. Uses color artwork only. Works on assignment only. Reviews ms/illustration packages from artists. Contact: Mike Lyons, art director. Illustration only: Query; send résumé, tearsheets. Reports only if interested. Credit line given.

Photography: Looks for "spontaneous, *real* kids in action shots."

Terms: Pays on acceptance. Buys all rights for mss. Buys first rights for artwork. "Features range in payment from $300-450; fiction from $250-500. We pay higher rates for stories exceptionally well-written or well-researched. Regular contributors get bigger bucks, too." Additional payment for ms/illustration packages "but we prefer to acquire our own illustrations." Pays illustrators $400-800/page. Pays photographers by the project (range: $300-1,000) or per photo (range: $100-500). Sample copies for $3.25. Writer's guidelines free for SASE.

Tips: "Make your manuscript good, relevant and playful. No preachy stories about Bible-toting children. *Guideposts for Kids* is not a beginner's market. Study our magazine. (Sure, you've heard that before—but it's *necessary*!) Neatness *does* count. So do creativity and professionalism. SASE essential." (See listing for *Guideposts for Teens*.)

⟦N⟧ GUIDEPOSTS FOR TEENS, Guideposts, P.O. Box 638, Chesterton IN 46304. (219)929-4429. Fax: (219)926-3839. E-mail: GP4T@aol.com. **Articles Editor:** Tanya Dean. **Art Director:** Michael Lyons. **Photo Editor:** Julie Brown. Bimonthly magazine. Estab. 1998. "We are a value-centered magazine that offers teens advice, humor and true stories—lots of true stories. These first-person stories feature teen protagonists and are filled with action, adventure, overcoming and growth—set against the backdrop of God at work in everyday life."

Nonfiction: Young adults: how-to, humorous, interview/profile, social issues, sports, true stories, most embarrassing moments. Average word length: 300-1,500. Byline sometimes given.

How to Contact/Writers: Nonfiction: Query. Reports on queries/mss in 4-6 weeks. Will consider simultaneous submissions or electronic submission via disk or modem. Send SASE for writer's guidelines.

Illustration: Uses color artwork only. Works on assignment only. Reviews ms/illustration packages from artists. Query. Contact: Michael Lyons, art director. Illustrations only: Query with samples. Reports back only if interested. Samples kept on file. Credit line given.

Photography: Buys photos separately. Wants location photography and stock; digital OK. Uses color prints; and 35mm, 2¼×2¼, 4×5 or 8×10 transparencies. Query with samples; provide web address. Reports back only if interested.

Terms: Pays on acceptance. Buys all rights for mss. Buys one-time rights for artwork. Original artwork returned at job's completion. Pays $300-500 for true stories; $100-300 for articles. Additional payment for photos accompanying articles. Pays illustrators $125-1,500 for color inside (depends on size). Pays photographers by the project (range: $100-1,000). Sample copies for $4.50 from: Guideposts, 39 Seminary Hill Rd., Carmel NY 10512. Attn: Special Handling.

Tips: "Language and subject matter should be current and teen-friendly. No preaching, please!" (See listing for *Guideposts for Kids*.)

HIGHLIGHTS FOR CHILDREN, 803 Church St., Honesdale PA 18431. (717)253-1080. **Manuscript Coordinator:** Beth Troop. **Art Director:** Janet Moir. Monthly magazine. Estab. 1946. Circ. 2.8 million. "Our motto is 'Fun With a Purpose.' We are looking for quality fiction and nonfiction that appeals to children, encourages them to read, and reinforces positive values. All art is done on assignment."

• *Highlights* ranked number 5 on *Writer's Digest's* Fiction 50, the magazine's annual list of the most writer-friendly publications.

Fiction: Picture-oriented material, young readers, middle readers: adventure, animal, contemporary, fantasy, folktales, history, humorous, multicultural, problem-solving, sports. Multicultural needs include first person accounts of children from other cultures and first-person accounts of children from other countries. Does not want to see war, crime, violence. "We see too many stories with overt morals." Would like to see more suspense/stories/articles with world culture settings, sports pieces, action/adventure and stories with children in contemporary settings. Buys 150 mss/year. Average word length: 400-800. Byline given.

Nonfiction: Picture-oriented material, young readers, middle readers: animal, arts/crafts, biography, careers, games/puzzles, geography, health, history, hobbies, how-to, interview/profile, multicultural, nature/environment, problem solving, science, sports. Multicultural needs include articles set in a country *about* the people of the country. "We have plenty of articles with Asian and Spanish settings. We also have plenty of holiday articles." Does not want to see trendy topics, fads, personalities who would not be good role models for children, guns, war, crime, violence. "We'd like to see more nonfiction for younger readers—maximum of 600 words. We still need older-reader material, too—600-900 words." Buys 75 mss/year. Maximum word length: 900. Byline given.

How to Contact/Writers: Send complete ms. Reports on queries in 1 month; mss in 4-6 weeks.

Illustration: Buys 25-30 illustrations/issue. Preferred theme or style: Realistic, some stylization, cartoon style acceptable. Works on assignment only. Reviews ms/illustration packages from artists. Illustrations only: photocopies, promo sheet, tearsheets, or slides. Résumé optional. Portfolio only if requested. Contact: Janet Moir, art director. Reports on art samples in 4-6 weeks. Samples returned with SASE; samples filed. Credit line given.

Terms: Pays on acceptance. Buys all rights for mss. Pays $100 and up for unsolicited articles. Pays illustrators $1,000 for color cover; $25-200 for b&w inside, $100-500 for color inside. Sample copies $3.95 and 9×11 SASE with 4 first-class stamps. Writer's/illustrator's guidelines free on request.

Tips: "Know the magazine's style before submitting. Send for guidelines and sample issue if necessary." Writers: "At *Highlights* we're paying closer attention to acquiring more nonfiction for young readers than we have in the past." Illustrators: "Fresh, imaginative work encouraged. Flexibility in working relationships a plus. Illustrators presenting their work need not confine themselves to just children's illustrations as long as work can translate to our needs. We also use animal illustrations, real and imaginary. We need party plans, crafts and puzzles—any activity that will stimulate children mentally and creatively. We are always looking for imaginative cover subjects. Know our publication's standards and content by reading sample issues, not just the guidelines. Avoid tired themes, or put a fresh twist on an old theme so that its style is fun and lively. We'd like to see stories with subtle messages, but the fun of the story should come first. Write what inspires you, not what you think the market needs."

HOLIDAYS & SEASONAL CELEBRATIONS, Teaching & Learning Company, 1204 Buchanan, P.O. Box 10, Carthage IL 62321. (217)357-2591. Fax: (217)357-6789. **Contact:** Articles Editor or Art Director. Quarterly magazine. Estab. 1995. "Every submission must be seasonal or holiday-related. Materials need to be educational and consistent with grades pre-K through 3 development and curriculum."

Fiction: Young readers: health, multicultural, nature/environment; must be holiday or seasonal-related. Buys 8 mss/year. Byline given.

Nonfiction: Young readers: arts/crafts, cooking, games/puzzles, geography, how-to, math, multicultural, nature/environment, science. "We need holiday and seasonally related ideas from all cultures that can be used in the classroom." Buys 150 mss/year. Byline given.

Poetry: Reviews holiday or seasonal poetry.

How to Contact/Writers: Fiction: Query. Nonfiction: Send complete ms. Reports on queries in 2 months; mss in 3 months. Publishes ms 4-12 months after acceptance. Will consider electronic submissions via disk or modem.

Illustration: Buys 70 illustrations/issue; 300 illustrations/year. Uses b&w and color artwork. Works on assignment only. "Prefers school settings with lots of children; b&w sketches at this time." Reviews ms/illustration packages from artists. Submit ms with rough sketches. Illustrations only: submit résumé, promo sheet, tearsheets, sketches of children. Reports in 1 month. Samples returned with SASE; samples filed. Credit line sometimes given.

Terms: Pays on publication. Buys all rights. Pays $20-75 for stories; $10-125 for articles. Additional payment for ms/illustration packages. Pays illustrators $150-300 for color cover; $10-15 for b&w inside. Pays photographers per photo. Sample copy available for $4.95. Writer's/illustrator's guidelines for SASE.

Tips: "95% of our magazine is written by freelancers. Writers must know that this magazine goes to teachers for use in the classroom, grades pre-K through 3. Also 90% of our magazine is illustrated by freelancers. We need illustrators who can provide us with 'cute' kids grades pre-K through 3. Representation of ethnic children is a must. Because our magazine is seasonal, it is essential that we receive manuscripts approximately 8-12 months prior to the publication of that magazine. Too often we receive a holiday-related article way past the deadline."

N THE HOME ALTAR, Meditations for Families with Children, Augsburg Fortress, 426 S. Fifth St., Box 1209, Minneapolis MN 55440. E-mail: grinerr@augsburgfortress.org. **Editor:** Randi Sundet Griner. Quarterly magazine. Circ. approximately 70,000. This is a booklet of interactive conversations and activities related to daily devotional material. Used primarily by Lutheran families with elementary school-aged children.

Fiction: Young readers, middle readers: adventure, contemporary, faith-related conversations, nature/environment, problem-solving, religious, service activities. Byline given.

Nonfiction: Young readers, middle readers: faith-related conversations and activities, narrative, nature/environment, problem-solving, religious, social issues. Byline given.

How to Contact/Writers: Fiction/nonfiction: Query with published clips. Reports on unsolicited mss in 2-3 months. Mss are accepted for review only. Published material is 100% assigned.

Illustration: Buys approximately 4 illustrations/issue; 16 illustrations/year. Reports back on artist's submissions only if interested. Samples returned with SASE. Credit line given. Works on assignment only.

How to Contact/Illustrators: Reports on art samples only if interested.

Terms: Pays on acceptance of final ms assignment. Buys all rights. Pays $300 for 1 month of devotional writing on assignment. Free sample and information for prospective writers. Include 6×9 SAE and 98¢ postage.

Tips: "Pay attention to details in the sample devotional. Follow the process laid out in the information for prospective writers.

HOPSCOTCH, The Magazine for Girls, The Bluffton News Publishing and Printing Company, 103 N. Main St., Bluffton OH 45817. (419)358-4610. **Editor:** Marilyn Edwards. **Contact:** Becky Jackman, editorial assistant. Bimonthly magazine. Estab. 1989. Circ. 10,000. For girls from ages 6-12, featuring traditional subjects—pets, games, hobbies, nature, science, sports, etc.—with an emphasis on articles that show girls actively involved in unusual and/or worthwhile activities."

Fiction: Picture-oriented material, young readers, middle readers: adventure, animal, history, humorous, nature/environment, science fiction, sports, suspense/mystery. Does not want to see stories dealing with dating, sex, fashion, hard rock music. Buys 30 mss/year. Average word length: 300-700. Byline given.

Nonfiction: Picture-oriented material, young readers, middle readers: animal, arts/crafts, biography, cooking, games/puzzles, geography, hobbies, how-to, humorous, math, nature/environment, science. Does not want to see pieces dealing with dating, sex, fashion, hard rock music. "Need more nonfiction with quality photos about a *Hopscotch*-age girl involved in a worthwhile activity." Buys 46 mss/year. Average word length: 400-700. Byline given.

Poetry: Reviews traditional, wholesome, humorous poems. Maximum word length: 300; maximum line length: 20. Will accept 6 submissions/author.

How to Contact/Writers: Fiction: Send complete ms. Nonfiction: Query, send complete ms. Reports on queries in 2 weeks; on mss in 2 months. Will consider simultaneous submissions.

Illustration: Buys illustrations for 6-8 articles/issue; buys 50-60 articles/year. "Generally, the illustrations are assigned after we have purchased a piece (usually fiction). Occasionally, we will use a painting—in any given medium—for the cover, and these are usually seasonal." Uses b&w artwork only for inside; color for cover. Review ms/illustration packages from artists. Query first or send complete ms with final art. Illustrations only: Send résumé, portfolio, client list and tearsheets. Reports on art samples with SASE in 2 weeks. Credit line given.

Photography: Purchases photos separately (cover only) and with accompanying ms only. Looking for photos to accompany article. Model/property releases required. Uses 5×7, b&w prints; 35mm transparencies. Black and white photos should go with ms. Should have girl or girls ages 6-12.

Terms: For manuscripts, pays a few months ahead of publication. For mss, artwork and photos, buys first

North American serial rights; second serial (reprint rights). Original artwork returned at job's completion. Pays 5¢/word and $5-10/photo. "We always send a copy of the issue to the writer or illustrator." Text and art are treated separately. Pays $150-200 for color cover. Photographers paid per photo (range: $5-15). Sample copy for $3. Writer's/illustrator's/photo guidelines free for #10 SASE.

Tips: "Remember we publish only six issues a year, which means our editorial needs are extremely limited. Please look at our guidelines and our magazine . . . and remember, we use far more nonfiction than fiction. If decent photos accompany the piece, it stands an even better chance of being accepted. We believe it is the responsibility of the contributor to come up with photos. Please remember, our readers are 6-12 years—most are 7-10—and your text should reflect that. Many magazines try to entertain first and educate second. We try to do the reverse of that. Our magazine is more simplistic like a book, to be read from cover to cover. We are looking for wholesome, non-dated material." (See listing for *Boys' Quest*.)

✓ HUMPTY DUMPTY'S MAGAZINE, Children's Better Health Institute, 1100 Waterway Blvd., P.O. Box 567, Indianapolis IN 46206. (317)636-8881. Fax: (317)684-8094. **Editor:** Nancy S. Axelrad. **Art Director:** Rebecca Ray. Magazine published 8 times/year—Jan/Feb; Mar; April/May; June; July/Aug; Sept; Oct/Nov; Dec. *HDM* is edited for children ages 4-6. It includes fiction (easy-to-reads; read alouds; rhyming stories; rebus stories), nonfiction articles (some with photo illustrations), poems, crafts, recipes, and puzzles. Content encourages development of better health habits.

• *Humpty Dumpty's* publishes material promoting health and fitness with emphasis on simple activities, poems and fiction.

Fiction: Picture-oriented stories: adventure, animal, contemporary, fantasy, folktales, health, humorous, multicultural, nature/environment, problem-solving, science fiction, sports. Does not want to see "bunny-rabbits-with-carrot-pies stories! Also, talking inanimate objects are very difficult to do well. Beginners (and maybe everyone) should avoid these." Buys 15-20 mss/year. Maximum word length: 300-400. Byline given.

Nonfiction: Picture-oriented articles: animal, arts/crafts, concept, games/puzzles, health, how-to, humorous, nature/environment, no-cook recipes, science, social issues, sports. Does not want to see long, boring, encyclopedia rehashes. "We're open to almost any subject (although it must have a health angle), but it must be presented creatively. Don't just string together some facts." Looks for a fresh approach. Buys 6-10 mss/year. Prefers very short nonfiction pieces—200 words maximum. Byline given.

How to Contact/Writers: Send complete ms. Nonfiction: Send complete ms with bibliography if applicable. "No queries, please!" Reports on mss in 1-2 months. Send seasonal material at least 8 months in advance.

Illustration: Buys 13-16 illustrations/issue; 90-120 illustrations/year. Preferred theme or style: Realistic or cartoon. Works on assignment only. Illustrations only. Query with slides, printed pieces or photocopies. Contact: Rebecca Ray, art director. Samples are not returned; samples filed. Reports on art samples only if interested. Credit line given.

Terms: Writers: Pays on publication. Artists: Pays within 1-2 months. Buys all rights. "One-time book rights may be returned if author can provide name of interested book publisher and tentative date of publication." Pays up to 22¢/word for stories/articles; payment varies for poems and activities. 10 complimentary issues are provided to author with check. Pays $250 for color cover illustration; $35-90 per page b&w inside; $70-155 for color inside. Sample copies for $1.75. Writer's/illustrator's guidelines free with SASE.

Tips: Writers: "Study current issues and guidelines. Observe word lengths and adhere to requirements. Submit what you do best. Don't send your first, second, or even third drafts. Polish your piece until it's as perfect as you can make it." Illustrators: "Please study the magazine before contacting us. Your art must have appeal to three- to seven-year-olds." (See listings for *Child Life, Children's Digest, Children's Playmate, Jack and Jill, Turtle Magazine* and *U*S* Kids*.)

Ⓝ INSIGHT MAGAZINE, Review & Herald Pub. Assoc., 55 W. Oak Ridge Dr., Hagerstown MD 21740. (301)393-4037. E-mail: insight@rhpa.org. Website: http://www.insightmagazine.org. **Articles Editor:** Lori Peckham. Weekly magazine. Estab. 1970. Circ. 20,000. "We print only true stories written about the author's or author's subject's teen years that portray a spiritual truth. This magazine is aimed at teens ages 14-19.

Nonfiction: Teens: animal, biography, concept, health, history, humorous, interview/profile, multicultural, religion, science, social issues, sports, travel, (all these topics must have a spiritual slant.) Buys 200-300 mss/year. Average word length: 500-1,500. Byline given.

How to Contact/Writers: Nonfiction: Send complete ms. Reports on mss in 6 weeks. Publishes ms 6 months after acceptance. Will consider simultaneous submissions, electronic submissions via disk or modem or previously published work.

Terms: Pays on acceptance. Buys first rights or one-time rights for mss. Pays $25-100 for stories.

This winter watercolor illustration by Phyllis Polema-Cahill appeared on the back cover of *Jack and Jill* magazine. She used the listing in *Children's Writer's & Illustrator's Market* to send samples of her work to the Art Director at *Jack and Jill*, Andrea O'Shea. Since then she has received subsequent assignments from the magazine. To market her work to art directors, Polema-Cahill mails an 8½ × 11 sheet that she had offset printed with five images, then follows up with quarterly printed postcards.

☑ **JACK AND JILL**, Children's Better Health Institute, 1100 Waterway Blvd., P.O. Box 567, Indianapolis IN 46206. (317)636-8881. **Editor**: Daniel Lee. **Art Director**: Andrea O'Shea. Magazine published 8 times/year. Estab. 1938. Circ. 360,000. "Write entertaining and imaginative stories *for* kids, not just *about* them. Writers should understand what is funny to kids, what's important to them, what excites them. Don't write from an adult 'kids are so cute' perspective. We're also looking for health and healthful lifestyle stories and articles, but don't be preachy."

Fiction: Young readers and middle readers: adventure, contemporary, folktales, health, history, humorous, nature, sports. Buys 30-35 mss/year. Average word length: 700. Byline given.

Nonfiction: Young readers, middle readers: animal, arts/crafts, cooking, games/puzzles, history, hobbies, how-to, humorous, interview/profile, nature, science, sports. Buys 8-10 mss/year. Average word length: 500. Byline given.
Poetry: Reviews poetry.
How to Contact/Writers: Fiction/nonfiction: Send complete ms. Reports on mss in 3 months.
Illustration: Buys 15 illustrations/issue; 120 illustrations/year. Reports back only if interested. Samples not returned; samples filed. Credit line given.
Terms: Pays on publication; minimum 17¢/word. Pays illustrators $275 for color cover; $35-90 fr b&w, $70-155 for color inside. Pays photographers negotiated rate. Sample copies $1.25. Buys all rights.
Tips: See listings for *Child Life, Children's Digest, Children's Playmate, Humpty Dumpty's Magazine, Turtle Magazine* and *U*S* Kids.* Publishes writing/art/photos by children.

Ⓝ JUMP, For Girls Who Dare to be Real, Weider Publications, 21100 Erwin St., Woodland Hills CA 91367. Fax: (818)594-0972. E-mail: letters@jumponline.com. Website: http://www.jumponline.com.
Contact: Elizabeth Sosa, editorial assistant. **Editor:** Kiru Berger. **Managing Editor:** Maureen Meyers. Monthly magazine for a female teen audience. Estab. 1997. Circ. 300,000.
Nonfiction: Young adults/teens: general interest, how-to, interview/profile, new product, personal experience. *Jump* columns include Busted! (quirky, bizarre and outrageous trends, news, quotes—6 items, 50 words each); The Dish (food and nutrition for teens—1,500 words); Jump On . . . In, Music, Sports, Body & Soul (small news and trend items on sports, health, music, etc.—6 items, 75 words each).
How to Contact/Writers: Nonfiction: Query with published clips. Reports on queries in 1 month. Publishes ms 4 months after acceptance. Will consider simultaneous submissions.
Terms: Pays on publication. Buys all rights. Pays 50¢-$1/word.
Tips: "Writers must read our magazine before submitting queries. We'll turn away queries that clearly show the writer isn't familiar with the content of the magazine."

KEYNOTER, Key Club International, 3636 Woodview Trace, Indianapolis IN 46268. (317)875-8755.
Articles Editor: Julie A. Carson. **Art Director:** James Patterson. Monthly magazine. Estab. 1915. Circ. 133,000. "As the official magazine of the world's largest high school service organization, we publish nonfiction articles that interest teenagers and will help our readers become better students, better citizens, better leaders."
Nonfiction: Young adults/teens: careers, health, hobbies, how-to, humorous, nature/environment, problem-solving, social issues. Does not want to see first-person accounts; short stories. Buys 15 mss/year. Average word length: 1,200-1,400. Byline given.
How to Contact/Writers: Nonfiction: Query. Reports on queries/mss in 1 month. Will consider simultaneous submissions.
Illustration: Buys 2-3 illustrations/issue; 15 illustrations/year. Works on assignment only. Reviews ms/ illustration packages from artists. Ms/illustration packages and illustration only: "Because of our publishing schedule, we prefer to work with illustrators/photographers within Indianapolis market." Reports on art samples only if interested. Samples returned with SASE. Credit line given.
Terms: Pays on acceptance. Buys first North American serial rights. Pays $150-350 for assigned/unsolicited articles. Original artwork returned at job's completion if requested. Sample copy for 8½×11 SAE and 65¢ postage. Writer's guidelines for SAE and 1 first-class stamp.
Tips: "Review a sample copy of the magazine before querying. Write a strong query, complete with persons to be interviewed, angle, lead paragraph, etc."

KIDS' WALL STREET NEWS, Kids' Wall Street News, Inc., P.O. Box 1207, Rancho Santa Fe CA 92067. (760)591-7681. Fax: (760)591-3731. E-mail: info@kwsnews.com. Website: http://www.kwsnews.-com. **Contact:** Kate Allen, editor-in-chief. Bimonthly magazine. Estab. 1996. *"Kids' Wall Street News* hopes to empower and educate America's youth so they will be better prepared for today and their future. This bimonthly magazine covers world and business news, financial information, computer updates, the environment, adventure and much more."
Nonfiction: Young adults/teens: animal, biography, careers, finance, geography, health, history, interview/ profile, nature/environment, science, social issues, sports, travel. Buys 130 mss/year. Average word length: 250-550. Byline given.
How to Contact/Writers: Nonfiction: Query with published clips. Reports on queries in 2-3 months. Will consider simultaneous submissions and electronic submission via disk or modem.
Terms: Pays on publication. Buys exclusive magazine rights for mss. Samples copies for 9×12 SAE and $1.70 postage (6 first-class stamps).
Tips: *"Kids' Wall Street News* generally assigns specific subject matter for articles. There is a heavy financial slant to the magazine."

Empowering teens with information

Being a teenage girl may be more difficult today than ever. Girls still worry about boys, clothes and make-up, but the modern teen is also faced with problems like pregnancy, date rape, drugs, smoking, eating disorders, low self-esteem, abuse and AIDS. And while information is certainly the best way to arm teens against these threats, sermons and lectures will likely fall on deaf ears. No one understands this better than Lori Berger, who has spent the majority of her 17-year publishing career in the youth market working for such venerable teen institutions as *Sassy, YM* and MTV. Berger is now busy as the editor of a relative newcomer to the teen scene, *Jump* magazine.

Lori Berger

On the newsstand *Jump* doesn't look so different from other lifestyle magazines aimed at teenage girls. But the magazine's tag line, "for girls who dare to be real," offers a clue about what waits inside. "We decided to put together a magazine that was lifestyle oriented with an emphasis on feeling good and making girls feel better about themselves," Berger explains. "A lot of that obviously involves the idea of self-esteem; however, we would never talk directly about self-esteem to teenagers."

From the beginning, the *Jump* editors wanted to use a new set of rules for crafting a teen magazine that challenged the old formulas. "Never define girls through boys, which a lot of the teen magazines have traditionally done," Berger says. "Don't feed on their insecurities by just featuring perfect, waify-thin models. Let's incorporate a real girl aspect into this magazine." But keeping the magazine "real" demands a careful balance between what girls need to read about and what they want to read about.

Jump defines being "real" as not being afraid to be yourself and holding true to what your heart tells you to do in difficult situations. But Berger knows part of being a teenager, even an intelligent, connected one, involves make-up, boys and clothes. So while each monthly issue features articles on sports, fitness and self-image, there are also stories about beauty and relationships, with a *Jump*-twist, of course.

"We do a boy feature every month, for example, called 'Guys Unplugged.' It's a group of real guys around the country and we have them discuss girls, our goal being to enlighten girls and show the softer, more vulnerable side of guys," Berger says. "We never, ever ask something like, 'what's your favorite thing to see girls wear?' " Past issues have featured guys spilling their guts about what makes them fall in love, what makes them get jealous, and why they're not always faithful.

If keeping girls responsibly informed and enthusiastically entertained sounds like a big job, it is. And Berger relies on freelancers to create 60% of *Jump*'s editorial content. "If someone sends me a query and they've got some clips that show me strength as a writer, I'm there," she says. But make sure you've studied *Jump* carefully before you approach her. "I will be turned off by the fact that a writer did not take the time to understand who

JUMP

JAN. FEB. 1998

For girls who dare to be real

the smart **sex** report
How to be safe, not sorry

body image blues: What *boys* see when they look in the mirror — (it ain't pretty)

21st CENTURY GIRL
She's brainy, brave & buff

1998 Horoscope Bonus
A whole year's worth of cosmic clues

Stylin' Snowboarders
Girls who rock the slopes
Plus: cool board giveaway

$2.95 U.S./$3.60 Canada

0 71896 47987 4

Display until February 9, 1998

Disaster Dates 14 Girls reveal their worst ever!

Jump cover reprinted with permission of Weider Publications, Inc.

"We decided to put together a magazine that was lifestyle oriented with an emphasis on feeling good and making girls feel better about themselves," says *Jump* editor Lori Berger. The magazine "for girls who dare to be real" offers a careful balance between what teenage girls need to read about and what they want to read about. *Jump* defines being "real" as not being afraid to be yourself and holding true to what your heart tells you to do in difficult situations.

we are and what we're trying to do. It's really crucial." It's also the most frequent mistake writers make when approaching the magazine.

A close read will reveal that half of the stories in *Jump* are first-person accounts. But you don't need to be a teenage girl to take advantage of the format. Though *Jump* does work with teenage writers, the editors are very happy to take on professional writers who can work with a real teen to craft a gripping "as told to" story.

Male voices are welcome in *Jump's* pages. Girls love hearing what guys think, Berger says. One of the magazine's most popular articles was written by a guy. "Confessions of an Ex-Jerk" revealed how true love tamed the writer's once wild heart. "I've gotten hundreds of letters from girls on that. They loved it," Berger says. "I think girls love to hear from guys who can show a vulnerable side, who have a great appreciation of women."

Though a large part of *Jump* is made up of real girls' stories, fashion and beauty features and relationship essays, there is still plenty of room for the facts. And Berger doesn't shy away from difficult stories. Past issues have featured articles like "The Smart Sex Report," which included explanations of STD's and birth control; "Kickin' Butt," where teen smokers revealed why they wanted to lose the nasty habit; and "Bad Love," a story about teenagers in abusive relationships. "We are very service oriented," Berger explains. "We are always looking to provide readers with information." But freelancers have to remember they're writing for a unique audience. Berger's "difficult story" rules include:

• Do not preach. "Don't ever sound like parents. The second we sound like readers' parents we lose them."

• Never take a position. "We did the nonsmoking story and we never came out and said 'Do not smoke.' But the story was such that it conveyed, 'Oh my God, look what smoking really does to you.' Our hope was that it would be such a turn off, that the message was really there."

• Be incredibly responsible in your reporting. "Recognize that you're writing to a very impressionable audience who looks to this magazine as a confidant and a friend."

Presenting teens with the facts empowers them to make their own decisions, exactly what Berger hopes her readers will do.

Above all, whether you're writing a feature about the latest fitness craze, the best new fashions or the worst drug problem, remember you're writing for teenagers. And most teens have short attention spans. "We can never present a 2,500 word piece of straight text. A 2,500 word piece for us, which would be one of our issue pieces, is typically a 300 word intro, 4 first-person stories that are 300 words a piece, and 3 sidebars that are 250 words a piece or less. When writers pitch us, I want to know that they're also pitching sidebars. Even the most enlightened teenagers I know won't sit down and read 2,500 words of hard text."

But the girls who read *Jump* are enlightened. They are active and involved and spend their time doing things other than going to the mall. You'll have to tell them the truth without talking down to them or they won't believe you. You'll have to use a voice that's fresh and optimistic but free of "teen" lingo or they'll see right through you. If you can do these things, Berger will welcome you on her mission. "Let's not treat girls like boy-crazed teenyboppers," she says. "Let's give them a smarter magazine."

—Megan Lane

✓ **KIDZ CHAT**, (formerly *R-A-D-A-R*), Standard Publishing, 8121 Hamilton Ave., Cincinnati OH 45231. (513)931-4050. **Editor:** Gary Thacker. Weekly magazine. Circ. 80,000. *Kidz Chat* is a weekly take-home paper for boys and girls who are in grades 3 and 4. "Our goal is to reach these children with the truth of God's Word, and to help them make it the guide of their lives. Most of our features, including our stories, correlate with the Sunday school lesson themes. Send SASE for a quarterly theme list and sample copies of *Kidz Chat*."

• At press time, the change from *R-A-D-A-R* to *Kidz Chat* was just enacted—contact the magazine for up-to-date guidelines before submitting.

Fiction: Young readers, middle readers: adventure, animal, humorous, nature/environment, sports, suspense/mystery, travel. Does not want to see fantasy or science fiction. Buys 52 mss/year. Average word length: 400-1,000. Byline given.

Nonfiction: Young readers, middle readers: animal, arts/crafts, games/puzzles, health, how-to, humorous, nature/environment, science, social issues. Buys 50 mss/year. Average word length: 400-500. Byline given.

Poetry: Reviews poetry. Maximum length: 16 lines.

How to Contact/Writers: Fiction/nonfiction: Send complete ms. Reports on mss in 2-3 weeks. Will consider simultaneous submissions (but prefers not to). "No queries or manuscript submissions via fax, please."

Illustration: Buys 2-3 illustrations/issue; 156 illustrations/year. Works on assignment only. Illustrations only: Send résumé, tearsheets or promo sheets; samples of art can be photocopied. Reports in 2-3 weeks. Samples returned with SASE; samples filed. Credit line given. Send SASE for artists' guidelines.

Terms: Pays on acceptance. Buys first rights, one-time rights, second serial, first North American rights for mss. Purchases all rights for artwork. Originals not returned at job's completion. Pays 3-7¢/word for unsolicited articles. Contributor copies given not as payment, but all contributors receive copies of their art/articles. Pays $150 for color (cover); $70-100 for color (inside). Sample copy and writer's guidelines free with business SASE and 1 first-class stamp.

Tips: "Write about current topics, issues that elementary-age children are dealing with. Keep illustrations/ photos current. Children are growing up much more quickly these days than ever before. This is seen in illustrations and stories. Send an SASE for sample copies, guidelines, and theme sheet. Be familiar with the publication for which you wish to write." (See listings for *Live Wire* and *Straight*.)

LADYBUG, THE MAGAZINE FOR YOUNG CHILDREN, Carus Publishing Company, P.O. Box 300, Peru IL 61354. (815)224-6656. **Editor-in-Chief**: Marianne Carus. **Editor:** Paula Morrow. **Art Director:** Suzanne Beck. Monthly magazine. Estab. 1990. Circ. 130,000. Literary magazine for children 2-6, with stories, poems, activities, songs and picture stories.

Fiction: Picture-oriented material: adventure, animal, fantasy, folktales, humorous, multicultural, nature/ environment, problem-solving, science fiction, sports, suspense/mystery. "Open to any easy fiction stories." Buys 50 mss/year. Average word length 300-850 words. Byline given.

Nonfiction: Picture-oriented material: activities, animal, arts/crafts, concept, cooking, humorous, math, nature/environment, problem-solving, science. Buys 35 mss/year.

Poetry: Reviews poems, 20-line maximum length; limit submissions to 5 poems. Uses lyrical, humorous, simple language.

How to Contact/Writers: Fiction/nonfiction: Send complete ms. Queries not accepted. Reports on mss in 3 months. Publishes ms up to 2 years after acceptance. Does not like, but will consider simultaneous submissions.

Illustration: Buys 12 illustrations/issue; 145 illustrations/year. Prefers "bright colors; all media, but use watercolor and acrylics most often; same size as magazine is preferred but not required." To be considered for future assignments: Submit promo sheet, slides, tearsheets, color and b&w photocopies. Reports on art samples in 3 months.

Terms: Pays on publication for mss; after delivery of completed assignment for illustrators. For mss, buys first publication rights; second serial (reprint rights). Buys first publication rights plus promotional rights for artwork. Original artwork returned at job's completion. Pays up to 25¢/word for prose; $3/line for poetry; $25 minimum for articles. Pays $750 for color (cover) illustration, $50-100 for b&w (inside) illustration, $250/page for color (inside). Sample copy for $4. Writer's/illustrator's guidelines free for SASE.

Tips: Writers: "Get to know several young children on an individual basis. Respect your audience. Wants less cute, condescending or 'preach-teachy' material. Less gratuitous anthropomorphism. More rich, evocative language, sense of joy or wonder. Set your manuscript aside for at least a month, then reread critically." Illustrators: "Include examples, where possible, of children, animals, and—most important—action and narrative (i.e., several scenes from a story, showing continuity and an ability to maintain interest). Keep in mind that people come in all colors, sizes, physical conditions. Be inclusive in creating characters." (See listings for *Babybug*, *Cicada*, *Cricket*, *Muse* and *Spider*.)

LISTEN, Drug-Free Possibilities for Teens, Health Connection, 55 West Oak Ridge Dr., Hagerstown MD 21740. (301)791-7000, ext. 2535. Fax: (301)790-9734. E-mail: lsteed@rhpa.org. **Editor:** Lincoln Steed. Monthly magazine. Estab. 1948. Circ. 50,000. *Listen* offers positive alternatives to drug use for its teenage readers.

Fiction: Middle readers, young adults: animal, contemporary, health, humorous, nature/environment, problem solving activities, sports. Buys 50 mss/year. Average word length: 1,000-1,200. Byline given.

Nonfiction: Middle readers, young adults: biography, careers, cooking, hobbies, how-to, health. Wants to see more factual articles on drug abuse. Buys 50 mss/year. Average word length: 1,000-1,200. Byline given.

How to Contact/Writers: Fiction/nonfiction: Query. Reports on queries in 6 weeks. Will consider simultaneous submissions, electronic submission via disk or modem, and previously published work.

Illustration: Buys 4 illustrations/issue; 48 illustrators/year. Reviews ms/illustration packages from artists. Ms/illustration packages and illustration only: Query. Contact: Ed Guthero, designer. Reports in 1 month. Samples returned with SASE. Credit line given.

Photography: Purchases photos from freelancers. Photos purchased with accompanying ms only. Uses color and b&w photos; 35mm, 2¼ × 2¼. Query with samples. Looks for "youth oriented—action (sports, outdoors), personality photos."

Terms: Pays on acceptance. Buys exclusive magazine rights for ms. Buys one-time rights for artwork and photographs. Pays $50-200 for stories/articles. Additional payment for ms/illustration packages and photos accompanying articles. Sample copy for $1 and SASE. Writer's guidelines free with SASE.

Tips: "*Listen* is a magazine for teenagers. It encourages development of good habits and high ideals of physical, social and mental health. It bases its editorial philosophy of primary drug prevention on total abstinence from alcohol and other drugs. Because it is used extensively in public high school classes, it does not accept articles and stories with overt religious emphasis. Four specific purposes guide the editors in selecting materials for *Listen*: (1) To portray a positive lifestyle and to foster skills and values that will help teenagers deal with contemporary problems, including smoking, drinking and using drugs. This is *Listen*'s primary purpose. (2) To offer positive alternatives to a lifestyle of drug use of any kind. (3) To present scientifically accurate information about the nature and effects of tobacco, alcohol and other drugs. (4) To report medical research, community programs and educational efforts which are solving problems connected with smoking, alcohol and other drugs. Articles should offer their readers activities that increase one's sense of self-worth through achievement and/or involvement in helping others. They are often categorized by three kinds of focus: (1) Hobbies. (2) Recreation. (3) Community Service."

LIVE WIRE, Standard Publishing Co., 8121 Hamilton Ave., Cincinnati OH 45231. (513)931-4050. Fax: (513)931-0950. E-mail: standardpub@attmail.com. **Articles Editor:** Carla J. Crane. **Art Director:** Sandy Wimmer. **Photo Editor:** Sandy Wimmer. Newspaper published quarterly in weekly parts. Estab. 1997. Circ. 40,000. "*Live Wire* is a weekly publication geared to preteens (10-12 year olds). 'who want to connect to Christ.' Articles are in a news brief format. We publish true stories about kids, puzzles, activities, interview."

Nonfiction: Middle readers: animal, arts/crafts, biography, games/puzzles, geography, health, history, hobbies, how-to, humorous, interview/profile, multicultural, nature/environment, science, special issues, sports, travel. Buys 50-70 mss/year. Average word length: 250-350. Byline given.

Poetry: Reviews poetry. Limit submissions to 5 poems.

How to Contact/Writers: Nonfiction: Send complete ms. Reports on queries in 1-3 weeks; mss in 2-3 months. Ms published 1 year after acceptance. Accepts simultaneous submissions and previously published work.

Illustration: Buys 8 illustrations/issue; 400 illustrations/year. Uses color artwork only. Works on assignment only. Reviews ms/illustration packages from artists. Ms/illustration packages: query first.

Terms: Pays on acceptance. Buys first rights or reprint rights for mss. Buys full rights for artwork; one-time use for photos. Additional payment for photos accompanying articles. Pays illustrators $100-200 for color cover, $40-200 for color inside. Pays photographers per photo (range: $75-200). Writer's guidelines for SASE.

Tips: "Articles should be appealing and fun. Multicultural material should deal specifically with missionary families or kids." (See listings for *Kidz Chat* and *Straight*.)

N: MAGIC REALISM, Pyx Press, P.O. Box 922648, Sylmar CA 91392-2648. Editor and Publisher: C. Darren Butler. Editor: Julie Thomas. Associate Editor: Patricia Hatch. Associate Publisher: Lisa S. Laurencot. Quarterly magazine. Estab. 1990. Circ. 600. "We publish magic, realism, exaggerated realism, literary fantasy; glib fantasy of the sort found in folktales, fables, myth." 10% of publication aimed at juvenile market.

Fiction: Middle readers and young adults: "primarily folktales and glib fantasy." Sees too much of wizards, witches, card readings, sword-and-sorcery, silly or precious tales of any sort, sleight-of-hand magicians. Especially needs short-shorts. Buys approximately 80 mss/year. Byline given.

Poetry: Reviews poetry. Length: prefers 3-30 lines. Limit submissions to 3-8 poems.

How to Contact/Writers: Fiction: send complete ms. Reports on queries in 1 month; mss in 3-6 months. Publishes ms 4 months-2 years after acceptance. "Simultaneous and previously published submissions are welcome if clearly labeled as such."

Illustration: Uses b&w or color covers; b&w inside. Reviews ms/illustration packages from artists. Query; submit complete package with final art or submit ms with rough sketches. Illustrations only: Query or send résumé and portfolio. Reports in 3 months. Samples returned with SASE. Original work returned at job's completion. Credit line given.

Photography: "We consider photos, but have received very few submissions." Model/property releases preferred. Photographers should query with samples and résumé of credits; submit portfolio for review.

Terms: Pays on acceptance. Buys first North American serial rights or one-time rights and reprint rights for ms, artwork and photographs; also buys worldwide Spanish language rights for Spanish edition published 1-2 years after English edition. Pays ¢4¢/word plus 3 copies for stories; $3 per magazine page and 1 copy for poetry. Pays illustrators $50 for b&w or $100 for color cover; $3-10 for b&w inside. Photographers paid per photo (range: $3-10). Sample copies for $4.95 (back issue); $5.95 (current issue). Writer's guidelines for SASE.

Tips: "Only a fraction of the material we publish is for children. We rarely use anthropomorphic tales. Most material for children is related to folklore.

MUSE, Carus Publishing, 332 S. Michigan Ave, Suite 1100, Chicago IL 60604. (312)939-1500. Fax: (312)939-8150. E-mail: muse@caruspub.com. Website: http://www.musemag.com **Editor:** Diane Lutz. **Art Director:** John Grandits. **Photo Editor:** Carol Parden. Estab. 1996. Circ. 100,000. "The goal of *Muse* is to give as many children as possible access to the most important ideas and concepts underlying the principal areas of human knowledge. It will take children seriously as developing intellects by assuming that, if explains clearly, the ideas and concepts of an article will be of interest to them. Articles should meet the highest possible standards of clarity and transparency aided, wherever possible, by a tone of skepticism, humor, and irreverence."

● *Muse* is published in cooperation of the Cricket Magazine Group and *Smithsonian* magazine. The magazine will change frequency from 6 to 10 issues in 1999.

Nonfiction: Middle readers, young adult: animal, biography, history, interview/profile, math, multicultural, nature/environment, problem-solving, science, social issues. Buys 60-75 mss/year. Word length for articles: 500 words minimum. Work on commision only. "Each article must be about a topic that children can understand. the topic must be a 'large' one that somehow connects with a fundamental tennet of some discipline or area of practical knowledge. The topic and presentation must lead to further questioning and exploration; it must be open-ended rather than closed. The treatment of the topic must be of the competence one would expect of an expert in the field in which the topic resides. It must be interesting and hold the reader's attention, not because of the way it is written, but because of the compelling presentation of the ideas it describes."

How to Contact/Writers: Nonfiction: Query with résumé, writing samples, published clips, detailed story ideas and SASE. Will consider simultaneous submissions, electronic submissions via disk or modem or previously published work.

Illustration: Buys 6 illustrations/issue; 40 illustrations/year. Uses color artwork only. Works on assignment only. Reviews ms/illustration packages. Send ms with dummy. Illustrations only: Query with samples. Send résumé, promo sheet and tearsheets. Reports back only if interested. Samples returned with SASE. Credit line given.

Photography: Needs vary. Query with samples. Reports back only if interested.

Terms; Pays within 60 days of acceptance. Buys first publications rights; all rights for feature articles. Pays 50¢/word for assigned articles; 25¢/word for unsolicited manuscripts. Writer's guidelines and sample copy available for $5.

Tips: "*Muse* many on occasion publish unsolicited manuscripts, but the easiest way to be printed in *Muse* is to send a query. However, manuscripts may be submitted to the Cricket Magazine Group for review, and any that are considered suitable for *Muse* will be forwarded. Such manuscripts will also be considered

---

MARKET CONDITIONS are constantly changing! If you're still using this book and it is 2000 or later, buy the newest edition of *Children's Writer's & Illustrator's Market* at your favorite bookstore or order directly from Writer's Digest Books.

INSIDER REPORT

Making finance fun for kids

Kate Allen

Wall Street. The name conjures up visions of stock traders scurrying along the floor of the New York Stock Exchange, waving paper and yelling at anyone who will listen. Hypertension is as common as guys in suits. Such a rat race is no place for kids. Or is it?

The Exchange may not be the proper learning center for children, but teaching kids early about finance is essential to their understanding of business. Kate Allen says it is this main philosophy that sparked the birth of her magazine, *Kids' Wall Street News*.

"It's an area that a lot of people aren't wisely educated on," says Allen, the magazine's editor-in-chief. "People assume kids learn this information at home as they grow up, but a lot of times they don't get even basic information."

Allen admits to having an interest in finances without being a "hard-core financial person." As a result, *Kids' Wall Street News* (founded in 1996) frequently branches out into non-financial areas. This is important for freelancers interested in approaching this market. A peek inside reveals a strong environmentally friendly, animal rights, socially conscious editorial tone.

"The name denotes some finance and news, but it's more about empowering kids and giving them a sounding board," says Allen. "Kids are great and they do a lot of great things, and we don't often have places to highlight those things."

Allen encourages submissions from kids, and in fact, often some of the best features are written by today's youth. "We love to have kid writers. If they've done something in their school or something personally, we always try to run it if we can," she says. Not a real stickler for proper submission formats, Allen says queries can be sent via e-mail or snail mail as long as the story idea is clearly spelled out. As a general rule, most freelance work is assigned and articles are short (300-400 words) in order to squeeze in as many stories as possible.

As an author of three children's books from Kumquat Press, Allen knows the challenges writers face in getting published. Her books, *Li'L Miss Fuss Budget* (1996), *The Lizard Who Followed Me Home* (1995) and *The Legend of the Whistle Pig Wrangler* (1995) are meant to provide underlying lessons for kids. A former kindergarten teacher, Allen believes it is important to educate children while letting them have fun. This is a theme she carries over to her magazine, but it's also a lesson she shares with other writers.

And on the subject of "fun," *Kids' Wall Street News* definitely gets a passing grade. Headlines are snappy and youthful. They find some oddball subjects to cover, such as two guys who wrote a book about duct tape or a contest to see who can ride a roller coaster the longest. There's even a monthly feature from the staff hound, Muffy.

A Benji look-alike that Allen and her family adopted, Muffy inks her own column (sort of) each issue. The column focuses on different businesses, such as a company that

INSIDER REPORT, *Allen*

Kids' Wall Street News editor Kate Allen feels teaching kids early about finances is essential to their understanding of business. "It's an area that a lot of people aren't wisely educated on," she says. "People assume kids learn this information at home as they grow up, but a lot of times they don't get even basic information." The issue shown here features articles like "The Sweet Story of Hershey," "What Makes the U.S. Stock Market Go Up and Down?," "Collectible Coins" and "Tobacco Companies Under Fire."

manufactures hard hats shaped like Stetsons, or a guy who catches and sells ants for ant farms. "It's a fun way for kids to read and learn about different businesses," says Allen.

Another bit of advice for freelancers is the importance of relating to kids from their level. "Find the kid inside you and work with that." Many of the submissions Allen rejects are from people who have a hard time relating to kids and, as a result, they write down to younger audiences.

One of the magazine's safeguards against inappropriate submissions is Allen's 13-year-old daughter, Lauren, who serves as the magazine's Kids Editor. She reviews a lot of the material that comes in and provides a younger perspective. "We put a lot in front of her, because we feel we need to hear what she has to say," Allen says of her daughter. Lauren tells which stories work and don't work from a kid's point of view. In fact, it was Lauren who came up with the magazine's motto: Be kind, be wise and be prepared for your future.

In reading the material submitted by kids, it's obvious the magazine's readers are interested in larger social issues and animal rights—subjects that some new writers may assume are too heavy for kids to comprehend. A true animal lover who owns eight dogs, a pot bellied pig, an iguana, ducks, chickens and horses, Allen believes animals and kids are somewhat kindred spirits. "Animals can do incredible things just like kids can do a lot of incredible things. Many times people don't give either one of those categories nearly enough credit," she says.

Allen prefers features that provide strong role models for kids and show them a cause and effect. For instance, how a drought in another part of the world affects them. "I want kids to think and learn about the world around them and not be so self-oriented—as we all can be, no matter how old we are."

—Michael Willins

for publication in *Cricket, Spider* or *Ladybug*." (See listing for *Babybug, Cicada, Cricket, Ladybug* and *Spider*.)

MY FRIEND, The Catholic Magazine for Kids, Pauline Books & Media, 50 St. Paul's Ave., Jamaica Plain, Boston MA 02130. (617)522-8911. E-mail: myfriendsk@aol.com. Website: http://www.pauline.org. **Articles/Fiction Editor:** Sr. Kathryn James, FSP. **Art Director:** Sister Helen Rita Lane, FSP. Monthly magazine. Estab. 1979. Circ. 12,000. "*My Friend* is a 32-page monthly Catholic magazine for boys and girls. Its' goal is to celebrate the Catholic Faith—as it is lived by today's children and as it has been lived for centuries. Its pages are packed with fun, learning, new experiences, information, crafts, global awareness, friendships and inspiration. Together with it's web-page KidStuff. *My Friend* provides kids and their families a wealth of information and contacts on every aspect of the Faith."
Fiction: Young readers, middle readers: adventure, Christmas, contemporary, humorous, multicultural, nature/environment, problem-solving, religious, science fiction. Does not want to see poetry, animals as main characters in religious stories, stories whose basic thrust would be incompatible with Catholic values. Buys 50 mss/year. Average word length: 450-750. Byline given.
Nonfiction: Young readers, middle readers: games/puzzles, humorous, interview/profile, media literacy, nature/environment, problem-solving, religious, social issues. Does not want to see material that is not compatible with Catholic values; no "New Age" material. Buys 10 mss/year. Average word length: 450-750. Byline given.
How to Contact/Writers: Fiction/nonfiction: Send complete ms. Reports on queries/mss in 2 months.
Illustration: Buys 8 illustrations/issue; buys 60-80 illustrations/year. Preferred theme or style: Realistic depictions of children, but open to variety! "We'd just like to hear from more illustrators who can do *humans*! (We see enough of funny cats, mice, etc.)" Looking for a "Bible stories" and comic book style artist, too. Reviews ms/illustration packages from artists. Send complete ms with copy of final art. Contact: Sister Helen Rita Lane, art director. Illustrations only: Query with samples. Send résumé, promo sheet and tearsheets. Reports only if interested in 2 months. Credit line given.
Photography: Wants photos of "children at play or alone; school scenes; also, sports."
Terms: Pays on acceptance for mss. Buys first rights for mss; variable for artwork. Original artwork returned at job's completion. Pays $60-150 for stories/articles. Pays illustrators $250/color (cover); $50-150/b&w (inside); $75-175/color (inside). Pays photographers $15-250/photo. Sample copy $2.75 with 9 × 12 SAE and 4 first-class stamps. Writer's guidelines free with SAE and 1 first-class stamp.
Tips: Writers: "We are looking for fresh perspectives into a child's world that are imaginative, unique, challenging, informative, current and fun. We prefer articles that are visual, not necessarily text-based—articles written in "windows" style with multiple points entry. Biographies are accepted if they emphasize the childhood of the subject and are written from a slant that emphasizes a theme or a particular issue. A biography should be written by someone who shows a rich mastery in the field in question. It should not be re-written from an encyclopedia. Please accompoany biographies with a bibliography. Fiction can entertain, inspire, or teach. Fiction stories do not have to do all three. We have a need for each of these types at different times. Illustrators: "Please contact us! For the most part, we need illustrations for fiction stories." In the future, sees children's magazines "getting more savvy, less sappy. Suspect that electronic media styles will penetrate a greater number of magazines for kids and adults alike; literary or intellectual publications would be less affected."

☑ NASCAR/RFT, (formerly *Racing for Kids*), RaceWay Marketing, LLC, P.O. Box 588, Concord NC 28026. (704)786-7132. Fax: (704)795-4460. **Editor:** Gary McCredie. Estab. 1990. Nonfiction publication caters to young adults/teens ages 12-18 interested in racing.
Nonfiction: Young adults: sports (motor sports). Multicultural needs include: sensitivity to minorities in racing—women and African-Americans; with foreign drivers, tell a little about their home country. Buys 12-20 mss/year. Average word length: 400-1,200. Byline given.
How to Contact/Writers: Query. Reports on queries in 2-4 weeks only if interested. Publishes ms 6-12 months after acceptance.
Illustration: Buys 5-10 illustrations/issue; 30-60 illustrations/year. Works on assignment only. Reviews ms/illustration packages from artists. Query. Contact: Gary McCredie, editor. Illustrations only: Query with samples and tearsheets. Contact: Bob Vlasich, art director. Reports in 2-4 weeks. Samples returned with SASE. Originals returned at job's completion if requested. Credit line given.
Terms: Pays on publication. Buys exclusive magazine rights for mss. Pays $50-150 for stories; $50-150 for articles. Additional payment for photos that accompany article ($10-125). Sample copies free for 10 × 12 SAE and 5 first-class stamps.
Tips: "Know the subject matter, study publication. All stories are racing-related. We like stories about NASCAR, NHRA and Monster Truck drivers. No fiction please."

NATIONAL GEOGRAPHIC WORLD, National Geographic Society, 1145 17th St. NW, Washington DC 20036-4688. (202)857-7000. Fax: (202)425-5712. **Editor:** Susan Tejada. **Art Director**: Ursula Vosseler. **Photo Editor**: Chuck Herron. Monthly magazine. Estab. 1975. Circ. 1.1 million.
Nonfiction: Young readers, middle readers, young adult/teens: animal, arts/crafts, biography, cooking, games/puzzles, geography, history, hobbies, how-to, interview/profile, multicultural, nature/environment, science, sports, travel. Middle readers, young adult/teens: social issues. "We do not review or buy unsolicited manuscripts, but do use freelance writers."
Illustration: Buys 100% of illustrations from freelancers. Works on assignment only. Query. Illustrations only: Query with samples. Reports in 2 months. Samples returned with SASE; samples filed. Credit line given.
Photography: Buys photos separately. Looking for active shots, funny, strange animal close-ups. Uses 35mm transparencies. Query with samples. Reports in 2 months.
Terms: Pays on acceptance. Buys all rights for mss and artwork. Originals returned to artist at job's completion. Writers get 3 copies of issue their work appears in. Pays photographers by the project. Sample copies for 9×12 SAE and 2 first-class stamps; photo guidelines available free for SASE.
Tips: "Most story ideas are generated in-house and assigned to freelance writers. Query with cover letter and samples of your writing for children or young adults. Keep in mind that *World* is a visual magazine. A story will work best if it has a very tight focus and if the photos show children interacting with their surroundings as well as with each other."

☑ **NATURE FRIEND MAGAZINE**, 2727 Press Run Rd., Sugarcreek OH 44681. (330)852-9922. Fax: (330)852-3285. **Articles Editor:** Marvin Wengerd. Monthly magazine. Estab. 1983. Circ. 9,000.
Fiction: Picture-oriented material, young readers, middle readers: animal.
Nonfiction: Picture-oriented material, young readers, middle readers, young adults: animal, how-to, nature. Does not want to see evolutionary material. Buys 50-80 mss/year. Average word length: 350-1,500. Byline given.
How to Contact/Writers: Nonfiction: Send complete ms. Reports on mss in 2 months. Will consider simultaneous submissions.
Illustration: Buys approximately 4 illustrations/issue from freelancers; 50 illustrations/year. Reports on artist's submissions in 1 month. Works on assignment only. Credit line given.
Terms: Pays on publication. Buys one-time rights. Pays $15-75. Payment for illustrations: $15-80/b&w, $50-100/color inside. Two sample copies and writer's guidelines for $5 with 7½×10½ SAE and $1.47 postage. Writer's/illustrator's guidelines for $2.50.
Tips: Looks for "main articles, puzzles and simple nature and science projects. Please examine samples and writer's guide before submitting."

NEW MOON: The Magazine For Girls & Their Dreams, New Moon Publishing, Inc., P.O. Box 3620, Duluth MN 55803-3620. (218)728-5507. Fax: (218)728-0314. E-mail: newmoon@computerpro.com. Website: http://www.newmoon.org. **Articles Editor/Art Director:** Barbara Stretchberry. Bimonthly magazine. Estab. 1992. Circ. 25,000. *New Moon* is for every girl who wants her voice heard and her dreams taken seriously. *New Moon* portrays strong female role models of all ages, backgrounds and cultures now and in the past. 100% of publication aimed at juvenile market.
Fiction: Middle readers, young adults: adventure, animal, contemporary, fantasy, folktales, history, humorous, multicultural, nature/environment, problem-solving, religious, science fiction, sports, suspense/mystery, travel. Buys 6 mss/year. Average word length: 300-1,200. Byline given.
Nonfiction: Middle readers, young adults: animal, arts/crafts, biography, careers, cooking, games/puzzles, health, history, hobbies, humorous, interview/profile, math, multicultural, nature/environment, problem-solving, science, social issues, sports, travel, stories about real girls. Does not want to see how-to stories. Wants more stories about real girls doing real things. Buys 6 mss/year. Average word length: 300-900. Byline given.
How to Contact/Writers: Fiction/Nonfiction: send complete ms. Reports on queries/mss in 6 months. Will consider simultaneous submissions and electronic submission via disk or modem.
Illustration: Buys 6-12 illustrations/year from freelancers. *New Moon* seeks 4-color cover illustrations as well as b&w illustrations for inside. Reviews ms/illustrations packages from artists. Query. Submit ms with rough sketches. Illustration only: Query; send portfolio and tearsheets. Samples returned with SASE; samples filed. Reports in 6 months only if interested. Credit line given.
Photography: Buys photos from freelancers. Model/property releases required; captions required. Uses color, b&w, glossy prints. Query with samples. Reports only if interested.
Terms: Pays on publication. Buys first rights, one-time rights, reprint rights for mss. Buys one-time rights, reprint rights, first rights for artwork and photographs. Original artwork returned at job's completion. Pays 5-12¢/word for stories; 5-12¢/word for articles. Pays in contributor's copies. Additional payment for ms/

Samantha Walker received $400 for her cover illustration for the science issue of *New Moon: The Magazine for Girls & Their Dreams*. Walker says she used the listing in *Children's Writer's & Illustrator's Market* to send out a promotional mailer and *New Moon* asked her to submit sketches. She advises new illustrators to "keep knocking on doors, and update your portfolio with fresh work often." To see more of Walker's work, check out http://www.geocities.com/SoHo/Studios/5717/.

illustration packages and for photos accompanying articles. Pays illustrators $200-400 for color cover; $50-125 for b&w inside. Pays photographers $15-30 per photo. Sample copies for $6.50. Writer's/illustrator's/photo/cover art guidelines for SASE.

Tips: "Please refer to a copy of *New Moon* to understand the style and philosophy of the magazine. Writers and artists who understand our goals have the best chance of publication. We're looking for stories about real girls; women's careers, and historical profiles." Publishes writing/art/photos by children.

☑ **ODYSSEY, Adventures in Science**, Cobblestone Publishing, Inc., 30 Grove St., Suite C, Peterborough NH 03458. (603)924-7209. Fax: (603)924-7380. E-mail: odyssey@cobblestonepub.com. Website: http://www.odyssey-mag.com. **Editor:** Elizabeth E. Lindstrom. **Managing Editor:** Denise L. Babcock. **Art Director**: Ann Dillon. Magazine published 10 times/year. Estab. 1979. Circ. 25,000. Magazine covers astronomy and space exploration for children ages 10-16. All material must relate to the theme of a specific upcoming issue in order to be considered.

Fiction: Middle readers and young adults/teens: adventure, folktales, history, biographical fiction. Does not want to see anything not theme-related. Average word length: 750-1,000 words.

Nonfiction: Middle readers and young adults/teens: arts/crafts, biography, cooking, games/puzzles (no word finds), science (space). Don't send anything not theme-related. Average word length: 200-750, depending on section article is used in.

How to Contact/Writers: "A query must consist of all of the following to be considered (please use nonerasable paper): a brief cover letter stating the subject and word length of the proposed article; a detailed one-page outline explaining the information to be presented in the article; an extensive bibliography of materials the author intends to use in preparing the article; a SASE. Writers new to *Odyssey* should send a writing sample with query. If you would like to know if your query has been received, please also include a stamped postcard that requests acknowledgment of receipt. In all correspondence, please include your complete address as well as a telephone number where you can be reached. A writer may send as many queries for one issue as he or she wishes, but each query must have a separate cover letter, outline, bibliography, and SASE. Telephone queries are not accepted. Handwritten queries will not be considered. Queries may be submitted at any time, but queries sent well in advance of deadline *may not be answered* *for several months.* Go-aheads requesting material proposed in queries are usually sent five months prior to publication date. Unused queries will be returned approximately three to four months prior to publication date."

Illustration: Buys 3 illustrations/issue; 27 illustrations/year. Works on assignment only. Reviews ms/illustration packages from artists. Query. Contact: Beth Lindstrom, editor. Illustration only: Query with samples. Send tearsheets, photocopies. Reports in 2 weeks. Samples returned with SASE; samples not filed. Original artwork returned upon job's completion (upon written request).

Photography: Wants photos pertaining to any of our forthcoming themes. Uses b&w and color prints; 35mm transparencies. Photographers should send unsolicited photos by mail on speculation.

Terms: Pays on publication. Buys all rights for mss and artwork. Pays 20-25¢/word for stories/articles. Covers are assigned and paid on an individual basis. Pays photographers per photo ($15-100 for b&w; $25-100 for color). Sample copy for $3.95 and SASE with $1.05 postage. Writer's/illustrator's/photo guidelines for SASE. (See listings for *Calliope, Cobblestone* and *Faces.*)

✔ **ON COURSE, A Magazine for Teens**, General Council of the Assemblies of God, 1445 Boonville Ave., Springfield MO 65802-1894. (417)862-2781. Fax: (417)866-1146. E-mail: oncourse@ag.org. **Editor:** Melinda Booze. **Art Director:** David Danielson. Quarterly magazine. Estab. 1991. Circ. 166,000. *On Course* is a religious quarterly for teens "to encourage Christian, biblical discipleship; to promote denominational post-secondary schools; to nurture loyalty to the denomination."

● *On Course* works on assignment only. Each issue focuses on a theme. Send for theme list along with writers guidelines. Accepts résumés and writing samples for publication's writer's file. Manuscripts not returned.

Fiction: Young adults: Christian discipleship, contemporary, humorous, multicultural, problem-solving, sports. Average word length: 1,000. Byline given.

Nonfiction: Young adults: careers, interview/profile, multicultural, religion, social issues, college life, Christian discipleship.

How to Contact/Writers: Works on assignment basis only.

Illustration: Buys 4 illustrations/issue; 16 illustrations/year. Uses color artwork only. Reviews ms/illustration packages from artists. Query. Illustration only: Query with samples or send résumé, promo sheet, slides, client list and tearsheets. Contact Melinda Booze, editor. Reports back only if interested. Originals not returned at job's completion. Credit line given.

Photography: Buys photos from freelancers. "Teen life, church life, college life; unposed; often used for illustrative purposes." Model/property releases required. Uses color glossy prints and 35mm or 2¼ × 2¼ transparencies. Query with samples; send business card, promotional literature, tearsheets or catalog. Reports only if interested.

Terms: Pays on acceptance. Buys first or reprint rights for mss. Buys one-time rights for photographs. Pays 10¢/word for stories/articles. Pays illustrators and photographers "as negotiated." Sample copies free for 9 × 11 SAE. Writer's guidelines for SASE.

✔ **ON THE LINE**, Mennonite Publishing House, 616 Walnut Ave., Scottdale PA 15683. (724)887-8500. Fax: (724)887-3111. E-mail: otl@mph.org. **Editor:** Mary Clemens Meyer. Magazine published monthly. Estab. 1970. Circ. 6,000. "*On The Line* is a children's magazine for ages 9-14, emphasizing self-esteem and Christian values. Also emphasizes multicultural awareness, care of the earth and accepting others with differences."

Fiction: Middle readers, young adults: contemporary, history, humorous, nature/environment, problem-solving, religious, science fiction, sports. "No fantasy or fiction with animal characters." Buys 45 mss/year. Average word length: 1,000-1,800. Byline given.

Nonfiction: Middle readers, young adults: arts/crafts, biography, cooking, games/puzzles, health, history, hobbies, how-to, humorous, sports. Does not want to see articles written from an adult perspective. Average word length: 200-600. Byline given.

Poetry: Wants to see light verse, humorous poetry.

How to Contact/Writers: Fiction/nonfiction: Send complete ms. "No queries, please." Reports on mss in 1 month. Will consider simultaneous submissions.

Illustration: Buys 5-6 illustrations/issue; buys 60 illustrations/year. "Inside illustrations are done on assignment only, to accompany our stories and articles—our need for new artists is limited." Looking for new artists for cover illustrations—full-color work. Illustrations only: "Prefer samples they do not want returned; these stay in our files." Reports on art samples only if interested.

Terms: Pays on acceptance. For mss buys one-time rights; second serial (reprint rights). Buys one-time rights for artwork and photos. Pays 3-5¢/word for assigned/unsolicited articles ($60 maximum for stories, $35 maximum for articles). Pays $50 for full-color inside illustration; $150 for full-color cover illustration.

Photographers are paid per photo, $25-50. Original artwork returned at job's completion. Sample copy free with 7×10 SAE. Free writer's guidelines.

Tips: "We focus on the age 12-13 group of our age 9-14 audience. Publishes writing/art/photos by readers."

OWL COMMUNICATIONS, 179 John St., Suite 500, Toronto, Ontario M5T 3G5 Canada. See listings for *Chickadee*, *Chirp* and *OWL*.

OWL, The Discovery Magazine for Children, 179 John St., Suite 500, Toronto, Ontario M5T 3G5 Canada. (416)971-5275. Fax: (416)971-5294. E-mail: owl@owlkids.com. Website: http://www.owlkids.com. **Editor:** Keltie Thomas. **Creative Director:** Tim Davin. **Photo Editor:** Katherine Murray. Monthly magazine. Circ. 110,000. "*OWL* helps children over eight discover and enjoy the world of science, nature and technology. We look for articles that are fun to read, that inform from a child's perspective, and that motivate hands-on interaction. *OWL* explores the reader's many interests in the natural world in a scientific, but always entertaining, way."

Nonfiction: Middle readers: animal, biology, games/puzzles, high-tech, humor, nature/environment, science, social issues, sports, travel. Especially interested in puzzles and game ideas: logic, math, visual puzzles. Does not want to see religious topics, anthropomorphizing. Buys 20 mss/year. Average word length: 500-1,500. Byline given.

How to Contact/Writers: Nonfiction: Query with published clips. Reports on queries/mss in 3-4 months.

Illustration: Buys 3-5 illustrations/issue; 40-50 illustrations/year. Uses color artwork only. Preferred theme or style: lively, involving, fun, with emotional impact and appeal. "We use a range of styles." Works on assignment only. Illustrations only: Send tearsheets and slides. Reports on art samples only if interested. Original artwork returned at job's completion.

Photography: Looking for shots of animals and nature. "Label the photos." Uses 2¼×2¼ and 35mm transparencies. Photographers should query with samples.

Terms: Pays on publication. Buys first North American and world rights for mss, artwork and photos. Pays $200-500 (Canadian) for assigned/unsolicited articles. Pays up to $650 (Canadian) for illustrations. Photographers are paid per photo. Sample copies for $4. Free writer's guidelines.

Tips: Writers: "*OWL* is dedicated to entertaining kids with contemporary and accurate information about the world around them. *OWL* is intellectually challenging but is never preachy. Ideas should be original and convey a spirit of humor and liveliness." (See listings for *Chickadee* and *Chirp*.)

POCKETS, Devotional Magazine for Children, The Upper Room, 1908 Grand, P.O. Box 189, Nashville TN 37202-0189. (615)340-7333. Fax: (615)340-7006. E-mail: pockets@upperroom.org. Website: http://www.upperroom.org/pockets. **Articles/Fiction Editor:** Lynn W. Gilliam. **Art Director**: Chris Schechner, Suite 207, 3100 Carlisle Plaza, Dallas TX 75204. Magazine published 11 times/year. Estab. 1981. Circ. 96,000. "*Pockets* is a Christian devotional magazine for children ages 6-12. Stories should help children experience a Christian lifestyle that is not always a neatly wrapped moral package but is open to the continuing revelation of God's will."

• *Pockets* ranked number 41 on *Writer's Digest*'s Fiction 50, the magazine's annual list of the most writer-friendly publications.

Fiction: Picture-oriented, young readers, middle readers: adventure, contemporary, folktales, multicultural, nature/environment, problem-solving, religious. Does not want to see violence or talking animal stories. Buys 40-45 mss/year. Average word length: 800-1,600. Byline given.

Nonfiction: Picture-oriented, young readers, middle readers: cooking, games/puzzles, interview/profile, religion. Does not want to see how-to articles. "Our nonfiction reads like a story." Multicultural needs include: stories that feature children of various racial/ethnic groups and do so in a way that is true to those depicted. Buys 10 mss/year. Average word length: 800-1,600. Byline given.

How to Contact/Writers: Fiction/nonfiction: Send complete ms. "Prefer not to deal with queries." Reports on mss in 6 weeks. Will consider simultaneous submissions.

Illustration: Buys 40-50 illustrations/issue. Preferred theme or style: varied; both 4-color and 2-color. Works on assignment only. Illustrations only: Send promo sheet, tearsheets.

POWER AND LIGHT, Children's Ministries, 6401 The Paseo, Kansas City MO 64131. (816)333-7000. Fax: (816)333-4439. E-mail: mprice@nazarene.org. Website: http://www.nazarene.org. **Editor:** Beula Postlewait. **Associate Editor:** Matt Price. Weekly story paper. "*Power and Light* is a leisure-reading piece for fifth and sixth graders. It is published weekly by the Department of Children's Ministries of the Church of the Nazarene. The major purposes of *Power and Light* are to provide a leisure-reading piece which will build Christian behavior and values; provide reinforcement for Biblical concepts taught in the Sunday School curriculum. The focus of the reinforcement will be life-related, with some historical appreciation.

Power and Light's target audience is children ages 11-12 in grades 5 and 6."

Fiction: Middle readers, young adults: adventure, contemporary, humorous, multicultural, preteen issues, problem solving, religious. "Avoid fantasy, science fiction, abnormally mature or precocious children, personification of animals. Also avoid extensive cultural or holiday references, especially those with a distinctly American frame of reference. Our paper has an international audience. We need stories involving multicultural preteens in realistic settings dealing with realistic problems with God's help." Average word length: 500-700. Byline given.

Nonfiction: Middle readers, young adults: archaeological, games/puzzles, how-to, interview/profile, problem-solving, multicultural, religion, social issues, travel. Multicultural needs include: ethnics and cultures—other world areas especially English-speaking.

How to Contact/Writers: Send complete ms. Reports on queries/mss in 2 months. Publishes ms 2 years after acceptance.

Illustration: Buys 1 illustration/issue; 14 illustrations/year. *Power and Light* publishes a wide variety of artistic styles, i.e., cartoon, realistic, montage, etc., but whatever the style, artwork must appeal to 11- to 12-year-old children. Illustrations only: Query; send résumé, promo sheet and portfolio. Reports back only if interested. Credit line given.

Photography: Buys "b&w archaeological/Biblical for inside use.

Terms: Pays on publication. "Payment is made approximately one year before the date of issue." Buys multiple use rights for mss. Purchases all rights for artwork and first/one-time rights for photographs. Pays 5¢/word for stories/articles. Pays illustrators $40 for b&w, $75 for color cover; $40 for b&w, $50-75 for color inside. Photographers paid per photo (range: $35-45; $200 maximum for cover color photo). Writer's/illustrator's guidelines for SASE.

Tips: Writers: "Themes and outcomes should conform to the theology and practices of the Church of the Nazarene, Evangelical Friends, Free Methodist, Wesleyan and other Bible-believing Evangelical churches." We look for bright, colorful illustrations; concise, short articles and stories. Keep it realistic and contemporary. Request guidelines first!" (See listing for *Discoveries*.)

N POWER STATION, Scripture Press Publications, 4050 Lee Vance View, Colorado Springs CO 80918. (719)536-0100. Fax: (719)536-3243. E-mail: burtonj@cookministries.org. **Articles/Fiction Editor:** Jan Burton. **Art Director:** Randy Maid. Quarterly newspaper. Estab. 1999. "We are a Sunday School take-home paper for fifth and sixth graders. Our papers correlate with the Scripture Press Sunday School curriculum. The purpose of our papers is to show children how Bible truths relate to their everyday life experiences. We seek to disciple children in Christian living."

Fiction: Middle readers: adventure, history, humorous, multicultural (stories set in other countries or ethnic settings in the US), nature/environment, problem-solving, religious, sports. All stories must have Christian context. Buys 26-30 mss/year. Average word length: 800-850. Byline given.

Nonfiction: Middle readers: arts/crafts, biography, games/puzzles, history, hobbies, how-to, humorous, interview/profile, multicultural, nature/environment, problem-solving, religion, science, social issues, sports. Buys 50 mss/year. Average word length: 300-350. Byline given.

How to Contact/Writers: Fiction/nonfiction: send complete ms. Reports on mss in 1-2 months.

Terms: Pays on acceptance. Buys first North American serial rights, first rights, one-time rights, reprint rights or all rights. Pays 8-10¢/word for stories and articles. Additional payment for photos accompanying article. Sample copies free for SAE and 1 first-class stamp. Writer's guidelines free for SASE.

Tips: "Pay attention to the Writers Tips or Guidelines. Write for sample copies so you know the flavor of the papers. Send manuscripts in acceptable form. Proofread all submissions carefully. Be sure submissions have a Christian emphasis, moral slant. Stories need to show God's work in a child's life or situation."

RANGER RICK, National Wildlife Federation, 8925 Leesburg Pike, Vienna VA 22184. (703)790-4000. Website: http://www.nwf.org. **Editor:** Gerald Bishop. **Design Director:** Donna Miller. Monthly magazine. Circ. 650,000. "Our audience ranges from ages 6 to 12, though we aim the reading level of most material at 9-year-olds or fourth graders."

Fiction: Middle readers: animal (wildlife), fables, fantasy, humorous, multicultural, plays, science fiction. Buys 3-4 mss/year. Average word length: 900. Byline given.

Nonfiction: Middle readers: animal (wildlife), conservation, humorous, nature/environment, outdoor adventure, travel. Buys 15-20 mss/year. Average word length: 900. Byline given.

How to Contact/Writers: Fiction: Send complete ms. Nonfiction: Query with published clips. Reports on queries/mss in 6 weeks.

Illustration: Buys 5-7 illustrations/issue. Preferred theme: nature, wildlife. Works on assignment only. Illustrations only: Send résumé, tearsheets. Reports on art samples in 2 months.

Terms: Pays on acceptance. Buys exclusive first-time worldwide rights and non-exclusive worldwide rights thereafter to reprint, transmit, and distribute the work in any form or medium. Original artwork returned at job's completion. Pays up to $600 for full-length of best quality. For illustrations, buys one-time rights. Pays $150-250 for b&w; $250-1,200 for color (inside, per page) illustration. Sample copies for $2.15 plus a 9×12 SASE. Writer's guidelines for SASE.

Tips: "Fiction and nonfiction articles may be written on any aspect of wildlife, nature, outdoor adventure and discovery, domestic animals with a 'wild' connection (such as domestic pigs and wild boars), science, conservation or related subjects. To find out what subjects have been covered recently, consult our cumulative index on our website and the *Children's Magazine Guide*, which is available in many libraries. The National Wildlife Federation (NWF) discourages the keeping of wildlife as pets, so the keeping of such pets should not be featured in your copy. Avoid stereotyping of any group. For instance, girls can enjoy nature and the outdoors as much as boys can, and mothers can be just as knowledgeable as fathers. The only way you can write successfully for *Ranger Rick* is to know the kinds of subjects and approaches we like. And the only way you can do that is to read the magazine. Recent issues can be found in most libraries or are available from our office for $2.15 plus 9×12 SASE."

REACT MAGAZINE, The magazine that raises voices, Parade Publications, 711 Third Ave., New York NY 10017. (212)450-0900. Fax: (212)450-0978. **Editor:** Lee Kravitz. **Managing Editor:** Susan Byrne. **Art Director:** Linda Rubes. **Photo Editor:** Margaret Kemp. Weekly magazine. Estab. 1995. Circ. 3.6 million. 100% publication aimed at teen market.

Nonfiction: Young adult: animal, entertainment, games/puzzles, health, hobbies, interview/profile, nature/environment, news, science, social issues, sports. Average word length: 250-600. Byline given.

How to Contact/Writers: Query with published clips.

Illustration: Works on assignment only. Illustration only: arrange portfolio review. Contact: Linda Rubes, art director. Credit given.

Photography: Query with résumé or credits. Arrange portfolio review. Reports only if interested.

Terms: Pays on acceptance. Buys all rights for mss, artwork and photographs. Pays writers by the project. Additional payment for photos accompanying articles. Pays photographers by the project. Writer's guidelines and sample issue for SAE and 80¢ postage.

Tips: "Do not submit work. Query with clips only."

READ, Weekly Reader Corporation, 200 First Stamford Place, P.O. Box 120023, Stamford CT 06912-0023. Fax: (203)705-1661. E-mail: edread@weeklyreader.com. Website: http://www.weeklyreader.com. **Editor:** Kate Davis. Magazine published 18 times during the school year. Language arts periodical for use in classrooms for students ages 12-16; motivates students to read and teaches skills in listening, comprehension, speaking, writing and critical thinking.

Fiction: Wants short stories, narratives and plays to be used for classroom reading and discussions. Middle readers, young adult/teens: adventure, animal, contemporary, fantasy, folktales, history, humorous, multicultural, nature/environment, problem solving, sports. Average word length: 1,000-2,500.

Nonfiction: Middle readers, young adult/teen: animal, games/puzzles, history, humorous, problem solving, social issues.

How to Contact: Reports on queries/mss in 6 weeks.

Illustration: Buys 2-3 illustrations/issue; 20-25 illustration jobs/year. Reports back only if interested. Samples returned with SASE. Credit line given.

Terms: Pays on publication. Rights purchased varies. Pays writers $200-1,000 for stories/articles. Pays illustrators $650-850 for color cover; $125-750 for b&w and color inside. Pays photographers by the project (range: $450-650); per photo (range: $125-650). Samples copies free for digest sized SAE and 3 first-class stamps.

Tips: "We especially like plot twists and surprise endings. Stories should be relevant to teens and contain realistic conflicts and dialogue. Plays should have at least 12 speaking parts for classroom reading. Avoid formula plots, trite themes, underage material, stilted or profane language, and sexual suggestion. Get to know the style of our magazine as well as our teen audience. They are very demanding and require an engaging and engrossing read. Grab their attention, keep the pace and action lively, build to a great climax, and make the ending satisfying and/or surprising. Make sure characters and dialogue are realistic. Do not use cliché, but make the writing fresh—simple, yet original."

THE AGE-LEVEL INDEX, located in the back of this book, lists book publishers and magazines according to the age-groups for which they need material.

SCIENCE WEEKLY, Science Weekly Inc., P.O. Box 70638, Chevy Chase MD 20813. (301)680-8804. Fax: (301)680-9240. E-mail: kids@scienceweekly.com. **Editor:** Deborah Lazar. Magazine published 16 times/year. Estab. 1984. Circ. 200,000.

• *Science Weekly* uses freelance writers to develop and write an entire issue on a single science topic. Send résumé only, not submissions. Authors must be within the greater DC, Virginia, Maryland area. *Science Weekly* works on assignment only.

Nonfiction: Young readers, middle readers, (K-8th grade): science/math education, education, problem-solving.

Terms: Pays on publication. Prefers people with education, science and children's writing background. *Send résumé.* Samples copies free with SAE and 2 first-class stamps. Follow what is asked for by a publication when submitting materials—if it says résumé only, just send a résumé. If it says a specific locale only, don't send if you are outside of this area. It is a waste of your valuable time and the time of the publication to go through materials it cannot use.

☑ **SCIENCE WORLD**, Scholastic Inc., 555 Broadway, New York NY 10012-3999. (212)343-6456. Fax: (212)343-6333. E-mail: scienceworld@scholastic.com. **Editor:** Mark Bregman. **Art Director:** Susan Kass. Magazine published biweekly during the school year. Estab. 1959. Circ. 350,000. Publishes articles in Life Science/Health, Physical Science/Technology, Earth Science/Environment/Astronomy for students in grades 7-10. The goal is to make science relevant for teens.

• *Science World* publishes a separate teacher's edition with lesson plans and skills pages to accompany feature articles.

Nonfiction: Young adults/teens: animal, concept, geography, health, nature/environment, science. Multicultural needs include: minority scientists as role models. Does not want to see stories without a clear news hook. Buys 20 mss/year. Average word length: 500-1,000. Byline sometimes given.

How to Contact/Writers: Nonfiction: Query with published clips. Reports on queries/mss in 2 weeks. Publishes ms 2 months after acceptance.

Illustration: Buys 2 illustrations/issue; 28 illustrations/year. Works on assignment only. Illustration only: Query with samples, tearsheets. Contact: Susan Kass, art director. Reports back only if interested. Samples returned with SASE; samples filed "if we use them." Credit line sometimes given.

Photography: Model/property releases required; captions required including background information. Provide résumé, business card, promotional literature or tearsheets to be kept on file. Reports back only if interested.

Terms: Pays on acceptance. Buys all right for mss/artwork. Originals returned to artist at job's completion. For stories/articles, pays $200. Pays photographers per photo. Sample copies free for 9×12 SAE and 2 first-class stamps. Writer's guidelines for SASE.

☑ **SEVENTEEN MAGAZINE**, K-III Magazines, 850 Third Ave., New York NY 10022. (212)407-9700. **Editor-in-Chief:** Meredith Berlin. **Fiction Editor:** Susan Brenna. **Senior Editor:** Heidi Parker. **Art Director:** Florence Sicard. Monthly magazine. Estab. 1944. Circ. 2.5 million. "*Seventeen* is a young women's first fashion and beauty magazine."

• *Seventeen* ranked number 7 on *Writer's Digest*'s 1998 Fiction 50, the magazine's annual list of the most writer-friendly publications.

Fiction: Young adults: animal, contemporary, fantasy, folktales, health, history, humorous, religious, romance, science fiction, sports, spy/mystery/adventure. "We consider all good literary short fiction." Buys 12-20 mss/year. Average word length: 800-2,500. Byline given.

Nonfiction: Young adults: animal, fashion, careers, health, hobbies, how-to, humorous, interview/profile, multicultural, religion, social issues, sports. Buys 150 mss/year. Word length: Varies from 800-1,000 words for short features and monthly columns to 800-2,500 words for major articles. Byline given.

How to Contact/Writers: Fiction: Send complete ms. Nonfiction: Query with published clips or send complete ms. "Do not call." Reports on queries/mss in 6-12 weeks. Will consider simultaneous submissions.

Terms: Pays on acceptance. Pays $20-100 for articles; $50 for columns. Writer's guidelines available for SASE.

SHARING THE VICTORY, Fellowship of Christian Athletes, 8701 Leeds, Kansas City MO 64129. (816)921-0909. Fax: (816)921-8755. **Articles/Photo Editor:** John Dodderidge. **Art Director:** Frank Grey. Magazine published 9 times a year. Estab. 1982. Circ. 60,000. "Purpose is to present to coaches and athletes, and all whom they influence, the challenge and adventure of receiving Jesus Christ as Savior and Lord."

Nonfiction: Young adults/teens: interview/profile, sports. Buys 15-20 mss/year. Average word length: 500-1,000. Byline given.

Poetry: Reviews poetry. Maximum length: 50-75 words.

How to Contact/Writers: Nonfiction: Query with published clips. Reports in 6 weeks. Publishes ms 3 months after acceptance. Will consider simultaneous submissions, electronic submissions via disk or modem and previously published work.

Photography: Purchases photos separately. Looking for photos of sports action. Uses color, b&w prints and 35mm transparencies.

Terms: Pays on publication. Buys first rights and second serial (reprint) rights. Pays $50-200 for assigned and unsolicited articles. Photographers paid per photo (range: $50-100). Sample copies for 9×12 SASE and $1. Writer's/photo guidelines for SASE.

Tips: "Be specific—write short. Take quality photos that are useable." Wants interviews and features. Interested in colorful sports photos.

SHOFAR, 43 Northcote Dr., Melville NY 11747. (516)643-4598. **Managing Editor:** Gerald H. Grayson. Magazine published monthly October through May—double issues December/January and April/May. Circ. 17,000. For Jewish children ages 9-13.

Fiction: Middle readers: cartoons, contemporary, humorous, poetry, religious, sports. All material must be on a Jewish theme. Buys 10-20 mss/year. Average word length: 500-700. Byline given.

Nonfiction: Middle readers: history, humorous, interview/profile, puzzles, religious. Buys 10-20 mss/ year. Average word length: 600-1,000. Byline given.

How to Contact/Writers: Fiction/nonfiction: Send complete ms (preferred) with SASE. Queries welcome. Publishes special holiday issues. Submit holiday theme pieces at least 4 months in advance. Reports on queries/mss in 1 month. Will consider simultaneous submissions.

Illustration: Buys 3-4 illustrations/issue; buys 15-20 illustrations/year. Works on assignment only. Reviews ms/illustration packages from artists. Query first. Illustrations only: Send tearsheets. Works on assignment only. Reports on art samples only if interested. Original artwork returned at job's completion.

Terms: Buys first North American serial rights or first serial rights for mss and artwork. Pays on publication. Pays 10¢/word plus 5 contributor's copies. Photos purchased with mss at additional fees. Pays $25-100/b&w cover illustration; $50-150/color (cover). Sample copy free with 9×12 SAE and 98¢ postage. Free writer's/illustrator's guidelines.

Tips: Submit holiday material at least 4 months in advance.

SKIPPING STONES, A Multicultural Children's Magazine, P.O. Box 3939, Eugene OR 97403. (541)342-4956. E-mail: skipping@efn.org. Website: http://www.nonviolence.org/skipping. **Articles/Photo/ Fiction Editor:** Arun N. Toké. Bimonthly magazine. Estab. 1988. Circ. 3,000. "*Skipping Stones* is a multicultural, nonprofit children's magazine designed to encourage cooperation, creativity and celebration of cultural and ecological richness. We encourage submissions by minorities and under-represented populations."

• Send SASE for *Skipping Stones* guidelines and theme list for detailed descriptions of the topics they're looking for.

Fiction: Middle readers, young adult/teens: contemporary, humorous. All levels: folktales, multicultural, nature/environment. Multicultural needs include: bilingual or multilingual pieces; use of words from other languages; settings in other countries, cultures or multi-ethnic communities.

Nonfiction: All levels: animal, biography, cooking, games/puzzles, history, humorous, interview/profile, multicultural, nature/environment, creative problem-solving, religion and cultural celebrations, sports, travel, social and international awareness. Does not want to see preaching or abusive language; no poems by authors over 18 years old; no suspense or romance stories for the sake of the same. Average word length: 500-750. Byline given.

How to Contact/Writers: Fiction: Query. Nonfiction: Send complete ms. Reports on queries in 1 month; mss in 4 months. Will consider simultaneous submissions; reviews artwork for future assignments. Please include your name on each page.

Illustration: Prefers color and/or b&w drawings, especially by teenagers and young adults. Will consider all illustration packages. Ms/illustration packages: Query; submit complete ms with final art; submit tearsheets. Reports back in 4 months. Credit line given.

Photography: Black & white photos preferred, but color photos with good contrast is welcome. Children 7-17, international, nature, celebration.

Terms: Buys first or reprint rights for mss and artwork; reprint rights for photographs. Pays in copies for authors, photographers and illustrators. Sample copies for $5 with SAE and 4 first-class stamps. Writer's/ illustrator's guidelines for 4×9 SASE.

Tips: "We want material meant for children and young adults/teenagers with multicultural or ecological awareness themes. Think, live and write as if you were a child. Let the 'inner child' within you speak out—naturally, uninhibited." Wants "material that gives insight on cultural celebrations, lifestyle, custom and tradition, glimpse of daily life in other countries and cultures. Photos, songs, artwork are most welcome if they illustrate/highlight the points. Translations are invited if your submission is in a language other than English. In 1999, our themes will include cultural celebrations, living abroad, challenging disability, rewards and punishments, hospitality customs of various cultures, modern technology and its impact on human societies, cross-cultural communications, African, Asian and Latin American cultures, indigenous architecture, humor international, creative problem solving and turning points in life."

SOCCER JR., The Soccer Magazine for Kids, Triplepoint Inc., 27 Unquowa Rd., Fairfield CT 06430-5015. (203)259-5766. Fax: (203)256-1119. E-mail: soccerjrol@aol.com. **Articles/Fiction Editor:** Jill Schoff. Bimonthly magazine. Estab. 1992. Circ. 120,000. *Soccer Jr.* is for soccer players 8-16 years old. "The editorial focus of *Soccer Jr.* is on the fun and challenge of the sport. Every issue contains star interviews, how-to tips, lively graphics, action photos, comics, games, puzzles and contests. Fair play and teamwork are emphasized in a format that provides an off-the-field way for kids to enjoy the sport."

Fiction: Middle readers, young adults/teens: sports (soccer). Does not want to see "cute," preachy or "moralizing" stories. Buys 3-4 mss/year. Average word length: 1,000-2,000. Byline given.

Nonfiction: Young readers, middle readers, young adults/teens: sports (soccer). Buys 10-12 mss/year.

How to Contact/Writers: Fiction/nonfiction: Send complete ms. Reports on mss in 4-6 weeks. Publishes ms 3-12 months after acceptance. Will consider simultaneous submissions.

Illustration: Buys 2 illustrations/issue; 20 illustrations/year. Uses color artwork only. Works on assignment only. Illustrations only: Send samples to be filed. Samples not returned; samples kept on file. "We have a small pool of artists we work from, but look for new freelancers occasionally, and accept samples for consideration." Credit line given.

Terms: Pays on acceptance. Buys first rights for mss. Pays $50-600 for stories. Pays illustrators $250-300 for color cover; $50-200 for b&w, $75-300 for color inside. Pays photographers per photo (range: $75-125). Sample copies for 9×12 SAE and 5 first-class stamps.

Tips: "We ask all potential writers to understand *Soccer Jr.*'s voice. We write to kids, not to adults. We request a query for any feature ideas, but any fiction pieces can be sent complete. All submissions, unless specifically requested, are on a speculative basis. Please indicate if a manuscript has been submitted elsewhere or previously published. Please give us a brief personal bio, including your involvement in soccer, if any, and a listing of any work you've had published. We prefer manuscripts in Microsoft Word, along with an attached hard copy." The magazine also accepts stories written by children.

SPIDER, The Magazine for Children, Carus Publishing Company, P.O. Box 300, Peru IL 61354. **Editor-in-Chief:** Marianne Carus. **Associate Editor:** Laura Tillotson. **Art Director**: Tony Jacobson. Monthly magazine. Estab. 1994. Circ. 85,000. *Spider* publishes high-quality literature for beginning readers, primarily ages 6-9.

• *Spider* ranked number 50 on *Writer's Digest*'s Fiction 50, the magazine's annual list of the most writer-friendly publications.

Fiction: Young readers: adventure, animal, contemporary, fantasy, folktales, history, humorous, multicultural, nature/environment, problem-solving, science fiction, sports, suspense/mystery. "Authentic, well-researched stories from all cultures are welcome. We would like to see more multicultural material. No didactic, religious, or violent stories, or anything that talks down to children." Average word length: 300-1,000. Byline given.

Nonfiction: Young readers: animal, arts/crafts, cooking, games/puzzles, geography, history, math, multicultural, nature/environment, problem-solving, science. "Well-researched articles on all cultures are welcome. Would like to see more games, puzzles and activities, especially ones adaptable to *Spider*'s takeout pages. No encyclopedic or overtly educational articles." Average word length: 300-800. Byline given.

Poetry: Serious, humorous, nonsense rhymes. Maximum length: 20 lines.

How to Contact/Writers: Fiction/nonfiction: Send complete ms. Reports on mss in 3 months. Publishes ms 1-2 years after acceptance. Will consider simultaneous submissions and previously published work.

Illustration: Buys 20 illustrations/issue; 240 illustrations/year. Uses color artwork only. "Any medium— preferably one that can wrap on a laser scanner—no larger than 20×24. We use more realism than cartoon-style art." Works on assignment only. Reviews ms/illustration packages from artists. Submit ms with rough sketches. Illustrations only: Send promo sheet and tearsheets. Reports in 6 weeks. Samples returned with SASE; samples filed. Credit line given.

Photography: Buys photos from freelancers. Buys photos with accompanying ms only. Model/property releases required; captions required. Uses 35mm or $2\frac{1}{4} \times 2\frac{1}{4}$ transparencies. Send unsolicited photos by mail; provide résumé and tearsheets. Reports in 6 weeks.

Terms: Pays on publication for text; within 45 days from acceptance for art. Buys first, one-time or reprint rights for mss. Buys first and promotional rights for artwork; one-time rights for photographs. Original artwork returned at job's completion. Pays 25¢/word for stories/articles. Authors also receive 2 complimentary copies of the issue in which work appears. Additional payment for ms/illustration packages and for photos accompanying articles. Pays illustrators $750 for color cover; $200-300 for color inside. Pays photographers per photo (range: $25-75). Sample copies for $4. Writer's/illustrator's guidelines for SASE. **Tips:** Writers: "Read back issues before submitting." (See listings for *Babybug*, *Cicada*, *Cricket*, *Muse* and *Ladybug*.)

STANDARD PUBLISHING, 8121 Hamilton Ave., Cincinnati OH 45231. See listings for *Kidz Chat*, *Live Wire* and *Straight*.

☑ STORY FRIENDS, Mennonite Publishing House, 616 Walnut Ave., Scottdale PA 15683. (724)887-8500. Fax: (724)887-3111. E-mail: RSTUTZ@mph.org. **Editor:** Rose Mary Stutzman. **Art Director:** Jim Butti. Estab. 1905. Circ. 7,000. Monthly story paper that reinforces Christian values for children ages 4-9.
Fiction: Picture-oriented material: contemporary, humorous, multicultural, nature/environment, problem-solving, religious, relationships. Multicultural needs include fiction or nonfiction pieces which help children be aware of cultural diversity and celebrate differences while recognizing similarities. Buys 45 mss/year. Average word length: 300-800. Byline given.
Nonfiction: Picture-oriented: animal, humorous, interview/profile, multicultural, nature/environment. Buys 10 mss/year. Average word length: 300-800. Byline given.
Poetry: Average length: 4-12 lines.
How to Contact/Writers: Fiction/nonfiction: Send complete ms. Reports on mss in 5-6 weeks. Will consider simultaneous submissions.
Illustration: Works on assignment only. Send tearsheets with SASE. Reports in 2 months. Samples returned with SASE; samples filed. Credit line given.
Photography: Occasionally buys photos from freelancers. Wants photos of children ages 4-8.
Terms: Pays on acceptance. Buys one-time rights or reprint rights for mss and artwork. Original artwork returned at job's completion. Pays 3-5¢/word for stories and articles. Pays photographers $15-30 per photo. Writer's guidelines free with SAE and 2 first-class stamps.
Tips: "Become immersed in high quality children's literature."

STRAIGHT, Standard Publishing, 8121 Hamilton Ave., Cincinnati OH 45231. (513)931-4050. Fax: (513)931-0950. **Articles/Fiction Editor:** Heather Wallace. Magazine published quarterly in weekly parts. Circ. 25,000. *Straight* is a magazine designed for today's Christian teenagers.
  • *Straight* ranked number 27 on *Writer's Digest*'s 1998 Fiction 50, the magazine's annual list of the most writer-friendly publications.
Fiction: Young adults/teens: adventure, contemporary, health, humorous, multicultural, nature/environment, problem solving, religious, romance, sports. Does not want to see science fiction, fantasy, historical. "All should have religious perspective." Buys 100-115 mss/year. Average word length: 1,100-1,500. Byline given.
Nonfiction: Young adults/teens: biography, careers, health, hobbies, how-to, humorous, interview/profile, multicultural, nature/environment, problem-solving, religion, social issues, sports. Does not want to see devotionals. Buys 24-30 mss/year. Average word length: 900-1,100. Byline given.
Poetry: Reviews poetry from teenagers only.
How to Contact/Writers: Fiction/nonfiction: Query or send complete ms. Reports on queries in 1-2 weeks; mss in 1-2 months. Will consider simultaneous submissions.
Illustration: Buys 40-45 illustrations/year. Uses color artwork only. Preferred theme or style: Realistic, cartoon (full-color only). Works on assignment only. Query first. Illustrations only: Submit promo sheets or tearsheets. Samples returned with SASE. Reports back only if interested. Credit line given.
Photography: Buys photos from freelancers. Looking for photos of contemporary, modestly dressed teenagers. Model/property release required. Uses 35mm transparencies. Photographer should request themes.
Terms: Pays on acceptance. Buys first rights and second serial (reprint rights) for mss. Buys full rights for artwork; one-time rights for photos. Pays 5-7¢ per word for stories/articles. Pays illustrators $150-325/ color inside. Pays photographers per photo (range: $75-125). Sample copy free with business SASE and 2 first-class stamps. Writer's/illustrator's guidelines for business SASE.
Tips: "Remember we are a publication for Christian teenagers. Each fiction or nonfiction piece should address modern-day issues from a religious perspective. We are trying to become more racially diverse. Writers, illustrators and photographers should keep this in mind and submit more material with African-Americans, Hispanics, Asian-Americans, etc. as the focus. The main characters of all pieces should be contemporary teens who cope with modern-day problems using Christian principles. Stories should be uplifting, positive and character-building, but not preachy. Conflicts must be resolved realistically, with

thought-provoking and honest endings. Accepted length is 1,100 to 1,500 words. Nonfiction is accepted. We use articles on current issues from a Christian point of view and humor. Nonfiction pieces should concern topics of interest to teens, including school, family life, recreation, friends, part-time jobs, dating and music." This magazine publishes writing/art/photos by children. (See listing for *Live Wire*.)

TEEN LIFE, Gospel Publishing House, 1445 Boonville Ave., Springfield MO 65802-1894. (417)862-2781, ext. 4370. Fax: (417)862-6059. E-mail: tbicket@ag.org. **Articles/Fiction Editor:** Tammy Bicket. **Art Director:** Sonny Carder. Quarterly magazine. Estab. 1920. Circ. 50,000. "Slant articles toward the 15- to 19-year-old teen. We are a Christian publication, so all articles should focus on the Christian's responses to life. Fiction should be realistic, not syrupy nor too graphic. Fiction should have a Christian slant also."
  • *Teen Life* is not currently accepting freelance writing.
Fiction: Young adults/teens: adventure, contemporary, history, humorous, multicultural, problem-solving, religious, romance, science fiction, sports (all with Christian slant). Also wants fiction based on true stories. Buys 50 mss/year. Average word length 700-1,500. Byline given.
Nonfiction: Young adults/teens: biography, careers, games/puzzles, history, how-to, humorous, interview/profile, multicultural, problem-solving, religion, social issues, sports, "thoughtful treatment of contemporary issues (i.e., racism, preparing for the future); interviews with famous Christians who have noteworthy stories to tell." Multicultural needs include: material on missions. Buys 50 mss/year. "Looking for more articles and fewer stories." Average word length: 1,000. Byline given.
Illustration: Buys 50-100 illustrations/issue, 200 illustrations/year. Uses color artwork only. Prefers to review youth-oriented styles. Art director will assign freelance art. Works on assignment only. Reviews ms/illustration packages from artists. Send portfolio. "We are Mac literate." Illustration only: arrange portfolio review or send promo sheet, slides, client list, tearsheets or on disk (Mac). Illustrations and design: "We are interested in looking at portfolios consisting of illustration and design work that is teen-oriented." Reports in 3-4 weeks. Samples returned with SASE. Originals returned to artist at job's completion. Credit line given.
Photography: Buys photos from freelancers. Wants "teen photos that look spontaneous. Ethnic and urban photos urgently needed." Uses color prints, 35mm, 2¼×2¼, 4×5 transparencies. Send unsolicited photos by mail.
Terms: Pays on acceptance. For mss, buys first North American serial rights, first rights, one-time rights, second serial (reprint rights), simultaneous rights. For artwork, buys one-time rights for cartoons; one-time rights for photos. Rights for illustrations negotiable. Pays $25-75 for stories; $25-100 for articles. Pays illustrators: $75-100 for color cover or $50-60 for color inside. Pays photographers $25-100. Sample copy free with 9×12 SASE for 3 first-class stamps. Writer's/photo guidelines for SASE.
Tips: "We want contemporary, real life articles, or fiction that has the same feel. Try to keep it teen-oriented—trendy, hip, interesting perspectives; current, topical situations that revolve around teens. We work on specific themes for each quarter, so interested writers should request current writers guidelines and topic list."

☑ TEEN MAGAZINE, Petersen Publishing Co., 6420 Wilshire Blvd., Los Angeles CA 90048-5515. (213)782-2950. **Editor:** Roxanne Camron. **Managing Editor:** Elizabeth Turner. **Fiction Editor:** Michelle Sullivan. **Art Director:** Laurel Finnerty. Monthly magazine. Estab. 1957. Circ. 1,100,000. "We are a pure high school female audience. *'TEEN* teens are upbeat and want to be informed."
Fiction: Young adults: contemporary, humorous, problem-solving, romance, suspense/mystery. Does not want to see "that which does not apply to our market—i.e., science fiction, history, religious, adult-oriented." Buys 12 mss/year. Length for fiction: 10-15 pages typewritten, double-spaced.
Nonfiction: Young adults: careers, cooking, health, multicultural, problem-solving, social issues, travel. Does not want to see adult-oriented, adult point of view." Buys 25 mss/year. Length for articles: 10-20 pages typewritten, double-spaced. Byline given.
How to Contact/Writers: Nonfiction: Query. Reports on queries in 3 weeks; mss in 3-4 weeks. Prefer submissions hard copy and disk. Fiction: Submit story.

**FOR EXPLANATIONS OF THESE SYMBOLS,
SEE THE INSIDE FRONT AND BACK COVERS OF THIS BOOK**

Illustration: Buys 0-4 illustrations/issue. Uses various styles for variation. Uses a lot of b&w illustration. "Light, upbeat." Reviews ms/illustration packages from artists. "Query first." Illustrations only: "Want to see samples whether it be tearsheets, slides, finished pieces showing the style." Reports back only if interested. Credit line given.

Terms: Pays on acceptance. Buys all rights. Pays $100-400 for stories; $50-500 for articles. Pays $25-250/b&w inside; $100-400/color inside. Writer's/illustrator's guidelines free with SASE.

Tips: Illustrators: "Present professional finished work. Get familiar with magazine and send samples that would be compatible with the style of publication." There is a need for artwork with "fiction/specialty articles. Send samples or promotional materials on a regular basis."

N: TEENS ON TARGET, United Pentecostal Church International, 8855 Dunn Rd., Hazelwood MO 63042. (314)837-7300. **Articles Editors:** R.M. Davis and P.D.Buford. Weekly leaflet. Estab. 1994. Circ. 6,000.

Fiction: Young adults: religious. Buys 52-70 mss/year. Average word length: 1,200-1,600. Byline given.

Nonfiction: Young adults: religion. Buys 26-40 mss/year. Average word length: 1,200-1,600. Byline given.

How to Contact/Writers: Fiction/nonfiction: Send complete ms. Reports on mss in 3-12 months. Publishes ms 3-12 months after acceptance. Will consider simultaneous submissions or previously published work.

Illustration: Samples returned with SASE.

Terms: Pays on publication. Buys reprint rights for mss. Pays $12-20 for stories; $12-20 for articles. Sample copies for #10 SAE and 1 first-class stamp.

3-2-1 CONTACT, Children's Television Workshop, One Lincoln Plaza, New York NY 10023. (212)595-3456.
- *3-2-1 Contact* uses a small amount of freelance material. They do not accept unsolicited manuscripts.

N: TODAY'S CHRISTIAN TEEN, Marketing Partners Inc., 162 E. Main St., Elverson PA 19520. (610)286-8800. Fax: (610)286-8881. E-mail: tcpubs@mkpt.com. **Articles Editor:** Elaine Williams. Publishes issues of interest to teenagers from a conservative biblical view.

Nonfiction: Young adults: health, religion, social issues. Buys 10 mss/year. Average word length: 800-1,100. Byline given.

How to Contact/Writers: Nonfiction: send complete ms. Reports on queries in 1 week; mss in 2-3 months. Publishes ms 1 year after acceptance. Will consider simultaneous submissions, electronic submissions via disk or modem and previously published work.

Terms: Pays on publication. Pays $150 for articles. Sample copies free for 9×12 SAE with 4 first-class stamps. Writer's guidelines for SASE.

Tips: "Make articles applicable to teens—something they can use, not just entertainment."

✓ TOGETHER TIME, WordAction Publishing Co., 6401 The Paseo, Kansas City MO 64131. (816)333-7000. Fax: (816)333-4439. E-mail: mhammer@nazarene.com. Website: http://www.nazarene.org or http://www.nphdirect.com. **Contact:** Melissa Hammer. Weekly magazine. Estab. 1981. Circ. 27,000. "*Together Time* is a story paper that correlates with the WordAction Sunday School Curriculum. Each paper contains a story, a poem, an activity, and an article directed to the parents. It is designed to connect Sunday School learning with the daily living experiences and growth of children three and four years old. All submissions must agree with the theology and practices of the Nazarene and other holiness denominations."

Fiction: Picture-oriented material: religious. "We would like to see more realistic stories. We don't like them to seem staged. We also do not purchase stories that give life and feeling to inanimate objects." Buys 50 mss/year. Average word length: 100-150. Byline given.

Nonfiction: Picture-oriented material: arts/crafts.

Poetry: Reviews poetry. Maximum length: 8 lines. Limit submissions to 10 poems.

How to Contact/Writers: Fiction: Send complete ms. Reports on queries in 6-8 weeks; mss in 2 months. Publishes ms 1 year after acceptance.

Illustration: Buys 52 illustrations/year. "We do assignment only and like both realistic and cartoon. Must be age-appropriate." Works on assignment. Reviews ms/illustration packages from artists. Illustration only: Query with samples. Send résumé slides and tearsheets. Reports back only if interested. Sample returned with SASE. Credit line given.

Photography: Buys photos from freelancers. Looks for outdoor or indoor pictures of 3- and 4-year-old children. Uses color and b&w prints; 35mm transparencies. Query with samples. Reports in 1 month.

Terms: Pays on publication. Buys all rights for mss. Buys all rights for artwork; multi-use rights for photographs. "Writers receive payment and contributor copies." Sample copies for #10 SAE and 1 first-class stamp. Writer's/illustrator's/photo guidelines for SASE.

Tips: "Make sure the material you submit is geared to three- and four-year-old children. Request a theme list with the guidelines and try to submit stories that correlate with specific issues."

☑ **TOUCH**, GEMS Girls' Clubs, Box 7259, Grand Rapids MI 49510. (616)241-5616. Fax: (616)241-5558. **Editor:** Jan Boone. **Managing Editor:** Carol Smith. **Art Director:** Joan Hall. Monthly (with combined issues May/June, July/August) magazine. Circ. 16,000. "*Touch* is designed to help girls ages 9-14 see how God is at work in their lives and in the world around them."

Fiction: Middle readers, young adults/teens: adventure, animal, contemporary, fantasy, folktales, health, history, humorous, multicultural, nature/environment, problem-solving, religious, romance. Does not want to see unrealistic stories and those with trite, easy endings. Buys 30 mss/year. Average word length: 400-1,000. Byline given.

Nonfiction: Middle readers, young adults/teens: animal, careers, fashion, games/puzzles, hobbies, how-to, humorous, interview/profile, multicultural, problem-solving, religious, social issues, sports, travel. Buys 9 mss/year. Average word length: 200-800. Byline given.

How to Contact/Writers: Send for annual update for publication themes. Fiction/nonfiction: Send complete ms. Reports on mss in 1 month. Will consider simultaneous submissions.

Illustration: Buys 3 illustrations/year. Prefers ms/illustration packages. Works on assignment only. Reports on submissions in 3 weeks. Samples returned with SASE. Credit line given.

Terms: Pays on publication. Buys first North American serial rights, first rights, second serial (reprint rights) or simultaneous rights. Original artwork not returned at job's completion. Pays $5-50 for stories; $20-50 for assigned articles; $5-30 for unsolicited articles. "We send complimentary copies in addition to pay." Pays $25-75 for color cover illustration; $25-50 for color inside illustration. Pays photographers by the project ($25-75 per photo). Writer's guidelines for SASE.

Tips: Writers: "The stories should be current, deal with adolescent problems and joys, and help girls see God at work in their lives through humor as well as problem-solving."

TURTLE MAGAZINE, For Preschool Kids, Children's Better Health Institute, 1100 Waterway Blvd., P.O. Box 567, Indianapolis IN 46206. (317)636-8881. **Editor:** Terry Harshman. **Art Director:** Bart Rivers. Monthly/bimonthly magazine published January/February, March, April/May, June, July/August, September, October/November, December. Circ. 300,000. *Turtle* uses read-aloud stories, especially suitable for bedtime or naptime reading, for children ages 2-5. Also uses poems, simple science experiments, and health-related articles. All but 2 pages aimed at juvenile audience.

Fiction: Picture-oriented material: adventure, animal, contemporary, fantasy, folktales, health-related, history, holiday themes, humorous, multicultural, nature/environment, problem-solving, sports, suspense/mystery. "We need very simple experiments illustrating basic science concepts. Also needs action rhymes to foster creative movement. We no longer buy stories on 'generic' turtles because we now have Pokey Toes, our own trade-marked turtle character." Do not want stories about monsters or scary things. Avoid stories in which the characters indulge in unhealthy activities like eating junk food. Buys 50 mss/year. Average word length: 150-300. Byline given.

Nonfiction: Picture-oriented material: animal, arts/crafts, cooking, games/puzzles, geography, health, multicultural, nature/environment, science, sports. Buys 24 mss/year. Average word length: 150-300. Byline given.

Poetry: "We're especially looking for action rhymes to foster creative movement in preschoolers. We also use short verse on our back cover."

How to Contact/Writers: Fiction/nonfiction: "Prefer complete manuscript to queries." Reports on mss in 3 months.

Photography: Buys photos from freelancers with accompanying ms only.

Terms: Pays on publication. Buys all rights for mss/artwork; one-time rights for photographs. Pays up to 22¢/word for stories and articles (depending upon length and quality) and 10 complimentary copies. Pays $30-70 for b&w inside. Sample copy $1.25. Writer's guidelines free with SASE.

Tips: "We're beginning to edit *Turtle* more for the very young preschooler (ages 2-5), so we're looking for stories and articles that are written more simply than those we've used in the past. Our need for health-related material, especially features that encourage fitness, is ongoing. Health subjects must be age-appropriate. When writing about them, think creatively and lighten up! Fight the tendency to become boringly pedantic. Nobody—not even young kids—likes to be lectured. Always keep in mind that in order for a story or article to educate preschoolers, it first must be entertaining—warm and engaging, exciting, or genuinely funny. Understand that writing for *Turtle* is a difficult challenge. Study the magazine to see if your manuscript is right for *Turtle*. Magazines have distinct personalities which can't be understood by only reading market listings. Here the trend is toward leaner, lighter writing. There will be a growing need for interactive activities. Writers might want to consider developing an activity to accompany their concise manuscripts." (See listings for *Child Life, Children's Digest, Children's Playmate, Humpty Dumpty's Magazine, Jack and Jill* and *U*S* Kids.*)

TWIST, Bauer Publishing Company, 270 Sylvan Ave., Englewood Cliffs NJ 07632. (201)569-6699. Fax: (201)569-4458. E-mail: twistmail@aol.com. **Articles Editors:** Jeannie Kim and Jena Hofstedt. **Art Director:** Robin Zachary. Monthly magazine. Estab. 1997. Circ. 700,000. "We capture the energy, attitude and interests of young women today. We stress reality over fantasy and serve as a forum for the concerns and passions of our 14- to 19-year-old readers."
Nonfiction: Young teens: health, humorous, interview/profile, social issues, relationships/dating, "real life" experiences, quizzes. Average word length: 100-1,800. Byline given.
How to Contact/Writers: Nonfiction: query with published clips. Reports on queries in 1-4 weeks. Will consider simultaneous submissions.
Illustration: Buys 4 illustrations/issue. Uses color artwork only. Works on assignment only. Query; send promo sheet and tearsheets; "follow with a phone call." Contact: Robin Zachary, creative director. Reports only if interested. Samples not returned; samples not filed.
Photography: Uses 35mm, 2¼×2¼ transparencies. Query with samples; provide promotional literature or tearsheets.
Terms: Pays on acceptance. Buys first North American serial rights. Pays $50 minimum and up to $1/word for articles. Pays illustrators $100-500 for color inside. Pays photographers by the project (range: $30/day up to $400); or per photo (range: $75 minimum). Sample copies not available. Writer's guidelines free for SASE.

U*S* KIDS, Children's Better Health Institute, 1100 Waterway Blvd., P.O. Box 567, Indianapolis IN 46206. (317)636-8881. **Editor:** Jeff Ayres. **Art Director:** Matthew Brinkman. Magazine published 8 times a year. Estab. 1987. Circ. 250,000.
Fiction: Young readers and middle readers: adventure, animal, contemporary, health, history, humorous, multicultural, nature/environment, problem-solving, sports, suspense/mystery. "We see too many stories with no real story line. We'd like to see more mysteries and contemporary humor stories." Buys approximately 8-16 mss/year. Average word length: 500-800. Byline given.
Nonfiction: Young readers and middle readers: animal, arts/crafts, cooking, games/puzzles, health, history, hobbies, how-to, humorous, interview/profile, multicultural, nature/environment, science, social issues, sports, travel. Wants to see interviews with kids ages 5-10, who have done something unusual or different. Buys 30-40 mss/year. Average word length: 500-600. Byline given.
Poetry: Maximum length: 32 lines.
How to Contact/Writers: Fiction: Send complete ms. Nonfiction: Query or submit complete ms. Reports on queries and mss in 1 month. Publishes ms 6 months after acceptance. Will consider simultaneous submissions, electronic submissions via disk or modem and previously published work.
Illustration: Buys 8 illustrations/issue; 70 illustrations/year. Color artwork only. Works on assignment only. Reviews ms/illustration packages from artists. Query. Illustrations only: Send résumé and tearsheets. Reports back only if interested. Samples returned with SASE; samples kept on file. Does not return originals. Credit line given.
Photography: Purchases photography from freelancers. Looking for photos that pertain to children ages 5-10. Model/property release required. Uses color and b&w prints; 35mm, 2¼×2¼, 4×5 and 8×10 transparencies. Photographers should provide résumé, business card, promotional literature or tearsheets to be kept on file. Reports back only if interested.
Terms: Pays on publication. Buys all rights for mss. Purchases all rights for artwork. Purchases one-time rights for photographs. Pays 10¢/word minimum. Additional payment for ms/illustration packages. Pays illustrators $140/page for color inside. Photographers paid by the project or per photo (negotiable). Sample copies for $2.50. Writer's/illustrator/photo guidelines for SASE.
Tips: "Write clearly and concisely without preaching or being obvious." (See listings for *Child Life, Children's Digest, Children's Playmate, Humpty Dumpty's Magazine, Jack and Jill* and *Turtle Magazine.*)

✔ **W.O.W. (Wild Outdoor World)**, 44 N. Last Chance Gulch, Suites 16-20, P.O. Box 1249, Helena MT 59624. (406)449-1335. Fax: (406)442-9197. **Editorial Director:** Carolyn Zieg Cunningham. **Executive Editor:** Kay Morton Ellerhoff. **Design Editor:** Bryan Knaff. Bimonthly magazine. Estab. 1993. Circ. 100,000. "A magazine for young conservationists (age 8-12)." W.O.W. is distributed in fourth grade classrooms throughout the US.
Nonfiction: Middle readers: adventure (outdoor), animal, nature/environment, sports (outdoor recreation), travel (to parks, wildlife refuges, etc.). Average word length: 800 maximum. Byline given.
How to Contact/Writers: Fiction/nonfiction: Query. Reports in 6 months.

Illustration: Buys 2 illustrations/issue; 12-15 illustrations/year. Prefers work on assignment. Reviews ms/illustration packages from artists. Illustrations only: Query; send slides, tearsheets. Reports in 2 months. Samples returned with SASE; samples sometimes filed. Credit line given.

Photography: *Must* be submitted in 20-slide sheets and individual protectors, such as KYMAC. Looks for "children outdoors—camping, fishing, doing 'nature' projects." Model/property releases required. Photo captions required. Uses 35mm transparencies. Does not accept unsolicited photography. Contact: Theresa Morrow Rush, photo editor. Reports in 2 months.

Terms: Pays 30-60 days after publication. Buys one-time rights for mss. Purchases one-time rights for photographs. Original work returned at job's completion. Pays $100-300 for articles; $50 for fillers. Pays illustrators variable rate for b&w inside; $250 color cover; $35-100 color inside. Pays photographers by the project ($35 minimum); per photo (range: $35-100); $250 for cover photo. Sample copies for $3.95 and 8½×11 SAE. Writer's/illustrator's/photo guidelines for SASE.

Tips: "We are seriously overloaded with manuscripts and do not plan to buy very much new material in the next year."

☑ 🔲 WHAT! A MAGAZINE, What! Publishers Inc. 108-93 Lombard Ave., Winnipeg, Manitoba R3B 3B1 Canada. (204)985-8160. Fax: (204)943-8991. E-mail: stu.slayen@m2ci.mb.ca. **Articles Editor:** Stuart Slayen. **Art Director:** Brian Kauste. Magazine published 5 times/year. Estab. 1987. Circ. 200,000. "Informative and entertaining teen magazine for both genders. Articles deal with issues and ideas of relevance to Canadian teens. The magazine is distributed through schools so we aim to be cool and responsible at the same time."

Nonfiction: Young adults (14 and up): biography, careers, concept, health, how-to, humorous, interview/profile, nature/environment, science, social issues, sports. "No cliché teen stuff. Also, we're getting too many heavy pitches lately on teen pregnancy, AIDS, etc." Buys 8 mss/year. Average word length: 675-2,100. Byline given.

How to Contact/Writers: Nonfiction: Query with published clips. Reports on queries/mss in 2 months. Publishes ms 2 months after acceptance.

Terms: Pays on publication plus 30 days. Buys first rights for mss. Pays $100-500 (Canadian) for articles. Sample copies when available for 9×12 and $1.45 (Canadian). Writer's guidelines free for SASE.

Tips: "Teens are smarter today than ever before. Respect that intelligence in queries and articles. Aim for the older end of our age-range (14-19) and avoid cliché. Humor works for us almost all the time."

WITH, The Magazine for Radical Christian Youth, Faith & Life Press, 722 Main, P.O. Box 347, Newton KS 67114. (316)283-5100. Fax: (316)283-0454. E-mail: deliag@gcmc.org. **Editor:** Carol Duerksen. Published 8 times a year. Circ. 5,800. Magazine published for teenagers, ages 15-18, in Mennonite, Brethren and Mennonite Brethren congregations. "We deal with issues affecting teens and try to help them make choices reflecting a radical Christian faith."

● *With* ranked number 36 on *Writer's Digest*'s Fiction 50, the magazine's annual list of the most writer-friendly publications.

Fiction: Young adults/teens: contemporary, fantasy, humorous, multicultural, problem-solving, religious, romance. Multicultural needs include race relations, first-person stories featuring teens of ethnic minorities. Buys 15 mss/year. Average word length: 1,000-2,000. Byline given.

Nonfiction: Young adults/teens: first-person teen personal experience (as-told-to), how-to, humorous, multicultural, problem-solving, religion, social issues. Buys 15-20 mss/year. Average word length: 1,000-2,000. Byline given.

Poetry: Wants to see religious, humorous, nature. "Buys 1-2 poems/year." Maximum length: 50 lines.

How to Contact/Writers: Send complete ms. Query on first-person teen personal experience stories and how-to articles. (Detailed guidelines for first-person stories, how-tos, and fiction available for SASE.) Reports on queries in 2-3 weeks; mss in 3-6 weeks. Will consider simultaneous submissions.

Illustration: Buys 6-8 assigned illustrations/issue; buys 64 assigned illustrations/year. Uses b&w and 2-color artwork only. Preferred theme or style: candids/interracial. Reviews ms/illustration packages from artists. Query first. Illustrations only: Query with portfolio (photocopies only) or tearsheets. Reports back only if interested. Credit line given.

Photography: Buys photos from freelancers. Looking for candid photos of teens (ages 15-18), especially ethnic minorities. Uses 8×10 b&w glossy prints. Photographers should send unsolicited photos by mail.

Terms: Pays on acceptance. For mss buys first rights, one-time rights; second serial (reprint rights). Buys one-time rights for artwork and photos. Original artwork returned at job's completion upon request. Pays 6¢/word for unpublished manuscripts; 4¢/word for reprints. Will pay more for assigned as-told-to stories. Pays $10-25 for poetry. Pays $50-60 for b&w cover illustration and b&w inside illustration. Pays photographers per project (range: $120-180). Sample copy for 9×12 SAE and 4 first-class stamps. Writer's/illustrator's guidelines for SASE.

Tips: "We want stories, fiction or nonfiction, in which high-school-age youth of various cultures/ethnic groups are the protaganist. Stories may or may not focus on cross-cultural relationships. We're hungry for stuff that makes teens laugh—fiction, nonfiction and cartoons. It doesn't have to be religious, but must be wholesome. Most of our stories would not be accepted by other Christian youth magazines. They would be considered too gritty, too controversial, or too painful. Our regular writers are on the *With* wavelength. Most writers for Christian youth magazines aren't." For writers: "Fiction and humor are the best places to break in. Send SASE and request guidelines." For photographers: "If you're willing to line up models and shoot to illustrate specific story scenes, send us a letter of introduction and some samples of your work."

WONDER TIME, WordAction Publications, 6401 The Paseo, Kansas City MO 64131. (816)333-7000. Fax: (816)333-4439. **Editor:** Donna Fillmore. Weekly magazine. Circ. 45,000. "*Wonder Time* is a full-color story paper for first and second graders. It is designed to connect Sunday School learning with the daily living experiences and growth of the primary child. Since *Wonder Time*'s target audience is children ages six to eight, the readability goal is to encourage beginning readers to read for themselves. The major purposes of *Wonder Time* are to: Provide a life-related paper that will build Christian values, encourage ethical behavior and provide reinforcement for the biblical concepts taught in the WordAction Sunday School curriculum."

Fiction: Picture-oriented material: adventure, contemporary, multicultural, nature/environment, religious. "We need ethnic balance—stories and illustrations from a variety of ethnic experiences." Buys 52 mss/year. Average word length: 250-350. Byline given.

Nonfiction: Picture-oriented material: problem solving, religious, social issues.

How to Contact/Writers: Fiction/nonfiction: Send complete ms. Reports on queries/mss in 6 weeks. Will consider simultaneous submissions.

Illustration: Buys 50 illustrations/year. Works on assignment only. Reviews ms/illustration packages from artists. Illustrations only: Submit samples of work. Reports on art samples in 6 weeks. Samples returned with SASE; samples kept on file. Credit line given.

Terms: Pays on acceptance. Original artwork not returned. Pays $25 per story for rights which allow the publisher to print the story multiple times without repayment. Pays illustrators $40 for b&w cover or inside; $75 for color cover or inside. Photographers paid per photo (range: $25-75). Sends complimentary contributor's copies of publication. Sample copy and writer's guidelines with 9½×12 SAE and 2 first-class stamps.

Tips: "Basic themes reappear regularly. Please write for a theme list. Also be familiar with what *Wonder Time* is all about. Ask for guidelines, sample copies, theme list *before* submitting."

☑ **WRITER'S INTL. FORUM, "For Those Who Write to Sell,"** Bristol Services Intl., P.O. Box 516, Tracyton WA 98393-0516. Website: http://www.bristolservicesintl.com. **Editor:** Sandra E. Haven. Monthly (10 times/year, excluding December and August) newsletter. Estab. 1990. Up to 25% aimed at writers of juvenile literature. "We offer authors the unique chance of having a short story or essay published plus receiving a free professional critique. If published, author must agree to allow both the manuscript and our professional critique to be published in our Featured Manuscript section. Each issue includes writing lessons and markets information."

Fiction: Middle readers, young adults/teens: adventure, contemporary, fantasy, humorous, nature/environment, problem-solving, religious, romance, science fiction, suspense/mystery. "No experimental formats; no picture books; no poetry. No stories for children under age eight. We see too many anthropomorphic characters. We would like to see more mysteries, problem-solving and adventures." Buys approximately 12 mss/year. Maximum word length: 1,000. Byline and bio information printed.

How to Contact/Writers: Fiction: Reports on mss in 2 months. Publishes ms 4-6 months after acceptance.

Terms: Pays on acceptance. Buys first North American serial rights. Pays $30, 1 contributor copy plus a written professional critique for stories and essays. Sample copy for $3.

Tips: "We want well-crafted stories with traditional plots which are written in clear language, have fully developed characters and an interesting storyline. Essays must have a tight focus, make a distinct point, and back up that point with specific facts and/or experiences. Always state the age group for which the children's manuscript is intended and be certain your material is suitable specifically for that audience."

N̲ YES MAG, Canada's Science Magazine for Kids, Peter Piper Publishing Inc., 4175 Francisco Place, Victoria, British Columbia V8N 6H1 Canada. Phone/fax: (250)477-5543. E-mail: shannon@yesmag. bc.ca. Website: http://www.yesmag.bc.ca. **Articles Editor:** Shannon Hunt. **Art/Photo Director:** David Garrison. Quarterly magazine. Estab. 1996. Circ. 12,000. "*YES Mag* is designed to make science accessible, interesting, exciting, and FUN. Written for children ages 8 to 14, *YES Mag* covers a range of topics including science and technology news, environmental updates, do-at-home projects, and articles about Canadian students and scientists."

Nonfiction: Middle readers: animal, math, nature/environment, science. Buys 70 mss/year. Average word length: 250-1,250. Byline given.

How to Contact/Writers: Nonfiction: Query with published clips or send complete ms (on spec only). Reports on queries/mss in 3 weeks. Publishes ms 3 months after acceptance. Will consider simultaneous submissions, electronic submission via disk or modem, previously published work.

Illustration: Buys 2 illustrations/issue; 10 illustrations/year. Uses color artwork only. Works on assignment only. Reviews ms/illustration packages from artists. Query. Contact: Shannon Hunt, managing editor. Illustration only: Query with samples. Contact: David Garrison, art/photo editor. Reports in 3 weeks. Samples returned with SASE; samples filed. Credit line given.

Photography: "Looking for science, technology, nature/environment photos based on current editorial needs." Photo captions required. Uses color prints. Provide résumé, business card, promotional literature, tearsheets if possible. Reports in 3 weeks.

Terms: Pays on publication. Buys one-time rights for mss. Buys one-time rights for artwork/photos. Original artwork returned at job's completion. Pays $25-125 for articles. Sample copies for $3.50. Writer's guidelines for SASE.

Tips: "We do not publish fiction or science fiction. Visit our web site for more information, sample articles and writers guidelines. We accept queries via e-mail. Articles relating to the physical sciences and mathematics are encouraged."

YM, 685 Third Ave., New York NY 10017. Fax: (212)499-1698. E-mail: lesleyym@aol.com. **Editor:** Lesley Seymour. "*YM* is a national magazine for young women ages 15-24 to help guide them through the many exciting and often rough aspects of young adulthood."

Nonfiction: "We buy articles on topics of interest to young women. All articles should be lively and informative. In the past year, we have tackled everything from interracial dating to sexual abuse to eating disorders. Expert opinions should be included as a supplement to the feelings and experiences of young women. We do not publish fiction or poetry." Word length: up to 2,500 words.

How to Contact/Writers: Nonfiction: Query with SASE. (Write "query" on envelope.) Reports on queries in 4-6 weeks; mss in 1-2 months. Credit line sometimes given.

Terms: Pays on acceptance. Rates vary. Sample copies available for $2.50.

[N] YOUNG ENTREPRENEUR, The News Magazine of Business, Careers, Finance, and Entrepreneurship, KidsWay Inc., Editorial Office: 1350 Nasa Rd. 1, Suite 101, Houston TX 77058. (281)333-8313. Fax: (281)333-9173. E-mail: YEmag@kidsway.com. Website: http://www.kidsway.com. **Articles Editor:** Bonnie Drew. Bimonthly magazine. Estab. 1996. Circ. 200,000. "*Young Entrepreneur,* is a business and career publication that promotes entrepreneurship education for ages 8-18. Our goal is to show teens and preteens how to prepare for careers, manage money and think like entrepreneurs."

Nonfiction: Young adults: careers, how-to, interview/profile, business entrepreneurship. Buys 50 mss/year. Average word length: 400-600. Byline given.

How to Contact/Writers: Nonfiction: Query with published clips. Reports on queries/mss in 2 months. Publishes ms 3 months after acceptance. Will consider electronic submission via disk or modem.

Illustration: Uses color artwork only. Works on assignment only. Illustrations only: Query with samples. Send résumé, client list, tearsheets. Contact: Bonnie Drew, editor. Reports back only if interested. Samples returned. Credit line given.

Photography: Looking for photos of teens involved in hands-on activity running a business that other teens would find intriguing. Model/property release required with submissions. Uses color 4×5 and 8×10 glossy prints. Query with samples; provide résumé, tearsheets. Reports in 2 months.

Terms: Pays on publication. Buys first North American serial rights. Buys first rights for artwork; first rights/all rights for photos. Original artwork returned at job's completion. Pays $80-250 for stories/articles. Additional payment for ms/illustration packages and for photos accompanying articles only if writer is also the photographer. Pays illustrators $100-200 for color cover; $25-75 for color inside. Pays photographers by the project (range: $50-250); per photo (range: $25-175). Sample copies for 9×12 SAE and 5 first-class stamps. Writer's guidelines for SASE.

THE SUBJECT INDEX, located in the back of this book, lists book publishers and magazines according to the fiction and nonfiction subjects they seek.

Tips: "Look for teens who are involved in money-making enterprises and submit articles that fit with the theme and style of our publication."

☑ **YOUNG SALVATIONIST**, The Salvation Army, 615 Slaters Lane, P.O. Box 269, Alexandria VA 22313. (703)684-5500. Published 10 times/year. Estab. 1984. Circ. 50,000. **Managing Editor:** Tim Clark. "We accept material with clear Christian content written for high school age teenagers. *Young Salvationist* is published for teenage members of The Salvation Army, an evangelical part of the Christian Church."

Fiction: Young adults/teens: contemporary religious. Buys 12-20 mss/year. Average word length: 750-1,200. Byline given.

Nonfiction: Young adults/teens: religious—careers, health, interview/profile, social issues, sports. Buys 40-50 mss/year. Average word length: 750-1,200. Byline given.

How to Contact/Writers: Fiction/nonfiction: Query with published clips or send complete ms. Reports on queries/mss in 1 month. Will consider simultaneous submissions.

Illustrations: Buys 3-5 illustrations/issue; 20-30 illustrations/year. Reviews ms/illustration packages from artists. Send ms with art. Illustrations only: Query; send résumé, promo sheet, portfolio, tearsheets. Reports back only if interested. Samples returned with SASE; samples filed. Credit line given.

Photography: Purchases photography from freelancers. Looking for teens in action.

Terms: Pays on acceptance. Buys first North American serial rights, first rights, one-time rights or second serial (reprint) rights for mss. Purchases one-time rights for artwork and photographs. Original artwork returned at job's completion "if requested." For mss, pays 15¢/word; 10¢/word for reprints. Pays $100-150 color (cover) illustration; $50-100 b&w (inside) illustration; $100-150 color (inside) illustration. Sample copy for 9×12 SAE and 4 first-class stamps. Writer's guidelines for #10 SASE.

Tips: "Ask for theme list/sample copy! Write 'up,' not down to teens. Aim at young *adults*, not children." Wants "less fiction, more 'journalistic' nonfiction."

YOUR BIG BACKYARD, National Wildlife Federation, 8925 Leesburg Pike, Vienna VA 22184. (703)790-4515. Fax: (703)827-2585. E-mail: johnsond@nwf.org. **Articles/Fiction Editor:** Donna Johnson. **Art Director:** Tamara Tylenda. **Photo Editor:** Stephen B. Freligh. Monthly magazine (includes a parents newsletter bound into the center to be pulled out.) Estab. 1980. Circ. 400,000. Purpose of the magazine is to educate young children (ages 3-6) about nature and wildlife in a fun, interactive and entertaining way. 90% of publication aimed at juvenile market (10% is parents' newsletter).

• *Your Big Backyard* cannot accept submissions of fiction and nonfiction until 2000. They are still open to receiving brief poetry. See Reaching the Youngest Audience: Writing for Babies and Toddlers on page 64 for more from *Your Big Backyard* editor Donna Johnson.

Fiction: Picture-oriented material: animal, fantasy, humorous, multicultural, nature/environment. Young readers: adventure, animal, humorous, multicultural, nature/environment. "We do not want fiction that does not involve animals or nature in some way." Buys 12 mss/year. Average word length: 200-1,000. Byline given.

Nonfiction: Picture-oriented material, young readers: animal, arts/crafts, games/puzzles, nature/environment. Wants no articles that deal with subjects other than nature. Buys 2 mss/year. Average word length: 50-100.

Poetry: Reviews poetry. Buys 5-6 poems/year. Maximum length: 15 words or 25 lines.

How to Contact/Writers: Fiction: send complete ms. Nonfiction: Query with published clips; send complete ms. Reports on queries/mss in 2 weeks. Publishes ms 4 months after acceptance. Will consider simultaneous submissions, electronic submission via disk or modem and previously published work.

Illustration: Buys 5 illustrations/issue 60 illustrations/year. Uses color artwork only. Reviews ms/illustration packages from artists. Send ms with dummy. Contact: Donna Johnson, art director. Illustrations only: Send promo sheet, portfolio, slides, tearsheets. Contact: Tammy Tylenda, art director. Reports back only if interested. Samples not returned; filed. Credit line given.

Photography: Wants animal photos. Uses 35mm transparencies. Send unsolicited photos by mail ("professional photographers only"). Reports in 2 months.

Terms: Pays on acceptance. Buys one-time rights, reprint rights for mss. Buys one-time rights for artwork and photographs. Original artwork returned at job's completion. Pays $250-750 for stories; $50-200 for articles. Additional payment for ms/illustration packages and for photos accompanying articles. Pays illustrators $200-500 for color inside. Pays photographers per photo (range: $200-600). Sample copies for $1.

Tips: "With regard to fiction, we accept stories in which the main characters can be talking animals; however, the storyline should deal with some aspect of the animal's natural history or habitat. The book *Stellaluna* is an example of the type or good fiction we want to see more of."

[N] YOUTH CHALLENGE, United Pentecostal Church International, 8855 Dunn Rd., Hazelwood MO 63042. (314)837-7300. **Articles Editors:** R.M. Davis and P.D. Buford. Weekly leaflet. Estab. 1994. Circ. 4,500.

Fiction: Young adults: religious. Buys 52-70 mss/year. Average word length: 1,200-1,600. Byline given.

Nonfiction: Young adults: religion. Buys 26-40 mss/year. Average word length: 1,200-1,600. Byline given.

How to Contact/Writers: Fiction/nonfiction: send complete ms. Reports on mss in 3-12 months. Publishes ms 3-12 months after acceptance. Will consider simultaneous submissions.

Illustration: Samples returned with SASE.

Terms: Pays on publication. Buys reprint rights for mss. Sample copies for #10 SAE and 1 first-class stamp. Writer's guidelines for SASE.

[N] YOUTH UPDATE, St. Anthony Messenger Press, 1615 Republic St., Cincinnati OH 45210. (513)241-5615. E-mail: carolann@americancatholic.org. Website: http://www.AmericanCatholic.org. **Articles Editor:** Carol Ann Morrow. **Art Director:** June Pfaff Daley. Monthly newsletter. Estab. 1982. Circ. 23,000. "Each issue focuses on one topic only. *Youth Update* addresses the faith and Christian life questions of young people and is designed to attract, instruct, guide and challenge its audience by applying the gospel to modern problems and situations. The students who read *Youth Update* vary in their religious education and reading ability. Write for average high school students. These students are 15-year-olds with a C+ average. Assume that they have paid attention to religious instruction and remember a little of what 'sister' said. Aim more toward 'table talk' than 'teacher talk.' "

Nonfiction: Young adults/teens: religion. Buys 12 mss/year. Average word length: 2,200-2,300. Byline given.

How to Contact/Writers: Nonfiction: Query. Reports on queries/mss in 2 months. Will consider computer printout and electronic submissions via disk.

Photography: Buys photos from freelancers. Uses photos of teens (high-school age) with attention to racial diversity and with emotion.

Terms: Pays on acceptance. Buys first North American serial rights for mss. Buys one-time rights for photographs. Pays $300-500 for articles. Pays photographers per photo ($50-75 minimum). Sample copy free with #10 SASE. Writer's guidelines free on request.

Tips: "Read the newsletter yourself—3 issues at least. In the past, our publication has dealt with a variety of topics including: dating, Lent, teenage pregnancy, baptism, loneliness, violence, confirmation and the Bible. When writing, use the *New American Bible* as translation. Interested in church-related topics."

ZILLIONS For Kids From Consumer Reports, Consumers Union, 101 Truman Ave., Yonkers NY 10703-1057. (914)378-2551. Fax: (914)378-2904. **Articles Editor:** Karen McNulty. **Art Director:** Rob Jenter. Bimonthly magazine. Estab. 1980. Circ. 300,000. "*Zillions* is the consumer reports for kids (with heavy emphasis on fun!) We offer kids information on product tests, ads and fads, money smarts, and more."

• *ZILLIONS* works on assignment only. They do not accept unsolicited manuscripts; query first.

Nonfiction: Children/young adults: arts/crafts, careers, games/puzzles, health, hobbies, how-to, humorous, nature/environment, problem-solving, social issues, sports. "Will consider story ideas on kid money matters, marketing to kids and anything that educates kids to be smart consumers." Buys 10 mss/year. Average word length: 800-1,000.

How to Contact/Writers: Nonfiction: Query with résumé and published clips. "We'll contact if interested (within a few months probably)." Publishes ms 2 months after acceptance.

Terms: Pays on publication. Buys all rights for ms. Pays $1,000 for articles. Writer's guidelines for SASE.

Tips: "Read the magazine!"

Greeting Cards, Puzzles & Games

In this section you'll find companies that produce puzzles, games, greeting cards and other items (like coloring books, stickers and giftwrap) especially for kids. These are items you'll find in children's sections of bookstores, toy stores, departments stores and card shops.

Because these markets create an array of products, their needs vary greatly. Some may need the service of freelance writers for greeting card copy or slogans for buttons and stickers. Others are in need of illustrators for coloring books or photographers for puzzles. Artists should send in copies of their work that art directors can keep on file—never originals. Carefully read through the listings to find a company's needs, and send for guidelines and catalogs if they're available, just as you would for a book or magazine publisher. For more submission tips, be sure to read the Insider Report with illustrator Joe Lacey on page 266.

If you'd like to find out more about the greeting card industry beyond the market for children, there are a number of resources to help you. *Greetings Today* is the official publication of the Greeting Card Association. For information call (800)627-0932. Illustrators should check out *The Complete Guide to Greeting Card Design & Illustration*, by Eva Szela (North Light Books) and *Greeting Card Designs*, by Joanne Fink (PBC Intl. Inc.). For a complete list of companies, consult the latest edition of *Artist's & Graphic Designer's Market* (Writer's Digest Books). Writers should see *How to Write & Sell Greeting Cards, Bumper Stickers, T-shirts and Other Fun Stuff*, by Molly Wigand (Writer's Digest Books).

☑ **AMCAL**, 2500 Bisso Lane, #500, Concord CA 94520. (925)689-9930. Fax: (925)689-0108. Vice President/Creative Development: Judy Robertson. Estab. 1975. Cards, calendars, desk diaries, boxed Christmas cards, limited edition prints and more.
Illustration: Receives over 150 submissions/year. "AMCAL publishes high quality full color, narrative and decorative art for a wide market from traditional to contemporary. "Currently we are very interested in country folk art and decorative styles. Know the trends and the market. Juvenile illustration should have some adult appeal. We don't publish cartoon, humorous or gag art, or bold graphics. We sell to mostly small, exclusive gift retailers. Submissions are always accepted for future lines." To contact, send samples, photocopies, slides and SASE for return of submission. Reports in approx. 1 month. Pays on publication. Pay negotiable/usually advance on royalty. Rights purchased negotiable. Guideline sheets for #10 SASE and 1 first-class stamp.

A/V CONCEPTS CORP., 30 Montauk Blvd., Oakdale NY 11769. (516)567-7227. Fax: (516)567-8745. Editor: Laura Solimene. President: Philip Solimene. Estab. 1969. "We are an educational publisher. We publish books for the K-12 market—primarily language arts and math and reading." 20% of products are made for kids or have kids' themes.
Writing: Needs freelance writing for classic workbooks only: adaptations from fine literature. Makes 5-10 assignments/year. To contact, send cover letter and writing samples and 9×12 SASE. Reports in 3 weeks. For writing assignments, pays by the project ($700-1,000). Pays on publication. Buys all rights.
Illustration: Needs freelance illustration for classic literature adaptations, fine art, some cartoons, super heroes. Makes 15-20 illustration assignments/year. Needs "super hero-like characters in four-color and b&w." To contact, send cover letter and photocopies. Reports back in 3 weeks. For artwork, pays by the project (range: $200-1,000). Pays on publication. Buys all rights.
Tips: Submit seasonal material 4 months in advance. "We're getting into CD-ROM development."

☑ **AVANTI PRESS, INC.**, 2500 Penobscot Bldg., Detroit MI 48226. (313)961-0022. Submit images to this address: Avanti, Suite 602, 134 Spring St., New York NY 10012. (212)941-9000. Website: http://www.avantipress.com. Contact: Editing Dept.. Estab. 1979. Greeting card company. Publishes photographic greeting cards—nonseasonal and seasonal.
Photography: Purchases photography from freelancers. Buys stock and assigns work. Buys approximately 150 stock images/year. Makes approximately 150 assignments/year. Wants "narrative, storytelling images,

graphically strong and colorful!" Uses b&w/color prints; 35mm, 2¼×2¼ and 4×5 transparencies. "Call for submission guidelines or visit our Website." Pays either a flat fee or a royalty which is discussed at time of purchase. Pays on acceptance. Buys exclusive product rights (world-wide card rights). Credit line given. Photographer's guidelines for SASE.

Tips: At least 75% of products have kids' and pets themes. Submit seasonal material 9 months-1 year in advance. "All images submitted should express some kind of sentiment which either fits an occasion or can be versed and sent to the recipient to convey some feeling."

THE BEISTLE COMPANY, P.O. Box 10, Shippensburg PA 17257. (717)532-2131. Fax: (717)532-7789. E-mail: beistle@mail.cvn.net. Website: http://www.beistle.com. Product Manager: C. Michelle Luhrs-Wiest. Estab. 1900. Paper products company. Produces decorations and party goods, posters—baby, baptism, birthday, holidays, educational, wedding/anniversary, graduation, ethnic themes, and New Year parties. 50% of products are made for kids' or have kids themes.

Illustration: Needs freelance illustration for decorations, party goods, school supplies, point-of-purchase display materials and gift wrap. Makes 100 illustration assignments/year. Prefers fanciful style, cute 4- to 5-color illustration in gouache and/or computer illustration. To contact, send cover letter, résumé, client list, promo piece. To query with specific ideas, phone, write or fax. Reports only if interested. Materials returned with SASE; materials filed. Pays by the project or by contractual agreement; price varies according to type of project. Pays on acceptance. Buys all rights. Artist's guidelines available for SASE.

Photography: Buys photography from freelancers. Buys stock and assigns work. Makes 30-50 assignments/year. Uses 35mm, 2¼×2¼, 4×5 transparencies. To contact, send cover letter, résumé, slides, client list, promo piece. Reports only if interested. Materials returned if accompanied with SASE; materials filed. Pays on acceptance. Buys first rights. Credit line sometimes given—depends on project. Guidelines available for SASE.

Tips: Submit seasonal material 6-8 months in advance.

BEPUZZLED/LOMBARD MARKETING, INC., 22 E. Newberry Rd., Bloomfield CT 06002. (860)769-5723. Fax: (860)769-5799. Creative Services Manager: Sue Tyska. Estab. 1987. Publishes mystery jigsaw puzzles, mystery dinner games. 30% of products are for kids or have kids' themes.

Writing: Needs freelance writing for short mystery stories. Makes 15-20 writing assignments/year. To contact, send cover letter and writing samples. Reports back in 3 weeks. Pays by the project ($1,800). Pays on publication. Buys all rights. No credit line given.

Photography: Needs freelance photographers for mystery jigsaw puzzles. Makes 20-30 photography assignments/year. Preferences announced when needed. To contact, send cover letter, résumé, client list and color promo pieces. Reports back in 2 months. Pays by the project. Pays on publication. Buys all rights.

Tips: "Send seasonal material six months in advance. Send SASE for guidelines. Submissions should be short and include idea of writing style, and an outline of ideas for visual and literal clues (six each, some with red herrings)."

BURGOYNE INC., 2030 E. Byberry Rd., Philadelphia PA 19116. (215)677-8000. Art Studio Manager: Mary Beth Burgoyne. Contact: Christine Cathers Donohue. Estab. 1907. Greeting card company. Publisher of Christmas and everyday cards.

Illustration: Interested in illustrations for greeting cards. To contact, send cover letter. To query with specific ideas, send slides, published samples. Be sure to include a SASE. Reports in 2 months. Materials filed. Pays on acceptance. Buys greeting card US and worldwide rights. Credit line sometimes given. Artist's guidelines for SASE.

Tips: "We are looking for new traditional Christmas artwork with a detailed children's book look. We are also looking for juvenile birthday and all-occasion artwork year round."

CREATE-A-CRAFT, P.O. Box 941293, Plano TX 75094-1293. Contact: Editor. Estab. 1967. Produces greeting cards, giftwrap, games, calendars, posters, stationery and paper tableware products for all ages.

**FOR EXPLANATIONS OF THESE SYMBOLS,
SEE THE INSIDE FRONT AND BACK COVERS OF THIS BOOK**

INSIDER REPORT

Mixing it up: Landing illustration assignments from Silly Putty to *Crayola Kids*

Though his name may not be familiar, you've probably seen Joe Lacey's art. He's carved out a lucrative career creating colorful, imaginative characters kids love. But instead of residing in storybooks, Lacey's quirky characters pop out at you from coloring books, kids' magazines, game boards and Silly Putty packages. Here, the Allentown, Pennsylvania illustrator, who taught illustration at both Syracuse and Kutztown Universities, lets you in on some trade secrets for landing assignments.

Joe Lacey

Is there a particular style or medium that lands more assignments than others?
The fact that I use a variety of mediums—gouache, acrylic, airbrush, oil, etc.—increases the amount of work I can get. To some art directors I am an airbrush illustrator, to others I am a computer illustrator. I asked some of my clients if my work would increase if I bought a computer. All of them said yes, so I went out and bought one. I didn't know how to use it, but today it counts for 50% of my work. The very first computer illustration I did was for *Crayola Kids* magazine. Like anything new, I made sure it was simple and not beyond my limited experience at the time. Today the illustrations I do on the computer are much more complex, but are no different in essence than illustrations I paint by hand. The computer is no different than the airbrush or technical pen. It is just another tool. Your work should look like it belongs to you, no matter what medium you use.

What's the best way to launch a career in children's product illustration?
I recommend working anywhere, doing anything, as long as it is in a field related to illustration. This is where you make contacts and learn about the field.

So often artists are advised to work in one medium and style, and limit their marketing to one niche, but I've been successful doing many different things and constantly changing. When I started out, many people told me my work was not focused enough and that I would not make it. But sometimes, a more general portfolio is useful when you're just starting out. I know it's the reason I first began getting jobs.

Find an area of illustration you like and focus on that. Bring more to the picture than just technique. So many students are impressed with technique, but never learn how to put a good illustration together. Study what other illustrators have done. Learn to see the big picture first before moving onto detail and technique. Technique is like following a recipe. But designing a good picture or coming up with creative ideas is difficult.

INSIDER REPORT, *Lacey*

JOE LACEY·ILLUSTRATION

"The Nine Nolan Brothers" Find what each has in common, left to right, up & down and diagonally. Copyright 1995 Crayola Kids Magazine.

1137 NORTH 19TH STREET ALLENTOWN, PENNSYLVANIA 18104 TEL/FAX 610-433-4696

Joe Lacey's illustration of "The Nine Nolan Brothers" first appeared in *Crayola Kids* magazine. (Readers look for what each brother has in common, left to right, up and down, and diagonally.) With the addition of his logo and contact information, Lacey turned the assignment into a promo piece. "Primarily I send out postcards with a single illustration reproduced on the front and my name and phone number on the back. It is an inexpensive way to promote yourself. An art director has to look at a postcard, even for a few seconds."

What types of promotional samples do you send?

Primarily I send out postcards with a single illustration reproduced on the front and my name and phone number on the back. It is an inexpensive way to promote yourself. An art director has to look at a postcard, even for a few seconds. Most art directors keep a file of samples for future reference. I try to do mailings three to four times a year. It's important to mail frequently; an art director may not have a need for your style today, but could have a need for it in the future. Between mailings I make color copies of recent jobs or jobs I feel meet a specific need of a client and send those off. Not every potential client receives the same samples. I have also found the Internet to be a good source for promotion and finding new clients.

I do very few portfolio drop-offs or interviews. If you have enough printed samples, drop-offs become less necessary. The key is getting your work seen by the right people. When I first started out, I was sending to the wrong people and not doing any follow-up mailings. Most of the time it takes multiple mailings to get a job. You can't stop after one mailing and you have to constantly update your mailing list. *Children's Writer's & Illustrator's Market* is great because it gives me enough general information about a company's needs so I can target them better. I also find sending out cards to existing clients, even if the card has nothing to do with what they produce, helps remind them you have worked for them before. I mail to all my clients regardless of how steady the work is from them. I know that is why I get some callbacks from old clients.

How do you get your foot in the door with big clients like Binney & Smith or Fisher-Price?

Though portfolio reviews aren't necessary to land most clients, I always try to set up interviews with the larger companies. Because of the wide range of services I offer, I find it much easier to show the work in person. I drove seven hours for my interview with Fisher-Price. They had never even seen my work and I was taking a big chance. The interview lasted about an hour with roughly ten art directors in one room. I remember driving home because it was the hottest day of the year and my car had no air conditioning. Had I not gotten any work, that would have been a horrible story. It took about nine months and several mailings before I got my first assignment with them. I have been working steadily with them for five years now. But for every successful interview I had about ten that were not. Once you get your foot in the door, make sure you find out exactly what that client needs and see if you can offer it to them.

Do you advertise in sourcebooks?

I advertised in a major sourcebook this year for the first time. Sourcebooks offer a great way to get your work seen by clients you would never think of. When I do my mailings, I research and choose the clients I would like to work with. When I advertise, clients choose me directly. I receive calls from agencies and book publishers I would have never thought to approach on my own. I was assigned one of the biggest jobs of my career as a result of my advertisement, so the ads can more than pay off.

On the down side, advertising can be very expensive, up to $3,000. I really can't say that an illustrator should or shouldn't advertise right away. It all depends upon how developed your art is—if it's strong and original, an ad will generate calls. Research many different sourcebooks and decide which is best. Try to be objective when comparing your art to those already in the book. If you feel your work is not strong enough, wait until

INSIDER REPORT, *Lacey*

next year. It took me five years to finally decide my work was strong enough.

Do you have an agent?

I have never had an agent. I enjoy having control over every aspect of my business. If you don't like doing your own mailings or calling clients to ask for money, then maybe an agent is for you. I don't like giving up 20-30% for this service. If I felt an agent could get me the type of work I want at a higher pay scale, I might reconsider my position.

What are you working on now and what are your plans for the future?

I just finished working on several illustrations for some children's magazines (*Crayola Kids* and *Kid City*) and some educational spot illustrations for Fisher-Price. Name recognition is becoming more and more important to me. Working for toy companies is great and pays very well, but most of the work remains anonymous. So I've begun working on some of my own holiday illustrations which I hope to license. I also have some ideas jotted down in the computer for a children's book I plan to write and illustrate. I can't wait to get started—if I can ever find the time!

—*Mary Cox*

One of Joe Lacey's favorite assignments was four package illustrations for Silly Putty—Original and Glitter (pictured), Florescent and Glow-in-the-Dark. "I felt really close to those characters," Lacey says. "Character development, when you are free to put some of yourself into the characters, is very satisfying."

Illustration: Works with 3 freelance artists/year. Buys 3-5 designs/illustrations/year. Primary age concentration is 4-8 year old market. Prefers artists with experience in cartooning. Works on assignment only. Buys freelance designs/illustrations mainly for greetings cards and T-shirts. Also uses freelance artists for calligraphy, P-O-P displays, paste-up and mechanicals. Considers pen & ink, watercolor, acrylics and colored pencil. Prefers humorous and "cartoons that will appeal to families. Must be cute, appealing, etc. No religious, sexual implications or off-beat humor." Produces material for all holidays and seasons. Contact only through artist's agent. Some samples are filed; samples not filed are not returned. Reports only if interested. Write for appointment to show portfolio of original/final art, final reproduction/product, slides, tearsheets, color and b&w. Original artwork is not returned. "Payment depends upon the assignment, amount of work involved, production costs, etc. involved in the project." Buys all rights. For guidelines and sample cards, send $2.50 and #10 SASE.

Tips: Submit 6 months in advance. "Demonstrate an ability to follow directions exactly. Too many submit artwork that has no relationship to what we produce. No phone calls accepted. Follow directions given. Do not ignore them."

CREATIF LICENSING CORP., 31 Old Town Crossing, Mt. Kisco NY 10549. (914)241-6211. E-mail: creatiflic@aol.com. President: Paul Cohen. Estab. 1975. Gift industry licensing agency. Publishes greeting cards, puzzles, posters, calendars, fabrics, home furnishings, all gifts. 75% of products are made for kids or have kids' themes.

Illustration: Needs freelance illustration for children's greeting cards, all gift and home furnishings. Makes many illustration assignments/month. Uses both color and b&w artwork. To contact, send cover letter, résumé, client list, published samples, photocopies, portfolio, promo piece and SASE. Reports in 1 month. Materials returned with SASE; materials filed. For greeting cards, pays royalty and advance. For other artwork, pays royalty and advance. Pays on acceptance or publication. Artist's guidelines available for SASE.

Tips: Submit seasonal material 8-12 months in advance.

DESIGN DESIGN INC., P.O. Box 2266, Grand Rapids MI 49501. (616)774-2448. Fax: (616)774-4020. President: Don Kallil. Creative Director: Tom Vituj. Estab. 1986. Greeting card company. 5% of products are made for kids or have kids themes.

Writing: Needs freelance writing for children's greeting cards. Makes 15 freelance writing assignments/month; 200/year. For greeting cards, prefers both rhymed and unrhymed verse ideas. To contact, send cover letter and writing samples. Materials returned with SASE; materials not filed. For greeting cards, pays flat fee. Buys all rights or exclusive product rights; negotiable. No credit line given. Writer's guidelines for SASE.

Illustration: Needs freelance illustration for children's greeting cards and related products. Makes 15 freelance illustration assignments/month; 200/year. To contact, send cover letter, published samples, color or b&w photocopies, color or b&w promo pieces or portfolio. Reports in 1 month. Returns materials with SASE. Pays by royalty. Buys all rights or exclusive product rights; negotiable. Artist's guidelines available for SASE.

Photography: Buys stock and assigns work. Looking for the following subject matter: babies, animals, dog, cats, humorous situations. Uses 4×5 transparencies or high quality 35mm slides. To contact, send cover letter with slides, stock photo list, published samples and promo piece. Materials returned with SASE; materials not filed. Pays royalties. Buys all rights or exclusive product rights; negotiable. Photographer's guidelines for SASE.

Tips: Seasonal material must be submitted 1 year in advance.

☑ EVERYTHING GONZO!, P.O. Box 1322, Roslyn Heights NY 11577. (516)488-8825. Fax: (516)826-4353. E-mail: polygonzo@aol.com. Owner: H.J. Fleischer. Toy designer, licensing agent and manufacturer. Designs, licenses, manufactures toys, gifts and related products. Manufactures novelties (educational, impulse, creative), puzzles, games; publishes booklets. 100% of products are made for kids or have kids' themes.

Illustration: Needs freelance illustration for toy concepts. Makes 100 illustration assignments/year. Uses both color and b&w artwork. To contact, send cover letter, résumé, published samples, portfolio, photocopies, promo pieces. To query with specific ideas, write to request disclosure form first. Reports only if interested. Materials returned with SASE; materials filed. For other artwork, pays by the hour($10); negotiable royalty. Pays on acceptance. Credit line sometimes given.

Photography: Buys photography from freelancers. Works on assignment only. Uses transparencies. To contact, send cover letter, published samples, portfolio, promo piece. Reports only if interested. Materials returned; materials filed. Pays on acceptance. Credit line sometimes given.

Tips: Submit seasonal material 6 months in advance. "Interested in unique toy/game/product concepts."

C. Michelle Luhrs-Weist, product manager for The Beistle Company, used the Wayne, Pennslyvania-based Brookins Group, a company that represents a range of artists, to create these festive Christmas illustrations. The gouache illustrations were used to make Glass Magnets™ for decorating windows. She chose the designs because they were "cute, whimiscal but tight illustrations." Luhrs-Weist sees continued growth in the gift product market and a "greater juvenile product demand due to the recent baby boom."

FAX-PAX USA, INC., 37 Jerome Ave., Bloomfield CT 06002. (203)242-3333. Fax: (203)242-7102. Editor: Stacey L. Savin. Estab. 1990. Buys 1 freelance project/year. Publishes art and history flash cards. Needs include US history, natural history.

Writing/Illustration: Buys all rights. Pays on publication. Cannot return material.

Tips: "We need concise, interesting, well-written 'mini-lessons' on various subjects including U.S. and natural history."

Ⓝ GALLERY GRAPHICS, INC., 227 Main St., P.O. Box 502, Noel MO 64854. (417)475-6191. Fax: (417)475-6494. Marketing Director: Terri Galvin. Estab. 1979. Greeting card, paper products company. Specializes in products including prints, cards, calendars, stationery, magnets, framed items, books, flue covers and sachets. We market towards all age groups. Publishes reproductions of children's books from the 1800's.

Illustration: Needs freelance illustration for children's greeting cards, other children's products. Makes 2 illustration assignments/year. Prefers children, angels, animals in any medium. Uses color artwork only. To contact, send cover letter, published samples, photocopies (prefer color), promo pieces. Reports in 4-6 weeks. "We'll return materials at our cost." Materials not filed. "I'll usually make copies." For greeting cards, pays flat fee of $100-700, or royalty of 5-7% for life of card. Pays on sales. Buys exclusive product rights. Credit line sometimes given.

Tips: "We've significantly increased our licensing over the last year. Most of these are set up on a 5% royalty basis. Submit various art subjects."

GREAT AMERICAN PUZZLE FACTORY, INC., 16 S. Main St., S. Norwalk CT 06854. (203)838-4240. Fax: (203)838-2065. E-mail: gapfctad@aol.com. Website: http://www.greatamericanpuzzle.com. Art Director: Anne Mulligan. Estab. 1976. Produces puzzles. 70% of products are made for kids or have kids' themes.

Illustration: Needs freelance illustration for puzzles. Makes over 20 freelance assignments/year. To contact, send cover letter, color photocopies and color promo pieces (no slides or original art) with SASE. Reports in 1 month. Artists guidelines available for SASE. Rights purchased vary. Buys all rights to puzzles. Pays on publication. Pay varies.

Photography: Needs local cityscapes for regional puzzles. "Photos that we have used have been of wildlife. We do occasionally use city skylines. These are only for custom jobs, though, and must be 4×5 or larger format."

Tips: Targets ages 4-12 and adult. "Go to a toy store and look at puzzles. See what is appropriate. No slides. Send color copies (3-4) for style. Looking for whimsical, fantasy and animal themes with a bright, contemporary style. Not too washy or cute. We often buy reprint rights to existing work. Graphic, children's-book style work is ideal for puzzles." Submit seasonal material 1 year in advance.

☑ INTERNATIONAL PLAYTHINGS, INC., 120 Riverdale Rd., Riverdale NJ 07457. (973)831-1400. Fax: (973)616-7775. Product Manager: Linda Golowko. Estab. 1968. Toy/game company. Distributes and markets children's toys, games and puzzles in specialty toy markets. 100% of products are made for kids or have kids' themes.

Illustration: Needs freelance illustration for children's puzzles and games. Makes 20-30 illustration assignments/year. Prefers fine-quality, original illustration for children's puzzles. Uses color artwork only. To contact, send published samples, slides, portfolio, or color photocopies or promo pieces. Reports in 1 month only if interested. Materials filed. For artwork, pays by the project (range: $500-2,000). Pays on publication. Buys one-time rights, negotiable.

Tips: "Mail correspondence only, please. No phone calls."

☑ JILLSON & ROBERTS GIFT WRAP, 5 Watson Ave., Irvine CA 92618. (949)859-8781. Art Director: Josh Neufeld. Estab. 1973. Paper products company. Makes gift wrap/gift bags. 20% of products are made for kids or have kids' themes.

Illustration: Needs freelance illustration for children's gift wrap. Makes 6-12 illustration assignments/ year. Wants children/baby/juvenile themes. To contact, send cover letter. Reports in 1 month. Returns material with SASE; materials filed. For wrap and bag designs, pays flat fee of $250. Pays on publication. Rights negotiable. Artist's guidelines for SASE.

Tips: Seasonal material should be submitted up to 3½ months in advance. "We produce two lines of gift wrap per year: one everyday line and one Christmas line. The closing date for everyday is June 30th and Christmas is September 15."

☑ NOVO CARD PUBLISHERS, INC., 3630 W. Pratt Ave., Lincolnwood IL 60645. (847)763-0077. Fax: (847)763-0020. Contact: Thomas Benjamin, art production. Estab. 1926. Greeting card company.

Company publishes greeting cards, note/invitation packs and gift envelopes for middle market. Publishes greeting cards (Novo Card/Cloud-9). 20% of products are made for kids or have kids' themes.
Writing: Needs freelance writing for children's greeting cards. Makes 400 writing assignments/year. Other needs for freelance writing include invitation notes. To contact send writing samples. To query with specific ideas, write to request disclosure form first. Reports back in 1 month only if interested. Materials returned only with SASE; materials filed. For greeting cards, pays flat fee of $2/line. Pays on acceptance. Buys all rights. Credit line sometimes given. Writer's guidelines available for SASE.
Illustration: Needs freelance illustration for children's greeting cards. Makes 1,000 illustration assignments/year. Prefers just about all types: traditional, humor, contemporary, etc. To contact, send published samples, slides and color photocopies. To query with specific ideas write to request disclosure form first. Reports in 1 month. Materials returned with SASE; materials filed. For greeting cards, pay negotiable. Pays on acceptance. Rights negotiable. Credit line sometimes given. Artist's guidelines available for SASE.
Photography: Buys stock and assigns work. Buys 30-40 stock images/year. Wants all types: prefers contemporary images for the time being. Uses color and b&w prints; 35mm transparencies. To contact, send slides, stock photo list, published samples, paper copies acceptable. Reports in 1 month. Materials returned with SASE; materials filed. Pays negotiable rate. Pays on acceptance. Rights negotiable. Credit line sometimes given. Guidelines for SASE.
Tips: Submit seasonal material 10-12 months in advance. "Novo has extensive lines of greeting cards: everyday, seasonal (all) and alternative lives (over 24 separate lines of note card packs and gift enclosures). Our lines encompass all types of styles and images."

P.S. GREETINGS/FANTUS PAPER PRODUCTS, 5060 N. Kimberly Ave., Chicago IL 60630. (773)725-9308. Art Director: Jennifer Dodson. Greeting card company. Publishes boxed and individual counter greeting cards. Seasons include: Christmas, every major holiday and everyday.
Writing: Needs freelance writing for children's greeting cards. To contact, send writing samples. Reports in 6 weeks. Material returned only if accompanied with SASE. For greeting cards, pays flat fee. Pays on acceptance. Buys all rights. Credit line given. Writer's guidelines free with SASE.
Illustration: Needs freelance illustration for children's greeting cards. Makes about 100 illustration assignments/year. Open to all mediums, all themes. To contact, send published samples and photocopies only. Reports in 6 months. Returns materials with SASE; materials filed. For greeting cards, pays flat fee. Pays on acceptance. Buys all rights. Credit line given. Artist's guidelines free with SASE.
Photography: Buys photography from freelancers. Buys stock. Wants florals, animals, seasonal (Christmas, Easter, valentines, etc.). Uses transparencies (any size). To contact, send slides. Reports in 6 weeks. Materials returned with SASE; materials filed. Pays on acceptance. Buys all rights. Credit line given. Photographer's guidelines free with SASE.
Tips: Seasonal material should be submitted 6 months in advance.

PANDA INK, P.O. Box 5129, West Hills CA 91308-5129. (818)340-8061. Fax: (818)883-6193. Owner: Art/Creative Director: Ruth Ann Epstein. Estab. 1981. Greeting card company and producer of clocks, magnets, bookmarks. Produces Judaica—whimsical, metaphysical, general, everyday. Publishes greeting cards. 15% of products are made for kids or have kids' themes.
Writing: Needs freelance writing for children's greeting cards. Makes 1-2 writing assignments/year. For greeting cards, accepts both rhymed and unrhymed verse ideas. Looks for greeting card writing which is Judaica or metaphysical. To contact, send cover letter, ask for guidelines, send SASE. To query with specific ideas, write to request disclosure form first. Reports in 1 month. Materials returned with SASE; materials filed. For greeting cards, pays flat fee of $3-20. Pays on acceptance. Rights negotiable. Credit line sometimes given.
Illustration: Needs freelance illustration for children's greeting cards, magnets, bookmarks. Makes 1 illustration assignment/year. Needs Judaica (Hebrew wording), metaphysical themes. Uses color artwork only. To contact, send cover letter. To query with specific ideas, write to request disclosure form first. Reports in 2 months. Materials returned with SASE; materials filed. Payment is negotiable. Pays on acceptance. Rights negotiable. Credit line sometimes given. Artist's guidelines available for SASE.
Tips: Submit seasonal material 1 year in advance. "Always send SASE."

A SELF-ADDRESSED, STAMPED ENVELOPE (SASE) should always be included with submissions within your own country. When sending material to other countries, include a self-addressed envelope (SAE) and International Reply Coupons (IRCs).

PLUM GRAPHICS INC., P.O. Box 136, Prince St. Station, New York NY 10012. Phone/fax: (212)337-0999. Owner: Yvette Cohen. Estab. 1983. Greeting card company. Produces die-cut greeting cards for ages 5-105. Publishes greeting cards and message boards.

Writing: Needs freelance writing for greeting cards. Makes 4 writing assignments/year. Looks for "greeting card writing which is fun. Tired of writing which is boring." To contact, send SASE for guidelines. Contact: Michelle Ingram. Reports in 2 months. Materials returned with SASE; materials filed. For greeting cards, pays flat fee of $40. Pays on publication. Buys all rights. Writer's guidelines available for SASE.

Illustration: Needs freelance illustration for greeting cards. Makes 10-15 freelance illustration assignments/year. Prefers very tight artwork, mostly realism. Uses color artwork only. To contact, send b&w photocopies. Contact: Yvette Cohen. Reports only if interested. Materials returned with SASE; materials filed. For greeting cards, pays flat fee of $350-450 "plus $50 each time we reprint." Pays on publication. Buys exclusive product rights. Credit line given.

Tips: Submit seasonal material 1 year in advance. "Go to a store and look at our cards and style before submitting work."

☑ **POCKETS OF LEARNING LTD.**, 30 Cutler St., Suite 101, Warren RI 02885. (800)635-2994. Fax: (800)370-1580. Product Manager: Darlene Fratelli. Estab. 1989. Educational soft toy company. Specializes in design, manufacture and distribution of high-quality educational cloth books, soft sculptures, wallhangings, travel bags and gifts. 100% of products are made for children ranging from birth to 6 years old.

Illustration: Needs freelance illustration for educational cloth toys. Makes 5 illustration assignments/year. "We introduce 20-30 new products per year, including cloth books, travel bags, soft sculpture and wallhangings." Uses both color and b&w artwork. To contact, send cover letter, slides, photocopies. To query with specific ideas, write to request disclosure form first. Pays on acceptance. Buys all rights.

N RED FARM STUDIO, 1135 Roosevelt Ave., P.O. Box 347, Pawtucket RI 02862. (401)728-9300. Contact: Production Coordinator. Estab. 1949. Greeting card company. Publishes coloring books and paintables.

Illustration: Needs freelance illustration for children's traditional subject greeting cards, coloring books and paintables. Makes 1 illustration assignments/month; 6-12/year. Prefers "watercolor, realistic styles yet cute." For first contact, request art guidelines with SASE. Reports in 2-4 weeks. Returns materials with SASE. Appropriate materials are kept on file. "We work on assignment using ink line work (coloring books) or pencil renderings (paintables)." Buys all rights. Credit line given and artist may sign artwork. Artist's guidelines for SASE.

Tips: 20% of products are made for kids or have kids' themes. Majority of freelance assignments made during January-May/yearly. "Research companies before sending submissions to determine whether your styles are compatible."

N SHULSINGER SALES, INC., 50 Washington St., Brooklyn NY 11201. (718)852-0042. Fax: (718)935-9691. President: Miriam Gutfeld. Estab. 1950. Greeting card and paper products company. "We are a Judaica company, distributing products such as greeting cards, books, paperware, puzzles, games, novelty items—all with a Jewish theme." Publishes greeting cards, novelties, coloring books and puzzles.

Writing: Looks for greeting card writing which can be sent by children to adults and sent by adults to children (of all ages). Makes 10-20 freelance writing assignments/year. To contact, send cover letter. To query with specific ideas, write to request disclosure form first. Reports in 2 weeks. Materials returned with SASE; materials filed. For greeting cards, pays flat fee (this includes artwork). Pays on acceptance. Buys exclusive product rights.

Illustration: Needs freelance illustration for children's greeting cards, books, novelties, games. Makes 10-20 illustration assignments/year. "The only requirement is a Jewish theme." To contact, send cover letter and photocopies, color if possible. To query with specific ideas, write to request disclosure form first. Reports in 2 weeks. Returns materials with SASE; materials filed. For children's greeting cards, pays flat fee (this includes writing). For other artwork, pays by the project. Pays on acceptance. Buys exclusive product rights. Credit line sometimes given. Artist's guidelines not available.

Tips: 60% of products are made for kids or have kids' themes. Seasonal material should be submitted 6 months in advance.

SMART ART, INC., P.O. Box 661, Chatham NJ 07928-0661. (973)635-1690. Fax: (973)635-2011. E-mail: smartart1@juno.com. Website: http://www.smartart.net. President: Barb Hauck-Mah. Estab. 1992. Greeting card company. Publishes photo-insert cards for card, gift and photo shops. About 10% of products are made for kids or have kids' themes.

Illustration: Needs freelance illustration for photo-insert cards. Makes 12-14 illustration assignments/year. Uses color artwork only. To contact, send color photocopies. To query with specific ideas, write to request confidentiality form. Reports in 2-3 months. Materials returned with SASE; materials not filed. For greeting cards, pays annual royalties for life of card or 5 years. Pays on publication. Credit line given. Artist's guidelines available for SASE.

Tips: Submit seasonal material 6-8 months in advance. "Smart Art specializes in a unique, premium quality line of photo-insert cards for the holidays, baby announcements, weddings and all-season occasions. Our cards feature watercolor or collage borders on textured, recycled paper. Designs should complement horizontal and vertical photos. Generally, our freelance designers are new to the greeting card/paper goods industry. Artists come from varied backgrounds, including an art teacher, a textile designer and several children's book illustrators. We are looking for 'border design' artwork rendered in pen & ink with watercolors or in cut/torn paper. We are interested in artists who can create interesting abstract textures as well as representational designs."

STANDARD PUBLISHING, 8121 Hamilton Ave., Cincinnati OH 45231. (513)931-4050. Fax: (513)931-0950. Director: Diane Stortz. Christian Education Editor: Ruth Frederick. Creative Director: Colleen Davis. Estab. 1866. Publishes children's books and teacher helps for the religious market. 75% of products are made for kids or have kids' themes.

● Standard also has a listing in Book Publishers.

Writing: Considers puzzle books, activity books and games. Reports in 3 months. Payment method varies. Credit line given.

Illustration: Needs freelance illustration for puzzle, activity books, teacher helps. Makes 6-10 illustration assignments/year. To contact, send cover letter and photocopies. Reports back in 3 months if interested. Payment method varies. Credit line given.

Photography: Buys a limited amount of photos from freelancers. Wants mature, scenic and Christian themes.

Tips "Many of our projects are developed inhouse and assigned. Study our catalog and products; visit Christian bookstores."

TALICOR, INC., 4741 Murriet St., Chino CA 91710. (909)517-0076. Fax: (909)517-0076. E-mail: webmaster@talicor.com. Website: http://www.talicor.com. President: Lew Herndon. Estab. 1971. Game and puzzle manufacturer. Publishes games and puzzles (adults' and children's). 70% of products are made for kids or have kids' themes.

Illustration: Needs freelance illustration for games and puzzles. Makes 14 illustration assignments/year. To contact, send promo piece. Reports only if interested. Materials returned with SASE; materials filed. For artwork, pays by the hour, by the project or negotiable royalty. Pays on acceptance. Buys negotiable rights.

Photography: Buys stock and assigns work. Buys 6 stock images/year. Wants photos with wholesome family subjects. Makes 6 assignments/year. Uses 4×5 transparencies. To contact, send color promo piece. Reports only if interested. Materials returned with SASE; materials filed. Pays per photo, by the hour, by the day or by the project (negotiable rates). Pays on acceptance. Buys negotiable rights.

Tips: Submit seasonal material 6 months in advance.

N: WARNER PRESS, P.O. Box 2499, Anderson IN 46018. Fax: (765)640-8005. Senior Editor: Jennie Bishop. Estab. 1880. Publishes church resources, coloring and activity books and children's supplies, all religious-oriented. 15% of products are made for kids.

Writing: To contact, request guidelines first. Contact: Jennie Bishop, senior editor. Reports in 4-6 weeks. Limited purchases of children's material right now. Materials may be kept on file for future use. Pays on acceptance. Buys all rights. Credit line sometimes given. Writer's guidelines for SASE.

Illustration: We purchase a very limited amount of freelance art at this time, but we are always looking for excellent coloring book artists.

Photography: Buys photography from freelancers for church bulletin covers. Contact: John Silvey, creative director.

Tips: Writers request guidelines before submitting. We purchase a very limited amount of children's material right now. Materials may be kept of file for future reference. Make sure to include SASE. Unsolicited material that does not follow guidelines will not be reviewed."

ZOLAN FINE ARTS, LTD., P.O. Box 656, Hershey PA 17033. (717)534-2446. Fax: (717)534-1095. E-mail: donaldz798@aol.com. Website: http://www.zolan.com. President: Jennifer Zolan. Estab. 1993. Commercial and fine art studio creating and marketing original oil paintings of early childhood. 100% of products are made for kids or have kids' themes.

Writing: Needs freelance writing for stories and poems about the art, and ad copy. Makes 7-8 writing assignments/month. To contact, send cover letter, client list and writing samples. Reports in 2-4 weeks only if interested. Materials returned with SASE; materials filed if interested. Pays $25-60/hour, or $50-150/project. Pays on acceptance. Rights: negotiable.

Photography: Buys stock and assigns work. Makes 8-12 assignments/year. Wants "candid, heart-warming and endearing photos of children with high emotional appeal between the ages of 2-4. Looking for human interest type of photographs evoking pleasant and happy memories at early childhood. Photos are used for artist reference only." Uses color and b&w prints; 35mm, 2¼×2¼, 4× 5 or 8×10 transparencies. To contact, send cover letter, client list. Reports only if interested. Materials returned if accompanied with SASE; materials not filed. Pays per photo (range: $200-1,000 for b&w and color). Pays on acceptance. Buys "exclusive artist reference rights." Guidelines available for SASE.

Tips: Submit seasonal material 6 months in advance. "Writers should have the love of early childhood capturing the essence and feelings of the artwork and have ability to write in various ranges from ad copy to stories. Photos should have high emotional appeal and tell a story. We are happy to work with amateur and professional photographers. Photos are used for artist reference only. Please write or e-mail for guidelines before submitting work.

Play Publishers & Producers

Writing plays for children and family audiences is a special challenge. Whether creating an original work or adapting a classic, plays for children must hold the attention of audiences that often include children and adults. Using rhythm, repetition and dramatic action are effective ways of holding the attention of kids. Pick subjects children can relate to, and never talk down to them.

Theater companies often have limited budgets so plays with elaborate staging and costumes often can't be produced. Touring companies want simple sets that can be moved easily. Keep in mind that they may have as few as three actors, so roles may have to be doubled up.

Many of the companies listed here produce plays with roles for adults and children, so check the percentage of plays written for adult and children's roles. Most importantly, study the types of plays a theater wants and doesn't want. Many name plays they've recently published or produced, and some have additional guidelines or information available. For more listings of theaters open to submissions of children's and adult material and information on contests and organizations for playwrights, consult *Dramatists Sourcebook* (Theatre Communications Group, Inc.).

Information on play publishers listed in the previous edition but not included in this edition of *Children's Writer's & Illustrator's Market* may be found in the General Index.

A.D. PLAYERS, 2710 W. Alabama, Houston TX 77098. (713)526-2721. Estab. 1967. Produces 4-5 children's plays/year in new Children's Theatre Series; 1-2 musical/year. Produces children's plays for professional productions.
- A.D. Players has received the Dove family approval stamp; an award from the Columbia International Film & Video Festival; and a Silver Angel Award.

Needs: 99-100% of plays/musicals written for adult roles; 0-1% for juvenile roles. "Cast must utilize no more than five actors. Need minimal, portable sets for proscenium or arena stage with no fly space and no wing space." Does not want to see large cast or set requirements or New Age themes.
How to Contact: Send script with SASE. No tapes or pictures. Will consider simultaneous submissions and previously performed work. Reports in 6-12 months.
Terms: Buys some residual rights. Pay negotiated. Submissions returned with SASE.
Tips: "Children's musicals tend to be large in casting requirements. For those theaters with smaller production capabilities, this can be a liability for a script. Try to keep it small and simple, especially if writing for theaters where adults are performing for children. We are interested in material that reflects family values, emphasizes the importance of responsibility in making choices, encourages faith in God and projects the joy and fun of telling a story."

N ALABAMA SHAKESPEARE FESTIVAL, #1 Festival Dr., Montgomery AL 36117. (334)271-5300. Fax: (334)271-5348. E-mail: pr4bard@wsnet.com. Website: http://www.asf.net. Artistic Director: Kent Thompson. Estab. 1972. Produces 2 children's plays/year.
Needs: Produces children's plays for professional LORT (League of Regional Theaters) theatre. 90% of plays/musicals written for adult roles; 10% for juvenile roles. Must have moderate sized casts (2-10 characters); have two stages (750 seat house/250 seat house). Musical needs: Interested in works for the Southern Writers' Project (contact ASF for information). Does not want to see plays exclusively for child actors. Recently produced plays: *Wiley and the Hairy Man*, by Susan Zeder (southern folk tale for elementary ages); *Androcles and the Lion*, by Aurand Harris (folktale for elementary ages); and *Alice's Adventures in Wonderland*, adaptation by Deborah Lynn Frockt.
How to Contact: Plays: Query first with synopsis, character breakdown and set description; scripts which meet/address the focus of the Southern Writers' Project. Musicals: Query with synopsis, character breakdown and set description; scripts which meet/address the focus of the Southern Writers' Project. Will consider previously performed work. Reports in 1 year.

Terms: Submissions returned with SASE.

Tips: "Created in 1991 by Artistic Director Kent Thompson, the Alabama Shakespeare Festival's Southern Writers' Project is an exploration and celebration of its rich Southern cultural heritage. In an attempt to reach this goal the project seeks: to provide for the growth of a 'new' voice for Southern writers and artists; to encourage new works dealing with Southern issues and topics including those that emphasize African-American experiences; to create theatre that speaks in a special way to ASF's unique and racially diverse audiences. In this way the Southern Writers' Project strives to become a window to the complexities and beauty found in this celebrated region of our country, the South."

✔ **AMERICAN STAGE**, P.O. Box 1560, St. Petersburg FL 33731. (813)823-1600. Producing Artistic Director: Jody Kielbasa. Artistic Associate: Ken Mitchell. Estab. 1977. Produces 3 children's plays/year. Produces children's plays for professional children's theater program, mainstage, school tour, performing arts halls.

Needs: Limited by budget and performance venue. Subject matter: classics and original work for children (ages K-12) and families. Recently produced plays: *A Christmas Carol*, by Doris Baisley (ages 5-up); *Puss-N-Boots*, by Bill Leavengood (ages 5-15). Does not want to see plays that look down on children. Approach must be that of the child or fictional beings or animals.

How to Contact: Query with synopsis, character breakdown and set description. Will consider simultaneous submissions and previously performed work. Reports in 6 months.

Terms: Purchases "professional rights." Pays writers in royalties (6-8%); $25-35/performance. SASE for return of submission.

Tips: Sees a move in plays toward basic human values, relationships and multicultural communities.

ANCHORAGE PRESS, INC., P.O. Box 8067, New Orleans LA 70182. (504)283-8868. Fax: (504)866-0502. Editor: Orlin Corey. Estab. 1935. Publishes 5-7 children's plays/year; 3-5 children's musicals/year.

Needs: "There is no genre, subject of preferred interest. We want plays of high literary/theatrical quality. Like music, such material—by nature of the stage—will appeal to any age capable of following a story. Obviously some appeal more to primary ages, some secondary." Does not want send-ups—cutesies—jargon-laden—pendantic/subject specific. "Plays—like ice cream—work only if they are superb. Teaching is not the purpose of theatre—entertainment is, and that may include serious subjects fascinatingly explored." Recently produced plays: *The Orphan Train*, by Aurand Harris (play about lives of 10 children who rode "orphan" trains of 1914 for ages 7-18); *Tokoloshe*, by Pieter Scholtz (Zulu tale of a water-sprite and a modern little Zulu girl seeking her father for ages 5-9).

How to Contact: Query for guidelines first. Will consider simultaneous submissions and previously performed work "essential to be proven." Reports 3 months.

Terms: Buys all stage rights. Pays royalty (varies extensively from 50% minimum to 80%). Submissions returned with SASE.

Tips: "Obtain guidelines and get a catalog first."

APPLE TREE THEATRE, 595 Elm Place, Suite 210, Highland Park IL 60035. (847)432-8223. Fax: (847)432-5214. Produces 3 children's plays/year.

Needs: Produces professional, daytime and educational outreach programs for grades 4-9. 98% of plays written for adult roles; 2% for juvenile roles. Uses a unit set and limited to 9 actors. No musicals. Straight plays only. Does not want to see: "children's theater," i.e. . . . Peter Rabbit, Snow White. Material *must* be based in social issues. Recently produced plays: *Devil's Arithmetic*, adapted from the novel by Jane Yolen (about the Holocaust, ages 10-up); *Roll of Thunder, Hear My Cry*, adapted from the novel by Mildred Taylor (about Civil rights, racial discrimination in Mississippi in 1930s, ages 10-up).

How to Contact: Query first. Query with synopsis, character breakdown and set description. Will consider simultaneous submissions and previously performed work. Reports in 2 months.

Terms: Pay negotiated per contract. Submissions returned with SASE.

Tips: "Never send an unsolicited manuscript. Include reply postcard for queries."

**FOR EXPLANATIONS OF THESE SYMBOLS,
SEE THE INSIDE FRONT AND BACK COVERS OF THIS BOOK**

BILINGUAL FOUNDATION OF THE ARTS, 421 N. Avenue 19th, Los Angeles CA 90031. (213)225-4044. Fax: (213)225-1250. Artistic Director: Margarita Galban. Estab. 1973. Produces 6 children's plays/year; 4 children's musicals/year.

Needs: Produces children's plays for professional productions. 60% of plays/musicals written for adult roles; 40% for juvenile roles. No larger than 8 member cast. Recently produced plays: *Second Chance*, by A. Cardona and A. Weinstein (play about hopes and fears in every teenager for teenagers); *The Circle*, by Liane Schirmer (play about violence for teenagers).

How to Contact: Plays: Query with synopsis, character breakdown and set description and submit complete ms. Musicals: Query with synopsis, character breakdown and set description and submit complete ms with score. Will consider simultaneous submissions and previously performed work. Reports in 4 months.

Terms: Pays royalty; per performance; buys material outright; "different with each play."

BOARSHEAD THEATER, 425 S. Grand Ave., Lansing MI 48933. (517)484-7800. Fax: (517)484-2564. Artistic Director: John Peakes. Director of P.R., Marketing and Outreach: Cathy Hansel. Estab. 1966. Produces 3 children's plays/year.

Needs: Produces children's plays for professional production. Majority of plays written for young adult roles. Prefers 5 characters or less for touring productions, 5 plus characters for mainstage productions; one unit set, simple costumes. Recently produced plays: *The Lion, the Witch & the Wardrobe*, by Joseph Robinette (fantasy for ages 6-12); *1,000 Cranes*, by Katharine Schultz Miller; *Step on a Crack*, by Susan Zeder (family play for ages 6-12); *The Planet of the Perfectly Awful People*; and *Patchwork*. Does not want to see musicals.

How to Contact: Query with synopsis, character breakdown and set description. Send to Education Director. Include 10 pages of representative dialogue. Will consider previously performed work. Reports in 2 weeks on queries; 4 months "if we ask for submissions."

Terms: Pays writers $15-25/performance. Submissions returned with SASE. If no SASE, send self-addressed stamped post card for reply.

CALIFORNIA THEATRE CENTER, P.O. Box 2007, Sunnyvale CA 94087. (408)245-2979. Artistic Director: Gayle Cornelison. Estab. 1975. Produces 15 children's plays and 3 musicals for professional productions.

Needs: 75% of plays/musicals written for adult roles; 20% for juvenile roles. Prefers material suitable for professional tours and repertory performance; one-hour time limit, limited technical facilities. Recently produced *Jungle Book*, adapted by Will Huddleston (Kipling's classic for ages 4th grade-up); *Heidi*, by Gayle Cornelison (classic for ages K-up). Does not want to see arcane, artsy, cute material.

How to Contact: Query with synopsis, character breakdown and set description. Send to: Will Huddleston. Will consider previously performed work. Reports in 6 months.

Terms: Rights negotiable. Pays writers royalties; pays $35-50/performance. Submissions returned with SASE.

Tips: "We sell to schools, so the title and material must appeal to teachers who look for things familiar to them. We look for good themes, universality. Avoid the cute."

CHILDREN'S STORY SCRIPTS, Baymax Productions, Suite 130, 2219 W. Olive Ave., Burbank CA 91506-2648. (818)563-6105. Fax: (818)563-2968. E-mail: baymax@earthlink.net. Editor: Deedra Bebout. Estab. 1990. Produces 1-10 children's scripts/year.

Needs: "Except for small movements and occasionally standing up, children remain seated in Readers Theatre fashion." Publishes scripts sold primarily to schools or wherever there's a program to teach or entertain children. "All roles read by children except K-2 scripts, where kids have easy lines, leader helps read the narration. Prefer multiple cast members, no props or sets." Subject matter: scripts on all subjects that dovetail with classroom subjects. Targeted age range—K-8th grade, 5-13 years old. Recently published plays: *A Clever Fox*, by Mary Ellen Holmes (about using one's wits, grades 2-4); *Memories of the Pony Express*, by Sharon Gill Askelson (grades 5-8). No stories that preach a point, no stories about catastrophic disease or other terribly heavy topics, no theatrical scripts without narrative prose to move the story along, no monologues or 1-character stories.

How to Contact: Submit complete ms. Will consider simultaneous submissions and previously performed work (if rights are available). Reports in 2 weeks.

Terms: Purchases all rights; authors retain copyrights. "We add support material and copyright the whole package." Pays writers in royalties (10-15% on sliding scale, based on number of copies sold). SASE for reply and return of submission.

Tips: "We're only looking for stories related to classsroom studies—educational topics with a freshness to them. Our scripts mix prose narration with character dialogue—we do not publish traditional, all-dialogue plays." Writer's guidelines packet available for business-sized SASE with 2 first-class stamps. Guidelines explain what Children's Story Scripts are, give 4-page examples from 2 different scripts, give list of suggested topics for scripts.

CIRCA '21 DINNER THEATRE, P.O. Box 3784, Rock Island IL 61204-3784. (309)786-2667. Producer: Dennis Hitchcock. Estab. 1977. Produces 3 children's musicals/year.
Needs: Produces children's plays for professional productions. 95% of musicals written for adult roles; 5% written for juvenile roles. "Prefer a cast of four to eight—no larger than ten. Plays are produced on mainstage sets." Recently produced plays: *Jack and the Beanstalk*, by Ted Morris and Bill Johnson (ages 6-10) and *Alice In Wonderland*, by Prince Street Players (ages 4-10).
How to Contact: Send complete script with audiotape of music. Reports in 3 months.
Terms: Payment negotiable.

I.E. CLARK PUBLICATIONS, P.O. Box 246, Schulenburg TX 78956. (409)743-3232. Fax: (409)743-4765. E-mail: ieclark@cvtv.net. General Manager: Donna Cozzaglio. Estab. 1956. Publishes 3 children's plays/year; 1 or 2 children's musicals/year.
Needs: Publishes plays for all ages. Published plays: *Little Women*, by Thomas Hischak (dramatization of the Alcott novel for family audiences); *Heidi*, by Ann Pugh, music by Betty Utter (revision of our popular musical dramatization of the Johanna Spyri novel). Does not want to see plays that have not been produced.
How to Contact: Submit complete ms and audio or video tape. Will consider simultaneous submissions and previously performed work. Reports in 2-4 months.
Terms: Pays writers in negotiable royalties. SASE for return of submission.
Tips: "We publish only high-quality literary works. Please send only one manuscript at a time."

N COLUMBIA ENTERTAINMENT COMPANY, % Betsy Phillips, 309 Parkade, Columbia MO 65202. (573)874-5628. Artistic Director: Betsy Phillips. Estab. 1988. Produces 3-6 children's plays/year; 0-2 children's musicals/year.
Needs: "We produce children's theatre plays. Our theatre school students act all the roles. We cast adult and children roles with children from theatre school. Each season we have 5 plays done by adults (kid parts possible)—3 theatre school productions." We need large cast plays-20+. Musical needs: Musicals must have songs written in ranges children can sing. Recently produced plays: *The King Who Stole Spring*, by Drew Hollywood, Brian Breen and Michael Cheertier (the king forbids flowers, but a feisty girl saves the day, for ages K-teen, but adults will enjoy it); *Zink: The Myth. The Legend. The Zebra*, by Cherie Bennett (a child deals with leukemia, for ages 10-adult).
How to Contact: Plays: Submit complete ms; use SASE to get form. Musicals: Submit complete ms and score; tape of music must be included, use SASE to get entry form. Will consider simultaneous submissions and previously performed work. Reports in 2-6 months.
Terms: Buys production (sans royalties) rights on mss. Pays $250 1st prize. Submissions returned with SASE.
Tips: "Please write a play/musical that appeals to all ages. We always need lots of parts, especially for girls."

N COMMUNITY CHILDREN'S THEATRE OF KANSAS CITY INC., 8021 E. 129th Terrace, Grandview MO 64030. (816)761-5775. Contact: Blanche Sellens. Estab. 1951. Produces 5 children's plays/year. Prefer casts of between 6-8 performed by women only. Produces children's plays for amateur productions for ages K-6. Produced play: *Red Versus the Wolf*, by Judy Wolferman, (musical, for K-6 audience). Submission method: Query first then submit complete ms. Reports in a matter of months. "Winning script is performed by one of the units for two years."
Tips: "Write for guidelines and details for The Margaret Bartle Annual Playwriting Award."

CONTEMPORARY DRAMA SERVICE, Division of Meriwether Publishing Ltd., 885 Elkton Dr., Colorado Springs CO 80907-3557. (719)594-4422. Fax: (719)594-9916. E-mail: merpads@aol.com. Executive Editor: Arthur L. Zapel. Estab. 1979. Publishes 60 children's plays/year; 10-15 children's musicals/year.
Needs: Prefer shows with a large cast. 15% of plays/musicals written for adult roles; 85% for juvenile roles. Recently published plays: *Fifties Flashback*, by Shirley Ullom and Ken Miller (rock music comedy, for ages 12-18); *The Velveteen Rabbit*, by Peterson/Nestor (on becoming real, for all ages). "We publish church plays for elementary level for Christmas and Easter. Most of our secular plays are for teens or college level." Does not want to see "full-length, three-act plays unless they are adaptations of classic works or have unique comedy appeal."

How to Contact: Query with synopsis, character breakdown and set description; "query first if a musical." Will consider simultaneous submissions or previously performed work. Reports in 6-8 weeks.
Terms: Purchases first rights. Pays writers royalty (10%) or buys material outright for $200-1,000. SASE for return of submission.
Tips: "If the writer is submitting a musical play an audiocassette of the music should be sent. We prefer plays with humorous action. A writer should provide credentials of plays published and produced. Writers should not submit items for the elementary age level."

THE COTERIE, 2450 Grand, Kansas City MO 64108. Phone/fax: (816)474-6785. Artistic Director: Jeff Church. Estab. 1979. Produces 7 children's plays/year; 1 children's musical/year.
Needs: "Prefer casts of between 5-7 no larger than 15." Produces children's plays for professional productions. 80% of plays/musicals written for adult roles; 20% for juvenile roles. "We produce original plays, musicals and literary adaptations for ages five through adult." Produced plays: *Amelia Lives*, by Laura Annawyn Shamas (one-woman show on Amelia Earhart, for 6th grade through adult); *Dinosaurus*, by Ed Mast and Lenore Bensinger (Mobil Oil workers discover cavern of dinosaurs, for ages 5 through adult). "We do *not* want to see 'camp' adaptations of fairytales."
How to Contact: Query with synopsis, sample scene, character breakdown and set description. Reports in 8-10 months.
Terms: Rights purchased "negotiable." Pays writers in royalties per play of approximately $1,000-1,500. SASE for return of submission.
Tips: "We're interested in adaptations of classic literature with small casts, simple staging requirements; also multicultural topics and biography plays of Latin and African-American figures. There is a need for non-condescending material for younger age groups (5-8) and for middle school (ages 9-13)."

CREEDE REPERTORY THEATRE, P.O. Box 269, Creede CO 81130. (719)658-2541. Fax: (719)658-2343. Artistic Director: Richard Baxter. Estab. 1966. Produces 1 children's play/year; 1 musical/year.
Needs: Limited to 4-6 cast members and must be able to tour. Produces children's plays for summer theater, school or professional productions. 100% of plays/musicals written for adult roles. Publishes plays for ages K-12. Recently produced plays: *Coyote Tales*, by Daniel Kramer and Company (Native American Coyote legend, for grades K-6); and *The Two of Us*, by Michael Frayn (contemporary relationship story, for ages 12-adult).
How to Contact: Query first, submit complete ms and score, or query with synopsis, character breakdown and set description. Will consider simultaneous submissions and previously performed work. Reports in 1 year.
Terms: Pays writers in royalties (5%); pays $15-30 per performance.
Tips: Sees trends in "non-sexist, non-traditional casting and Native American/Hispanic American interest. No fairy tales unless non-traditional."

N DALLAS CHILDREN'S THEATER, 2215 Cedar Springs, Dallas TX 75201. Artistic Director: Robyn Flatt. Estab. 1984. Produces 10 children's plays/year.
Needs: Produces children's plays for professional theater. 80% of plays/musicals written for adult roles; 20% for juvenile roles. Prefer cast size between 8-12. Musical needs: "We do produce musical works, but prefer non-musical. Availability of music tracks is a plus." Does not want to see: anything not appropriate for a youth/family audience. Recently produced plays: *Young King Arthur*, by Linda Daugherty (early life of Arthurian legend for students/family); *Bunnicula*, by Jon Klein from book by Deborah & James Howe (musical based on popular children's book series for students/family).
How to Contact: Plays: Query with synopsis, character breakdown and set description. Musicals: Query with synopsis, character breakdown and set description. Will consider previously performed work. Reports only if interested.
Terms: Rights are negotiable. Pay is negotiable. Submissions returned with SASE.
Tips: "We are most interested in substantive works for a student/youth/family audience. Material which enlightens aspects of the global community, diverse customs and perspectives, adaptations of classical and popular literature, myth, and folk tale. Topics which focus on the contemporary concerns of youth, families, and our diverse communities are also of great interest. Full-length works are preferred rather than one-acts or classroom pieces."

N ▼ DRAMATIC PUBLISHING, INC., 311 Washington St., Woodstock IL 60098. (815)338-7170. Fax: (815)338-8981. E-mail: plays@dramaticpublishing.com. Website: http://www.dramaticpublishing.com. Acquisitions Editor: Linda Habjan. Estab. 1885. Publishes 5-8 children's plays/year; 4-6 children's musicals. Recently published: *Still Life with Iris*, by Steven Dietz; *The Little Prince*, by Rick Cummins and John Scoullar; and *Amazing Grace*, by Shay Youngblood. Submission method: Submit complete ms/

score and cassette/video tape (if a musical); include SASE if materials are to be returned. Reports in 4-6 months. Pays writers in royalties.

● Dramatic Publishing's plays have won several awards recently. Both *A Women Called Truth* and *Song for the Navigator* won A.A.T.E. Distinguished Play Award. *A Play About the Mothers of Plaza de Mayo*, by Alisa Palmer, won the Canadian Children's Award for Best New Play.

Tips: "Scripts should be from ½ to 1½ hours long, and not didactic or condescending. Original plays dealing with hopes, joys and fears of today's children are preferred to adaptations of old classics."

EL CENTRO SU TEATRO, 4725 High, Denver CO 80216. (303)296-0219. Fax: (303)296-4614. Artistic Director: Anthony J. Garcia. Estab. 1971. Produces 2 children's plays/year.

Needs: "We are interested in plays by Chicanos or Latinos that speak to that experience. We do not produce standard musicals. We are a culturally specific company." Recently produced *Joaquim's Christmas*, by Anthony J. Garcia (children's Christmas play for ages 7-15); and *The Dragonslayer*, by Silviana Woods (young boy's relationship with grandfather for ages 7-15). Does not want to see "cutesy stuff."

How to Contact: Query with synopsis, character breakdown and set description. Will consider simultaneous submissions and previously performed work. Reports in 6 months. Buys regional rights.

Terms: Pays writers per performance: $35 1st night, $25 subsequent. Submissions returned with SASE.

Tips: "People should write within their realm of experience but yet push their own boundaries. Writers should approach social issues within the human experience of their character."

ELDRIDGE PUBLISHING CO. INC., P.O. Box 1595, Venice FL 34284. (941)496-4679. Fax: (941)493-9680. E-mail: info@histage.com. Website: http://www.histage.com or http://www.95church.com. Editor: Nancy Vorhis. Estab. 1906. Publishes approximately 25 children's plays/year; 2-3 children's musicals/year.

Needs: Prefers simple staging; flexible cast size. "We publish for junior and high school, community theater and children's theater (adults performing for children), all genres, also religious plays." Recently published plays: *Mother Goose Inc.*, by Steve Murray (fairytale characters go MTV, ages 12-14); *Agatha Christie Never Took Trig*, by Jeffrey Smart (comedy/mystery at a high school party, ages 12-18). Prefers work which has been performed or at least had a staged reading.

How to Contact: Submit complete ms, score and tape of songs (if a musical). Will consider simultaneous submissions ("please let us know, however"). Reports in 2 months.

Terms: Purchases all dramatic rights. Pays writers royalties of 50%; 10% copy sales; buys material outright for $200-800.

Tips: "Try to have your work performed, if at all possible, before submitting. We're always on the lookout for comedies which provide a lot of fun for our customers. But other more serious topics which concern teens, as well as intriguing mysteries, and children's theater programs are of interest to us as well. We know there are many new talented playwrights out there and we look forward to reading their fresh scripts."

ENCORE PERFORMANCE PUBLISHING, P.O. Box 692, Orem UT 84059. (801)225-0605. Fax: (807)765-0489. E-mail: encoreplay@aol.com. Website: http://www.Encoreplay.com. Contact: Mike Perry. Estab. 1978. Publishes 20-30 children's plays/year; 10-20 children's musicals/year.

Needs: Prefers close to equal male/female ratio if possible. Adaptations for K-12 and older. 60% of plays written for adult roles; 40% for juvenile roles. Recently published plays: *Boy Who Knew No Fear*, by G. Riley Mills/Mark Levenson (adaptation of fairy tale, ages 8-16); *Two Chains*, by Paul Burton (about drug abuse, ages 11-18).

How to Contact: Query first with synopsis, character breakdown, set description and production history. Will only consider previously performed work. Reports in 2 months.

Terms: Purchases all publication and production rights. Author retains copyright. Pays writers in royalties (50%). SASE for return of submission.

Tips: "Give us issue and substance, be controversial without offense. Use a laser printer! Don't send an old manuscript. Make yours look the most professional."

N THE FOOTHILL THEATRE COMPANY, P.O. Box 1812, Nevada City CA 95959. (530)265-9320. Fax: (530)265-9325. E-mail: garyw@foothilltheatre.org. Website: http://www.foothilltheatre.org. Literary

---

● **SPECIAL COMMENTS** by the editor of *Children's Writer's & Illustrator's Market* are set off by a bullet.

Manager: Gary Wright. Estab. 1977. Produces 0-2 children's plays/year; 0-1 children's musicals/year. Professional nonprofit theater.

Needs: 95% of plays/musicals written for adult roles; 5% for juvenile roles. "Small is better, but will consider anything." Produced *Peter Pan*, by J.M. Barrie (kids vs. grownups, for all ages); *The Lion, the Witch and the Wardrobe*, by Joseph Robinette (adapted from C.S. Lewis, for all ages). Does not want to see traditional fairy tales.

How to Contact: Query with synopsis, character breakdown and set description. Will consider simultaneous submissions and previously performed work. Reports in 6 months.

Terms: Buys negotiable rights. Payment method varies. Submissions returned with SASE.

Tips: "Trends in children's theater include cultural diversity, real life issues (drug use, AIDS, etc.), mythological themes with contemporary resonance. Don't talk down to or underestimate children. Don't be preachy or didactic—humor is an excellent teaching tool."

THE FREELANCE PRESS, P.O. Box 548, Dover MA 02030. (508)785-8250. Managing Editor: Narcissa Campion. Estab. 1979. Produces 3 musicals and/or plays/year.

Needs: Casts are comprised of young people, ages 8-15, and number 25-30. "We publish original musicals on contemporary topics for children and adaptations of children's classics (e.g., Rip Van Winkle)." Published plays: *The Tortoise and the Hare* (based on story of same name, for ages 8-12); *Monopoly*, 3 (young people walk through board game, for ages 11-15).

• The Freelance Press does not accept plays for adult performers.

How to Contact: Submit complete ms and score with SASE. Will consider simultaneous submissions and previously performed work. Reports in 3 months.

Terms: Pays writers 10% royalties on book sales, plus performance royalties. SASE for return of submission.

N GREAT PLATTE RIVER PLAYWRIGHTS FESTIVAL, Theatre, UNK, Kearney NE 68849. (308)865-8406. E-mail: greenj@platte.unk.edu. Artistic Director: Jeffrey Green. Estab. 1988. Produces 1 children's play/year; 1 children's musical/year.

Needs: Produces children's plays for university, summer theatre. 25% of plays/musicals written for adult roles; 75% for juvenile roles. Minimal props and scenery preferred; small pits. Recently produced plays: *Hansel & Gretel (the Opera)*, by Engelbert Humperdinck (for grades elementary-junior high); *Broken Hearts*, by Oscar Wilde (for grades elementary-junior high).

How to Contact: Plays: Submit complete ms with synopsis, character breakdown and set description. Musicals: Submit complete ms and score with tape, synopsis, character breakdown and set design. Will consider simultaneous submissions. "We close April 1—winner announced July 30."

Terms: Buys first performance rights. Pays contest prize of $500, $300, $200. Submissions returned with SASE.

THE GROWING STAGE THEATRE, In Residence at the Palace, Rt. 183, Netcong NJ 07857. (973)347-4946. Fax: (973)691-7069. Executive Director: Stephen L. Fredericks. Estab. 1982. Produces 5 mainstage children's shows, a summer production for the whole family and 3 children's musicals/year. Equity touring production to schools and other organizations. Professional actors work with community actors.

Needs: 60% of plays/musicals written for adult roles; 40% for juvenile roles. Produced: *Snow White*, by Stephen L. Fredericks (adaptation of classic tale, ages 5-up); *The Hobbit*, by Thomas Olsen (Tolkeine classic, for ages 10-up). Plays for young audiences only.

How to Contact: Query with synopsis, character breakdown and set description. Will consider previously performed work. Reports in 2 months.

Terms: "Contracts are developed individually." Pays $25-75/performance. Submissions returned with SASE.

Tips: "There's an overabundance on issue-oriented plays. Creativity, quality, the standards we place on theater aimed at adults should not be reduced in preparing a script for young people. We, together, are forming the audience of tomorrow. Don't repel young people by making the theater another resource for the infomercial—nurture, challenge and inspire them. Never write down to your intended audience."

HAYES SCHOOL PUBLISHING CO. INC., 321 Pennwood Ave., Wilkinsburg PA 15221. (412)371-2373. Fax: (412)371-6408. Estab. 1940.

Needs: Wants to see supplementary teaching aids for grades K-12. Interested in all subject areas, especially music, foreign language (French, Spanish, Latin), early childhood education.

How to Contact: Query first with table of contents, sample page of activities. Will consider simultaneous and electronic submissions. Reports in 4-6 weeks.

Terms: Purchases all rights. Work purchased outright. SASE for return of submissions.

N HEUER PUBLISHING COMPANY, P.O. Box 248, Cedar Rapids IA 52406. (319)364-6311. Fax: (319)364-1771. E-mail: editor@hitplays.com. Website: www.hitplays.com. Associate Editor: Geri Albrecht. Estab. 1928. Publishes 10-15 plays/year for young audiences and community theaters; 5 musicals/year.

Needs: "We publish plays and musicals for schools and community theatres (amateur)." 100% of plays/musicals written for juvenile roles. Single sets preferred. Props should be easy to find and costumes, other than modern dress, should be simple and easy to improvise. Stage effects requiring complex lighting and/or mechanical features should be avoided. Musical needs: "We need musicals with large, predominantly female casts. We publish plays and musicals for middle, junior and senior high schools." Recently published plays: *My Son the Rock*, by Martin Follose (medieval comedy for ages 11-18); *Out of the Frying Pan Into the Oven*, by Timothy Pechey (courtroom comedy with fairytale drama for ages 11-18).

How to Contact: Plays: Query with synopsis. Musicals: Query with synopsis. Will consider simultaneous submissions and previously performed work. Reports in 2 months.

Terms: Buys amateur rights. Pays royalty or purchases work outright. Submissions returned with SASE.

Tips: "We sell almost exclusively to junior and smaller senior high schools so the subject matter and language should be appropriate for schools and young audiences."

N LAGUNA PLAYHOUSE YOUTH THEATRE, P.O. Box 1747, Laguna Beach CA 92652. (949)497-2787. Fax: (949)376-8185. E-mail: lphjoe@gte.net. Artistic Director: Joe Lauderdale. Estab. 1986. Produces 4-6 children's plays/year; 1-2 children's musicals/year.

Needs: The Laguna Playhouse is a professional theatre company with an amateur youth theatre. 40% of plays/musicals written for adult roles; 60% for juvenile roles. "We especially look for small touring shows based on existing children's literature." Musical needs: Small combos of 4-7 people with some doubling of instruments possible. Recently produced plays: *Tuck Everlasting*, by Mark Frattaroli (eternal life for family audience); *You're A Good Man, Charlie Brown*, by Clark Gesner ("Peanuts" musical for family audience).

How to Contact: Plays: Submit complete ms. Musicals: Submit complete ms and score. Will consider simultaneous submissions and previously performed work. Reports in 3-6 months.

Terms: Pays 5-8% royalties.

Tips: "The majority of our work is literary based. We produce shows based on books for young people, however, we do on occasion produce original works. They must be intelligent and not condescending to the audience."

N MIDWEST THEATRE NETWORK/ROCHESTER PLAYWRIGHT FESTIVAL, 5031 Tongen Ave. NW, Rochester MN 55901. (507)281-8887. Executive Director/Dramaturg: Joan Sween. Estab. 1992. Produces 1-8 children's plays biennially; varying number of children's musicals/year (maximum 1 biennially).

Needs: "The Rochester Playwright Festival is an event wherein four to eight different theatres, usually amateur, all simultaneously produce a new play. The plays are generated by a play writing competition administered by Midwest Theatre Network. The festival is biennial on even years, the contest is biennial on odd years. The first festival was in 1996, the second will occur October, 1998, and the next will be October, 2000. The contest leading to the 2000 festival will run from January 1, 1999 to November 30, 1999. One of the participating theatres is usually specifically a children's theatre. Others may be community theatres with adjunct children's programs. Any of the other theatres, however, may elect to produce a children's play if one engages their enthusiasm. Our participating theatres are oriented toward theatre for children (product), as opposed to theatre by children (process). However, they remain motivated solely by the quality of the script. The age of the performer required is not an issue." No limitations such as cast, props, staging, etc. other than the resources of the various participating theatres, whose annual budgets vary from $500,000 to $20,000. Musical needs: "We have no specific musical needs or preferences—whatever engages. Generally, overly simplistic progressions and repetitive tempi are not competitive. We'll read anything, but there are certain types of plays that are never successful with our theatres: plays with bunny rabbits and other creatures using off-color language; plays full of adult double entendre, sly adult humor, and sexual orientation; uninspired rehashes of folk tales with no fresh direction or characters; plays with knives, poison, guns, torture, bigotry or humor based on disabilities and body shape; plays with no structure, no conflict, no point; plays of egregious length; plays that condescend to young people." Recently produced plays: *The Robin and the Raven*, by Scott Burroughs (adventure/Celtic mythological characters for ages 6-12).

How to Contact: Plays: Submit complete ms. Musicals: Submit complete ms and audio tape. Will consider simultaneous submissions. Send #10 SASE for guidelines and required entry form after January 1, 1999. The first submission from any author is free, succeeding submissions require a $10 (each) reading fee. Reports in 3-8 weeks.

Terms: All a winning author relinquishes is permission for one of our cooperating theatres to produce his/her play royalty-free at the festival, and permission for that theatre to make sufficient copies of the ms for actors, technicians, development people. The author receives expenses to attend festival and a cash prize.

Tips: "Best advice: (If I could do this in neon that would leap off the page and smack the playwright in the face, I would.) *Do not send your play in close to the contest deadline.* We receive 4% of our submissions in the first seven months of the contest and 96% during the last three months. The former receive thoughtful leisurely readings by our panel and are more likely to receive helpful feedback. The latter are read by panelists who are rushed and jaded and are less likely to receive any feedback at all. We are eager to receive children's scripts. We do not receive nearly as many as we'd like. We receive between 700 and 1,000 scripts each competition, but only 25-40 of them are children's scripts, and the majority of them are inept or offensively adult. Where are the good children's scripts?"

THE NEW CONSERVATORY THEATRE CENTER, 25 Van Ness Ave., San Francisco CA 94102-6033. (415)861-4914. Fax: (415)861-6988. Executive Director: Ed Decker. Estab. 1981. Produces 6 children's plays/year; 1 children's musical/year.
Needs: Limited budget and small casts only. Produces children's plays as part of "a professional theater arts training program for youths ages 4-19 during the school year and 2 summer sessions. The New Conservatory also produces educational plays for its touring company. We do not want to see any preachy or didactic material." Recently produced plays: *Charlie and The Chocolate Factory*, by Roald Dahl (good overcomes all, for ages 4-12); *Puss in Boots and Other Cat Tails*, by Stephanie Leverage (geography, for ages 4-12).
How to Contact: Query with synopsis, character breakdown and set description, or submit complete ms and score. Reports in 3 months.
Terms: Rights purchased negotiable. Pays writers in royalties. SASE for return of submission.
Tips: "Wants plays with name recognition, i.e., *The Lion, the Witch and the Wardrobe* as well as socially relevant issues."

NEW PLAYS INCORPORATED, P.O. Box 5074, Charlottesville VA 22905-0074. (804)979-2777. Fax: (804)984-2230. E-mail: patwhitton@aol.com. Website: http://www.newplaysforchildren.com. Publisher: Patricia Whitton. Estab. 1964. Publishes 3-4 plays/year; 1 or 2 children's musicals/year.
Needs: Publishes "generally material for kindergarten through junior high." Recently published: *Jungle Book*, by Rex Stephenson (adaptation from Kipling, for ages 5-12); *Time and Tide*, by Jennifer Hayes (Yorkshire fishing village life, for ages 10-15). Does not want to see "adaptations of titles I already have. No unproduced plays; no junior high improvisations. Read our catalog."
How to Contact: Submit complete ms and score. Will consider simultaneous submissions and previously performed work. Reports in 2 months (usually).
Terms: Purchases exclusive rights to sell acting scripts. Pays writers in royalties (50% of production royalties; 10% of script sales). SASE for return of submission.
Tips: "Write the play you really want to write (not what you think will be saleable) and find a director to put it on."

NEW YORK STATE THEATRE INSTITUTE, 155 River St., Troy NY 12180. (518)274-3200. Fax: (518)274-3815. E-mail: nysti@crisny.org. Website: http://www.crisny.org/not-for-profit/nysti. Artistic Director: Patricia B. Snyder. Estab. 1976. Produces 5 children's plays/year; 1-2 children's musicals/year.
Needs: Produces family plays for professional theater. 90% of plays/musicals are written for adult roles; 10% for juvenile roles. Does not want to see plays for children only. Produced plays: *The Snow Queen*, by Adrian Mitchell and Richard Penslee (ages 10-100); *A Canterville Ghost*, adapted by John Vreeke from Oscar Wilde (all ages).
How to Contact: Query with synopsis, character breakdown and set description; submit tape of songs (if a musical). Will consider simultaneous submissions and previously performed work. Reports in 1 month for queries. SASE for return of submission.
Tips: Writers should be mindful of "audience *sophistication.* We do not wish to see material that is childish. Writers should submit work that is respectful of young people's intelligence and perception—work that is appropriate for families, but that is also challenging and provocative."

THE OPEN EYE THEATER, P.O. Box 959, Margaretville NY 12455. Phone/fax: (914)586-1660. E-mail: openeye@catskill.net. Website: http://www.tchouse.com/artcenters. Producing Artistic Director: Amie Brockway. Estab. 1972 (theater). Produces 3 plays/year for a family audience. Most productions are with music, but are not musicals.
Needs: "Casts of various sizes. Technical requirements are kept to a minimum for touring purposes."

Produces professional productions combining professional artists and artists-in-training (actors of all ages). Recently produced plays: *The Nightingale*, by William E. Black and Amie Brockway (adaptation of Hans Christian Andersen story for ages 6-adult); and *Selkie*, by Laurie Brooks Gollobin (based on Selkie legend for ages 8-adult).

How to Contact: "No videos or cassettes. Letter of inquiry only." Will consider previously performed work. Reports in 6 months.

Terms: Rights agreement negotiated with author. Pays writers one-time fee or royalty negotiated with publisher. SASE for return of submission.

Tips: "Send letter of inquiry only. We are interested in plays for a multigenerational audience (eight-adult)."

PHOENIX THEATRE'S COOKIE COMPANY, 100E. McDowell, Phoenix AZ 85004. (602)258-1974. Fax: (602)253-3626. Artistic Director: Alan J. Prewitt. Estab. 1980. Produces 4 children's plays/year.

Needs: Produces theater with professional adult actors performing for family audiences. 95% of plays/musicals written for adult roles; 5% for juvenile roles. Requires small casts (4-7), small stage, mostly 1 set, flexible set or ingenious sets for a small space. "We're just starting to do plays with music—no musicals per se." Does not want to see larger casts, multiple sets, 2 hour epics. Recently produced *Mother Goose on the Loose*, by Alan J. Prewitt (Mother Goose gets a makeover, for ages 4-11); *Cinderella*, by Alan J. Prewitt (1950s version, for ages 4-12).

How to Contact: Plays/musicals: Query with synopsis, character breakdown and set description. Will consider simultaneous submissions. Reports back only if interested within 2 weeks.

Terms: Submissions returned with SASE.

Tips: "Only submit innovative, imaginative work that stimulates imagination and empowers the child. We specialize in producing original scripts based on classic children's literature."

☑ **PIONEER DRAMA SERVICE**, P.O. Box 4267, Englewood CO 80155. (303)779-4035. Fax: (303)779-4315. E-mail: piodrama@aol.com. Website: http://www.pioneerdrama.com. Submissions Editor: Beth Somers. Publisher: Steven Fendrich. Estab. 1960. Publishes 20 new plays and musicals/year.

Needs: "We are looking for plays up to 90 minutes long." Publishes plays for ages preschool-12th grade. Recently published plays/musicals: *The Story of Hansel and Gretel*, by Vera Morris, music/lyrics by Bill Francoer (based on work by Brothers Grimm, for young audiences); *Hyronomous A. Frog*, by Edith Weiss (classic tale of frog prince, for family theater). Wants to see "script, scores, tapes, pics and reviews."

How to Contact: Query with synopsis, character breakdown, running time and set description. Submit complete ms and score (if a musical) with SASE. Will consider simultaneous submissions, CAD electronic submissions via disk or modem, previously performed work. Contact: Beth Somers, submissions editor. Reports in 3-4 months. Send for writer's guidelines.

Terms: Purchases all rights. Pays writers in royalties (10% on sales, 50% royalties on productions). Research Pioneer through catalog and website.

PLAYERS PRESS, INC., P.O. Box 1132, Studio City CA 91614-0132. (818)789-4980. Vice President: R. W. Gordon. Estab. 1965. Publishes 10-20 children's plays/year; 3-10 children's musicals/year.

Needs: Subject matter: "We publish for all age groups." Published plays: *Silly Soup*, by Carol Kirty (comic children's play for ages 5-15); *Indian Tales*, by William-Alan Landes (American Indian musical).

How to Contact: Query with synopsis, character breakdown and set description; include #10 SASE with query. Considers previously performed work only. Reports on query in 2-4 weeks; submissions in 1-12 months.

Terms: Purchases stage, screen, TV rights. Payment varies; work purchased possibly outright upon written request. Submissions returned with SASE.

Tips: "Submit as requested—query first and send only previously produced material. Entertainment quality is on the upswing and needs to be directed at the world, no longer just the U.S. Please submit with two #10 SASEs plus ms-size SASE. Please do not call."

PLAYS, The Drama Magazine for Young People, 120 Boylston St., Boston MA 02116-4615. (617)423-3157. Managing Editor: Elizabeth Preston. Estab. 1941. Publishes 70-75 children's plays/year.

Needs: "Props and staging should not be overly elaborate or costly. There is little call among our subscrib-

---

VISIT THE WRITER'S DIGEST WEBSITE at http://www.writersdigest.com for hot new markets, daily market updates, writers' guidelines and much more.

ers for plays with only a few characters; ten or more (to allow all students in a class to participate, for instance) is preferred. Our plays are performed by children in school from lower elementary grades through junior-senior high." 100% of plays written for juvenile roles. Subject matter: Audience is lower grades through junior/senior high. Recently published plays: *Society Page*, by Joan and Pearl Allred (about a cynical reporter who falls for happy-go-lucky reporter, junior and senior high); *Medieval Madness*, by Jan Meriwether (melodrama about how the lovely Nellie triumphs over Count Snydley to save the family castle, middle and lower grades). "Send nothing downbeat—no plays about drugs, sex or other 'heavy' topics."

How to Contact: Query first on adaptations of folk tales and classics; otherwise submit complete ms. Reports in 2-3 weeks.

Terms: Purchases all rights. Pay rates vary. Guidelines available; send SASE. Sample copy $3.50.

Tips: "Get your play underway quickly. Above all, plays must be entertaining for young people with plenty of action, fast-paced dialogue and a satisfying conclusion. Any message imparted should be secondary to the entertainment value. No sex, drugs, violence, alcohol."

✓ STAGE ONE: THE LOUISVILLE CHILDREN'S THEATRE, 501 W. Main, Louisville KY 40202-2957. (502)589-5946. Fax: (502)588-5910. E-mail: kystageone@aol.com. Website: http://www.stageone.org. Producing Director: Moses Goldberg. Estab. 1946. Produces 6-8 children's plays/year; 1-4 children's musicals/year.

Needs: Stage One is an Equity company producing children's plays for professional productions. 100% of plays/musicals written for adult roles. "Sometimes we do use students in selected productions." Produced plays: *Pinocchio*, by Moses Goldbey, music by Scott Kasbann (ages 8-12); and *John Lennon & Me*, by Cherie Bennett (about cystic fibrosis; peer acceptance for ages 11-17). Does not want to see "camp or condescension."

How to Contact: Submit complete ms, score and tape of songs (if a musical); include the author's résumé if desired. Will consider simultaneous submissions, electronic submissions via disk or modem and previously performed work. Reports in 3-4 months.

Terms: Pays writers in royalties (5-6%) or $25-75/performance.

Tips: Looking for "stageworthy and respectful dramatizations of the classic tales of childhood, both ancient and modern; plays relevant to the lives of young people and their families; and plays directly related to the school curriculum."

TADA!, 120 W. 28th St., New York NY 10001-6109. (212)627-1732. Fax: (212)243-6736. E-mail: tada@ziplink.net. Website: http://www.tadatheater.com. Artistic Director: Janine Nina Trevens. Estab. 1984. Produces 5 staged readings of children's plays and musicals/year; 0-5 children's plays/year; 2-3 children's musicals/year.

Needs: "All actors are children, ages 8-17." Produces children's plays for professional, year-round theater. 100% of plays/musicals written for juvenile roles. Recently produced musicals: *The Little Moon Theater*, book by Michael Slade, music/lyrics by Joel Gelpe (traveling performance troupe travels around the country fulfilling wishes for ages 3 and up); *Maggie and the Pirate*, book/lyrics by Winnie Holzman, music by David Evans (Maggie and her friends search for her kidnapped cricket; when they find the kidnapper, disguised as a pirate, they also find a new friend for ages 3 and up). Does not want to see fairy tales or material that talks down to children.

How to Contact: Query with synopsis, character breakdown and set description; submit complete ms, score and tape of songs (if a musical). Reports in 6 months "or in October following the August deadline for our Annual Playwriting Competition. (Send two copies of manuscript if for competition)."

Terms: Rights purchased "depend on the piece." Pays writers in royalties of 1-6% and/or pays commissioning fee. SASE a must for return of submissions.

Tips: "For plays for our Annual Playwriting Competition, submit between January and August 15. We're looking for plays with current topics that specific age ranges can identify with, with a small cast of children and one or two adults. Our company is multi-racial and city-oriented. We are not interested in fairy tales. We like to produce material that kids relate to and that touches their lives today."

THE THEATRE STUDIO INC., 750 Eighth Ave., #200, New York NY 10036. (212)719-0500. Artistic Director: A.M. Raychel. Estab. 1980. Produces 6 children's plays/year. "We would like to produce more." Produces children's musicals.

Needs: Produces children's plays for professional productions. Minimal sets.

How to Contact: Plays: Submit complete ms. Prefers one act plays (up to 45 min.). Musicals: Query first. Prefers one act musicals (up to 45 min.). Will consider simultaneous submissions and previously performed work. Reports in several months.

Terms: No pay. Submissions returned with SASE.

✅ **THEATREWORKS/USA**, 151 W. 26th, 7th Floor, New York NY 10001. (212)647-1100. Fax: (212)924-5377. Associate Artistic Director: Barbara Pasternack. Estab. 1960. Produces 3-4 children's plays and musicals/year.

Needs: Cast of 5 or 6 actors. Play should be 1 hour long, tourable. Professional children's theatre comprised of adult equity actors. 100% of shows are written for adult roles. Produced plays: *Curious George*, book and lyrics by Thomas Toce, music by Tim Brown (adaptation, for grades K-3); *Little Women*, by Allan Knee, incidental music by Kim Oler and Alison Hubbard (adaptation, for grades 4-8). No fractured, typical "kiddy theater" fairy tales or shows written strictly to teach or illustrate.

How to Contact: Query first with synopsis, character breakdown and sample songs. Will consider previously performed work. Reports in 6 months.

Terms: Pays writers royalties of 6%. SASE for return of submission.

Tips: "Plays should be not only entertaining, but 'about something.' They should touch the heart and the mind. They should not condescend to children."

Young Writer's & Illustrator's Markets

The listings in this section are special because they publish work of young writers and artists (under age 18). Some of the magazines listed exclusively feature the work of young people. Others are adult magazines with special sections for the work of young writers. There are also a few book publishers listed that exclusively publish the work of young writers and artists. Many of the magazines and publishers listed here pay only in copies, meaning authors and illustrators receive one or more free copies of the magazine or book to which they contributed.

As with adult markets, markets for children expect writers to be familiar with their editorial needs before submitting. Many of the markets listed will send guidelines to writers stating exactly what they need and how to submit it. You can often get these by sending a request with a self-addressed, stamped envelope (SASE) to the magazine or publisher, or by checking a publication's website (a number of listings include web addresses). In addition to obtaining guidelines, read through a few copies of any magazines you'd like to submit to—this is the best way to determine if your work is right for them.

A number of kids' magazines are available on newsstands or in libraries. Others are distributed only through schools, churches or home subscriptions. If you can't find a magazine you'd like to see, most editors will send sample copies for a small fee.

Before you submit your material to editors, take a few minutes to read Before Your First Sale on page 6 for more information on proper submission procedures. You may also want to check out two other sections—Contests & Awards and Conferences & Workshops. Some listings in these sections are open to students (some exclusively)—look for the phrase **"open to students"** in bold. Additional opportunities for writers can be found in *Market Guide for Young Writers* (Writer's Digest Books) and *A Teen's Guide to Getting Published: the only writer's guide written by teens for teens*, by Danielle and Jessica Dunn (Prufrock Press). More information on these books are given in the Helpful Resources section in the back of this book.

Information on companies listed in the previous edition but not included in this edition of *Children's Writer's & Illustrator's Market* may be found in the General Index.

THE ACORN, 1530 Seventh St., Rock Island IL 61201. (309)788-3980. Newsletter. Estab. 1989. Audience consists of "kindergarten-12th grade students, parents, teachers and other adults. Purpose in publishing works for children: to expose children's manuscripts to others and provide a format for those who might not have one. We want to present wholesome writing, material that will entertain and educate—audience grades K-12." Children must be K-12 (put grade on manuscripts). Guidelines available for SASE.
Magazines: 100% of magazine written by children. Uses 6 fiction pieces (500 words); 20 pieces of poetry (32 lines). No payment; purchase of a copy isn't necessary to be printed. Sample copy $2. Subscription $10 for 4 issues. Submit mss to Betty Mowery, editor. Send complete ms. Will accept typewritten, legibly handwritten and/or computer printout. Include SASE. Reports in 1 week. Will not respond without SASE.
Artwork: Publishes artwork by children. Looks for "all types; size 4×5. Use black ink in artwork." No payment. Submit artwork either with ms or separately to Betty Mowery. Include SASE. Reports in 1 week.
Tips: "My biggest problem is not having names on the manuscripts. If the manuscript gets separated from the cover letter, there is no way to know whom to respond to. Always put name, age or grade and address on manuscripts, and if you want your material returned enclose a SASE. Don't send material with killing of humans or animals, or lost love poems or stories."

AMELIA MAGAZINE, 329 "E" St., Bakersfield CA 93304-2031. (805)323-4064. Magazine. Published quarterly. Strives to offer the best of all genres. Purpose in publishing works for children: wants to offer first opportunities to budding writers. Also offers the annual Amelia Student Award for high school students. Submissions from young writers must be signed by parent, teacher or guardian verifying originality. Guidelines are not specifically for young writers; they cover the entire gamut of publication needs. For sample of past winner send $3 and SASE.

Magazines: 3% of magazine written by children. Uses primarily poetry, often generated by teachers in creative writing classes. Uses 1 story in any fiction genre (1,500 words); 4 pieces of poetry, usually haiku (3 lines). Would like to receive more general poetry from young writers. Pays in copies for haiku; $2-10 for general poetry. Regular $35 rate for fiction or nonfiction. Submit mss to Frederick A. Raborg, editor. Submit complete ms (teachers frequently submit student's work). Will accept typewritten ms. Include SASE. Reports in 3 weeks.

Artwork: Publishes artwork and photography by children; "have not yet, however." Looks for photos no smaller than 5×7; artwork in any method; also cartoons. Pays $5-20 on publication. Submit well-protected artwork with SASE. Submit artwork/photos to Frederick A. Raborg, Jr., editor. Include SASE. Reports in 3 weeks. Sample issue: $9.95.

Tips: "Be neat and thorough. Photos should have captions. Cartoon gaglines ought to be funny; try them out on someone before submitting. We want to encourage young writers, because the seeds of literary creativity are sown quite young with strong desires to read and admiration for the authors of those early readings."

AMERICAN GIRL, 8400 Fairway Place, Middleton WI 53562. (608)836-4848. Fax: (608)831-7089. Website: http://www.americangirl.com. Bimonthly magazine. Audience consists of girls ages 8-12 who are joyful about being girls. Purpose in publishing works by young people: self-esteem boost and entertainment for readers. Young writers should be 8-12 years old. "We don't have writer's guidelines for children's submissions. Instruction for specific solicitations appears in the magazine."

Magazines: 5% of magazine written by young people. "A few pages of each issue feature articles that include children's answers to questions or requests that have appeared in a previous issue of *American Girl*." Pays in copies. Submit to address listed in magazine. Will accept legibly handwritten ms. Include SASE. Reports in 8-12 weeks.

Tips: "Please, no stories, poems, etc. about American Girls Collection Characters (Felicity, Samantha, Molly, Kirsten, Addy or Josefina)."

THE APPRENTICE WRITER, % Gary Fincke, Susquehanna University, Selinsgrove PA 17870-1001. (717)372-4164. Fax: (717)372-4310. E-mail: gfincke@susqu.edu. Magazine. Published annually. "Writing by high school students and for high school students." Purpose in publishing works by young people: to provide quality writing by students which can be read for pleasure and serve as a text for high school classrooms. Work is primarily from eastern and northeastern states, but will consider work from other areas of US. Students must be in grades 9-12. Writer's guidelines available for SASE.

Magazines: Uses 15 short stories (prefers under 5,000 words); 15 nonfiction personal essays (prefers under 5,000 words); 60 poems (no word limit) per issue. Pays in copies to writers and their schools. Submit mss to Gary Fincke, editor. Submit complete ms. Will accept typewritten mss. Include SASE. Submit ms by March 15. Responds by May of each year.

Artwork/Photography: Publishes artwork and photography by children. Looks for b&w. Pays in copies to artists and their schools. Submit originals or high quality copies. Submit art and photographs to Gary Fincke, editor. Include SASE. Submit artwork by March 15. Responds by May of each year.

N BEYOND WORDS PUBLISHING, INC., 20827 NW Cornell Rd., Suite 500, Hillsboro OR 97124. (503)531-8700. Fax: (503)531-8773. E-mail: marianne@beyondword.com. Book publisher. Managing Editor of Children's Department: Marianne Monson. Publishes 2-3 books by children/year. Looks for "books that encourage creativity and an appreciation of nature in children." Wants to "encourage children to write, create, dream and believe that it is possible to be published. The books must be unique, be of national interest and the child author must be personable and promotable." Writer's guidelines available with SASE.

Books: Holds yearly writing contests for activity/advice books written by and for children/teens. Also occasionally publishes nonfiction advice books for and by children such as joke books, or guides for kids about pertinent concerns.

Tips: "Write about issues that affect your life. Winners in the past have written chapters on great slumber parties, analyzing dreams, jokes and understanding peers with disabilities."

BOYS' LIFE, 1325 W. Walnut Hill Lane, P.O. Box 152079, Irving TX 75015-2079. (972)580-2366. Magazine published monthly. Audience consists of boys ages 7-18. *Boys' Life* is published by the Boy

Scouts of America to make available to children the highest caliber of fiction and nonfiction, to stimulate an interest in good reading and to promote the principles of Scouting. Writer's and illustrator's guidelines available for SASE. Send 9×12 SASE plus a check or money order for a sample issue as well as guidelines.

Magazines: Submissions from children: Small percentage of magazine written by young people under 18. Uses hobby and collecting tips for "Hobby Hows" and "Collecting" columns. Pays $10/tip. Uses jokes for "Think & Grin" column. Pays choice of $2 or copy of *Scout Handbook* or *Scout Fieldbook*/joke accepted. Several times/year uses personal stories (500 words maximum) for "Readers' Page." Pays $25. Submit mss to column. Submit complete ms. Will accept typewritten and legibly handwritten mss for consideration. Reports in 6-8 weeks. Submissions from adults: For nonfiction mss, *query first* to Mike Goldman, articles editor. All fiction mss should be double-spaced and typed copy, 1,000-1,500 words. Pays $750 and up for accepted stories. Story categories: humor, mystery, science fiction, adventure. Include SASE for return of materials. For fiction mss, send one copy of story plus cover letter. Submit to Shannon Lowry, associate editor. Include SASE.

Tips: "Study one year's worth of recent magazines before submitting."

N **CHICKADEE MAGAZINE,** 179 John St., Suite 500, Toronto, Ontario M5T 3G5 Canada. (416)340-2700. Magazine published 9 times/year. "*Chickadee* is for children ages 6-9. Its purpose is to entertain and educate children about science, nature and the world around them. We publish children's drawings to give readers the chance to express themselves. Drawings must relate to the topics that are given in the 'All Your Own' section of each issue."

Artwork: Publishes artwork by children. No payment given. Mail submissions with name, age and return address for thank you note. Submit to Mitch Butler, All Your Own Editor. Reports in 4 months.

CREATIVE KIDS, P.O. Box 8813, Waco TX 76714-8813. (800)998-2208. Fax: (254)756-3339. E-mail: creative_kids@prufrock.com. Website: http://www.prufrock.com. Editor: Libby Lindsey. Magazine published 4 times/year. Estab. 1979. "All material is by children, for children." Purpose in publishing works by children: "to create a product that provides children with an authentic experience and to offer an opportunity for children to see their work in print. *Creative Kids* contains the best stories, poetry, opinion, artwork, games and photography by kids ages 8-14." Writers ages 8-14 must have statement by teacher or parent verifying originality. Writer's guidelines available on request with SASE.

Magazines: Uses "about 6" fiction and nonfiction stories (800-900 words); poetry, plays, ideas to share (200-750 words) per issue. Pays "free magazine." Submit mss to submissions editor. Will accept typewritten mss. Include SASE. Reports in 1 month.

Artwork/Photography: Publishes artwork and photos by children. Looks for "any kind of drawing, cartoon, or painting." Pays "free magazine." Send original or a photo of the work to submissions editor. No photocopies. Include SASE. Reports in 1 month.

Tips: "*Creative Kids* is a magazine by kids, for kids. The work represents children's ideas, questions, fears, concerns and pleasures. The material never contains racist, sexist or violent expression. The purpose is to provide children with an authentic experience. A person may submit one piece of work per envelope. Each piece must be labeled with the student's name, birth date, grade, school, home address and school address. Include a photograph, if possible. Recent school pictures are best. Material submitted to *Creative Kids* must not be under consideration by any other publication. Items should be carefully prepared, proofread and double checked (perhaps also by a parent or teacher). All activities requiring solutions must be accompanied by the correct answers. Young writers and artists should always write for guidelines and then follow them. It is very frustrating to receive submissions that are not complete."

CREATIVE WITH WORDS, Thematic anthologies, Creative with Words Publications, P.O. Box 223226, Carmel CA 93922. Fax: (408)655-8627. E-mail: cwwpub@usa.net. Website: http://members.tripod .com/~CreativeWithWords. Editor: Brigitta Geltrich. Nature Editor: Bert Hower. Publishes 14 anthologies/ year. Estab. 1975. "We publish the creative writing of children (two anthologies written by children; two anthologies written by adults; ten anthologies written by all ages)." Audience consists of children, schools, libraries, adults, reading programs. Purpose in publishing works by children: to offer them an opportunity

FOR EXPLANATIONS OF THESE SYMBOLS,
SEE THE INSIDE FRONT AND BACK COVERS OF THIS BOOK

to get started in publishing. "Work must be of quality, original, unedited, and not published before; age must be given (up to 19 years old)." SASE must be enclosed with all correspondence and mss. Writer's guidelines and theme list available on request with SASE, via e-mail or on website.

Books: Considers all categories except those dealing with death, violence, pornography and overly religious. Uses fairy tales, folklore items (up to 1,500 words) and poetry (not to exceed 20 lines, 46 characters across). Published *Nature Series: Skies, Land, Forests, Seas*; *Dinosaurs & Dragons*; and *Relationships* (all children and adults). Pays 20% discount on each copy of publication in which fiction or poetry by children appears. Best of the month receives award, is published on website and author receives one free copy of issue. Submit mss to Brigitta Geltrich, editor. Query; child, teacher or parent can submit; teacher and/or parents must verify originality of writing. Will accept typewritten and/or legibly handwritten mss. SASE. "Will not go through agents." Reports in 2-4 weeks after deadline of any theme.

Artwork/Photography: Publishes artwork, b&w photos and computer artwork by children (language art work). Pays 20% discount on every copy of publication in which work by children appears. Submit artwork to Brigitta Geltrich, editor, and request info on payment.

Tips: "Enjoy the English language, life and the world around you. Look at everything from a different perspective. Be less descriptive and use words wisely. Let the reader experience a story through a viewpoint character, don't be overly dramatic."

☑ **FREE SPIRIT PUBLISHING INC.**, 400 First Ave. North, Suite 616, Minneapolis MN 55401-1730. (612)338-2068. Fax: (612)337-5050. E-mail: help4kids@freespirit.com. Website: http://www.freespirit.com. Publishes 15-20 books/year. "We specialize in SELF-HELP FOR KIDS®. We aim to help kids help themselves. We were the *first* publisher of self-help materials for children, and today we are the *only* publisher of SELF-HELP FOR KIDS® materials. Our main audience is children and teens, but we also publish for parents, teachers, therapists, youth workers and other involved in caring for kids. Our main interests include the development of self-esteem, self-awareness, creative thinking and problem-solving abilities, assertiveness and making a difference in the world. We do not publish fiction or poetry. We do accept submissions from young people ages 14 and older; however, please send a letter from a parent/guardian/leader verifying originality." Request catalog, author guidelines, and "student guidelines" before submitting work. Send SASE.

Books: Publishes self-help for kids, how-to, classroom activities. Pays advance and royalties. Submit mss to Caryn Pernu, acquisitions editor. Send query and sample table of contents. Will accept typewritten mss. SASE required. Reports in 3-4 months.

Artwork/Photography: Submit samples to Caryn Pernu, acquisitions editor.

Tips: "Free Spirit publishes very specific material, and it helps when writers request and study our catalog before submitting work to us, and refer to our author guidelines (our catalog and guidelines are available by mail or via our website.) We do not accept general self-help books, autobiographies or children's books that feature made-up stories. Our preference is books that help kids to gain self-esteem, succeed in school, stand up for themselves, resolve conflicts and make a difference in the world. We do not publish books that have animals as the main characters."

THE GOLDFINCH, Iowa History for Young People, 402 Iowa Ave., Iowa City IA 52240. (319)335-3916. Fax: (319)335-3935. Magazine published quarterly. Audience is 4th-8th graders. "Magazine supports creative work by children: research, art, writing. *The Goldfinch* puts the fun back into history. We publish young Iowans' work to show them that they and their creative efforts are an important part of Iowa history." Submitted work must go with the historical theme of each issue.

Magazines: 10-20% written by children. Uses at least 1 nonfiction essay, poem, story/issue (500 words). Pays complimentary copies. Submit mss with SASE to Millie K. Frese, interim editor. Submit complete ms. Will accept typewritten, legibly handwritten, computer disk (Apple) mss. Reports in 1 month.

Artwork/Photography: Publishes artwork/photographs by children. Art and photos must be b&w. Pays complimentary copies. Query first with SASE to Amy Ruth.

Tips: "We make the subject of Iowa history come alive through short features, games/puzzles/activities, fiction and cool historical photographs."

HIGHLIGHTS FOR CHILDREN, 803 Church St., Honesdale PA 18431. (717)253-1080. Magazine. Published monthly. "We strive to provide wholesome, stimulating, entertaining material that will encourage children to read. Our audience is children ages 2-12." Purpose in publishing works by young people: to encourage children's creative expression.

Magazines: 15-20% of magazine written by children. Uses stories and poems. Also uses jokes, riddles, tongue twisters. Features that occur occasionally: "What Are Your Favorite Books?" (8-10/year), Recipes (8-10/year), "Science Letters" (15-20/year). Special features that invite children's submissions on a specific topic occur several times per year. Recent examples include "Pet Stories," "Favorite Songs," "Kids at

Work," and "Help the Cartoonists." Pays in copies. Submit complete ms to the editor. Will accept typewritten, legibly handwritten and computer printout mss. Reports in 3-6 weeks.

Artwork: Publishes artwork by children. Pays in copies. No cartoon or comic book characters. No commercial products. Submit b&w or color artwork for "Our Own Pages." Features include "Creatures Nobody Has Ever Seen" (5-8/year) and "Illustration Job" (18-20/year). Reports in 3-6 weeks.

INK BLOT, 901 Day Rd., Saginaw MI 48609. Newsletter. Published monthly. "I want young writers to do their best work, learn proper form and have their work shared with others. We put our newsletter in libraries, hospitals, waiting rooms and copies to contributors." Purpose in publishing works by young people: to give children an outlet for publishing their talents; to have them write using their imagination and creativity and to share them with others. Accepts manuscripts from all ages. If student, please include age, grade and school name. Only print original works from contributors. Material is accepted from across the United States and Canada. Typewritten preferred—handwritten *neatly* OK. Please put name on each page submitted.

Magazines: Submit mss to Margaret Larkin. Responds in 6 months. Sample copy and guidelines available for $1 (check made out to M. Larkin, editor) and include SASE. Maximum length 500 words (stories). "Must fit on one side of typewritten page."

Artwork: Publishes artwork by children. Wants small 3 × 3 b&w ink drawings only; especially drawings that accompany poetry and short stories. No derogatory or obscene pictures accepted. Pays in copies. Submit art to Margaret Larkin, editor, or Vicki Larkin, assistant editor. Include SASE. Reports in 3 months.

N ⬧ **KWIL KIDS PUBLISHING, The Little Publishing Company That Kwil Built**, P.O. Box 29556, Maple Ridge, British Columbia V2X 2V0 Canada. Phone/fax: (604)466-5712. E-mail: kwil@bc.sympatico.ca. Publishes books, newspaper column, newsletter and web page. Publishes 10-20 books/year by children (at cost, nonprofit). Publishes weekly column in local paper starting autumn '98; monthly newsletter; books—2 launches/year. "*Kwil Kids* come in all ages, shapes and sizes—from 4-64 and a whole lot more! Kwil does not pay for or profit from the creative work of children but provides opportunity/encouragement. We want to promote literacy, creativity, and written 'connections'; to publish autobiographical, inspirational, fantastical, humorous stories of gentleness, compassion, truth and beauty." Must include name, age, school, address and parent signature (if a minor). Will send newsletter upon request as a sample.

Books: Publishes autobiographical, inspirational, creative stories (alliterative, rhyming refrains, juicy words), fiction; short rhyming and non-rhyming poems (creative, fun, original, expressive, poetry). Length: 1,000 words for fiction; 8-16 lines for poetry. No payment—self published and sold "at cost" only (2 free copies). Submit mss to Kwil publisher. Submit complete ms; send copy only—expect a reply but will not return ms. Will accept typewritten and legibly handwritten mss and e-mail. Include SASE. Reports in 1 month.

Newsletter: 95% of newsletter written by young people. Uses 15 short stories, poems, jokes (20-100 words). No payment—free newsletter subscription, contests with book/cash awards. Submit complete ms. Will accept typewritten and legibly handwritten mss and e-mail. Reports in 1 month.

Artwork: Publishes artwork and photography by children (only occasionally with writing). Looks for black ink sketches to go with writing, photos to go with writing. Nonprofit/at cost—free newsletter subscription. Submit by postal mail only; white background for sketches. Submit artwork/photos to Kwil publisher. Include SASE. Reports in 1 month.

Tips: "Just be who you are and do what you do—then all of life's treasures will come to you." In other words: be creative, have fun, and remember that we all have important thoughts, feelings, and ideas to share. Kwil very much wants to hear yours. Kwil's motto: 'Keep your pencil moving!' Kwil always writes back."

✓ **MERLYN'S PEN: Fiction, Essays, and Poems by America's Teens**, P.O. Box 1058, East Greenwich RI 02818. (800)247-2027. Fax: (401)885-5222. Website: http://www.merlynspen.com. Magazine. Published annually. "By publishing student writing, *Merlyn's Pen* seeks to broaden and reward the young author's interest in writing, strengthen the self-confidence of beginning writers and promote among all students a positive attitude toward literature. We publish 75 manuscripts annually by students in grades 6-12. The entire magazine is dedicated to young adults' writing. Our audience is classrooms, libraries and students from grades 6-12." Writers must be in grades 6-12 and must send a completed *Merlyn's Pen* cover sheet with each submission. When a student is accepted, he/she, a parent and a teacher must sign a statement of originality.

Magazines: Uses 20 short stories (no word limit); plays; 8 nonfiction essays (no word limit); 25 pieces of poetry; letters to the editor; editorials; reviews of previously published works. Published authors receive 3 contributor's copies and payment of $20-200. Also, a discount is offered for additional copies of the issue. Submit up to 3 titles at one time. Will only accept typewritten mss. Reports in 10 weeks.

Tips: "All manuscripts and artwork must be accompanied by a completed copy of *Merlyn's Pen* official cover sheet for submissions. Call to request cover sheet."

NATIONAL GEOGRAPHIC WORLD, 1145 17th St. NW, Washington DC 20036-4688. (202)857-7000. Magazine published monthly. Picture magazine for ages 8 and older. Purpose in publishing work by young people: to encourage in young readers a curiosity about the world around them.
Tips: Publishes art, letters, poems, games, riddles, jokes and craft ideas by children in mailbag section only. No payment given. Send by mail to: Submissions Committee. "Sorry, but *World* cannot acknowledge or return your contributions."

NEW MOON: The Magazine For Girls & Their Dreams, New Moon Publishing, Inc., P.O. Box 3620, Duluth MN 55803-3620. (218)728-5507. Fax: (218)728-0314. E-mail: newmoon@computerpro.com. Website: http://www.newmoon.org. Magazine. Published bimonthly. *New Moon*'s primary audience is girls ages 8-14. "We publish a magazine that listens to girls." More than 70% of *New Moon* is written by girls. Purpose in publishing work by children/teens: "We want girls' voices to be heard. *New Moon* wants girls to see that their opinions, dreams, thoughts and ideas counts." Writer's guidelines available for SASE.
Magazine: 75% of magazine written by young people. Uses 4 fiction mss (300-900 words); 12 nonfiction mss (300-900 words) per year. Submit to Barbara Stretchberry, managing editor. Submit query, complete mss for fiction and nonfiction. Will accept typewritten, legibly handwritten mss and disk (IBM compatible). "We do not return unsolicited material." Please include SASE. Reports in 6 months.
Artwork/Photography: Publishes artwork and photography by children. Looks for cover and inside illustrations. Pay negotiated. Submit art and photographs to Barbara Stretchberry, managing editor. "We do not return unsolicited material."
Tips: "Read *New Moon* to completely understand our needs."

POTLUCK CHILDREN'S LITERARY MAGAZINE, P.O. Box 546, Deerfield IL 60015-0546. Phone/fax: (847)948-1139. E-mail: nappic@aol.com. Website: http://members.aol.com/nappic. Quarterly magazine. "We look for works with imagery and human truths. Occasionally we will work with young authors on editing their work. We are available to the writer for questions and comments. The purpose of *Potluck* is to encourage creative expression and to supply young writers with a forum in which they can be heard. We also provide informative articles to help them become better writers and to prepare them for the adult markets. For example, recent articles dealt with work presentation, tracking submissions and rights." Writer's guidelines available on request.
Magazines: 99% of magazine written by young people. Uses fiction (300-400 words); nonfiction (300-400 words); poetry (30 lines); book reviews (150 words). Pays with copy of issue published. Submit mss to Susan Napoli Picchietti, editor. Submit complete ms; teacher may send group submissions, which have different guidelines and payment schedules. Will accept typewritten and e-mailed mss. Include SASE. Reports 4-6 weeks after deadline.
Artwork/Photography: Publishes artwork by children. Looks for all types of artwork—no textured works. Must be 8½×11 only. Pays in copies. Do not fold submissions. If you want your work returned, you must include proper postage and envelope. Submit artwork to Susan Napoli Picchietti, editor. Include SASE. Reports in 4-6 weeks.
Tips: "Relax—observe and acknowledge all that is around you. Life gives us a lot to draw on. Don't get carried away with style—let your words speak for themselves. If you want to be taken seriously as a writer, you must take yourself seriously. The rest will follow. Enjoy yourself and take pride in every piece, even the bad, they keep you humble."

SHOFAR MAGAZINE, 43 Northcote Dr., Melville NY 11747. (516)643-4598. Fax: (516)643-4598. E-mail: graysonpsc@aol.com. Managing Editor: Gerald H. Grayson. Magazine published 6 times/school year. Audience consists of American Jewish children age 9-13. Purpose in publishing works by young people: to give them an opportunity to get their work printed.
Magazines: 10% of magazine written by young people. Uses fiction/nonfiction (750-1,000 words), Kids Page items (50-150 words). Submit mss to Gerald Grayson, publisher. Submit complete ms. Will accept typewritten, legibly handwritten mss and computer disk (Mac only). SASE. Reports in 2 months.
Artwork/Photography: Publishes artwork and photography by children. Pays "by the piece, depending

SPECIAL COMMENTS by the editor of *Children's Writer's & Illustrator's Market* are set off by a bullet.

on size and quantity." Submit original with SASE. Reports in 1-2 months.

SKIPPING STONES, Multicultural Children's Magazine, P.O. Box 3939, Eugene OR 97403. (541)342-4956. Website: http://www.nonviolence.org/skipping. Articles/Poems/Fiction Editor: Arun N. Toké. 5 issues a year. Estab. 1988. Circulation 3,000. "*Skipping Stones* is a multicultural, nonprofit, children's magazine to encourage cooperation, creativity and celebration of cultural and environmental richness. It offers itself as a creative forum for communication among children from different lands and backgrounds. We prefer work by children under 18 years old. International, minorities and under represented populations receive priority, multilingual submissions are encouraged."

• *Skipping Stones*' theme for their Youth Honor Awards 1999 is multicultural and nature awareness.

Send SASE for guidelines and for more information on the awards.

Magazines: 50% written by children. Uses 5-10 fiction short stories and plays (500-750 words); 5-10 nonfiction articles, interviews, letters, history, descriptions of celebrations (500-750 words); 15-20 poems, jokes, riddles, proverbs (250 words or less) per issue. Pays in contributor's copies. Submit mss to Mr. Arun Toké, editor. Submit complete ms for fiction or nonfiction work; teacher may submit; parents can also submit their contributions. Submissions should include "cover letter with name, age, address, school, cultural background, inspiration for piece, dreams for future . . . " Will accept typewritten, legibly handwritten and computer/word processor mss. Include SASE. Responds in 3 months. Accepts simultaneous submissions.

Artwork/Photography: Publishes artwork and photography for children. Will review all varieties of ms/illustration packages. Wants comics, cartoons, b&w photos, paintings, drawings (preferably ink & pen or pencil), 8×10, color photos OK. Subjects include children, people, celebrations, nature, ecology, multicultural. Pays in contributor's copies.

Terms: "*Skipping Stones* is a labor of love. You'll receive complimentary contributor's (up to four) copies depending on the length of your contribution and illustrations." Reports back to artists in 3 months. Sample copy for $5 and 8½×11 SAE with 4 first-class stamps.

Tips: "Let the 'inner child' within you speak out—naturally, uninhibited." Wants "material that gives insight on cultural celebrations, lifestyle, custom and tradition, glimpse of daily life in other countries and cultures. Please, no mystery for the sake of mystery! Photos, songs, artwork are most welcome if they illustrate/highlight the points. Upcoming features: Turning points in life, cooperative games and sports, religions and cultures from around the world, modern technology and its impact, Native American cultures, street children, songs and recipes from around the world, resource conservation and sustainable lifestyles, indigenous architecture, building community and networking, grandparents, Humor Unlimited, Intl., creative problem-solving, rewards and punishments and fear and loss."

SKYLARK, Purdue University Calumet, 2200 169th St., Hammond IN 46323. (219)989-2262. Fax: (219)989-2750. Editor: Pamela Hunter. Young Writers' Editor: Shirley Jo Moritz. Annual magazine. Circ. 650-1,000. 15% of material written by juvenile authors. Presently accepting material by children. "*Skylark* wishes to provide a vehicle for creative writing of all kinds (with emphasis on an attractive synthesis of text and layout), especially by writers ages 5-18, who live in the Illinois/Indiana area and who have not ordinarily been provided with such an outlet. Children need a place to see their work published alongside that of adults." Proof of originality is required from parents or teachers for all authors. "We feel that creativity should be nurtured as soon as possible in an individual. By publishing young, promising authors and illustrators in the same magazine which also features work by adults, perhaps we will provide the impetus for a young person to keep at his/her craft." Writer's guidelines available upon request with a SASE.

Magazines: 15% of magazine written by young people. In previous issues, *Skylark* has published mysteries, fantasy, humor, good narrative fiction stories (400-800 words), personal essays, brief character sketches, nonfiction stories (400-650 words), poetry (no more than 16 lines). Does not want to see material that is obviously religious or sexual. Pays in contributor's copies. Submit ms to Shirley Jo Moritz, Young Writers' editor. Submit complete ms. Prefers typewritten ms. Must include SASE for response or return of material. Reports in 4 months. Byline given.

Artwork/Photography: Publishes artwork and photographs by children. Looks for "photos of animals, landscapes and sports, and for artwork to go along with text." Pays in contributor's copies. All artwork and photos must be b&w, 8½×11, unlined paper. Do not use pencil and no copyrighted characters. Markers are advised for best reproduction. Include name and address on the back of each piece. Package properly to avoid damage. Submit artwork/photos to Pamela Hunter, editor-in-chief. Include SASE. Reports in 5 months.

Tips: "We're looking for literary work. Follow your feelings, be as original as you can and don't be afraid to be different. Some of our children or perhaps their teachers and parents don't understand that a SASE must accompany the submission in order to get a response or reply."

STONE SOUP, The Magazine by Young Writers and Artists, Children's Art Foundation, P.O. Box 83, Santa Cruz CA 95063. (408)426-5557. Fax: (408)426-1161. E-mail: editor@stonesoup.com. Website: http://www.stonesoup.com. Articles/Fiction Editor, Art Director: Ms. Gerry Mandel. Magazine published 6 times/year. Circ. 20,000. "We publish fiction, poetry and artwork by children through age 13. Our preference is for work based on personal experiences and close observation of the world. Our audience is young people through age 13, as well as parents, teachers, librarians." Purpose in publishing works by young people: to encourage children to read and to express themselves through writing and art. Writer's guidelines available upon request with a SASE.

Magazines: Uses animal, contemporary, fantasy, history, problem-solving, science fiction, sports, spy/mystery/adventure fiction stories. Uses 5-10 fiction stories (100-2,500 words); 5-10 nonfiction stories (100-2,500 words); 2-4 poems per issue. Does not want to see classroom assignments and formula writing. Buys 65 mss/year. Byline given. Pays on publication. Buys all rights. Pays $10 each for stories and poems, $15 for book reviews. Contributors also receive 2 copies. Sample copy $2. Free writer's guidelines. "We don't publish straight nonfiction, but we do publish stories based on real events and experiences." Send complete ms to Ms. Gerry Mandel, editor. Will accept typewritten and legibly handwritten mss. Include SASE. Reports in 1 month.

Artwork/Photography: Publishes any type, size or color artwork/photos by children. Pays $10 for b&w illustrations. Contributors receive 2 copies. Sample copy $2. Free illustrator's guidelines. Send originals if possible. Send submissions to Ms. Gerry Mandel, editor. Include SASE. Reports in 1 month. Original artwork returned at job's completion. All artwork must be by children through age 13.

Tips: "Be sure to enclose a SASE. Only work by young people through age 13 is considered. Whether your work is about imaginary situations or real ones, use your own experiences and observations to give your work depth and a sense of reality. Read a few issues of our magazine to get an idea of what we like."

STRAIGHT MAGAZINE, Standard Publishing, 8121 Hamilton Ave., Cincinnati OH 45231. (513)931-4050. Fax: (513)931-0950. Magazine published quarterly in weekly parts. Estab. 1951. Magazine includes fiction pieces and articles for Christian teens 13-19 years old to inform, encourage and uplift them. "*Straight* is a magazine for today's Christian teenagers. We use fiction and nonfiction to address modern-day problems from a Christian perspective." Purpose in publishing works by young people: to provide them with an opportunity to express themselves and communicate with their peers through poetry, fiction and nonfiction. Children must submit their birth dates and Social Security numbers. Writer's guidelines available on request, "included in regular guidelines."

Magazines: Uses fiction (900-1,500 words), personal experience pieces (900-1,100 words), poetry. Pays flat fee for poetry; 5-7¢/word for stories/articles. Submit complete mss to Heather E. Wallace, editor. Will accept typewritten and computer printout mss. Reports in 1-2 months.

Artwork/Photography: Publishes artwork and photography by children. Send samples for review for consideration for assignment. Send samples for file to Heather Wallace, editor.

Tips: "Remember that we are a religious publication. Any submissions, including poetry should have a religious slant."

⊞ TEXAS YOUNG WRITERS' NEWSLETTER, P.O. Box 942, Adkins TX 78101-0942. E-mail: susancurrie@yahoo.com. Newsletter. Published bimonthly during school year, monthly during summer. "Our audience is young writers 12-19, their teachers and their parents." Purpose in publishing works by young people: to give them an opportunity to publish their work in a reputable publication along with other talented young writers, and to show them that they can be published authors. Children must be 12-19 years old. "We do send a form for them to sign after their work is accepted that states that their work is original." Writer's guidelines available on request.

Magazines: 50% of magazine written by young people. Uses 1 fiction story (400-800 words) or 1 opinionated essay, personal experience, etc. (400-800 words), 2 poems (maximum 30 lines) per issue. "Very experienced young writers may submit articles discussing the art and business of writing; relate experience in cover letter." Pays 5 copies for stories, essays and articles; 2 copies for poetry. Submit mss to Susan Currie, editor. Include SASE. Reports in 1 month. Work must be typed.

Tips: "Be persistent and careful in your submissions! Keep trying until you've published. We also need articles on the art and business of writing from adults. Send SASE for guidelines. We appreciate cover letters!"

VIRGINIA WRITING, Longwood College, 201 High St., Farmville VA 23909. (804)395-2160. Magazine published twice yearly. "*Virginia Writing* publishes prose, poetry, fiction, nonfiction, art, photography, music and drama from Virginia high school students and teachers. The purpose of the journal is to publish 'promise,' giving the talented young people of Virginia an opportunity to have their works published. Our audience is mainly Virginia high schools, Virginia public libraries, Department of Education offices, and private citizens. It is also used as a supplementary text in many of Virginia's high school classrooms. The children must be attending a Virginia high school, preferably in no less than 9th grade (though some work has been accepted from 8th graders). Originality is strongly encouraged. The guidelines are in the front of our magazine or available with SASE." No profanity or racism accepted.

● *Virginia Writing* is the recipient of 14 national awards, including the 1997 Golden Shoestring Honor Award, eight Distinguished Achievement Awards for Excellence in Educational Journalism, and the Golden Lamp Honor Award as one of the top four educational magazines in the U.S. and Canada.

Magazines: 85% of magazine written by children. Uses approximately 7 fiction and nonfiction short stories and essays, 56 poems per issue. Submit mss to Billy C. Clark, founder and editor. Submit complete ms. Will accept typewritten mss. Reports in 1-4 months, "but must include SASE to receive a reply in the event manuscript is not accepted."

Artwork/Photography: Publishes artwork by children. Considers all types of artwork, including that done on computer. Color slides of artwork are acceptable. All original work is returned upon publication in a non-bendable, well protected package. Submit artwork to Billy C. Clark. Reports as soon as possible.

Tips: "All works should be submitted with a cover letter describing student's age, grade and high school currently attending. Submit as often as you like and in any quantity. We cannot accept a work if it features profanity or racism."

WHOLE NOTES, P.O. Box 1374, Las Cruces NM 88004-1374. (505)541-5744. Magazine published twice yearly. "We look for original, fresh perceptions in poems that demonstrate skill in using language effectively, with carefully chosen images, clear ideas and fresh perceptions. Our audience (general) loves poetry. We try to recognize excellence in creative writing by children as a way to encourage and promote imaginative thinking." Writer's guidelines available for SASE.

Magazines: Every fourth issue is 100% by children. Writers should be 21 years old or younger. Uses 30 poems/issue (length open). Pays complimentary copy. Submit mss to Nancy Peters Hastings, editor. Submit complete ms. "No multiple submissions, please." Will accept typewritten and legibly handwritten mss. SASE. Reports in 3 weeks.

Artwork/Photography: Publishes artwork and photographs by children. Looks for b&w line drawings which can easily be reproduced; b&w photos. Pays complimentary copy. Send clear photocopies. Submit artwork to Nancy Peters Hastings, editor. SASE. Reports in 3 weeks.

Tips: Sample issue is $3. "We welcome translations. Don't send your only copy of your poem. Keep a photocopy."

WORD DANCE, Playful Productions, Inc., P.O. Box 10804, Wilmington DE 19850. (302)322-6699. Website: http://www.worddance.com. Magazine. Published quarterly. "We're a magazine of creative writing and art that is for *and* by children in kindergarten through grade eight."

Magazines: Uses adventure, fantasy, humorous, etc. (fiction); travel stories, poems and stories based on real life experiences (nonfiction). Publishes 250 total pieces of writing/year; maximum length: 3 pages. Submit mss to Stuart Ungar, articles editor. Sample copy $3. Free writer's guidelines and submissions form. SASE. Reports in 6-8 months.

Artwork: Illustrations accepted from young people in kindergarten through grade 8. Accepts illustrations of specific stories or poems and other general artwork. Must be high contrast. Query. Submit complete package with final art to art director. SASE. Reports in 6-8 months.

☑ **WRITERS' INT'L FORUM FOR YOUNG AUTHORS**, (also see Writers' Int'l Forum), P.O. Box 516, Tracyton WA 98393-0516. Website: http://www.bristolservicesintl.com. Newsletter published monthly (except December, July and August). Purpose in publishing works by young people (under 17): to promote strong communications skills, both in essays and in traditional fiction formats. Guidelines available for SASE.

Magazines: Publication contains a "Featured Manuscript" section in which both a young author's manuscript and our professional comments on that manuscript are published. Seeks short stories and essays (1,000 word maximum). Any genre or subject (except no horror or violence). We want well-crafted stories with traditional plots which are written in clear language, have fully developed characters and an interesting storyline. Essays must have a tight focus, make a distinct point, and back up that point with specific facts and/or experiences (preferably experiences of the young author). Pays $10 upon our receipt of completed acceptance form, 1 complimentary copy and provides a written professional comment. Author's biographical information printed for every accepted manuscript. Submit mss to Sandra E. Haven, Editor. Submit complete ms with cover letter stating author's age. Will accept only typewritten mss. Please send SASE for full guidelines *before* submitting or visit website to request guidelines. Reports in 2 months.

This illustration by a fourth grade student appeared in *Word Dance*, a magazine of creative writing and art by children in kindergarten through eighth grade. "Schools and parents submit work to us on a quarterly basis," says editor Stuart Ungar. "We look for simple pieces that are high in contrast and dynamic." The art is reprinted in the magazine in a two-color format. "It is wonderful to see how one young artist illustrates a story by a young author," says Ungar. "The effects of the writing can often be seen in the images that are produced."

© 1998 *Word Dance*

☑ **THE WRITERS' SLATE**, (The Writing Conference, Inc.), P.O. Box 664, Ottawa KS 66067-0664. (913)242-0407. Fax: (913)242-0407. E-mail: wjbushman@writingconference.com. Website: http://www.writingconference.com. Magazine. Publishes 3 issues/year. *The Writers' Slate* accepts original poetry and prose from students enrolled in kindergarten-12th grade. The audience is students, teachers and librarians. Purpose in publishing works by young people: to give students the opportunity to publish and to give students the opportunity *to read* quality literature written by other students. Writer's guidelines available on request.

Magazines: 90% of magazine written by young people. Uses 10-15 fiction, 1-2 nonfiction, 10-15 other mss per issue. Submit mss to Dr. F. Todd Goodson, editor, Kansas State University, 364 Bluemont Hall, Manhattan KS 66506-5300. Submit complete ms. Will accept typewritten mss. Reports in 1 month. Include SASE with ms if reply is desired.

Artwork: Publishes artwork by young people. Bold, b&w, student artwork may accompany a piece of writing. Submit to Dr. F. Todd Goodson, editor. Reports in 1 month.

Tips: "Always accompany submission with a letter indicating name, home address, school, grade level and teacher's name. If you want a reply, submit a SASE."

☑ **WRITES OF PASSAGE**, 345 Lorton Ave., Burlingame CA 94010. (650)558-0276. E-mail: wpusa@aol.com. Website: http://www.writes.org. Contact: Wendy Mass. Journal. Publishes 2 issues/year by children (spring/summer and fall/winter). "Our philosophy: 'It may make your parents cringe, your teacher blush, but your best friend will understand.' " Purpose in publishing works by young people: to give teenagers across the country a chance to express themselves through creative writing. "We publish poems and short stories written by teens across the U.S. providing an outlet for their thoughts and feelings. We provide a forum in which teenagers can share their words. It gives teens an opportunity to see that they are not alone with their fears and confusion and rewards them for creative writing. It sends a message that

A SELF-ADDRESSED, STAMPED ENVELOPE (SASE) should always be included with submissions within your own country. When sending material to other countries, include a self-addressed envelope (SAE) and International Reply Coupons (IRCs).

their thoughts are important." Writers must be 12-18 years old, work must be original, short biography should be included. "We are also accepting columns of tips and advice for our young readers to be posted on the website."

Magazines: Uses short stories (up to 4 double-spaced pages) and poetry. Pays in 2 copies. Submit to Laura Hoffman, president. Will accept typewritten and legibly handwritten mss. SASE. Reports in 2 months. Sample copies available for $6. Writer's guidelines for SASE.

Tips: "We began *Writes of Passage* to encourage teenage reading and writing as fun and desirable forms of expression and to establish an open dialogue between teenagers in every state. Our selection process does not censor topics and presents submissions according to the authors' intentions. It gives teens an opportunity to expand on what they have learned in reading and writing classes in school by opening up a world of writing in which they can be free. As a result, submissions often reveal a surprising candidness on the part of the authors, including topics such as love, fear, struggle and death and they expose the diverse backgrounds of contributors."

Resources
Clubs & Organizations

Contacts made through organizations such as the ones listed in this section can be quite beneficial for children's writers and illustrators. Professional organizations provide numerous educational, business and legal services in the form of newsletters, workshops or seminars. Organizations can provide tips about how to be a more successful writer or artist, as well as what types of business records to keep, health and life insurance coverage to carry and competitions to consider.

An added benefit of belonging to an organization is the opportunity to network with those who have similar interests, creating a support system. As in any business, knowing the right people can often help your career, and important contacts can be made through your peers. Membership in a writer's or artist's organization also shows publishers you're serious about your craft. This provides no guarantee your work will be published, but it gives you an added dimension of credibility and professionalism. For tips on networking, see Only Connect: A Beginner's Guide to Networking, on page 53.

Some of the organizations listed here welcome anyone with an interest, while others are only open to published writers and professional artists. Organizations such as the Society of Children's Book Writers and Illustrators (SCBWI) have varying levels of membership. SCBWI offers associate membership to those with no publishing credits, and full membership to those who have had work for children published. Many national organizations such as SCBWI also have regional chapters throughout the country. Write or call for more information regarding any group that sounds interesting, or check the websites of the many organizations that list them. Be sure to get information about local chapters, membership qualifications and services offered.

Information on organizations listed in the previous edition but not included in this edition of *Children's Writer's & Illustrator's Market* **may be found in the General Index.**

AMERICAN ALLIANCE FOR THEATRE & EDUCATION, Theatre Department, Arizona State University, Box 872002, Tempe AZ 85287-2002. (602)965-6064. E-mail: aateinfo@asuvm.inre.asu.edu. Website: http://www.aate.com. Administrative Director: Christy M. Taylor. Purpose of organization: to promote standards of excellence in theatre and drama education by providing the artist and educator with a network of resources and support, a base for advocacy, and access to programs and projects that focus on the importance of drama in the human experience. Membership cost: $90 annually for individual in US and Canada, $120 annually for organization, $55 annually for students, $65 annually for retired people; add $20 outside Canada and US. Annual conference. Newsletter published quarterly; must be member to subscribe. Contests held for unpublished play reading project and annual awards for best play for K-8 and 1 for secondary audience. Awards plaque and stickers for published playbooks. Publishes list of unpublished plays deemed worthy of performance in newsletter and press release, and staged readings at conference.

■■ **CANADIAN SOCIETY OF CHILDREN'S AUTHORS, ILLUSTRATORS AND PERFORMERS, (CANSCAIP)**, 35 Spadina Rd., Toronto, Ontario M5R 2S9 Canada. (416)515-1559. Fax: (416)515-7022. E-mail: canscaip@interlog.com. Website: http://www.interlog.com/~canscaip. Office Manager: Nancy Prasad. Purpose of organization: development of Canadian children's culture and support for authors, illustrators and performers working in this field. Qualifications for membership: Members—professionals who have been published (not self-published) or have paid public performances/records/tapes to their credit. Friends—share interest in field of children's culture. Membership cost: $60 (members dues), $25 (friends dues), $30 (institution dues). Sponsors workshops/conferences. Publishes newsletter: includes profiles of members; news round-up of members' activities countrywide; market news; news on awards, grants, etc; columns related to professional concerns.

LEWIS CARROLL SOCIETY OF NORTH AMERICA, 18 Fitzharding Place, Owingsmills MD 21117. (410)356-5110. E-mail: eluchin@erols.com. Website: http://www.lewiscarroll.org/carroll.html. Secretary: Ellie Luchinsky. "We are an organization of Carroll admirers of all ages and interests and a center for Carroll studies." Qualifications for membership: "An interest in Lewis Carroll and a simple love for Alice (or even the Snark)." Membership cost: $20/year. There is also a contributing membership of $50. Publishes a quarterly newsletter.

THE CHILDREN'S BOOK COUNCIL, INC., 568 Broadway, New York NY 10012. (212)966-1990. Website: http://www.cbcbooks.org. Purpose of organization: "A nonprofit trade association of children's and young adult publishers, CBC promotes the enjoyment of books for children and young adults, and works with national and international organizations to that end. The CBC has sponsored National Children's Book Week since 1945." Qualifications for membership: US trade publishers and packagers of children's and young adult books and related literary materials are eligible for membership. Membership cost: "Individuals wishing to receive mailings from the CBC (our semi-annual newsletter *CBC Features*—and our materials brochures) may be placed on our mailing list for a one-time-only fee of $60. Publishers wishing to join should contact the CBC for dues information." Sponsors workshops and seminars. Publishes a newsletter with articles about children's books and publishing, and listings of free or inexpensive materials available from member publishers. Sells reading encouragement graphics and informational materials suitable for libraries, teachers, booksellers, parents, and others working with children.

FLORIDA FREELANCE WRITERS ASSOCIATION, Cassell Network of Writers, P.O. Box A, North Stratford NH 03590. (603)922-8338. Fax: (603)922-8339. E-mail: danakcnw@moose.ncia.net. Executive Director: Dana K. Cassell. Purpose of organization: To act as a link between Florida writers and buyers of the written word; to help writers run more effective communications businesses. Qualifications for membership: "None—we provide a variety of services and information, some for beginners and some for established pros." Membership cost: $90/year. Publishes a newsletter focusing on market news, business news, how-to tips for the serious writer. Non-member subscription: $39—does not include Florida section—includes national edition only. Annual *Directory of Florida Markets* included in FFWA newsletter section. Publishes annual *Guide to CNW/Florida Writers*, which is distributed to editors around the country. Sponsors contest: annual deadline March 15. Guidelines available fall of each year. Categories: juvenile, adult nonfiction, adult fiction. Awards include cash for top prizes, certificate for others. Contest open to non-members.

GRAPHIC ARTISTS GUILD, 90 John St., Suite 403, New York NY 10038. (212)791-3400. Fax: (212)791-0333. E-mail: pbasista@nac.net. Website: http://www.gag.org/. Executive Director: Paul Basista, CAE. Purpose of organization: "to promote and protect the economic interests of member artists. It is committed to improving conditions for all creators of graphic arts and raising standards for the entire industry." Qualification for full membership: 50% of income derived from artwork. Associate members include those in allied fields, students and retirees. Initiation fee: $25. Full memberships $120, $165, $215, $270; student membership $55/year. Associate membership $115/year. Publishes *Graphic Artists Guild Handbook, Pricing and Ethical Guidelines* and quarterly *Guild News* (free to members, $12 to non-members). "The Guild is an egalitarian union that embraces all creators of graphics arts intended for presentation as originals or reproductions at all levels of skill and expertise. The long-range goals of the Guild are: to educate graphic artists and their clients about ethical and fair business practices; to educate graphic artists about emerging trends and technologies impacting the industry; to offer programs and services that anticipate and respond to the needs of our members, helping them prosper and enhancing their health and security, to advocate for the interests of our members in the legislative, judicial and regulatory arenas; to assure that our members are recognized financially and professionally for the value they provide; to be

FOR EXPLANATIONS OF THESE SYMBOLS,
SEE THE INSIDE FRONT AND BACK COVERS OF THIS BOOK

responsible stewards for our members by building an organization that works efficiently on their behalf."

THE INTERNATIONAL WOMEN'S WRITING GUILD, P.O. Box 810, Gracie Station, New York NY 10028. (212)737-7536. Executive Director and Founder: Hannelore Hahn. IWWG is "a network for the personal and professional empowerment of women through writing." Qualifications: open to any woman connected to the written word regardless of professional portfolio. Membership cost: $35 annually; $45 annually for foreign members. "IWWG sponsors several annual conferences a year in all areas of the US. The major conference is held in August of each year at Skidmore College in Saratoga Springs NY. It is a week-long conference attracting more than 400 women internationally." Also publishes a 32-page newsletter, *Network*, 6 times/year; offers health insurance at group rates, referrals to literary agents.

JEWISH PUBLICATION SOCIETY, 1930 Chestnut St., Philadelphia PA 19103-4599. (215)564-5925. Editor-in-Chief: Dr. Ellen Frankel. Children's Editor: Bruce Black. Purpose of organization: "To publish quality Jewish books and to promote Jewish culture and education. We are a non-denominational, nonprofit religious publisher. Our children's list specializes in fiction and nonfiction with substantial Jewish content for pre-school through young adult readers." Qualifications for membership: "One must purchase a membership of at least $50, which entitles the member to a 20% discount off every book purchase. Our membership is nondiscriminatory on the basis of religion, ethnic affiliation, race or any other criteria." "*The JPS Bookmark* reports on JPS Publications; activities of members, authors and trustees; JPS projects and goals; JPS history; children's books and activities." All members receive *The Bookmark* with their membership.

LEAGUE OF CANADIAN POETS, 54 Wolseley St., 3rd Floor, Toronto, Ontario M5T 1A5 Canada. (416)504-1657. Fax: (416)504-0096. Executive Director: Edita Petrauskaite. President: Roger Nash. Inquiries to Program Manager: Sandra Drzewiecki. The L.C.P. is a national organization of published Canadian poets. Our constitutional objectives are to advance poetry in Canada and to promote the professional interests of the members. Qualifications for membership: full—publication of at least 1 book of poetry by a professional publisher; associate membership—an active interest in poetry, demonstrated by several magazine/periodical publication credits, student—an active interest in poetry, 12 sample poems required; supporting—any friend of poetry. Membership fees: full—$175/year, associate—$60, student—$30, supporting—$100. Holds an Annual General Meeting every spring; some events open to nonmembers. "We also organize reading programs in schools and public venues. We publish a newsletter which includes information on poetry/poetics in Canada and beyond. Also publish the books *Poetry Markets for Canadians*; *Who's Who in the League of Canadian Poets*; *Poets in the Classroom* (teaching guide) and its accompanying anthology of Canadian poetry *Vintage*; plus a series of cassettes. We sponsor a National Poetry Contest, open to Canadians living here and abroad." Rules: Unpublished poems of any style/subject, under 75 lines, typed, with name/address on separate sheet. $6 entry fee (includes GST) per poem. $1,000-1st prize, $750-2nd, $500-3rd; plus best 50 published in an anthology. Inquire with SASE. Contest open to Canadian nonmembers. Sponsors an annual chapbook ms contest. Organizes 2 annual awards: The Gerald Lampert Memorial Award for the best first book of poetry published in Canada in the preceding year and The Pat Lowther Memorial Award for the best book of poetry by a Canadian woman published in the preceding year. Deadline for poetry contest is January 31 each year, for awards December 31. Send SASE for more details. Sponsors youth poetry competition. Deadline March 1 of each year. Send SASE for details.

LITERARY MANAGERS AND DRAMATURGS OF THE AMERICAS, Box 355, CASTA, CUNY Grad Center, 33 W. 42nd St., New York NY 10036. (212)642-2657. Fax: (212)642-1977. E-mail: hbc3@col umbia.edu. LMDA is a not-for-profit service organization for the professions of literary management and dramaturgy. Student Membership: $20/year. **Open to students in dramaturgy, performing arts and literature programs, or related disciplines.** Proof of student status required. Includes national conference, New Dramaturg activities, local symposia, job phone and select membership meetings. Active Membership: $45/year. Open to full-time and part-time professionals working in the fields of literary management and dramaturgy. All privileges and services including voting rights and eligibility for office. Associate Membership: $35/year. Open to all performing arts professionals and academics, as well as others interested in the field. Includes national conference, local symposia and select membership meetings. Institutional Membership: $100/year. Open to theaters, universities, and other organizations. Includes all privileges and services except voting rights and eligibility for office. Publishes a newsletter featuring articles on literary management, dramaturgy, LMDA program updates and other articles of interest.

THE NATIONAL LEAGUE OF AMERICAN PEN WOMEN, 1300 17th St. N.W., Washington D.C. 20036-1973. (202)785-1997. Fax: (202)452-6868. E-mail: nlapw@juno.com. Website: http://members .aol.com/penwomen/pen.htm. National President: Judith E. LaFourest. Purpose of organization: to promote professional work in art, letters, and music since 1897. Qualifications for membership: An applicant must show "proof of sale" in each chosen category—art, letters, and music. Membership cost: $40 ($10 processing fee and $30 National dues); Annual fees—$30 plus Branch/State dues. Different levels of membership include: Active, Associate, International Affiliate, Members-at-Large, Honorary Members (in one or more of the following classifications: Art, Letters, and Music). Holds workshops/conferences. Publishes magazine 6 times a year titled *The Pen Woman*. Nonmember subscription $18 per year. Sponsors various contests in areas of Art, Letters, and Music. Awards made at Biennial Convention. Biannual scholarships awarded to non-Pen Women for mature women. Awards include cash prizes—up to $1,000. Specialized contests open to non-members.

N NATIONAL WRITERS ASSOCIATION, 1450 S. Havana, Suite 424, Aurora CO 80012. (303)751-7844. Fax: (303)751-8593. E-mail: sandywrter@aol.com. Website: http://www.nationalwriters.com. Executive Director: Sandy Whelchel. Purpose of organization: association for freelance writers. Qualifications for membership: associate membership—must be serious about writing; professional membership—must be published and paid writer (cite credentials). Membership cost: $65-associate; $85-professional. Sponsors workshops/conferences: TV/screenwriting workshops, NWA Annual Conferences, Literary Clearinghouse, editing and critiquing services, local chapters, National Writer's School. Open to non-members. Publishes industry news of interest to freelance writers; how-to articles; market information; member news and networking opportunities. Nonmember subscription $20. Sponsors poetry contest; short story contest; article contest; novel contest. Awards cash for top 3 winners; books and/or certificates for other winners; honorable mention certificate places 11-20. Contests open to nonmembers.

PEN AMERICAN CENTER, 568 Broadway, New York NY 10012. (212)334-1660. Fax: (212)334-2181. E-mail: jm@pen.org. Purpose of organization: "To foster understanding among men and women of letters in all countries. International PEN is the only worldwide organization of writers and the chief voice of the literary community. Members of PEN work for freedom of expression wherever it has been endangered." Qualifications for membership: "The standard qualification for a writer to join PEN is that he or she must have published, in the United States, two or more books of a literary character, or one book generally acclaimed to be of exceptional distinction. Editors who have demonstrated commitment to excellence in their profession (generally construed as five years' service in book editing), translators who have published at least two book-length literary translations, and playwrights whose works have been professionally produced, are eligible for membership." An application form is available upon request from PEN Headquarters in New York. Candidates for membership should be nominated by 2 current members of PEN. Inquiries about membership should be directed to the PEN Membership Committee. Friends of PEN is also open to writers who may not yet meet the general PEN membership requirements. PEN sponsors public events at PEN Headquarters in New York, and at the branch offices in Boston, Chicago, New Orleans, San Francisco and Portland, Oregon. They include tributes by contemporary writers to classic American writers, dialogues with visiting foreign writers, symposia that bring public attention to problems of censorship and that address current issues of writing in the United States, and readings that introduce beginning writers to the public. PEN's wide variety of literary programming reflects current literary interests and provides informal occasions for writers to meet each other and to welcome those with an interest in literature. Events are all open to the public and are usually free of charge. The Children's Book Authors' Committee sponsors biannual public events focusing on the art of writing for children and young adults and on the diversity of literature for juvenile readers. The PEN/Norma Klein Award was established in 1991 to honor an emerging children's book author. The bimonthly *PEN Newsletter* covers PEN activities, features interviews with international literary figures, transcripts of PEN literary symposia, reports on issues vital to the literary community. All PEN publications are available by mail order directly from PEN American Center. Individuals must enclose check or money order with their order. Subscription: $8 for 6 issues; sample issue $2. Pamphlets and brochures all free upon request. Sponsors several competitions per year. Monetary awards range from $700-7,500.

PUPPETEERS OF AMERICA, INC., #5 Cricklewood Path, Pasadena CA 91107. (818)797-5748. Membership Officer: Gayle Schluter. Purpose of organization: to promote the art of puppetry. Qualifications for membership: interest in the art form. Membership cost: single adult, $40; youth member, $25; retiree, $25 (65 years of age); family, $60; couple, $50. Membership includes a bimonthly newsletter. Sponsors workshops/conferences. Publishes newsletter. *The Puppetry Journal* provides news about puppeteers, puppet theaters, exhibitions, touring companies, technical tips, new products, new books, films, television, and events sponsored by the Chartered Guilds in each of the 8 P of A regions. Subscription: $35 (libraries only).

SOCIETY OF CHILDREN'S BOOK WRITERS AND ILLUSTRATORS, 345 N. Maple Dr., Suite 296, Beverly Hills CA 90210. (310)859-9887. E-mail: info@scbwi.org (autoresponse). Website: http://

www.scbwi.org. President: Stephen Mooser. Executive Director: Lin Oliver. Chairperson, Board of Directors: Sue Alexander. Purpose of organization: to assist writers and illustrators working or interested in the field. Qualifications for membership: an interest in children's literature and illustration. Membership cost: $50/year plus one time $10 initiation fee. Different levels of membership include: full membership—published authors/illustrators; associate membership—unpublished writers/illustrators. Holds 100 events (workshops/conferences) around the country each year. Open to nonmembers. Publishes a newsletter focusing on writing and illustrating children's books. Sponsors grants for writers and illustrators who are members.

☑ **SOCIETY OF ILLUSTRATORS**, 128 E. 63rd St., New York NY 10021-7303. (212)838-2560. Fax: (212)838-2561. Director: Terrence Brown. Purpose of organization: to promote interest in the art of illustration for working professional illustrators and those in associated fields. Membership cost: Initiation fee—$250. Annual dues for non-resident members (those living more than 125 air miles from SI's headquarters) are $248. Dues for Resident Artist Members are $428 per year; Resident Associate Members $496. Different levels of membership: *Artist Members* "shall include those who make illustration their profession" and through which they earn at least 60% of their income. *Associate Members* are "those who earn their living in the arts or who have made a substantial contribution to the art of illustration." This includes art directors, art buyers, creative supervisors, instructors, publishers and like categories. "All candidates for membership are admitted by the proposal of one active member and sponsorship of four additional members. The candidate must complete and sign the application form which requires a brief biography, a listing of schools attended, other training and a résumé of his or her professional career." Candidates for *Artist* membership, in addition to the above requirements, must submit examples of their work. Sponsors "The Annual of American Illustration." Awards include gold and silver medals. Open to nonmembers. Deadline: October 1. Sponsors "The Original Art: The Best of Children's Book Illustration." Deadline: mid-September. Call for details.

VOLUNTEER LAWYERS FOR THE ARTS, 1 E. 53rd St., 6th Floor, New York NY 10022-4201. (212)319-2787 (administration), ext. 10 (the Art Law Line). Fax: (212)752-6575. E-mail: vlany@bway.net. Executive Director: Amy Schwartzman. Purpose of organization: Volunteer Lawyers for the Arts is dedicated to providing free arts-related legal assistance to low-income artists and not-for-profit arts organizations in all creative fields. Over 800 attorneys in the New York area donate their time through VLA to artists and arts organizations unable to afford legal counsel. There is no membership required for our services. Everyone is welcome to use VLA's Art Law Line, a legal hotline for any artist or arts organization needing quick answers to arts-related questions. VLA also provides clinics, seminars and publications designed to educate artists on legal issues which affect their careers. Membership is through donations and is not required to use our services. Members receive discounts on publications and seminars as well as other benefits. Some of the many publications we carry are *All You Need to Know About the Music Business*; *Business and Legal Forms for Fine Artists, Photographers & Authors & Self-Publishers*; *Contracts for the Film & TV Industry*, plus many more. Please call Matt M. Morrow at ext. 10 to order. VLA's Seminars include "Not-for-Profit Incorporation and Tax Exemption Seminar" and "Copyright Basics for all Seminars."

WESTERN WRITERS OF AMERICA, INC., 1012 Fair St., Franklin TN 37064. (615)791-1444. Fax: (615)791-1444. Secretary/Treasurer: James A. Crutchfield. Purpose of organization: to further all types of literature that pertains to the American West. Membership requirements: must be a *published* author of Western material. Membership cost: $75/year ($90 foreign). Different levels of membership include: Active and Associate—the 2 vary upon number of books published. Holds annual convention. Publishes bimonthly magazine focusing on market trends, book reviews, news of members, etc. Non-members may subscribe for $30 ($40 foreign). Sponsors contests. Spur awards given annually for a variety of types of writing. Awards include plaque, certificate, publicity. Contest open to nonmembers.

WRITERS CONNECTION, P.O. Box 24770, San Jose CA 95154-4770. (408)445-3600. Fax: (408)445-3609. Purpose of organization: to provide services and resources for script writers. Sponsors annual Selling to Hollywood scriptwriting conference in the Los Angeles area each August.

VISIT THE WRITER'S DIGEST WEBSITE at http://www.writersdigest.com for hot new markets, daily market updates, writers' guidelines and much more.

WRITERS' FEDERATION OF NEW BRUNSWICK, Box 37, Station A, 404 Queen St., Fredericton, New Brunswick E3B 4Y2 Canada. (506)459-7228. E-mail: aa821@fan.nb.ca. Website: http://www.sjfn .nb.ca/community_hall/W/Writers_FEDERATION_NB/index.htm. Project Coordinator: Anna Mae Snider. Purpose of organization: "to promote the work of New Brunswick writers and to help them at all stages of their development." Qualifications for membership: interest in writing. Membership cost: $30, basic annual membership; $20, student/unemployed; $40, family membership; $50, institutional membership; $100, sustaining member; $250, patron; and $1,000, lifetime member. Holds workshops/conferences. Publishes a newsletter with articles concerning the craft of writing, member news, contests, markets, workshops and conference listings. Sponsors annual literary competition (for New Brunswick residents). Categories: fiction, nonfiction, poetry, children's literature—3 prizes per category of $150, $75, $30; Alfred Bailey Prize of $400 for poetry ms; The Richards Prize of $400 for short novel, collection of short stories or section of long novel; The Sheree Fitch Prize for writing by young people (14-18 years of age). Contest open to nonmembers (residents of New Brunswick only).

WRITERS GUILD OF ALBERTA, 11759 Groat Rd., 3rd Floor, Percy Page Centre, Edmonton, Alberta T5M 3K6 Canada. (403)422-8174. Fax: (403)422-2663. E-mail: wga@oanet.com. Website: http:// www.writersguildofalberta.ca. Executive Director: Mr. Miki Andrejevic. Purpose of organization: to provide meeting ground and collective voice for the writers in Alberta. Membership cost: $60/year; $20 for seniors/students. Holds workshops/conferences. Publishes a newsletter focusing on markets, competitions, contemporary issues related to the literary arts (writing, publishing, censorship, royalties etc.). Nonmembers may subscribe to newsletter. Subscription cost: $60/year. Sponsors annual literary awards program in 7 categories (novel, nonfiction, short fiction, children's literature, poetry, drama, best first book). Awards include $500, leather-bound book, promotion and publicity. Open to nonmembers.

Conferences & Workshops

Writers and illustrators eager to expand their knowledge of the children's publishing industry should consider attending one of the many conferences and workshops held each year. Whether you're a novice or seasoned professional, conferences and workshops are great places to pick up information on a variety of topics and network with experts in the publishing industry, as well as your peers. For tips on networking, see Only Connect: A Beginner's Guide to Networking, on page 53.

Many conferences and workshops included here focus on children's writing or illustrating and related business issues. Others appeal to a broader base of writers or artists, but still provide information that can be useful in creating material for children. Illustrators may be interested in painting and drawing workshops, for example, while writers can learn about techniques and meet editors and agents at general writing conferences.

Listings in this section provide details about what conference and workshop courses are offered, where and when they are held, and the costs. Some of the national writing and art organizations also offer regional workshops throughout the year. Write or call for information.

Artists can find a detailed directory of annual art workshops offered around the globe in the March, June, September and December issues of *The Artist's Magazine*. Writers should consult the May issue of *Writer's Digest*.

Members of the Society of Children's Book Writers and Illustrators can find information on conferences in national and local SCBWI newsletters. Nonmembers may attend SCBWI events as well. A number of local SCBWI conferences are listed in this section. For information on SCBWI's annual national conference, contact them at (310)859-9889 or check their website for a complete calendar of national and regional events (http://www.scbwi.org).

Information on conferences listed in the previous edition but not this edition of *Children's Writer's & Illustrator's Market* may be found in the General Index.

AMERICAN CHRISTIAN WRITERS CONFERENCE, P.O. Box 110390, Nashville TN 37222. 1(800)21-WRITE or (615)834-0450. Website: http://www.ecpa.org/acw. Director: Reg Forder. Writer and illustrator workshops geared toward beginner, intermediate and advanced levels. Classes offered include: fiction, nonfiction, poetry, photography, music, etc. Workshops held in two dozen US cities. Call or write for a complete schedule of conferences. 75 minutes. Maximum class size: 30 (approximate). Cost of conference: $99, 1-day session; $169, 2-day session; $229, 3-day session (discount given if paid 30 days in advance).

[N] ARKANSAS WRITERS' CONFERENCE, 6817 Gingerbread Lane, Little Rock AR 72204. (501)565-8889. Fax: (501)565-7220. Counselor: Peggy Vining. Writer workshops geared toward beginner, intermediate and advanced levels. **Open to students.** Annual conference. Conference always held the first full weekend in June. "1999 will be our 55th annual conference." Cost of conference: $5/day; includes registration and workshops. Contest fees, lodging and food are not included. Write for more information. Offers 34 different awards for various types of writing, poetry and essay.

[N] AUSTIN WRITERS' LEAGUE CONFERENCE WORKSHOP SERIES, 1501 W. Fifth St., Suite #E-2, Austin TX 78703. (512)499-8914. Fax: (512)499-0441. E-mail: awl@eden.com. Executive Director: Jim Bob McMillan. Writer and illustrator workshops and conferences geared toward all levels for children and adults. Sessions include writing children's books and marketing children's books. Annual conferences. Workshops usually held March, April and May; September, October and November. Write for more information. The Austin Writers' League has available audiotapes of past workshop programs.

AUTUMN AUTHORS' AFFAIR XV, 1507 Burnham Ave., Calumet City IL 60409. (708)862-9797. President: Nancy McCann. Writer workshops geared toward beginner, intermediate, advanced levels. **Open to students.** Emphasizes writing for children and young adults. Sessions include children/teen/young adult writing, mysteries, romantic suspense, romance, nonfiction, etc. Annual workshop. Workshops held in October. Cost of workshop: $75 for 1 day, $120 for weekend, includes meals Friday night, Saturday morning and Saturday afternoon; dessert buffet Saturday night and breakfast/brunch Sunday morning. Write for more information.

BE THE WRITER YOU WANT TO BE—MANUSCRIPT CLINIC, Villa 30, 23350 Sereno Court, Cupertino CA 95014. (415)691-0300. Contact: Louise Purwin Zobel. Writer workshops geared toward beginner, intermediate and advanced levels. "Participants may turn in manuscripts at any stage of development to receive help with structure and style, as well as marketing advice. Manuscripts receive some written criticism and an oral critique from the instructor, as well as class discussion." Annual workshop. Usually held in the spring. Registration limited to 20-25. Cost of workshop: $45-65/day, depending on the campus; includes an extensive handout. SASE for more information.

BUTLER UNIVERSITY CHILDREN'S LITERATURE CONFERENCE, 4600 Sunset Drive, Indianapolis IN 46208. (317)940-9861. Fax: (317)940-9644. E-mail: sdaniell@butler.edu. Contact: Shirley Daniell. Writer and illustrator conference geared toward intermediate level. **Open to college students.** Annual conference, held January 30, 1999. Includes sessions such as The Joy of Writing Nonfiction, Creating the Children's Picture Book and Nuts and Bolts for Beginning Writers. Registration limited to 300. Cost of conference: $80; includes meals, registration, 3 plenary addresses, 2 workshops, book signing, reception and conference bookstore. Write for more information. "The conference is geared toward three groups: teachers, librarians and writers/illustrators."

CELEBRATION OF CHILDREN'S LITERATURE, Montgomery College, 51 Mannakee St., Office of Continuing Education, Room 220, Rockville MD 20850. (301)251-7914. Fax: (301)251-7937. E-mail: ssonner@cc.mc.md.us. Senior Program Director: Sandra Sonner. Writer and illustrator workshops geared toward all levels. **Open to students.** Past topics included The Publisher's Perspective, Successful Picture Book Design, The Oral Tradition in Children's Literature, The Best and Worst Children's Books, Websites for Children, The Pleasures of Nonfiction and The Book as Art. Annual workshop. Will be held April 24, 1999. Registration limited to 200. Writing/art facilities, continuing education classrooms and large auditorium. Cost of workshop: approximately $65; includes workshops, box lunch and coffee. Write for more information.

CHILDREN'S LITERATURE CONFERENCE, 250 Hofstra University, U.C.C.E., Hempstead NY 11549. (516)463-5016. Fax: (516)463-4833. E-mail: dcelcs@hofstra.edu. Writers/Illustrators Contact: Lewis Shena, associate dean, Liberal Arts Studies. Writer and illustrator workshops geared toward all levels. Emphasizes: fiction, nonfiction, poetry, submission procedures, picture books. Workshops will be held April 24, 1999. Length of each session: 1 hour. Registration limited to 35/class. Cost of workshop: approximately $65; includes 2 workshops, reception, lunch, 2 general sessions, and panel discussion with guest speakers and/or critiquing. Write for more information. Co-sponsored by Society of Children's Book Writers & Illustrators.

CHILDREN'S WRITER'S CONFERENCE, St. Charles County Community College, P.O. Box 76975, 103 CEAC, St. Peters MO 63376-0975. (314)213-8000 ext. 4108. E-mail: suebe@inlink.com. SCBWI MO Regional Advisor: Sue Bradford Edwards. Writer and illustrator conference geared toward all levels. Speakers include editors, writers and other professionals, mainly from the Midwest. Topics vary from year to year, but each conference offers sessions for both writers and illustrators as well as for newcomers and published writers. Previous topics include: "What Happens When Your Manuscript is Accepted" by Dawn Weinstock, editor; "Writing—Hobby or Vocation?" by Chris Kelleher; "Mother Time

**FOR EXPLANATIONS OF THESE SYMBOLS,
SEE THE INSIDE FRONT AND BACK COVERS OF THIS BOOK**

Gives Advice: Perspectives from a 25 Year Veteran" by Judith Mathews, editor; "Don't Be a Starving Writer" by Vicki Berger Erwin, author; and "Words & Pictures: History in the Making" by author-illustrator Cheryl Harness. Annual conference held in late October/early November. Registration limited to 50-70. Cost of conference: $50-70; includes one day workshop (8:00 a.m. to 5:00 p.m.) plus lunch. Write for more information.

N CHILDREN'S WRITERS' INTENSIVE WORKSHOP, Rice University, Houston TX 77251-1892. (713)527-4803. Fax: (713)285-5213. E-mail: scs@rice.edu. Website: http://www.rice.edu/scs. Contact: School of Continuing Studies. Writer and illustrator workshops geared toward all levels. Topics include Issues in Children's Publishing, Censorship, Multiculturalism, Dealing with Sensitive Subjects, Submissions/Formatting, The Journal as Resource, The Markets—Finding Your Niche, Working with an Editor, The Agent/Author Connection, The Role of Research, Contract Negotiation. Annual workshop held every July. Registration limited to 40. Cost of workshop: $325; includes study materials and a continental breakfast and lunch on the first day. Manuscripts must be received by the School of Continuing Studies by 3 p.m., Friday, June 26. Picture books should not exceed eight double-spaced pages. Novel submissions should consist of the first two chapters, a synopsis, and a plot summary. These should not exceed a total of 20 double-spaced pages. Offers discount fee: $275 for two or more participants who register together.

N CLEVELAND HEIGHTS/UNIVERSITY HEIGHTS WRITER'S MINI-CONFERENCE, 34200 Ridge Rd., #110, Willoughby OH 44094-2954. (440)943-3047. E-mail: fa837@po.cwru.edu. Writer workshops geared toward all levels. **Open to students.** Conference will cover children's writing, fiction, nonfiction, poetry, articles, writing for educators and other topics of interest to the beginning or advanced writer. Annual conference. Conference held October 23, 1999 at Taylor Academy in Cleveland Heights, OH. Cost of conference: $39; includes coffee and handouts.

✓ THE COLLEGE OF NEW JERSEY WRITERS' CONFERENCE, English Dept., The College of New Jersey, P.O. Box 7718, Ewing NJ 08628-0718. (609)771-3254. Director: Jean Hollander. Writer workshops geared toward all levels. Offers workshop in children's literature. Workshops held in April of every year. Length of each session: 2 hours. Registration limited to 50. Cost of workshop: $50 (reduced rates for students); includes conference, workshop and ms critique. Write for more information.

THE COLUMBUS WRITERS CONFERENCE, P.O. Box 20548, Columbus OH 43220-0176. (614)451-3075. Fax: (614)451-0174. E-mail: angelapl28@aol.com. Director: Angela Palazzolo. Writer workshops geared toward all levels. "Since its inception in 1993, the conference has offered a wide variety of topics including writing in the following markets: children's, young adult, movie/television, humor, suspense, science fiction/fantasy, travel, educational and greeting card. Other topics have included writing the novel, the short story, the nonfiction book; playwriting; finding and working with an agent; independent publishing; book reviewing; technical writing; and time management for writers. Specific sessions that have pertained to children: children's writing, children's markets, writing and publishing children's poetry and stories. Annual conference. Conference held in September. Cost of full conference: $129 for early registration (includes a day-and-a-half of sessions, Friday night dinner program, Saturday continental breakfast, lunch and refreshments); $145 regular registration. Saturday only: $89 for early registration; $105 regular registration. Friday night dinner program is $29. Call, e-mail or write for more information.

PETER DAVIDSON'S HOW TO WRITE A CHILDREN'S PICTURE BOOK SEMINAR, 982 S. Emerald Hills Dr., P.O. Box 497, Arnolds Park IA 51331-0497. Fax: (712)362-8363. Seminar Presenter: Peter Davidson. "This seminar is for anyone interested in writing and/or illustrating children's picture books. Beginners and experienced writers alike are welcome. If participants have a manuscript in progress, or have an idea, they are welcome to bring it along to discuss with the seminar presenter." *How to Write a Children's Picture Book* is a one-day seminar devoted to principles and techniques of writing and illustrating children's picture books. Topics include Definition of a Picture Book, Picture Book Sizes, Developing an Idea, Plotting the Book, Writing the Book, Illustrating the Book, Typing the Manuscript, Copyrighting Your Work, Marketing Your Manuscript and Contract Terms. Seminars are presented year-round at community colleges. Even-numbered years, presents seminars in Minnesota, Iowa, Nebraska, Kansas, Colorado and Wyoming. Odd-numbered years, presents seminars in Illinois, Minnesota, Iowa, South Dakota, Missouri, Arkansas and Tennessee (write for a schedule). One day, 9 a.m.-4 p.m. Cost of workshop: varies from $40-59, depending on location; includes approximately 35 pages of handouts. Write for more information.

N DOWN EAST MAINE WRITER'S WORKSHOPS, P.O. Box 446, Stockton Springs ME 04981. (207)567-4317. Fax: (207)567-3023. E-mail: redbaron@lme.net. Website: http://www.agate.net/~herrick/writers. Director: Janet J. Barron. Writing workshops geared towards beginning writers. **Open to students.**

We hold 3-day "modular" workshops (writers can attend complete workshops, or for the specific days they find most valuable) during the summer each year. Workshop usually held the first or second Friday-Sunday in August. Workshops topics include Writing for the Children's Market, Creative Writing (basics of Fiction & Nonfiction), How to Get Your Writing Published, and a Sampler (a half day gourmet taste of Fiction, Nonfiction, Writing for the Children's Market, Poetry, Scriptwriting, and How to Get Published). Tuition (includes lunch): by-the-day, $115; 3-day, $295 (we accept Visa and MC) plus $19.95 for 300 page textbook. Reasonable local accommodations additional. Expert, individual, personal, practical instruction on the fundamentals of writing for publication. We also offer a writer's clinic for writing feedback if participants seek this type of guidance. No requirements prior to registration. For more information, contact DEMWW.

FISHTRAP, INC., P.O. Box 38, Enterprise OR 97828. (541)426-3623. Fax: (541)426-3324. Director: Rich Wandschneider. Writer workshops geared toward beginner, intermediate, advanced and professional levels. **Open to students.** Not specifically writing for children, although we have offered occasional workshops such as "The Children's Picture Book." A series of eight writing workshops (enrollment 12/workshop) and a writers' gathering is held each July; a winter gathering concerning writing and issues of public policy (e.g. "Violence," "Fire") is held in February. For February 19-21, 1999, the conference will focus on "Children" with writer Jim Heyreen plus a public policy person working with children's issues and a psychologist/historian. During the school year Fishtrap brings writers into local schools and offers occasional workshops for teachers and writers of children's and young adult books. Also brings in "Writers in Residency" (10 weeks). Cost of workshops: $175-220 for 1-4 days; includes workshop only. Food and lodging can be arranged. College credit is available. Please contact for more information.

FLORIDA CHRISTIAN WRITERS CONFERENCE, 2600 Park Ave., Titusville FL 32780. (407)269-6702, ext. 202. Fax: (407)383-1741. E-mail: writer@digital.net. Website: http://www.Kipertek.com/writer. Conference Director: Billie Wilson. Writer workshops geared toward all levels. **Open to students.** "We offer 48 one-hour workshops and 7 five-hour classes. Approximately 24 of these are for the children's genre: Seeing Through the Eyes of an Artist; Characters . . . Inside and Out; Seeing Through the Eyes of a Child; Picture Book Toolbox; and CD-ROM & Interactive Books for Children. Annual workshop held January 28-February 1, 1999. We have 30 publishers and publications represented by editors teaching workshops and reading manuscripts from the conferees. The conference is limited to 200 people. Usually workshops are limited to 25-30. Advanced or professional workshops are by invitation only via submitted application." Cost of workshop: $400; includes food, lodging, tuition and manuscript critiques and editor review of your manuscript. Write for more information.

GREAT LAKES WRITER'S WORKSHOP, Alverno College, 3401 S. 39th St., P.O. Box 343922, Milwaukee WI 53234-3922. (414)382-6176. Fax: (414)382-6332. Assistant Director: Cindy Jackson. Writing workshops geared toward beginner and intermediate levels; subjects include writing techniques/focuses such as character development, scene development, etc.; techniques for getting over writer's block; marketing strategies; and publishing strategies. Annual workshop. Workshop held on a weekend in June. Average length of each session: 2 hours. Workshop is currently being redeveloped into a weekend format. Write for more information.

GREEN RIVERS WRITERS NOVELS-IN-PROGRESS WORKSHOP, 11906 Locust Rd., Middletown KY 40243-1413. (502)245-4902. President: Mary O'Dell. Writer workshops geared toward intermediate and advanced levels. Workshops emphasize novel writing. Format is 6 novelist instructors working with small groups (5-7 people); one of these novelists may be young adult novelist. Workshop held March 14-21, 1998. Registration limited to 49. Participants will need to bring own computers, typewriters, etc. Private rooms are available for sleeping, working. No art facilities. Cost of workshop: $350; includes organization membership, buffet banquet with agents and editors, registration, manuscript reading fee (60 pages approximately with outline/synopsis). Writers must supply 40-60 pages of manuscript with outline, synopsis or treatment. Write for more information. Conference held on Shelby Campus at University of Louisville; private rooms with bath between each 2 rooms. Linens furnished. $20 per night.

☑ **THE HEIGHTS WRITER'S CONFERENCE**, Sponsored by Writer's World Press, 35 N. Chillicothe Rd. #D, Aurora OH 44202-8741. (330)562-6667. Fax: (330)562-1216. E-mail: writersworld@juno.com. Conference Director: Lavern Hall. Writer workshops geared toward beginner and intermediate. **Open to students.** Program includes 1-hour seminars and 4 2½-hour workshops. "Our workshop topics vary yearly. We *always* have children's literature." Annual workshop held first Saturday in May. Registration is open for seminars. The 2 teaching workshops are limited to 25 and pre-registration is a must. Cost of conference: $85; includes continental breakfast, registration packet, lunch, seminars and/or workshops, general session and networking reception at the end of the day. SASE for brochure.

"HELP! I'M A WRITER" SEMINAR, (formerly "Writing for the Local Church . . . and Beyond"), P.O. Box 12624, Roanoke VA 24027. (540)342-7511. Fax: (540)342-7929. E-mail: ccmbbr@juno.com. Director: Betty Robertson. Writer and illustrator workshops geared toward beginner and intermediate levels. Includes sessions on stories for children, puppet scripts, puzzles, curriculum. Workshops held on invitation; various locations. Cost of workshop: $24.95-34.95; includes comprehensive handbook, refreshments, free magazine samples. Write for more information.

✓ **HOFSTRA UNIVERSITY SUMMER WRITERS' CONFERENCE**, 250 Hofstra University, UCCE, Hempstead NY 11549. (516)463-5016. Fax: (516)463-4833. E-mail: dcelcs@hofstra.edu. Associate Dean: Lewis Shena. Writer workshops geared toward all levels. Classes offered include fiction, nonfiction, poetry, children's literature, stage/screenwriting and other genres. Children's writing faculty has included Pam Conrad, Johanna Hurwitz, Tor Seidler and Jane Zalben, with Maurice Sendak once appearing as guest speaker. Annual workshop. Workshops held for 2 weeks July 12-23, 1999. Each workshop meets for 2½ hours daily for a total of 25 hours. Students can register for 2 workshops, schedule an individual conference with the writer/instructor and submit a short ms (less than 10 pages) for critique. Enrollees may register as certificate students or credit students. Cost of workshop: certificate students enrollment fee is approximately $375 plus $26 registration fee; 2-credit student enrollment fee is approximately $1,000 undergraduate and $1,750 graduate; 4-credit student enrollment fee is approximately $1,750 undergraduate and $1,850 graduate. On-campus accommodations for the sessions are available for approximately $350/person. Students may attend any of the ancillary activities, a private conference, special programs and social events.

Ⓝ HUDSON WRITERS MINI CONFERENCE, 34200 Ridge Rd., #110, Willoughby OH 44094-2954. (440)943-3047. E-mail: fa837@po.cwru.edu. Coordinator: Lea Leever Oldham. Writer workshops geared toward all levels. **Open to students.** Covers children's writing, young adult, fiction, nonfiction, poetry, science fiction and other topics of interest. Annual conference. Conference held at Hudson High School in Hudson, OH, February 6, 1999. Cost of conference: $39; includes coffee and sessions.

INSPIRATIONAL WRITERS ALIVE, Rt. 4, Box 81-H, Rusk TX 75785. Director: Maxine E, Holder. Guest speaker for 1998: Pam Zollman. Other speakers include Sally E. Stuart, Holly G. Miller, Deborah White-Smith. Topics: Focus and Writing for Children. Annual conference held 1st Saturday in August. **Open to students and adults.** Registration usually 60-75 conferees. Writing/art facilities available: First Baptist Church, Christian Life Center, Houston TX. Cost of conference: approximately $90. Write for more information. "Annual IWA Contest presented. Manuscripts critiqued along with one-on-one 15 minute sessions with speaker(s). (Extra ms. if there is room.)" For more information send for brochure: Attn: Martha Roger, 6038 Greenmont, Houston TX 77092, (713)686-7209 or Maxine Holder, or call Pat Vance, (713)477-4968.

Ⓝ INSTITUTE OF PUBLISHING AND WRITING: CHILDREN'S BOOKS IN THE MARKETPLACE, Vassar College, 124 Raymond Ave., Poughkeepsie NY 12604. (914)437-5903. Fax: (914)437-7209. E-mail: mabruno@vassar.edu. Website: http://www.vassar.edu. Associate Director of College Relations: Maryann Bruno. Writer workshops geared toward all levels. **Open to students.** Conference covers writing fiction and nonfiction, the picture book, editing, production process, how to get your work published. Annual conference. Conference held June 13-18; directed by Jean Marzollo. Registration limited to 30-35. Writing/art facilities available: computer center. Cost of conference: $800; includes tuition, room and full board, use of Vassar's athletic facilities. Write for more information.

INTERNATIONAL WOMEN'S WRITING GUILD "REMEMBER THE MAGIC" ANNUAL SUMMER CONFERENCE, P.O. Box 810, Gracie Station, New York NY 10028. (212)737-7536. Executive Director: Hannelore Hahn. Writer and illustrator workshops geared toward all levels. Offers 65 different workshops—some are for children's book writers and illustrators. Also sponsors 13 other events throughout

---

MARKET CONDITIONS are constantly changing! If you're still using this book and it is 2000 or later, buy the newest edition of *Children's Writer's & Illustrator's Market* at your favorite bookstore or order directly from Writer's Digest Books.

the US. Annual workshops. Workshops held 2nd or 3rd week in August. Length of each session: 1 hour-15 minutes; sessions take place for an entire week. Registration limited to 450. Cost of workshop: $350 (plus $350 room and board). Write for more information. "This workshop always takes place at Skidmore College in Saratoga Springs NY."

I'VE ALWAYS WANTED TO WRITE BUT—BEGINNERS' CLASS, Villa 30, 23350 Sereno Ct., Cupertino CA 95014. (415)691-0300. Contact: Louise Purwin Zobel. Writer workshops geared toward beginner and intermediate levels. "This seminar/workshop starts at the beginning, although the intermediate writer will benefit, too. There is discussion of children's magazine and book literature today, how to write it and how to market it. Also, there is discussion of other types of writing and the basics of writing for publication." Annual workshops. "Usually held several times a year; fall, winter and spring." Sessions last 1-2 days. Cost of workshop: $45-65/day, depending on the campus; includes extensive handout. Write with SASE for more information.

☑ **LIGONIER VALLEY WRITERS CONFERENCE**, P.O. Box B, Ligonier PA 15658-1602. (724)537-3341. Fax: (724)537-0482. Conference Director: Tina Thoburn. Contact: Sally Shirey. Writer programs geared toward all levels. Annual conference features fiction, nonfiction, poetry and other genres. Conference held July 9-11, 1999. Write or call for more information.

🆕 **LORAIN COUNTY COMMUNITY COLLEGE WRITER'S MINI-CONFERENCE**, 34200 Ridge Rd., #110, Willoughby OH 44094-2954. (440)943-3047. E-mail: fa837@po.cwru.edu. Coordinator: Lea Leever Oldham. Writer workshops geared toward all levels. **Open to students.** Offers sessions on children's writing, poetry, self-publishing, fiction, nonfiction, articles and other topics of interest to the beginning to advanced writer. Annual conference, held May 8, 1999. Cost of conference: $39.

☑ **MANHATTANVILLE WRITERS' WEEK**, Manhattanville College, 2900 Purchase St., Purchase NY 10577-2103. (914)694-3425. Fax: (914)694-3488. E-mail: rdowd@mville.edu. Dean, Adult and Special Programs: Ruth Dowd. Writer workshops geared toward beginner, intermediate and advanced levels. Writers' week offers a special workshop for writers interested in children's/young adult writing. We have featured such workshop leaders as: Patricia Gauch, Patricia Horner, Elizabeth Winthrop and Lore Segal. Annual workshop held last week in June. Length of each session: one week. Cost of workshop: $560 (non-credit); includes a full week of writing activities, 5-day workshop on children's literature, lectures, readings, sessions with editors and agents, etc. Workshop may be taken for 2 graduate credits. Write for more information.

☑ **MAPLE WOODS COMMUNITY COLLEGE WRITERS' CONFERENCE**, 2601 NE Barry Rd., Kansas City MO 64156. (816)437-3011. Fax: (816)437-3049. E-mail: schumacp@maplewoods.cc.mo. us. Director Community Education: Paula Schumacher. Contact: Sherry Skinner. Writer workshops geared toward beginner, intermediate levels. Various writing topics and genres covered. Covers where do you get your ideas for children books; how to write childrens books and get published; panels comprised of childrens books authors, librarians and book sellers. Conference held September 1999. Registration limited to 350. Cost of workshop: $78; includes continental breakfast, refreshments and two networking sessions.

🆕 **MARITIME WRITERS' WORKSHOP**, Department Extension & Summer Session, P.O. Box 4400, University of New Brunswick, Fredericton, New Brunswick E3B 5A3 Canada. (506)453-4646. Fax: (506)453-3572. E-mail: extensin@unb.ca. Website: http://www.unb.ca/web/coned/writers/marritrs.html. Coordinator: Glenda Turner. Week-long workshop on writing for children, general approach, dealing with submitted material, geared to all levels and held in July. Annual workshop. 3 hours/day. Group workshop plus individual conferences, public readings, etc. Registration limited to 10/class. Cost of workshop: $350 tuition; meals and accommodations extra. 10-20 ms pages due before conference (deadline announced). Scholarships available.

MIDWEST WRITERS' CONFERENCE, 6000 Frank Ave. NW, Canton OH 44720-7599. (330)499-9600. Fax: (330)494-6121. E-mail: druhe@stark.kent.edu. Assistant Director: Debbie Ruhe. Writer workshops geared toward beginner, intermediate and advanced levels. Topics include: Fiction, Nonfiction, Juvenile Literature, Poetry and a rotating category. Titles for Juvenile Literature have included Writing as Power, Writing for Children, and Lifting Them Up to Our Windows: Writing for Kids. Annual conference. Conference held early October. Length of each session: 1 hour. Registration limited to 400 total people. Cost of workshop: $95; includes Friday afternoon workshops, keynote address, Saturday workshops, box lunch, up to 2-ms entries in contest. Write for more information.

☑ **MIDWEST WRITERS WORKSHOP**, Department of Journalism, Ball State University, Muncie IN 47306. (765)285-5587. Fax: (765)285-7997. Director: Earl L. Conn. Writer workshops geared toward intermediate level. Topics include fiction and nonfiction writing. Past workshop presenters include Joyce Carol Oates, James Alexander Thom, Bill Brashler and Alice Friman. Workshop also includes ms evaluation and a writing contest. Annual workshop. Workshop held July 28-31, 1999. Registration tentatively limited to 135. Cost of workshop: $205; includes everything but room and meals. Offers scholarships. Write for more information.

MISSISSIPPI VALLEY WRITERS CONFERENCE, 3403 45th St., Moline IL 61265. E-mail: kimseuss @aol.com. Conference Director: David R. Collins. Writer workshops geared toward all levels. Conference open to students. Classes offered include Juvenile Writing—1 of 9 workshops offered. Annual workshop. Workshops held June 6-11, 1999; usually it is the second week in June each year. Length of each session: Monday-Friday, 1 hour each day. Registration limited to 20 participants/workshop. Writing facilities available: college library. Cost of workshop: $25 registration; $50 to participate in 1 workshop, $90 in 2, $40 for each additional; $25 to audit a workshop. Write for more information.

MONTROSE CHRISTIAN WRITER'S CONFERENCE, 5 Locust St., Montrose PA 18801-1112. (717)278-1001. Fax: (717)278-3061. E-mail: mbc@epix.net. Executive Director: Jim Fahringer. Writer workshops geared toward beginner, intermediate and advanced levels. **Open to students.** Annual workshop. Workshop held in July. Cost of workshop: $100; includes tuition. Write for more information.

☑ **MOUNT HERMON CHRISTIAN WRITERS CONFERENCE**, Mount Hermon Christian Conference Center, P.O. Box 413, Mount Hermon CA 95041-0413. (831)335-4466. Fax: (831)335-9218. E-mail: davidtalbott@mhcamps.org. Website: http://www.mountherman.org. Director of Specialized Programs: David R. Talbott. Writer workshops geared toward all levels. **Open to students over 16 years.** Emphasizes religious writing for children via books, articles; Sunday school curriculum; marketing. Classes offered include: Suitable Style for Children; Everything You Need to Know to Write and Market Your Children's Book; Take-Home Papers for Children. Workshops held annually over Palm Sunday weekend: March 26-30, 1999. Length of each session: 5-day residential conferences held annually. Registration limited 45/class, but most are 10-15. Conference center with hotel-style accommodations. Cost of workshop: $500-700 variable; includes tuition, resource notebook, refreshment breaks, full room and board for 13 meals and 4 nights. Write for more information.

THE NATIONAL WRITERS ASSOCIATION CONFERENCE, Suite 424, 1450 S. Havana, Aurora CO 80012. (303)751-7844. Executive Director: Sandy Whelchel. Writer workshops geared toward all levels. Classes offered include marketing, agenting, "What's Hot in the Market." Annual workshop. "In 1997 the workshop will be held in Denver, Colorado, June 13-15. Write for more information.

NEW ENGLAND WRITERS' WORKSHOP AT SIMMONS COLLEGE, 300 The Fenway, Boston MA 02115. (617)521-2220. Fax: (617)521-3199. Conference Administrator: Cynthia Grady. Writers' workshops geared toward intermediate and advanced levels. Writing workshops focusing on novels and short stories. We may be adding a children's literature section for 1998. Annual workshop. Workshop held early-June, Monday-Friday. Registration limited to 45. Writing facilities available: computer labs and equipment in library. Cost of workshop: $550; includes workshop, individual ms consultation. Write for more information.

NORTH CAROLINA WRITERS' NETWORK FALL CONFERENCE, P.O. Box 954, Carrboro NC 27510. (919)967-9540. Fax: (919)929-0535. E-mail: ncwn@sunsite.unc.edu. Website: http://sunsite.unc. edu/ncwriters. Writer workshops geared toward beginner, intermediate, advanced and professional levels. "We offer workshops and critique sessions in a variety of genres: fiction, poetry, children's. Past young adult and children's writing classes include: 'Everybody's Got a Story to Tell—or Write!' with Eleanora Tate, 'Writing Young Adult Fiction' with Sarah Dessen." Annual conference. Conference held November 20-22, 1998 (Winston-Salem, NC). Cost of workshop: approximately $130-145, includes workshops, panel discussions, 3 meals.

NORTHWEST OKLAHOMA WRITERS WORKSHOP, P.O. Box 5994, Enid OK 73702-5994. (405)237-2744. E-mail: scrybr8@enid.com or enidwriters@hotmail.com. Website: http://www.freeyellow. com/members2/enidwriters/index.html. Workshop Chair: Bev Walton-Porter. Writer workshops geared toward beginner, intermediate, advanced and professional levels. Workshop open to students. Annual workshop. Workshop held in spring (usually March). Cost of workshop: $40; includes registration, handouts and lunch. Write or call for more information. "Our workshops are not geared, per se, to children's writers.

We generally have one speaker for the day. Past speakers were Norma Jean Lutz, Mary Elizabeth Lynn, Deborah Bouziden, Anna Meyers (the only time we've had a children's writer), Jean Hager, Sandra Soli and Marcia Preston. The speaker for the 1999 workshop has not yet been determined. Workshop covers general mechanics of writing, query letters, creativity, proposals, attracting agents/editors, revision/rewriting, basic tools/skills all writers should have. "Look for details around February in *Writer's Digest* or *Byline Magazine*."

☑ **OHIO KENTUCKY INDIANA CHILDREN'S LITERATURE CONFERENCE**, % Greater Cincinnati Library Consortium, 3333 Vine St., Suite 605, Cincinnati OH 45220. (513)751-4422. Fax: (513)751-0463. E-mail: gclc@one.net. Website: http://www.libraries.uc.edu/gclc/. Staff Development Coordinator: Judy Malone. Writer and illustrator conference geared toward all levels. Annual workshop. Emphasizes multicultural literature for children and young adults. 1998 conference keynote speakers: George Ella Lyon and Patricia Reilly Giff. Tristate Authors & Illustrators Showcase; workshops by children's literature specialists/authors/illustrators including: Sue Eades, Ann Olson, Darwin Henderson, Harriet Arrington, Miriam McKenney, Fred Shaw, Nina Strauss, Charlotte Decker and Tina Moore. Annual conference. Conference held November 13, 1999. Registration limited to 250. Cost of conference: $35; includes registration/attendance at all workshop sessions, coffee break, lunch, author/illustrator signings. Write for more information.

☑ **OKLAHOMA FALL ARTS INSTITUTES**, P.O. Box 18154, Oklahoma City OK 73154. (405)842-0890. Fax: (405)848-4538. Website: okarts@telepath.com. Assistant Program Director: Christina Newendorp. Writer and illustrator workshops geared toward intermediate, advanced and professional levels. Writing topics include children's writing, fiction, nonfiction, poetry, art of teaching writing, painting, drawing, printmaking. Annual workshop, Visual arts workshop held in early October; writing workshops in late October. Registration is limited to 20 participants per workshop; 5 workshops each weekend. Cost of workshop: $450; includes tuition, double-occupancy room and board. Write for more information. "Catalogues are available. Each workshop is taught by a professional artist of national reputation."

OUTDOOR WRITERS ASSOCIATION OF AMERICA ANNUAL CONFERENCE, 2155 E. College Ave., State College PA 16801-7204. (814)234-1011. Fax: (814)234-9692. E-mail: eking4owaa@compuserve.com. Meeting Planner: Eileen King. Writer workshops geared toward all levels. Annual workshop. Workshop held in June. Cost of workshop: $130; includes attendance at all workshops and most meals. Attendees must have prior approval from Executive Director before attendance is permitted. Write for more information.

OZARK CREATIVE WRITERS, INC. CONFERENCE, 6817 Gingerbread Lane, Little Rock AR 72204. (501)565-8889. Fax: (510)565-7220. Director: Peggy Vining. Writer's workshops geared to all levels. "All forms of the creative process dealing with the literary arts. We sometimes include songwriting. We invite excellent speakers who are selling authors. We also promote writing by providing competitions in all genres." Always the second full weekend in October at Inn of the Ozarks in Eureka Springs AR (a resort town). Morning sessions are given to main attraction author . . . 6 1-hour satellite speakers during each of the 2 afternoons. Two banquets. "Approximately 200 attend the conference yearly . . . many others enter the creative writing competition." Cost of registration/contest entry fee approximately $40-50. Includes entrance to all sessions, contest entry fees. "This does not include meals or lodging. We block off 70 rooms prior to August 15 for OCW guests." Send #10 SASE for brochure by May 1st. "Reserve early."

PHOTOGRAPHY: A DIVERSE FOCUS, 895 W. Oak St., Zionsville IN 46077-1220. Phone/fax: (317)873-0738. Director: Charlene Faris. Writer and illustrator workshops geared to beginners. "Conferences focus primarily on children's photography; also literature and illustration. Annual conferences are held very often throughout year." Registration is not limited, but "sessions are generally small." Cost of conference: $150 (2 days), $75 (1 day). "Inquiries with an SASE only will receive information on seminars."

☑ **GARY PROVOST'S WRITERS RETREAT WORKSHOP**, % Write It/Sell It, P.O. Box 139, South Lancaster MA 01561. (800)642-2494 (for brochure). Fax: (978)368-0237. E-mail: wrwwisi@aol.com. Website: http://www.channel1.com/wisi. Director: Gail Provost Stockwell. Writer workshops geared toward beginner, intermediate and advanced levels. Workshops are appropriate for writers of full length novels for children/YA. Also, for writers of all novels or narrative nonfiction. Annual workshop. Workshops held in May. Registration limited to small groups: beginners and advanced. Writing facilities available: private rooms with desks. Cost of workshop: $1,620; includes tuition, food and lodging for nine nights, daily classes, writing space, time and assignments, consultation and instruction. Requirements: short synopsis required to determine appropriateness of novel for our nuts and bolts approach to getting the work in shape for publication. Write for more information. For complete details, call 800 number.

ROBERT QUACKENBUSH'S CHILDREN'S BOOK WRITING AND ILLUSTRATING WORKSHOP, 460 E. 79th St., New York NY 10021-1443. Phone/fax: (212)744-3822. E-mail: rqstudios @aol.com. (E-mail inquirers please include mailing address). Website: http://www.rquackenbush.com. Contact: Robert Quackenbush. Writer and illustrator workshops geared toward all levels and open to students. Emphasizes picture books from start to finish. Also covered is writing fiction and nonfiction for middle grades and young adults, if that is the attendees' interest. Current trends in illustration are also covered. Workshops held fall, winter and summer. Courses offered fall and winter include 10 weeks each— 1½ hour/week; July workshop is a full 5-day (9 a.m.-4 p.m) extensive course. Next workshop July 12-16, 1999. Registration limited to 10/class. Writing and/or art facilities available; work on the premises; art supply store nearby. Cost of workshop: $650 for instruction. Cost of workshop includes instruction in preparation of a ms and/or book dummy ready to submit to publishers. Attendees are responsible for arranging their own hotel and meals, although suggestions are given on request for places to stay and eat. "This unique five-day workshop, held annually since 1982, provides the opportunity to work with Robert Quackenbush, a prolific author and illustrator of children's books with more than 160 fiction and nonfiction books for young readers to his credit, including mysteries, biographies and song-books."

N **READER'S DIGEST WRITER'S WORKSHOP**, Northern Arizona University, P.O. Box 6024, Flagstaff AZ 86011-6024. (602)523-3559. Workshop Director: Ray Newton. Writer workshops geared toward all levels. Classes offered include major emphasis on nonfiction magazine articles for major popular publications. Annual workshops in various locations in US. Time of year varies, depending on location. Registration limited to 250. Cost of workshop: $150 registration fee; includes three meals. Does not include travel or lodging. "Participants will have opportunity for one-on-one sessions with major editors, writers representing national magazines, including the *Reader's Digest*." Write for more information.

N **ST. DAVIDS CHRISTIAN WRITERS CONFERENCE**, % Audrey Stallsmith, Registrar, 87 Pines Rd. E, Hadley PA 16130. (412)253-2738. Registrar: Audrey Stallsmith. Writer workshops geared toward all levels. **Open to students.** Annual conference. Conference held in June. Writing/art facilities available: college computer lab. Cost of conference: $425; includes tuition with room and board (double room, $25 extra for single room). Write for more information.

SAN DIEGO STATE UNIVERSITY WRITERS' CONFERENCE, The College of Extended Studies, San Diego CA 92182-1920. (619)594-2517. Fax: (619)594-8566. E-mail: ealcaraz@mail.sdsu.edu. Website: http://www.ces.sdsu.edu. Conference Facilitator: Erin Grady Alcaraz. Writer workshops geared toward beginner, intermediate and advanced levels. Emphasizes nonfiction, fiction, screenwriting, advanced novel writing; includes sessions specific to writing and illustrating for children. Workshops offered by children's editors, agents and writers. Workshops held third weekend in January each year. Registration limited. Cost of workshop: approximately $225. Write for more information or see our home page at the above Website.

SEATTLE CHRISTIAN WRITERS CONFERENCE, sponsored by Writers Information Network, P.O. Box 11337, Bainbridge Island WA 98110. (206)842-9103. Fax: (206)842-0536. Director: Elaine Wright Colvin. Writer workshops geared toward all levels. Conference open to students. Past conferences have featured subjects such as 'Making It to the Top as a Children's Book Author,' featuring Debbie Trafton O'Neal. Quarterly workshop (4 times/year). Workshop dates to be announced. Cost of workshop: $25. Write for more information and to be added to mailing list.

N **SELF PUBLISHING YOUR OWN BOOK**, 34200 Ridge Rd., #110, Willoughby OH 44094-2954. (440)943-3047. E-mail: fa837@po.cwru.edu. Coordinator: Lea Leever Oldham. **Open to students.** Covers options for publishing, ISBN, copyright, fair use, pricing, bar codes, size and binding and other topics of interest to the potential self publisher. Quarterly workshop. Workshop will be offered at several locations in Cleveland Heights, Kirtland, Euclid and Chardon, Ohio, on February 9, 1999; April 14, 1999; July 12, 1999; and October 7, 1999. Cost of workshop varies.

N **SKYLINE WRITERS' CONFERENCE**, P.O. Box 33343, N. Royalton OH 44133. (440)234-0763. Conference Director: Lilie Kilburn. Writer workshops geared toward all levels. **Open to students.** Conference covers writing and marketing children's literature. Annual conference. Conference held the first Saturday in August. Writing/art facilities available: classrooms for writing exercises. Cost of conference: $50; includes conference fee, continental breakfast, lunch, door prizes. Write for more information.

☑ **SOCIETY OF CHILDREN'S BOOK WRITERS AND ILLUSTRATORS—CAROLINAS ANNUAL FALL CONFERENCE**, 104 Barnhill Place, Chapel Hill NC 27514-9224. (919)967-2452. Fax: (919)929-6643. E-mail: earl-frandavis@prodigy.net. Coordinator: Stephanie Greene. Writer and illustrator conference geared toward beginner, intermediate, advanced and professional levels. **Open to students.** Sessions include Character-Driven Writing; Picture Book Writing; Middle Grade Writing; What's Hot and What's Not; illustration techniques, etc. Annual conference held October or early November. Cost of conference is $60 for SCBWI members; $65 for NCWN members; $70 for non-members before October 1st. Critiques for writing. Portfolios will be displayed, not critiqued. Write for more information.

SOCIETY OF CHILDREN'S BOOK WRITERS AND ILLUSTRATORS—FLORIDA REGION, 2158 Portland Ave., Wellington FL 33414. (561)798-4824. E-mail: barcafer@aol.com. Florida Regional Advisor: Barbara Casey. Writer and illustrator workshops geared toward beginner, intermediate, advanced and professional levels. Workshops open to students. Subjects to be announced. Annual workshop. Workshop held second Saturday of September in the meeting rooms of the Palm Springs Public Library, 217 Cypress Lane, Palm Springs FL. Registration limited to 100/class. Cost of workshop: $50 for members, $55 for non-members. Special rates are offered through the West Palm Beach Airport Hilton Hotel for those attending the conference who wish to spend the night. Write for more information.

SOCIETY OF CHILDREN'S BOOK WRITERS AND ILLUSTRATORS—HAWAII, 2355 Ala Wai Blvd. #502, Honolulu HI 96815-3404. (808)926-0115. E-mail: dmasters@sprynet.com. Website: http://www.scbwi.org. Regional Advisor: Elaine Masters. Writer and illustrator conferences geared toward all levels. **Open to students.** Conferences feature general topics—writing, illustrating, publishing and marketing; also specific skills workshops teach "plotting, characterization, etc. Cost varies. Reduced rate for SCBWI members. Open to nonmembers. Next workshop: February 1999. SASE or e-mail for more information.

ℕ **SOCIETY OF CHILDREN'S BOOK WRITERS AND ILLUSTRATORS—HOUSTON**, 8826 Rowen, Houston TX 27036. (713)777-5394. Fax: (713)266-0961. Regional Advisor: Mary Wade. Writer and illustrator workshops geared toward all levels. **Open to students.** Conference covers picture books and middle grade novels. Offers 3-4 small workshops throughout the year. Contact Mary Wade for more information.

SOCIETY OF CHILDREN'S BOOK WRITERS AND ILLUSTRATORS—ILLINOIS SPRING RETREAT—THE WRITE CONNECTION: 3 ACQUIRING EDITORS, 2408 Elmwood, Wilmette IL 60091. (847)256-4494. Fax: (847)256-9462. E-mail: esthersh@aol.com. Regional Advisor, SCBWI-Illinois: Esther Hershenhorn.
  • The workshop is held in Woodstock, Illinois. Next scheduled retreat in Spring 2000.
Writer workshops geared toward intermediate, advanced and professional levels. Offers teaching sessions; open mike; ms critiques; panel discussions; editor presentations. Biannual workshop.

☑ **SOCIETY OF CHILDREN'S BOOK WRITERS AND ILLUSTRATORS—INDIANA SPRING & FALL WRITERS' AND ILLUSTRATORS' CONFERENCE**, 934 Fayette St., Indianapolis IN 46202. E-mail: s_murray@iquest.net. Conference Director: Sara Murray-Plumer. Writer and illustrator workshops geared toward all levels. All are geared toward children's writers and illustrators. Two conferences held annually in June and October. Length of each session: 45 minutes to 1½ hours. Cost of workshop: approximately $55; includes meal and workshops. Write or e-mail for more information.

ℕ **SOCIETY OF CHILDREN'S BOOK WRITERS AND ILLUSTRATORS—IOWA CONFERENCE**, 1007 Oakwood Blvd., Fairfield IA 52556. (515)472-2996. Iowa SCBWI Regional Advisor: Cheryl Fusco Johnson. Writer workshops geared toward all levels. Illustrator workshops geared towards beginners. "Usually speakers include one to two acquiring book editors who discuss the needs of their publishing house and manuscripts that caught their attention. Also, we usually have several published Iowa authors discussing specific genres and/or topics like promotion, marketing, school visits, etc." Annual conference. Iowa has 1 or 2 conferences a year, usually in May and October. Registration limited to 100 or less. Cost of conference: usually about $60; less for SCSWI members; includes lunch and snacks. Individual critique costs $30 extra. Work must be submitted in advance.

☑ **SOCIETY OF CHILDREN'S BOOK WRITERS AND ILLUSTRATORS—MICHIGAN ANNUAL WRITERS AND ILLUSTRATORS RETREAT**, 1152 Stellma Lane, Rochester Hills MI 48309. Fax: (248)651-6489. E-mail: bsz@flash.net. Retreat Chairs: Brenda Yee and Anna Celenza. Writer and illustrator workshops geared toward intermediate and advanced levels. Topics include peer critique groups for both writers or illustrators of children's literature. This year will feature writing and illustration workshops and editors' workshops (workshop subjects vary from year to year). Past topics include plot/character development, use of computer illustration and what editors look for. Retreat held October 22-24. Registration limited. Cost of retreat $235 (to members); includes meals, lodging, linens, registration. Those wishing an individual ms or portfolio critique by a member of the faculty should send a copy of their ms, neatly typed and double-spaced, with a check for $35 to Brenda Yee before September 6. (Limit: complete picture book text, or 1 chapter of a novel or nonfiction work, or a complete magazine story.) Write or e-mail for more information.

☑ SOCIETY OF CHILDREN'S BOOK WRITERS AND ILLUSTRATORS—MIDSOUTH, (formerly Society of Children's Book Writers and Illustrators—Tennessee/Kentucky Spring Conference), Box 3342, Clarksville TN 37043-3342. (931)358-9849. E-mail: czauthor@aol.com. Regional Advisor: Cheryl Zach. Writer workshop geared toward all levels. Illustrator workshops geared toward beginner and intermediate levels. Previous workshop topics have included Editor's Perspective, Writing Query Letters, Writing Picture Books, Marketing Your Artwork, Mining History for Ideas, What Books Do Children's Librarians Want To See?, Whodunit: Writing Juvenile Mysteries, Writing About Koalas and Quantum Physics, Writing a Series, Successful School Visits, Book Contracts, Writing for Magazines. Workshop held in April. 1 day. Cost of workshop: $65 SCBWI members, $70 nonmembers; includes all day of workshops and lunch. Registration limited to 100. "SCBWI-Midsouth 1999 is scheduled for April 24 in Nashville." Send SASE for flier.

SOCIETY OF CHILDREN'S BOOK WRITERS AND ILLUSTRATORS—MINNESOTA, 7060 Valley Creek Rd., Suite 115215, Woodbury MN 55125. (612)739-0119. E-mail: kidlit@isd.net. Minnesota Regional Advisor: Peg Helminski. Writer and illustrator workshops geared toward beginner, intermediate, advanced and professional levels. All of our workshops and conferences focus on the needs of children's writers and illustrators. Critique sessions and portfolio reviews are often available. "We try to have at least one full day conference and one evening event per year." Conferences are held in April and October. Cost of conference: varies $20-85. Full day conferences usually include luncheon, coffee breaks and snack. Evening workshops usually include snack. SASE for more information 6 weeks prior to each event.

☑ SOCIETY OF CHILDREN'S BOOK WRITERS AND ILLUSTRATORS—NEW YORK— CONFERENCE IN CHILDREN'S LITERATURE, P.O. Box 20233, Park West Finance Station New York NY 10025-1511. Conference Co-chair: Frieda Gates. Writer and illustrator conference geared toward all levels. Annual conference. Workshop held usually the first or second Saturday in November. Length of each session: 45 minutes. Registration limited to 400. Cost of conference: $70, nonmembers; $65, members; includes continental breakfast, and a day of meeting authors, illustrators, publishers, editors and agents. Write for more information.

SOCIETY OF CHILDREN'S BOOK WRITERS AND ILLUSTRATORS—NORCAL RETREAT AT ASILOMAR, 1316 Rebecca Dr., Suisun CA 94585-3603. (707)426-6776. Fax: (707)427-2885. Regional Advisor: Bobi Martin Downey. Writer and illustrator workshops geared toward beginner, intermediate, advanced and professional levels. Emphasizes various topics from writing or illustrating picture books to young adult novels. Past speakers include agents, publishers, editors, published authors and illustrators. Annual workshop. Workshop generally held last weekend in February; Friday evening through Sunday lunch. Registration limited to 65. Rooms are shared with 1 other person. Desks available in most rooms. All rooms have private baths. Cost of workshop: $225 SCBWI members; $250 nonmembers; includes shared room, 6 meals, ice breaker party and conference. A full scholarship is available to SCBWI members. Call Bobi Martin Downey for application procedure. Registration opens October 1st and usually is full by October 31st. A waiting list is formed. SASE for more information. "This is a small retreat with a relaxed pace."

**FOR EXPLANATIONS OF THESE SYMBOLS,
SEE THE INSIDE FRONT AND BACK COVERS OF THIS BOOK**

Ⓝ SOCIETY OF CHILDREN'S BOOK WRITERS AND ILLUSTRATORS—NORTH CEN-TRAL CALIFORNIA; MARCH IN MODESTO, 8931 Montezuma Rd., Jamestown CA 95327. (209)984-5556. Fax: (209)984-0636. E-mail: trigar@mlode.com. SCBWI North Central CA Regional Advisor: Tricia Gardella. Writer and illustrator workshops geared toward all levels. **Open to students.** Offers talks on different genres, illustration evaluations and afternoon question breakout sessions. Annual conference. Conference held March 20, 1999; 8:30-4. Cost of conference: $50. Write for more information.

Ⓝ SOCIETY OF CHILDREN'S BOOK WRITERS AND ILLUSTRATORS—POCONO MOUNTAINS WRITERS' RETREAT, 708 Pine St., Moscow PA 18444. Conference Director: Susan Campbell Bartoletti. Workshop held third weekend in April, depending upon Easter and Passover. Registration limited to 75. Cost of workshop: tuition about $350; includes tuition, room and board. Send SASE in December or January for more information.

SOCIETY OF CHILDREN'S BOOK WRITERS AND ILLUSTRATORS—SOUTHERN BREEZE (ALABAMA/GEORGIA/MISSISSIPPI REGION), P.O. Box 26282, Birmingham AL 35260. Fax: (205)979-0274. E-mail: joanbroer@aol.com. Regional Advisor: Joan Broerman. "The fall conference, Writing and Illustrating for Kids, offers more than 20 workshops on craft, from entry level to professional track, picture books to young adult. This year also includes a panel discussion titled 'Tracking the Trends.' Annual workshop. Workshop held October 16, 1999. Cost of workshop: $50-60 for SCBWI members; $60-80 for nonmembers; ms critiques and portfolio review available for additional cost. Write for more information (include SASE). "Our spring conference, Springmingle!, is in different parts of the three-state region. Springmingle '99! will be held in Gulf Shores, Alabama, February 26-28, 1999." This workshop is geared towards intermediate to professional level. Preregistration important for both conferences.

SOCIETY OF CHILDREN'S BOOKS WRITERS AND ILLUSTRATORS—SOUTHERN CALI-FORNIA; ILLUSTRATOR'S DAY, 5632 Van Nuys Blvd., #292, Van Nuys CA 91401. (818)785-7282. Co-regional Advisors: Julie Williams and Marilyn Morton. Illustrators sessions geared toward all levels. Emphasizes illustration and illustration markets. Conference includes presentations by art director, children's book editor, and artist/author-illustrators. This conference has been held annually in the fall, but will be in February beginning with 1999. Conference held February 27, 1999. Great day for picture book authors as well. "Editors and art directors will view portfolios. We want to know whether or not each conferee is bringing a portfolio." Cost of conference: $70-85; included entire day of speakers and portfolio sharing ($10 extra for private portfolio review for beginning illustrators.)

SOCIETY OF CHILDREN'S BOOKS WRITERS AND ILLUSTRATORS—SOUTHERN CALI-FORNIA; WRITER'S DAY, 5632 Van Nuys Blvd., #292, Van Nuys CA 91401. (818)785-7282. Fax: (818)787-2104. E-mail: JULSCHIME@aol.com. Co-regional Advisors: Julie Williams and Marilyn Morton. A one-day conference for children's book writers geared toward all levels. Emphasizes fiction and nonfiction writing for children from picture books through young adult. Conference includes presentations by a children's book editor and children's book authors. Annual conference, next held May 8, 1999. Cost of conference: $70-80; includes entire day of speakers, lunch and a Writer's Day Contest.

Ⓝ SOCIETY OF CHILDREN'S BOOK WRITERS AND ILLUSTRATORS—UTAH/IDAHO; SPRING INTO ACTION, 819 E. Verbenia Ave., Sandy UT 84094. (801)523-6311. Fax: (801)523-6311. E-mail: kimorchid@aol.com. Website: http://members.aol.com/kimorchid/utahscbw.htm. Utah/Idaho SCBWI Regional Advisor: Kim Williams-Justesen. Writer workshops geared toward all levels. Illustrator workshops geared toward beginners and intermediate. **Open to students.** Topics include writing for magazines, improving plot, promoting your book and working with the art department. Annual conference. Conference held in April. Cost of conference: $30 SCBWI members; $40 nonmembers; includes workshops, lunch, registration packet. Additional $10 critique fee (limit 3 pages per ms); $10 art critique (limit 2 illustrations). Write for more information.

SOCIETY OF CHILDREN'S BOOK WRITERS AND ILLUSTRATORS—VENTURA/SANTA BARBARA FALL CONFERENCE, 100 Hillveiw Lane, Simi Valley CA 93065. (805)581-1906. E-mail: alexisinca@aol.com. Regional Advisor: Alexis O'Neill. Writers conference geared toward all levels. "We invite editors, authors and author/illustrators and agents. We have had speakers on the picture book, middle grade, YA, magazine and photo essay books. Both fiction and nonfiction are covered." Conference held in October from 9:00 a.m.-4 p.m. on Saturdays. Cost of conference $55; includes all sessions and lunch. Write for more information.

N: SOCIETY OF CHILDREN'S BOOK WRITERS AND ILLUSTRATORS—WASHINGTON STATE, 4037 56th Ave. SW, Seattle WA 98116. (206)932-3157. Regional Advisor: D. Bergman. Writer workshops geared toward all levels. **Open to students.** "In the past we have covered writing the picture book, easy-reader, middle grade novel, poetry magazine writing, promotion, illustration and illustrator's critique, etc." Annual conference. Conference held April 24, 1999. Registration limited to about 200. Cost of conference: $55-70; includes registration and lunch. The conference is a one-day event held at Seattle Pacific University. Hour to hour and ½ sessions run back-to-back so attendees have 2 or 3 choices. "In this way we can meet the needs of both those at the entry-level and those more advanced."

SOCIETY OF CHILDREN'S BOOK WRITERS & ILLUSTRATORS—WISCONSIN ANNUAL FALL RETREAT, Rt. 1, Box 137, Gays Mills WI 54631. (608)735-4707. Fax: (608)735-4700. E-mail: pfitsch@mwt.net. Co-Regional Advisor: Patricia Pfitsch. Writer workshops geared toward working writers. Some years we offer group critique sessions with faculty and participant participation—each full time participant receives critique from well-known editors, writers and or agents as well as other participants. Also talks by faculty on various aspects of writing and selling your work. "We try to have major New York editors, agents and well-known writers on the faculty. The entire retreat is geared *only* to children's book writing." Annual workshop. Retreat held in October or November, from Friday evening to Sunday afternoon. Registration limited to approximately 60. Cost of workshop: about $225; includes room, board and program. Critique may be extra. "We strive to offer an informal weekend with an award-winning children's writer, an agent or illustrator and an editor from a trade house in New York in attendance." There's usually a waiting list by mid-July. Send SASE for flier.

☑ SOFER, THE JEWISH WRITERS WORKSHOP, 555 Skokie Blvd., Suite 225, Northbrook IL 60062. (847)509-0990 ext. 12. Fax: (847)509-0970. E-mail: dunnfried@aol.com. Website: http://www.uahc .org/camps/osrui. Assistant Director: Deanne Dunn Friedman. Writers conference geared toward the intermediate, advanced and professional levels. Sessions cover creative nonfiction, poetry, fiction and playwriting. Speakers have included Roger Kamenetz and Howard Schwartz. Annual workshop held in August. Registration limited to 100. Cost of workshop is $255-350, depending on chosen lodging and includes programming, lodging and meals. "We do ask for a writing sample, but acceptance is not based on it. Though most workshop leaders are not children's writers, they can advise on writing for children. We usually have several attendees who are children's writers." Write for more information.

SOUTHWEST WRITERS WORKSHOP, Suite B, 1338 Wyoming Blvd. NE, Albuquerque NM 87112. (505)293-0303. Fax: (505)237-2665. E-mail: swriters@aol.com. Website: http://www.US1.net/sww. Contact: Carol Bruce-Fritz, executive director. Writer workshops geared toward all genres at all levels of writing. Various aspects of writing covered. Examples from conferences: Preconference workshops on the juvenile/young adult/novel taught by Penny Durant; on picture books by April Halprin Wayland; on Writing a Juvenile Novel in 6 weeks by Shirley Raye Redmond; on writing for children's magazines by C. Walskel (of Cricket). Annual conference. Conference held September 17-19, 1999 at Alburquerque Convention Center. Length of each session: Friday-Sunday. Cost of workshop: $250 (approximately); includes all workshops and meals. Also offers critique groups (for $40/year, offers 2 monthly meetings, monthly newsletter, annual writing contest and occasional workshops). Write for more information.

☑ SPLIT ROCK ARTS PROGRAM, University of Minnesota, 335 Nolte Center, 315 Pillsbury Dr., SE, Minneapolis MN 55455-0139. (612)624-6800. Fax: (612)625-5891. E-mail: srap@mail.cee.umn.edu. Registrar: Danielle Porter. Writer and illustrator workshops geared toward intermediate, advanced and professional levels. Workshops offered in writing and illustrating books for children and young people. Workshops begin in July for 5 weeks. Two college credits available. Registration limited to 16 per class. Workshops held on the University of Minnesota-Duluth campus. Cost of workshop: $440; includes tuition and fees. Amounts vary depending on course fee, determined by supply needs, etc. "Moderately priced on-campus housing available." Complete catalogs available in March. Call or write anytime to be put on mailing list. Some courses fill very early.

☑ STATE OF MAINE WRITERS' CONFERENCE, 36 Winona Ave., P.O. Box 7146, Ocean Park ME 04063-7146. (207)934-9806 (summer). (413)596-6734 (winter). Fax: (413)796-2121. E-mail: rburns0 @wnec.edu. Chairman: Richard F. Burns. Writers' workshops geared toward beginner, intermediate, advanced levels. **Open to students.** Emphasizes poetry, prose, mysteries, editors, publishers, etc. Annual conference held August 17-20, 1999. Cost of workshop: $100; includes all sessions and banquet, snacks, poetry booklet. Send SASE for more information.

[N] STEAMBOAT SPRINGS WRITERS CONFERENCE, P.O. Box 774284, Steamboat Springs CO 80477. (970)879-8079. E-mail: freiberger@compuserve.com. Conference Director: Harriet Freiberger. Writers' workshops geared toward intermediate levels. **Open to students.** Annual conference since 1982. Workshops held July 24, 1999. Registration limited to 25-30. Cost of workshop: $45; includes 4 seminars and luncheon. Write or e-mail for more information.

[✓] TO WRITE, WRITERS' GUILD OF ACADIANA, P.O. Box 51532, Lafayette LA 70505-1532. Contact: Marilyn Continé (318)981-5153 or Ro Foley (318)234-8694. Fax: (318)367-6860. E-mail: lbsimmons@aol.com. Writer conference geared toward beginner and intermediate levels. "We invite children's writers and agents, among other genres. The conference is not geared only to children's writings." Annual conference. Conference held March 19-20, 1999. Registration limited to 150. Cost of workshop: $100 member/$125 nonmember; includes 2 days of about 20 various sessions, some geared to children's writers; Friday night dinner, Saturday continental breakfast and luncheon; Friday and Saturday autograph teas; a chance to have your ms looked at by agents. Also includes a year membership to Writer's Guild of Acadiana. Write for more information or call.

UMKC/WRITERS PLACE WRITERS WORKSHOPS, University of Missouri—Kansas City, 5100 Rockhill Rd., 215 55B, Kansas City MO 64110-2499. (816)235-2736. Fax: (816)235-5279. E-mail: mckinleym@umkc.edu. Continuing Education Manager: Mary Ann McKinley. Writer workshops geared toward intermediate, advanced and professional levels. Workshops open to students. Semi-annual workshops. Workshops held in fall and spring. Registration limited to 25. Cost of workshop: $45. Write for more information.

[🍁] VANCOUVER INTERNATIONAL WRITERS FESTIVAL, 1243 Cartwright St., Vancouver, British Columbia V6H 4B7 Canada. (604)681-6330. Fax: (604)681-8400. E-mail: vifw@axionet.com. Website: http://www.writersfest.bc.ca. Artistic Director: Alma Lee. Annual literary festival. The Vancouver International Writers Festival strives to encourage an appreciation of literature and to promote literacy by providing a forum where writers and readers can interact. This is accomplished by the production of special events and an annual Festival which feature writers from a variety of countries, whose work is compelling and diverse. The Festival attracts over 11,000 people and presents approximately 40 events in four venues during five days on Granville Island, located in the heart of Vancouver. The first 3 days of the festival are programmed for elementary and secondary school students. Held third week in October (5-day festival). All writers who participate are invited by the A.D. The events are open to anyone who wishes to purchase tickets. Cost of events ranges from $10-25.

VASSAR INSTITUTE OF PUBLISHING AND WRITING: CHILDREN'S BOOKS IN THE MARKETPLACE, Box 300, Vassar College, Poughkeepsie NY 12604-0540. (914)437-5903. Fax: (914)437-7209. E-mail: mabruno@vassar.edu. Website: http://www.vassar.edu. Program Coordinator: Maryann Bruno. Director: Jean Marzollo. Writer and illustrator conference geared toward all levels. Emphasizes "the editorial, production, marketing and reviewing processes, on writing fiction and nonfiction for all ages, creating the picture book, understanding the markets and selling your work." Workshop held June 14-19, 1999. Length of each session: 3½-hour morning critique sessions, afternoon and evening lectures. Registration limited to 30-35/class (with 2 instructors). Cost of conference: approximately $800, includes room, board and tuition for all critique sessions, lectures and social activities. Proposals are pre-prepared and discussed at morning critique sessions. Art portfolio review given on pre-prepared works. Write for more information. "This conference gives a comprehensive look at the publishing industry as well as offering critiques of creative writing and portfolio review."

[🍁] [✓] THE VICTORIA SCHOOL OF WRITING, P.O. Box 8152, Victoria, British Columbia V8V 3R8 Canada. (250)598-5300. Fax: (250)598-0066. E-mail: writeawy@islandnet.com. Website: http://www.islandnet.com/writeawy. Director: Margaret Dyment. Writer conference geared toward intermediate level. In the 1999 conference there may be 1 workshop on writing for children and young adults. Annual conference. Workshop held July 20-23. Registration limited to 100. Conference includes close mentoring from established writers. Cost of conference: $445 (Canada); includes tuition and some meals. To attend, submit 3-10 pages of writing samples. Write for more information.

WESLEYAN WRITERS CONFERENCE, Wesleyan University, Middletown CT 06459. (860)685-3604. Fax: (860)685-2441. E-mail: agreene@wesleyan.edu. Website: http://www.wesleyan.edu/writing/conferen.html. Director: Anne Greene. Writer workshops geared toward all levels. "This conference is useful for writers interested in how to structure a story, poem or nonfiction piece. Although we don't always offer classes in writing for children, the advice about structuring a piece is useful for writers of any sort, no matter who their audience is." Classes in the novel, short story, fiction techniques, poetry, journalism and literary nonfiction. Guest speakers and panels offer discussion of fiction, poetry, reviewing, editing and publishing. Individual ms consultations available. Conference held annually the last week in June. Length of each session: 6 days. "Usually, there are 100 participants at the Conference." Classrooms, meals, lodging and word processing facilities available on campus. Cost of workshop: tuition—$450, room—$105, meals (required of all participants)—$185. "Anyone may register; people who want financial aid must submit their work and be selected by scholarship judges." Call for a brochure or look on the web at address above.

☑ **WESTERN RESERVE WRITERS AND FREELANCE CONFERENCE**, 34200 Ridge Rd., #110, Willoughby OH 44094-2954. E-mail: fa837@po.cwru.edu. Coordinator: Lea Leever Oldham. Writer workshops geared toward all levels. **Open to students.** Emphasizes fiction, nonfiction, articles, children's writing, poetry, marketing, tax for freelancers, copyright issues and other topics of interest to the beginning or advanced writer. All-day conference, September 11, 1999. Cost of workshop: $59 includes lunch. Held at Lakeland Community College, Kirtland, OH.

WESTERN RESERVE WRITERS MINI CONFERENCE, 34200 Ridge Rd. #110, Willoughby OH 44094-2954. E-mail: fa837@po.cwru.edu. Coordinator: Lea Leever Oldham. Writer workshops geared toward beginner, intermediate and advanced levels. **Open to students.** Topics include children's writing, fiction, nonfiction, poetry, articles, marketing and other topics of interest to the beginning or advanced writer. Annual conference March 27, 1999. Held at Lakeland Community College, Kirtland OH. Cost of conference: $39. Write for more information.

WILLAMETTE WRITERS ANNUAL WRITERS CONFERENCE, 9045 SW Barbur Blvd., Suite 5A, Portland OR 97219. (503)452-1592. Fax: (503)452-0372. E-mail: wilwrite@teleport.com. Office Manager: Bill Johnson. Writer workshops geared toward all levels. Emphasizes all areas of writing, including children's and young adult. Opportunities to meet one-on-one with leading literary agents and editors. Workshops held in August. Cost of conference: $231; includes membership.

☑ **WRITE FOR SUCCESS WORKSHOP: CHILDREN'S BOOKS**, 3748 Harbor Heights Dr., Largo FL 33774. (813)581-2484. Workshop Leader: Theo Carroll. Writer and illustrator workshops geared toward intermediate levels. **Open to students and adults.** Program covers: writing and defining the picture book; finding and developing ideas; creating characters; plotting; writing dialogue; trends in publishing; developing conflict; revising. Annual workshop in March. Registration limited to 50-110. Cost of workshop: $85; includes hand outs and writers magazines. Write for more information.

WRITE PEOPLE LITERARY CONFERENCE, P.O. Box 188, Scottville, MI 49454. Conference held at West Shore Community College, 3000 Stiles Rd, Scottville, MI 49454. (616)757-9432. Fax: (616)757-3801. E-mail: jeter@t-one.net. Website: http://www.t-one.net/~ghol. Director: Jacky Jeter. Writer and illustrator conference geared toward: beginner, intermediate, advanced and professional levels. **Open to students.** Conference held every other year on the first or second weekend in October. Registration to conference is not limited; however, individual sessions may be limited. Cost of conference is under $75 and includes continental breakfast Saturday, luncheon, coffee/tea/cookie breaks morning and afternoon. Friday evening is free to public. Write for more information.

WRITERS' FORUM, 1570 E. Colorado Blvd., Pasadena CA 91106-2003. (818)585-7608. Coordinator of Forum: Meredith Brucker. Writer workshops geared toward all levels. Workshops held March 20, 1999. Length of sessions: 1 hour and 15 minutes including Q & A time. Cost of day: $100; includes lunch. Write for more information to Extended Learning, Pasadena City College, 1570 E. Colorado Blvd., Pasadena CA 91106-2003.

WRITING FOR MONEY, Lakeland Community College, 7700 Clocktower Dr., Mentor OH 44060. (440)943-3047. E-mail: fa837@po.cwru.edu. Contact: Lea Leever Oldham. **Open to students.** Covers query letters, characterization, editing, leads, ms preparation, marketing and multiple use of ideas. Quarterly workshop. Held January 23, 1999; April 24, 1999; July 17, 1999; October 23, 1999. Cost of workshop: $39; includes handouts. For information send SASE to 34200 Ridge Rd., #110, Willoughby OH 44094.

Contests & Awards

Publication is not the only way to get your work recognized. Contests can also be viable vehicles to gain recognition in the industry. Placing in a contest or winning an award validates the time spent writing and illustrating. Even for those who don't place, many competitions offer the chance to obtain valuable feedback from judges and other established writers or artists.

When considering contests, be sure to study guidelines and requirements. Regard entry deadlines as gospel and note whether manuscripts and artwork should be previously published or unpublished. Also, be aware that awards vary. While one contest may award a significant amount of money or publication, another may award a certificate or medal instead.

Note that some contests require nominations. For published authors and illustrators, competitions provide an excellent way to promote your work. Your publisher may not be aware of local competitions such as state-sponsored awards—if your book is eligible, have the appropriate person at your publishing company nominate or enter your work for consideration.

To select potential contests for your work, read through the listings that interest you, then send for more information about the types of written or illustrated material considered and other important details, such as who retains the rights to prize-winning material. A number of contests offer such information through websites given in their listings. If you are interested in knowing who has received certain awards in the past, check your local library or bookstores or consult *Children's Books: Awards & Prizes*, compiled and edited by the Children's Book Council (http://www.cbcbooks.org). Many bookstores have special sections for books that are Caldecott and Newbery Medal winners.

Information on contests listed in the previous edition but not included in this edition of *Children's Writer's & Illustrator's Market* may be found in the General Index.

☑ **AIM Magazine Short Story Contest**, P.O. Box 1174, Maywood IL 60153-8174. (773)874-6184. Contest Directors: Ruth Apilado, Mark Boone. Annual contest. **Open to students.** Estab. 1983. Purpose of contest: "We solicit stories with social significance. Youngsters can be made aware of social problems through the written word and hopefully they will try solving them." Unpublished submissions only. Deadline for entries: August 15. SASE for contest rules and entry forms. SASE for return of work. No entry fee. Awards $100. Judging by editors. Contest open to everyone. Winning entry published in fall issue of *AIM*. Subscription rate $12/year. Single copy $4.50.

☑ **ALCUIN CITATION AWARD**, The Alcuin Society, P.O. Box 3216, Vancouver, British Columbia V6B 3X8 Canada. (604)888-9049. Fax: (604)888-9052. Secretary: Doreen E. Eddy. Annual award. Estab. 1983. **Open to students.** Purpose of contest: Alcuin Citations are awarded annually for excellence in Canadian book design. Previously published submissions only, "in the year prior to the Awards Invitation to enter; i.e., 1996 awards went to books published in 1995." Submissions made by the author, publishers and designers. Deadline for entries: March 15. SASE. Entry fee is $10. Awards certificate. Judging by professionals and those experienced in the field of book design. Requirements for entrants: Winners are selected from books designed and published in Canada. Awards are presented annually at the Annual General Meeting of the Alcuin Society held in late May or early June each year.

AMERICA & ME ESSAY CONTEST, Farm Bureau Insurance, Box 30400, 7373 W. Saginaw, Lansing MI 48909-7900. (517)323-7000. Fax: (517)323-6615. Contest Coordinator: Lisa Fedewa. Annual contest. Estab. 1968. Purpose of the contest: to give Michigan 8th graders the opportunity to express their thoughts/feelings on America and their roles in America. Unpublished submissions only. Deadline for entries: mid-November. SASE for contest rules and entry forms. "We have a school mailing list. Any school located in Michigan is eligible to participate." Entries not returned. No entry fee. Awards savings bonds and plaques for state top ten ($500-1,000), certificates and plaques for top 3 winners from each school. Each school may submit up to 10 essays for judging. Judging by home office employee volunteers. Requirements for entrants: "Participants must work through their schools or our agents' sponsoring schools. No individual submissions will be accepted. Top ten essays and excerpts from other essays are published in booklet form following the contest. State capitol/schools receive copies."

AMERICAN ASSOCIATION OF UNIVERSITY WOMEN, NORTH CAROLINA DIVISION, AWARD IN JUVENILE LITERATURE, North Carolina Literary and Historical Association, 109 E. Jones St., Raleigh NC 27601-2807. (919)733-9375. Fax: (919)733-8807. Award Director: Dr. Jerry C. Cashion. Annual award. Purpose of award: To reward the creative activity involved in writing juvenile literature and to stimulate in North Carolina an interest in worthwhile literature written on the juvenile level. Must be published during the year ending June 30 of the year of publication. Submissions made by author, author's agent or publisher. Deadline for entries: 15 July. SASE. for contest rules. Awards a cup to the winner and winner's name inscribed on a plaque displayed within the North Carolina Division of Archives and History. Judging by Board of Award selected by sponsoring organization. Requirements for entrants: Author must have maintained either legal residence or actual physical residence, or a combination of both, in the State of North Carolina for three years immediately preceding the close of the contest period.

AMERICAS AWARD, Consortium of Latin American Studies Programs (CLASP), CLASP Committee on Teaching and Outreach, % Center for Latin America, University of Wisconsin-Milwaukee, P.O. Box 413, Milwaukee WI 53201. (414)229-5986. Fax: (414)229-2879. E-mail address: cla@csd.uwm.edu. Website: http://www.uwm.edu/Dept/CLA/outreach_americas.html. Coordinator: Julie Kline. Annual award. Estab. 1993. Purpose of contest: "Two awards are given each spring in recognition of a U.S. published work (from the previous year) of fiction, poetry, folklore or selected nonfiction (from picture books to works for young adults) in English or Spanish which authentically and engagingly relate to Latin America, the Caribbean, or to Latinos in the United States. By combining both and linking the "Americas," the intent is to reach beyond geographic borders, as well as multicultural-international boundaries, focusing instead upon cultural heritages within the hemisphere." Previously published submissions only. Submissions open to anyone with an interest in the theme of the award. Deadline for entries: January 15. SASE for contest rules and any committee changes. Awards $200 cash prize, plaque and a formal presentation at the Library of Congress, Washington DC. Judging by a review committee consisting of individuals in teaching, library work, outreach and children's literature specialists.

✓ **AMHA LITERARY CONTEST**, American Morgan Horse Association Youth, P.O. Box 960, Shelburne VT 05482. (802)985-4944. Website: http://www.morganhorse.com. Contest Director: Susan Bell. Annual contest. **Open to students.** Purpose of contest: "to award youth creativity." The contest includes categories for both poetry and essays. The 1998 theme was "Morgans-Link to the Past, a Bridge to the Future" Entrants should write to receive the 1999 entry form and theme. Unpublished submissions only. Submissions made by author. Deadline for entries: October 1. SASE for contest rules and entry forms. No entry fee. Awards $50 cash and ribbons to up to 5th place. "Winning entry will be published in *AMHA News and Morgan Sales Network*, a monthly publication."

AMHA MORGAN ART CONTEST, American Morgan Horse Association, Box 960, Shelburne VT 05482. (802)985-4944. Fax: (802)985-8897. E-mail: amha@together.net. Website: http://www.morganhors e.com. Membership Recognition Coordinator: Susan Bell. Annual contest. The art contest consists of two categories: Morgan art (pencil sketches, oils, water colors, paintbrush), Morgan specialty pieces (sculptures, carvings). Unpublished submissions only. Deadline for entries: October 1. Contest rules and entry forms available for SASE. Entries not returned. Entry fee is $2. Awards $50 first prize in 2 divisions (for adults) and AMHA gift certificates to top 6 places (for children). Judging by *The Morgan Horse* magazine staff. "All work submitted becomes property of The American Morgan Horse Association. Selected works may be used for promotional purposes by the AMHA." Requirements for entrants: "We consider all work submitted." Works displayed at the annual convention and the AMHA headquarters; published in *AMAHA*

**FOR EXPLANATIONS OF THESE SYMBOLS,
SEE THE INSIDE FRONT AND BACK COVERS OF THIS BOOK**

News and *Morgan Sales Network* and in color in the *Morgan Horse Magazine* (TMHA). The contest divisions consist of Junior (to age 17), Senior (18 and over) and Professional (commercial artists). Each art piece must have its own application form and its own entry fee. Matting is optional.

HANS CHRISTIAN ANDERSEN AWARD, IBBY International Board on Books for Young People, Nonnenweg 12, Postfach, CH-4003 Basel Switzerland. Phone: (004161)272 29 17. Fax: (004161)272 27 57. E-mail: lbby@eye.ch. Website: http://www.ibby.org. Award offered every two years. Purpose of award: A Hans Christian Andersen Medal shall be awarded every two years by the International Board on Books for Young People (IBBY) to an author and to an illustrator, living at the time of the nomination, who by the outstanding value of their work are judged to have made a lasting contribution to literature for children and young people. The complete works of the author and of the illustrator will be taken into consideration in awarding the medal, which will be accompanied by a diploma. Previously published submissions only. Submissions are nominated by National Sections of IBBY in good standing. The National Sections select the candidates. The Hans Christian Andersen Award, named after Denmark's famous storyteller, is the highest international recognition given to an author and an illustrator of children's books. The Author's Award has been given since 1956, the Illustrator's Award since 1966. The Andersen Award is often called the "Little Nobel Prize." Her Majesty Queen Margrethe of Denmark is the Patron of the Hans Christian Andersen Awards. At the discretion of the jury the distinction "Highly Commended" may also be awarded. The Hans Christian Andersen Jury judges the books submitted for medals according to literary and artistic criteria. The awards are presented at the biennial congresses of IBBY.

☑ ARTS RECOGNITION AND TALENT SEARCH (ARTS), National Foundation for Advancement in the Arts, 800 Brickell Ave., Suite 500, Miami FL 33131. (305)377-1147. Fax: (305)377-1149. E-mail: nfaa@nffa.org. Website: http://www.nfaa.org. Contact: Dena Willman. **Open to students/high school seniors or 17 and 18-year-olds.** Annual award. Estab. 1981. "Created to recognize and reward outstanding accomplishment in dance, music, jazz, theater, photography, visual arts and/or writing. Arts Recognition and Talent Search (ARTS) is an innovative national program of the National Foundation for Advancement in the Arts (NFAA). Established in 1981, ARTS touches the lives of gifted young people across the country, providing financial support, scholarships and goal-oriented artistic, educational and career opportunities. Each year, from a pool of more than 8,000 applicants, an average of 400 ARTS awardees are chosen for NFAA support by panels of distinguished artists and educators. Deadline for entries: June 1 and October 1. Entry fee is $25/35. Fee waivers available based on need. Awards $100-3,000—unrestricted cash grants. Judging by a panel of authors and educators recognized in the field. Rights to submitted/winning material: NFAA/ARTS retains the right to duplicate work in an anthology or in Foundation literature unless otherwise specified by the artist. Requirements for entrants: Artists must be high school seniors or, if not enrolled in high school, must be 17 or 18 years old. Applicants must be US citizens or residents, unless applying in jazz. Works will be published in an anthology distributed during ARTS Week, the final adjudication phase which takes place in Miami.

Ⓝ ☑ ATLANTIC WRITING COMPETITION, Writer's Federation of Nova Scotia, 901, 1809 Barrington St., Halifax, Nova Scotia B3J 3K8 Canada. (902)423-8116. Fax: (902)422-0881. E-mail: writers1@fox.nstn.ca. Website: http://www.chebucto.ns.ca/Culture/WFNS/. **Open to students.** Annual contest. Estab. 1970s. Purpose is to encourage new and emerging writers. Unpublished submissions only. Submissions made by author. Deadline for entries: August 1, 1999. SASE for contest rules and entry forms. Entry fee is $15 (Canadian). Judging by a team of a writer, bookseller and publisher. Only open to residents of Atlantic Canada who are unpublished in category they enter. Judges return comments to all entrants.

Ⓝ MARGARET BARTLE ANNUAL PLAYWRITING AWARD, Community Children's Theatre of Kansas City, 8021 E. 129th Terrace, Grandview, MO 64030. (816)761-5775. Chairperson: Blanche Sellens. Annual contest. Estab. 1947. "Community Children's Theatre of Kansas City, Inc. was organized in 1947 to provide live theater for elementary aged children. We are now recognized as being one of the country's largest organizations providing this type of service." Unpublished submissions only. Deadline for entries: end of January. SASE for award rules. SASE for return of entries. No entry fee. Awards $500. Judging by a committee of 5. "CCT reserves the right for one of the units to produce the prize winning play for two years. The plays are performed before students in elementary schools. Although our 5- to 12-year-old audiences are sophisticated, gratuitous violence, mature love stories, or slang are not appropriate—cursing is *not acceptable*. In addition to original ideas, subjects that usually provide good plays are legends, folklore, historical incidents, biographies and adaptations of children's classics."

☑ BAY AREA BOOK REVIEWER'S ASSOCIATION (BABRA), %*Poetry Flash*, 1450 Fourth St., #4, Berkeley CA 94710. (510)525-5476. Fax: (510)525-6752. Contact: Joyce Jenkins. Annual award for outstanding book in children's literature, open to Bay Area authors, northern California from Fresno north. Annual award. Estab. 1981. "BABRA presents annual awards to Bay Area (northern California) authors annually in fiction, nonfiction, poetry and children's literature. Purpose is to encourage Bay Area writers and stimulate interest in books and reading." Previously published submissions only. Must be published the calendar year prior to spring awards ceremony. Submissions nominated by publishers; author or agent could also nominate published work. Deadline for entries: December. No entry forms. Send 3 copies of the book to Jonathan Sharp. No entry fee. Awards $100 honorarium and award certificate. Judging by voting members of the Bay Area Book Reviewer's Association. Books that reach the "finals" (usually 3-5 per category) displayed at annual award ceremonies (spring). Nominated books are displayed and sold at BABRA's annual awards ceremonies, in the spring of each year.

☑ **THE IRMA S. AND JAMES H. BLACK BOOK AWARD**, Bank Street College of Education, 610 W. 112th St., New York NY 10025-1898. (212)875-4450. Fax: (212)875-4558. E-mail: lindag@bnkst.edu. Website: http://www.bnkst.edu/library/clib/isb.html. Contact: Linda Greengrass. Annual award. Estab. 1972. Purpose of award: "The award is given each spring for a book for young children, published in the previous year, for excellence of both text and illustrations." Entries must have been published during the previous calendar year (between January '98 and December '98 for 1998 award). Deadline for entries: January 1. "Publishers submit books to us by sending them here to me at the Bank Street library. Authors may ask their publishers to submit their books. Out of these, three to five books are chosen by a committee of older children and children's literature professionals. These books are then presented to children in selected second, third and fourth grade classes here and at a few other cooperating schools on the East Coast. These children are the final judges who pick the actual award. A scroll (one each for the author and illustrator, if they're different) with the recipient's name and a gold seal designed by Maurice Sendak are awarded in May."

☑ **WALDO M. AND GRACE C. BONDERMAN/IUPUI NATIONAL YOUTH THEATRE PLAYWRITING COMPETITION AND DEVELOPMENT WORKSHOP AND SYMPOSIUM**, Indiana University-Purdue University at Indianapolis, 425 University Blvd. #309, Indianapolis IN 46202. (317)274-2095. Fax: (317)278-1025. E-mail: dwebb@.iupui.edu. Director: Dorothy Webb. Entries should be submitted to Priscilla Jackson, Literary Manager. Contest every two years; next competition will be 2000. Estab. 1983. Purpose of the contest: "to encourage writers to create artistic scripts for young audiences. It provides a forum through which each playwright receives constructive criticism of his/her work and, where selected, writers participate in script development with the help of professional dramaturgs, directors and actors." Unpublished submissions only. Submissions made by author. SASE for contest rules and entry forms. No entry fee. "Awards will be presented to the top ten finalists. Four cash awards of $1,000 each will be received by the top four playwrights whose scripts will be given developmental work culminating in polished readings showcased at the symposium held on the IUPUI campus. This symposium is always held opposite years of the competition. Major publishers of scripts for young audiences, directors, producers, critics and teachers attend this symposium and provide useful reactions to the plays. If a winner is unable to be involved in preparation of the reading and to attend the showcase of his/her work, the prize will not be awarded. Remaining finalists will receive certificates." Judging by professional directors, dramaturgs, publishers, university professors. Write for guidelines and entry form.

☑ **BOOK OF THE YEAR FOR CHILDREN**, Canadian Library Association, 200 Elgin St., Suite 206, Ottawa, Ontario K2P 1L5 Canada. (613)232-9625. Fax: (613)563-9895. Contact: Chairperson, Canadian Association of Children's Librarians. Annual award. Estab. 1947. "The main purpose of the award is to encourage writing and publishing in Canada of good books for children up to and including age 14. If, in any year, no book is deemed to be of award calibre, the award shall not be made that year. To merit consideration, the book must have been published in Canada and its author must be a Canadian citizen or a permanent resident of Canada." Previously published submissions only; must be published between January 1 and December 1 of the previous year. Deadline for entries: January 1. SASE for award rules. Entries not returned. No entry fee. Awards a medal. Judging by committee of members of the Canadian Association of Children's Librarians. Requirements for entrants: Contest open only to Canadian authors or residents of Canada. Winning books are on display at CLA headquarters.

☑ **BOOK PUBLISHERS OF TEXAS, Children's/Young People's Award**, The Texas Institute of Letters, % TCU Press, P.O. Box 298300, Ft. Worth TX 76129. (817)257-7822. Fax: (817)257-5075. E-mail: j.alter@tcu.edu. Website: http://www.prs.tcu.edu/prs/TIL/. Contact: Judy Alter. Send SASE to above address for list of judges to whom entries should be submitted. Annual award. Purpose of the award: "to recognize notable achievement by a Texas writer of books for children or young people or by a writer whose work deals with a Texas subject. The award goes to the author of the winning book, a work published during the calendar year before the award is given. Judges list available each July. Submissions go directly to judges, so current list of judges is necessary. Write to above address. Deadline is first postally operative day of January." Previously published submissions only. SASE for award rules and entry forms. No entry fee. Awards $250. Judging by a panel of 3 judges selected by the TIL Council. Requirements for entrants: The writer must have lived in Texas for 2 consecutive years at some time, or the work must have a Texas theme.

☑ **THE BOSTON GLOBE-HORN BOOK AWARDS**, The Boston Globe & The Horn Book, Inc., The Horn Book, 56 Roland St., Suite 200, Boston MA 02129. (800)325-1170. E-mail: info@hbook.com. Website: http://www.hbook.com. Award Directors: Stephanie Loer and Roger Sutton. Writing Contact: Stephanie Loer, children's book editor for *The Boston Globe*, 298 North St., Medfield MA 02052. Annual award. Estab. 1967. Purpose of award: "To reward literary excellence in children's and young adult books. Awards are for picture books, nonfiction and fiction. Up to two honor books may be chosen for each category." Books must be published between June 1, 1998 and May 31, 1999. Deadline for entries: May 15. "Publishers usually submit books. Award winners receive $500 and silver engraved bowl, honor book winners receive a silver plate." Judging by 3 judges involved in children's book field who are chosen by Roger Sutton, editor-in-chief for The Horn Book, Inc. (*The Horn Book Magazine* and *The Horn Book Guide*) and Stephanie Loer, children's book editor for *The Boston Globe*. "*The Horn Book Magazine* publishes speeches given at awards ceremonies. The book must have been published in the U.S. The awards are given at the fall conference of the New England Library Association."

BUCKEYE CHILDREN'S BOOK AWARD, State Library of Ohio, 65 S. Front St., Columbus OH 43215-4163. (614)644-7061. Fax: (614)728-2788. E-mail: rmetcalf@winslo.state.oh.us. Website: http://www.wpl.lib.oh.us:80/buckeyebook/. Nancy Smith, Chairperson. Correspondence should be sent to Ruth A. Metcalf at the above address. Award every two years. Estab. 1981. Purpose of the award: "The Buckeye Children's Book Award Program was designed to encourage children to read literature critically, to promote teacher and librarian involvement in children's literature programs, and to commend authors of such literature, as well as to promote the use of libraries. Awards are presented in the following three categories: grades K-2, grades 3-5 and grades 6-8." Previously published submissions only. Deadline for entries: February 1. "The nominees are submitted by this date during the even year and the votes are submitted by this date during the odd year. This award is nominated and voted upon by children in Ohio. It is based upon criteria established in our bylaws. The winning authors are awarded a special plaque honoring them at a banquet given by one of the sponsoring organizations. The BCBA Board oversees the tallying of the votes and announces the winners in March of the voting year in a special news release and in a number of national journals. The book must have been written by an author, a citizen of the United States and originally copyrighted in the U.S. within the last three years preceding the nomination year. The award-winning books are displayed in a historical display housed at the Columbus Metropolitan Library in Columbus, Ohio."

☑ **BYLINE MAGAZINE CONTESTS**, P.O. Box 130596, Edmond OK 73013-0001. E-mail: bylinemp@aol.com. Website: http://www.bylinemag.com. Contest Director: Marcia Preston. Purpose of contest: *ByLine* runs 4 contests a month on many topics to encourage and motivate writers. Past topics include first chapter of a novel, children's fiction, children's poem, nonfiction for children, personal essay, general short stories, valentine or love poem, etc. Send SASE for contest flier with topic list. Unpublished submissions only. Submissions made by the author. "We do not publish the contests' winning entries, just the names of the winners." SASE for contest rules. Entry fee is $3-4. Awards cash prizes for first, second and third place. Amounts vary. Judging by qualified writers or editors. List of winners will appear in magazine.

BYLINE MAGAZINE STUDENT PAGE, P.O. Box 130596, Edmond OK 73013. (405)348-5591. E-mail: bylinemp@aol.com. Website: http://www.bylinemag.com. Contest Director: Marcia Preston, publisher. Estab. 1981. "We offer writing contests for students in grades 1-12 on a monthly basis, September through May, with cash prizes and publication of top entries." Previously unpublished submissions only. "This is not a market for illustration." Deadline for entries varies. "Entry fee usually $1." Awards cash and publication. Judging by qualified editors and writers. "We publish top entries in student contests. Winners' list published in magazine dated 2 months past deadline." Send SASE for details.

☑ **CALIFORNIA YOUNG PLAYWRIGHTS CONTEST**, Playwrights Project, 450 B St., Suite 480, San Diego CA 92101. (619)239-7483. E-mail: youth@playwright.com. Director: Deborah Salzer. Open to Californians under age 19. Annual contest. Estab. 1985. "Our organization, and the contest, is designed to nurture promising young writers. We hope to develop playwrights and audiences for live theater. We also teach playwriting." Submissions required to be unpublished and not produced professionally. Submissions made by the author. Deadline for entries: April 1. SASE for contest rules and entry form. No entry fee. Award is professional productions of 3-5 short plays each year, participation of the writers in the entire production process, with a royalty award of $100 per play. Judging by professionals in the theater community, a committee of 5-7; changes somewhat each year. Works performed in San Diego at the Cassius Carter Centre Stage of the Old Globe Theatre. Writers submitting scripts of 10 or more pages receive a detailed script evaluation letter.

N CALLIOPE FICTION CONTEST, Writers' Specialized Interest Group (SIG) of American Mensa, Ltd., P.O. Box 466, Moraga CA 94556-0466. E-mail: cynthia@theriver.com. Submit entries to Sandy Raschke, fiction editor. **Open to students.** Annual contest. Estab. 1991. Purpose of contest: To promote good writing and opportunities for getting published. To give our member/subscribers and others an entertaining and fun exercise in writing. Unpublished submissions only (all genres, no violence, profanity or extreme horror). Submissions made by author. Deadline for entries: changes annually, but usually around September 15. Entry fee is $2 for non-subscribers; subscribers get first entry fee. Awards small amount of cash (up to $25 for 1st place, to $5 for 3rd), certificates, full or mini-subscriptions to *Calliope*) and various premiums and books, depending on donations. All winners are published in subsequent issues of *Calliope*. Judging by fiction editor, with concurrence of other editors, if needed. Requirements for entrants: one-time rights. Open to all writers. No special considerations—other than following the guidelines. Contest theme, due dates and sometimes entry fees change annually. Always send SASE for complete rules; available after April 1 each year.

N RAYMOND CARVER SHORT STORY CONTEST, English Dept. Humboldt State University, Arcata CA 95521. (707)826-5946, ext. 1. Website: http://www.humboldt.edu/~ams20/carver/. Submit entries to Student Coordinator. **Open to students**, US citizens and writers living in the US. Annual contest. Estab. 1982. Unpublished submissions only. Submissions made by author. Deadline for entries: December 1. SASE for contest rules and entry forms. Entry fee is $10. Awards $1,000 1st place and publication in TOYON; $500 2nd place and honorable mention in TOYON; 3rd place honorable mention. Judges change every year. Must be US citizen or writers living in US.

☑ REBECCA CAUDILL YOUNG READERS' BOOK AWARD, Illinois Reading Council, Illinois School Library Media Association, Illinois Association of Teachers of English, P.O. Box 6536, Naperville IL 60567-6536. (630)420-6378. Fax: (630)420-3241. Award Director Bonita Slovinski. Annual award. Estab. 1988. Purpose of contest: to award the Children's Choice Award for grades 4-8 in Illinois. Submissions nominated by students. Must be published within the last 5 years. Awards honorarium, plaque. Judging by children, grades 4-8.

CHILDREN'S BOOK AWARD, Federation of Children's Book Groups. The Old Malt House, Aldbourne Marlborough, Wiltshire SN8 2DW England. 01672 540629. Fax: 01672 541280. E-mail: 106311.12 05@compuserve.com. Coordinator: Marianne Adey. Purpose of the award: "The C.B.A. is an annual prize for the best children's book of the year judged by the children themselves." Categories: (I) picture books, (II) short novels, (III) longer novels. Estab. 1980. Previously unpublished submissions only. Deadline for entries: December 31. SASE for rules and entry forms. Entries not returned. Awards "a magnificent silver and oak trophy worth over $6,000 and a portfolio of children's work." Silver dishes to each category winner. Judging by children. Requirements for entrants: Work must be fiction and published during the current year (poetry is ineligible). Work will be published in current "Pick of the Year" publication.

☑ CHILDREN'S WRITERS FICTION CONTEST, Goodin Williams Goodwin Literary Associates, P.O. Box 8863, Springfield MO 65801. (417)863-7670 or (417)866-0744. Coordinator: V.R. Williams. Annual contest. Estab. 1994. Purpose of contest: To promote writing for children, by giving children's writers an opportunity to submit work in competition. Unpublished submissions only. Submissions made by the author. Deadline for entries: July 31st. SASE for contest rules and entry forms. Entry fee is $5. Awards cash prize and publication in newsletter; certificates for Honorable Mention. Judging by Goodin, Williams and Goodwin. First rights to winning material acquired or purchased. Requirements for entrants: Work must be suitable for children and no longer than 1,000 words. "Send SASE for list of winners."

MR. CHRISTIE'S BOOK AWARD® PROGRAM, Christie Brown & Co., Division of Nabisco Ltd., 2150 Lakeshore Blvd., Toronto, Ontario M8V 1A3 Canada. (416)503-6050. Fax: (416)503-6034. E-mail: myustin@nabisco.ca. Coordinator: Marlene Yustin. Competition is open to Canadian citizens, landed immigrants and students. Books must be published in Canada in 1998. Annual award. Estab. 1990. Purpose of award: to honor Canadian authors and illustrators of good English/French Canadian published children's books. Contest includes three categories: Best Book for 7 and under; 8-11; and 12 and up. Submissions are made by the author, made by the author's agent, publishers. Deadline for entries: January 31. SASE for contest rules and entry forms. No entry fee. Awards a total of $45,000. Judging by a panel consisting of people in the literary/teaching community across Canada. Requirements for entrants: must be published children's literature in English or French.

⚠ THE CHRISTOPHER AWARD, The Christophers, 12 E. 48th St., New York NY 10017. (212)759-4050. E-mail: tci@idt.net. Website: http://www.christophers.org. Christopher Awards Coordinators: Peggy Flanagan and Virginia Armstrong. Annual award. Estab. 1969 (for young people; books for adults honored since 1949). "The award is given to works, published in the calendar year for which the award is given, that 'have achieved artistic excellence, affirming the highest values of the human spirit.' They must also enjoy a reasonable degree of popular acceptance." Previously published submissions only; must be published between January 1 and December 31. "Books should be submitted all year. Two copies should be sent to Peggy Flanagan, 12 E. 48th St., New York NY 10017 and two copies to Virginia Armstrong, 22 Forest Ave., Old Tappan NJ 07675." Entries not returned. No entry fee. Awards a bronze medallion. Books are judged by both reading specialists and young people. Requirements for entrants: "only published works are eligible and must be submitted during the calendar year in which they are first published."

CHRISTOPHER COLUMBUS SCREENPLAY DISCOVERY AWARDS, Christopher Columbus Society of the Creative Arts, #600, 433 N. Camden Dr., Beverly Hills CA 90210. (310)288-1988. Fax: (310)288-0257. E-mail: awards@screenwriters.com. Website: http://screenwriters.com. Award Director: Mr. Carlos Abreu. Annual and monthly awards. Estab. 1990. Purpose of award: to discover new screenplay writers. Unpublished submissions only. Submissions are made by the author or author's agent. Deadline for entries: August 1st and monthly (last day of month). Entry fee is $45. Awards: (1) Feedback—development process with industry experts. (2) Financial rewards—option moneys up to $10,000. (3) Access to key decision makers. Judging by entertainment industry experts, producers and executives.

✔ THE COMMONWEALTH CLUB'S BOOK AWARDS CONTEST, The Commonwealth Club of California, 595 Market St., San Francisco CA 94105. (415)597-6700. E-mail: cwc@sirius.com. Website: http://www.commonwealthclub.org. Attn: James Wilson. Chief Executive Officer: Gloria Duffy. Annual contest. Estab. 1932. Purpose of contest: the encouragement and production of literature in California. Juvenile category included. Previously published submission; must be published from January 1 to December 31, previous to contest year. Deadline for entries: January 31. SASE for contest rules and entry forms. No entry fee. Awards gold and silver medals. Judging by the Book Awards Jury. The contest is only open to California writers/illustrators (must have been resident of California when ms was accepted for publication). "The award winners will be honored at the Annual Book Awards Program." Winning entries are displayed at awards program and advertised in newsletter.

✔ CRICKET LEAGUE, *Cricket Magazine*, P.O. Box 300, 315 Fifth St., Peru IL 61354. (815)224-6633. Website: http://www.cricketmag.com. Address entries to: Cricket League. Monthly. Estab. 1973. "The purpose of Cricket League contests is to encourage creativity and give young people an opportunity to express themselves in writing, drawing, painting or photography. There is a contest each month. Possible categories include story, poetry, art or photography. Each contest relates to a *specific theme* described on each *Cricket* issue's Cricket League page. Signature verifying originality, age and address of entrant required. Entries which do not relate to the current month's theme cannot be considered." Unpublished submissions only. Deadline for entries: the 25th of each month. Cricket League rules, contest theme, and submission deadline information can be found in the current issue of *Cricket*. "We prefer that children who enter the contests subscribe to the magazine, or that they read *Cricket* in their school or library." No entry fee. Awards certificate suitable for framing and children's books or art/writing supplies. Judging by *Cricket* editors. Obtains right to print prizewinning entries in magazine. Refer to contest rules in current *Cricket* issue. Winning entries are published on the Cricket League pages in the *Cricket* magazine 3 months subsequent to the issue in which the contest was announced. Current theme, rules, and prizewinning entries also posted on the website.

MARGUERITE DE ANGELI PRIZE, Bantam Doubleday Dell Books for Young Readers, 1540 Broadway, New York NY 10036. Estab. 1992. Fax: (212)782-9452 (note re: Marguerite De Angeli Prize). Annual award. Purpose of the award: to encourage the writing of fiction for children aged 7-10, either contemporary or historical; to encourage unpublished writers in the field of middle grade fiction. Unpublished submissions only. Length: between 40-144 pages. Submissions made by author or author's agent. Entries should be postmarked between April 1st and June 30th. SASE for award rules. No entry fee. Awards a $1,500 cash prize plus a hardcover and paperback book contract with a $3,500 advance against a royalty to be negotiated. Judging by Bantam Doubleday Dell Books for Young Readers editorial staff. Open to US and Canadian writers who have not previously published a novel for middle-grade readers (ages 7-10). Works published in an upcoming Bantam Doubleday Dell Books for Young Readers list.

DELACORTE PRESS PRIZE FOR A FIRST YOUNG ADULT NOVEL, Delacorte Press, Books for Young Readers Department, 1540 Broadway, New York NY 10036. (212)354-6500. Fax: (212)782-9452. Annual award. Estab. 1982. Purpose of award: to encourage the writing of contemporary young adult fiction. Previously unpublished submissions only. Mss sent to Delacorte Press may not be submitted to other publishers while under consideration for the prize. "Entries must be submitted between October 1 and New Year's Day. The real deadline is a December 31 postmark. Early entries are appreciated." SASE for award rules. No entry fee. Awards a $1,500 cash prize and a $6,000 advance against royalties on a hardcover and paperback book contract. Works published in an upcoming Bantam Doubleday Dell Books for Young Readers list. Judged by the editors of the Books for Young Readers Department of Bantam Doubleday Dell. Requirements for entrants: The writer must be American or Canadian and must *not* have previously published a young adult novel but may have published anything else. Send SASE for new guidelines.

MARGARET A. EDWARDS AWARDS, American Library Association, 50 East Huron St., Chicago IL 60611-2795. (312)944-6780 or (800)545-2433. Fax: (312)664-7459. Annual award administered by the Young Adult Library Services Association (YALSA) of the American Library Association (ALA) and sponsored by *School Library Journal* magazine. Purpose of award: "ALA's Young Adult Library Services Association (YALSA), on behalf of librarians who work with young adults in all types of libraries, will give recognition to those authors whose book or books have provided young adults with a window through which they can view their world and which will help them to grow and to understand themselves and their role in relationships, society and the world." Previously published submissions only. Submissions are nominated by young adult librarians and teenagers. Must be published five years before date of award. SASE for award rules and entry forms. No entry fee. Judging by members of the Young Adult Library Services Association. "The award will be given annually to an author whose book or books, over a period of time, have been accepted by young adults as an authentic voice that continues to illuminate their experiences and emotions, giving insight into their lives. The book or books should enable them to understand themselves, the world in which they live, and their relationship with others and with society. The book or books must be in print at the time of the nomination."

N **ARTHUR ELLIS AWARD**, Crime Writers of Canada, 3007 Kingston Rd., Box 113, Scarborough, Ontario M1M 1P1 Canada. (416)466-9826. Fax: (416)406-6141. E-mail: ap113@torfree.net.on.ca. Submit entries to: Secretary/Treasurer. Annual contest. Estab. 1984. Purpose of contest: to honor the best juvenile writing with a theme of crime, detective, espionage, mystery, suspense and thriller, fictional or factual accounts of criminal doings. Includes novels with a criminous theme. Previously published submissions only. Submissions made by author or by author's agent or publisher. Must be published during year previous to award. Deadline for entries: January 31. SASE for contest rules and entry forms. Awards a statuette of a hanged man—with jumping jack limbs. Judging by 2 nonmembers and one member per category. Must be first publication, regardless of language, by a writer, regardless of nationality, resident in Canada or a Canadian writer resident abroad.

JOAN FASSLER MEMORIAL BOOK AWARD, Association for the Care of Children's Health, 7910 Woodmont Ave., Suite 300, Bethesda MD 20814. (301)654-6549. Fax: (301)986-4553. E-mail: acch@clark .net. Website: http://www.acch.org. Membership Manager: Jennifer Fincken. Competition open to adults and children. Annual award. Estab. 1989. "Award is given to the author(s) of the trade book that makes the most distinguished contribution to a child's or young person's understanding of hospitalization, illness, disabling conditions, dying and death and preventive care." Previously published submissions only. Submissions made by the author, author's agent. Must be published between 1996 and 1997. Deadline for entries: December 1. SASE for award rules and entry forms. No entry fee. Award $1,000 honorarium, plaque. Judging by multidisciplinary committee of ACCH members. Requirements for entrants: open to any writer. Display and book signing opportunities at annual conference.

MARKET CONDITIONS are constantly changing! If you're still using this book and it is 2000 or later, buy the newest edition of *Children's Writer's & Illustrator's Market* at your favorite bookstore or order directly from Writer's Digest Books.

☑ **DOROTHY CANFIELD FISHER CHILDREN'S BOOK AWARD**, Vermont Department of Libraries, Vermont State PTA, % Northeast Regional Library, RR2, 304244, St. Johnsburg VT 05819. (802)828-3261. Fax: (802)828-2199. E-mail: ggreene@dol.state.vt.us. Website: http://www.dol.state.vt.us. Chairman: Sandra S. Roy. Annual award. Estab. 1957. Purpose of the award: to encourage Vermont children to become enthusiastic and discriminating readers by providing them with books of good quality by living American authors published in the current year. Deadline for entries: December of year book was published. SASE for award rules and entry forms. No entry fee. Awards a scroll presented to the winning author at an award ceremony. Judging is by the children grades 4-8. They vote for their favorite book. Requirements for entrants: "Titles must be original work, published in the United States, and be appropriate to children in grades 4 through 8. The book must be copyrighted in the current year. It must be written by an American author living in the U.S."

☑ **FLICKER TALE CHILDREN'S BOOK AWARD**, Flicker Tale Award Committee, North Dakota Library Association, 1107 Airport Rd., Bismarck ND 58504. (701)221-3597. Fax: (701)221-3454. Award Director: Konnie Wightman. Estab. 1979. Purpose of award: to give children across the state of North Dakota a chance to vote for their book of choice from a nominated list of 10: 5 in the picture book category; 5 in the juvenile category. Also, to promote awareness of quality literature for children. Previously published submissions only. Submissions nominated by a person or group of people. Awards a plaque from North Dakota Library Association and banquet dinner. Judging by children in North Dakota. Entry deadline in July.

FLORIDA STATE WRITING COMPETITION, Florida Freelance Writers Assocociation, P.O. Box A, North Stratford NH 03590. (603)922-8338. Fax: (603)922-8339. E-mail: danakcnw@moose.ncia.net. Executive Director: Dana K. Cassell. Annual contest. Estab. 1984. Categories include children's literature (length appropriate to age category). Entry fee is $5 (members), $10 (nonmembers). Awards $75 first prize, membership second prize, book third prize, certificates for honorable mentions. Judging by teachers, editors and published authors. Judging criteria: interest and readability within age group, writing style and mechanics, originality, salability. Deadline: March 15. For copy of official entry form, send #10 SASE.

Ⓝ **FOR A GOOD TIME THEATRE COMPANY'S ANNUAL SCRIPT CONTEST**, For A Good Time Theatre Company, P.O. Box 5421, Saginaw MI 48603-0421. (517)753-7891. Fax: (517)753-5890. E-mail: theatreco@aol.com. Contest Director: Lee-Perry Belleau, artistic director. Annual contest. Estab. 1997. Purpose of contest: To award top-notch playwrights in theater for young audiences with a production by a critically acclaimed regional theater company. Unpublished submissions only. Submissions made by author or by author's agent. Deadline for entries: May 1 (postmark). SASE for contest rules and entry forms. Entry fee is $10. Awards production of the winning script; cash award or $1,000; and a videotape of the produced script. Judging by For A Good Time Theatre's staff dramaturg (prescreening). Screening is then done by the producer. Final judging is done by the artistic director. Acquires regional production rights for the year of the contest. Plays must be 50 minutes long; must be a musical (composed music is not necessary, jsut song lyrics); written for multiple characters played by three actors, with roles for men and women. Other criteria, such as subject matter, varies from year to year. Send SASE for details.

4-H ESSAY CONTEST, American Beekeeping Federation, Inc., P.O. Box 1038, Jesup GA 31598. (912)427-4233. Fax: (912)427-8447. E-mail: info@abfnet.org. Website: http://www.abfnet.org. Contest Director: Troy H. Fore. Annual contest. **Open to students.** Purpose of contest: to educate youth about the beekeeping industry. For complete rules and details on topic, see website. The assignment for the 1999 essay will be to create a lesson plan and activity sheet to teach 3rd grade elementary school students about bees and beekeeping. Unpublished submissions only. Deadline for entries: before March 1. No entry fee. Awards 1st place: $250; 2nd place: $100; 3rd place: $50. Judging by American Beekeeping Federation's Essay Committee. "All national entries become the property of the American Beekeeping Federation, Inc., and may be published or used as it sees fit. No essay will be returned. Essayists *should not* forward essays directly to the American Beekeeping Federation office. Each state 4-H office is responsible for selecting the state's winner and should set its deadline so state judging can be completed at the state level in time for the winning state essay to be mailed to the ABF office before March 1, 1999. Each state winner receives a book on honey bees, beekeeping or honey. The National Winner will announced by May 1, 1999." Requirements for entrants: Contest is open to active 4-H Club members only.

DON FREEMAN MEMORIAL GRANT-IN-AID, Society of Children's Book Writers and Illustrators, 345 N. Maple Dr. #296, Beverly Hills CA 90210. (310)859-9887. Website: http://www.scbwi.org. Estab. 1974. Purpose of award: to "enable picture book artists to further their understanding, training and work in the picture book genre." Applications and prepared materials will be accepted between January 15 and

February 15. Grant awarded and announced on June 15. SASE for award rules and entry forms. SASE for return of entries. No entry fee. Annually awards one grant of $1,000 and one runner-up grant of $500. "The grant-in-aid is available to both full and associate members of the SCBWI who, as artists, seriously intend to make picture books their chief contribution to the field of children's literature."

AMELIA FRANCES HOWARD GIBBON AWARD FOR ILLUSTRATION, Canadian Library Association, Suite 602, 200 Elgin St., Ottawa, Ontario K2P 1L5 Canada. (613)232-9625. Contact: Chairperson, Canadian Association of Children's Librarians. Annual award. Estab. 1971. Purpose of the award: "to honor excellence in the illustration of children's book(s) in Canada. To merit consideration the book must have been published in Canada and its illustrator must be a Canadian citizen or a permanent resident of Canada." Previously published submissions only; must be published between January 1 and December 31 of the previous year. Deadline for entries: January 1. SASE for award rules. Entries not returned. No entry fee. Awards a medal. Judging by selection committee of members of Canadian Association of Children's Librarians. Requirements for entrants: illustrator must be Canadian or Canadian resident. Winning books are on display at CLA Headquarters.

GOLD MEDALLION BOOK AWARDS, Evangelical Christian Publishers Association, 1969 East Broadway Rd., Suite Two, Tempe AZ 85282. (602)966-3998. Fax: (602)966-1944. E-mail: jmeegan@ecpa.org. Website: http://www.ecpa.org. President: Doug Ross. Annual award. Estab. 1978. Categories include Preschool Children's Books, Elementary Children's Books, Youth Books. "All entries must be evangelical in nature and cannot be contrary to ECPA's Statement of Faith (stated in official rules)." Deadlines for entries: December 1. SASE for award rules and entry form. "The work must be submitted by the publisher." Entry fee is $250 for nonmembers. Awards a Gold Medallion plaque.

GOLDEN ARCHER AWARD, Wisconsin Educational Media Association, 1300 Industrial Dr., Fennimore WI 53809. Website: http://www.marshfield.k12.wi.us/WEMA. Award Director: Annette R. Smith. **Open to students.** Annual award. Estab. 1974. Purpose of award: to encourage young readers to become better acquainted with quality literature written expressly for them, to broaden students' awareness of reading and literature as life-long pleasure and to honor favorite books and their authors. Previously published submissions only. Submissions nominated by Wisconsin students. No entry fee. Three awards are given—one in each of 3 categories, Primary, Intermediate and Middle/Junior High.

GOLDEN KITE AWARDS, Society of Children's Book Writers and Illustrators, 345 N. Maple Dr., #296, Beverly Hills CA 90210. (310)859-9887. Website: http://www.scbwi.org. Coordinator: Sue Alexander. Annual award. Estab. 1973. "The works chosen will be those that the judges feel exhibit excellence in writing, and in the case of the picture-illustrated books—in illustration, and genuinely appeal to the interests and concerns of children. For the fiction and nonfiction awards, original works and single-author collections of stories or poems of which at least half are new and never before published in book form are eligible—anthologies and translations are not. For the picture-illustration awards, the art or photographs must be original works (the texts—which may be fiction or nonfiction—may be original, public domain or previously published). Deadline for entries: December 15. SASE for award rules. Self-addressed mailing label for return of entries. No entry fee. Awards statuettes and plaques. The panel of judges will consist of two children's book authors, a children's book artist or photographer (who may or may not be an author), a children's book editor and a librarian." Requirements for entrants: "must be a member of SCBWI." Winning books will be displayed at national conference in August. Books to be entered, as well as further inquiries, should be submitted to: The Society of Children's Book Writers and Illustrators, above address.

HIGHLIGHTS FOR CHILDREN FICTION CONTEST, 803 Church St., Honesdale PA 18431. (717)253-1080. Mss should be addressed to Fiction Contest. Editor: Kent L. Brown Jr. Annual contest. Estab. 1980. Purpose of the contest: to stimulate interest in writing for children and reward and recognize excellence. Unpublished submissions only. Deadline for entries: February 28; entries accepted after January 1 only. SASE for contest rules and return of entries. No entry fee. Awards 3 prizes of $1,000 each in cash and a pewter bowl (or, at the winner's election, attendance at the Highlights Foundation Writers Workshop at Chautauqua). Judging by *Highlights* editors. Winning pieces are purchased for the cash prize of $1,000 and published in *Highlights*; semifinalists go to out-of-house judges (educators, editors, writers, etc.). Requirements for entrants: open to any writer. Winners announced in June. "The 1999 theme is 'contemporary action/adventure stories.' Length up to 900 words. Stories for beginning readers should not exceed 500 words. Stories should be consistent with *Highlights* editorial requirements. No violence, crime or derogatory humor. Send SASE for further rules and guidelines."

☑ **HRC'S ANNUAL PLAYWRITING CONTEST**, Hudson River Classics, Inc., P.O. Box 940, Hudson NY 12534. (518)851-6840. Fax: (518)851-2631. President: W. Keith Hedrick. Annual contest. Estab. 1992. Hudson River Classics is a not-for-profit professional theater company dedicated to the advancement of performing in the Hudson River Valley area through reading of plays and providing opportunities for new playwrights. Unpublished submissions only. Submissions made by author and by the author's agent. Deadlines for entries: June 1st. SASE for contest rules and entry forms. Entry fee is $5. Awards $500 cash plus concert reading by professional actors. Judging by panel selected by Board of Directors. Requirements for entrants: Entrants must live in the northeastern US.

☒ ☘ **INFORMATION BOOK AWARD**, Children's Literature Roundtables of Canada, Dept. of Language Education, University of British Columbia, 2125 Main Mall, Vancouver, British Columbia V6T 1Z4 Canada. (604)822-5788. Fax: (604)822-3154. Award Directors: April Gill and Dr. Ron Jobe. Estab. 1987. Purpose of contest: The Information Book Award recognizes excellence in the writing of information books for young people from 5 to 15 years. It is awarded to the book that arouses interest, stimulates curiosity, captures the imagination, and fosters concern for the world around us. The award's aim is to recognize excellence in Canadian publishing of nonfiction for children. Previously published submissions only. Submissions nominated by a person or group of people. Work must have been published the calendar year previous to the award being given. Deadline for entries: June. SASE for contest rules. Certificates are awarded to the author and illustrator and they share a cash prize of $500 (Canadian). Judging by members of the children's literature roundtables of Canada. In consultation with children's bookstores across Canada, a national committee based in Vancouver sends out a selective list of over 20 titles representing the best of the information books from the preceding year. The Roundtables consider this preliminary list and send back their recommendations, resulting in 5-7 finalists. The Roundtables make time at their Fall meetings to discuss the finalists and vote on their choices, which are collated into one vote per Roundtable. Winning work is displayed at Serendipity Children's Literature Conference held in February in Vancouver British Columbia.

☑ **INSPIRATIONAL WRITERS ALIVE! OPEN WRITERS COMPETITION**, Texas Christian Writer's Forum, 6038 Greenmont, Houston TX 77092. E-mail: mrogers353@aol.com or patav@aol.com. Contact: Contest Director. Annual contest. Estab. 1990. Purpose of contest: to help aspiring writers in the inspirational/religion markets. Unpublished submissions only. Submissions made by author. Deadline: May 15. SASE for contest rules. Entry fee is $5 (devotional, short story or article); $5 (3 poems). Awards certificate of merit for 1st, 2nd and 3rd place. Requirements for entrants: Cannot enter published material. "We want to aid especially new and aspiring writers." Contest has 5 categories—to include short story (adult), short story (for children and teens) article, daily devotions, and poetry and book proposal. Entry forms and info available after December 1, 1998. "*Must* include a cover sheet with every category."

EZRA JACK KEATS/KERLAN COLLECTION MEMORIAL FELLOWSHIP, University of Minnesota, 109 Walter Library, 117 Pleasant St. SE, Minneapolis MN 55455. (612)624-4576. Fax: (612)625-5525. E-mail: clrc@tc.umn.edu. Website: http://www.lib.umn.edu/special/kerlan. Competition open to adults. Offered annually. Deadline for entries: first Monday in May. Send request with SASE, including 52¢ postage. The Ezra Jack Keats/Kerlan Collection Memorial Fellowship from the Ezra Jack Keats Foundation will provide $1,500 to a "talented writer and/or illustrator of children's books who wishes to use the Kerlan Collection for the furtherance of his or her artistic development. Special consideration will be given to someone who would find it difficult to finance the visit to the Kerlan Collection." The fellowship winner will receive transnportation and per diem. Judging by the Kerlan Award Committee—3 representatives from the University of Minnesota faculty, one from the Kerlan Friends, and one from the Minnesota Library Association.

☒ **KENTUCKY BLUEGRASS AWARD**, Northern Kentucky University & Kentucky Reading Association, c/o Janet A. Miller, School of Education, Northern Kentucky University, Highland Heights KY 41099. (606)572-5239. Fax: (606)572-6096. E-mail: miller@ku.edu. Award Directors: Janet A. Miller and Jennifer Smith. Submit entries to: Janet A. Miller. Annual award. Estab. 1983. Purpose of award: to promote readership among young children and young adolescents. Also to recognize exceptional creative efforts of authors and illustrators. Previously published submissions only. Submissions made by author, made by author's agent, nominated by teachers or librarians. Must be published between 1996 and 1999. Deadline for entries: March 31. SASE for contest rules and entry forms. No entry fee. Awards a framed certificate and invitation to be recognized at the annual luncheon of the Kentucky Reading Association for KBA. Judging by children who participate through their schools or libraries. "Books are reviewed by a panel of teachers and librarians before they are placed on a list of Bluegrass Award books for the year. These books must have been published within a three year period prior to the review. Winners are chosen from this list of pre-selected books. Books are divided into two divisions, K-3 and 4-8 grades. Picture books with considerable text are included in the 4-8 division. Winners are chosen by children who either read the books or have the books read to them. Children from the entire state of Kentucky are involved in the selection of the annual winners for each of the divisions."

KENTUCKY STATE POETRY SOCIETY ANNUAL CONTEST, Kentucky State Poetry Society, % *Pegasus* editor Miriam L. Woolfolk, 3289 Hunting Hills Dr., Lexington KY 40515. (606)271-4662. Annual contest. Estab. 1966. Purpose of award: To encourage the creative mind and the continuing appreciation of poetry. Unpublished poems only. Deadline for entries: June 30. SASE for contest rules and entry forms. Student categories are free; Grand Prix, $5; all others $1. Offers more than 30 categories and awards certificates of merit and cash prizes from $3 to $200. Sponsors pick judges. Contest open to all. "One-time printing rights acquired for publication of first prize winner in the Prize Poems Issue of *Pegasus*, our annual journal (late fall/early winter issue). All other winners will be displayed at our October annual awards banquet."

ANNE SPENCER LINDBERGH PRIZE IN CHILDREN'S LITERATURE, The Charles A. and Anne Morrow Lindbergh Foundation, 708 S. Third St., Suite 110, Minneapolis MN 55415. (612)338-1703. Fax: (612)338-6826. E-mail: lindfdtn@mtn.org. Website: http://www.mtn.org/lindfdtn. Contest Director: Gene Bratsch. Competition open to adults. Contest is offered every 2 years. Estab. 1996. Purpose of contest: To recognize the children's fantasy novel judged to be the best published in the English language during the year. Prize program honors Anne Spencer Lindbergh, author of a number of acclaimed juvenile fantasies, who died in late 1993 at the age of 53. Previously published submissions only. Submissions made by author, author's agent or publishers. Must be published between January 1 and December 31. Deadline for entries: November 1. Entry fee is $25. Awards $5,000 to author of winning book. Judging by panel drawn from writers, editors, librarians and teachers prominent in the field of children's literature. Requirements for entrants: Open to all authors of children's fantasy novels published during the year. Entries must include 4 copies of books submitted. Winner announced in January.

LONGMEADOW JOURNAL LITERARY COMPETITION, % Rita and Robert Morton, 6750 N. Longmeadow, Lincolnwood IL 60646. (312)726-9789. Fax: (312)726-9772. Contest Director: Rita and Robert Morton. Competition open to students (anyone age 10-19). Held annually and published every year. Estab. 1986. Purpose of contest: to encourage the young to write. Submissions are made by the author, made by the author's agent, nominated by a person or group of people, by teachers, librarians or parents. Deadline for entries: June 30. SASE. No entry fee. Awards first place, $175; second place, $100; and five prizes of $50. Judging by Rita Morton and Robert Morton. Works are published every year and are distributed to teachers and librarians and interested parties at no charge.

N JUDY LOPEZ MEMORIAL AWARD FOR CHILDREN'S LITERATURE, Women's National Book Assoc. Los Angeles Chapter, P.O. Box 7034, Beverly Hills CA 90212-0034. Award Director: Margaret Flanders. Annual award. Estab. 1985. Purpose of contest: To recognize excellence in writing for children ages 9-12. The awards are made in remembrance of Judy Lopez, a founding member of the Los Angeles chapter of the Women's National Book Assoc. who was deeply interested in seeing that children's literature of quality is recognized and rewarded. Previously published submissions only. Submissions made by author, author's agent or nominated by a person or group of people (most are made by publishers). Work must have been published within the year of the award. Deadline for entries: December 31. Medal and cash award to 1 winner; 2 runners-up receive honor certificates. Judging by committee of librarians, educators, editors. Requirements for entrants: Author must be citizen or resident of US. Book must be published in US during award year (e.g. 1998 award books must be published January-December 1998, award is presented in 1999). Book must be for ages 9-12. No picture books. Winning work displayed at the award banquet held traditionally in June at the University of Southern California campus.

LOUISE LOUIS/EMILY F. BOURNE STUDENT POETRY AWARD, Poetry Society of America, 15 Gramercy Park, New York NY 10003-1705. (212)254-9628. Fax: (212)673-2352. E-mail: timothyd@poetrysociety.org. Website: http://www.poetrysociety.com. Award Director: Timothy Donnelly. Annual award. Purpose of the award: Award is for the best unpublished poem by a high or preparatory school student (grades 9-12) from the US and its territories. Unpublished submissions only. Deadline for entries: Oct. 1 to Dec. 21. SASE for award rules and entry forms. Entries not returned. "High schools can send an unlimited number of submissions with one entry per individual student for a flat fee of $10." Award: $100. Judging by a professional poet. Requirements for entrants: Award open to all high school and preparatory students from the US and its territories. School attended, as well as name and address, should be noted. PSA submission guidelines must be followed. These are printed in our fall calendar, and are readily available if those interested send us a SASE. Line limit: none. "The award-winning poem will be included in a sheaf of poems that will be part of the program at the award ceremony and sent to all PSA members."

MAGAZINE MERIT AWARDS, Society of Children's Book Writers and Illustrators, 345 N. Maple Dr. #296, Beverly Hills CA 90210. (310)859-9887. Website: http://www.scbwi.org. Award Coordinator: Dorothy Leon. Annual award. Estab. 1988. Purpose of the award: "to recognize outstanding original magazine work for young people published during that year and having been written or illustrated by members of SCBWI." Previously published submissions only. Entries must be submitted between January 31 and December 15 of the year of publication. For brochure (rules) write Award Coordinator. No entry fee. Must be a SCBWI member. Awards plaques and honor certificates for each of the 3 categories (fiction, nonfiction, illustration). Judging by a magazine editor and two "full" SCBWI members. "All magazine work for young people by an SCBWI member—writer, artist or photographer—is eligible during the year of original publication. In the case of co-authored work, both authors must be SCBWI members. Members must submit their own work." Requirements for entrants: 4 copies each of the published work and proof of publication (may be contents page) showing the name of the magazine and the date of issue. The SCBWI is a professional organization of writers and illustrators and others interested in children's literature. Membership is open to the general public at large.

MAJESTIC BOOKS WRITING CONTEST, Majestic Books, P.O. Box 19097, Johnston RI 02919-0097. Contest Director: Cindy MacDonald. Open to Rhode Island students only. Annual contest. Estab. 1992. Purpose of contest: to encourage students to write to the best of their ability and to be proud of their work. Unpublished submissions only. Submissions made by the author or teacher. Deadline for entries: second Friday in October. No entry fee, however, we do ask for a large SASE (9 × 12) for our reply and certificate. Winners are published in an anthology. All entrants receive a certificate acknowledging their efforts. Judging by a panel of published writers and an English teacher. One-time publishing rights to submitted material required or purchased. Our contest is open to all students, age 6-17 in Rhode Island. *Anthology* comes off the press in December and a presentation ceremony is held for all winning students. Students must include their age, grade, school and statement of authenticity signed by the writer and a parent or teacher. Entries must be neat and will not be returned. In order to encourage all children, every entrant receives a personalized award acknowledging their efforts.

☑ **N.C. WRITERS' NETWORK INTERNATIONAL LITERARY PRIZES**, N.C. Writers' Network, 3501 Hwy. S4 W, Studio C, Chapel Hill NC 27516. (919)967-9540. Fax: (919)929-0535. E-mail: ncwn@sunsite.unc.edu. Website: http://sunsite.unc.edu/ncwriters. Program Coordinator: Frances Dowell. **Open to students.** Annual contest. *Thomas Wolfe Fiction Prize* (TWFP), est. 1994, awards $500 prize for best piece of fiction (short story or novel excerpt not to exceed 12 pp.), winning entry will be considered for publication in Carolina quarterly; *Paul Green Playwrights Prize* (PGPP), est. 1995, awards $500 prize for best play, any length, no musicals, winning entry will be considered for production by a consortium of North Carolina theaters. *Randall Jarrell Poetry Prize* (RJPP), est. 1990, awards $500 prize, publication and reading/reception for best poem, winning poem published in Parnassus: Poetry in Review. Unpublished submissions only. Submissions made by the author. Deadline for entries: TWFP—Aug. 31; PGPP—Sept. 30; RJPP—Nov. 1. SASE for award rules and entry forms. Entry fee is $7-TWFP; $7-RJPP; $10-PGPP ($7.50 for NCWN members). Judging by published writers or editors. Previous judges have included: Anne Tyler, Barbara Kingsolver, Donald Hall, Lucille Clifton, Romulus Linney.

🍁 **THE NATIONAL CHAPTER OF CANADA IODE VIOLET DOWNEY BOOK AWARD**, Suite 254, 40 Orchard View Blvd., Toronto, Ontario M5R 1B9 Canada. (416)487-4416. Award Director: Marty Dalton. Annual award. Estab. 1985. Purpose of the award: to honor the best children's English language book, by a Canadian, published in Canada for ages 5-13, over 500 words. Fairy tales, anthologies and books adapted from another source are not eligible. Previously published submissions only. Books must have been published in Canada in previous calendar year. Submissions made by author, author's agent; anyone may submit. Three copies of each entry are required. Must have been published during previous calendar year. Deadline for entries: January 31, 1999. SASE for award rules and entry forms. No entry fee. Awards $3,000 for the year 1999 for books published in 1998. Judging by a panel of 6, 4 IODE members and 2 professionals.

Ⓝ NATIONAL PARENTING PUBLICATIONS AWARD (NAPPA), National Association of Parenting Publications, 443 E. Irving Dr., Suite D, Burbank CA 91504. (818)864-0400, ext. 250. E-mail: laparent@family.com. Website: http://www.laparent.com. Contact person: NAPPA Coordinator. Annual contest. Estab. 1991. Purpose of award: To recognize high-quality media and toys that enrich the educational and entertainment experiences of children. Submissions made by author, author's agent, nominated by a person or group, or may be submitted by anyone. Deadline for entries: July 31. SASE for contest rules and entry forms. Entry fee is $95. Gold winners receive editorial mention in each of the participating parenting publications throughout the US. Judged by distinguished reviewers, educators, editors and authors. The most important criteria is that each product must enrich both the educational and entertainment experiences of children, helping today's kid prepare for tomorrow. Call for categories and entry forms.

 **NATIONAL PEACE ESSAY CONTEST**, United States Institute of Peace, 1200 17th St. NW, Washington DC 20036. (202)429-3854. Fax: (202)429-6063. E-mail: usip_requests@usip.org. Website: http://www.usip.org. Contest Director: Heather Kerr-Stewart. Annual contest. Estab. 1987. "The contest gives students the opportunity to do valuable research, writing and thinking on a topic of importance to international peace and conflict resolution. Submissions, instead of being published, can be a classroom assignment." Deadline for entries is January 27, 1999. "Interested students, teachers and others may write or call to receive free contest kits. Please do not include SASE." No entry fee. State Level Awards are college scholarships in the following amounts: first place $1,000. National winners are selected from among the 1st place state winners. National winners receive scholarships in the following amounts: first place $10,000; second $5,000; third $2,500. Judging is conducted by education professionals from across the country and by the Board of Directors of the United States Institute of Peace. "All submissions become property of the U.S. Institute of Peace to use at its discretion and without royalty or any limitation. Students grades 9-12 in the U.S., its territories and overseas schools may submit essays for review by completing the application process. U.S. citizenship required for students attending overseas schools. National winning essays for each competition will be published by the U.S. Institute of Peace for public consumption."

NATIONAL WRITERS ASSOCIATION NONFICTION CONTEST, 1450 S. Havana, Suite 424, Aurora CO 80012. (303)751-7844. Executive Director: Sandy Whelchel. Annual contest. Estab. 1971. Purpose of contest: "to encourage writers in this creative form and to recognize those who excel in nonfiction writing." Submissions made by author. Deadline for entries: December 31. SASE for contest rules and entry forms. Entry fee is $15. Awards three cash prizes; choice of books; Honorable Mention Certificate. "Two people read each entry; third party picks three top winners from top five." Top 3 winners are published in an anthology published by National Writers Association, if winners agree to this. Judging sheets sent if entry accompanied by SASE.

NATIONAL WRITERS ASSOCIATION NOVEL WRITING CONTEST, 1450 S. Havana, Suite 424, Aurora CO 80012. (303)751-7844. Executive Director: Sandy Whelchel. Annual contest. Estab. 1971. Purpose of contest: "to encourage writers in this creative form and to recognize those who excel in novel writing." Submissions made by the author. Deadline for entries: April 1. SASE for contest rules and entry forms. Entry fee is $35. Awards top 3, cash prizes; 4 to 10, choice of books; 10 to 20, Honorable Mention Certificates. Judging: "two people read the manuscripts; a third party picks the three top winners from the top 5. We display our members' published books in our offices." Judging sheets available for SASE.

NATIONAL WRITERS ASSOCIATION SHORT STORY CONTEST, 1450 Havana St., Suite 424, Aurora CO 80012. (303)751-7844. Executive Director: Sandy Whelchel. Annual contest. Estab. 1971. Purpose of contest: "To encourage writers in this creative form and to recognize those who excel in fiction writing." Submissions made by the author. Deadline for entries: July 1. SASE for contest rules and entry forms. Entry fee is $15. Awards 3 cash prizes, choice of books and certificates for Honorable Mentions. Judging by "two people read each entry; third person picks top three winners." Judging sheet copies available for SASE. Top three winners are published in an anthology published by National Writers Association, if winners agree to this.

THE NATIONAL WRITTEN & ILLUSTRATED BY . . . AWARDS CONTEST FOR STUDENTS, Landmark Editions, Inc., P.O. Box 270169, Kansas City MO 64127-0169. (816)241-4919. Fax: (816)483-3755. Website: http://www.landmarkeditions.com. Contest Director: Teresa Melton. Annual awards contest with 3 published winners. Estab. 1986. Purpose of the contest: to encourage and celebrate the creative efforts of students. There are 3 age categories (ages 6-9, 10-13 and 14-19). Unpublished submissions only. Deadline for entries: May 1. For a free copy of the contest rules, send a self-addressed, business-sized envelope, stamped with 64¢ postage. "Need to send a self-addressed, sufficiently stamped (at least $3 postage) book mailer with book entry for its return. All entries which do not win are mailed back in November or December of each contest year." Entry fee is $2. Awards publication of book. Judging by national panel of educators, editors, illustrators, authors and school librarians. "Each student winner receives a publishing contract allowing Landmark to publish the book. Copyright is in student's name and student receives royalties on sale of book. Books must be in proper contest format and submitted with entry form signed by a teacher or librarian. Students may develop their illustrations in any medium of their choice, as long as the illustrations remain two-dimensional and flat to the surface of the paper." Winners are notified by phone by October 15 of each contest year. During November/December all other book entries are returned, accompanied by a list of winners and finalists. By September of the following year, all winners' books are published—after several months of pre-production work on the books by the students and the editorial and artistic staff of Landmark editions. Works are published in Kansas City, Missouri for distribution nationally and internationally.

THE NENE AWARD, Hawaii State Library, 478 S. King St., Honolulu HI 96813. (808)586-3510. Fax: (808)586-3584. E-mail: hslear@netra.lib.state.hi.us. Estab. 1964. "The Nene Award was designed to help the children of Hawaii become acquainted with the best contemporary writers of fiction, become aware of the qualities that make a good book and choose the best rather than the mediocre." Previously published submissions only. Books must have been copyrighted not more than 6 years prior to presentation of award. Work is nominated. Ballots are usually due around the beginning of March. Awards Koa plaque. Judging by the children of Hawaii in grades 4-6. Requirements for entrants: books must be fiction, written by a living author, copyrighted not more than 6 years ago and suitable for children in grades 4, 5 and 6. Current and past winners are displayed in all participating school and public libraries. The award winner is announced in April.

NEW ENGLAND BOOK AWARDS, New England Booksellers Association, 847 Massachusetts Ave., Cambridge MA 02139. (617)576-3070. Fax: (617)576-3091. E-mail: neba@neba.org. Award Director: Nan Sorensen. Annual award. Estab. 1990. Purpose of award: "to promote New England authors who have produced a body of work that stands as a significant contribution to New England's culture and is deserving of wider recognition." Previously published submissions only. Submissions made by New England booksellers; publishers. "Award given to authors 'body of work' not a specific book." Entries must be still in print and available. Deadline for entries: October 31. SASE for contest rules and entry forms. No entry fee. Judging by NEBA membership. Requirements for entrants: Author/illustrator must live in New England. Submit written nominations only; actual books should not be sent. Member bookstores receive materials to display winners' books.

OHIOANA BOOK AWARDS, Ohioana Library Association, 65 S. Front St., Suite 1105, Columbus OH 43215. (614)466-3831. Fax: (614)728-6974. E-mail: ohioana@winslo.ohio.gov. Website: http://www.o plin.lib.oh.us/OHIOANA/. Director: Linda R. Hengst. Annual award. "The Ohioana Book Awards are given to books of outstanding literary quality. Purpose of contest: to provide recognition and encouragement to Ohio writers and to promote the work of Ohio writers. Up to six are given each year. Awards may be given in the following categories: fiction, nonfiction, juvenile, poetry and books about Ohio or an Ohioan. Books must be received by the Ohioana Library during the calendar year prior to the year the award is given and must have a copyright date within the last two calendar years." Deadline for entries: December 31. SASE for award rules and entry forms. No entry fee. Winners receive citation and glass sculpture. "Any book that has been written or edited by a person born in Ohio or who has lived in Ohio for at least five years" is eligible. The Ohioana Library Association also awards the "Ohioana Award for children's literature." Send SASE for more information.

OKLAHOMA BOOK AWARDS, Oklahoma Center for the Book, 200 NE 18th, Oklahoma City OK 73105. (405)521-2502. Fax: (405)525-7804. E-mail: gcarlile@oltn.odl.state.ok.us. Website: http://www.sta te.ok.us.~odl.oc. Annual award. **Open to students.** Estab. 1989. Purpose of award: "to honor Oklahoma writers and books about our state." Previously published submissions only. Submissions made by the author, author's agent, or entered by a person or group of people, including the publisher. Must be published during the calendar year preceding the award. Awards are presented to best books in fiction, nonfiction, childrens, design and illustration, and poetry to books about Oklahoma or books written by an author who was born, is living or has lived in Oklahoma. Deadline for entries: January. SASE for award rules and entry forms. No entry fee. Awards a medal—no cash prize. Judging by a panel of 5 people for each category—a librarian, a working writer in the genre, editors, etc. Requirements for entrants: author must be an Oklahoma native, resident, former resident or have written a book with Oklahoma theme. Book will be displayed at banquet at the Cowboy Hall of Fame in Oklahoma City.

[N] ONCE UPON A WORLD BOOK AWARD, Simon Wiesenthal Center's Museum of Tolerance, 9786 W. Pico Blvd., Los Angeles CA 90035. (310)772-2502. Award Director: Janet N. Garfinkle. Submit entries to: Janet Garfinkle, coordinator of youth education. Annual award. Estab. 1996. Previously published submissions only. Submissions made by author or by author's agent. Must be published January-December of previous year. Deadline for entries: March 31, 1999. SASE for contest rules and entry forms. Awards $1,000 and award. Judging by 3 judges familiar with children's literature. Award open to any writer with work on subject of tolerance for children 6-10 years old.

THE ORIGINAL ART, Society of Illustrators, 128 E. 63rd St., New York NY 10021-7303. (212)838-2560. Fax: (212)838-2561. Annual contest. Estab. 1981. Purpose of contest: to celebrate the fine art of children's book illustration. Previously published submissions only. Deadline for entries: August 20. SASE for contest rules and entry forms. Entry fee is $20/book. Judging by seven professional artists and editors. Works will be displayed at the Society of Illustrators Museum of American Illustration in New York City October-November annually. Medals awarded.

HELEN KEATING OTT AWARD FOR OUTSTANDING CONTRIBUTION TO CHILDREN'S LITERATURE, Church and Synagogue Library Association, P.O. Box 19357, Portland OR 97280-0357. (503)244-6919. Fax: (503)977-3734. E-mail: csla@worldaccessnet.com. Website: http://www.worldaccess net.com/~csla. Chair of Committee: Alrene Hall. Annual award. Estab. 1980. "This award is given to a person or organization that has made a significant contribution to promoting high moral and ethical values through children's literature." Deadline for entries: April 1. "Recipient is honored in July during the conference." Awards certificate of recognition and a conference package consisting of registration, all meals day of awards banquet, two nights' housing and a complementary 1 year membership. "A nomination for an award may be made by anyone. It should include the name, address and telephone number of the nominee plus the church or synagogue relationship where appropriate. Nominations of an organization should include the name of a contact person. A detailed description of the reasons for the nomination should be given, accompanied by documentary evidence of accomplishment. The person(s) making the nomination should give his/her name, address and telephone number and a brief explanation of his/her knowledge of the nominee's accomplishments. Elements of creativity and innovation will be given high priority by the judges."

[symbol] [check] OWL MAGAZINE CONTESTS, Writing Contest, Photo Contest, Poetry Contest, Cover Contest, *OWL Magazine*, 179 John St., Suite 500, Toronto, Ontario M5T 3G5 Canada. (416)340-2700. Fax: (416)340-9769. E-mail: owl@owlkids.com. Website: http://www.owlkids.com. Contact: Children's Page editor. Annual contest. Purpose of contest: "to encourage children to contribute and participate in the magazine. *Owl* also recognizes excellence in an individual or group effort to help the environment. Unpublished submissions only. Deadlines change yearly. Prizes/awards "change every year. Often we give books as prizes." Winning entries published in the magazine. Judging by art and editorial staff. Entries become the property of Bayard Press. "The contests and awards are open to children up to 14 years of age."

[N] PATERSON PRIZE FOR BOOKS FOR YOUNG PEOPLE, Poetry Center at Passaic County Community College, One College Blvd., Paterson NJ 07505-1179. (973)684-6555. Fax: (973)684-5843. E-mail: mgillan@pccc.cc.nj.us. Website: http://www.pccc.cc.nj.us/poetry. Award Director: Maria Mazziotti Gillan. **Open to students.** Estab. 1996. Previously published submissions only. Submissions made by author, author's agent or publisher. Must be published between January 1, 1998-December 31, 1998. Deadline for entries: March 15, 1999. SASE for contest rules and entry forms. Awards $500 for the author in either of 3 categories: PreK-Grade 3; Grades 4-6, Grades 7-12. Judging by a professional writer selected by the Poetry Center. Contest is open to any writer/illustrator. Write for guidelines.

[N] PENNSYLVANIA YOUNG READER'S CHOICE AWARDS, Pennsylvania School Librarians Association, 148 S. Bethelehem Pike, Ambler PA 19002-5822. (215)643-5048. Coordinator: Jean B. Bellavance. Annual award. Estab. 1991. Submissions nominated by a person or group. Must be published within 5 years of the award—for 1999-2000 books published 1995 to present. Deadline for entries: September 15, 1999. SASE for contest rules and entry forms. No entry fee. Framed certificate to winning authors. Judging by children of Pennsylvania (they vote). Requirements for entrants: currently living in North America. Reader's Choice Award is to promote reading of quality books by young people in the Commonwealth of Pennsylvania, to promote teacher and librarian involvement in children's literature, and to honor authors whose work has been recognized by the children of Pennsylvania. Three awards are given, one for each of the following grade level divisions: K-3, 3-6, 6-8.

POCKETS MAGAZINE FICTION CONTEST, The Upper Room, P.O. Box 189, Nashville TN 37202-0189. (615)340-7333. Fax: (615)340-7006. E-mail: pockets@upperroom.org. Website: http://www.upperro om.org/pockets. Associate Editor: Lynn Gilliam. **Open to students.** Annual contest. Estab. 1990. Purpose of contest: "to discover new freelance writers for our magazine and to encourage freelance writers to become familiar with the needs of our magazine." Unpublished submissions only. Submissions made by the author. Deadline for entries: August 15. SASE for contest rules and entry forms. No entry fee. Awards $1,000 and publication. Judging by *Pockets*' editors and 3 other editors of other Upper Room publications. Winner published in the magazine.

☑ **EDGAR ALLAN POE AWARD**, Mystery Writers of America, Inc., 6th Floor, 17 E. 47th St., New York NY 10017. (212)888-8171. Fax: (212)888-8107. Website: http://www.mysterywriters.org. President: Stuart Kaminsky. Annual award. Estab. 1945. Purpose of the award: to honor authors of distinguished works in the mystery field. Previously published submissions only. Submissions made by the author, author's agent; "normally by the publisher." Work must be published/produced the year of the contest. Deadline for entries: November 30 "except for works only available in the month of December." SASE for award rules and entry forms. No entry fee. Awards ceramic bust of "Edgar" for winner; scrolls for all nominees. Judging by professional members of Mystery Writers of America (writers). Nominee press release sent after first Wednesday in February. Winner announced at the Edgar Banquet, held in late April.

:N: ☑ **THE PRISM AWARDS**, The Kids Netword, 1235 Williams Park, 68532, Brampton, Ontario L6S 4S0 Canada. (905)451-1725. Fax: (908)451-2035. Award Manager: Sylvia Chirco. Annual award. Estab. 1989. Purpose of the award: Children have an opportunity to submit mss for review. Winners are chosen based on originality of ideas and self-expression. Unpublished submissions only. Deadline for entries: January 1999. SASE for award rules and entry forms. Entry fee is $2. Award consists of $500 cash and editorial training and possible publication. Judging by more than 40 independent judges. Requirements for entrants: a Native Indian, Canadian or landed immigrant in Canada, ages 7-14; story must be written solely by the submitter. No less than 4 pages, no more than 16 pages. Copyright to winning ms acquired by The Kids Netword upon winning.

☑ **PRIX ALVINE-BELISLE**, Association pour l'avancement des sciences et des techniques de la documentation (ASTED) Inc., 3414 Avenue Du Parc, Bureau 202, Montreal, Québec H2X 2H5 Canada. (514)281-5012. Fax: (514)281-8219. E-mail: info@asted.org. Award President: Josée Valiquette. Award open to children's book editors. Annual award. Estab. 1974. Purpose of contest: To recognize the best children's book published in French in Canada. Previously published submissions only. Submissions made by publishing house. Must be published the year before award. Deadline for entrie: June 1. Awards $500. Judging by librarians jury.

QUILL AND SCROLL INTERNATIONAL WRITING/PHOTO CONTEST, *Quill and Scroll*, School of Journalism, University of Iowa, Iowa City IA 52242. (319)335-5795. Contest Director: Richard Johns. Annual contest. Previously published submissions only. Submissions made by the author or school newspaper adviser. Must be published February 6, 1998 to February 4, 1999. Deadline for entries: February 5. SASE for contest rules and entry forms. Entry fee is $2/entry. Awards engraved plaque to junior high level sweepstakes winners. Each high school sweepstakes winner receives electric typewriter. Judging by various judges. *Quill and Scroll* acquires the right to publish submitted material in the magazine if it is chosen as a winning entry. Requirements for entrants: must be students in grades 9-12 for high school division.

:N: **THE ERIN PATRICK RABORG POETRY AWARD**, *AMELIA Magazine*, 329 E St., Bakersfield CA 93304-2031. (805)823-4064. Fax: (805)323-5326. E-mail: amelia@lightspeed.net. Submit entries to: Frederick A. Raborg, Jr., Editor. **Open to students.** Estab. 1992. Purpose of contest: To draw attention to childhood lifestyles and consequences. Also, to explore the humor as well as the bathos of childhood. Unpublished submissions only. Submissions made by author. Deadline for entries: December 1 annually. SASE for contest rules. Entry fee is $3 each entry. Award consists of $50 and publication in *AMELIA*. Judging is done in-house. Rights to winning material acquired: first North American serial only. "Be consistent within the form chosen."

☑ **READ ESSAY CONTEST**, (formerly Read Writing & Art Awards), *Read* Magazine, Weekly Reader Corp., 200 First Stamford Place, P.O. Box 120023, Stamford CT 06912-0023. (203)705-3406. Fax: (203)705-1661. Website: http://www.weeklyreader.com/read.html. Annual award. **Open to students.** Estab. 1998. "We're looking for essays about something or someone or some moment that was important to you, as well as your insights into that subject." Must include entry coupon and signature of teacher, parent or guardian and student. Deadline for entries: December. SASE for contest/award rules and entry forms. No entry fee. Awards first prize ($500), second prize ($75), third prize ($50). Prizes are given in each category, plus publication of first place winners. Judging by *Read* editorial staff.

N: RIP VAN WINKLE AWARD, School Library Media Specialists of Southeastern NY, 85 Rocky Hill Rd., New Paltz NY 12561. (914)255-9090. Award Director: Maxine Kamin. Annual award. Purpose of award: given to reward an author, illustator or author/illustrator residing in the seven county SLMSSENG region (Dutchess, Putnam, Orange, Rockland, Sullivan, Ulster and Westchester Counties, NY) for his/her outstanding contributions in the field of children's/young adult literature. Previously published submissions only. Submissions nominated by a person or group. Judging by Executive Board of Organization.

TOMÁS RIVERA MEXICAN AMERICAN CHILDREN'S BOOK AWARD, Southwest Texas State University, EDU, 601 University Dr., San Marcos TX 78666-4613. (512)245-8539. Fax: (512)245-8345. E-mail: vm04@academia.swt.edu. Award Director: Dr. Velma Menchaca. Competition open to adults. Annual contest. Estab. 1995. Purpose of award: "To encourage authors, illustrators and publishers to produce books that authentically reflect the lives of Mexican American children and young adults in the American Southwest." Previously published submissions only. Submissions made by "any interested individual." Must be published during the year of consideration. Deadline for entries: February 1 post publication year. Contact Dr. Menchaca for nomination forms. No entry fee. Awards $3,000 per book. Judging of nominations by a regional committee, national committee judges finalists. Annual ceremony honoring the book and author/illustrator is held during Hispanic Heritage Month at Southwest Texas State University.

☑ **ANNA DAVIDSON ROSENBERG AWARD FOR POEMS ON THE JEWISH EXPERIENCE**, Judah L. Magnes Museum, 2911 Russell St., Berkeley CA 94705. (510)549-6950. Poetry Award Director: Paula Friedman. Annual award. Estab. 1986-87. Purpose of the award: to encourage poetry in English on the Jewish experience (writer does not need to be Jewish). Previously unpublished submissions only. Deadline for entries: August 31. SASE for award rules and entry forms by July 31. Entry forms must be included with submissions. SASE for mandatory list of winners. Awards $100-first prize, $50-second prize, $25-third prize; honorable mention certificates; $25 Youth Commendation (poets under 19); $25 Emerging Poet Award. Judging by committee of 3 well-published poets with editing/teaching experience. There will be a reading of top award winners in December at Magnes Museum. Write for entry form and guidelines *first*; entries must follow guidelines and be accompanied by entry form. *Please do not phone.* Note: "We are not a contest for works for children—though our Youth Commendation is for authors under 19 (winners have been as young as 9 years old).

PLEASANT T. ROWLAND PRIZE FOR FICTION FOR GIRLS, Pleasant Company Publications, 8400 Fairway Place, Middleton, WI 53562. Contact: Submissions Editor. Purpose of contest: "The mission of the competition is to encourage writers to turn their talents to the creation of high-quality fiction for girls and to reward talented authors of novles that successfully capture the spirit of contemporary American girls and illuminate the ways in which their lives may be personally touched by events and concerns shaping the United States today. Stories should feature a female protagonist between the ages of 8 and 12. Characters of varying cultural backgronds and family situations are welcome." Unpublished submissions only. Submissions made by author or author's agent. Deadline for entries: September. No entry fee. Awards $10,000 in cash and a standard contract with advance and royalty for publication of the winning book. Judging by the editors of Pleasant Company Publications, publisher of The American Girls Collection, American Girl Library, and *American Girl* magazine. Requirement for entrants: Must be U.S. resident. "Authors whose work is now being published by Pleasant Company are not eligible. Manuscripts sent to Pleasant Company Publications may not be submitted to other publishers while under consideration for the Pleasant T. Rowland Prize."

VISIT THE WRITER'S DIGEST WEBSITE at http://www.writersdigest.com for hot new markets, daily market updates, writers' guidelines and much more.

SASKATCHEWAN BOOK AWARDS: CHILDREN'S LITERATURE, Saskatchewan Book Awards, Box 1921, Regina, Saskatchewan S4P 3E1 Canada. (306)569-1585. Fax: (306)569-4187. Award Director: Joyce Wells. Annual award. Estab. 1995. Previously published submissions only. Submissions made by author, author's agent or publisher by September 30. SASE for contest rules and entry forms. Entry fee is $15 (Canadian). Awards $1,000 (Canadian). Judging by two children's literature authors outside of Saskatchewan. Requirements for entrants: Must be Saskatchewan resident; book must have ISBN number; book must have been published within the last year. Award winning book will appear on TV talk shows, and be pictured on book marks distributed to libraries, schools and bookstores in Saskatchewan.

SEEDHOUSE MAGAZINE'S SUMMER WRITING CONTEST, Seedhouse Magazine, P.O. Box 883009, Steamboat Springs CO 80488. **Open to students.** Annual contest. Purpose of contest: "In our first writing contest, we are not looking for specific genre or form, but rather for fresh perspectives on whatever 'unlimbers' your keyboard. The contest is open to all genres of fiction and all types of poetry. We welcome entries from published and non-published writers. The winning story and poem will appear in the September/October issue of *Seedhouse Magazine*. Prizes will be awarded in both categories. First place $50, Second place $30, Third place $20." Submissions made by author. Deadline for entries: July 4th, 1999. SASE for contest rules and entry forms. Non-subscribers should include a $2 reading fee per entry. Subscribers who enter more than one short story should include a $2 reading fee for each additional entry. Requirements for entrants: "Please put your name, address and telephone number on a separate piece of paper and include a two-three-sentence bio. Your name must not appear anywhere on your entry. Short story: 5,000 words or less. Poetry: two page maximum, up to three poems may be submitted as one entry."

SEVENTEEN FICTION CONTEST, 850 Third Ave., 9th Floor, New York NY 10022. Fiction Editor: Ben Schrank. Annual contest. Estab. 1945. Fax: (212)407-9899. E-mail: seventeenm@aol.com. Unpublished submissions only. Deadline for entries: April 30. SASE for contest rules and entry forms; contest rules also published in November issue of *Seventeen*. Entries not returned. No entry fee. Awards cash prize and possible publication in *Seventeen*. Judging by "inhouse panel of editors, external readers." If first prize, acquires first North American rights for piece to be published. Requirements for entrants: "Our annual fiction contest is open to anyone between the ages of 13 and 21 who submit on or before April 30 (check November issue of *Seventeen* for details). Submit only original fiction that has not been published in any form other than in school publications. Stories should be between 1,500 and 3,000 words in length (6-12 pages). All manuscripts must be typed double-spaced on a single side of paper. Submit as many original stories as you like, but each story must include your full name, address, birth date and signature in the top right-hand corner of the first page. Your signature on submission will constitute your acceptance of the contest rules."

SHUBERT FENDRICH MEMORIAL PLAYWRIGHTING CONTEST, Pioneer Drama Service, Inc., P.O. Box 4267, Englewood CO 80155-4267. Fax: (303)779-4315. E-mail: piodrama@aol.com. Website: http://www.pioneerdrama.com. Director: Beth Somers. Annual contest. **Open to students.** Estab. 1990. Purpose of the contest: "to encourage the development of quality theatrical material for educational and family theater." Previously unpublished submissions only. Deadline for entries: March 1. SASE for contest rules and entry forms. No entry fee. Application must accompany all submissions. Awards $1,000 royalty advance and publication. Upon receipt of signed contracts, plays will be published and made available in our next catalog. Judging by editors. All rights acquired with acceptance of contract for publication. Restrictions for entrants: Any writers currently published by Pioneer Drama Service are not eligible.

SKIPPING STONES YOUTH HONOR AWARDS, *Skipping Stones*, P.O. Box 3939, Eugene OR 97403-0939. (541)342-4956. E-mail: skipping@efn.org. Website: http://www.nonviolence.org/skipping. Annual award. Purpose of contest: "to recognize youth, 7 to 17, for their contributions to multicultural awareness, nature and ecology, social issues, peace and nonviolence. Also to promote creativity, self-esteem and writing skills, and to recognize important work being done by youth organizations." Submissions made by the author. For 1999, the theme is "Multicultural and Nature Awareness." Deadline for entries: June 20, 1999. SASE for contest rules. Entries must include certificate of originality by a parent and/or teacher, and background information on the author written by the author. Entry fee is $3. Judging by *Skipping Stones*' staff. "Up to ten awards are given in three categories: (1) Compositions—(essays, poems, short stories, songs, travelogues, etc.) should be typed (double-spaced) or neatly handwritten. Fiction or nonfiction should be limited to 750 words; poems to 30 lines. Non-English writings are also welcome. (2) Artwork—(drawings, cartoons, paintings or photo essays with captions) should have the artist's name, age and address on the back of each page. Send the originals with SASE. Black & white photos are especially welcome. Limit: 8 pieces. (3) Youth Organizations—Tell us how your club or group works to: (a) preserve the nature and ecology in your area, (b) enhance the quality of life for low-income, minority or disabled, or (c) improve racial or cultural harmony in your school or community. Use the same format as for compositions." The 1999 winners will be published in Vol. 11, #4 (September-October 1999) issue of *Skipping Stones*.

KAY SNOW WRITERS' CONTEST, Williamette Writers, 9045 SW Barbur Blvd. #5A, Portland OR 97219-4027. (503)452-1592. Fax: (503)452-0372. E-mail: wilwrite@teleport.com. Website: http://www.tel eport.com/~wilwrite/. Contest Director: Martha Miller. Annual contest. **Open to students.** Purpose of contest: "to encourage beginning and established writers to continue the craft." Unpublished, original submissions only. Submissions made by the author or author's agent. Deadline for entries: May 15. SASE for contest rules and entry forms. Entry fee is $10, Williamette Writers' members; $15, nonmembers; free for student writers 6-18. Awards cash prize of $200 per category (fiction, nonfiction, juvenile, poetry, script writing), $50 for students in three divisions: 1-5, 6-8, 9-12. "Judges are anonymous."

N SPUR AWARDS, Western Writers of America, 60 Sandpiper Court, Conway AR 72032. (501)450-0086. Fax: (501)450-9870. Award Director: W.C. Jameson. Annual award. Estab. 1953. Previously published submissions only. Submissions made by author, author's agent or publisher. Must be published the year previous to the award. SASE for contest rules and entry forms. Entry fee is $10 Awards plaque. Judging by panel of 3 published writers. Awards given in June 1999 at Colorado Springs CO.

N THE STANLEY DRAMA AWARD, Stanley-Tomolat Foundation, Wagner College, One Campus Rd., Staten Island NY 10301. (718)390-3325. Fax: (718)390-3323. E-mail: lterry@wagner.eou. Award Director: Liz Terry. **Open to students.** Annual award. Estab. 1957. Purpose of contest: to support new works and playwrights. Unpublished submissions only. Submissions made by author. Deadline for entries: October 1. SASE for contest rules and entry forms. Entry fee is $20. Awards $2,000. Judging by committee. Award is to a full-length play or musical, previously unpublished and/or produced. One-act plays must be a full evening of theater; accepts series of one-acts related to one theme.

GEORGE G. STONE CENTER FOR CHILDREN'S BOOKS RECOGNITION OF MERIT AWARD, George G. Stone Center for Children's Books, Claremont Graduate University, 131 E. 10th St., Claremont CA 91711-6188. (909)607-3670. Fax: (909)621-8390. Award Director: Doty Hale. Annual award. Estab. 1965. Purpose of the award: to recognize an author or illustrator of a children's book or a body of work exhibiting the "power to please and expand the awareness of children and teachers as they have shared the book in their classrooms." Previously published submissions only. SASE for award rules and entry forms. Entries not returned. No entry fee. Awards a scroll. Judging by a committee of teachers, professors of children's literature and librarians. Requirements for entrants: "Nominations are made by students, teachers, professors and librarians. Award made at annual Claremont Reading Conference in spring (March)."

N SWW ANNUAL CONTEST, Southwest Writers Workshop, 1338 B Wyoming NE, Albuquerque NM 87112. (505)293-0303. Fax: (505)237-2665. E-mail: swriters@aol.com. Website: http://www.us1.net/ sww. Submit entries to: Contest Chair. Annual contest. Estab. 1982. Purpose of contest: to encourage writers of all genres. Previously unpublished submissions only. Submissions made by author. Deadline for entries: May 1, 1999. SASE for contest rules and entry forms. Entry fee. Award consists of cash prizes in each of over 15 categories. Judging by national editors and agents. Official entry form is required.

✓ SYDNEY TAYLOR MANUSCRIPT COMPETITION, Association of Jewish Libraries, 1327 Wyntercreek Lane, Dunwoody GA 30338-3816. Fax: (770)394-2060. E-mail: m-psand@mindspring.com. Website: http://aleph.Ohio-State.edu/www/xajl.html. Coordinator: Paula Sandfelder. Annual contest. Estab. 1985. Purpose of the contest: "This competition is for unpublished writers of fiction. Material should be for readers ages 8-11, with universal appeal that will serve to deepen the understanding of Judaism for all children, revealing positive aspects of Jewish life." Unpublished submissions only. Deadline for entries: January 15. SASE for contest rules and entry forms. No entry fee. Awards $1,000. Award will be given at the Association of Jewish Libraries annual convention. Judging by qualified judges from within the Association of Jewish Libraries. Requirements for entrants: must be an unpublished fiction writer; also, books must range from 64 to 200 pages in length. "AJL assumes no responsibility for publication, but hopes this cash incentive will serve to encourage new writers of children's stories with Jewish themes for all children."

TREASURE STATE AWARD, Missoula Public Library, Missoula County Schools, Montana Library Assoc., 301 E. Main, Missoula MT 59802. (406)721-2005. Fax: (406)728-5900. E-mail: bammon@missoul a.lib.mt. Website: http://www.missoula.lib.mt. Award Directors: Bette Ammon and Carole Monlux. Annual award. Estab. 1990. Purpose of the award: Children in grades K-3 read or listen to a ballot of 5 picture books and vote on their favorite. Previously published submissions only. Submissions made by author, nominated by a person or group of people—children, librarians, teachers. Must be published in previous 5 years to voting year. Deadline for entries: March 20. SASE for contest rules and entry forms. No entry fee. Awards a plaque or sculpture. Judging by popular vote by Montana children grades K-3.

VEGETARIAN ESSAY CONTEST, The Vegetarian Resource Group, P.O. Box 1463, Baltimore MD 21203. (410)366-VEGE. Fax: (410)366-8804. E-mail: vrg@vrg.org. Website: http://www.vrg.org. Address to Vegetarian Essay Contest. Annual contest. Estab. 1985. Purpose of contest: to promote vegetarianism in young people. Unpublished submissions only. Deadline for entries: May 1 of each year. SASE for contest rules and entry forms. No entry fee. Awards $50 savings bond. Judging by awards committee. Acquires right for The Vegetarian Resource Group to reprint essays. Requirements for entrants: age 18 and under. Winning works may be published in *Vegetarian Journal*, instructional materials for students. "Submit 2-3 page essay on any aspect of vegetarianism, which is the abstinence of meat, fish and fowl. Entrants can base paper on interviewing, research or personal opinion. Need not be vegetarian to enter."

VFW VOICE OF DEMOCRACY, Veterans of Foreign Wars of the U.S., 406 W. 34th St., Kansas City MO 64111. (816)968-1117. Fax: (816)968-1157. Website: http://www.vfw.org. Annual contest. Estab. 1960. Purpose of contest: to give high school students the opportunity to voice their opinions about their responsibility to our country and to convey those opinions via the broadcast media to all of America. Deadline for entries: November 1st. No entry fee. Winners receive awards ranging from $1,000-20,000. Requirements for entrants: "Tenth-twelfth grade students in public, parochial and private schools in the United States and overseas are eligible to compete. Former national and/or first place state winners are not eligible to compete again. Contact your high school counselor or your local VFW Post to enter."

VOLUNTEER STATE BOOK AWARD, Tennessee Library Association, P.O. Box 158417, Nashville TN 37215-8417. (615)297-8316. Award Co-Chairs: Dr. Beverly N. Youree, Sue Thetford. Competition open to adults only. Annual award. Estab. 1978. Purpose of award: to promote awareness, interest, and enjoyment of good new children's and young adult literature and to promote literacy and life-long reading habits by encouraging students to read quality contemporary literature which broadens understanding of the human experience and provides accurate, factual information. Previously published submissions only. Submissions made by author, by the author's agent and nominated by a person or group of people. Must be published in 5 years prior to year of voting. SASE for contest rules and entry forms. No entry fee. Awards plaque. Judging by children. Any public or private school in Tennessee is eligible to participate. It is not required that the entire school be involved. Each participating school must have a minimum of twelve of the twenty titles per division available.

☑ **VSA (VERY SPECIAL ARTS) PLAYWRIGHT DISCOVERY PROGRAM**, (formerly Very Special Arts Playwright Discovery), VSA, 1300 Connecticut Ave., NW, Suite 700, Washington DC 20036. (202)628-2800 or 1-800-933-8721. TTY: (202)737-0645. Fax: (202)737-0725. E-mail: playwright@vsarts. org. Website: http://www.vsarts.org. Program Manager: Elena Widder. Annual contest. Estab. 1984. "All scripts must document the experience of living with a disability." Unpublished submissions only. Deadline for entries: April 30, 1999. Write to Playwright Discovery Program Manager for contest rules and entry forms. No entries returned. No entry fee. Judging by Artists Selection Committee. Entrants must be people with disabilities. "Script will be selected for production at The John F. Kennedy Center for the Performing Arts, Washington DC. The winning play(s) is presented each fall."

THE STELLA WADE CHILDREN'S STORY AWARD, *Amelia* Magazine, 329 E St., Bakersfield CA 93304. (805)323-4064. Fax: (805)323-5326. E-mail: amelia@lightspeed.net. Editor: Frederick A. Raborg, Jr. Annual award. Estab. 1988. Purpose of award: "With decrease in the number of religious and secular magazines for young people, the juvenile story and poetry must be preserved and enhanced." Unpublished submissions only. Deadline for entries: August 15. SASE for award rules. Entry fee is $7.50 per adult entry; there is no fee for entries submitted by young people under the age of 17, but such entry must be signed by parent, guardian or teacher to verify originality. Awards $125 plus publication. Judging by editorial staff. Previous winners include Maxine Kumin and Sharon E. Martin. "We use First North American serial rights only for the winning manuscript." Contest is open to all interested. If illustrator wishes to enter only an illustration without a story, the entry fee remains the same. Illustrations will also be considered for cover publication. Restrictions of mediums for illustrators: Submitted photos should be no smaller than 5×7; illustrations (drawn) may be in any medium. "Winning entry will be published in the most appropriate issue of either *Amelia*, *Cicada* or *SPSM&H*—subject matter would determine such. Submit clean, accurate copy." Sample issue: $9.95.

N WASHINGTON CHILDRENS' CHOICE PICTURE BOOK AWARD, Washington Library Media Association, P.O. Box 99121, Seattle WA 98199-0121. E-mail: galantek@edmonds.wednet.edu. Award Director: Kristin Galante. Submit entries to: Kristin Galante, chairman. Annual award. Estab. 1982. Previously published submissions only. Submissions nominated by a person or group. Must be published within 3 years prior to year of award. Deadline for entries: February 1. SASE for contest rules and entry forms. Awards pewter plate, recognition. Judging by WCCPBA committee.

✓ WASHINGTON POST/CHILDREN'S BOOK GUILD AWARD FOR NONFICTION, % Kristi Beavin, President of the Children's Book Guild of Washington, D.C., Head, Central Library Children's Room, 1015 Quincy St., Arlington VA 22201. Annual award. Estab. 1977. Purpose of award: "to encourage nonfiction writing for children of literary quality. Purpose of contest: "to call attention to an outstanding nonfiction author of several works, judged on the author's total output, to encourage authors to write nonfiction." Awarded for the body of work of a leading American nonfiction author." Awards $1,000 and an engraved crystal paperweight. Judging by a jury of Children's Book Guild librarians and authors and a *Washington Post* book critic. "One doesn't enter. One is selected. Authors and publishers mistakenly send us books. Our jury annually selects one author for the award."

WE ARE WRITERS, TOO!, Creative With Words Publications, P.O. Box 223226, Carmel CA 93922. Fax: (408)655-8627. E-mail: cwwpub@usa.net. Website: http://members.tripod.com/~CreativeWithWords. Contest Director: Brigitta Geltrich. Semi-annual contest. Estab. 1975. Purpose of award: to further creative writing in children. Unpublished submissions only. Deadline for entries: June 1 and December 1. SASE for contest rules and entry forms. SASE for return of entries "if not winning poem." No entry fee. Awards publication in an anthology, on website and a free copy for "Best of the Month." Judging by selected guest editors and educators. Contest open to children only (up to and including 19 years old). Writer should request contest rules. SASE with all correspondence. Age of child must be stated and manuscript must be verified of its authenticity. Each story or poem must have a title. Creative with Words Publications publishes the top 100 manuscripts submitted to the contest, and also publishes anthologies on various themes throughout the year to which young writers may submit. Request theme list, include SASE, or visit our website at above address.

WESTERN HERITAGE AWARDS, National Cowboy Hall of Fame, 1700 NE 63rd St., Oklahoma City OK 73111-7997. (405)478-2250. Fax: (405)478-4714. E-mail: nchf@aol.com. Website: http://www.cowboyhalloffame.com. Director of Public Relations: Lynda Haller. Annual award. Estab. 1961. Purpose of award: The WHA are presented annually to encourage the accurate and artistic telling of great stories of the West through 15 categories of western literature, television and film, including fiction, nonfiction, children's books and poetry. Previously published submissions only; must be published the calendar year before the awards are presented. Deadline for literary entries: November 30. Deadline for film, music and television entries: December 31. SASE for award rules and entry forms. Entries not returned. Entry fee is $35. Awards a Wrangler bronze sculpture designed by famed western artist, John Free. Judging by a panel of judges selected each year with distinction in various fields of western art and heritage. Requirements for entrants: The material must pertain to the development or preservation of the West, either from a historical or contemporary viewpoint. Literary entries must have been published December 1 and November 30 of calendar year. Film, music or television entries must have been released or aired between January 1, 1997 and December 31, 1998 of calendar year of entry. Works recognized during special awards ceremonies held annually at the museum. There is an autograph party preceding the awards. Film clips of award winner are shown during the awards presentation. Awards ceremonies are sometimes broadcast.

N WESTERN WRITERS OF AMERICA AWARD, Western Writers of America, Inc., 60 Sandpiper, Conway AR 72032. (501)450-0086. Award Director: W.C. Jameson. Submit entries to: W.C. Jameson. Annual award. Purpose of award: to recognize the best western writing. Western material is defined by the WWA, Inc. as that which is set in the territory west of the Mississippi River or on the early frontier. Previously published submissions only. Submissions made by author. Must be published in the previous year. Deadline for entries: December 31. SASE for contest rules and entry forms. Entry fee is $10. Awards include the Spur Awards, the Medicine Pipe Bearer Award for Best First Novel and the Storyteller Award for the Best Children's Picture Book of the West.

JACKIE WHITE MEMORIAL NATIONAL CHILDREN'S PLAY WRITING CONTEST, Columbia Entertainment Company, 309 Parkade Blvd., Columbia MO 65202-1447. (573)874-5628. Contest Director: Betsy Phillips. Annual contest. Estab. 1988. Purpose of contest: to find good plays for 30-45 theater school students, 6-9 grade, to perform in CEC's theater school. Previously unpublished submissions only. Submissions made by author. Deadline for entries: June 1. SASE for contest rules and entry forms. Entry fee is $10. Awards $250, production of play, travel expenses to come see production. Judging by board members of CEC and at least one theater school parent. Play is performed during the following season, i.e. 1997 winner to be presented during CEC's 1997-98 season. We reserve the right to award 1st place and prize monies without a production.

☑ **PAUL A. WITTY OUTSTANDING LITERATURE AWARD**, International Reading Association, Special Interest Group, Reading for Gifted and Creative Learning, School of Education, P.O. Box 297900, Fort Worth TX 76129. (817)921-7660. Award Director: Dr. Cathy Collins Block. Annual award. Estab. 1979. Categories of entries: poetry/prose at elementary, junior high and senior high levels. Unpublished submissions only. Deadline for entries: February 1. SASE for award rules and entry forms. SASE for return of entries. No entry fee. Awards $25 and plaque, also certificates of merit. Judging by 2 committees for screening and awarding. Works will be published in International Reading Association publications. "The elementary students' entries must be legible and may not exceed 1,000 words. Secondary students' prose entries should be typed and may exceed 1,000 words if necessary. At both elementary and secondary levels, if poetry is entered, a set of five poems must be submitted. All entries and requests for applications must include a self-addressed, stamped envelope."

N WOMEN IN THE ARTS ANNUAL CONTESTS, Women In The Arts, P.O. Box 2907, Decatur IL 62524-2907. Phone/fax: (217)763-3311. E-mail: jagusch@novanet1.com. Submit entries to Vice President. **Open to students.** Annual contest. Estab. 1995. Purpose of contest: to encourage beginning writers, as well as published professionals by offering a contest for well-written material in fiction and poetry. Submissions made by author. Deadline for entries: November 15 annually. SASE for contest rules and entry forms. Entry fee is $2/item. Prize consists of $30 1st place; $25 2nd place; $15 3rd place—plus publication in anthology titled "Spring Fantasy." Send SASE for complete rules.

ALICE LOUISE WOOD OHIOANA AWARD FOR CHILDREN'S LITERATURE, Ohioana Library Association, 65 S. Front St., Suite 1105, Columbus OH 43215. (614)466-3831. Fax: (614)728-6974. E-mail: ohioana@winslo.ohio.gov. Website: http://www.oplin.lib.oh.us/OHIOANA/. Director: Linda R. Hengst. Annual award. Estab. 1991. Purpose of award: "to recognize an Ohio author whose body of work has made, and continues to make, a significant contribution to literature for children or young adults." SASE for award rules and entry forms. Award: $1,000. Requirements for entrants: "must have been born in Ohio, or lived in Ohio for a minimum of five years; established a distinguished publishing record of books for children and young people; body of work has made, and continues to make, a significant contribution to the literature for young people; through whose work as a writer, teacher, administrator, or through community service, interest in children's literature has been encouraged and children have become involved with reading."

CARTER G. WOODSON BOOK AWARD, National Council for the Social Studies, 3501 Newark St. NW, Washington DC 20016-3167. (202)966-7840. Fax: (202)966-2061. E-mail: excellence@ncss.org. Website: http://www.ncss.org. Contact: Manager of Recognition Programs. Annual award, named after Carter G. Woodson (1875-1950), a distinguished African-American historian, educator and social activist. Purpose of contest: to recognize books relating to ethnic minorities and authors of such books. NCSS established the Carter G. Woodson Book Awards for the most distinguished social science books appropriate for young readers which depict ethnicity in the United States. This award is intended to "encourage the writing, publishing, and dissemination of outstanding social studies books for young readers which treat topics related to ethnic minorities and race relations sensitively and accurately." Submissions must be previously published. Submissions generally made by publishers "because copies of the book must be supplied to each member of the committee and copies of winning books must be provided to NCSS headquarters." Eligible books must be published in the year preceding the year in which award is given, i.e., 1997 for 1998 award. Books must be received by members of the committee by February 1. Rules, criteria and requirements are available for SASE. No entry fee. Award consists of: an announcement published in NCSS periodicals and forwarded to national and Council affiliated media. The publisher, author and illustrator receive written notification of the committee decision. Reviews of award-winning books and "honor books" are published in the NCSS official journal, *Social Education*. The award is presented at the NCSS Annual Conference in November. Judging by committee of social studies educators (teachers, curriculum supervisors and specialists, college/university professors, teacher educators—with a specific interest in multicultural education and the use of literature in social studies instruction) appointed from the NCSS membership at large.

WORK-IN-PROGRESS GRANTS, Society of Children's Book Writers and Illustrators, 345 N. Maple Dr. #296, Beverly Hills CA 90210. Fax: (310)859-4877. Website: http://www.SCBWI.org. Annual award. "The SCBWI Work-in-Progress Grants have been established to assist children's book writers in the completion of a specific project." Five categories: (1) General Work-in-Progress Grant. (2) Grant for a Contemporary Novel for Young People. (3) Nonfiction Research Grant. (4) Grant for a work whose author has never had a book published. (5) Grant for a picture book writer. Requests for applications may be made beginning October 1. Completed applications accepted February 1-May 1 of each year. SASE for applications for grants. In any year, an applicant may apply for any of the grants except the one awarded for a work whose author has never had a book published. (The recipient of this grant will be chosen from entries in all categories.) Five grants of $1,000 will be awarded annually. Runner-up grants of $500 (one in each category) will also be awarded. "The grants are available to both full and associate members of the SCBWI. They are not available for projects on which there are already contracts." Previous recipients not eligible to apply.

N ☑ WRITER'S BLOCK LITERARY CONTEST, *Writer's Block Magazine*, #32, 9944-33 Ave., Edmonton, Alberta T6N 1E8 Canada. (403)464-6623. Fax: (403)464-5524. Contest Director: Shaun Donnelly. Submit entries to: Shaun Donnelly, editor. **Open to students.** Biannual contest. Estab. 1994. Unpublished submissions only. Submissions made by author. Deadline for entries: March 30 and September 30. SASE for contest rules and entry forms. Entry fee is $5. Prize consists of publication, $100-150 cash, hardcover books in author's genre. Judging by independent judges (usually writers).

☑ WRITER'S EXCHANGE POETRY CONTEST, 100 Upper Glen Dr., Blythewood SC 29016. E-mail: eboone@aol.com. Website: http://members.aol.com/WriterNet or http://members.aol.com/WEBBAS E1. Contest Director: Gene Boone. Quarterly contest. **Open to students.** Estab. 1985. Purpose of the contest: to promote friendly competition among poets of all ages and backgrounds, giving these poets a chance to be published and win an award. Submissions are made by the author. Continuous deadline; entries are placed in the contest closest to date received. SASE for contest rules and entry forms. Entry fee is $2 first poem, $1 each additional poem. Awards 50% of contest proceeds, usually $35-100 varying slightly in each quarterly contest due to changes in response. Judging by Gene Boone or a guest judge such as a widely published poet or another small press editor. "From the entries received, we reserve the right to publish the winning poems in an issue of *Writer's Exchange*, a literary newsletter. The contest is open to any poet. Poems on any subject/theme, any style, to 30 lines, may be entered. Poems should be typed, single-spaced, with the poet's name in the upper left corner."

☑ WRITER'S INT'L FORUM FOR YOUNG AUTHORS CONTESTS, (formerly Writer's International Forum Contests), *Writer's Int'l Forum for Young Authors*, P.O. Box 516, Tracyton WA 98393-0516. Website: http://www.bristolservicesintl.com. Contest Director: Sandra E. Haven. Estab. 1997. Purpose of contest: to inspire excellence in the traditional short story format and for tightly focused essays. "In fiction we like identifiable characters, strong storylines, and crisp, fresh endings. Open only to young writers." Unpublished submissions only. Submissions made by the author with verification from parent or guardian that this is the student's own efforts. Deadlines, fees, and cash award prizes vary per contest. SASE for dates of each upcoming contest, contest rules and entry forms. Judging by *Writer's Int'l Forum* staff. "We reserve the right to publish cash award winners." Please state age of author and birth date in cover letter. Contest winners announced in future issue. Word count restrictions vary with each contest. Some contests require following a theme or other stipulation. Please request guidelines for contest you want to enter or visit website to request guidelines.

WRITING CONFERENCE WRITING CONTESTS, The Writing Conference, Inc., P.O. Box 664, Ottawa KS 66067-0664. (913)242-0407. Fax: (913)242-0407. E-mail: jbushman@writingconference.com. Website: http://www.writingconference.com. Contest Director: John H. Bushman. Annual contest. Estab. 1988. Purpose of contest: to further writing by students with awards for narration, exposition and poetry at the elementary, middle school and high school levels. Unpublished submissions only. Submissions made

"WE WANT TO PUBLISH YOUR WORK."

Completely Updated Each Year

Now includes more information for illustrators

Children's Writer's & Illustrator's Market

800 EDITORS & ART DIRECTORS WHO BUY YOUR WRITING & ILLUSTRATIONS

150 new markets
250 book publishers
125 magazines
500 e-mail addresses & websites
120 contests & awards
100 conferences & workshops

OVER 300,000 COPIES SOLD

You would give anything to hear an editor speak those 6 magic words. So you work hard for weeks, months, even years to make that happen. You create a brilliant piece of work and a knock-out presentation, but there's still one vital step to ensure publication. You still need to submit your work to the right buyers. With rapid changes in the publishing industry it's not always easy to know who those buyers are. That's why each year thousands of writers and illustrators turn to the most current edition of this indispensable market guide.

Keep ahead of the changes by ordering *2000 Children's Writer's & Illustrator's Market* today! You'll save the frustration of getting your work returned in the mail stamped MOVED: ADDRESS UNKNOWN. And of NOT submitting your work to new listings because you don't know they exist. All you have to do to order the upcoming 2000 edition is complete the attached order card and return it with your payment. Order now and you'll get the 2000 edition at the 1999 price—just $19.99—no matter how much the regular price may increase!

2000 Children's Writer's & Illustrator's Market will be published and ready for shipment in January 2000.

More books to help you get published

☐ **Yes!** I want the most current edition of *Children's Writer's & Illustrator's Market*. Please send me the 2000 edition at the 1999 price—$19.99.* (NOTE: *2000 Children's Writer's & Illustrator's Market* will be ready for shipment in January 2000.) #10626

Additional books from the back of this card:

Book	Price
#	$
#	$
#	$
#	$
Subtotal	$

*Add $3.50 postage and handling for one book; $1.50 for each additional book.

Postage & Handling	$

Payment must accompany order. Ohioans add 6% sales tax. Canadians add 7% GST.

Total	$

VISA/MasterCard orders call
TOLL FREE 1-800-289-0963
8:30 to 5:00 Mon.-Fri. Eastern Time
or FAX 1-888-590-4082

☐ Payment enclosed $_____ (or)
Charge my: ☐ Visa ☐ MasterCard Exp._____

Account #_____

Signature_____

Name_____

Address_____

City_____

State/Prov._____ Zip/PC _____

30-Day Money Back Guarantee on every book you buy!

6501

Mail to: Writer's Digest Books • 1507 Dana Avenue • Cincinnati, OH 45207

Get Your Children's Stories Published with help from these Writer's Digest Books!

1999 Guide to Literary Agents
edited by Donya Dickerson
Agents can open doors for you in the publishing industry. You can team up with an agent using this invaluable directory (now in its 8th year). Over 500 listings of literary and script agents, plus inside information on the industry will help you choose the right agent to represent you.
#10583/$19.99/300 pgs/pb

Writing For Young Adults
Award-winning novelist Sherry Garland reveals the secrets of writing successfully for the young adult market. You'll learn how to write for this special audience by conducting research, writing an outline/synopsis, and using plot dialogue and characterization effectively. Plus, you'll get an inside look at current publishing trends, including the popularity of multi-cultural literature and packaged books.
#10568/$14.99/240 pgs/pb

You Can Write Children's Books
Writer and editor Tracey Dils gives you the essential writing and submission guidelines you need to get your work in print. She reveals the hot trends in children's publishing, how to maintain a structured format, ways to target the right age group, how to produce a professional package, and more.
#10547/$12.99/128 pgs/pb

Children's Writer's Word Book
Even the most original children's story won't get published if its language usage or sentence structure doesn't speak to young readers. You'll avoid these pitfalls with this quick-reference guide full of word lists, reading levels for synonyms and more!
#10316/$19.99/352 pages

Writing and Illustrating Children's Books for Publication
Create a good, publishable manuscript in eight weeks using this self-taught writing course. Easy-to-follow lessons and exercises cover everything from getting ideas to writing, polishing and publishing.
#10448/$24.95/128 pages/200 illus.

How To Write and Illustrate Children's Books and Get Them Published
Find everything you need to break into the lucrative children's market. You'll discover how to write a sure-fire seller, create captivating illustrations, get your manuscript into the right buyer's hands and more!
#30082/$24.99/144 pages/115 illus.

How To Write and Sell Children's Picture Books
If you yearn to put smiles on little faces, you need this charming guide. You'll discover how to put your picture book on paper and get it published—whether you're retelling a wonderful old tale, or spinning a splendid new yarn.
#10410/$17.99/192 pages

Ten Steps to Publishing Children's Books
Discover vital information on children's publishing as you polish your writing skills. You'll find advice from professionals, case histories, checklists, exercises and more.
#10534/$24.95/128 pages/150 illus.

by the author or teacher. Deadline for entries: January 11. SASE for contest rules and entry form or consult website. No entry fee. Awards plaque and publication of winning entry in *The Writers' Slate*, March issue. Judging by a panel of teachers. Requirements for entrants: must be enrolled in school—K-12th grade.

YEARBOOK EXCELLENCE CONTEST, *Quill and Scroll*, School of Journalism, University of Iowa, Iowa City IA 52242. (319)335-5795. Executive Director: Richard Johns. Annual contest. Estab. 1987. Previously published submissions only. Submissions made by the author or school yearbook adviser. Must be published between November 1, 1997 and November 1, 1998. Deadline for entries: November 1. SASE for contest rules and entry form. Entry fee is $2 per entry. Awards National Gold Key; sweepstakes winners receive plaque; seniors eligible for scholarships. Judging by various judges. Winning entries may be published in *Quill and Scroll* magazine.

YOUNG ADULT CANADIAN BOOK AWARD, The Canadian Library Association, Suite 602, 200 Elgin St., Ottawa, Ontario K2P 1L5 Canada. (613)232-9625. Fax: (613)563-9895. Contact: Committee Chair. Annual award. Estab. 1981. Purpose of award: "to recognize the author of an outstanding English-language Canadian book which appeals to young adults between the ages of 13 and 18 that was published the preceding calendar year. Information is available for anyone requesting. We approach publishers, also send news releases to various journals, i.e., *Quill & Quire*." Entries are not returned. No entry fee. Awards a leather-bound book. Requirement for entrants: must be a work of fiction (novel or short stories), the title must be a Canadian publication in either hardcover or paperback, and the author must be a Canadian citizen or landed immigrant. Award given at the Canadian Library Association Conference.

Helpful Books & Publications

The editor of *Children's Writer's & Illustrator's Market* suggests the following books and periodicals to keep you informed on writing and illustrating techniques, trends in the field, business issues, industry news and changes, and additional markets.

BOOKS

CHILDREN'S WRITER GUIDE TO 1998, (annual), The Institute of Children's Literature, 95 Long Ridge Rd., West Redding CT 55104. (800)443-6078.

CHILDREN'S WRITER'S WORD BOOK, by Alijandra Mogilner, Writer's Digest Books, 1507 Dana Ave., Cincinnati OH 45207. (800)289-0963.

GETTING STARTED AS A FREELANCE ILLUSTRATOR OR DESIGNER, by Michael Fleischman, North Light Books, 1507 Dana Ave., Cincinnati OH 45207. (800)289-0963.

GUIDE TO LITERARY AGENTS, (annual) edited by Donya Dickerson, Writer's Digest Books, 1507 Dana Ave., Cincinnati OH 45207. (800)289-0963.

Ν **HOW TO GET YOUR TEACHING IDEAS PUBLISHED**, by Jean Stangl, Walker and Company, 435 Hudson St., New York NY 10014. (212)727-8300.

HOW TO SELL YOUR PHOTOGRAPHS & ILLUSTRATIONS, by Elliot & Barbara Gordon, North Light Books, 1507 Dana Ave., Cincinnati OH 45207. (800)289-0963.

HOW TO WRITE A CHILDREN'S BOOK & GET IT PUBLISHED, by Barbara Seuling, Charles Scribner's Sons, 1230 Avenue of the Americas, New York NY 10020. (212)702-2000.

HOW TO WRITE AND ILLUSTRATE CHILDREN'S BOOKS AND GET THEM PUBLISHED, edited by Treld Pelkey Bicknell and Felicity Trottman, Writer's Digest Books, 1507 Dana Ave., Cincinnati OH 45207. (800)289-0963.

HOW TO WRITE AND SELL CHILDREN'S PICTURE BOOKS, by Jean E. Karl, Writer's Digest Books, 1507 Dana Ave., Cincinnati OH 45207. (800)289-0963.

Ν **HOW TO WRITE ATTENTION-GRABBING QUERY & COVER LETTERS**, by John Wood, Writer's Digest Books, 1507 Dana Ave., Cincinnati OH 45207. (800)289-0963.

HOW TO WRITE, ILLUSTRATE, AND DESIGN CHILDREN'S BOOKS, by Frieda Gates, Lloyd-Simone Publishing Company, distributed by Library Research Associates, Inc., Dunderberg Rd. RD 6, Box 41, Monroe NY 10950. (914)783-1144.

LEGAL GUIDE FOR THE VISUAL ARTIST, by Tad Crawford, North Light Books, 1507 Dana Ave., Cincinnati OH 45207. (800)289-0963.

MARKET GUIDE FOR YOUNG WRITERS, Fifth Edition, by Kathy Henderson, Writer's Digest Books, 1507 Dana Ave., Cincinnati OH 45207. (800)289-0963.

A TEEN'S GUIDE TO GETTING PUBLISHED, by Danielle Dunn & Jessica Dunn, Prufrock Press, P.O. Box 8813, Waco TX 76714-8813. (800)998-2208.

TEN STEPS TO PUBLISHING CHILDREN'S BOOKS, by Berthe Amoss & Eric Suben, Writer's Digest Books, 1507 Dana Ave., Cincinnati OH 45207. (800)289-0963.

THE ULTIMATE PORTFOLIO, by Martha Metzdorf, North Light Books, 1507 Dana Ave., Cincinnati OH 45207. (800)289-0963.

THE WRITER'S DIGEST GUIDE TO MANUSCRIPT FORMATS, by Dian Dincin Buchman & Seli Groves, Writer's Digest Books, 1507 Dana Ave., Cincinnati OH 45207. (800)289-0963.

THE WRITER'S ESSENTIAL DESK REFERENCE, Second Edition, Writer's Digest Books, 1507 Dana Ave., Cincinnati OH 45207. (800)289-0963.

WRITING AND ILLUSTRATING CHILDREN'S BOOKS FOR PUBLICATION: TWO PERSPEC-TIVES, by Berthe Amoss and Eric Suben, Writer's Digest Books, 1507 Dana Ave., Cincinnati OH 45207. (800)289-0963.

WRITING & PUBLISHING BOOKS FOR CHILDREN IN THE 1990s: THE INSIDE STORY FROM THE EDITOR'S DESK, by Olga Litowinsky, Walker & Co., 435 Hudson St., New York NY 10014. (212)727-8300.

WRITING BOOKS FOR YOUNG PEOPLE, Second Edition, by James Cross Giblin, The Writer, Inc., 120 Boylston St., Boston MA 02116-4615. (617)423-3157.

WRITING FOR CHILDREN & TEENAGERS, Third Edition, by Lee Wyndham and Arnold Madison, Writer's Digest Books, 1507 Dana Ave., Cincinnati OH 45207. (800)289-0963.

N: WRITING FOR YOUNG ADULTS, by Sherry Garland, Writer's Digest Books, 1507 Dana Ave., Cincinnati OH 45207. (800)289-0963.

N: WRITING TOGETHER, by Dawn Denham Haines, Susan Newcomer and Jacqueline Raphael, The Berkley Publishing Group, Penguin Putnam, Inc., 375 Hudson St., New York NY 10014. (212)366-2000.

WRITING WITH PICTURES: HOW TO WRITE AND ILLUSTRATE CHILDREN'S BOOKS, by Uri Shulevitz, Watson-Guptill Publications, 1515 Broadway, New York NY 10036. (212)764-7300.

YOU CAN YOU CAN WRITE CHILDREN'S BOOKS, by Tracey Dils, Writer's Digest Books, 1507 Dana Ave., Cincinnati OH 45207. (800)289-0963.

PUBLICATIONS

BOOK LINKS, editor Judith O'Malley, American Library Association, 50 E. Huron St., Chicago IL 60611. (800)545-2433. *Magazine published 6 times a year (September-July) for the purpose of connecting books, libraries and classrooms. Features articles on specific topics followed by bibliographies recommending books for further information. Subscription: $18.95/year.*

✓ CHILDREN'S BOOK INSIDER, editor Laura Backes, 901 Columbia Rd., Ft. Collins CO 80525-1838. (970)495-0056 or (800)807-1916. E-mail: mail@write4kids.com. Website: http://www.write4kids.com. *Monthly newsletter covering markets, techniques and trends in children's publishing. Subscription: $29.95/year. Official update source for* Children's Writer's & Illustrator's Market, *featuring quarterly lists of changes and updates to listings in CWIM.*

CHILDREN'S WRITER, editor Susan Tierney, The Institute of Children's Literature, 95 Long Ridge Rd., West Redding CT 55104. (800)443-6078. *Monthly newsletter of writing and publishing trends in the children's field. Subscription: $24/year; special introductory rate: $15.*

THE FIVE OWLS, editor Susan Stan, Hamline University Crossroads Center, MS-C1924, 1536 Hewitt Ave., St. Paul MN 55104. (612)644-7377. Fax: (612)641-2956. *Bimonthly newsletter for readers personally and professionally involved in children's literature. Subscription: $35/year.*

✓ THE HORN BOOK MAGAZINE, editor-in-chief Robert Sutton, The Horn Book Inc., 56 Roland St., Suite 200, Boston MA 02129. (800)325-1170. E-mail: info@hbook.com. Website: http://www.hbook.com. *Bimonthly guide to the children's book world including views on the industry and reviews of the latest books. Subscription: $42/year; special introductory rate: $24.95.*

THE LION AND THE UNICORN: A CRITICAL JOURNAL OF CHILDREN'S LITERATURE, editors Jack Zipes and Louisa Smith, The Johns Hopkins University Press—Journals Publishing Division, 2175 N. Charles St., Baltimore MD 21218-4319. (410)516-6987. *Magazine published 3 times a year serving as a forum* *for discussion of children's literature featuring interviews with authors, editors and experts in the field. Subscription: $26/year.*

☑ **ONCE UPON A TIME . . .**, editor Audrey Baird, 553 Winston Court, St. Paul MN 55118. (651)457-6233. Fax: (651)457-9565. Website: http://members.aol.com/OUATMAG/. *Quarterly support magazine for children's writers and illustrators and those interested in children's literature. Subscription: $23/year.*

PUBLISHERS WEEKLY, editor-in-chief Nora Rawlinson, Bowker Magazine Group, Cahners Publishing Co., 249 W. 17th St., New York NY 10011. (800)278-2991. *Weekly trade publication covering all aspects of the publishing industry; includes coverage of the children's field (books, audio and video) and spring and fall issues devoted solely to children's books. Subscription: $139/year. Available on newsstands for $4/issue. (Special issues are higher in price.)*

N RIVERBANK REVIEW of books for young readers, editor Martha Davis Beck, University of St. Thomas, 2115 Summit Ave., CHC-131, St. Paul MN 55105. (612)962-5373. Fax: (612)962-5169. *Quarterly publication exploring the world of children's literature including book reviews, articles and essays. Subscription: $20/year.*

SOCIETY OF CHILDREN'S BOOK WRITERS AND ILLUSTRATORS BULLETIN, editors Stephen Mooser and Lin Oliver, SCBWI, 22736 Vanowen St., Suite 106, West Hills CA 91307. (818)888-8760. *Bimonthly newsletter of SCBWI covering news of interest to members. Subscription with $50/year membership.*

Websites of Interest

The editor of *Children's Writer's & Illustrator's Market* suggests the following websites to keep you informed on writing and illustrating techniques, trends in the field, business issues, industry news and changes, and additional markets.

⊞ AMAZON.COM: http://www.amazon.com
Calling itself "A bookstore too big for the physical world," Amazon.com has more than 3 million books available on their website at discounted prices, plus a personal notification service of new releases, reader reviews, bestseller and suggested book information. Be sure to check out Amazon.com Kids.

⊞ BARNES & NOBLE ONLINE: http://www.barnesandnoble.com
The world's largest bookstore chain's website contains 600,000 in-stock titles at discount prices as well as personalized recommendations, online events with authors and book forum access for members.

⊞ BOOKWIRE: http://www.bookwire.com
A gateway to finding information about publishers, booksellers, libraries, authors, reviews and awards. Also offers frequently asked publishing questions and answers, a calendar of events, a mailing list and other helpful resources.

⊞ CANADIAN CHILDREN'S BOOK CENTRE: http://www3.sympatico.ca/ccbc/
The site for the CCBC includes profiles of illustrators and authors, information on recent books, a calendar of upcoming events, information on CCBC publications, and tips from Canadian children's authors.

CBONLINE, THE WEBSITE OF THE CHILDREN'S BOOK COUNCIL: http://www.cbcbooks.org/
This site includes a complete list of CBC members with addresses, names and descriptions of what each publishes, and links to publishers' websites. Also offers previews of upcoming titles from members; articles from CBC Features, the Council's newsletter; and their catalog.

CHILDREN'S LITERATURE WEB GUIDE: http://www.ucalgary.ca/~dkbrown/index.html
This site includes stories, poetry, resource lists, lists of conferences, links to book reviews, lists of awards (international), and information on books from classic to contemporary.

CHILDREN'S WRITERS RESOURCE CENTER: http://www.write4kids.com
This site includes highlights from the newsletter Children's Book Insider*; definitions of publishing terms; answers to frequently asked questions; information on trends; information on small presses; a research center for Web information; and a catalog of material available from* CBI.

⊞ THE DRAWING BOARD: http://members.aol.com/thedrawing
This site for illustrators features articles, interviews, links and resources for illustrators from all fields.

⊞ EDITOR & PUBLISHER: http://www.mediainfo.com
The Internet source for Editor & Publisher, *this site provides up-to-date industry news, with other opportunities such as a research area and bookstore, a calendar of events and classifieds.*

⊞ INKSPOT: http://www.inkspot.com
An elaborate site that provides information about workshops, how-to information, copyright, quotations, writing tips, resources, contests, market information (including children's writers marketplace), publishers, booksellers, associations, mailing lists, newsletters, conferences and more.

KIDS 'N STUFF WRITING FOR CHILDREN HOMEPAGE: http://pages.prodigy.com/childrens_writers/
Site coordinator Jody Blosser includes articles for writers, lists of resources, lists of clubs and organizations, and links to other sites including companion site A World of Pictures. Blosser is looking for articles from writers to include on the page.

ONCE UPON A TIME: http://members.aol.com/OUATMAG
This companion site to Once Upon A Time *magazine offers excerpts from recent articles, notes for prospective contributors, and information about OUAT's 11 regular columnists.*

N **PUBLISHERS' CATALOGUES HOME PAGE:** http://www.lights.com/publisher/index.html
A mammoth link collection of publishers around the world arranged geographically. This site is one of the most comprehensive directories of publishers on the Internet.

THE PURPLE CRAYON: http://www.users.interport.net/~hdu/
Editor Harold Underdown's site includes articles on trends, business, and cover letters and queries as well as interviews with editors and answers to frequently asked questions. He also includes links to a number of other sites helpful to writers.

THE SLUSH PILE: http://www.theslushpile.com/
Editor Laura Belgrave's site offers a wealth of tips for writers such as information on submissions, agents, copyright, cover and query letters, a glossary of publishing terms, online and offline resources and frequently asked questions.

SOCIETY OF CHILDREN'S BOOK WRITERS AND ILLUSTRATORS: http://www.scbwi.org
Site coordinator Bruce Balan includes information on awards and grants available to SCBWI members, a calendar of events listed by date and region, a list of publications available to members, and a site map for easy navigation. Balan welcomes suggestions for the site from visitors.

N **UNITED STATES POSTAL SERVICE:** http://www.usps.gov/welcome.htm
Domestic and International postage rate calculator, stamp ordering, zip code look up, express mail tracking, etc.

N **WRITERSDIGEST.COM:** http://www.writersdigest.com
Brought to you by Writer's Digest magazine and Writer's Market, this site features a hot list, markets of the day, and a searchable database of more than 1,000 writer's guidelines.

WRITES OF PASSAGE: http://www.writes.org
Run by Writes of Passage (a literary magazine for teens), this site includes features from the magazine; links to a list of teen resources on the Web, including high school and college newspapers and online dictionaries; and a database of high school websites.

Glossary

Advance. A sum of money a publisher pays a writer or illustrator prior to the publication of a book. It is usually paid in installments, such as one half on signing the contract; one half on delivery of a complete and satisfactory manuscript. The advance is paid against the royalty money that will be earned by the book.

All rights. The rights contracted to a publisher permitting the use of material anywhere and in any form, including movie and book club sales, without additional payment to the creator. (See The Business of Writing & Illustrating.)

Anthology. A collection of selected writings by various authors or gatherings of works by one author.

Anthropomorphization. The act of attributing human form and personality to things not human (such as animals).

ASAP. As soon as possible.

Assignment. An editor or art director asks a writer, illustrator or photographer to produce a specific piece for an agreed-upon fee.

B&W. Black & white.

Backlist. A publisher's list of books not published during the current season but still in print.

Biennially. Occurring once every 2 years.

Bimonthly. Occurring once every 2 months.

Biweekly. Occurring once every 2 weeks.

Book packager. A company that draws all elements of a book together, from the initial concept to writing and marketing strategies, then sells the book package to a book publisher and/or movie producer. Also known as book producer or book developer.

Book proposal. Package submitted to a publisher for consideration usually consisting of a synopsis, outline and sample chapters. (See Before Your First Sale.)

Business-size envelope. Also known as a #10 envelope. The standard size used in sending business correspondence.

Camera-ready. Refers to art that is completely prepared for copy camera platemaking.

Caption. A description of the subject matter of an illustration or photograph; photo captions include persons' names where appropriate. Also called cutline.

CD-ROM. Compact disc read-only memory. Non-erasable electronic medium used for digitalized image and document storage capable of holding enormous amounts of information. A computer user must have a CD-ROM drive to access a CD-ROM.

Clean-copy. A manuscript free of errors and needing no editing; it is ready for typesetting.

Clips. Samples, usually from newspapers or magazines, of a writer's published work.

Concept books. Books that deal with ideas, concepts and large-scale problems, promoting an understanding of what's happening in a child's world. Most prevalent are alphabet and counting books, but also includes books dealing with specific concerns facing young people (such as divorce, birth of a sibling, friendship or moving).

Contract. A written agreement stating the rights to be purchased by an editor, art director or producer and the amount of payment the writer, illustrator or photographer will receive for that sale. (See The Business of Writing & Illustrating.)

Contributor's copies. The magazine issues sent to an author, illustrator or photographer in which her work appears.

Co-op publisher. A publisher that shares production costs with an author, but, unlike subsidy publishers, handles all marketing and distribution. An author receives a high percentage of royalties until her initial investment is recouped, then standard royalties.

Copy. The actual written material of a manuscript.

Copyediting. Editing a manuscript for grammar usage, spelling, punctuation and general style.

Copyright. A means to legally protect an author's/illustrator's/photographer's work. This can be shown by writing ©, the creator's name, and year of work's creation. (See The Business of Writing & Illustrating.)

Cover letter. A brief letter, accompanying a complete manuscript, especially useful if responding to an editor's request for a manuscript. May also accompany a book proposal. (See Before Your First Sale.)

Cutline. See caption.

Disk. A round, flat magnetic plate on which computer data may be stored.

Division. An unincorporated branch of a company.

Dummy. Handmade mock-up of a book.

Electronic submission. A submission of material by modem or on computer disk.

E-mail. Electronic mail. Messages sent from one computer to another via a modem or computer network.

Final draft. The last version of a polished manuscript ready for submission to an editor.

First North American serial rights. The right to publish material in a periodical for the first time, in the United States or Canada. (See The Business of Writing & Illustrating.)

Flat fee. A one-time payment.

Galleys. The first typeset version of a manuscript that has not yet been divided into pages.

Genre. A formulaic type of fiction, such as horror, mystery, romance, science fiction or western.

Glossy. A photograph with a shiny surface as opposed to one with a non-shiny matte finish.

Gouache. Opaque watercolor with an appreciable film thickness and an actual paint layer.

Halftone. Reproduction of a continuous tone illustration with the image formed by dots produced by a camera lens screen.

Hard copy. The printed copy of a computer's output.

Hardware. All the mechanically-integrated components of a computer that are not software—circuit boards, transistors and the machines that are the actual computer.

Hi-Lo. High interest, low reading level. Pertains mostly to books for beginning adult readers.

Home page. The first page of a World Wide Web document.

Imprint. Name applied to a publisher's specific line of books.

Interactive. A type of computer interface that takes user input, such as answers to computer-generated questions, and acts upon them.

Internet. A worldwide network of computers that offers access to a wide variety of electronic resources.

IRC. International Reply Coupon. Sold at the post office to enclose with text or artwork sent to a foreign buyer to cover postage costs when replying or returning work.

Keyline. Identification, through signs and symbols, of the positions of illustrations and copy for the printer.

Layout. Arrangement of illustrations, photographs, text and headlines for printed material.

Line drawing. Illustration done with pencil or ink using no wash or other shading.

Mass market books. Paperback books directed toward an extremely large audience sold in supermarkets, drugstores, airports, newsstands and chain bookstores.

Mechanicals. Paste-up or preparation of work for printing.

Middle reader. The general classification of books written for readers ages 9-11.

Modem. A small electrical box that plugs into the serial card of a computer, used to transmit data from one computer to another, usually via telephone lines.

Ms (mss). Manuscript(s).

One-time rights. Permission to publish a story in periodical or book form one time only. (See The Business of Writing & Illustrating.) ·

Outline. A summary of a book's contents in 5-15 double-spaced pages; often in the form of chapter headings with a descriptive sentence or two under each heading to show the scope of the book.

Package sale. The sale of a manuscript and illustrations/photos as a "package" paid for with one check.

Payment on acceptance. The writer, artist or photographer is paid for her work at the time the editor or art director decides to buy it.

Payment on publication. The writer, artist or photographer is paid for her work when it is published.

Photostat. Black & white copies produced by an inexpensive photographic process using paper negatives; only line values are held with accuracy. Also called stat.

Picture book. A type of book aimed at preschoolers to 8-year-olds that tells a story primarily or entirely with artwork.

Print. An impression pulled from an original plate, stone, block, screen or negative; also a positive made from a photographic negative.

Proofreading. Reading a typescript to correct typographical errors.

Query. A letter to an editor designed to capture her interest in an article or book you propose to write. (See Before Your First Sale.)

Reading fee. Money charged by some agents and publishers to read a submitted manuscript.

Reprint rights. Permission to print an already published work whose first rights have been sold to another magazine or book publisher. (See The Business of Writing & Illustrating.)

Response time. The average length of time it takes an editor or art director to accept or reject a query or submission and inform the creator of the decision.

Rights. The bundle of permissions offered to an editor or art director in exchange for printing a manuscript, artwork or photographs. (See The Business of Writing & Illustrating.)

Rough draft. A manuscript that has not been checked for errors in grammar, punctuation, spelling or content.

Roughs. Preliminary sketches or drawings.

Royalty. An agreed percentage paid by a publisher to a writer, illustrator or photographer for each copy of her work sold.

SAE. Self-addressed envelope.

SASE. Self-addressed, stamped envelope.

SCBWI. The Society of Children's Book Writers and Illustrators. (See listing in Clubs & Organizations section.)

Second serial rights. Permission for the reprinting of a work in another periodical after its first publication in book or magazine form. (See The Business of Writing & Illustrating.)

Semiannual. Occurring once every 6 months.

Semimonthly. Occurring twice a month.

Semiweekly. Occurring twice a week.

Serial rights. The rights given by an author to a publisher to print a piece in one or more periodicals. (See The Business of Writing & Illustrating.)

Simultaneous submissions. Queries or proposals sent to several publishers at the same time. (See Before Your First Sale.)

Slant. The approach to a story or piece of artwork that will appeal to readers of a particular publication.

Slush pile. Editors' term for their collections of unsolicited manuscripts.

Software. Programs and related documentation for use with a computer.

Solicited manuscript. Material that an editor has asked for or agreed to consider before being sent by a writer.

Speculation (spec). Creating a piece with no assurance from an editor or art director that it will be purchased or any reimbursements for material or labor paid.

Stat. See photostat.

Subsidiary rights. All rights other than book publishing rights included in a book contract, such as paperback, book club and movie rights. (See The Business of Writing & Illustrating.)

Subsidy publisher. A book publisher that charges the author for the cost of typesetting, printing and promoting a book. Also called a vanity publisher.

Synopsis. A brief summary of a story or novel. Usually a page to a page and a half, single-spaced, if part of a book proposal.

Tabloid. Publication printed on an ordinary newspaper page turned sideways and folded in half.

Tearsheet. Page from a magazine or newspaper containing your printed art, story, article, poem or photo.

Thumbnail. A rough layout in miniature.

Trade books. Books sold strictly in chain bookstores, aimed at a smaller audience than mass market books, and printed in smaller quantities by publishers.

Transparencies. Positive color slides; not color prints.

Unsolicited manuscript. Material sent without an editor's or art director's request.

Vanity publisher. See subsidy publisher.

Word processor. A computer that produces typewritten copy via automated text-editing, storage and transmission capabilities.

World Wide Web. An Internet resource that utilizes hypertext to access information. It also supports formatted text, illustrations and sounds, depending on the user's computer capabilities.

Work-for-hire. An arrangement between a writer, illustrator or photographer and a company under which the company retains complete control of the work's copyright. (See The Business of Writing & Illustrating.)

Young adult. The general classification of books written for readers ages 12-18.

Young reader. The general classification of books written for readers ages 5-8.

Age-Level Index

This index lists book and magazine publishers by the age-groups for which they publish. Use it to locate appropriate markets for your work, then carefully read the listings and follow the guidelines of each publisher. Use this index in conjunction with the Subject Index to further narrow your list of markets. **Picture Books** are for preschoolers to 8-year-olds; **Young Readers** are for 5- to 8-year-olds; **Middle Readers** are for 9- to 11-year-olds; and **Young Adults** are for ages 12 and up.

BOOK PUBLISHERS

MAGAZINES

Picture-oriented material

Subject Index

This index lists book and magazine publishers by the fiction and nonfiction subject area in which they publish. Use it to locate appropriate markets for your work, then carefully read the listings and follow the guidelines of each publisher. Use this index in conjunction with the Age-Level Index to further narrow your lists of markets.

Fantasy

Folktales

BOOK PUBLISHERS: NONFICTION

MAGAZINES: FICTION

MAGAZINES: NONFICTION

Poetry Index

This index lists markets that are open to poetry submissions and is divided into book publishers and magazines. It's important to carefully read the listings and follow the guidelines of each publisher to which you submit.

Photography Index

This index lists markets that buy photos from freelancers, and is divided into book publishers, magazines and greeting cards. It's important to carefully read the listings and follow the guidelines of each publisher to which you submit.

General Index

Companies that appeared in the 1998 edition of *Children's Writer's & Illustrator's Market* but do not appear in this edition are identified with a two-letter code explaining why the market was omitted: (**ED**)—Editorial Decision; (**NR**)—No (or late) Response to Listing Request; (**OB**)—Out of Business; (**RR**)—Removed by Market's Request.

Companies that appeared in the 1998 edition of *Children's Writer's & Illustrator's Market,* **but do not appear this year, are listed in this General Index with the following codes explaining why these markets were omitted: (ED)—Editorial Decision, (NS)—Not Accepting Submissions, (NR)—No (or late) Response to Listing Request, (OB)—Out of Business, (RR)—Removed by Market's Request, (UC)—Unable to Contact.**